Beyond Bilateralism

EAST-WEST CENTER
SERIES ON

CONTEMPORARY ISSUES IN ASIA AND THE PACIFIC

Series Editor, Muthiah Alagappa

Beyond Bilateralism

U.S.-JAPAN RELATIONS
IN THE NEW ASIA-PACIFIC

Edited by Ellis S. Krauss and T. J. Pempel

STANFORD UNIVERSITY PRESS
STANFORD, CALIFORNIA
2004

Stanford University Press
Stanford, California

© 2004 by the Board of Trustees
of the Leland Stanford Junior University.

Printed in the United States of America
on acid-free, archival-quality paper

Library of Congress Cataloging-in-Publication Data

Beyond bilateralism : U.S.-Japan relations in the new Asia-Pacific /
edited by Ellis S. Krauss and T. J. Pempel.
    p.   cm. — (Contemporary issues in Asia and the Pacific)
Includes bibliographical references and index.
ISBN 0-8047-4909-4 (alk. paper)
ISBN 0-8047-4910-8 (pbk. : alk. paper)
    1. United States—Foreign relations—Japan.
    2. Japan—Foreign relations—United States.
    3. United States—Foreign relations—1989–
        4. Asia—Economic conditions.
        5. Pacific Area—Economic conditions.
        6. Asia—Politics and government—1945–
        7. Pacific Area—Politics and government.
                8. Geopolitics.
        9. International economic relations.
            10. International agencies.
I. Krauss, Ellis S.   II. Pempel, T. J., date–   III. Series.
        E183.8.J3 B5155   2004
        327.73052—dc22   2003018028

Original Printing 2004

Last figure below indicates year of this printing:

13   12   11   10   09   08   07   06   05   04

Typeset by Heather Boone in 10/12 Sabon

CONTEMPORARY ISSUES IN ASIA AND THE PACIFIC

Series Editor, Muthiah Alagappa

A collaborative effort by Stanford University Press and the East-West Center, this series addresses issues of policy and scholarly concern affecting the Asia Pacific region. It focuses on understanding the dynamics of key changes in regional political, sociocultural, economic, demographic, environmental, and technological landscapes, as well as their implications for building an Asia Pacific community that is peaceful, just, and prosperous. Preference is given to comparative, regional, or single-country studies that are conceptual in orientation and emphasize underlying processes and broad implications.

The East-West Center, located in Honolulu, Hawai'i is a public, non-profit educational and research institution established by the US Congress in 1960 to foster understanding and cooperation among the governments and peoples of the Asia Pacific, including the United States.

Also available in this series:

Political Legitimacy in Southeast Asia: The Quest for Moral Authority
Edited by Muthiah Alagappa

Chiefs Today: Traditional Pacific Leadership and the Postcolonial State
Edited by Geoffrey M. White and Lamont Lindstrom

Making Majorities: Constituting the Nation in Japan, Korea, China, Malaysia, Fiji, Turkey, and the United States
Edited by Dru C. Gladney

Capital, Coercion, and Crime: Bossism in the Philippines
By John T. Sidel

Population Change and Economic Development in East Asia: Challenges Met, Opportunities Seized
Edited by Andrew Mason

For
Martha Anne Leche and Kaela Kory
Our Wives and Best Friends

Contents

Illustrations

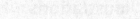

Acknowledgments

This project and the idea of reexamining the U.S.-Japan relationship in light of the momentous changes occurring in the Asia-Pacific region began when Ellis S. Krauss and T. J. Pempel decided to organize a relatively straightforward ninety-minute panel at the annual meeting of the Association for Asian Studies. Rather quickly the idea sparked plans for a conference, which in turn generated a two-year grant proposal that eventually spawned several formal meetings on three continents. More than three years after the original panel proposal, we can finally bring forth this volume. Birthing this book has of course left us in deep debt to the many who helped along the way.

Most important, we wish to thank the Japan-U.S. Friendship Commission and its executive director, Eric Gangloff, for providing the bulk of our research support. In addition, Eric was particularly generous in offering us organizational guidance and administrative flexibility that proved invaluable in our ongoing attempts to improve the conceptualization and shaping of the project.

Early versions of most of the chapters in this volume were presented at meetings in several venues. Each venue allowed the authors and the editors to test and refine their arguments. The Mauna Kea Resort in Kona, Hawaii, was a productive and pleasant context for collective inspiration in the early stages and allowed for personal and intellectual bonding among the members that carried on throughout the project. International House of Japan provided another such opportunity. Koishi Izumi and the rest of the "I House" staff were exceptionally generous and attentive in the support they provided for all of the participants. The Institute of Social Science Research (Shaken) at Tokyo University offered another early and invaluable forum within which to present versions of the chapters. Nobuhiro Hiwatari organized a particularly adept group of scholars to reflect on our papers. We wish to thank all of them for their insights and suggestions.

The U.S. Embassy in Tokyo, and in particular Warren Soiffer and Alexei Kral of the Public Affairs Section, made it possible for a number of us to present our ideas and to get feedback from a diversity of Japanese audiences made up largely of policymakers, journalists, and businesspeople directly involved in various aspects of the U.S.-Japan relationship. A similar venue was provided for us in Washington, D.C., by the Woodrow Wilson Center, where Robert Hathaway and Amy McCreedy of the Asia Program offered us their particularly valuable organizational talents.

The Research Institute of Economy, Trade and Industry (RIETI) also provided several of us with an opportunity to test our ideas before an extremely insightful group of Japanese and European researchers and policymakers. We wish to thank in particular Nobuo Tanaka and Akiko Kumagai of RIETI for organizing this meeting.

Finally, the British Association for Japanese Studies and its chairman, J.A.A. Stockwin of the Nissan Institute, invited Krauss and Pempel to present the major ideas from this project at their 2002 annual convention in Oxford. Once again, a different venue generated alternative perspectives and additional insights.

Robert Pekkanen, Eiichi Katahara, and Eric Gangloff participated in early meetings and contributed to our conceptualization of the project. Mary Alice Pickert served as a meticulous note taker during our Tokyo meetings. Glen Fukushima, Sheila Smith, Nobuo Tanaka, and Muthiah Alagappa read early versions of most of the chapters and provided many of the authors with exceptionally insightful and useful feedback. Muthiah Alagappa and Elisa W. Johnston of the East-West Center along with Muriel Bell and Carmen Borbon-Wu of Stanford University Press have been speedy, gracious, and insightful in their oversight of the processes of editorial review and manuscript preparation. We thank all of them along with the various anonymous reviewers from the East-West Center for their many insights and suggestions. The anonymous reviewer for Stanford University Press has our respect and gratitude for a balanced, insightful, and very useful review.

The Jackson School at the University of Washington; the University of California, San Diego; the Shaken at Tokyo University; and the University of California, Berkeley (UCB), provided important supplementary financing and organizational support. Jere Bacharach, former director of the Jackson School, along with John Rowe and the very helpful Business Relations Office at the Graduate School of International Relations and Pacific Studies of the University of California, San Diego (UCSD), deserve special thanks. Krauss is also grateful to the Center for Global Partnership and the Social Science Research Council, which provided him with Abe Fellowship funding for his research on Asia Pacific Economic Cooperation.

This sparked his initial interest in the issues this volume addresses. Several research assistants at both UCSD and UCB helped us gather data and provided bibliographic and other research assistance at various times. Kumi Sawada Hadler of the Institute of East Asian Studies at Berkeley was meticulous in transforming an infinite number of presentational styles and editorial scribblings into a cohesive and well-edited whole. Mariana Raykov, our production editor at Stanford University Press, earned our sincere gratitude and appreciation for her most efficient and friendly shepherding of the manuscript into a published volume.

We apologize to any others whose contributions we have failed to acknowledge adequately. But certainly our thanks would not be complete if as editors we did not recognize the wonderfully cooperative spirit of our contributors, an unusually talented group of junior and senior scholars from several countries. Both of us have been involved in several such projects in the past and we know how easily collective enterprises can be stymied or sidetracked. Without question the participants in this project have been unfailingly supportive of one another's work and equally responsive to the editors' seemingly arbitrary deadlines and stylistic punctiliousness. They have made the never-fun work of whip cracking far less necessary than usual. Working with them has been a delightful and insightful experience for both of us.

Last, we wish to thank our wives, Martha Leche and Kaela Kory, for the patience and support they have given to us throughout this project. A work such as this invariably makes time demands that are even more inflexible than those that usually occur in the academic world. Both of them have been unfailingly tolerant of our incessant e-mail traffic, convoluted travel schedules, and the seemingly never-ending working lunches and editorial meetings that continued to force last-minute changes in plans for evenings, weekends, and vacations. It is to them that we lovingly dedicate this book.

Contributors

JENNIFER A. AMYX is assistant professor in the Department of Political Science at the University of Pennsylvania. She joined the faculty in 2002, having taught and carried out research previously as a postdoctoral fellow (1998–99) and research fellow (2000–01) at the Australian National University, Canberra. Amyx received her doctorate in political science in 1998 from Stanford University. Her research focuses primarily on three areas: the politics of financial regulation and reform in Japan after the end of its speculative "bubble," the political dynamics of regional financial cooperation in East Asia since 1997, and the comparative analysis of the politics of privatizing Japan's postal savings and government-backed financial institutions in Japan. She has coedited (with Peter Drysdale) *Japanese Governance: Beyond Japan Inc.* (Routledge Curzon Press, 2003) and is author of *Japan's Financial Crisis: Institutional Rigidity and Reluctant Change* (Princeton University Press, forthcoming).

KUNIKO P. ASHIZAWA is a doctoral candidate at the Fletcher School of Law and Diplomacy, Tufts University, and is currently a visiting scholar at the Graduate School of International Relations and Pacific Studies, University of California, San Diego. Her dissertation examines U.S. and Japanese policymaking toward the creation of APEC and the ARF, affording special consideration to the impact of the two countries' relative influence over the direction and pace of regional multilateral institution-building in the Asia-Pacific. Her research interests also encompass Japanese foreign and security policy, the international relations of Northeast Asia, and regionalism in Asia. Following several years as a journalist in Tokyo, she occasionally consults and provides research in international issues to Japanese media firms, such as the *Asahi* newspaper and NHK, Japan's public service broadcaster.

AKIKO FUKUSHIMA is director of policy studies and senior fellow at the National Institute for Research Advancement, Tokyo. She received her doctorate in International Public Policy from Osaka University in 1998 and is recognized as one of Japan's top experts on international peace and security, in which capacity she frequently participates in government-sponsored two-track dialogues in the Asia-Pacific region, in policy deliberation councils that advise the Japanese government, and in many international forums. Her fields of specialization include international security, conflict prevention, and multilateralism. Among her many publications are *Japanese Foreign Policy: The Emerging Logic of Multilateralism* (Macmillan, 1999) and *Lexicon: Asia Taiheiyō Anzenhoshō Taiwa* (Lexicon: Asia-Pacific security dialogue) (Nihon Keizai Hyōronsha, 2002).

NATASHA HAMILTON-HART is assistant professor in the Southeast Asian Studies Programme at the National University of Singapore. She received her doctorate from Cornell University in 1999. Her research interests include the comparative political economy of Southeast Asia; international political economy; state structures and administrative systems of Southeast Asia, especially Indonesia and Malaysia; and regionalism in Asia. She recently published *Asian States, Asian Bankers: Central Banking in Southeast Asia* (Cornell University Press, 2002).

WALTER HATCH is assistant professor of government at Colby College in Waterville, Maine, as well as editor of *The Japanese Economy*, a journal published by Sharpe. He has been assistant professor at the University of Tokyo and lecturer at the University of Washington in Seattle, where he received his doctorate in political economy in 2000. Hatch is coauthor (with Kozo Yamamura) of *Asia in Japan's Embrace: Building a Regional Production Alliance* (Cambridge University Press, 1996), as well as author of numerous journal articles and book chapters. His research focuses on Asian regionalism, on the slow pace of change in the Japanese political economy, and most recently on Sino-Japanese relations.

CHRISTOPHER W. HUGHES is senior research fellow and deputy director at the Centre for the Study of Globalisation and Regionalisation, University of Warwick, United Kingdom. He received his bachelor of arts degree from Oxford University and his doctorate from Sheffield University. Formerly visiting professor at the Faculty of Law, University of Tokyo, and research fellow at Hiroshima University, his research interests include Japanese security policy, Japanese international political economy, regionalism in East Asia, and North Korea's external political and economic relations. He is author of *Japan's Economic Power and Security: Japan and North Korea* (Routledge, 1999) and *Japan's Security Agenda: The Search for Regional Stability* (Lynne Rienner, 2004); coauthor of *Japan's Interna-*

tional Relations: Politics, Economics and Security (Routledge, 2001); and coeditor of *New Regionalisms in the Global Political Economy* (Routledge, 2002). He is associate editor of the *Pacific Review*, and a participant in the Council for Security Cooperation in the Asia-Pacific.

G. JOHN IKENBERRY is Peter F. Krogh Professor of Geopolitics and Global Justice at Georgetown University. He received his doctorate in political science from the University of Chicago in 1984 and previously taught at Princeton University and the University of Pennsylvania. His fields of specialization are international relations, international political economy, American foreign policy, and theories of the state. He is author of, among others, *After Victory: Institutions, Strategic Restraint, and the Rebuilding of Order After Major Wars* (Princeton University Press, 2001); editor of *America Unrivaled: The Future of the Balance of Power* (Cornell University Press, 2002); coauthor of *State Power and World Markets: The International Political Economy* (Norton, 2002); and coeditor of *The Nation-State in Question* (Princeton University Press, 2003), *International Relations Theory and the Asia Pacific* (Columbia University Press, 2003), and *Reinventing the Alliance: The U.S.-Japan Security Partership in an Era of Change* (Palgrave, 2003).

SAORI N. KATADA is associate professor at the School of International Relations, University of Southern California (USC). She is author of *Banking on Stability: Japan and the Cross-Pacific Dynamics of International Financial Crisis Management* (University of Michigan Press, 2001), which was awarded the Masayoshi Ohira Memorial Book Award in 2002. She has also published articles on Japanese foreign aid, international financial crises, and development issues of Asia and Latin America. Her current research is on regionalism in Asia. She received her bachelor of arts degree from Hitotsubashi University, Tokyo, and her doctorate in political science from the University of North Carolina at Chapel Hill in 1994. Before joining USC, she worked for the World Bank in Washington, D.C., and for the United Nations Development Programme in Mexico City.

ELLIS S. KRAUSS is professor at the Graduate School of International Relations and Pacific Studies, University of California, San Diego. He received his doctorate in political science from Stanford University in 1973 and taught previously at the University of Pittsburgh and at Western Washington University. His fields of specialization are Japanese politics, especially political elites and media and politics; comparative politics; U.S.-Japan relations; and Japanese foreign policy. He is author of, among others, *Broadcasting Politics in Japan: NHK and Television News* (Cornell University Press, 2000); and coeditor of *Media and Politics in Japan* (University of Hawaii Press, 1996) and *Democracy in Japan* (University of Pittsburgh Press, 1989). His current research projects include a collaborative study of the consequences of Japan's electoral reform and a planned comparative study of U.S. security and economic relationships with key partners such as Japan.

ANDREW MACINTYRE is professor and director of the Asia Pacific School of Economics and Government, Australian National University. His previous position, until 2002, was professor, Graduate School of International Relations and Pacific Studies, University of California, San Diego. MacIntyre received his doctorate in political science in 1989 from Australian National University. His specialties are comparative politics, Southeast Asia, and international relations of the Asia-Pacific region. He is author of *The Power of Institutions: Political Architecture and Governance* (Cornell University Press, 2002); *Business and Politics in Indonesia* (Allen & Unwin, 1991); and "Institutions and Investors: The Politics of the Financial Crisis in Southeast Asia," *International Organization* (55:1, 2001); and editor of *Business and Government in Industrializing Asia* (Cornell University Press, 1994).

MIKE M. MOCHIZUKI received his doctorate from Harvard University and is associate professor of political science and international affairs, director of the Sigur Center for Asian Studies, and holder of the Japan-U.S. Relations Chair at the Elliott School, George Washington University. His previous positions were senior fellow at the Brookings Institution and codirector of the Center for Asia-Pacific Policy at RAND. He has taught at the University of Southern California and at Yale University. His recent publications include *Japan Reorients: The Quest for Wealth and Security in East Asia* (Brookings Institution, forthcoming); *Crisis on the Korean Peninsula: How to Deal with a Nuclear North Korea* (with Michael O'Hanlon; McGraw Hill, 2003), *Toward a True Alliance: Restructuring U.S.-Japan Security Relations* (Brookings Institution, 1997); and *Japan: Domestic Change and Foreign Policy* (RAND, 1995). He is currently writing a book entitled *The New Strategic Triangle: The U.S.-Japan Alliance and the Rise of China*.

SAADIA M. PEKKANEN received her doctorate from Harvard University in 1996. She is presently assistant professor at Middlebury College and was previously a postdoctoral fellow at the Harvard Academy for International and Area Studies. She is author of *Picking Winners? From Technology Catch-up to the Space Race* (Stanford University Press, 2003); is coeditor of *Late Liberalizers: Japan and China in the World Political Economy* (under review); and presently has a book manuscript, *International Law and Foreign Trade Politics: Japan and the WTO*, under consideration for review. She is recipient of an Abe Fellowship, and her present research interests lie at the intersection of international law, the World Trade Organization, and domestic judicial politics in the United States, Europe, and Japan.

T. J. PEMPEL is director of the Institute of East Asian Studies and Il Han New Professor of Asian Studies and professor of political science at the University of California, Berkeley. He received his doctorate in political science at Columbia University and taught previously at Cornell University, the University of Washington, the University of Colorado, and the University of Wisconsin. His fields of expertise are Japanese politics, comparative politics, and Asian regionalism. He is author of, among other works, *Regime Shift* (Cornell University Press, 1998); and editor of *The Politics of the Asian Economic Crisis* (Cornell University Press, 1999), *Uncommon Democracies: The One-Party Dominant Regimes* (Cornell University Press, 1990), and a volume on Asian regionalism entitled *Remapping Asia* (Cornell University Press, forthcoming).

Beyond Bilateralism

1

Challenges to Bilateralism

CHANGING FOES, CAPITAL FLOWS, AND COMPLEX FORUMS

T. J. PEMPEL

For most of the period since the signing of the San Francisco Peace Treaty in 1951, relations between Japan and the United States were overwhelmingly characterized by bilateralism. Each country extended to the other special privileges that they did not extend to other countries. Moreover, the key economic, political, and security relationships between the two nations were primarily dyadic links between the two governments; little influence was allowed to nongovernmental actors or other nations.[1] Most academic studies of U.S.-Japan relations correspondingly concentrated on this bilateralism.

Starting in the mid- to late 1980s, however, and accelerating since then, these once unambiguously bilateral ties have become far more complex and, consequently, ambiguous. Three forces account for the bulk of these changes: (1) alterations in geopolitics, (2) the enhanced role of private capital flows, and (3) the rise in number and importance of multilateral organizations. We argue in this volume that these three major trends have combined to restructure the previously bilateral nature of the U.S.-Japan relationship in fundamental ways, moving it "beyond bilateralism." Bilateralism has by no means vanished completely, nor has it been replaced by some equally easy-to-label alternative. Nonetheless, relations between Japan and the United States now manifest a panoply of new traits, directions, and managerial complexity that have unquestionably reshaped the relationship. Even where bilateral management continues to prevail—and we find this more in the security than in the economic or financial realms—

elites from both countries must face more complicated choices and implications than their predecessors faced. This book analyzes the three major structural forces that have changed the relationship and explores the myriad ways in which relations between the United States and Japan have consequently been restructured. In the argot of social science, the book analyzes the complex ways in which these three independent variables have reshaped the dependent variable, namely, the U.S.-Japan relationship.

These forces, individually and in combination, have come to exert powerful and transformative influence over relations between the two countries. Such deep structural shifts by no means eliminate the role of choice by powerful actors in Japan and the United States. These actors' preferences and behaviors still count mightily in the shaping of policies. However, these new contexts have reshaped both the arenas in which these leaders act and the incentives that guide their choices, dramatically reducing the appeal of certain previous choices while making other alternatives increasingly appealing. The chapters in this book analyze the altered interplay between these three structural changes and the political and economic choices that have been made in response.

Our argument and the evidence of our contributors is that neither the relationship between the United States and Japan nor its consequences are any longer characterized primarily by bilateral ties. It no longer suffices to study the relationship or its consequences in isolation from the relationship's increasingly multilateral context. We therefore use the integrating theme of the volume, "beyond bilateralism," in three ways. First, we show that the economic, security, and political relationships have changed as the result of the forces noted earlier.[2] Second, we apply the theme as well to the consequences of the changed relationship. The current character of relations between the two countries has unmistakably wider impacts on both the Asian region and the global political economy than it did a decade or more ago. These more comprehensive consequences reverberate well beyond the Washington Beltway and Kasumigaseki, its Japanese equivalent. Such broader implications—that is, the ripple effects of interactions between the United States and Japan on the broad regional and global canvas—are thus the second dimension to our use of the concept "beyond bilateralism."

There is now a rich and extensive literature on the ways in which the Asia-Pacific context, among others, has been transformed since the late 1980s toward greater multilateralism in economics and security.[3] There is also, as is discussed later, a large amount of literature on U.S.-Japan relations. Rarely, however, have the changed context of the relationship and its resulting consequences for the region been closely linked or fully explored, as we explicitly and directly attempt to do in this volume. The third implication, therefore, of the expression "beyond bilateralism" is the analytic approach taken in this book. Almost all previous treatments of U.S.-Japan ties have reflected the preponderantly bilateral nature of the relationship, concentrating on the particularistic interactions between the two countries and their governments. Occasionally some studies have gone further, analyzing the ways in which the two governments confronted common problems, threats, or opportunities. Nevertheless, such studies have taken for granted the primacy of the bilateral nature of the relationship.

This bilateral approach to the relationship prevailed across three broad streams in the literature. One such stream, by far the largest, focused on the bilateral implications of Japan's rise to economic superpower between 1960 and the early 1980s. Especially salient were studies of the trade friction that resulted from Japan's success and the perceived decline of the United States.[4]

The second approach involved work on the all-important military alliance that undergirded the political relationship.[5] Most of these works analyzed the domestic political forces that helped constrain and shape Japan's military role in the alliance, and Japan's attempt to satisfy American pressure for greater armament while maintaining some autonomy from its American partner. Even when the regional consequences of the relationship were discussed, they were usually examined in terms of contributions to American postwar foreign policy and military goals.

The third stream was the literature on each country's foreign policy. There the United States was treated as a major component of Japan's foreign policy and at least customary lip service was paid to the importance of the bilateral relationship as part of American global strategy.[6] Such works usually emphasized either a one-sided view of the relationship or a strictly bilateral one. The United States was taken to be the driving focus of Japan's foreign policy while Japan was seen as one of the key Pacific spokes in the bilateral "hub-and-spoke" alliance strategy of the United States. Even the burgeoning literature on Japan's economic relations and foreign policy toward Asia[7] rarely considered in depth the consequences of these trends for the U.S.-Japan relationship.

Thus, the economic, alliance, and foreign policy literatures, as well as the literature on regionalism and Japan's Asian relations, have all tended to move forward on separate tracks; but in dealing with the relationship, the vast majority share the approach of bilateralism. Such an approach made eminent sense when the relationship and its consequences were indeed primarily bilateral. Yet despite what we believe are strikingly new conditions, bilateralism has continued to characterize even the best of the most recent studies of U.S.-Japan relations.[8] The focus and consequences of the relationship continue to be observed primarily within an analytical "cocoon" of bilateralism, and each country's influence on the other is treated as the primary "independent variable." When external, multilateral events impinge on the relationship, they are seen as punctuations in the more prevalent bilateral equilibrium. When multilateral trends and new directions in Japan's foreign policy are analyzed, they are rarely related back to their impact on the U.S.-Japan relationship. The result has been a failure to explore systematically, or in many cases even to note, how the relationship has been and is being fundamentally transformed by the three major trends noted earlier.

In contrast, this volume explicitly embeds the relationship within a broader global and regional context. It is our contention that the new "equilibrium" in U.S.-Japan relations is increasingly multilateral and no longer bilateral, although to different degrees in different issue areas. We demonstrate how changes in international security and economics along with the rise of regional multilateral institutions have fundamentally reconfigured the previously bilateral U.S.-Japan relationship. Most especially we show how this reconfiguration has put new pressures on, and created new problems for, policymakers in both countries.

These changes create more than problems, however. They also provide both countries with new policy contexts as well as with new tools for advancing their respective interests. They thus present new opportunities along with the new challenges. We evaluate these changes across the financial, trade, and security realms, and examine as well their important consequences for the region. We believe that in all three of these areas the book breaks important new ground in the examination of U.S.-Japan ties.

The rest of this chapter analyzes the forces that have been changing the relationship for more than a decade, but first it outlines the character and management of the bilateral relationship for roughly the first three and a half decades after the American occupation (1945–52). This background serves as a comparative touchstone for recent patterns of interaction. The chapter then explores the three fundamental changes that have transformed the context of that interaction. Finally, the chapter anticipates some of the volume's key conclusions. Both here and in the concluding chapter, specific findings from the contributors' chapters provide illustrative examples.

The Bilateral Relationship

Prior to the last decade and a half, on which this volume concentrates, bilateralism permeated both the character of the U.S.-Japan relationship and the process by which it was managed and maintained. This section examines both of these dimensions and maps the previously bilateral character of U.S.-Japan relations that we contend no longer prevails.

The Character of the Relationship

Bilateralism means that two countries, in this case Japan and the United States, cede particular privileges to one another that they do not give to other countries. Bilateralism also involves the normative belief among policymakers from both countries that dealings between them on most issues should be primarily dealt with through one-to-one governmental links; they should not generally involve the private sector, nor should they be settled in multilateral arenas. At its most basic level, bilateralism in U.S.-Japan relations was characterized by several specific features. First, in most matters of foreign affairs the two countries shared a common and distinctive set of priorities. Without surrendering their particular national objectives, the two nations typically pursued broadly compatible objectives in international and regional affairs. Second, a set of clear and well-defined bilateral institutional mechanisms existed for negotiations about key issues in the relationship. Third, although changes on this point began to appear as early as the 1970s, for the most part the relationship was characterized by what could be thought of as a "non-linkage rule." Both sides avoided mixing negotiations on different kinds of issues. In particular, the economic and security dimensions of the relationship were kept independent of one another. Fourth, although they generally worked toward common goals, the two sides were by no means equal in the resources they could muster toward achieving them. An unmistakable structural asymmetry prevailed. The United States was the more powerful senior partner and Japan was the weaker junior partner.

In terms of priorities, from at least the end of the U.S. occupation, Japan and the United States were in basic accord in their quest for several key objectives. Most fundamentally, the two shared the same side in the bipolar international arena, including an unmistakable commitment to the military containment of Soviet Union, China, and other Communist regimes in Asia. Their bipolar ties were most formally expressed in the U.S.-Japan Security Treaty initially effected in 1951 and then revised in 1960. The treaty was the starting point for both countries in their security dealings. Bilateralism also played out in the hub-and-spoke alliance structures built by the United States across Asia. Closely linked to this military goal was the embrace of intimate economic relations between the two countries even as both pursued their own distinctive but compatible versions of capitalism. In a related vein, the countries were similar in their sharing and seeking to maintain (admittedly imperfect) democratic political systems domestically and occasionally elsewhere.

Nowhere was agreement on goals clearer than in the military sphere. In the bipolar world that prevailed until the collapse of the Soviet Union in 1989, Japan was America's single most important anti-Communist ally in Asia. The country was integral to what Cumings has described as America's grand crescent of Communist containment—military bases that stretched south from the Aleutian Islands through Japan, South Korea, Taiwan, and the Philippines and on to Southeast Asia, ending in New Zealand and Australia.[9] Fundamental to the bargain was the U.S.-Japan alliance built first around the San Francisco Peace Treaty and the U.S.-Japan Security Treaty that went into effect immediately after the end of the U.S. occupation in 1952, and later around the renegotiated version of that treaty that has been in effect since 1960.[10] Marking these and other alliance documents throughout the postwar period was Japan's unquestionable reliance on U.S. military force, including the so-called nuclear umbrella, as the primary component of its own defense policies, combined with the unchallenged role that Japan played as America's foremost ally in Asia. This included quite explicitly the stationing of large numbers of American troops on Japanese soil from the end of the occupation in 1952 until today. Japan served as what Prime Minister Nakasone frequently referred to as an "unsinkable aircraft carrier" off the coast of Asia. Japan had no military alliance arrangements with any country other than the United States, and although the United States had numerous alliances throughout the world, in Asia all of its alliances were based on bilateral ties rather than on multimember alliance structures such as the North Atlantic Treaty Organisation (NATO). The single most important of these alliances was with Japan.

These defense ties were part of the larger bilateral bargain that Ikenberry describes in his contribution to this volume: "The United States would provide Japan and other countries with security protection and access to American markets, technology, and supplies within an open world economy. In return, Japan and other countries in the region would become stable partners who would provide diplomatic, economic, and logistical support for the United States as it led the wider American-centered, anti-Communist postwar order."[11]

Predicated on these American guarantees of its security as well as access to U.S. markets, Japan pursued a systematic strategy of rapid economic development at home and a low posture abroad in areas both diplomatic and military. The result came to be known as the "Yoshida Doctrine."[12] Its economic focus was most explicitly articulated by Prime Minister Ikeda's 1960 plan to double the national income and was clearly manifested in Japanese gross national product (GNP) growth rates, which from 1952 until 1990 were typically double that of the other Organisation for Economic Development (OECD) countries.

Without question, Japanese and American approaches to capitalism were characterized by numerous important differences. Most notably, the United States was far more laissez-faire than Japan, which in turn embraced policies that elsewhere have been labeled "embedded mercantilism."[13] Despite such differences, however, Japan and the United States were closely aligned as unmistakable advocates of private ownership, limited government, and a selective mixture of market mechanisms and oligopoly in contrast to the Communist bloc. From direct economic assistance in the early postwar years and continuing on to a disproportionately low-value yen, low-cost technology transfers, and a disproportionately open market for Japanese exports through much of the 1970s and into the 1980s, the United States provided Japan with widespread economic assistance. This was all calculated to assist Japan in becoming an economic success story that could be projected as a model for much of the rest of Asian development.

Japan was marked by a deep-seated pacifism and by official rejection of an enhanced and active role for its own military forces. Policymakers sought to demonstrate Japan's broad commitment to U.S. aims while at the same time doing little to redirect resources from civilian to military spending and resisting any rapid shift toward a more active and strategic use of its military force as an instrument of foreign policy.[14] The United States in turn concentrated on keeping Japanese policies compatible with U.S. aims while at the same time systematically encouraging Japan to expand its military spending and to take a more active (albeit far from independent) military posture. With its low defense budget and concentration on economic growth, Japan left it to the United States to take the lead on most issues of foreign policy, willingly adding its support to the broad direction of U.S. policy actions as requested and needed, as long as such support required little overt military activity by Japan.[15]

Finally, and not to be forgotten in the global context, Japan and the United States shared democratic political systems at home. Each system had its flaws and shortcomings.[16] Still, as is becoming increasingly clear, democracies rarely if ever go to war with one another. As Nau has phrased it, their common domestic political systems meant that the "United States and Japan form an incipient democratic security community in Asia. . . . "[17]

Beyond shared goals, the bilateral institutional mechanisms established for management of the relationship formed another important feature of the relations between the two countries, which were defined primarily in diplomatic and governmental terms. Relatedly, the specific agencies in both governments that were charged with analyzing and managing the relationship were those whose principal responsibilities involved the other country. The executive branches in both countries dominated this process—in the United States it was primarily the Department of State, the Department of Defense, and later the U.S. Trade Representative (USTR); in Japan, it was the Ministries of Foreign Affairs (MOFA), the Ministry of International Trade and Industry (MITI), the Ministry of Finance (MOF), and periodically the Japan Defense Agency (JDA).[18] Broadly speaking, the bilateral trajectory was defined almost exclusively by the interactions of these agencies and their leaders. Rarely did actors other than the two governments' official agencies exert more than marginal influence over policymaking. Particularly limited in their influence were Japanese parliamentarians, but so for the most part were American congressional representatives.

Most important, these institutions were distinctively not multilateral, in contrast to the institutions that were structuring relations between the United States and its Western European allies during the same period. America's European allies were embedded in a series of multilateral organizations, including NATO, the European Coal and Steel Community, and eventually the European Union (EU). At the core of such policies were American, British, and French efforts to enmesh Germany in a series of linkages with its immediate neighbors so as to preclude the reemergence of the combustible national brittleness that had catalyzed the two world wars.[19] These multilateral organizations gave the various European allies a series of formats within which to forge temporary alliances on specific issues or bundle issues and engage in trade-offs from one issue to another. Sometimes this meant agreement with, but sometimes opposition to, the United States. From the very start the major institutions that managed U.S.-European relations were unambiguously multilateral. In contrast, those that dealt with relations between the United States and Japan were categorically bilateral—Asian countries allied with the United States, including Japan, were connected not to one another but through separate spokes back to the hub in Washington.

A third feature of the bilateral relationship involved the functional separation of issues, particularly those of security and economics. Perhaps the most overt articulation of this orientation came with Japanese Prime Minister Ikeda's explicit policy of "separating economics from politics," articulated in the aftermath of the 1960 Security Treaty crisis. For Ikeda, and for subsequent conservative governments, it was critical that any popular Japanese frustrations with the military aspects of the treaty not interfere with the country's focus on high-speed growth. The U.S. defense and foreign policy establishments correspondingly did their best to keep issues of economics subordinate to those of security.

Institutional arrangements facilitated this separation. In effect, institutions devoted to military problems did not deal with trade organizations, and monetary issues were dealt with along another, separate track. Similarly separated were environmental, cultural, and foreign aid organizations. Functionally specific agencies in both countries worked with their counterparts on matters within their joint domains relatively independently of agencies dealing with issues in other areas. On the relatively rare occasions when broader coordination was necessary, the White House or the prime minister's office became the fulcrum on which the relationship hinged. But multiple issues rarely became part of any common package of discussions. Additionally, no multilateral alliance structures or regional institutions existed to complicate these bilateral and functionally specific interactions.

The fourth and final characteristic of the bilateral relationship was its structural asymmetry. As one of the world's two superpowers, the United States possessed vastly more military and economic resources than did Japan. Moreover, the United States pursued its foreign policy goals globally, while for the most part Japan, even after its GNP became the second largest in the world, remained at best a regional power. In the bilateral relationship, Japan was typically dependent on the United States and locked into a complex and embedded relationship. For example, inequality in security was demonstrated by the fact that the United States typically spent five to six times more than Japan did on its military budget. Despite polite fictions about joint consultation, the United States had a relatively free hand in the use of its troops in Asia. Moreover, the United States was committed to defending Japan despite the fact that Japan had no reciprocal responsibility to defend the United States. Article 9 of the Japanese Constitution was consistently interpreted to restrict military expenditures for most of the postwar years at below 1 percent of GNP. It also constricted actions by Japan's Self-Defense Forces, which, as Hughes and Fukushima point out in their contribution to this volume, concentrated on Article 5 of the Security Treaty, stressing the treaty's role in ensuring the defense of the Japanese homeland. Japan also signed the Nuclear Non-Proliferation Treaty and endorsed the so-called Three Non-Nuclear Principles, marking the country as a clear contrast to the hypernuclearized United States. A final measure of Japan's military ties to, and dependence on, the United States can be found in arms sales. As Samuels has summarized it, "In the 1970s and 1980s, the United States transferred more weapons to Japan than to any other ally except Germany. But these transfers were not sales of finished products. To the contrary, Japanese defense contractors licensed and co-produced twenty-nine major U.S. weapons systems, more than any nation in the world."[20] Japan's self-defined role as a non-nuclear, nonbelligerent, low-posture military power, however, left it highly dependent on the United States for its own security.

Economic relations between the two nations were also bilateral and unequal. The United States was Japan's most important trade partner throughout the postwar years. In 1960, 35 percent of Japan's imports came from the United States. The United States has also remained Japan's largest single export market, typically accepting between one-quarter and one-third of all of Japan's exports.[21] Most striking is that into the early 1990s, Japan's number two export market (usually Germany or South Korea) rarely received more than one-forth or one-fifth of the amounts sent by Japan to the United States. This represented a level of singular dependence on one national market much more akin to the dependence of the former Eastern European satellites on the U.S.S.R. than to the ties among the other industrialized democracies.

Important as imports from the United States were to Japan, the Japanese market represented a far smaller proportion of U.S. trade. Japan rarely received more than 8 percent of U.S. exports, and even at its high point in 1990, Japanese imports constituted only 14 percent of the total of U.S. imports.

In a similar vein, Japanese outgoing foreign direct investment (FDI), which was largely insignificant until the early 1970s, also went disproportionately to the United States in the years that followed. Thus, in the early 1990s somewhat more than 20 percent of incoming U.S. FDI came from Japan, making the country one of America's largest investors.[22] At the same time, however, U.S. FDI into Japan was as high as 57 percent of Japan's total incoming FDI in 1989 and reached 60 percent in 1998.[23]

One of the most blatant examples of the economic inequality between the two countries came in their two governments' official reactions to trade problems. U.S. trade policy initiatives toward Japan, including dumping cases, numbered in the hundreds during the postwar period. Japan in turn, despite numerous protectionist provocations from the United States, never challenged such practices officially. Nor did Japan impose any antidumping penalties on American-made goods, even though such provisions are part of Japanese law.

Problems and Their Management

Bilateralism characterized the resolution of problems between the two countries. Again, country-to-country ties prevailed. Despite broad agreement on major goals, the relationship, not surprisingly, encountered a series of problems. For the most part, these were managed largely by mid-level bureaucrats on both sides of the Pacific. Solutions were typically the outgrowth of functionally specific arrangements that kept issues unlinked and allowed specific bargains to be struck on an ad hoc basis. Also, following virtually any such specific bargain, as well as during moments of external crisis affecting either country, the two governments would go through a ritualistic exchange of highly publicized reassurances about their overarching and unaltered commitments to one another.

For the most part, regardless of how messy the security relationship may have appeared at times, in relative terms and in retrospect such affairs remained under the rather tight supervision of civilian and military bureaucrats in both countries; only rarely did they involve the chief executives of the two countries, except for symbolic ratification of decisions made at lower levels. Equally important, on few occasions did problem resolution involve nongovernmental actors[24] or other states. Rather, a network of connectors ran from one country's government to that of the other. Nonmilitary, nongovernmental, and extranational influences over the military relationship were minimal.[25]

Problems in economics were more frequent than those in security and became even more nettlesome as the economic goals and strengths of the two countries began to diverge. Yet as such economic problems arose, military officials from both countries were particularly keen to ensure that economics not be allowed to undermine the bilateral security ties. The high priority given to the maintenance of close military ties allowed for the continuation of an increasingly asymmetrical economic relationship in which Japan exported far more heavily to the (relatively) open markets of the United States than the United States did to the substantially more closed markets of Japan. Only when the United States began to experience domestic economic problems did its officials begin to press Japan to alter its economic policies.

The key turning point came in the early 1970s when, for the first time in the twentieth century, the U.S. current account went deeper and deeper into the red, turning the country from the world's largest creditor nation to its largest debtor. Conversely, Japan began to experience a major shift in its international balance of payments, which peaked in 1993 at nearly $132 billion.[26] The overall trade balances of the two countries—but more importantly their bilateral trade balances—reflected this shift. Throughout the 1970s and 1980s, the size of the Japanese bilateral trade surplus with the United States was a continually reported statistic in America. No single country accounted for more of the perceived imbalance in U.S. trade than Japan, making this a key issue for alliance management.

In most such instances, the solution was bilaterally governmental, despite the more general predisposition of the U.S. government to deal with trade issues in multilateral forums such as the General Agreement on Tariffs and Trade (GATT). In U.S.-Japan trade disputes, officials from the two countries could typically cut a deal that would resolve the discord, usually at the expense of domestic industries or consumers in one country or the other. Crises were at least temporarily "managed," regardless of how dissatisfied one side or both sides felt with the outcome. This was the pattern in a host of trade disputes between Japan and the United States, including the painful "textile wrangle" of the early 1970s,[27] the so-called voluntary export restraints (VER) imposed in 1981 on Japanese automobile exports to the United States, stringent bargaining on citrus fruits and beef,[28] the MOSS (market-oriented, sector specific) talks, the Semiconductor Agreement in the mid- to late 1980s, and the SII (Structural Impediments Initiative) negotiations of 1989–90. In all of these cases, government-to-government bargaining was the critical driver in the process of resolution, while security issues were largely kept off the negotiation table.

The two governments' management of bilateral relations was also in evidence during the reconfiguring of international exchange rates in 1971, 1985, and 1987.[29] It was prominent in the coordination of foreign aid policies by both countries, in many joint macroeconomic manipulations, and in mutual government efforts to encourage foreign direct investment in the United States by Japanese auto and electronics companies, among other issues. Not until the summit meeting between Prime Minister Hosokawa and President Clinton in February 1994 did the two governments clearly and publicly fail to reach an accommodation on a critical economic matter. At that time, Hosokawa publicly refused to accede to U.S. demands for what Japan claimed were numerical quotas on autos and auto parts, and negotiations failed.

Throughout most of the postwar period, a close and multifaceted relationship was thus forged and fostered. It has lasted for more than fifty years, the longest bilateral relationship in modern history and one that former ambassador to Japan Mike Mansfield frequently characterized as the most important bilateral relationship in the world, bar none. Nevertheless, by the late 1980s and early 1990s, as subsequent sections of this chapter demonstrate, the relationship ran headlong into three complicating challenges that have altered its underlying character and supplied new contexts, pressures, and opportunities for the methods of its management. The first of these changes involved the radical alteration of the global security climate.

Changes in the Security Climate

Bilateralism was based on an Asia-Pacific in which the security tableau was starkly clear. Friends and enemies were easily identifiable; ambiguities were few. Moreover, Japan was far and away the richest and most industrially developed democracy in Asia, making it a necessary and logical starting point for U.S. policies in the region.

The bilateral character of the U.S.-Japan relationship has been seriously challenged by alterations in the security climate in the Asia-Pacific. Without a doubt, some of Asia's long-standing trouble spots, most notably the Korean Peninsula and the Taiwan Straits, remain mired in the vestiges of the Cold War. But the changes since then are far more striking than the continuities. Four demand particular attention. First, the Cold War has ended in most parts of the world, along with the overt threat of nuclear war but also with the bipolar clarity that allowed the United States and its allies to demarcate friend and foe. Second, numerous countries in Asia have achieved considerable levels of economic development, and several—most particularly South Korea and Taiwan, and to some extent Thailand, the Philippines, and Malaysia—have become more politically democratic than they were before. A third important change concerns China, which has enjoyed extensive economic growth while at the same time expanding its military spending geometrically, giving it a vastly more complex role in the region than it has enjoyed for many decades. Finally, the Asia-Pacific has been dramatically reshaped by the events of September 11, 2001 and the growing problems of international rogue states and organized nonstate terror. In combination, these forces have restructured the bilateral nature of the U.S.-Japan relationship.

As late as 1985, the Japanese Defense White Paper spelled out what that government saw as the three major goals of its security arrangements with the United States: (1) establish an airtight defense posture, (2) deter invasions, and (3) contribute to international peace and security in the Far East.[30] The probability that the alliance would be needed for either of the first two goals declined dramatically as the Soviet Union and its Eastern European alliance structure collapsed from within. The Soviet Union had always been treated by both the United States and Japan as the most probable source of any external military threat to Japan. As the world entered the twenty-first century, however, Russia had become a pale military and economic successor to the U.S.S.R. Several of its Eastern European allies in the Warsaw Pact had joined NATO. Russia had become a member of the Group of Eight (G8) and had at least a nominally democratic domestic regime. The Northern Territories issue between Russia and

Japan remained unresolved. But only the most paranoid would consider a Russian military threat to, let alone an invasion of, Japan to be remotely plausible in the medium-to-short term.

Simultaneously, as the sharp lines of Cold War conflict have been blurred, there has been a rapid rise in the number and importance of intrastate conflicts, particularly those involving religious or ethnic splits and failed states. Rwanda, Congo, the Balkans, Sierra Leone, and Sri Lanka are but a few of the more prominent cases. Within the East Asia region, Cambodia and East Timor saw major intrastate military confrontations; separatist movements in the Philippines, Indonesia, and the Central Asian Republics posed similar threats. None of these were easily subject to solution through traditional alliances such as that between Japan and the United States. Far more important have been United Nations (UN) peacekeeping operations. Of a total of fifty-five such missions throughout the postwar period, fully forty-two were begun since 1989. Both Japan and the United States have shifted elements of their military and strategic thinking to be more responsive to these new forms of conflict.

Furthermore, with the increased economic well-being and democratization of several other Asian powers, Japan was no longer the sole outpost of industrialization and democratization in the region. Rather, the regional ground was fertile for the expanded development of a broader economic and security community in Asia that was not wedded to the past structures of bilateralism and that did not require Japan to be the automatic starting point for action. The economic implications of these changes are explored more fully in the next section as well as in several chapters linked to the implications of the rise in global finance. The security community, meanwhile, has been developing through a variety of new multilateral forums such as the ASEAN Regional Forum (ARF) and through the rising number of Track II dialogues that sought to take up difficult issues in nonofficial forums and to encourage the collective pursuit of confidence-building measures. As shown by Ashizawa as well as by Hughes and Fukushima in their respective chapters in this volume, such processes have, along with economic integration, contributed significantly to the reduction of military tensions across the Asia-Pacific. Both processes have substantially reshaped earlier bilateralism. They are explored more fully in the two sections that follow.

China has also changed, but in ways that give it a highly ambiguous character in the region and much more influence over the U.S.-Japan relationship, as well as over developments in the region. On the one hand, open rivalry between China and the U.S.S.R. had long ago created a rift within the previous Communist alliance, which was so critical to the early postwar bipolarity. Subsequent clashes between China and Vietnam made it even clearer that national interests and traditional territorial disputes drove actions by these governments at least as powerfully as any presumed commitment to some purportedly overarching Communist strategy. Following this split, any notion of a bipolar Asia—with the Soviet Union and China on a common side—was difficult to sustain.

Even more complicating, China subsequently changed domestically and economically. From the consolidation of Communist control in 1949 through the Great Leap Forward in 1958–60 and the Great Proletarian Cultural Revolution in 1965, the People's Republic of China (PRC) was mired in ideologically driven disasters that left it falling economically further and further behind many of its neighbors, as well as enhanced its image as a potential regional destabilizer. Once the United States and Japan normalized their diplomatic ties with China, the latter began to undergo a major change in its domestic and strategic policies. China's leaders began the tentative embrace of more pro-Western and capitalist-friendly policies, contributing to an improved regional security climate and opening the way to a host of previously implausible diplomatic and economic ties between China and its non-Communist neighbors. China also normalized relations with Indonesia, Singapore, and South Korea. It also opened parts of its territory to regional and worldwide investment and trade, further reducing the perception of China as a direct military threat, particularly to Japan but also, with the undeniable exception of Taiwan, to most of the rest of Asia. In all of these ways, Chinese actions reduced the probability that China would continue to pose a military threat to both Japan and the United States, making it less likely to need "containment." Instead, as Mochizuki's analysis in Chapter 3 of this volume makes clear, China began to emerge as a potentially beneficial trade partner and market for both countries. National differences among Japan, China, and the United States have hardly disappeared, and many American and Japanese strategic planners still anticipate that China will eventually become a territorial rival to either Japan or the United States or to both. Yet the old images of a militarily hostile China have given way to far greater ambiguities. Indeed, to the extent that it has been willing to do so, the United States and Japan have encouraged China to mediate in other Asian trouble spots where it has influence, most notably with North Korea, as well as to help reduce Islamic terrorism and halt arms exports to other potential trouble spots in the Middle East and Central Asia.

Yet the China picture is more complicated. China has been proactive in much of its regional diplomacy. It built up its neighborhood ties through the Shanghai Cooperative Organization (SCO), which linked China, Russia, and four Central Asian states. China also signed a Friendship Treaty with Russia in 2001 and engaged in summit exchanges with North Korea during the same year. Such moves, combined with the increased economic prowess of China, have challenged the automatic presumption of Japan's leadership in Asia. Japanese concerns were enhanced by the American warming toward China and its SCO allies as a result of the U.S. post-September 11 antiterrorism campaign, as well as by China's willingness to utilize the antiterrorism label to justify actions against domestic dissidents. Such moves improved Chinese political and security ties with the United States at the potential expense of Japan. Even more worrisome has been the growth in China's defense budget, which has increased by double digits every year since 1988, amounting to some 200 percent over the fourteen-year period, including 55 percent since 1998.[31]

Japanese concerns about China clearly had their military and diplomatic dimensions, but anxiety about a stronger and more diplomatically active China also grew out of economics. First, both U.S. and Japanese policymakers have begun to express concern about China's rapid economic liberalization and growth, which could make it a potential security rival and economic threat. Second, as Mike Mochizuki's chapter in this volume makes clear, President Clinton's policy of "strategic engagement" with China, along with his separation of human rights and trade issues and increased U.S. investments in China, paralleled by the United States' diminished economic interest in Japan, combined to raise another kind of worry among Japanese policymakers, namely that of "Japan passing." This clichéd phrase grew out of Tokyo's perceptions that for a host of reasons the United States no longer felt any particular necessity to approach Asia through Japan; it could instead deal directly with other Asian countries, most particularly China, whether diplomatically or economically.

In addition, increasing numbers of Japanese high-tech companies began to invest heavily in both the engineering and design of products within China, taking advantage not only of that country's unskilled workforce but also of its talented workers. Such moves became the source of escalating fears about the further hollowing out of Japan's manufacturing capabilities, as well as the possibility that sophisticated Japanese technologies would quickly find their way into Chinese civilian and military products. China's entry into the World Trade Organization (WTO) early in 2002 and its growing integration into the world economy heightened Japanese fears. Rapid economic growth by China thus became not only an opportunity but also a threat to Japan. As Gilbert Rozman has put it, "As the 1990s began, China overtook the former Soviet Union as Japan's most significant other after the United States."[32]

China poses equally complex problems for American policies. Throughout the bulk of the 1990s, the United States encouraged China's economic

growth as a probable prelude to increased democratization and civil liber-
ties. At the same time, however, strong voices in the Congress, in various
nongovernmental organizations (NGOs), and particularly within the Bush
administration have been critical of China as a potential military threat,
particularly to Taiwan, as well as a political human rights repressor at
home. Just as in Japan, so in America: as China's economy has grown, so
have worries about its rising capability for military expenditure. Similarly,
Chinese exports to the United States have now begun to outstrip those
from Japan, giving rise to additional macroeconomic concerns.

The Bush administration, following what many have labeled its ABC
(anything but Clinton) policies, initially took a hard line against China
and a more favorable line toward Japan. In particular, arms sales to Taiwan were exceptionally liberalized and the American commitment to defend Taiwan in the event of a Chinese attack was strongly articulated.
While maintaining firmness during the crisis over an American spy plane
colliding with a Chinese fighter plane and landing on Hainan Island,
however, the Bush administration also demonstrated patience and the desire not to provoke China further to avoid worsening the confrontation.
Further, in the wake of its war on terrorism, the United States has downplayed earlier concerns about both Chinese domestic politics and China's
military buildup, and simultaneously accepted China's definition of the
separatist East Turkestan Islamic movement in western Xinjiang as a terrorist group.

For the three countries, the relationship has clearly become trilateral, as
Mochizuki's analysis in Chapter 3 shows. U.S. unilateralism pushes Japan
and China closer together, while any warming of ties between either Japan
or China on the one hand and the United States on the other forces a recalibration of interests by the party left out. Japan fears that closer U.S.
ties to China may come at Japan's expense. Japan-China ties remain the
triangle's weakest link, but American policymakers have long worried that
closer links between those two countries would come at the expense of
American influence in Asia. And as China grows economically, some people in Japan feel similarly threatened, despite the short-term profitability
to many Japanese corporations derived from investment in and trade with
China. Thus, the recent "mushroom war" between the two countries that
Pekkanen describes in her chapter in this volume may be only a precursor
of future Japan-China trade tensions.

U.S.-Japan relations have also become more complicated because of
changes on the Korean Peninsula. On the one hand, China's normalization
of relations with South Korea undermined China's unquestioned support
for North Korea. The Democratic People's Republic of Korea (DPRK)

continued to be treated by Japan, the United States, and South Korea as a potentially problematic regime, but the three have differed substantially on how best to deal with the regime. North Korea's independent nuclear weapons capabilities were checked in March 1995 with the creation of the Korean Energy Development Organization (KEDO), thereby preventing a likely military confrontation between the United States and North Korea. Involving as it did Japan, the United States, South Korea, and recently as well the EU, the KEDO seems an excellent example of one way in which U.S. and Japanese policymakers have moved beyond bilateralism. Indeed, in the subsequent nuclear crisis of 2002–03, even the United States was pressing for a multilateral rather than a bilateral approach to the problem.

Also important have been agreements between Japan and South Korea. In 1994, a defense policy dialogue was established as a byproduct of previous trilateral meetings among Japan, the United States, and the Republic of Korea. The dialogue was then broadened in 1998. Military-to-military contacts have since burgeoned, with mutual port visits beginning in 1994, the establishment of a ROKAF-JASDF hotline in 1995, the launching of joint search-and-rescue exercises in 1999, and other measures. Such changes also take Japanese security activities beyond bilateralism.

As Ikenberry makes clear in Chapter 1 of this volume, the Bush administration is internally divided over how best to weave Asia into its overall liberal grand strategy. One side (gathered around the State Department and Colin Powell) prefers pragmatic engagement; the other side (gathered around Vice President Richard Cheney and Secretary of Defense Donald Rumsfeld) favors an aggressive unilateralism that is deeply skeptical about operating within a rule-based international order. The Bush administration's efforts to paint North Korea as part of an international "axis of evil" derailed the "Sunshine Policy" of South Korean President Kim Dae-jung and soured relations between the United States and South Korea as well as with Japan, a strong supporter of Kim's approach. Relations with Kim's successor, Roh Moo-hyun, were somewhat of an improvement, but the two countries are clearly pursuing differently calibrated moves toward the DPRK. Meanwhile, U.S. actions toward North Korea have also challenged Japan's long-standing efforts to facilitate closer ties between the two Koreas and have added fuel to debates in Asia about the impending pressures to introduce missile defense systems in Japan and Taiwan. The differences in approach between Japan and the United States toward the DPRK remained particularly sharp in September 2002, when President Bush rearticulated his condemnation of Kim Il Sung and the North at about the same time that Japanese Prime Minister Koizumi was making an official state visit to the DPRK and attempting to normalize relations. Clearly, Korean issues, such as those connected to China, transcend earlier

U.S.-Japan bilateralism, and as of this writing it is clear that the two countries see the DPRK regime through very different lenses.

Also important in changing the relationship has been America's emerging military doctrine. As a presidential candidate, George W. Bush promised a rethinking of U.S. military commitments abroad and a revolution in military affairs that would include skipping a generation of weapons systems to concentrate on more advanced systems such as missile defense. By 2002, the number of U.S. troops stationed abroad was down to 250,000, with approximately 100,000 in the Asia-Pacific. The United States in 1995 and then again in May 1997 committed itself to maintaining that 100,000 figure. But clearly the general trend was for a diminution of total U.S. military forces in Asia. By 2002, however, U.S. military expenditures were rising rapidly. Not counting emergency funds for the Afghan war and later for the Iraq war, the U.S. defense budget jumped by $20 billion between 2001 and 2002. By that time the United States was spending more for its military than the next twenty largest military spending nations combined.

This U.S. military buildup, along with the explicit actions designed to isolate the DPRK, has put pressure on Japan to shift its own security and defense policies. Among other things, and in dramatic contrast to the slowness with which Japan acted during the Persian Gulf War a decade earlier, Japan reacted quickly to American demands for assistance in the war on terrorism. It quickly passed the Anti-Terrorism Special Measures Law and acceded to U.S. requests to dispatch Japanese warships to the Indian Ocean in conjunction with American military actions against the Taliban. Hughes and Fukushima's chapter in this volume examines these measures in considerable detail and shows the ways in which they restructured the relationship.

The September 11 attacks changed American thinking concerning terrorism, nonstate military threats, and asymmetrical warfare. Japan went through a similar rethinking following the domestic terrorist attack by Aum Shinrikyō using sarin gas[33] and the 1997 hostage-taking in Peru. For both the United States and Japan, such events have combined to make clear the limitations of conventional military alliances and of a singular focus on traditional state-to-state conflicts. Both Japan and the United States have consequently broadened their notions of security and have taken actions to cope with such threats in Asia in ways that have little to do with their formal bilateral alliance.[34] But their reactions to such threats have been quite different.

Thus, despite the growing importance of economic ties in Asia, military force and security problems have by no means been eradicated from the region; numerous serious flash points remain. At the same time, the

bipolarity and the pervasive military threats that for a long time were the
rationale for the formation of the U.S.-Japan Security Treaty have given
way to a substantially more complex climate in the region. Asia now represents not a bipolar map defined largely by armies and alliances but
rather a vastly more complex tableau marked by residual territorial
claims, intensified national concerns over economic as well as military security, a region in which military issues are no longer defined in clearly
bipolar terms, and a region with far more multipolarity than at any other
time in the last hundred years. In Mochizuki's phrasing in Chapter 3 of
this volume, U.S-Japan relations have developed a far more complex mix
of "competitive and cooperative bilateralism."

Escalating Global Capital Flows

In the early years of the two countries' bilateral ties, economic relations
between the United States and Japan were largely compatible and remained heavily under national governmental control. Since the early
1980s, there has been an explosive increase in the amount of capital that
moves across national borders. As is now widely reported, between $1.2
and $2 trillion in capital crossed national borders on a typical day in
2002, compared to a daily turnover of $590 billion in 1989, and this fig-
ure was expanding geometrically. In 1998, trading and derivative activities
of seventy-one of the world's leading banks and securities firms reached a
total of more than $130 trillion.[35] Capital flows are now roughly seventy
times larger than the amounts involved in trade flows. Cross-national capital flows now represent by the far the most consistent and pervasive
transnational economic interactions. Such money moves far more often
with a computer key click than physically as pieces of official script. By far
the largest proportion of these capital movements is private rather than
governmental. These monumental amounts compromise the powers of national governments to shape monetary policies.
    Such high volumes of fast-moving money have affected the previously
bilateral relationship between the United States and Japan in at least two
critical ways. First and most important, they have altered the balance between governments and the private sector when it comes to monetary
transactions. In 1983, five major central banks (in the United States, Germany, Japan, Britain, and Switzerland) held $139 billion in foreign-ex-
change reserves, whereas the average daily turnover in the major foreign-
exchange markets was $39 billion. The combined firepower of these
governments dwarfed the marketplace by more than three to one. By
1986, the official foreign-exchange reserves were about equal to daily

trading in foreign-exchange markets. By 1998, the balance of power was reversed. The major central banks had $278 billion in reserves against $1.8 trillion in daily trading activity. Private markets had gained a four to one advantage over the central banks.[36]

These shifts have enhanced the autonomy that private sector actors now have over the use of their capital. As Cohen phrased it, " . . . the key is the wider range of options that comes to more privileged elements of the private sector with the globalization of financial activity. For societal actors who can take advantage of the opportunities afforded by market integration, capital mobility means more degrees of freedom—more room to maneuver in response to the actual or potential decisions of government."[37]

This expanding flow of private capital has had a major impact on both the Japanese and the American political economies, enhancing the choices of private capital holders, reducing government control, and reshaping the nature of the U.S.-Japan bilateral relationship. Most fundamental, it has made the Japanese economy far more regional than it was previously, while sparking a series of closer economic ties across the region. For the United States, such changes have meant an explosion of influence by investment banks, bond rating agencies, mutual fund managers, and multinational investors. These have begun to play an enhanced role in U.S.-Japan economic relations and in broader Asia-Pacific economic integration.

Until at least the late 1970s, Japan's capital markets and the Japanese currency had been heavily insulated from world capital markets; they were essentially "national" in character, reflecting Japan's system of "embedded mercantilism."[38] Enhanced internationalization of capital began with the breakdown in 1971 of the Bretton Woods system, ending the regime of fixed currency exchange rates linked to the U.S. dollar and ultimately to gold. This internationalization accelerated when Japanese financial markets were substantially liberalized, particularly with the revision of the Foreign Exchange and Control Law in 1980 and with deregulation of the corporate bond market. It became even greater following the efforts of the previously secret Group of Five (G5) finance ministers to coordinate monetary rates in the Plaza Accord of 1985 and the Louvre Accord of 1987. With Japan's "big bang" reforms in 1998, an even broader integration scrapped most of the barriers separating banks and brokerages in Japan while opening Japanese finance to waves of incoming global investment. Such global integration reduced the ability of Japanese government officials and the Bank of Japan to set exchange rates while vastly expanding the power of international markets and currency speculators, particularly those housed in the United States and Europe. This overall internationalization, combined with important liberalizations of the domestic currency regime, eroded many of the economic foundations that had previously underpinned "Japan, Inc." and expanded greatly the significance of global finance in U.S.-Japan relations.

As the yen appreciated in value, an outflow of Japanese capital followed, moving in two major directions—east toward the United States and south and west toward Asia. By the mid-1990s, individual Japanese companies and financial institutions had become free to issue overseas bonds in whatever was the most suitable currency, and then to swap the proceeds into yen. Japan had become the world market's major supplier of capital. By the late 1980s, Japanese banks dominated Eurobond underwriting, and Japan became the world's largest creditor nation. In 1996, the country had 16.7 percent of its gross domestic product (GDP), or $742 billion in net foreign assets.[39] Numerous Japanese firms, including many of their subcontractors, became more truly multinational in their manufacturing and distribution.

Some 40 percent of Japanese outward investment went to North America, principally the United States, but roughly one-quarter was targeted for the rest of Asia. Numerous Japanese firms, particularly in consumer electronics and automobile production, began an expanded, intra-industry division of labor throughout the Asian region. As Hatch and Yamamura have argued elsewhere, and as Hatch demonstrates for both autos and computers in his chapter in this volume, many Japanese companies regionalized their formerly national networks of production.[40]

Japanese investment expansion was phenomenal. By 1989, Japanese firms were investing four times as much money in Taiwan as they had in 1985, five times as much in Malaysia, five times as much in South Korea, six times as much in Singapore, fifteen times as much in Hong Kong, and twenty-five times as much in Thailand.[41] These trends continued into the 1990s, as Hamilton-Hart makes clear in her chapter in this book. Some $35 billion in Japanese investment went into Asia from 1992 to 1995. The consequent increase in regional economic integration was profound.

The result was a twofold shift in Japanese foreign economic policy. First, FDI and globalized production networks began to outweigh simple production and trade from Japan's home islands. Second, Asia gained importance within the corporate strategies of numerous Japanese-owned companies.

Although many Japanese-owned companies remained international export powerhouses, their products were no longer manufactured exclusively—or in some cases predominantly—within Japan. From 1990 to the first quarter of 1996, Japanese exports grew at the lowest rate in one twelve-country OECD survey. Conversely, Japanese imports grew by 41 percent, the third largest figure in the survey.[42] Even more symbolic, by

1995 Japan was manufacturing more overseas (¥41.2 trillion) than it was exporting from the home islands (¥39.6 trillion).[43]

Japanese financial institutions also stepped up their overseas operations during this period, expanding equities outflows, bond outflows, and short-term bank outflows.[44] Between 1991 and 1997, Japanese banks doubled the proportion of their overseas lending to Asia; by the late 1990s, they held 37 percent of Asia's private external liabilities. Hamilton-Hart explores this soaring role of Japanese bank lending across Asia in her chapter in this book.

All of these movements of Japanese money into Asia contributed to a bottom-up process of economic regionalization. The various national economies of Asia became increasingly interlinked with one another. Similarly, intra-Asian trade expanded considerably. Japanese exports to the rest of Asia rose from 25.7 percent in 1980 to 42.1 percent in 1995; by this time, for the first time in decades, Japanese exports to Asia were greater than those to the United States. ASEAN trade with the United States also gave way to intra-Asian trade. When the U.S. Congress eliminated General Special Preference (GSP) status for several ASEAN countries in 1991, East Asian newly industrializing economies (NIEs) and the ASEAN countries began to absorb one another's products. Between 1986 and 1992, for example, the intraregional share of exports from Asian countries increased from 31 percent to 43 percent while dependence on the U.S. market fell from 34 percent to 24 percent.[45] Finally, soaring Japanese trade with China helped Japan reach a different milestone: for the first time, Japanese imports from China and the rest of Asia (42 percent) as a percentage of total imports exceeded the value of purchases from North America and Europe (35 percent).[46] Japan's prior market dependence on the United States, once so critical to the bilateral relationship and to Japan's relative vulnerability to U.S. trade pressures, was being counterbalanced by Japanese trade with Asia. As a result of these and similar developments, by 1999 Asia had the second largest proportion of intraregional trade of the major regions of the world (see Figure 1.1).

As Ikenberry notes in his chapter in this volume and as Solingen has also argued,[47] the internationalization of the Japanese and Asian-Pacific economies through freer trade and enhanced capital movements, as well as through multilateral norms and policies, strengthened the position of internationally oriented sectors as well as internationally oriented elites who were supportive of greater integration and stable multilateral relations. It also made for a much more economically diverse region, where both the United States and Japan were major players, other Asian countries and "pan-Chinese" networks had an increasing and integrating role,[48] and even European banks and firms became active.

FIGURE I.I. Intraregional Trade as Percentage of Total, 2001

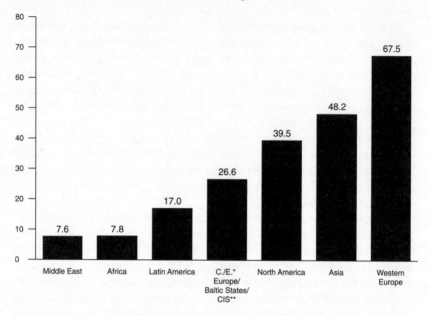

SOURCE: World Trade Organization, Intra- and Interregional Merchandise Trade (Washington, D.C.: WTO, 2001), http://www.wto.org/english/res_e/statis_e/its2002_e/section3_e/iii03.xls. Cited in Park, "Policy Ideas and Crisis." The author thanks Gene Park for providing the original data for this graph.
  *Central and Eastern Europe
  **Commonwealth of Independent States

The United States was quicker than Japan to respond domestically to global financial integration. Several steps were vital to this adjustment. Most important, U.S. corporations were quick to substitute the fast-moving, cheaper capital for slow-moving, expensive labor. The U.S. government simultaneously expanded tax incentives for investments in services. The result was a rocketing rise in service sector employment as U.S. manufacturing facilities moved abroad or closed down. In addition, the Federal Reserve Board, first under Paul Volker and then under Alan Greenspan, with strong support from a sequence of administrations, introduced exceptionally tight discipline over the American money supply, thereby reducing the country's double-digit inflation of the 1970s.[49] Subsequently, very rigid fiscal discipline under the first Bush and the Clinton administrations reversed the spiraling budget deficits and burgeoning national debt that had taken place under Reagan. The cumulative result was that by the mid-1990s, the U.S. government, along with American financial and manufacturing firms, had adjusted to global financial changes far more substantially and quickly than did their counterparts in the rest of the industrialized world.[50]

At least two important consequences of these changes in America were felt in U.S.-Japan relations. First, U.S. financial institutions, enjoying a substantial competitive edge over their Japanese competitors, pressed both the Japanese and U.S. governments for changes that would enhance their ability to compete in the Japanese market. The result has been a drumbeat of demands since the early 1990s for various adjustments in Japanese corporate, accounting, and financial practices, many of which have been strongly resisted by domestic Japanese political and corporate policymakers. For most of the last decade, and into the current one, bilateral and global financial issues gained substantial weight in relations between Japan and the United States, as trade and defense issues faded into the background.

A second major consequence of U.S. changes came in the form of increasingly mobile American capital. Much of this money flowed into the markets of developing Asia during the region's rapid expansion in the early and mid-1990s. A considerable portion was short-term "hot money" that flowed into equities and into foreign exchange speculation, further catalyzing growth and enhancing Asian regionalism. Equally important, however, this money was quick to flow out at the first signs of exchange rate instability; it was a major source of the currency and market collapses of several Asian countries in 1997–98.[51]

The cumulative result of both U.S. and Japanese adjustments to global capital pressures has been at least twofold. First, these adjustments have benefited the most dynamic sectors and economic well-being in both Japan and the United States. In doing so, however, a wedge has been driven between the most and least dynamic corporations and sectors in both countries. It has become much more difficult in both countries to generate and sustain a truly national economic policy to put forward in bilateral negotiations. Simultaneously, dynamic corporations in both countries have gained enhanced power to act with far less sensitivity to the particular policy goals of either government.

A second set of consequences are concerned with the growing economic integration of Asia as a result of new cross-border Asian production networks. Both Japan and the United States have been intimately involved in this integration. At the same time, as Hamilton-Hart makes clear in her chapter in this volume, in the aftermath of the Asian economic crisis of 1997–98, Japan's economic presence within the Asian region has been shrinking, in large part due to Japan's own domestic economic problems and the slowdown in regional economic dynamism. In her phrasing, Asia has become a "more globalized region." Moreover, the American role in the crisis of 1997–98 has spurred demands for a variety of Asia-specific adjustments to the rising power of global capital. In all of these ways, the preeminence of bilateralism between the United States and Japan has been diluted. In particular, as economic ties have deepened and spread, the overall security climate in the Asian region has improved, and thus the singular importance given to bilateral economic and security ties has lost much of its intensity and rationale.

Increasing Multilateralism

Unilateralism is the luxury of only the most powerful, the most desperate, or the most marginal states in the international system. Historically, nation-states have generally opted for one or another form of allegiance with one another. In more recent times, the presence of formalized international and regional organizations has provided even more regularized arenas within which nation-states can pursue their interests. Japan and the United States have pursued their postwar policy goals through substantially different mixtures of unilateralism, bilateralism, and multilateralism.

The United States has been highly selective in its approaches to multilateralism. At one level, the United States led the way in creating the sweeping array of multilateral structures—most notably the UN, the OECD, the Bretton Woods system, GATT, the World Bank, and the International Monetary Fund—that came into being at the end of World War II. Broadly inclusive in membership, such institutions were in practice originally responsive to, and dominated by, U.S. goals.

Furthermore, such organizations often fell short of being truly liberal vehicles for a more internationalized world system, particularly in the economic area. Thus, the U.S. Congress blocked the introduction of the WTO that the United States initially sought after World War II, while the GATT that survived "was less extensive, contained escape clauses and exemptions, and left agriculture trade outside the multilateral framework."[52] Furthermore, maritime trade and shipping were also left outside the multilateral framework. Such illiberalities were an outgrowth of U.S. domestic politics, making many multilateral organizations, in practical terms, simply arenas within which the United States advanced its own unilaterally determined objectives, rather than bodies within which U.S. policies were shaped by the constraints endemic to genuine multilateral cooperation. America embraced only soft versions of multilateralism.

The U.S. approach to multilateral organizations ebbed and flowed over the postwar period, often with changes in presidential administrations, but it is difficult to find many instances in which U.S. actions were actually constrained by the country's multilateral memberships. Far more reflective of U.S. policies was the Reagan administration's decision to end coopera-tion with a number of UN bodies, such as the UN Educational, Scientific, and Cultural Organization (UNESCO), and to cease paying its UN dues until the organization returned to being one that was more responsive to U.S. priorities. The Clinton administration was more favorable to multi-lateralism, and it was Clinton who personally took the initiative to up-grade the Asia-Pacific Economic Cooperation (APEC) to include a national leaders' meeting. Yet the George W. Bush administration was adamantly opposed to any multilateral arrangements that it has seen as interfering with its policy objections, abridging a dozen or more multilateral treaties and agreements in its first year in office. As Richard Haass, director of pol-icy planning in the U.S. Department of State, put it, the administration would pursue "a la carte multilateralism," a code phrase for "multilater-alism when it suits our national purposes."[53] The administration's refusal to allow its attack on Iraq to be slowed by the United Nations underscored its overall willingness to pursue unilateralism.

As was noted earlier, postwar American policies toward Europe and Asia were quite different from each other. Interactions in Europe were largely multilateral. By way of contrast, in Asia, where deep ideological and postcolonial divisions prevailed across the region, U.S. policy was built around a series of parallel bilateral alliances. The only noteworthy exception was the ANZUS Pact among Australia, New Zealand, and the United States. As a consequence, security linkages among the Asian na-tion-states were virtually absent until the creation of ASEAN in 1967, and with the exception of the relatively weak ARF, also lacking thereafter.

Even in the economic arena, multilateralism was far slower to evolve in Asia than in several other parts of the world. The creation of ASEAN in 1967 was followed by establishment of the Asia-Pacific Economic Coop-eration (APEC) forum, which grew out of a 1987 proposal by Australia, with behind-the-scenes encouragement from Japan, a process described in detail by Ashizawa later in this volume. APEC provides a trans-Pacific organization, loosely organized and with no binding powers, that has aimed at removing barriers to trade in manufactured goods and eventu-ally in investment flows, and at aiding countries in economic and techni-cal development.

It was in the economic arena that U.S. policy toward multilateralism shifted most noticeably. The first big step in this direction came with the Blake Island meeting of APEC in 1993, when President Clinton gave a strong push to that organization. It was followed quickly by the January 1994 launching of the North American Free Trade Agreement (NAFTA). NAFTA was a regional organizational response to the growing trade and monetary regionalization taking place in Europe with the EU and later with the European Monetary Union. It also reflected a growing U.S. frustration with the limitations faced by GATT in creating a more liberal trade regime, as well as U.S. concerns about the rise in Asian imports into the United States.

The NAFTA is a preferential trade arrangement and its scope of activity remains largely limited to trade and investment, although it has also been used as a forum for discussing and implementing standards for labor and the environment. NAFTA has a dispute settlement mechanism and its panel decisions create a binding obligation under national law.[54] In all of these ways, the U.S. decision to join NAFTA imposed significant restrictions on its own ability to act unilaterally.

As NAFTA was gaining momentum in the United States, the country also began to show increased interest in APEC, although as Ashizawa argues in her chapter in this volume, "U.S. policymaking toward regional multilateral institution-building [in Asia] was largely reactive." The United States took little initiative in the creation of such institutions within Asia, and indeed strongly resisted any Asian regional proposals that might create a closed Asia (such as the proposal for an East Asian Economic Caucus, which would have excluded the United States, Australia, New Zealand, and Canada). Unlike the more enthusiastic Asian members of APEC, the United States was initially ambivalent toward APEC as well, up to APEC's inauguration in November 1989. Yet at APEC's Seattle meeting of 1993, President Clinton, through his presence and enthusiastic embrace of the forum, credentialed it, at least for a time, as one more multilateral regional body within which the United States would seek to advance its trade liberalization and investment goals. APEC, however, was far less deeply institutionalized and far less constrictive of its member countries' behavior than was NAFTA. As such, it subjected the United States (and its other members) to far fewer constraints on its behaviors.

On security matters, the reluctance of the United States to encourage Asian multilateral organizations was even more striking. Secretary of State Baker resisted any alteration in the preexisting hub-and-spoke arrangements that kept the United States at the core of Asian security. Only with the arrival of the Clinton administration did the United States commit itself to the development of multilateral forums for security consultation as one of ten major goals for U.S. policy in the Asia-Pacific. It should also be noted that the U.S. commitment was to "forums for consultation" rather than to a full embrace of multilateral security institutions. As Ikenberry stresses in his chapter in this volume, however, by 2002 the United States had indeed accepted various forms of what he calls "minilateralism." Hughes and Fukushima explore similar phenomena in their chapter in what they label America's "bilateralism plus."

Japan has historically been far more receptive to multilateralism than has the United States. Thus, Japan has relied far more overtly on participation in and cooperation with the various international organizations that had been put in place by the United States at the end of World War II. Still, as Green has put it, "The multilateral impulse has been strong in Japan's postwar foreign policy thinking, but in practice it has often been elusive."[55] On the one hand, multilateral involvement allowed Japan to temper residual images of its prewar military aggression and to convince the rest of the world that contemporary Japan could be counted on to pursue its national interests in accord with internationally established procedures and with sensitivity to global consensus. At the same time, Japan remained heavily dependent on America. Thus, the United States was Japan's early sponsor in acquiring such multilateral memberships, and Japan initially followed the lead of the United States in most such bodies. One of the first results of this combination came with Japan's accession to the United Nations in 1956, after which Japan officially committed itself to the pursuit of a "UN-centered diplomacy." A year later, Japan made UN-centric policies one of three pillars of its foreign policy.[56] Japan also became an active and supportive member of such global institutions as the World Bank, the International Monetary Fund, G7 (later G8) summit meetings, and GATT and its successor, the WTO, although as Pekkanen points out in this volume, it was initially wary of the former, although quite proactive in the latter.

Japanese commitment to global organizations, however, was continually modulated by Japan's deep reliance on close bilateral ties with the United States. Nevertheless, in a host of ways, Japan endeavored, as Hughes and Fukushima describe in their chapter, to use its membership in multilateral organizations to validate its transition from a military state to a merchant state and a market democracy.

The persistence of bilateralism typically left Japanese managers in a far weaker bargaining position than their U.S. counterparts, particularly on trade issues. Thus, after the many trade frictions of the mid- to late-1980s, Japan was anxious to reduce its dependence on the United States and also on those global multilateral organizations in which U.S. influence was overwhelming. As a consequence, Japan became increasingly proactive in fostering regional organizations as mechanisms to deal with a host of problems on an Asia-specific, multilateral basis. Thus, as Katada's chapter in this volume demonstrates, multilateralism in Asia offered Japan a means to reassert enhanced regional influence in ways far less threatening than any unilateral steps might have been. Japan was consequently an early and strong supporter of such Asian regional multilateral institutions as the Asian Development Bank, ARF, the APEC forum, and a host of informal, nonofficial institutions such as the Pacific Economic Cooperation Council (PECC), the Pacific Basin Economic Council (PBEC), and the Pacific Trade and Development Conference (PAFTAD), all of which helped lead to APEC's formation, as well as dozens, if not hundreds, of so-called Track II dialogue processes.

Furthermore, the downside of its bilateral security relationship with the United States was made clear to Japan in the first Bush administration's deeply critical reaction to Japan's behavior in the Gulf War. Despite what was perceived within Japan as exceptionally generous support of U.S. actions—Japan raised taxes to pay for what was eventually a $13 billion contribution to the war effort—the United States reacted with pique to what was widely castigated as mere "checkbook diplomacy." Indeed, the United States continued to squeeze Japan for additional funds beyond its original pledge, ultimately demanding a supplement to cover fluctuations in the dollar-yen exchange rate. Within Japan, U.S. behavior was seen as ungrateful, crass, and mercenary. But while Japan tried to earn alliance credit and international prestige through its economic contributions, the 1990–91 Gulf War demonstrated to Japan that the United States in particular still measured security in the traditional currency of military force.[57]

The breakup of the Soviet Union and its European empire revitalized Japan's impulse toward multilateralism and multilateral diplomacy.[58] Japanese policymakers began to search for increased regional security arrangements, particularly with Asia but also in enhanced ties to Europe, that would allow it to claim a more active contribution to burden sharing while at the same time reducing its dependence on the bilateral relationship alone. Japan, as Ashizawa discusses at length in this volume, moved toward a more multilevel approach to its own, and to Asian regional, security. One result was ARF, the first meeting of which was held in Brunei in July 1994. Such organizations and processes enhanced the potential arenas for dispute resolution and clearly reduced the singularity of Japan's dependence on bilateral bargaining with the U.S. government. In the process, Japan expanded its pursuit of goals in ways that broke the long-standing separation of security and economic issues. Japanese trade, investment, and Official Development Assistance (ODA) all became tools, along with traditional military force, of enhancing Japan's own regional security.

Ironically, Japan's moves toward greater regionalism were reinforced by continued U.S. pressures on Japan about trade. Before 1995 some U.S. politicians and business leaders argued that the alliance was overrated and had prevented the United States from pursuing its economic interests in the U.S.-Japan relationship. Some specifically argued that the United States should use the security relationship as leverage to open Japanese trade and financial markets to American firms.[59] In this view, Japan had for too long been allowed a free ride on defense while the American concern with security had kept the economic relationship between the two nations unbalanced in favor of Japan. Even the generally more multilateral Clinton administration slipped steadily back into the familiar bilateral economic ruts of the past. It continued to focus on bilateral trade deficits rather than on the U.S. global trade imbalance; it increasingly blamed trade barriers rather than domestic disequilibria for those bilateral trade deficits; and despite its earlier disclaimers it appeared to be moving toward managed trade, with indices becoming targets and targets sliding toward quotas.[60] All of this reinforced the increased Japanese warming toward multilateral organizations.

Overall, both the United States and Japan began to rely increasingly on multilateral organizations as an additional set of tools with which to manage their financial and economic relations. For the United States, this typically meant pressuring Japan to behave in accord with American interpretations of the international norms of global organizations such as GATT or the WTO. This was shown, for example, in U.S. pressures on forestry and fisheries products during the early voluntary sector liberalization (EVSL) negotiations within APEC, as demonstrated by Krauss. At the same time, Japan, while resisting legalization and the creation of any binding authority in a regional forum such as APEC, could, as Pekkanen's chapter in this volume details, use legal and binding multilateralism against the United States in the WTO. Katada's analysis in this volume of similar successes in Japan's pursuit of its "counterweight strategies" within monetary forums such as the ASEAN+3 format—the ten ASEAN countries plus Japan, China, and South Korea—as well as ASEM similarly demonstrates how Japan was able to work through multilateral organizations to bypass bilateral U.S. pressures in areas where Japan's legal or moral case might be far stronger than its bilateral political leverage. Interestingly, both Japan and the United States have sought on various occasions to pursue their trade issues not through direct negotiations, as had once been the case, but rather through the WTO dispute settlement system.[61] Japan also increased its efforts to spawn Asian regional finance organizations in an effort to avoid what were increasingly becoming problems caused by escalating global capital flows, as Katada and Amyx show in this volume with regard to ASEAN+3.

In these and other ways, therefore, multilateral organizations—both those focused primarily on Asia and those that are truly global—now provide a totally new array of forums within which both Japan and the United States are reshaping their previously bilateral relations. To date there is little clarity on which side is the more likely to "win" through such bodies; but preliminary results suggest that Japan has used them to considerable advantage to counterbalance its previous weaknesses under bilateralism.

Breakdowns in Bilateralism

These three big trends—security shifts, enhanced private capital flows, and multilateralism—have shifted the context and basis for the previously bilateral U.S.-Japan relationship, as well as the means through which the two sides now manage their relations. The remaining chapters in this volume provide detailed examinations of the various ways in which the bilateral relationship has been reshaped as a result. Several of these chapters also explore the global and regional consequences of these changes. In the concluding chapter, Ellis Krauss and I provide an analysis of the major new trends that we see being woven into the relationship, as well as their broader implications. But as a prelude to the remaining chapters, three broad trends in the changed character of the relationship and the way it is managed deserve to be noted.

First, far more interactions that affect the U.S.-Japan relationship arise outside diplomatic and governmental circles than before. Many of the most important of these interactions are no longer being channeled through or monopolized by governments. Private sector actors—such as banks, corporations, trade associations, NGOs, and global bond rating agencies—as well as members of international organizations are now sufficiently powerful to prevent the two governments from monopolizing developments in their bilateral relationship. The very game of relationship management has become vastly more difficult for both governments.

Second, the arenas within which the relationship is managed have become vastly more numerous. No longer do Kasumigaseki and the Washington Beltway define the outer boundaries of national decision making. Rather, multilateral organizations in various parts of the region and the world provide dozens of alternative arenas within which the two governments can now pursue their objectives. In a similar way, the breakdown of international and regional bipolarity means that the lines of national cooperation and conflict can differ from issue to issue or on the same issue over short periods of time. New alternatives previously blocked by bilateral interactions are sometimes opened up; in other cases, multilateral organizations create enhanced pressures on one or the other country to behave in ways that are different than if bilateralism were still dominant.

Third and finally, the very targets of the alliance have subtly shifted. Where once the alliance was explicitly directed at providing an airtight defense for Japan and only secondarily at providing peace and security in East Asia, that secondary goal has gained in explicit significance, particularly since 1995. And as this goal has changed, so have the security positions not only of Japan and the United States but also of China. So too have the military orientations of both Japan and the United States, as Japan begins to take on a more active and overt role in military security and as the United States moves to press the case for missile defense. It remains to be seen whether the two governments will more explicitly acknowledge these changes in future discussions of their relationship.

The chapters that follow describe and analyze specific aspects of and changes in the relationship and include discrete case studies. Each chapter emphasizes some but not all of the aims of the volume. Together, however, they allow us to begin an initial attempt to assess how these alterations in geopolitics, the enhanced role of private capital flows, and the rise in number and importance of multilateral organizations have influenced the U.S.-Japan relationship. All are united in showing how the transformed environment has more or less, directly and subtly, transformed the character of the previously bilateral relationship, bringing to policymakers in both countries new opportunities and challenges. We return in the conclusion to an assessment of how the relationship has changed in each of these realms, the ways it has been enhanced, and the important problems it faces, as well as the implications of these changes for the Asia-Pacific region.

PART I

STRATEGY AND SECURITY

America in East Asia

POWER, MARKETS, AND GRAND STRATEGY

G. JOHN IKENBERRY

Introduction

American foreign policy toward East Asia—and the geopolitical organization of the region—is a creature of the Cold War. Yet despite the end of
that great conflict, American policy toward the region has remained
largely unchanged. In the decade since the end of the Cold War, the United
States has reaffirmed its alliance commitments and made clear its geopolitical and economic interests. This is partly because the Cold War has not
fully ended in East Asia. The Berlin Wall came down in Europe, but the
walls—real and imagined—remain in place across the Taiwan straits and
the Korean peninsula. Indeed, the strategic warming of relations with
China during the 1970s was primarily a product of America's bipolar
struggle with the Soviet Union, but since the disappearance of the Soviet
threat, this rationale for strategic partnership with China has been lost. In
the meantime, the U.S.-Japan alliance has remained the organizational
center of the region. In Asia, the end of the Cold War was less a grand historical transition than it was elsewhere in the world.

The explanation for continuity in American policy is also due to a larger
reality, however. The United States is a global hegemonic power that has
constructed a political-security order in East Asia—as it has around the
world—and in practical terms there is no alternative order that it or the
countries in the region can conjure up that is more stable or mutually beneficial than the current order. Perhaps a new order will someday emerge,
but it has not yet. American policy toward East Asia and the regional order that has evolved over the decades reflects this hegemonic reality: key

countries in the region are dependent on American military protection and the American market. American deterrence and regional trade linkages are at the heart of this U.S.-East Asian order. Moreover, this order—and American foreign policy toward the region—is also supported by America's ideas and intellectual traditions about how to build regional and global order. These are realist ideas about power and containment, but also liberal ideas about how best to build an international order and how to engage the region in the economic, political, and security spheres.

The George W. Bush administration's policy toward the region—as well as its wider global vision—is still emerging, but it already exhibits both realist and liberal logic. The administration's unilateralist tendencies are manifest in the rejection of a host of treaties and agreements. Yet in the aftermath of September 11, officials in the Bush administration seem to have discovered some usefulness in coalitions, alliances, and multilateral cooperation. The American campaign to fight terrorism should reinforce cooperative relations with U.S. allies in East Asia and create incentives for accommodating relations with China. Likewise, in confronting North Korea over its nuclear program, the United States will be pressured to coordinate its position with Beijing, Seoul, and Tokyo. These developments will reinforce the continuity of America's presence in the region and the existing regional structures.

This chapter does three things. First, it sketches American policy toward East Asia, built as it is around hegemony, bilateral security ties, and soft multilateralism, and it traces how American policy has been evolving since the early 1990s. Second, it looks at the broader realist and liberal grand strategies that the United States wields in the region. Finally, it examines recent efforts to maintain a hegemonic leadership position in the region by reinvigorating the bilateral U.S.-Japan alliance, pursuing multilateral cooperative arrangements in security and economic areas, and searching for a lasting rationale for the American presence in the region.

American Policy Toward East Asia

American policy toward East Asia is built on hard bilateral security ties and soft multilateral economic relations. Embedded in this policy are a set of political bargains between the United States and the countries in East Asia. The U.S.-Japan alliance is the cornerstone of the security order, and the Asia-Pacific Economic Cooperation (APEC) forum and the trans-Pacific trade and investment system are the cornerstone of the economic order. The hub-and-spoke defense system has its roots in the early Cold War and in the failure of multilateral security arrangements that were intended to mirror the Atlantic security pact.[1] The U.S.-Japan alliance was established to deter the expansion of Soviet power and of Communism more generally in the Asia-Pacific. This Cold War anti-Communist goal led the United States to use its occupation of Japan and military victory in the Pacific to actively shape the region—and it did so more successfully in Northeast Asia than in Southeast Asia. The United States offered Japan, and the region more generally, a postwar political bargain: it would provide Japan and other countries with security protection and access to American markets, technology, and supplies within an open world economy; in return, Japan and other countries in the region would become stable partners that would provide diplomatic, economic, and logistical support for the United States as it led the wider, American-centered, anti-Communist postwar order.

From the beginning, this bilateral security order has been intertwined with the evolution of regional economic relations. The United States facilitated Japanese economic reconstruction after the war and sought to create markets for Japanese exports, particularly after the closing of China in 1949.[2] It prompted the import of Japanese goods into the United States during the 1950s so as to encourage Japanese postwar economic growth and political stability.[3] The American military guarantee to its partners in East Asia (and Western Europe) provided a national security rationale for Japan and the Western democracies to open their markets. Free trade helped cement the alliance, and in turn the alliance helped settle economic disputes. In Asia, the export-oriented development strategies of Japan and the smaller Asian "tigers" depended on America's willingness to accept the imports of these countries and to live with huge trade deficits; alliances with Japan, South Korea, and other Southeast Asian countries made this politically tolerable.[4]

The alliance system—and the U.S.-Japan security pact in particular—has also played a wider stabilizing role in the region. The American alliance with Japan has solved Japan's security problems, allowing it to forego building up its military capability, thereby making it less threatening to its neighbors. This has served to solve or reduce the security dilemmas that would surface within the region if Japan were to rearm and become a more autonomous and unrestrained military power than it currently is. At the same time, the alliance makes American power more predictable than it would be if it were a free-standing superpower. This too reduces the instabilities and risk premiums that countries in the region would need to incur if they were to operate in a more traditional balance of power order.[5] Even China has seen the virtues of the U.S.-Japan alliance. During the Cold War the alliance was at least partially welcome as a tool to balance Soviet power—an objective that China shared with the United States. Even today, however, as long as the alliance does not impinge on China's other regional goals—most important, the reunification with Taiwan—it reduces the threat of a resurgent Japan.

In the late 1940s, in an echo of today's situation, the United States was the world's dominant state, with 45 percent of the world's gross national product, leadership in military power, technology, finance, and industry, and brimming with natural resources. It nevertheless found itself building world order around stable regional partnerships. Its calling card was its offer of Cold War security protection, but the intensity of political and economic cooperation between the United States and its partners went well beyond what was necessary to counter Soviet threats. As historian Geir Lundstadt has observed, the expanding American political order in the half century after World War II was in important respects an "empire by invitation."[6] The remarkable global reach of American postwar hegemony has been driven, at least in part, by the efforts of European and Asian governments to harness American power, to render that power more predictable, and to use it to overcome their own regional insecurities. The result has been a vast system of U.S.-centered economic and security partnerships.

The political bargain behind the East Asian regional hegemonic order was also aimed at making American power more predictable and user-friendly. If the United States worried about finding partners to help wage the Cold War and build a U.S.-centered world order, these partners worried about American power—both its domination and its abandonment. Thus the East Asian regional bargain was also about the restraint and commitment of American power. The United States agreed to operate within bilateral and multilateral institutional frameworks and the junior partners agreed to operate within and support the American order.[7] American hegemony became more open, predictable, reciprocal, and institutionalized—and therefore more benign and tolerable. But the United States was able to lock other countries into operating within a legitimate and U.S.-centered order.

The end of the Cold War and the shifting economic and political environment in East Asia has altered the region and presented challenges to this postwar regional hegemonic order. The geopolitical landscape has changed. The Soviet Union has collapsed and Russia is now a weakened power—too weak to play a dominant role in the region. The peace negotiations between the Koreas are also likely to lead to the reassessment of relationships and bargains. The end of the Cold War has made it difficult for some Americans to understand why the United States continues to provide security protection to Japan and the wider region; but in other ways the relations and bargains remain critical to regional order—and largely intact. The United States is even more powerful today than it was in the past, particularly in relation to the ongoing economic malaise in Japan and because of the growth of America's new economy during the 1990s. It is still the world's leading military power. Fifty percent of world military spending takes place in the United States, as does 80 percent of world military research and development. The United States also remains the leading destination for East Asian exports. In the late 1990s, the United States passed Japan as the largest trade partner of the Association of Southeast Asian Nations (ASEAN). A wide array of regional vested interests—on both sides of the Pacific—are in favor of open trade and investment. This creates powerful and ongoing incentives for the countries of the region to engage the United States and encourage it to establish credible restraints on and commitments to its power. The U.S. government clearly is convinced that its security and political presence in the region are as important as they were in the past, despite the end of the Cold War. The Nye Commission of the mid-1990s provides a critical intellectual and policy rationale for continuation of the U.S. leadership role in the region. The asymmetries of power and prevailing strategic interests thus make the basic bargain between the United States and its partners as relevant and valued as ever before.

As argued later in this chapter, American policy toward the U.S.-Japan alliance, APEC, and other regional multilateral dialogues reflects this view. The alliance may have lost its Cold War function, but it remains critical in forestalling security dilemma-driven conflict and arms races in the region, and it makes the United States a more predictable and institutionalized superpower. APEC also serves this function. The United States gets some insurance through APEC that regional economic relations will remain trans-Pacific (rather than intra-Asian) and move in the direction of liberalization and openness. In exchange, other countries in the region get some insurance against American bilateral discrimination and they get an institutionalized forum for helping to shape how the United States operates within the region. The bargains behind the regional hegemonic order are evolving, but they are also being recreated.

America's Realist and Liberal Grand Strategies

Behind American thinking toward East Asia stand at least two intellectual traditions. One is realist, of course, and is exhibited in the balance of power and containment policies that the United States has pursued. America's hegemonic bargain with East Asia reflects this logic: the United States provides security protection and access to its technology and markets in exchange for diplomatic, logistical, and economic support from its partners as the United States leads the wider postwar order. America's wars in Asia and its forward military presence are all manifestations of this realist geopolitical orientation.

There is also, however, a liberal orientation that has informed policies that have sought to create various sorts of integrative, reciprocal, and highly institutionalized political orders. This tradition has stressed the importance of multilateral organization of economic relationships and has placed a premium on the encouragement of democratic reform in defeated or transitional states. The liberal orientation toward order is also concerned with the management of power, but it brings a rich set of ideas about how economic interdependence, democratic community, political socialization, and binding institutions can contribute to stable and mutually agreeable order.[8] The liberal orientation has taken America's experience with building order—in the founding fathers' period and after the civil war—and brought it to bear on regional and global problems of order building. The United States has not tended to make sharp distinctions between the logics of domestic order and international order—both can be anarchic arenas of coercion and violence, and both can potentially be legitimate, reciprocal, institutionalized, and stable. America's "liberal grand strategy"—grounded in a particular reading of history, economics, and politics—is built around at least three elements of policy engagement that seek to *open up*, *tie down*, and *bind together* countries so as to generate stable order.[9]

Opening up means directing the forces of trade and investment, cultural exchange, and transnational society into the closed politics of strong state rule. "These linkages bring with them powerful forces for change. Computers and the Internet, fax machines and photocopiers, modems and satellites all increase exposure to people, ideas, and the world beyond China's border," as former President Bill Clinton explained in a speech in October 1998. This concept can be called "strategic interdependence." The idea is to create realms of wealth and autonomy within the economy and society, thus encouraging political pluralism and eroding the iron-fisted control of the Communist party. Expanding trade and investment also create new and more vocal vested interests in closed societies that want to maintain continuous and stable relations with the outside world. Strategic interdependence is meant to accomplish at least two objectives. The first is to help activate and reward internal groups and factions within the economy and society and strengthen their domestic position, thereby giving a boost to political forces that favor democracy and a pluralistic political system. Trade and investment in China are meant to bolster the position of civil society and the nonstate sectors, thereby creating more political counterweight to the party and the military. The other objective of strategic interdependence is to create dependencies and vested interests within the country who favor stable and continuous relations. This is often seen most clearly in the economic realm: international business leaders grow in number and importance in the target country and raise their collective voices in favor of political and economic openness and friendly relations. Again in regard to China, the anticipation is that rising economic dependence on the flow of trade and investment will restrain China's geopolitical actions.[10] As Jean-Pierre Cabestan, director of the French Center for Research on Contemporary China in Hong Kong, sees it: "The more China's economy is integrated with the world economy, the more dependent she is on the outside world and the less she can afford to embark upon some adventurous course."[11] This view is shared by foreign policy experts in both American political parties.

Tying down means inviting other governments to get involved in international organizations such as the World Trade Organization (WTO) and APEC. Here the idea is to create expectations and obligations for governments through membership in regional and global institutions. Political conditionality for gaining membership in these organizations can itself create leverage, but the expectation is also that once the government is inside the institution, its officials will slowly be socialized into embracing the institution's principles and norms. The variety of multilateral security forums in East Asia—the most important being the ASEAN Regional Forum (ARF)—are seen as playing a small role in socializing regional governments, providing mechanisms for conflict resolution, and fostering at least a small sense of common identity.

Binding together means establishing formal institutional links between countries that are potential adversaries, thereby reducing the incentives for each state to balance against the other.[12] This is the security component of a liberal grand strategy. Rather than responding to a potential strategic rival by organizing a counterbalancing alliance against it, member countries invite the threatening state to participate in a joint security association or alliance. By binding nations to one another, such alliances reduce surprises and create expectations of stable future relations that dampen the security dilemmas that trigger worst-case preparations, arms races, and dangerous strategic rivalry. Also, by creating institutional connections among potential rivals, alliances establish channels of communication that provide opportunities for each country to influence the other's evolving security policy. The binding logic of the North Atlantic Treaty Organisation (NATO) allowed France and the other Western partners to acquiesce in Germany's military rearmament during the Cold War. Even today, the United States and its European and Japanese partners ward off rivalry and balancing among themselves by maintaining their security alliances. It is the binding logic more than the response to external threats that makes these institutions attractive today.

American-led economic and security institutions provide Germany and Japan with a political bulwark of stability that far transcends their more immediate and practical purposes. Germany has had more opportunities to bind itself to Western Europe and the Atlantic order than Japan has had opportunities in East Asia. The European Community—and later the European Union (EU)—and the NATO alliance have given Germany a layer of institutions through which to bind itself to neighbors and thereby reduce security-dilemma instabilities. Japan—because of geography, history, and politics—does not have as many regional institutional options. The U.S.-Japan alliance is currently the only serious institution with which Japan can signal restraint and commitment. As a result, the bilateral alliance has become even more indispensable to Japan and to the region.[13] Seen in this light, the security alliance between the United States and Japan remains a critical piece of the region's geopolitical architecture, even if the external threats disappear. The binding logic of the alliance allows Japan to maintain a "civilian" great-power role and remain faithful to its postwar political identity as a nonnuclear, nonbelligerent major power.[14]

China may not be ready for security binding, but some of the benefits of binding are being sought in more modest institutional relationships, such as attending annual meetings of Chinese and American defense officials, working with other states in the region on the nonproliferation regime, and participating in regional security forums. The idea is to respond to potential external threats from neighboring states by staying close to them, thereby reducing untoward surprises, curtailing these states' autonomy of action, and providing at least some opportunities to influence what these states do in the future. This is a classic and enduring choice of states when confronted by potentially dangerous or threatening states: either to isolate them, contain them, and organize an alliance of states to ensure against threats from them; or to include them within existing institutions, co-opt them, monitor them closely, and limit their opportunities to act aggressively. This debate continues within the current Bush administration, but most observers agree that a hard-line containment approach to China is unsustainable.

These tactics and strategies work together, of course. The more that trade, investment, and political exchange work to open up a country to the outside, the more opportunities there are to tie them down and bind them with other states. This observation follows from a rather simple argument: the more open a state is—the more democratic, liberal, pluralist, and decentralized—the more points of contact it can have with the outside world. Private actors in society can directly connect to international organizations and build extensive nongovernmental relationships with similar actors in other states. The more connecting points and institutionalized relationships a state has, the less arbitrary and sudden are shifts in state policy likely or possible to be. Webs of interdependence are created that mitigate the security dilemmas, lower the incentives to balance, and render shifts in power more tolerable than they would otherwise be.

America's liberal grand strategy is not really new—it was pursued quietly during the Cold War among the industrial democracies, and with remarkable if unheralded success. Promoting economic interdependence, institutional cooperation, and binding commitments are this country's secret weapons for creating a stable world political order. They allow the United States to unleash the thousands of eager multinational companies, transnational organizations, and governmental representatives who stand ready to envelope a country and bring it into the wider liberal international order. The basic point is this: the United States does have a general liberal orientation toward order building, which is manifest in various ways in U.S. foreign policy toward East Asia. This foreign policy strategy is not triggered by external security threats as such and it allows us to explain why the United States may be pursuing a more continuous and coherent foreign policy in East Asia than would otherwise be expected.

America's East Asian Policies in the Post-Cold War Era

Since the end of the Cold War, the United States has pursued a variety of realist and liberal policies in East Asia, and together these policies have reinforced continuity in the country's overall commitment to regional leadership and engagement. The Clinton administration may not have had a fully formed grand strategy in place, but its policies were informed by both traditional realist security objectives and liberal aspirations. Clinton officials described their policy toward China at one point as "constructive engagement," but it did so without loosening its commitment to the security of Taiwan. The warming of relations with China did not preclude the Clinton administration from sending two carriers to patrol the waters off Taiwan, and it was willing to debate how to press China on human rights and trade problems. Obviously, distinctions between *containment* and *engagement* are too simple to capture the mix of policies available to the United States.[15] We can look at American foreign policy on East Asia in this light.

The George W. Bush administration is still shaping a strategy toward the region. The so-called Armitage Report of October 2000 is still probably the best indicator of how the administration's policy will evolve.[16]

There has been an attempt to reestablish Japan as America's core strategic partner in the region and to dispense with the notion of a strategic partnership with China. Indeed, the ambition appears to be to make Japan a heavier and more involved military partner, to share intelligence and expand Japanese functional duties in the region. The initial steps by the Bush team have also included signaling a hard-line position toward North Korea. The surprising language in President Bush's state of the union address portraying North Korea as part of a global "axis of evil" is a continuation of this hard-line approach to what the administration sees as rogue states.[17] Missile defense is also an issue that is creating controversy, and how it plays out will do more than any other issue to shape the balance of continuity and change in American policy toward the region. But the major thrusts of the new administration also involve ideas of liberal grand strategy: the bilateral alliances will remain the core of America's commitment to the region, the United States will support soft multilateral dialogues in the region, trans-Pacific regional economic relations will be championed, and trade and investment flows will be encouraged in American relations with China. The wider sweep of American policy toward East Asia in the 1990s can thus be identified.

In the economic arena, the United States has had a consistent policy of fostering expanded economic ties with China, encouraging cross-cutting trade and investment patterns within the region among the various economic centers, and raising the level of multilateral political management of intraregional economic relations. In many ways, the evolution of the East Asian region is already being driven by the forces of trade and investment. Japanese foreign investment exploded in the mid-1980s within Asia, reversing the earlier Western orientation of Japanese economic relations. At the same time, the overseas Chinese in Southeast Asia have created a complex production and trade network in the region. The result is a growing intraregional economy, not dominated by either the United States or Japan. The very complexity and cross-cutting character of these relations is driving greater political and security engagement in the region.[18] American policy appears to be aimed at deepening trade and investment interdependence, and encouraging institutional groupings such as APEC, to reinforce the open and "soft" character of Asia-Pacific economic regionalism. The United States has also consistently sought to make sure that Asia-Pacific regionalism encompasses the Western Hemisphere and not just Asia.

The internationalization of the Asia-Pacific economies is important not just because the expansion of trade and investment promotes growth and raises living standards. The expansion of the internationally oriented sectors in Japan, China, and Korea also strengthens the position of internationally oriented elites who are supportive of greater integration and stable multilateral relations. The rise of international business and banking in Japan, for example, has strengthened the internationalist coalition within Tokyo and added voices in favor of more extensive domestic economic reform and political pluralism.[19] The same trajectory of internationalization, expanded vested interests, and domestic reform is anticipated for the whole region.

APEC, which was launched in 1989, shows the evolving American economic bargain with East Asia. A multilateral economic dialogue was possible within East Asia because of the long-term shift in the developmental orientation of the emerging economies of the region. Japan and Australia were the initiators of the APEC process, but the United States quickly lent its support. At least part of the appeal of APEC within the region was that it was a counterweight to American unilateral trade tendencies: the multilateral process would help restrain the worst impulses of American trade policy, symbolized in the authority granted by the Super 301 provisions of the Omnibus Trade and Competitiveness Act of 1988. In return, the United States would encourage an open East Asian economic regionalism and reinforce the market reforms that were unfolding across Asia and the Western hemisphere. The actual ability of APEC to lock in policy orientations in the region was limited, and the restraints on American policy autonomy were also more symbolic than real, but APEC reveals the basic orientation of American economic relations with East Asia. The United States wants to remain "inside" the region, and to support a region that identifies itself with democracy and open markets.

In the political arena, the United States has supported the expansion of wider and deeper institutional relations among China, Japan, Korea, the United States, and the ASEAN countries—at least as much as these contacts are manifest as dialogues or policy consultations. The United States has reaffirmed its commitment to bilateral security ties, but it has also offered support for multilateral and minilateral dialogues that are consistent with these underlying bilateral security commitments. Support for Chinese membership in the WTO and various regional dialogues are meant to provide ways to foster agreement on regional norms and standards of conduct. One argument made by American officials during the Clinton administration was that institutions should be arrayed so as to enmesh the regional powers in a series of regional and global institutions that serve to establish explicit standards and expectations on government behavior in regard to human rights, political accountability, property rights, and business law. Yardsticks are erected that, often in subtle and indirect ways, allow governments and private groups to both support and criticize government policy and politics in neighboring countries. This in turn helps foster political community. Another argument is that a dense set of regional institutions provides forums and arenas for governmental and political elites to interact, thereby providing opportunities for the socialization of these elites into common regional norms and expectations.[20] Finally, dialogues can also provide functional problem-solving mechanisms that bring together leaders and specialists across the region to find common solutions to problems. This is the old liberal argument about functional integration and the spillover of technical problem solving into more widely shared political bonds.[21]

In terms of Track II dialogues, the United States government has backed the Northeast Asia Cooperation Dialogue (NEACD), a consultation grouping aimed at enhancing mutual understanding and cooperation through unofficial dialogue among China, Japan, Russia, the United States, and the two Koreas. Although North Korea has not participated, this forum has brought together officials and policy experts from the five countries to talk about political, security, and economic issues. The Clinton administration was closely involved in the launching of this dialogue and secured government funding for it. Together, these various multilateral mechanisms serve various purposes. NEACD brings Russia and Japan into discussions of regional issues without involving them in the more narrow four-power talks (involving the United States, China, and the two Koreas) over North Korea. These multilateral venues are also a useful way to defuse Chinese and Russian suspicion of the bilateral alliances.

The United States has at various moments talked in lofty terms about building "political community" in East Asia. Secretary of State James Baker called for a new political community in East Asia in a prominent *Foreign Affairs* article during the earlier Bush administration. Similar statements were made by Clinton administration officials. What these statements actually mean in terms of new political institutions or architecture has never been fully clarified. The United States has been more comfortable working within the traditional bilateral alliances and in ad hoc minilateral groupings, such as those that have brought together Tokyo, Seoul, and Washington over policy toward North Korea. The Korean Peninsula Energy Development Organization and the Perry Commission process are examples of this minilateral approach that continues to be manifest in American policy.

The final arena is regional security relations. The U.S.-Japan alliance (as well as the other bilateral pacts) provides a vehicle for the United States to play an active role in the region. In this sense, it serves the same function as NATO does for American involvement in Europe. These alliances also stabilize relations between the United States and its Asian partners. The deepening of the U.S.-Japan alliance does appear to be driven by these multiple logics of tying down and binding together. The United States and

Japan agreed to enhance security cooperation in the U.S.-Japan Joint Declaration on Security in 1996, and Japan enacted the U.S.-Japan Defense Guidelines in 1998 to make the security treaty effective. The Taiwan Straits crisis in 1996 and North Korea's missile launching in 1998 both served to intensify American and Japanese efforts to reaffirm and update the alliance.

An important development in American thinking about its post-Cold War security involvement in East Asia came with the 1995 Nye Initiative, which argued that America's military umbrella in the region had real and important consequences for the stability and functioning of regional political and economic relations, and for the success of America's economic, political, and security goals, including issues such as nonproliferation. Its famous phase that "security is like oxygen" sums up the rationale that was advanced.[22] The report made the case that maintaining the U.S.-Japan alliance and engaging China remain among the long-run interests of the United States—that America's security presence had both direct and indirect impacts on the stability of the region and on the ability of the United States to achieve its interests. Serious intellectual and policy challenges to this view have been raised from time to time but have not lasted, at least within the American defense and foreign policy community. At the end of the decade, the thinking remained the same. The 1998 Defense Department strategic report on East Asia argued that "maintaining an overseas military presence is a cornerstone of U.S. National Security Strategy and a key element of U.S. military policy to 'shape, respond, and prepare.'" It again makes the direct link between the bilateral alliances and their "critical practical and symbolic contributions to regional security."[23] Despite the end of the Cold War, it is the widely held view of the American foreign policy community that the United States needs to be permanently engaged with a forward-deployed military presence in East Asia.

The American view toward multilateral military cooperation has fluctuated over the decades but it has generally been supportive of initiatives, as long as they do not undermine the core bilateral security order. The 1995 Pentagon report on East Asia used more space than the 1998 report to discuss the positive contributions of these multilateral cooperative initiatives, but overall the United States has warmed up to soft security multilateralism. In 1991, when Japanese Foreign Minister Nakayama proposed at an ASEAN postministerial conference that a forum be created to discuss regional security, American officials responded coolly. The American attitude warmed up in later years. The Clinton administration signaled its interest in multilateral security dialogues in April 1993 during the confirmation hearings for Assistant Secretary of State for East Asia and Pacific Affairs Winston Lord, who identified such initiatives as one of the major policy goals of the new administration for Asia. President Clinton himself gave voice to the multilateral vision in a speech before the Korean National assembly in July 1993, when he called for the creation of a "new Pacific community, built on shared strength, shared prosperity, and a shared commitment to democratic values."[24] He identified four aspects to this vision of community: continued U.S. military presence and commitment, stronger efforts to combat the proliferation of weapons of mass destruction, support for democracy and open societies, and the promotion of new multilateral regional dialogues on the full range of common security challenges.

In the years since this speech, the United States has signaled its interest in organizing "coalitions of the willing" to address various regional security problems and to cautiously foster closer ties between the United States and its partners. It has given support to the ARF as a mechanism for dialogue. But the United States has also backed minilateral initiatives among its allies, including the U.S.-Japan-Republic of Korea (ROK) Trilateral Coordination and Oversight Group; the U.S.-Japan-ROK Trilateral Defense Talks; the Pacific Command's (PACOM) dialogue with Australia, Japan, ROK, and Singapore on establishing greater interoperability for future collective humanitarian operations; and PACOM's Asia Pacific Security Center, where Asian militaries study the conceptual and operational aspects of confidence-building measures and cooperative security. These cooperative security undertakings reflect the general American government view that the bilateral alliances should be strengthened and coordinated as much as possible. "Foremost," argues the 1998 Pentagon strategic statement of East Asia, "the U.S. will continue to strengthen its strategic partnerships with allies, which serve as important pillars from which to address regional political and military challenges. All of our alliance relationships promise to expand both in scope and degree in coming years to encompass more comprehensive concepts of security cooperation."[25]

Going beyond these minilateral groupings, the new Bush administration is focusing on even greater cooperation among America's security partners in the region. This is an idea championed by Admiral Dennis Blair, commander-in-chief of the U.S. Pacific Command, and he calls it a proposal to build a "security community" in the region.[26] The idea is to enrich bilateralism with increased cooperation and shared strategic purpose among the East Asian security partners. These cooperative ties would build on the example of ASEAN, the ARF, and the Five-Power Defense Arrangements (United Kingdom, Australia, New Zealand, Malaysia, and Singapore), and on America's bilateral ties with Australia, the Philippines, Singapore, and Thailand to provide a foundation for expanding shared expectations of peaceful relations among East Asian countries. This proposal for building community security ties in the region excludes, of course, China. The danger is that in the name of the liberal idea of security communities, the United States will actually end up building a containment ring around China.

The United States has shown some inclination to go beyond bilateral security alliances in Asia, but it is less certain how and if to attempt to incorporate China into an agreed-upon regional security order. This order might simply involve regular security talks among Chinese, Japanese, Korean, and American defense and foreign ministry officials. More ambitiously, it might include formal security commitments and collective security guarantees. Thinking through the character, organization, and phasing of this sort of regional security architecture is perhaps the most challenging area of American foreign policy today. Ideas from many quarters have already been suggested. Former Secretary of State Warren Christopher has recently suggested that discussion of a regional security organization be added to American foreign policy thinking on Asia.

The major question today is how America's post-September 11 global campaign against terrorism will influence the American presence in the region as well as the wider set of regional great-power relationships. It does appear that at least two competing visions of American grand strategy coexist within the Bush administration. The multilateral vision of Secretary of State Powell and others emphasizes traditional military partnerships and multilateral cooperation. It is a pragmatic vision that essentially represents continuity with the broad thrusts of American grand strategies—both realist and liberal—over the postwar era. The other vision is an aggressive unilateralism that is deeply skeptical about operating within a rule-based international order. It is an imperial view of America's role that was largely pushed to the sidelines during the Cold War and the Clinton era. It is a vision of a country that is big enough, powerful enough, and remote enough to go it alone, free from the dangerous and corrupting conflicts festering in all the other regions of the world.[27] The dynamics of American foreign policy since September 11 are paradoxical. The unilateral wing of the Bush administration has been strengthened by the success of the military campaign in Afghanistan and Iraq. American military capacity has been demonstrated, and many in the administration want to assert that unipolar military power in new operations around the world. At the same time, however, the administration's antiterrorism campaign has led to closer ties with Russia and China. The great powers—the United States, Europe, Russia, Japan, and China—are now as closely aligned as they have been since the Concert of Europe in 1815. Whether this new great power accord lasts or America's unilateralist impulses trigger a global backlash will shape the future of America's role in East Asia.

Conclusion

American foreign policy toward East Asia is based on America's position as a hegemonic and status quo power in the region. It wants continuity more than change, and its security and economic strategies toward the region reflect this reality. The American presence in the region exhibits both realist and liberal logics. American security protection and market access are part of a practical convergence of interests between the United States and its partners in the region, but a more diffuse liberal orientation is also manifest in that American policy seeks to open up and tie together countries in the region so as to realize a more stable and integrative order. These realist and liberal impulses have coexisted for decades and together have reinforced continuity in America's role within the region.

There are at least five underlying challenges to this policy continuity. The first challenge is *the problem of a weak Japan.* The United States, as reflected in the Armitage Report, wants Japan to play a more active role in the region, but will the weakness of Japan's economic and political situation allow it to do so? The weakness of Japan might seem to favor a continuation of the bilateral alliance structure of the region because there is no prospect in sight of a transformed regional security order organized around Japan or a Japanese-Chinese accord; but that weakness makes it difficult for Japan to step up and expand its security role. A weak Japanese government might also be unable to explain and defend the American troop presence when some future incident creates a crisis and domestic outrage over the military bases grows. If Japan does move in the direction envisaged by the Bush administration, the question is whether an expanded Japanese military role in the region will antagonize China and other countries and destabilize the very order that the United States seeks to preserve. American officials should also worry about how prolonged economic stagnation might affect Japanese political identity, which in the postwar decades was transformed from military great power to economic achiever. If Japan can no longer see itself as a great economic power, what sort of national identity will replace that self-image? The problem of a too-strong Japan has long been appreciated in the region, but the problem of a too-weak Japan is just beginning to be understood.

The second challenge is *redefining the patron-client character of the alliance.* More so than within NATO, the American role in the U.S.-Japan alliance is that of the asymmetrical senior partner. Can this relationship be put on a more equal and reciprocal footing without unraveling the political bargain on which the partnership is based? When Japan and the United States talk about alliance reform, Japan thinks more about increasing political equality and the United States thinks more about increasing burden sharing. On the one hand, can Japan have more voice in the alliance without the United States deciding that the political gains from being in the alliance are not worth the costs of tying itself to Japan and restricting its policy autonomy? On the other hand, a more equal alliance will necessarily make Japan a more salient and active security player in the region, and again the question is whether this can be accomplished without unleashing new security dilemmas and arms races in the region, particularly with China.

A third, related challenge is *fostering increased cooperation among America's bilateral security partners without turning the security community impulses of multilateral security cooperation into a threatening new containment belt around China*. Enhancing multilateral cooperation among the United States, Japan, South Korea, Singapore, Australia, and other allies could look very provocative from Beijing's perspective, even if it is cooperation dressed up in the liberal rhetoric of security community. After all, what is that enhanced cooperation aimed at? The form and content of great regional cooperation—at least cooperation that does not include China—will matter a great deal in determining if that cooperation is stabilizing or destabilizing. It would be a nice irony if hub-and-spoke security bilateralism were actually more congenial to regional stability than alliance multilateralism.

A fourth challenge to the existing order in East Asia is the *stickiness of the American military commitment in the wake of future political reconciliation in Korea and the settlement of Cold War territorial disputes elsewhere in the region*. Even if the United States is able to maintain a steady security commitment to East Asia, the question is how and where that military commitment will be forward deployed.

A final challenge is *American power itself*. The rise of a unipolar American order after the Cold War has not triggered a global backlash but it has unsettled relationships worldwide. Asians and Europeans worry about the steadiness of American leadership. Some governments and peoples around the world resent the extent and intrusiveness of American power, markets, and culture. Some intellectuals in the West even suggest that an arrogant and overbearing America brought the terrorism of September 11 on itself.[28] Aside from diffuse hatreds and resentments, the practical reality for many states around the world is that they need the United States more than it needs them—or so it would seem. In the early months of the Bush administration the political consequences of a unipolar superpower seemed all too obvious. It could walk away from treaties and agreements with other countries—on global warming, arms control, trade, business regulation, and so forth—and suffer fewer consequences than its partners; but to conduct a successful campaign against terrorism, the United States now needs the rest of the world. This is a potential boon to cooperation across the board. To pursue its objects—fighting terrorism but also managing the world economy and maintaining stable security relations—the United States will need to rediscover and renew the political bargains on which its hegemonic leadership is based. East Asia will be a critical location for this process.

In the final analysis, the hegemonic order is probably a stable one. Alternative institutions are not likely to emerge to rival the U.S.-led bilateral security structure. The ARF is not a template for a wider security system. The multilateral dialogues that are proliferating in the region seem to be actually serving to defuse antagonism toward the alliance pacts rather than to replace them. Just as there is no political coalition, within the United States or the wider region, that could support and sustain an American hard-line, containment-oriented approach to China, there is also no political coalition that could support or sustain a transformed regional order.

U.S.-Japan Security Relations

TOWARD BILATERALISM PLUS?

CHRISTOPHER W. HUGHES AND AKIKO FUKUSHIMA

Japan's Strategic Choice for Alliance

More than half a century after the signing of the original Security Treaty Between the United States and Japan in September 1951, and despite the passing of the Cold War strategic environment and the adversaries and functions for which it was ostensibly designed, the U.S.-Japan security relationship remains firmly intact. Indeed, bilateral security cooperation has not only been maintained in the post-Cold War period, but by all accounts has also been strengthened, and the incremental rate of the expansion of its geographical and functional scope has been accelerated.

The revision of the U.S.-Japan Defense Guidelines between 1997 and 1999 that outlined for the first time Japan's military assistance for the United States in an East Asian regional contingency under the U.S.-Japan security treaty, and Japan's dispatch of Self-Defense Forces (SDF) to the Indian Ocean area to provide logistical support for the U.S.-led war on terrorism in Afghanistan since November 2001 under the Anti-Terrorism Special Measures Law (ATSML), are two clear indications that U.S.-Japan bilateral cooperation has evolved to take on strengthened regional and global security responsibilities.

Japanese policymakers continue to stress that the range of support Japan provides for the United States under the bilateral security treaty is designed for Japan's individual self-defense. However, they have also become more willing than in the past to acknowledge overtly the long-understood fact that the treaty simultaneously undergirds both the United States' regional and global military strategies. This fact is then used to ar-

gue that the U.S.-Japan security treaty is indispensable to the maintenance of the U.S. military presence in East Asia, and hence serves as a
public good and as the foundation for the region's security architecture
and stability. Japan therefore continues to place the U.S.-Japan security
relationship at the core of its individual national security policy in the
post-Cold War period. Concomitantly, Japan's commitment to the bilateral security treaty and its alliance relationship with the United States remains the principal basis of its declared contribution to regional and
global security at the start of the twenty-first century.

Japan's seemingly unswerving commitment to bilateralism in security
affairs stands in stark contrast to the changing nature of the other dimensions of its international relations vis-à-vis the United States and the rest
of the global political economy in the post-Cold War period. As observed
in the other chapters of this volume, in the political and economic dimensions, Japan has developed increasingly viable multilateral frameworks
and options at the regional and global levels for the conduct of its international relations, which in many instances have the potential to serve as
partial or near total alternatives to the U.S.-Japan bilateral framework. By
contrast, in its security relations, Japan has yet to develop such similarly
viable multilateral frameworks to defuse, dilute, or deflect U.S. power.

As discussed in later sections of this chapter, Japan has certainly been
involved in important multilateral security dialogue initiatives in East
Asia, such as the ASEAN Regional Forum (ARF) and Track II security dialogues, and it has been a staunch supporter of many United Nations
(UN)-centered security activities at the global level. Nevertheless, as most
commentators and even Japanese policymakers themselves would acknowledge, these multilateral frameworks have rarely been seen as viable
or sufficient options for Japan's own security and for Japan to carve out
a role in regional and global security separate from the alliance. More
usually, they have been accorded, at best, and especially in military security affairs and at the East Asian regional level, a role that is secondary,
supplementary, or subordinate to the primacy of the U.S.-Japan security
arrangements, and that can be called part of a "bilateralism plus" security policy.

Japan's reluctance or inability to move beyond bilateralism in military
security affairs gives rise to the central research problems of this chapter,
which seeks to answer the question of why Japan's security policy has
been and continues to be so strongly rooted in U.S.-Japan alliance bilateralism, in spite of the fact that the post-Cold War strategic environment
and the evidence from the other dimensions of Japan's international relations suggest that Japan may increasingly have need and recourse to develop alternative multilateral security options. Following this discussion,

the chapter examines whether the factors that account for Japan's past predilection for what has been called *entrenched bilateralism* are likely to continue to propel it toward not only maintaining the alliance in the future but also further strengthening its functional and geographical scope.[1]

At the same time, this chapter considers the flipside to the question about the continuing strength of U.S.-Japan bilateralism and why multilateralism has been so relatively weakly rooted in Japan's security policy to date. It further asks whether the types of changes in the international environment identified earlier and Japan's development of multilateral frameworks in other dimensions are yet likely to strengthen the role of multilateralism alongside bilateralism in shaping Japan's future security policy.

In turn, the chapter addresses the question that arises from the first two sets of questions about the interrelationship between bilateralism and multilateralism in Japan's security policy, and to what degree they are capable of reinforcing or undermining each other. Specifically, the chapter investigates whether the relative strength of bilateralism in Japanese security policy is accounted for not simply by some inherent weakness in multilateralism that has compelled reliance on the U.S.-Japan alliance, but also by a more complex dynamic whereby the strength of alliance bilateralism itself has restricted multilateral options for security.

In the post-Cold War period, a body of academic and policymaking opinion has arisen in Japan and the United States arguing that alliance bilateralism and certain varieties of multilateralism are largely compatible approaches for augmenting Japan's own security, and that they offer pathways for Japan to enhance its contribution to regional and global security. This type of argument employs the logic that the two approaches can either perform separate but mutually reinforcing security functions, or that the U.S.-Japan alliance, even if it stops short of integration with multilateral approaches, is capable of providing a stable platform on which "incipient" multilateral security frameworks can now be constructed in line with the more propitious post-Cold War strategic environment.[2]

In opposition to this view is a body of opinion, often derived from the experience of the Cold War but also given force by the noticeable lack of substantial progress in East Asian multilateral security frameworks since the mid-1990s, that argues that bilateralism and multilateralism are essentially incompatible. The argument runs that the two approaches are at loggerheads because they are based on different assumptions about with whom and against whom and by what means security is provided. In many cases they are seen to conflict outright, with bilateral alliance ties constraining Japan from full participation in any meaningful multilateral framework that could come to form a substitute for and threaten the continuation of the U.S.-Japan security arrangements. In other cases, they are seen to work in tandem only if multilateralism is subordinated in practice to alliance bilateralism.

The intention of this chapter is to engage with these contending arguments about the compatibility and relative strengths of bilateralism and multilateralism because they offer further explanation for Japan's enduring attachment to the U.S.-Japan alliance in the post-Cold War period. For if it can be discovered that in the past Japan's alliance bilateralism has played a large part in weakening confidence in multilateral approaches to security, then it will also be important to look to this quarter to understand Japan's contemporary attachment to the U.S.-Japan alliance, and to understand Japan's capacity and likelihood to move away from near-exclusive reliance on bilateralism and search for multilateral security options in the future.

Understanding Japan's Predilection for Bilateralism

This chapter argues that the best method for analyzing and uncovering the reasons that lie behind Japan's persistent attachment to bilateralism is to examine the strategic perceptions of Japanese policymaking elites, their corresponding evaluation of the relative security benefits and costs of alliance with the United States, and how their continuous calculus of the last fifty years that overall the alliance best serves Japan's national interests has made for its longevity and a disinclination to explore multilateral security options in depth. Japan's policymaking elite is taken to be composed of Ministry of Foreign Affairs (MOFA) and Japan Defense Agency (JDA) officials, as well as other elements of the central bureaucracy; politicians from the governing Liberal Democratic Party (LDP) and other main parties; and other actors from big business, the mass media, and the academic communities.

The chapter starts with and backtracks to the Cold War period, because this enables detailing of the component factors that made for Japan's original strategic choice in favor of alliance with the United States. The chapter then moves on to the post-Cold War period and uses these factors as a basis for comparing and thereby explaining the continuities of the U.S.-Japan alliance relationship across the supposed divide of the Cold War and post-Cold War periods. It argues that by understanding the factors that underlie Japan's alliance choice in the Cold War, and by understanding that many factors similar to these are still at work in the post-Cold War period, we can see why Japanese policymakers continue to adhere to the strategic calculus that a strong or even strengthened U.S.-Japan security relationship is necessary despite the changing international security environment. Moreover, this chapter argues in its concluding section that all current indications are that these factors are likely to continue to determine Japan's strong attachment to the alliance in the near to medium future.

Three factors, discussed in detail later, transcend the divide between the Cold War and post-Cold War periods, continue to shape Japan's strategic calculation in favor of the alliance in the present day, and are likely to drive it forward in the future. The first of these factors has been *Japan's assessment of the strategic environment that has surrounded it in these periods and the resulting debates among its policymakers about the challenges posed to Japan and the opportunities for guaranteeing national interests and security through the mechanism of alliance with the United States.* Japan's perception of its national interest is here taken to be conditioned by more than straight material defense and economic interests.[3] In addition, and particularly as the security relationship increasingly acquired the trappings of an alliance during the later stages of the Cold War, the role of bilateral security institutions and the function of bilateralism itself as an emerging norm must be seen as significant influences in buttressing perceptions of the indispensability of the alliance.

The second factor is *the assessment by Japanese policymakers of the costs alongside the likely benefits of bilateral alliance with the United States.* In particular, these costs for Japan are calculated in terms of the alliance security dilemmas of *entrapment* and *abandonment*—the former arising if Japan becomes too dependent on the United States for its security, thus leading to its overintegration into U.S. military strategy and the related risks of becoming embroiled in a conflict; and the latter arising if Japan attempts to push for too much security independence from the United States, thus leading to its abandonment by the United States as an ally that it is reliable and worth defending.[4]

Also included in the calculations of this second factor are the expectations of Japanese policymakers that they have at their disposal alternative security options and associated hedging tactics to alleviate security dilemmas. In the Cold War and post-Cold War periods, even while sustaining an ever-deepening bilateral alliance relationship, Japan has safeguarded key constitutional prohibitions and independent military capabilities that have allowed it to retain a measure, even if gradually diminishing in scope, of security autonomy vis-à-vis the United States. This has meant that Japan has been able to obfuscate or even refuse support for the United States in certain areas of bilateral alliance cooperation, and to keep in reserve the extreme option of striking out on a more independent security policy. Japan's subsequent ability to intimate the limits of its support for U.S. global and regional strategy has made for U.S. wariness in pushing too hard to enlist support from or abdicate support for Japan in a military conflict, thus reducing the probability of Japanese entrapment or abandonment resulting from unwanted conflict scenarios.

Added to these potential security options and hedges against the costs of alliance, and given special attention in this chapter as the third factor underlying strategic choice in favor of the bilateral alliance, is *the perception by Japanese policy actors of the utility or nonutility of multilateral security frameworks*. Multilateralism has clearly been one option that is capable of countering exclusive security dependence on the United States. As will be seen, however, Japan's eventual consideration that multilateral frameworks have not been sufficiently viable options has proved to be another component of the calculation that has governed its strategic preference for the bilateral alliance. Hence, taken together, Japan's careful assaying of the benefits but also the costs of alliance with the United States as well as its belief that it has the means to manage these costs through hedging options and that multilateralism has not been a viable alternative option are factors that can be used to explain its constant calculation from the Cold War through to the post-Cold War period that on balance the optimum choice available for its security is to adhere to alliance with the United States.

Japan's Cold War Strategic Calculus and the U.S.-Japan Alliance

Japanese Assessments of the Cold War Strategic Environment

Prime Minister Shigeru Yoshida's decision to seek and sign the original security treaty with the United States in 1951 was a demonstration of his conviction that alignment, if not alliance, with the United States was the best vehicle available for Japan to achieve its interrelated postwar objectives of regaining national independence from the U.S.-dominated occupation, countering the potential threat of Soviet Communism, gradually reintegrating itself into the East Asia region, and assuring economic recovery. The signing of the security treaty confirmed the grand "strategic bargain" between Japan and the United States alluded to in Ikenberry's chapter in this volume. Japan was able to pursue what was later to be called the Yoshida Doctrine of minimal rearmament and the concentration on economic restructuring, provided as it was by the United States with an effective guarantee of military security and access to special economic dispensations. Japan in return provided the United States with bases for projecting military power in support of its regional Cold War military strategy.

Japanese and U.S. policymakers and commentators at the time and since have been struck by the various unequal and lopsided provisions of the original security treaty. Most prominent was the absence of an explicit commitment on the part of the United States to defend Japan (although Yoshida had always been confident that the basing of U.S. forces in Japan would be a sufficient tripwire deterrent against the Soviet Union), and of any obligation for Japan to defend the United States in a collective self-defense arrangement despite the treaty acknowledging Japan's possession of this defensive right under the UN Charter. The 1951 U.S.-Japan security treaty thus lacked the mutuality of the other bilateral treaties signed by the United States with the Philippines, Australia and New Zealand, and South Korea in the early stages of the Cold War.

Prime Ministers Ichirō Hatoyama and Nobusuke Kishi sought over time to persuade the United States to accept the removal of the unequal provisions relating to Japan by offering to inject a greater degree of mutuality into the treaty. Kishi's negotiations for the revised Treaty of Mutual Cooperation and Security of 1960 set out more clearly Japan and U.S. security responsibilities toward each other. Article 5 of the treaty provided an explicit U.S. guarantee by stating that any attack on the territory of Japan was recognized as an attack on both treaty partners. Article 6 of the treaty pledged that Japan, in order to contribute to its own security, would supply bases to the United States for the maintenance of security in the Far East. However, Japan here again stopped short of full mutuality in the treaty by stressing that its support for the United States was predicated on the right of individual rather than collective self-defense.

Japan's Cold War Risk Calculation and Management

Japan was thus able to forge, through the device of the original and revised treaties, a security relationship with the United States, the asymmetrical nature of which was seen to function much to Japan's overall benefit. Japan's choice for the security relationship in this period, however, was not made without extensive calculation about the accompanying costs and the methods available to minimize these costs. Strategic alignment with the United States carried the logic that Japan could become a proxy target in conventional or nuclear conflict with the USSR. In addition, Japan's policymakers were aware that beyond acting as part of the U.S.-inspired defensive perimeter for the containment of communism, there was the constant risk that the United States might push for Japan to become a more direct actor in the Cold War struggle outside its own territory, in areas such as the Korean Peninsula or Taiwan.

In the negotiations running up to the conclusion of both the original and revised treaties, sections of the U.S. policy community demonstrated a persistent interest in encouraging Japan to participate in and develop the necessary military capabilities to support a genuine collective self-defense arrangement. Japan was first envisaged as a key member of a collective self-defense mechanism on a multilateral and regional basis, modeled along the lines of NATO and designed to complement the creation of the Southeast Asia Treaty Organization (SEATO), that would oblige it to assist militarily both the United States and other U.S.-aligned states. Second, Japan was envisaged as, at the very least, exercising the right of collective self-defense to come to the sole and direct assistance of the United States as its treaty partner through the overseas dispatch of the SDF to defend U.S. territory.[5]

Japan's policymakers were aware during the original and revised treaty negotiations that varying U.S. ambitions for a Japanese role in collective self-defense arrangement on a regional multilateral or bilateral basis, and above all for overseas dispatch of SDF, carried major risks of entrapment. Japan would face increased U.S. pressure for a rapid buildup of its military forces, and in particular of large ground forces designed for expeditionary purposes to complement U.S. naval and air forces deployed in the region.

Japanese policymakers instead sought, while continuing to accrue certain benefits of the security treaty, to minimize the associated risks by working to preserve a degree of autonomy in security cooperation with the United States. In Article 4 of the revised treaty and in the exchange of notes that took place afterward, Japan succeeded in negotiating a U.S. pledge to consult on combat operations from bases in Japan apart from those operations conducted under Article 5. Japanese policymakers have argued that this pledge has provided them with a final veto over U.S. military operations from Japan. In fact, they have never dared to exercise this veto due to fear of alienating the United States. Nevertheless, for Japan, the right to refuse cooperation under the security treaty has served as one latent means by which to rein in U.S. military operations from its territory if they are seen to impose too great a security cost.

In the revised treaty, Japan also succeeded in limiting the functional and geographic scope of bilateral cooperation, and the consequent risks of entrapment. Since 1954 the Japanese government had asserted that although Japan as a sovereign nation under Article 7 of the UN Charter possessed the right of collective self-defense, it could not exercise that right because it would exceed interpretations of Article 9 of the Constitution of Japan that limited the use of force to the minimum necessary for self-defense. During the negotiations for the revised treaty, Japan's policymakers held to this position and the United States was forced to accept that enhanced mutuality would mean neither a Japanese collective self-defense obligation nor the overseas dispatch of the SDF.

Japanese policymakers were further able to gain U.S. assent to drop plans for the geographic scope of Article 6 of the treaty to be designated as the Asia-Pacific and to accept the less extensive designation of the Far East, as in the original treaty. Prime Minister Kishi, in Diet interpellations in February 1960, limited the scope of U.S.-Japan security cooperation by stating that while the Far East was not necessarily a clearly designated geographical region to which the treaty could be restricted, it broadly included the areas north of the Philippines and surrounding Japan (*Nihon no shūhen*), and the areas under the control of South Korea and Taiwan.

Finally, Japan's determination to retain a degree of security autonomy was demonstrated in this period by its development of key independent military capabilities. Japanese policymakers were intent to retain control of the incremental buildup of their national military capabilities, not only to assist economic recovery and to satisfy U.S. demands for expanded cooperation, but also to ensure that this was done in a balanced manner that would ultimately make for cooperation rather than dependence in security affairs. Japan accepted Mutual Security Assistance (MSA) military aid from the United States from 1953 onward, but steadfastly refused to use this aid to develop the type of large-scale ground forces that could then identify it as a candidate possessing the requisite fighting capabilities to be press-ganged into U.S.-led conflicts in East Asia.[6] Although constricted by constitutional prohibitions and the need to consider U.S. expectations for assistance in the Cold War struggle, Japan sought to create more balanced naval, air, and ground forces and indigenous defense production capabilities that befitted the aspirations of an independent state.

Japan and the Nonviability of Multilateralism

During the periods of the treaty negotiations, Japan therefore sensed considerable risks of "satellization" and entrapment in U.S. military strategy. It also felt, however, that it could exert sufficient autonomy to minimize these risks, meaning that the aggregate cost-benefit analysis was still weighted toward partial strategic accommodation with the United States. Japan's strategic choice for the security treaty in this period was reinforced by its lack of perception of any viable multilateral alternative. The bipolar divisions of the early Cold War period offered few prospects for the development of cooperative multilateral security cooperation. Japan's principal and most realizable multilateral option was thought instead to be a collective self-defense framework, centered on the United Nations or the United States.

Throughout the Cold War, Japan emphasized the importance of the United Nations to the maintenance of global and regional security and in part attempted to locate its own security policy within UN multilateralism. The original and revised security treaties stress that the U.S.-Japan security arrangements are in conformity with UN principles and that they should remain in place only until such time as the United Nations can satisfactorily provide for Japan's defense. Japan, however, was in this period clearly reluctant to exploit the United Nations more fully as an alternative security framework. Japanese policymakers were concerned that the United Nations was rendered ineffective by superpower competition and that it was unlikely ever to function as a sufficient or supplementary guarantee of security. Moreover, an active Japanese attachment to the United Nations was thought to conflict with the U.S. bilateral security guarantee because it would subject Japan to the Cold War tensions within the organization and detract from its freedom of action to cooperate with the United States under the security treaty.

Any potential Japanese commitment to a UN option was then subordinated to the exigencies of the U.S.-Japan security arrangements, and the principal role of the UN multilateralism in this period was to provide domestic and international legitimacy for the bilateralism of the security treaty. Japan's diffidence toward UN multilateralism at this time was also an indication of the fundamental contradictions that were to continue to hamper its role in the United Nations and other multilateral security frameworks for the rest of the Cold War, and arguably into the post-Cold War period. The avowed aspiration of Japanese policymakers in the security treaties was for the growth of the United Nations as a reliable and eventually alternative multilateral security framework, but in practice they looked first to the United States for security, and without acknowledging that the U.S.-Japan bilateral security treaty may have actually undercut Japan's ability to support the development of the United Nations as a viable security institution.

Japan's other multilateral option, of a U.S.-centered collective self-defense framework in the East Asia region, was also in effect a nonoption in this period. Japan's policymakers were fully aware that this type of framework was unlikely to function effectively given that many of the partners that the United States projected for it had no shared security identity with Japan and were in fact former adversaries, such as Australia and South Korea, that were strongly disinclined to accept Japan's membership in any type of regional security community. Similarly, the increasingly apparent failure of the United States to mold a nascent collective self-defense organization in the form of SEATO, which lacked both genuine multilateral character and political and military coherence, did not inspire confidence.[7] Even more important, as noted earlier, Japanese policymakers were aware that U.S. plans for a collective self-defense framework in this period involved obligations for the overseas dispatch of the SDF, and thus entrapment in U.S. regional military strategy and the very antithesis of Japan's carefully calibrated strategic posture.

Japan's Strategic Calculus in the Mid- and Latter Stages of the Cold War

Japanese perceptions that the grand strategic bargain with the United States was the best available security option continued to hold, with some fluctuations, into the mid- and later stages of the Cold War. During the Vietnam War, Japan's immediate concern was to avoid entrapment in U.S. military strategy in Southeast Asia. Japan was prepared to provide diplomatic and economic assistance to South Vietnam, but avoided any position that suggested it could follow the United States' allies, Australia and South Korea, in dispatching military forces to assist the United States. Similarly, as the price of U.S. agreement on the eventual reversion of Okinawa to Japanese administration in 1972, Japan was obliged in the Satō-Nixon joint communiqué of November 1969 to acknowledge that South Korea and Taiwan were respectively essential and important factors for the security of Japan. Nevertheless, Japan was also cautious to ensure that in the communiqué and thereafter it never provided the United States with any explicit pledge to participate directly in a regional security arrangement to support other U.S.-aligned states.[8]

During the early 1970s, the United States' pursuit of détente with the USSR and its rapprochement with China clearly reduced the risks for Japan of becoming embroiled in a regional conflict, and created space for it to pursue diplomatic and economic engagement toward China. Japan's only fear in this period was possible abandonment by the United States as a security partner as the result of bilateral economic frictions and the apparent limits of the maintenance of U.S. military hegemony in the region. Japan moved to hedge against abandonment through the device of the National Defense Program Outline (NDPO) in 1976. The NDPO was the first attempt by Japan to set out the principles of its defense policy alongside the military force structure necessary to achieve them. It was notable in emphasizing not only a qualitative buildup of Japan's national military capabilities as an implicit demonstration of efforts to relieve the defensive burdens of the United States, but also its explicit stress that Japan would maintain forces sufficient to defend itself in the first instance from direct aggression but that if this proved impossible it would seek U.S. support.

Japan was thus beginning to develop a military doctrine premised on the closer coordination of Japanese and U.S. forces.

Japanese and U.S. strategic interests began to coincide more closely during the late 1970s and 1980s due to the enhanced and common threat of the USSR. Japan found itself threatened to a more direct and greater degree than it had been threatened before by the Soviet military buildup in East Asia. In this situation, Japanese and U.S. Cold War strategic interests overlapped more clearly than they had previously, and Japanese policymakers' fears of needless entrapment in a military conflict were lessened.

Under the security treaty, Japan and the United States discovered for the first time a robust division of labor for security cooperation. Japan expanded its national military capabilities in order to assist the United States in fulfilling its obligations to defend Japan under Article 5 of the security treaty. Japan's military buildup, although predicated only on the basis of its own individual self-defense, was encouraged by the United States because it was seen to provide a more solid defensive platform from which the United States could project power under Article 6 of the treaty. Japan and the United States also embarked on the first steps toward the direct coordination of their respective military roles through the formulation of the 1978 Guidelines for U.S.-Japan Defense Cooperation. These guidelines outlined areas for bilateral cooperation relating to Japan's immediate defense under Article 5 of the security treaty (including tactical planning, joint exercises, and logistical support) and for cooperation in regional contingencies in the Far East under Article 6 (including sea lane patrol). The fact that Japan's defense efforts were mainly focused on Japan itself, and that U.S. military activities, even if outside Japanese territory, were seen to contribute clearly to Japan's own security by countering the common Soviet threat meant that the issue of collective self-defense as a basis for bilateral cooperation was not seriously raised.

In turn, enhanced bilateral cooperation at the policy elite level among Japanese and U.S. politicians and bureaucrats, and at the operational level among the SDF and their U.S. military counterparts, led to the gradual inculcation of a norm of bilateralism into the security arrangements. This norm came to reinforce Japanese perceptions of the overall utility of the security treaty and of the importance of bilateral cooperation, to the point that in 1981 Prime Minister Zenkō Suzuki was for the first time able to refer to this relationship publicly as an alliance.

The conversion of the bilateral security treaty into an alliance did not, however, eliminate Japan's residual concerns about entrapment in U.S. military strategy, or its attempts to hedge against it. Japan retained its latent veto on the U.S. use of bases, the limitations of the geographic scope of the security treaty, and most of its key constitutional prohibitions, in-

cluding the ban on collective self-defense. The SDF's emphasis on the procurement of interceptor aircraft and antisubmarine warfare ships designed to complement and defend U.S. offensive military assets operating
from Japan meant that the structure of its defense force became highly
skewed, to the point that it lacked the balanced range of capabilities necessary to defend Japan independently of the United States. In this sense,
Japan had begun to move away from one of the key hedging strategies of
its policymakers in the early Cold War period. Yet Japanese policymakers
ensured that even though the SDF and the United States increasingly developed complementary capabilities, they were still fundamentally separate. Japan avoided the integration of the SDF's command structures with
those of the United States. It also studiously avoided in-depth research
into Article 6-type cooperation under the Guidelines for U.S.-Japan Defense Cooperation for fear that this could lead to operations outside
Japan's territory. Moreover, Japan continued to seek an indigenous defense production capacity, thereby keeping a degree of security autonomy
from the United States.[9]

Japan's Post-Cold War Strategic Calculations

Japan's Post-Cold War Security Environment and Strategic Debates

Japan's strategic bargain and calculus of alliance with the United States
began to come into question with the end of the Cold War. The collapse
of the USSR removed the prime rationale for the security treaty and the
dynamic that had influenced the evolution of the alliance in the 1980s.
U.S.-Japan bilateral security arrangements also appeared poorly suited to
deal with the vagaries of the new post-Cold War strategic environment.

During the Gulf War of 1990–91, Japan failed to respond to the U.S. expectation that as an ally Japan would provide a "human contribution" to
the war effort of the U.S.-led and UN-sanctioned international coalition
against Iraq. The Japanese government was unable to navigate the UN
Peace Cooperation Corps bill through the Diet in October 1990, which
would have enabled the dispatch of SDF to the Gulf region for noncombat
logistical operations. It was obliged instead to financially underwrite the
war with a total contribution of US$13 billion that was derided by much
of international opinion as "checkbook diplomacy."[10] The final outcome
of the international and domestic crisis generated by the Gulf War was to
provide political momentum for the enactment of the International Peace
Cooperation Law (IPCL) in June 1992, which has enabled the subsequent
dispatch of the SDF on UN peacekeeping operation (PKO) missions.

Japan's failure to support its U.S. ally in the Gulf War and to meet U.S. requests to participate more actively in security affairs at the global level suffered a repeat performance at the regional level in the North Korean nuclear crisis of 1994. In spite of its shared concerns about North Korea's suspected nuclear weapons program, Japan found itself politically hesitant and militarily incapable of supporting U.S. attempts to apply military pressure on North Korea during the crisis. The nuclear crisis exposed the fundamental lack of military operability of the U.S.-Japan alliance that resulted from Japan's reluctance since 1978 to study in depth Article 6-type bilateral cooperation for regional contingencies under the original Defense Guidelines, as pointed out in the previous section.[11]

U.S.-Japan alliance jitters in the mid-1990s were compounded by domestic questioning on both sides of the alliance's utility. Japanese domestic criticism of the alliance focused on renewed opposition to U.S. bases in Okinawa. Since reversion to Japanese administration in 1972, around 60 percent of the 37,000 U.S. troops in Japan have continued to be stationed in Okinawa, with U.S. bases accounting for close to 10 percent of the total land area of the prefecture. The necessity of this high concentration of U.S. forces in Okinawa came into question with the end of the Cold War. The protests of Okinawa's prefectural government and of sizeable sections of its civil society against this disproportionately heavy U.S. military presence obliged the Japanese and U.S. governments to create the Special Action Committee on Facilities and Areas in Okinawa (SACO) in November 1995. SACO's reports in 1996 recommended a general reduction of 20 percent in the land area of U.S. bases in Okinawa and the return of the Futenma Marine Corp air station at Ginowan. The SACO report assuaged Okinawan opposition to the bases, but as of early 2003 the issue has not been resolved because Futenma is yet to be relocated to an alternative site. Meanwhile, from the U.S. side, the utility of the alliance was brought into question due to trade frictions and accusations that Japan was a free rider in defense.

Since the mid-1990s, in addition to the global and regional security tests of the Gulf War and North Korea, as well as the domestic criticisms emanating from frictions over Okinawa and trade, the alliance has also been faced with a variety of new post-Cold War challenges to its continued functioning and viability. Japan is increasingly conscious of the looming military challenge of China. The preferred option of its policymakers has been and continues to be the political and economic engagement of China. Nevertheless, China's intimidation of Taiwan through military exercises and missile tests in 1995 and 1996 in the run up to presidential elections, and intensified bilateral tensions over the sovereignty of the Senkaku Islands since 1996, have been seen by Japanese policymakers as increasing evidence of China's willingness to project military power in pursuit of its national interests.

China represents for Japan and the United States a potential interstate regional security challenge to set alongside that of North Korea. It is also clear that in the future the alliance will have to adjust to deal with nonstate security challenges at the regional and global levels. Japan's policymakers have argued strongly that the events of September 11 (which claimed the lives of twenty-four Japanese citizens) are a demonstration of the threat posed to international stability by terrorist networks such as al-Qaeda. Japan has been made doubly aware of the threat of terrorism by the Aum Shinrikyō's sarin gas attack on the Tokyo underground in 1995 and by the bombing in Bali in October 2002.[12] Japan has consequently been faced with the expectation that it should find ways to respond to the threats of transnational terrorism in conjunction with its U.S. ally and as a member of international society.

The contemporary and emerging challenges posed for Japan's security by the changing post-Cold War international strategic environment, and related questions about the recent ability of the U.S.-Japan alliance to respond to these challenges, have created the conditions for an ongoing debate among Japanese policymakers about the future viability of the alliance, and about the necessity and means to upgrade its functions. Japanese policy continues to be strongly influenced by antimilitaristic norms and prohibitions. However, mainstream opinion has firmly shifted toward acceptance of Japan's need to play a more active or "normal" role in regional and global security. Japan's security debate was first framed in terms of its assuming a so-called normal role following its failure to respond to requests from the United States and the international community for military participation in the Gulf War. In particular, former LDP power-broker and later leader of the Liberal Party Ichirō Ozawa gave life to this debate with his argument from the time of the Gulf War onward that Japan should become a "normal state" (*futsū no kuni*).[13] Ozawa posited that Japan, in determining its reaction to the Gulf War, should have taken greater note of the Preamble of the Constitution of Japan, which obliges Japan to cooperate with the international community for the purposes of international stability. Utilizing this constitutional interpretation, Japan should thus have been free to exercise the right of *collective security* to support the United States and its other coalition partners in the UN-sanctioned war effort.

Collective security is seen to differ from collective self-defense in that the latter is an inherent right under the UN Charter that can be exercised without UN approval, whereas the former is a right that can be exercised only if sanctioned by the United Nations. Ozawa has argued ever since that the Preamble—preferably combined with a revision of Article 9 to acknowledge Japan's right to maintain military forces for the support of international stability—provides Japan with the ability to participate in any form of UN-sanctioned and centered multilateral military operation, from PKO to full combat peace enforcement.

Ozawa's concept of a normal Japanese security role and his radical UN-centered collective security option was rejected at the time of the Gulf War. Nevertheless, since the early 1990s the idea of the normal state has been explicitly and implicitly appropriated by other sections of the policymaking community in Japan and then taken in different directions with different implications for the U.S.-Japan alliance. Japanese Gaullist opinion has argued that Japan should assume a more normal security role by removing constitutional prohibitions, increasing its national military capacity, and eventually abrogating the security treaty with the United States, because this is the only way for Japan to break its security dependence on an external power and function as a truly independent sovereign state.[14]

The dominant strains of opinion about seeking a normal role for Japan, however, are those in favor of strengthening Japan's individual military capabilities in tandem with strengthening the alliance. Japan's most influential LDP, MOFA, and JDA policymakers have largely held to the position that the pathway to the normalization of Japanese security policy is the incremental expansion of national military capabilities and responsibilities within the framework of existing constitutional prohibitions and the U.S.-Japan alliance.[15] However, Japanese and U.S. policymakers both within and outside government have also increasingly debated whether there is need for a more radical expansion of Japan's military capabilities and simultaneous reinforcement of the alliance functions. Some commentators argue that Japan should take on enhanced capabilities and responsibilities to assist the United States, and that the United States should provide Japan with greater consultation on regional and global security affairs. In large part, this more equal partnership would involve Japan in reexamining its constitutional prohibitions and ending its ban on the exercise of the right of collective self-defense—thereby bringing to an end the asymmetries of the alliance in place since the Cold War.[16]

Japan's Readjusted Strategic Bargain with the United States

Japanese questioning of the future direction of national security policy and the U.S.-Japan alliance fed into official policy with the publication in August 1994 of the report of the Prime Minister's Advisory Group on Defense, known as the Higuchi Report. Designed to serve as a preparatory document for the revision of the 1976 NDPO, the report recommended that Japan should adapt its policy to the post-Cold War strategic environment not only by strengthening its military cooperation with the United States, but also by taking initiatives to increase SDF involvement in UN PKO activities, and by promoting multilateral security dialogue in East Asia.[17] The report, if fully implemented, would have produced a significant shift in Japanese security policy toward greater multilateralism.

Japan's wavering with regard to its commitment to the bilateral alliance (called "alliance drift" by *Asahi Shinbun* journalist Yōichi Funabashi) was arrested, however, by the intervention of U.S. and Japanese policymakers.[18] The first moves to strengthen the U.S.-Japan alliance came from the United States and the production of the East Asian Strategic Review (EASR) in February 1995. The Review stated that the United States would retain 100,000 troops in East Asia; it also focused on the rehabilitation of the U.S.-Japan alliance as one of the keystones of U.S. security strategy in the region. In turn, Japan's attempts to restructure its security policy were conducted in relative coordination with U.S. security initiatives. The revised NDPO of October 1995 mirrored the Higuchi Report in stressing the need for an enhanced SDF contribution to UN PKO and the promotion of multilateral security dialogue; but it was also formulated with the draft EASR in hand and with a view to strengthening the U.S.-Japan alliance. The revised NDPO differed from the original version in stating that Japan would now seek from the outset to repeal any form of direct aggression with U.S. assistance. It also stressed that Japan would seek to cooperate with the United States to deal with situations in areas surrounding Japan (*shūhen*) that affected Japan's security, thereby carrying over the purport of the unfinished research on U.S.-Japan cooperation under the 1978 Guidelines for U.S.-Japan Defense Cooperation and the conviction on the need for bilateral cooperation to respond to regional contingencies.

Japan and the United States next moved to strengthen the alliance through the issuance on April 17, 1996, of the U.S.-Japan Joint Declaration on Security: Alliance for the Twenty-First Century. This declaration stressed the importance of the bilateral alliance for the security not only of Japan but also, for the first time, of the entire Asia-Pacific. It outlined areas for future security cooperation, including technology exchange and Ballistic Missile Defense (BMD) research, and most important, for the revision of the 1978 guidelines and research into military cooperation to deal with situations in areas surrounding Japan (*shūhen*).

U.S.-Japan bilateral research produced the revised Guidelines for U.S.-Japan Defense Cooperation in September 1997. As noted in the introductory section of this chapter, the revised guidelines outlined for the first time Japan's military support for the United States in regional contingencies, including the provision of rear-end logistics, the enforcement of economic sanctions, and the use of SDF and civilian base facilities. Japan again stopped short of any form of support for the United States that involved combat or the breach of the ban on the exercise of collective self-defense, but the revised guidelines still represented a significant upgrading of the military operability of the alliance.

The NDPO, the Joint Declaration, and the revised guidelines are important adjustments to the U.S.-Japan strategic bargain. Japanese and U.S. policymakers are correct to point out that these developments constitute simply a reaffirmation of the alliance in the sense that the letter of the security treaty remains strictly intact and the revised guidelines fill in the gaps in the operability of the alliance left open since the Cold War period. Nevertheless, in other ways these policymakers are disingenuous in claiming that there has been no redefinition of the security treaty and alliance in terms of its practical emphasis and function. The revised guidelines are an indication that the division of labor between Japan and the United States that developed in the latter stages of the Cold War can no longer be strictly demarcated. Japan can no longer satisfy U.S. expectations of fulfilling an alliance defense burden by acting as a de facto front-line state against the USSR and by purely defending its own territory in line with Article 5 of the security treaty. U.S. strategic priorities and expectations for Japanese alliance cooperation have shifted to Article 6 of the treaty in order to meet regional contingencies, such as North Korea and Taiwan. The emphasis of the revised guidelines on military cooperation in areas surrounding Japan reflects this regionalization of alliance functions and adjusted strategic bargain; Japan retains U.S. security guarantees but it must reciprocate by supporting U.S. power projection capabilities more actively, both regionally and beyond.

Japan's awareness of the need to expand the range of support for the United States beyond the traditional functional and geographic confines of Cold War interpretations of the security treaty and the alliance has been demonstrated also by its reaction to the U.S. war on terrorism. As noted in the introductory section of this chapter, Japan's response has taken the form of the enactment of the ATSML and the dispatch of units of the Maritime Self-Defense Forces (MSDF) and the Air Self-Defense Force (ASDF) to support U.S. and other concerned states' efforts to combat transnational terrorism and the al-Qaeda network in Afghanistan. To take these steps, Japan was forced to circumvent the Constitution's prohibition of collective self-defense. The U.S. and NATO allies engaged in the Afghan campaign have primarily justified their involvement on the basis of the rights of individual and collective self-defense. Japanese policymakers might arguably have had the option to invoke the right of individual self-defense due to the number of Japanese fatalities in the events of September 11. Instead, their preference has been for a noncombat and logistical role in support of the Afghan campaign that neither invokes individual self-defense nor challenges the ban on collective self-defensive but is predicated on relevant UN resolutions. Japan has stressed UN resolutions that identify the September 11 attacks on the United States as a threat to international peace and call on all member states, and by implication Japan, to combat terrorism. Japan has been able to link these resolutions to its own Constitution in order to legitimize SDF dispatch. It has done this by switching emphasis from Article 9 of the Constitution to the Preamble, which states, as explained earlier, that Japan should work with international society for the preservation of peace. Japan has been able to use the Preamble to argue that it should support the United Nations as international society's highest representative and its relevant resolutions to combat terrorism by dispatching the SDF to the Indian Ocean area.[19]

Japan included provisions in the ATSML that enabled the MSDF and ASDF to provide logistical and refueling support for U.S. and other international forces across an area stretching from the Indian Ocean to Australia, Japan, and the United States, and that allowed the Ground Self-Defense Forces (GSDF) to operate in Pakistan and India to provide medical care and protection for refugees from the Afghan conflict and wounded U.S. personnel. In devising its response to the war on terrorism, Japan has stretched its constitutional interpretations to the utmost, and as many policymakers admit, it is now to all intents and purposes involved in an active war campaign with the United States. Yet even this role is indirect and distanced from the actual battlefield.

Japan's Post-Cold War Strategic Calculus

The turnaround in the propensity and level of Japan's commitment to provide active support for the United States to deal with regional and global security crises during the ten-year period from the Gulf War to the war on terrorism appears remarkable. Japan's overall strategic calculus, despite the doubts of the early post-Cold War period, clearly remains weighted toward the strategic benefits of continued alliance with the United States and can be accounted for by a number of factors. Japanese policymakers, faced in the short to medium term with the potential threat from North Korea and in the long term with the latent threat of China and in general with an uncertain strategic environment in East Asia, have concluded that the bilateral relationship with the United States remains the most reliable quantity in their overall security calculations. The alliance with the United States is perceived as continuing to provide a framework that enables Japan to gradually assume an enhanced regional and global security role, and it works to suppress, if not always resolve, many potential regional security threats. Moreover, Japanese policymakers are aware that if the alliance relationship were to fail, then one option Japan might be forced to pursue for its defense is a rapid qualitative and quantitative expansion of its independent national military capabilities. The outcome of this expansion could be to produce enhanced fears of Japan's remilitarization and militarism in East Asia, an action-reaction arms race dynamic in the region, and a costly downward spiral of insecurity.

Japanese perceptions of the utility of the alliance are also buttressed by increasingly deeply rooted norms of bilateralism among key sections of the policymaking community and by the growth of the alliance as a quasi-institution. Japan and U.S. interaction at the policy elite and military operation levels that began during the Cold War has gathered further momentum since the 1990s, leading to a greater coincidence of normative worldviews and Japanese acceptance of the central importance of bilateral cooperation as a means to safeguard regional and global political, economic, and security orders.[20] In short, Japan continues to view the alliance as its safest security bet, and its policymakers have acquired deeply ingrained normative habits of bilateral behavior.

Japan's acceptance of a strengthened bilateral alliance as the outcome of its post-Cold War strategic calculus is further confirmed by its policymakers' knowledge that a strengthened alliance carries strategic risks as well as benefits, but that they still have at their disposal the means to manage both the entrapment and abandonment alliance dilemmas. As they were during the Cold War, Japanese policymakers are aware that the United States can be a capricious superpower ally with a regional and global security agenda that may supersede its interests vis-à-vis Japan. Japanese concerns about abandonment by the U.S. surfaced momentarily during the period of so-called alliance drift in the early stages of the Clinton administration in the mid-1990s, and then again toward the later stages of the administration in the late 1990s as the United States appeared disaffected with Japan's economic malaise and instead to be prioritizing relations with a rising China. Japan's reaction to this potential abandonment by the United States has been to strengthen the alliance, but also to explore, as seen later, other bilateral and multilateral options for its security.

Given U.S.-Japan recognition, however, of the importance of the alliance and of the moves to strengthen it, the most probable alliance dilemma scenario for Japan is entrapment in U.S. regional and global military strategy. U.S. expectations that U.S.-Japan bilateral cooperation should shift from Article 5 to Article 6 and include contingencies such as the Korean Peninsula and Taiwan, combined with the adverse reaction of China to the strengthening of the alliance's regional contingency functions and the advent of the George W. Bush administration, which has fixed even more firmly on the U.S.-Japan alliance as the foundation of U.S. regional strategy, have intensified the entrapment dilemma. In particular, if the definition of *shūhen* in the revised guidelines were ever operationalized, Japan would be forced to choose between its engagement strategy toward China and its alliance with the United States, thereby upsetting its careful balancing act between its regional and global interests throughout the postwar period.

Nevertheless, Japan's policymakers have continued to deploy a number of traditional hedging tactics to minimize and manage the risks of entrapment. During the process of the revision of the defense guidelines, Japan took pains to stress that it still retained the option of saying no to the United States if it felt that Article 6-type cooperation did not function on behalf of the immediate security of Japan. The political costs of sustaining the alliance by using the final veto noted earlier are still too great to make it anything but a last-ditch option to check U.S. security behavior. Japan has instead fallen back on the option of continuing to manipulate the geographic scope of the security treaty to obfuscate and build in limitations to its security commitments. Japanese government policymakers maintain that the revised guidelines were not designed to counter the threat from any specific country, and that the term *shūhen* used in the guidelines as well as in the NDPO is situational rather than geographic. They argue that Prime Minister Kishi's 1960 definition of the Far East remains intact and that the revised guidelines contain a geographic element in that the range of action of the security treaty is most likely to be close to Japan. They also stress, however, Kishi's additional statements at the time that definitions of *shūhen* are not necessarily geographically rigid or restrictive of the security treaty's range of action, and they posit that it is not possible to draw a firm geographic line to demarcate Japan's security interests.

This concept of situational need introduces a valuable element of strategic ambiguity into the coverage of the U.S.-Japan security treaty and enables Japan to hedge against a regional contingency involving China and the United States. Utilizing the strengthened regional contingency functions of the revised guidelines, and in line with the 1960 definition of the Far East, Japan retains the option to support the United States in order to deter Chinese military action against Taiwan. At the same time, Japan's simultaneous utilization of the concept of situational need under the revised guidelines enables it to choose to deemphasize the clear-cut geographic specification of Taiwan as part of *shūhen* and as a concern of the U.S.-Japan security treaty and guidelines, and thereby deemphasize the designation of China as a threat and the risks of antagonizing it that could overturn its preferred strategy of engagement.

Japan has also minimized the risks of involuntary participation in U.S. regional military strategy by adhering to its own constitutional prohibitions. Throughout the revision of the guidelines, Japan's policymakers doggedly held the line that the legitimization for enhanced bilateral cooperation remained Japan's self-defense. The refusal to breach the prohibition on the exercise of the right of collective self-defense, despite the heightened domestic debate on this issue, has meant that Japanese policy elites have remained the final arbiters of which regional contingencies pose a sufficient security risk to warrant Japanese support for U.S. military action. Finally, Japan has again sought to hedge against entrapment by the careful structuring of its military forces and by the retention of key independent military capabilities. Japan and the United States have sought to coordinate their command and control systems more closely through a comprehensive mechanism in order to implement the revised guidelines. Japan has taken care, however, to ensure that these systems remain distinct and nonintegrated. It has also eschewed the development of power projection capabilities. This is in line with constitutional prohibitions and with the principle of "exclusively defense-oriented defense." At the same time, however, Japan's relative lack of long-range defensive expeditionary force capabilities that can complement U.S.-led coalitions (with the exception of its minesweeping functions) has also enabled it to evade U.S. demands for the dispatch of the SDF outside Japan's immediate area.

Japan has found it increasingly difficult to maintain indigenous production capabilities for key military technologies and has been obliged to explore with the United States greater joint research and development of key weapons such as the F-2 fighter aircraft and BMD systems. Even so, Japan has still attempted to maintain independent production capabilities, not only for reasons of military-civilian technology "spin-on" and "techno-nationalism," but also to ensure a degree of continued autonomy in military affairs that lessens dependence on the United States and the risks of entrapment.[21] Japan's decision since 1999, in reaction to North Korea's test-firing of a Taepondong-1 missile over Japan in September 1998, to acquire its own intelligence satellites, as inferior as these might be to U.S. off-the-shelf products, is a demonstration of this drive for a degree of security autonomy from the United States.

Japanese hedging tactics are also evident in its response to the war on terrorism. Contrary to speculation in both Japan and the United States, Japan has not yet "crossed the Rubicon" in dispatching the SDF to the Indian Ocean area and in terms of providing unequivocal military support for its U.S. ally in future operations in the war on terrorism or other conflicts. Japan's policymakers have again held the line on the nonexercise of collective self-defense and on limited SDF dispatch to noncombat functions, and they have made it clear that dispatch is outside the framework of the bilateral security treaty and the revised defense guidelines and is predicated instead on specific UN resolutions relating to September 11 and the Afghan conflict. In this way, even though it has in practice provided substantial military support for the United States in the Afghan campaign, Japan has retained the legal safeguard to avoid providing similar cooperation for the United States in other military operations relating to the war on terrorism that are not sanctioned by the UN, and to avoid providing similar support in the context of the bilateral security treaty in East Asia.

Aware that the possession and deployment of certain military capabilities in the military theater could lead to expanded requests for military cooperation from the United States, Japanese policymakers have also been cautious in deciding the actual composition of the SDF forces dispatched to the Indian Ocean area. Japan initially decided not to dispatch the MSDF's destroyers equipped with Kongō-class *Aegis* war-fighting systems (AWS) to the Indian Ocean area in its first deployments in November 2001, and then relented on this decision only in December 2002. Japanese policymakers were deeply divided on the issue of Aegis dispatch because, on the one hand, they recognized that the AWS destroyers are the MSDF's most capable asset and thus provide it with maximum flexibility and security in an uncertain theater of operations, while on the other hand they were concerned that the high degree of interoperability between MSDF and U.S. Navy warships equipped with the AWS might lead to U.S. requests for Japan to deploy its naval assets as substitutes for those of the United States, thus raising questions of the potential for the exercise of collective self-defense, and the risk of Japanese forces becoming directly involved in combat operations.

Japan's government eventually made the decision for *Aegis* dispatch only after persistent internal pressure from MOFA, JDA, and MSDF, which sought to maximize the safety of Japanese forces and the degree of visible support for the U.S.-led war effort, and after the damping down of hostilities in Afghanistan, which minimized the risks of the SDF becoming involved in combat operations. Japanese caution was also seen in the decision not to dispatch the GSDF to Pakistan under the ATSML. In part this decision was obviated by the relative lack of U.S. casualties in the Afghan war and by the ability of aid agencies to cope with refugee flows. In part, however, the government was also influenced by fears that the GSDF could become embroiled in land-combat operations in the volatile environment of Pakistan.

*Japan's Multilateral Options and Nonoptions in the
Post-Cold War Period*

In addition to their analysis of the relative benefits and costs of alliance and available hedging options, Japanese policymakers' strategic choice in favor of strengthening the U.S.-Japan alliance after the Cold War has been strongly influenced by their perceptions of the availability and viability of multilateral frameworks as alternative security options. Japan has undoubtedly sought to explore multilateralism as a security option far more deeply in the post-Cold War period than it did during the Cold War. Japan was especially encouraged in the early 1990s as the relaxation of regional tensions and the Clinton administration's own "multilateral moment" in regard to APEC and other regional organizations offered an environment conducive to multilateral frameworks. Japan's revised NDPO stresses that the bilateral U.S.-Japan security arrangements facilitate the promotion of multilateral security dialogue and cooperation, as well as support for UN activities. The U.S.-Japan Joint Declaration on Security asserts that the two states will cooperate with each other and with other states to further promote multilateral security dialogue bodies such as the ARF.

Japan is now known, as outlined in Chapter 11, to have played a major part in initiating ASEAN's moves to create the ARF and has been one of its most consistent supporters. Japan has matched its support for the ARF's Track I security dialogue with active participation in a variety of Track II dialogue bodies such as the Council on Security and Cooperation in Asia-Pacific (CSCAP), the Trilateral Forum on North Pacific Security, and the Northeast Asia Cooperation Dialogue (NEACD). The Japanese government further dabbled with multilateral security concepts in the region by suggesting since 1997 the possibility of a four-way dialogue on security among Japan, the United States, Russia, and China, and that Japan and Russia could be added to the four-way peace talks over the Korean Peninsula to create a six-way peace framework. The director general of the JDA in March 2002 also suggested (in what has become known as the Shangri-La initiative, after its Singapore hotel conference venue) that the ARF, which mainly involves foreign ministry officials in the region, could be complemented by a defense ministers' forum.

APEC has served for Japan as a type of security forum for the multilateral discussion of the Korean Peninsula and East Timor. Japan has also utilized the margins of APEC and the ASEAN+3 (APT) as a space for more informal, minilateral and multiple bilateral security dialogues with China, South Korea, Russia, the United States, and individual ASEAN states. In addition, Japan has been an active member of the U.S.-inspired Trilateral Coordination and Oversight Group (TCOG), which has func-

tioned to promote trilateral U.S.-Japan-South Korea diplomatic cooperation to respond to the North Korean security problem.

Japan's support for multilateral security cooperation at the regional
level via the United Nations has grown significantly in the post-Cold War
period with Japan's participation in UN PKO operations. Japan's human
contribution to the United National Transitional Authority Cambodia
(UNTAC) and PKO activities took the form of providing 600 GSDF engineers for supply and reconstruction projects from 1992 to 1993. In
2002, Japan also dispatched 680 GSDF personnel for reconstruction activities in East Timor, and unfroze provisions in the IPCL that now enable
the SDF to participate in core UN PKO activities, including the monitoring of ceasefires; the inspection, transport, and disposal of weapons; and
the exchange of prisoners.

Japan's participation in multilateral security frameworks thus represents a total reversal of its position during the Cold War with regard to
the acceptance of regional security dialogue, and a major expansion with
regard to UN-centered multilateral activities. Japan's support of the formation and maintenance of these frameworks, and the importance of
their contribution to confidence building and stability in East Asia,
should not be belittled. It is clear, however, that few Japanese policymakers really view multilateral frameworks as viable security options in terms
of their assuming a major and effective role in guaranteeing Japan's security over the medium to long terms. Moreover, in relation to the existing
U.S.-Japan security arrangements, few policymakers see multilateral
frameworks as capable of significantly bolstering the functions of the alliance, let alone developing as practical alternatives. Indeed, it is arguable
that, as is explained in this section, the factor of multilateralism is actually perceived in certain cases not to be such an effective hedge against
and to ameliorate the costs of the alliance with the United States, but to
potentially accentuate these costs by complicating the dilemmas of entrapment and abandonment—entrapment in the sense that multilateral
frameworks may actually work to reinforce Japan's dependence on a
U.S.-determined security agenda; and abandonment in the sense that multilateral frameworks may work for a divergence of U.S.-Japan security interests that undermines the alliance.

Therefore, contrary to the arguments of Japanese and U.S. policymakers and academics, as mentioned in the introduction to this chapter,
Japan's participation in multilateral security frameworks does not necessarily involve a straightforward development upward and outward from
the base of U.S.-Japan bilateral cooperation, nor does it imply that both
types of approaches to security are capable of developing equally or are
sustainable in conjunction. Instead, the recent record of Japan's support

for multilateral security frameworks suggests that bilateralism and multilateralism are in tension with each other, and that Japanese policymakers
have been reluctant to experiment too far with the latter for fear of undo-
ing the strategic bargain of the former and enhancing its associated risks.

That bilateralism and multilateralism make uncomfortable and even ir-
reconcilable bedfellows is illustrated by examining the limitations of
Japan's participation in extant and putative regional cooperative security,
in U.S.- and UN-centered collective self-defense, and in UN-centered collective multilateral security frameworks. Japan's commitment to the ARF
as a multilateral cooperative and regional security dialogue body has been
active, but this participation clearly remains a highly limited option for
Japan's security policy. This is because Japan's participation in this form of
multilateral cooperative security framework has been tailored to conform
to the overarching constraints of U.S.-Japan bilateral alliance objectives,
and because this framework is seen to have only moderate potential to develop into a practical framework for augmenting Japan's security.

Japan has been motivated to participate in the ARF to reassure regional
states about its security intentions in the fluid post-Cold War international
environment, and in large part, as noted in Chapter 11, to ensure its U.S.
ally's continued security engagement in the region. Japan is able to participate in the ARF because as a cooperative security dialogue body it involves no obligations for the exercise of military force, and thus is in line
with the principle of individual self-defense. Just as important, the absence
of any military commitment means that the multilateralism of the ARF
can in no way challenge Japan's present or future bilateral military commitments to the United States. Hence, for Japan the ARF serves as a multilateral framework that ensures the essential continuity and reinforcement
of the primacy of the U.S.-Japan alliance and limits the risks of abandonment. Not unsurprisingly, Japan has ascribed to the ARF the role of supplemental rather than alternative security framework to the alliance.

In turn, it can be argued that Japan's continued subordination of ARF
multilateralism to the demands of U.S.-Japan alliance bilateralism has ensured that the ARF is not just at best a supplement to the alliance, but it
also has had even these supplemental functions undercut by the alliance
relationship, thus demonstrating the essential incompatibility of multilateral and bilateral approaches in the case of cooperative security. Japanese
policymakers and commentators have asserted that they have no choice
but to prioritize the bilateral alliance because the ARF's security function
remains highly limited in both conception and practice for all involved
states. Most notable among the ARF's limitations has been its lack of a
mandate and of organizational capacity to tackle interstate tensions in
Northeast Asia with regard to North Korea and Taiwan and intrastate

conflict in Southeast Asia, and to move from its current state of confidence building and security measures to preventive diplomacy. It would not be reasonable to criticize Japanese policymakers for failing to rely on the ARF to deal with these issues, because few member states have envisaged the ARF as a body that can deal practically with these issues alone or substitute for existing individual national and alliance deterrence capabilities. Nevertheless, it is important for Japanese policymakers to acknowledge that the continued prioritization of the U.S.-Japan alliance has been not only the consequence but also the cause of the relative inability to date of the ARF to develop in order to fulfill even its more limited mandate of cooperative security.

Japan's strong attachment to bilateralism does not sit comfortably with multilateral security dialogue principles and in fact undermines the prospects for its development. Multilateral cooperative security relies on the principle that no attempt should be made to designate, explicitly or implicitly, certain states within a region as adversaries, and it stresses the need for all regional states, even those of potential concern, to cooperate with one another to eliminate sources of military conflict. Japanese and U.S. efforts to strengthen their alliance, and the well-understood fact in all states of the region, despite Japanese obfuscation and hedging tactics, that China is to all intents and purposes one of the most likely adversaries for alliance military cooperation, contravene these principles. China has often been seen as responsible for obstructing the progress of the ARF toward preventive diplomacy. It has most certainly been interested in restricting ARF functions to confidence-building measures since it joined the body in 1994, and even before the strengthening of the U.S.-Japan alliance in the mid-1990s. However, since the mid-1990s, the enhanced regional security functions of the U.S.-Japan alliance have clearly contributed to China's reluctance to push forward the ARF process with partners that see China as a potential adversary. In this sense, it can be said that in spite of the metaphorical talk of the U.S.-Japan alliance as a platform for the growth of ARF cooperative security, the bilateral alliance has actually proved to be a ceiling on the further development of these forms of regionwide multilateral frameworks.

Japan's potential participation in any type of collective self-defense and multilateral security arrangement can also be seen as conditioned by and meant to serve the purposes of alliance bilateralism, far more than serving as any type of viable alternative to the alliance. Japan would be able to consider participation in such a multilateral framework only if it were to lift its constitutional prohibition on the exercise of collective self-defense. As noted earlier, since the early 1990s Japan has faced increased domestic and international demands to exercise this right in order to move toward achieving a normal role in security. It is important to note, however, that the majority of those pushing for Japan to revise its constitutional prohibitions, especially the most influential figures in policymaking circles in Japan and the United States, advocate this course of action primarily because it is a means by which Japan can further expand its support for the bilateral alliance rather than a way of equalizing its security role in multilateral frameworks. Japanese and U.S. policymakers in favor of the exercise of collective self-defense do not deny the utility of Japan's participation in UN-centered or other multilateral frameworks, but this is clearly a secondary consideration to the prime one of upgrading the ease of bilateral alliance cooperation. Japan is seen as exercising the collective self-defense multilateral option in order to participate primarily in U.S.-led multilateral coalitions of the willing along the lines of the Gulf War and the war on terrorism that may or may not be under the sanction of the United Nations.

In practice, therefore, Japan's exercise of collective self-defense may simply serve to strengthen U.S.-Japan bilateral security linkages further, with participation in multilateral frameworks enhanced but still functioning as a secondary appendage to the alliance. Japan could then be faced with scenarios similar to the Cold War period of debate on collective self-defense—aware that the exercise of this right in the name of multilateralism will in actuality lead only to greater dependence on U.S. bilateralism and entrapment.

Japan's other conceivable multilateral security option is to explore enhanced UN-centered frameworks. Japan has shown an inclination to expand UN cooperation in a number of ways. It has been able to expand cooperation with the UN incrementally by keeping in place current constitutional prohibitions and utilizing the principle of individual self-defense. As already observed, this has enabled it to take on important UN PKOs and to exploit UN resolutions to expand the range of Japan's cooperation in the war on terrorism since 2001. Japan also has available the option of exercising collective self-defense in line with and to serve the principles of the UN Charter, and to enable full participation in UN activities.

Just as radical is the potential option of collective security. Japan rejected this Ozawa-inspired proposal for a normal role in security at the time of the Gulf War. Nevertheless, Japan's participation in the Afghan campaign, with its stress on the Preamble of the Japanese Constitution and on UN resolutions as the de jure basis for SDF dispatch, has edged Japan toward a latent, if not yet acknowledged, collective security option. If it were to take this option in the future, Japan could participate in all forms of UN-sanctioned security activities, both in conjunction with and independent of the United States. Japan's collective security option could thus make for greater U.S.-Japan bilateral cooperation in a new range of coalition missions and in scenarios like that of the first Gulf War. It could also, however, allow Japan, on the basis of UN resolutions, to remove its military capabilities from the context and control of the bilateral alliance, to place them under the control of the UN Security Council (UNSC), and actually to prevent U.S.-Japan cooperation in certain instances. Japan's careful use of UN resolutions to both expand and limit its role in the Afghan campaign in support of the United States is an example of how a multilateral collective security option under the auspices of the United Nations could check bilateral cooperation and undermine political confidence in the alliance.

Japan's strong interest in a UNSC permanent seat means that it will continue to deepen cooperation with UN-centered multilateral security activities. It is likely, however, to be ultracautious in expanding cooperation with the United Nations through the utilization of collective self-defense or collective security options. Japanese exercise of collective self-defense, given the realities of U.S. leadership in international coalitions, is likely, even under the sanction of the United Nations, to compound the risks of entrapment. Japanese exercise of collective security could accentuate the risks of entrapment, and more likely abandonment, especially if Japan is more beholden to the demands of the United Nations than to its U.S. ally. Instead, the most likely path of Japan's UN-centered multilateral activities is to continue to explore the current incremental path of expanding cooperation in PKO and in the types of measures contained in the ATSML and in similar legal frameworks in the future. This offers Japan the ability to make an active multilateral contribution to international security via the United Nations that is at times distinct from the function of the U.S.-Japan alliance, but also to maintain the bilateral alliance as the principal foundation of its security policy.

Indeed, it is apparent that in the post-Cold War period, as in the Cold War period, for Japanese policymakers one of the principal functions of the United Nations is to provide multilateral legitimization for the incremental expansion of U.S.-Japan bilateral security activities that are seen not to impose unmanageable risks of entrapment. The role of the United Nations as a "stalking horse" for recent developments in the expansion of alliance cooperation can be seen in a number of ways. The revised NDPO and the revised Guidelines for U.S.-Japan Defense Cooperation, although designed to facilitate bilateral cooperation, again both draw on the United Nations for their legitimacy. Japan's participation in PKO has been seen by some as a means to enable SDF dispatch to accomplish the goal that was not possible at the time of the first Gulf War of removing restrictions on the overseas dispatch of the SDF on an individual self-defense basis and then of preparing the domestic and international conditions for SDF dispatch on other missions that are non-UN-centered, including support for U.S. forces in East Asia. Japan's role in the war on terrorism has been a partial realization of this goal, and the clearest demonstration that UN multilateralism can be manipulated as the justification for bilateral objectives.

Japan's Security Policy Toward Bilateralism Plus

From the above discussion, Japan can be seen to have consistently prioritized alliance bilateralism over cooperative, collective self-defense, and collective security forms of multilateralism. Japanese policymakers have tried to graft cooperative security onto the bilateral alliance, but its viability has been sapped by the alliance itself. Collective self-defense engenders too many uncertainties and potential alliance costs. Collective security is a too-radical option that spells entrapment or abandonment. Hence, the alliance may have strengthened and regionalized its functions in the post–Cold War period, but this is yet to be accompanied by any serious multilateralization. Multilateralism is a "bolt on" and supplemental accessory that primarily serves the needs of bilateralism. The U.S.-Japan alliance embraces multilateralism only in the sense of "bilateralism plus."

Japan's continued preference for strengthened bilateralism and the underdevelopment of multilateral security options can be explained by its overall strategic calculation in the post–Cold War period. Japanese policymakers have concluded that in an uncertain strategic environment the U.S.-Japan alliance remains the most reliable form of security insurance, and that even though the strengthening of the bilateral security arrangements also carries potentially heavy risks, Japan can employ a variety of tactics to hedge against these. Multilateralism is one option that Japan's policymakers are prepared to experiment with in order to hedge against total security dependence on the United States, but at present multilateral frameworks are not seen as viable options because they lack efficacy or only exacerbate alliance risks. Therefore, Japan's highly complex strategic calculus has arrived at the simple outcome that, given its international and domestic circumstances, the bilateral alliance is still the best security option available.

In determining the future trajectory of its security policy, Japan is also unlikely to demonstrate much prospect of moving beyond bilateralism or into bilateralism plus. Its security policy will continue to be influenced by a strategic calculus and by component factors similar to the Yoshida doctrine that have driven it toward bilateralism in the past. Japanese perceptions of its immediate regional security environment continue to be dominated by North Korea and the rise of Chinese power. Japan will persist in moving toward engagement with China. However, the relative decline of its economic capacity to pursue engagement policies may force Japan to rely increasingly on its own national military capabilities in tandem with those of the bilateral alliance to hedge against a potential Chinese security threat. At the same time, Japan will face ever-increasing U.S. expectations for enhanced bilateral alliance cooperation to deal with regional contingencies involving North Korea and China, and for support in contingencies beyond East Asia.

Still lacking suitable alternatives, Japan is likely to see continued value in the further strengthening of the alliance. The ongoing growth of the norm of bilateral interaction among policy elites will also harden Japan's resolve in this task, even if Japanese policymakers persist with examining alternative options and hedging tactics to manage the potential costs of the alliance. Japan will continue to obfuscate the true extent of its military support for the alliance in East Asia; to separate its support for the United States in the context of the bilateral alliance from support in other contexts, such as the war on terrorism; to maintain many key constitutional prohibitions on the exercise of military force; to eschew certain types of power projection capacity that could be used to defend the United States; and to safeguard key indigenous military production capabilities. Nevertheless, Japan's room for maneuver to exercise these options is likely to shrink in the near future. Japan may find it politically hard to sustain the U.S.-Japan alliance while simultaneously placing different and, as possibly seen from the U.S. perspective, artificial restrictions on the support it can provide to the United States in the Afghan conflict under the ATSML and on a regional contingency under the revised Guidelines for U.S.-Japan Defense Cooperation. If it were to move from the stage of cooperative research to actual production and deployment of BMD systems, Japan would also find it difficult to continue to obfuscate its commitments to the United States and maintain its constitutional prohibitions. To construct an effective BMD, Japan will be forced to rely on U.S. sensor technology to track incoming ballistic missiles and to integrate increasingly its command and control systems with those of its ally.[22] In this instance, Japan will have to commit itself to more definite military contingency planning and joint military action with the United States, and will most probably have to end its ban on collective self-defense.

In plumping for a sea-based BMD option on its current class or on a new class of Aegis destroyers, Japan will also acquire a significant form of overseas expeditionary defensive capacity that could be used to support U.S.-led coalitions in Gulf War-type scenarios. Hence, the need for technology and the possession of military capabilities may push Japan toward ever tighter military integration with the United States—again drawing Japan into the very scenario feared by Yoshida at the start of the postwar period of involvement in U.S. expeditions and land wars.

Finally, Japan may find that multilateralism remains a security option that has too many unquantifiable risks to make it worth exercising. Japan is unlikely to seek the multilateral option unless the costs of alliance with the United States become so great that they outweigh the Japanese ability to manage them and associated alliance benefits. If Japan were to become potentially entrapped in a Sino-U.S. conflict it might need to reconsider the benefits of the alliance and opt for a UN-centered framework or even the independent Gaullist option. However, given Japanese policymakers' greater concerns about the unknown risks of the rise of China, and given the vagaries of multilateralism and complete security autonomy in a hostile region compared to the relatively known risks of alliance with the United States and the fear that if Japan does not support its ally the security treaty will in effect be nullified, Japan on balance might still acquiesce to the calculation that it is better to be entrapped than abandoned by alliance bilateralism.

4

Terms of Engagement

THE U.S.-JAPAN ALLIANCE AND THE RISE OF CHINA

MIKE M. MOCHIZUKI

How is the rise of China affecting the U.S.-Japanese relationship? Are the United States and Japan, as realists might predict, cooperating more and strengthening their alliance in order to balance, even contain, a more powerful China? Or are these two countries, as liberals might advocate, working more closely together to engage China and to expand areas of common interest and mutual cooperation with China? Or has the emergence of China as a global and regional actor caused strains in the relationship between Washington and Tokyo?

In analyzing how the United States and Japan have been responding to the rise of China and how the trilateral interaction among the United States, Japan, and China is affecting the U.S.-Japan alliance, this chapter examines the 1989–2001 period, from the Tiananmen crackdown and the end of the Cold War to the September 11 terrorist attacks. It argues that despite significant differences between American and Japanese interests, perspectives, and policy processes regarding China, there has been a partial convergence between the United States and Japan on China. While pursuing a general policy of engaging rather than containing China, both countries have also taken steps to hedge against a threatening China. Notwithstanding the minimal coordination between Washington and Tokyo on policy toward Beijing, their policies have tended to be more complementary than conflictual. The primary modality of engaging China continues to be two separate but parallel bilateral tracks. Despite some concerns that U.S. relations with China might undermine Japanese interests and that Japanese relations with China might undermine American interests, trilateral and multilateral approaches designed to minimize these concerns have remained relatively undeveloped.

Partial U.S.-Japan Convergence on China

At a general level, the United States and Japan have shared and do share common interests regarding China. In terms of security, both Washington and Tokyo have desired Beijing's moderation on military modernization and its restraint on the use of force to deal with international disputes. Regarding economics, both the United States and Japan have sought access to China's expanding market, greater transparency and predictability about the rules and norms for doing business in China, and the prevention of predatory trade practices. On China's domestic evolution, both countries have favored strengthening the rule of law and liberalizing China's political system. Finally, regarding Taiwan, both Washington and Tokyo have preferred peaceful management and resolution of the dispute between China and Taiwan. Regarding the actual pursuit of these interests and their relative priority, however, the United States and Japan have differed significantly, and many of these differences persist. What is also striking, however, is that the gap between the United States and Japan has begun to narrow somewhat.

In the security realm, U.S. and Japanese security perspectives toward China had diverged because of differences in geographic position and historical legacy as well as in the military balance of power. The United States historically tended to view China in broad geopolitical terms. At the beginning of the Cold War, Washington saw China as an ally of the Soviet Union that needed to be contained. During the 1970s, U.S. policymakers viewed China as a potential partner to counter the Soviet threat, and during the last decade American analysts have debated whether or not China will be a "peer competitor"[1] of the United States. Compared to the United States, China is still a weak military power. While large in terms of military personnel, the People's Liberation Army remains predominantly a ground force without much in the way of high-tech weaponry. Despite recent purchases of naval and air capabilities from Russia, China is no match for U.S. sea and air power. China does have a limited number of long-range nuclear strategic missiles that it could use to hit the United States, but America has overwhelming nuclear superiority in terms of number of warheads, their survivability, and their accuracy. Many analysts in fact argue that the United States has the counterforce missiles to destroy China's second-strike capability. At the very least, the logic of mutual assured destruction should apply to deter strategic nuclear strikes between the United States and China. Also, for some time there is likely to be an asymmetry regarding the credibility of deterrence in favor of the United States.

Therefore, the key Chinese security challenge for at least the next twenty-five years is not that China can threaten the American homeland, but rather that it can threaten Asian states in which the United States has a keen interest, such as Japan, Taiwan, and South Korea, and possibly endanger the critical sea lanes from Northeast Asia to South Asia. U.S. military planners would therefore like to prevent China from becoming a peer competitor, even in the waters and airspace off the Asian landmass. The United States has also been interested in getting China to play a constructive role on the Korean peninsula. But U.S. security interests regarding China have extended beyond East Asia. For example, Washington would like to get Beijing to support various international security regimes (such as nuclear nonproliferation) and to refrain from arms sales and military technology transfers that undermine U.S. interests in the Middle East and in South and Central Asia.

In contrast to the United States, Japan tended not to see China in broad strategic terms during the Cold War era. Despite China's involvement in the Korean War, few Japanese believed that China would launch an attack on Japan; nor did Japanese leaders embrace the notion of using China to balance against the Soviet threat. Therefore, for the most part, Japan's security perspective relative to China was relaxed and detached. The U.S. security guarantee was more than sufficient to deter China from threatening Japan, and Japan was skeptical of the American idea during the early 1980s of enhancing military cooperation with China as a way of enlisting China to help contain the Soviet Union. Given China's geographic proximity to Japan, a cordial and stable relationship between the two countries was critical, but on Japan's own terms rather than as a tool for a wider geopolitical agenda. In this regard, Japanese leaders believed that providing official development assistance and developing economic ties with China were effective means of fostering such a relationship and for overcoming the burden of Japan's militaristic past. Such a policy also harmonized with Japan's postwar pacifism.

Since the mid-1990s, however, Japan has become more concerned about China as a potential military threat. Japanese defense planners worry that China's air and naval modernization might threaten Japanese territorial waters and air space as well as the vital commercial sea lanes. The intrusion of what the Chinese unconvincingly referred to as "research vessels" into waters claimed by Japan as exclusive economic zones, as well as the huge military exercises in the Taiwan straits during 1995–96, indicated to the Japanese that China was becoming more militarily assertive. Such assertiveness could undermine the ability of the two countries to manage peacefully the territorial dispute over the Senkaku/Diaoyu Islands. Moreover, China is modernizing its medium-range nuclear ballistic missiles that can hit Japan, but Japan has no strategic capabilities that can target important assets in the Chinese homeland. One should not, however, exaggerate China's possible threat to Japan. Being an island country, Japan does not face an imminent threat from China's huge ground forces. The current configuration of Japan's Self-Defense Forces (SDF) could successfully repel an amphibious invasion, and China's navy and air force lag technologically behind the Japanese maritime and air SDF in terms of warships, fighter planes, antisubmarine warfare capability, early warning systems, and ship and air defense. For the foreseeable future, China would not have the ability to invade the Japanese home islands by using only conventional forces—even without U.S. military involvement.

Japanese and American perspectives on China's potential to become a military threat have certainly converged, but there are clear limits to this convergence. Despite the worrisome trends in the Sino-Japanese military balance, persistent pacifist sentiments as well as the burden of history are likely to make Japan more hesitant than the United States about confronting Chinese military power directly. Geographic proximity will also make the Japanese more sensitive than the Americans about the negative implications of an arms race with China, and unless Japan breaks out of its current strictly defensive and nonnuclear military doctrines, it will have to rely on America's extended deterrence and power projection capabilities to deter the Chinese. Such a breakout continues to face formidable domestic political obstacles in Japan, especially because the U.S. security commitment to Japan remains credible.

The United States and Japan have also differed regarding their respective economic interactions with China. After World War II, Japan's economic interest in China predated that of the United States. As early as the 1950s, Japan separated politics and economics to cultivate a commercial relationship with China. American business interest in China really did not blossom until after the normalization of relations in 1979. After China's economic opening, Japan focused on large-scale infrastructure projects and investments in heavy industry and raw materials extraction and provided large amounts of official development assistance and low-cost private capital for such endeavors. But because of some initial negative experiences in doing business in China, as well as the attraction of Southeast Asia, Japanese corporations did not invest heavily in the manufacturing sector in China until the latter half of the 1990s. Despite America's late start in developing economic ties with China, U.S. corporations were much more eager than their Japanese counterparts to utilize China's abundant cheap labor to manufacture goods for export—especially back to the American market. Japanese corporations, however, preferred to think in terms of regional production networks through which they could modulate trade between Japan and their overseas subsidiaries to minimize the dislocative effects of foreign direct investments on their own workforce at home.

This difference in international business strategies contributed to the difference in American and Japanese trade balances with China. Whereas the U.S. trade deficit with China skyrocketed during the 1990s, Japan's trade with China was, until recently, either balanced or only modestly in the red. Indeed, if one included Japan's trade with Hong Kong as part of Sino-Japanese bilateral trade, then a large portion of Japan's trade deficit would disappear. As a consequence, Tokyo has been much more lenient than Washington about the terms of China's accession to the World Trade Organization (WTO). Furthermore, reflecting its relative economic strengths, the United States has placed much greater emphasis than Japan on the reduction of Chinese barriers to agricultural trade and financial services and on the protection of intellectual property rights.

In recent years, the gap between Japan and the United States on economic relations with China has begun to narrow in the wake of China's stunning growth trajectory. After the East Asian economic crisis of 1997, Japanese investments in the manufacturing sector in China increased dramatically and the Japanese began to question publicly for the first time the need to continue large development assistance programs. Similar to the United States, Japan is now experiencing chronic trade deficits with China, and Japanese economic officials and business leaders see China no longer as simply a commercial opportunity, but as an economic challenger as well. Just as trade frictions have marred Sino-American relations, they have also begun to strain Sino-Japanese relations.

On the issue of China's internal politics, the United States and Japan also tended to diverge significantly. Domestic developments in China have had major implications for Sino-American relations. The Jackson-Vanik amendment required annual congressional consent for conferring most favored nation (MFN) trading status on Communist countries such as China. As a consequence, human rights violations in China always had the potential of derailing Sino-American relations. President Bill Clinton's initial effort to tie trade to Chinese progress on human rights was a logical extension of this traditional linkage between economics and politics. Consequently, in order to sell domestically the relaxation of trade restrictions toward China, U.S. administrations have had to argue, whether justified or not, that trade with China will ultimately lead to China's democratization.

Japan has generally refrained from using trade or other tools to compel China to stop human rights abuses and liberalize its political system. One reason for this restraint has been the historical issue. Because of the guilt that many Japanese leaders have felt about their country's past aggression against China, they have believed that Japanese criticisms of Chinese internal political behavior would only provoke Chinese wrath. Moreover, the Japanese have tended to stress the importance of political and social stability over premature democratization and to feel that external states can have little influence on China's domestic politics. In the final analysis, the best path to Chinese democratization would be through economic development and the creation of a large middle class. For most Japanese, American criticisms of China have appeared to be both self-righteous and impatient.

Even in the political realm, however, there has been a modest degree of Japanese-American convergence. More and more Japanese officials believe that China's democratization may ultimately be the only way to put Sino-Japanese relations on a stable footing and enhance both economic and security cooperation. At the same time, U.S. officials have started to shift away from heavy-handed criticisms of Chinese human rights abuses and to stress more institutional and technical assistance to promote the rule of law in China.

Regarding Taiwan, the divergence between the United States and Japan has been substantial. In the early years of the Cold War, the United States maintained a formal defense alliance with the Nationalist regime in Taiwan, including the forward deployment of U.S. military forces, and viewed Taiwan as a frontline state in containing Communism in Asia. With the Nixon-Kissinger opening to China in 1971, followed by full normalization of relations with Beijing in 1979, Washington terminated its alliance and formal diplomatic ties with Taiwan. Nevertheless, American political support for Taiwan remained strong, especially in Congress, compelling President Jimmy Carter to accept the Taiwan Relations Act as the condition for normalization of U.S.-China relations. As a consequence, the United States has continued to sell arms to Taiwan while acknowledging Beijing's position that there is "one China."

By contrast, Tokyo's diplomatic break with the Republic of China on Taiwan in 1972 was more complete. Japan does not have the equivalent of the United States' Taiwan Relations Act to govern relations with Taipei or to articulate formally an interest in Taiwan's security. There are no military contacts between Japan and Taiwan, and of course Japan does not provide arms to Taiwan. Much more than Washington, Japan has been careful not to irritate Beijing by avoiding visits by high-level Taiwan officials to Japan and comparable visits by Japanese officials to Taiwan.

Since the 1990s, there has been a partial convergence between the

United States and Japan on attitudes toward Taiwan, although actual policies remain fundamentally different. The Tiananmen massacre, the 1996 Chinese military exercises in the Taiwan strait, and Taiwan's successful democratization have made Japan more sympathetic to Taiwan relative to China. The Japanese appreciate that, unlike China, Taiwan is willing to move beyond the issue of Japan's militaristic past. Furthermore, deepening economic links with Taiwan have increased Japan's stake in that island regime. Although this growing affinity with Taiwan has not steered Japan to join the U.S. government in making explicit statements about helping to defend Taiwan against Chinese threats, Japanese leaders *are* becoming more sympathetic about enhancing Taiwan's participation in the international arena.

In addition to differing interests and perspectives vis-à-vis China, the United States and Japan have diverged in terms of their domestic politics regarding policies on China. Compared to Japan's policy process, the United States has been much more complex and pluralistic. Geopolitical calculations about containing the Soviet Union have dampened to some extent the contentious nature of China policymaking in the United States, but the secrecy surrounding Nixon's initiative toward Beijing and the enactment of the Taiwan Relations Act in the context of full normalization demonstrated the fragility or absence of consensus about how to relate to China even during the Cold War era. The end of the Cold War, the Tiananmen massacre in 1989, and the rise of Chinese power have only further complicated the situation. In addition to major policy disagreements, the myriad of issues related to China that are now on the American agenda has made the policy process even more unruly and volatile.

Without strong and clear presidential leadership, U.S. policy on China tends to be buffeted by congressional and interest group pressures; and even with such strong and clear leadership, the White House needs to forge and maintain congressional support through constant dialogue and compromise. Presidential electoral politics have also contributed to fluctuations in U.S. policy toward China. Since the early 1980s, presidential candidates from the nonincumbent party have challenged outgoing administrations for being too soft on China. Ronald Reagan criticized the Carter administration for betraying Taiwan in its eagerness to normalize relations with China. Bill Clinton criticized the Bush administration for coddling China's dictators responsible for the Tiananmen massacre. And most recently, George W. Bush argued that the Clinton administration was misguided in seeing China as strategic partner rather than as strategic competitor. But after ascending to the presidency, these leaders have moderated their rhetoric and pursued more cooperative policies, after confronting the reality of U.S.-China relations.[2]

In Japan, China policy has been controversial as well. In addition to the sharp ideological division between the conservative government and the progressive opposition, even the ruling Liberal Democratic Party (LDP) was divided between those who favored the Nationalist regime in Taipei and those who wanted to normalize relations with the Communist regime in Beijing. But after the 1972 normalization, a relatively stable consensus emerged in Japan for a conciliatory policy toward mainland China, backed by large amounts of economic aid. Primary responsibility for managing relations with China fell on the shoulders of the "China hands" in the foreign ministry, who were supported by powerful conservative politicians (such as Kakuei Tanaka, Masayoshi Ohira, and Noboru Takeshita) committed to good relations with China. The business community reinforced this consensus, and China policy tended to be insulated from competing interest-group pressures. Therefore, compared to the United States, politicization of China policy in Japan was relatively rare and episodic.

During the last decade, the politics of China policy in Japan has evolved in the direction of America's more pluralistic pattern. The postnormalization consensus on behalf of a conciliatory policy toward China has weakened considerably after Tiananmen and the end of the Cold War. Not only conservative Nationalists, but also even some in the progressive camp have become critical of China's harping on the history issue and its ingratitude for Japan's economic aid programs. Whereas in the past conservatives and progressives were on opposite sides of the China policy debate, now some conservatives and progressives have formed tacit alliances on behalf of a more assertive policy toward China. With the passing of influential politicians who favored strengthening relations with China, firm leadership to shield the professional diplomats in charge of China policy from political criticism has largely disappeared.

These trends, however, do not mean that the Japanese policy process regarding China has become as contentious, complicated, and volatile as that in the United States. Even with the increasing pluralization of policymaking in Japan, its policy on China continues to be more stable than China policy in the United States. Although some economic interest groups have started to push for tougher policies toward China, Japan lacks the numerous human rights organizations and their enthusiastic political patrons that influence the China policy agenda in the United States. The continuing U.S.-Japanese divergence on the politics of China policy is also evident on the Taiwan issue. In the United States, a heated debate has emerged between those who want to promote stronger political and defense ties with Taiwan, even at the risk of worsening relations with mainland China, and those who want to preserve the one-China policy developed during the 1970s and early 1980s. In Japan there is still little support for moving away from a one-China policy. A revealing indicator of Japanese political attitudes on Taiwan is the membership in the parliamentary associations for promoting relations with China and Taiwan. In the past, Japanese politicians tended to belong to one group or the other. Today, they tend to belong to both groups at the same time. In short, the overlapping memberships of the pro-China and pro-Taiwan groups demonstrate Japan's desire to finesse the Taiwan issue and avoid a military confrontation across the Taiwan strait.

Operationalizing Engagement

In addition to the partial convergence between the United States and Japan regarding interests in and perspectives on China, there is a general consensus in both countries that a policy of engaging China is preferable to one of either containing or ignoring China.[3] Despite its rapid economic ascendancy, China does not present a clear and present danger. Although it has the potential of becoming an acute military threat in the future, an explicit policy of containing China is now unnecessary. In fact, such an approach is likely to yield the outcome that Japan and the United States want to avoid: a China that is a powerful adversary. It is far better to engage China now in order to encourage it to be more cooperative and less threatening while its power capabilities are not as formidable as they could become in the future. China is also too important to ignore. For Japan, China's geographic proximity makes such a policy unthinkable. For the United States, China factors into so many economic and security interests that ignoring China is unreasonable.

At least for the moment, even hardliners in both the United States and Japan appear willing to give engagement a try. Rather than rejecting engagement outright, they advocate a hedging strategy. In case engagement fails to make China more cooperative and prevent it from becoming a threat, the United States and Japan should have in place the means to constrain, even contain, Chinese behavior. One analyst who is now a member of the Bush administration has called such an approach "congagement." It goes without saying that the future political sustainability of engagement in both the United States and Japan will depend on the achievements of this approach. But as long as both Tokyo and Washington generally pursue the engagement approach, there will not be a fundamental strategic break between Japan and the United States regarding China. This does not mean, however, that there have not been and will not be strains between these two countries over China policy.

First, despite the partial convergence on interests and perspectives with respect to China, differences between the United States and Japan do persist. Different priorities and even different diplomatic styles have the potential to cause each country to be irritated by the other. The key question is whether these differences will lead to complementary or contradictory policies.

Second, strains in the bilateral relationship could emerge because of the so-called alliance dilemma whereby allies are wary of being either abandoned or entrapped by the other.[4] Washington might be concerned that Tokyo might appease Beijing to the detriment of U.S. interests, or that Sino-Japanese relations might become so fraught with tension that the United States is dragged into an unwanted conflict. By the same logic, Tokyo might be anxious that Washington might bypass Japan in developing a cooperative Sino-American relationship or that U.S.-China relations could become so conflictual that Japan is caught in the crossfire and forced to choose between the United States and China.

Third, China could provoke strains in U.S.-Japan relations by attempting to play the two countries off of each other. Indeed, to counter the possibility of U.S.-Japanese collaboration to constrain or contain China, Beijing could pursue diplomatic tactics to accentuate differences between Washington and Tokyo.

How then have Japan and the United States put into practice their engagement policies toward China, and what implications have these policies had for U.S.-Japan relations?

Engaging China After Tiananmen: 1989–1993

Initially, the Americans and the Japanese reacted quite differently to the June 4, 1989, Tiananmen massacre. Most Americans expressed moral outrage about the military repression of the student democracy movement. The Bush administration promptly terminated military exports to and military exchanges with China, and suspended numerous commercial and government-to-government contracts. Although President Bush exercised some restraint in criticizing the Chinese crackdown so as to keep open communication channels to leaders in Beijing, congressional and public pressure for stiffer measures mounted. Faced with the prospect of Congress revoking MFN treatment for Chinese trade, the administration decided to halt all high-level diplomatic exchanges with Chinese leaders and block loans to China by international financial institutions such as the World Bank. But even as President Bush took these steps, he secretly dispatched National Security Advisor Brent Scowcroft and Deputy Secretary of State Lawrence Eagleburger to Beijing less than a month after the massacre to explore the possibility of getting Chinese leaders to work with Washington to reverse the downward slide in bilateral relations.[5]

Japanese public reaction to Tiananmen was more muted. Government leaders noted that "the heavy history of the past" constrained Japan from harshly criticizing China or imposing sanctions. During the first several days after the Tiananmen incident, Prime Minister Sosuke Uno emphasized the importance of recognizing that Sino-Japanese relations were different from Sino-American relations. He cautioned against seeing things in clear black-and-white terms. The reaction of the Japanese business community was mixed. Although some business leaders stressed the importance of keeping in step with the Western countries in condemning Chinese repression, many others felt that Japan should continue to assist China's economic development and capitalize on attractive business opportunities. Even as late as June 13, nine days after the incident, Japanese Foreign Ministry officials signaled their desire to keep economics and politics separated by noting that the promise to assist China's development was distinct from humanitarian questions. But a week later, on June 20, the Japanese government finally decided to freeze the third round of yen loans (the primary mode of economic aid) to China in response to Tiananmen.[6] This was the same day that Secretary of State James Baker informed Congress that he was recommending stronger measures against China.

To a large extent, Bush administration officials agreed with Japanese leaders about the need to maintain stable relations with China. What was different between the United States and Japan was the domestic politics of this issue. Whereas congressional and public outcries pushed President Bush to adopt a harder line than he had wanted, comparable pressure was absent in the Japanese case. If anything, there was greater support in Japan to keep economics and politics separated. Therefore, the main concern in Tokyo was how to adjust its response so that Japan would stay in step with the United States and the rest of the international community. Japan's initial reluctance to adopt economic reprisals against China reflected the dilemma between aligning firmly with the Western nations and preserving friendly relations with a critical neighboring power. Some Japanese officials may have even thought that by not completely embracing the harsh reaction from the United States and other Western countries, Japan might gain a diplomatic advantage by having a closer relationship with China than the United States and other advanced industrial democracies had.[7]

After the Tiananmen incident, China began to value relations with Japan as way of rescuing itself from international isolation. Although Chinese leaders rebuked the U.S. sanctions and the G7 summit statement condemning China, they refrained from explicitly mentioning Japan in their criticisms and used various channels to express their appreciation for Japan's relatively judicious response. In return, Japan moved briskly on the diplomatic front. In mid-September 1989, former foreign minister Masayoshi Ito headed a delegation of the Japanese Diet Members' League for Japan-China Friendship to China and met with China's top leaders, including Li Peng and Deng Xiaoping. On this occasion, Premier Li expressed his hope that Japan would play a role in breaking out of the current situation that China has with the Western states. Less than two weeks later, a group of some 150 LDP politicians visited China to reinforce the trend toward restoring Sino-Japanese relations. Again Chinese leaders assumed a conciliatory posture toward the Japanese visitors.[8]

When these exchanges did not lead Japan to lift the freeze on economic aid, however, Beijing began to exhibit some impatience, even irritation, with Tokyo. Professor Akihiko Tanaka of Tokyo University surmises that Chinese expectations about an opening in relations with the United States may have caused this mood shift.[9] Scowcroft and Eagleburger were scheduled to make a second post-Tiananmen secret visit to Beijing in early December 1989. Chinese leaders probably calculated that if this mission led to a normalization of Sino-American relations, Japan would eagerly restore aid anyway. In other words, from the Chinese perspective, the diplomatic value of Japan would diminish if relations with the United States got back on track. The Scowcroft-Eagleburger mission, however, did not produce the improvement in Sino-American relations that the Chinese leadership sought. Instead, when the mission became known, American public criticism of the Bush administration's overture to Beijing was fierce, delaying the possibility of a full restoration of Sino-American relations. The failure of the Scowcroft-Eagleburger mission probably steered Chinese leaders to emphasize again the Japanese path to reintegrating their country into the international community.

By the spring of 1990, the ruling LDP, the business community, and even government ministries like the Ministry of Finance were clamoring to unfreeze the yen loans to China. These domestic pressures in Japan and the frosty state of Sino-American relations, however, did not expedite an improvement in Sino-Japanese relations. Problems with the United States probably inhibited Japan from moving too quickly with China.[10] With the end of the Cold War and the burgeoning trade deficit with Japan, American opinion began to view Japan increasingly as a potential threat to U.S. interests. If Japan improved its relations with China in this context without demonstrating much concern about China's human rights violations, there was a danger that U.S.-Japan economic frictions could escalate into a new East-West conflict in which Japan would be associated with China in the minds of Americans. Anxious about the possible negative impact on relations with Washington, Tokyo therefore held back on resuming its yen loans to China until circumstances changed.

Circumstances finally did change in June 1990. Beijing agreed to permit astrophysicist Fang Lizhi and his family to leave China, and the United States extended MFN trading status to China. U.S.-Japan economic relations were also improved with the release of the final report related to the Structural Impediments Initiative (SII) talks. In this new diplomatic climate, Prime Minister Toshiki Kaifu informed the Bush administration on the eve of the Houston G7 summit of Japan's intention to resume economic aid to China. A succession of trips to China by Japanese officials (including career diplomat Hisashi Owada) in July and political leaders (including former Prime Minister Noboru Takeshita and education minister Kōsuke Hori) in September cleared the path for the restoration of the yen loans, which the Japanese Cabinet formally approved in early November 1990.[11]

After the resumption of the yen loans and Japan's support for China's reentry into the international community, Sino-Japanese relations became strikingly warm. This trend culminated in the Japanese imperial visit to China in October 1992 to mark "a new stage of development in friendly China-Japan relations."[12] As early as June 1991, Beijing expressed its desire to have the Japanese emperor visit China to celebrate the twentieth anniversary of the normalization of bilateral relations. Although Foreign Minister Michio Watanabe was eager to have the emperor accept this invitation, there was significant opposition within the LDP. First of all, given the controversy with South Korea about the "comfort women" issue (regarding female sexual slavery to provide "comfort" for Japanese soldiers during World War II), some conservatives were concerned that the "history issue" might also mar the emperor's trip to China. That is, Chinese leaders might criticize Japan for its past military aggression and wartime atrocities. Second, the passage by China in February 1992 of a territorial waters law that treated the Senkaku/Diaoyu Islands as Chinese territory provoked a hostile reaction among LDP politicians. Third, calls within China about seeking war reparations from Japan also raised concerns among Japanese leaders. These issues complicated Prime Minister Kiichi Miyazawa's efforts to forge a domestic consensus on behalf of an imperial visit. During this delicate period, Chinese leaders made a point of not provoking the Japanese with negative remarks. In contrast to previous warnings about the revival of Japanese militarism,"[13] China toned down its remarks about Japan's legislation to participate in UN peacekeeping operations. In fact, President Yang Shangkun declared in January 1992 that greater Japanese political contributions to regional peace and development would be welcome. To defuse domestic opposition to an im-

perial visit to China, Miyazawa had to genuflect to the Japanese nationalist right by indicating his willingness to make a private visit to the Yasukuni Shrine. After meticulous spadework, the Miyazawa Cabinet on
August 25 formally approved the imperial trip for late October.[14]

The emperor's historical visit went well, without any negative inci-
dents. Chinese leaders responded positively to the emperor's expression
of "profound personal sorrow" for the "untold hardships" that Japan
had inflicted on the people of China.[15] After the visit, Sino-Japanese relations continued to improve. Chinese officials applauded Japan's participation in the UN peacekeeping operation in Cambodia and expressed
their understanding of Japan's wish to assume a larger political role in international society. As evident in Chinese analyses of Japan's strategic significance, this positive view toward Japan probably reflected a calculation
that an increase in Japan's international influence would serve China's interests by restraining the United States.[16] On the Japanese side, Koji Kakizawa, who was later to become Foreign Minister in the Hata Cabinet,
heralded the arrival of a "new stage" in Sino-Japanese relations in which
friendship between Japan and China would become the foundation of an
East Asian stability comparable to that of the Franco-German relationship for West Europe.[17] On the economic front, after many years of hesi-
tation, Japan's direct investments in China finally began to take off in
1992. Japanese firms were now attracted by the increasing ability of Chinese consumers to buy higher value-added products.[18] All of this fed into
a flurry of Japanese commentary about a "new Asianism," a "re-Asianization" of Japan, or an Asian restoration.[19]

While Japan's relations with China recovered completely from the
Tiananmen crackdown, the Bush administration struggled to get Sino-
American relations back on track. Democratic Party politicians and various interest groups put the administration on the defensive by mobilizing anti-Chinese sentiments on a variety of issues ranging from China's
abortion practices, human rights violations, labor exploitation, and environmental degradation.[20] Given the political sensitivities about direct bilateral contacts, high officials focused on multilateral contexts to elicit
Chinese cooperation on issues of keen interest to the United States. Some
of these efforts paid off. Beijing did not use its veto power to block UN
support for actions against Iraq after its invasion of Kuwait. China
agreed to join the Non-Proliferation Treaty after almost twenty-five years
of resistance. Beijing also informed the U.S. government of its intention
to refrain from transferring M-11 missile technology or systems to Pakistan, and to observe the guidelines of the Missile Technology Control
Regime (MTCR). On economic and trade matters, in 1992 Beijing signed
an agreement to protect American intellectual property, and a memoran-

dum of understanding promising to discontinue the export of goods manufactured with prison labor.[21] Despite the progress on these fronts, President Bush's decision during the presidential election campaign to approve
the sale of 150 F-16 fighter planes to Taiwan pushed relations with China
back onto a downward course. Beijing saw this decision as a clear viola-
tion of the August 1982 communiqué on Taiwan arms sales.

Competitive and Cooperative Bilateralism: 1993–1998

By the time Bill Clinton became president, Sino-Japanese relations were
much better than Sino-American relations, and this trend looked as if it
would continue. During the 1992 election campaign, candidate Clinton accused then President George Bush of coddling Chinese dictators responsible for the Tiananmen massacre. Clinton vowed to use American diplomatic leverage to promote human rights and democratization in China.
This was in stark contrast to Japan's more detached policy regarding human rights in China and its willingness to keep economic cooperation with
China separate from political issues. From China's strategic perspective, a
further deepening of relations with Japan might be an effective way to
counter Clinton's hostile policies toward China. Also, in light of Clinton's
heavy-handed approach to Japan on trade issues, Japan might also enhance its diplomatic maneuverability vis-à-vis the United States by keeping
relations with China on a positive track. In others words, the logic of triangular diplomacy suggested that as Sino-American and Japanese-American relations became fraught with tensions, China and Japan might be
drawn closer together. In the end, however, the interaction of these three
states over the next four years yielded an entirely different outcome.

After Prime Minister Morihiro Hosokawa's frank statements in the fall
of 1993 that he regarded the Japanese war in Asia as a "war of aggression," it appeared as if Japan might finally be able to lay to rest the issue
of its militaristic past and put its relations with China on a more secure
footing. Moreover, during his visit to Beijing, Hosokawa made a point of
distancing Japan from the United States' views on human rights when he
questioned the notion of one country imposing democratic values on another. In sharp contrast to his conciliatory approach to China, Hosokawa
then went to Washington to say no to President Clinton's results-oriented
approach to trade negotiations. While its aggressive style on trade bred
Japanese resentment, the Clinton administration also angered Beijing in
May 1993 by linking the extension of MFN trade status for China to
progress on human rights. At this point, it looked as if the United States
was driving Japan and China toward each other at its own expense.

But before this trend could gain momentum, Clinton shifted gears on China policy. After its second China policy review in fall 1993, the administration initiated a policy of "comprehensive engagement," under which the United States would resume high-level meetings with Chinese leaders and military-to-military exchanges. A major motivation for this change appeared to be an interest in getting Beijing's support in dealing with the looming crisis regarding North Korea's nuclear program.[22] Then, in May 1994, President Clinton severed the link between human rights and trade after recognizing that conditionality on MFN trading status was not producing the desired results and had the potential of hurting American business opportunities in China.

As these moves improved the climate of Sino-American relations slightly, Sino-Japanese relations began to take a negative turn. A sequence of informal remarks by conservative Japanese Cabinet officers provoked the Chinese. In May 1994, off-the-record comments by Shigeto Nagano questioning the authenticity of the Nanking massacre and the appropriateness of characterizing the Japanese war in Asia as an aggressive one came to light soon after his appointment as Minister of Justice in the Hata Cabinet. In August 1994, Shin Sakurai, director-general of the Environmental Agency, made a similar statement; and in 1995, Education Minister Yoshinobu Shimamura declared that Japan did not have "aggressive intentions" during the Pacific War. Sino-Japanese relations slid back into the old pattern of Chinese protests and Japanese apologies and resignations of officials.[23] The Taiwan issue also resurfaced as an irritant in Sino-Japanese relations in the form of possible visits by Taiwan president Lee Teng-hui to Japan. In August 1993, Ichirō Ozawa, then leader of the political party Shinseitō, announced that he would welcome a visit by President Lee to Japan. Then a trip by a high-level Japanese trade official to Taiwan in December 1993 provoked protests from Beijing.[24] The problem escalated when the Asia Olympic Committee in October 1994 extended an invitation to President Lee to attend the Asian Athletic Meet to be held in Hiroshima. Although a Lee visit never materialized, these episodes soured Japan's ties with China.

In the context of a modest improvement in Sino-American relations and a slight deterioration in Sino-Japanese relations, the Pentagon in the fall of 1994 initiated a dialogue with Japan to reinvigorate the security alliance (the so-called Nye Initiative). At a time when North Korea's nuclear program and China's military modernization were making the East Asian security environment more uncertain, the United States could no longer take the alliance with Japan for granted while pursuing its trade agenda. Similarly, Japan was interested in getting U.S. reassurance about its security commitments in the region.

As Washington and Tokyo worked to strengthen defense cooperation and redefine the alliance for regional security, Sino-American relations again worsened while Sino-Japanese relations continued to drift downward. Under Congressional pressure, President Clinton decided in June 1995 to permit Taiwan President Lee Teng-hui to visit his alma mater, Cornell University, after U.S. officials had assured their Chinese counterparts that a visa would not be issued. Washington's explanation that this action did not constitute a shift away from a one-China policy was not enough to satisfy Beijing. In light of the Clinton administration's abrupt policy reversal on the visa issue, Chinese President Jiang Zemin noted the inadequacy of a "mere verbal promise by the U.S." Jiang urged the U.S. government to "take effective practical steps to undo the serious damage done to Sino-U.S. relations by President Lee Teng-hui's visit to the U.S., and see to it that there will no longer be a recurring serious problem affecting relations."[25]

As for Sino-Japanese relations, China's nuclear tests in 1995 damaged its image among the Japanese public. In response to the May test, the Japanese government scaled back its grant economic aid to China. When China tested another nuclear device in mid-August, right after the fiftieth anniversary of the Hiroshima and Nagasaki atomic bombings, Japanese reaction was more severe. A number of Diet members called on the government to go beyond a suspension of grant aid to a reduction of yen loans, which constituted a much larger part of Japan's economic aid to China. Put on the defensive, the Foreign Ministry decided to freeze all of the grant aid scheduled for 1995. The nuclear tests issue altered the political dynamics of Japanese policy toward China. Dovish political forces, which had heretofore been positive about expanding relations with Beijing, became more critical of China. To some extent, right-wing nationalists and left-wing pacifists had formed a tacit coalition in favor of a tougher policy toward China. Moreover, in stark contrast to Tokyo's traditional practice of separating politics and economics in its relations with Beijing, the suspension of grant aid signaled an explicit linkage of politics and economics.[26] China countered the Japanese move by raising the history issue. Chinese Premier Li Peng stated that "Japan should never try to apply pressure on China by economic means" when "Japanese militarist aggression inflicted such gigantic damage upon China as to dwarf the Japanese government credits so far extended."[27] But rather than appealing to Japan's sense of guilt, Li's statement seemed to infuriate the Japanese further.

By the time China held military exercises and missile tests in March 1996 to intimidate Taiwan during its presidential election, negative views of China were on the ascendancy in both the United States and Japan. Assessments that China was becoming a potential military threat appeared with greater frequency in both countries. When the Clinton administration sent two carriers into Taiwan's vicinity in response to the Chinese exercises, few Americans or Japanese questioned this display of military power. Some Japanese security analysts even referred to this episode as a watershed event because Japan cooperated logistically with the dispatch of the U.S. carrier homeported in Yokosuka.[28]

A month later, President Clinton and Prime Minister Ryutaro Hashimoto issued a joint security declaration reaffirming the alliance for the post-Cold War era and committing the two countries to review the 1978 bilateral guidelines on defense cooperation. U.S. and Japanese officials worked closely together to draft the appropriate language regarding China in the joint declaration. They decided against using the term *engagement* to characterize the Japanese and American approach to China, because Beijing might construe this concept negatively. They were also careful not to provoke China by even implying the future uncertainty of China's role in the region. According to Yōichi Funabashi's journalistic account, Japanese officials stated that "the American action [during the China-Taiwan missile crisis] was more than sufficiently effective, so let's not incite them any further."[29] The final text of the April 1996 declaration made the following reference to China: "[The prime minister and the president] emphasized that it is extremely important for the stability and prosperity of the region that China play a positive and constructive role, and, in this context, stressed the interest of both countries in furthering cooperation with China."[30]

With the reaffirmation of the bilateral alliance coming so soon after the Taiwan strait crisis, however, the Chinese not surprisingly feared that the U.S.-Japan security relationship was being redirected against China and might even encourage Taiwan to move toward independence. The new U.S.-Japan defense cooperation guidelines, which were released in September 1997, only reinforced this anxiety. According to the revised guidelines, the Japanese SDF could provide rear-area support for the United States in regional security contingencies beyond the defense of Japan proper. For the Chinese, this implied that Japan might cooperate militarily with the United States against China in a Taiwan crisis. Both Americans and Japanese quickly tried to reassure the Chinese, but because these reassurance messages were not coordinated between Washington and Tokyo, there were suspicions on both sides that the other might be appeasing Beijing at their expense.[31]

The applicability of the defense cooperation guidelines to Taiwan was especially contentious among Japanese political leaders, as Hughes and Fukushima's chapter in this volume indicates. Japanese officials contended that the concept of U.S.-Japanese cooperation in "situations in areas surrounding Japan" was not a geographic one and that a Taiwan contingency could not be assumed because China was pursuing a peaceful resolution of the Taiwan issue. Therefore, the issue of including or excluding Taiwan was irrelevant.[32] Despite strong pressure from Beijing to explicitly exclude Taiwan, Tokyo resisted and stuck to this ambiguous position.[33] Needless to say, China was not satisfied.

Fearing a joint Japanese-American containment strategy, China countered with a dazzling array of diplomatic initiatives toward Russia, India, Vietnam, the ASEAN states, and Central Asia. Russia was especially receptive to Chinese overtures, not only because China was an eager buyer of Russian weaponry, but also because Moscow feared Washington's support of NATO enlargement. About the same time that the United States and Japan issued its joint security declaration in April 1996, China and Russia announced their "strategic partnership." During their Moscow summit a year later, Jiang Zemin and Boris Yeltsin emphasized their collaboration to promote "multipolarization of the world"—their code language for constraining U.S. predominance.[34] This competitive bilateralism raised the possibility that a new cold war divide could emerge in Asia, with the United States and Japan in one camp and China and Russia in the other.

Although an enduring alliance between Russia and China seemed improbable, the Clinton administration did move on both the Russian and Chinese fronts to shift major power relations in a direction more favorable to the United States. Regarding Russia, President Clinton moved to reassure Moscow about NATO enlargement by forging a "founding agreement" with Russia and personally inviting Russian President Boris Yeltsin to attend the G7 summit held in Denver in summer 1997. The subsequent transformation of the G7 into the G8 summits symbolized Russia's membership in the community of Western democratic states. On China, the Clinton administration negotiated with Beijing to lay the groundwork for an exchange of presidential visits: first by Jiang Zemin to the United States, followed by Bill Clinton to China.[35]

Not to be left behind by America's diplomatic activity, Japan developed an initiative of its own. In August 1997, Prime Minister Hashimoto outlined his "Eurasian diplomacy" concept, which emphasized his desire to improve relations with Russia. He then followed up with a major speech calling for "the expansion of the cooperative relationship between China and Japan" and highlighting Japanese and Chinese contributions to "the formation of a common order." In addition to confirming that Japan understands and respects China's position that "Taiwan is an indivisible part of the People's Republic of China," Hashimoto explicitly stated that Japan does not support Taiwan's independence.[36] This reassurance to-

ward China set the stage for Sino-Japanese summitry to parallel that between China and the United States.

By reaching out to both Russia and China, the United States and Japan
shifted the competitive character of bilateralism in a more cooperative direction. Given the strategic importance of this diplomatic activity, what is
remarkable is that there was hardly any explicit coordination between
Washington and Tokyo about these initiatives and their desired objectives. Except for some perfunctory notification, the United States and
Japan moved independently to engage China at the summit level; but this
parallel pursuit of high-level engagement did not yield parallel results. In
the end, the Sino-American interaction went better than the Sino-Japanese one, raising some concerns in Japan that U.S.-China relations were
improving at Japan's expense.

For Japan and China, the exchange of summits took place in September 1997 with Prime Minister Hashimoto visiting China and in November 1998 with President Jiang Zemin visiting Japan to meet Prime Minister Keizō Obuchi in commemoration of twenty years since the signing of
the bilateral peace and friendship treaty. At the September 1997 meeting,
the two countries agreed to hold regular bilateral summits and to promote bilateral security dialogues in order to enhance transparency about
defense policy. Concerned about the lack of progress in U.S.-Chinese
talks about the terms of China's accession to the WTO, Prime Minister
Hashimoto took the lead in forging an agreement with China on the substantive package necessary for China's accession.[37] At the November
1998 summit in Tokyo, the two sides issued a joint declaration called
"Building a Partnership of Friendship and Cooperation for Peace and
Development" and announced a thirty-three-point agenda (drafted primarily by the Japanese) for bilateral cooperation.

The U.S.-China summits were held in October 1997, with Jiang visiting the United States, and in June 1998, with Clinton visiting China. Despite intense preparatory negotiations, the only concrete agreement to
emerge from the 1997 summit was a Chinese written promise to end nuclear cooperation with Iran in exchange for the U.S. government allowing American firms to sell nuclear power equipment and technology to
China. Moreover, during the joint press conference, in alluding to China's
democracy and human rights record, President Clinton argued that China
was "on the wrong side of history."[38] Despite these harsh words, however, the Clinton-Jiang meeting did clear the way for a broader U.S. engagement with China, because the Chinese leadership had finally succeeded in overcoming the legacy of the Tiananmen massacre to get a state
visit with full honors in Washington.[39]

During his June 1998 trip to China, Clinton publicly spelled out the so-called "three no's" about Taiwan: "we don't support independence for Taiwan, or two Chinas, or one Taiwan, one China, and we don't believe that Taiwan should be a member in any organization for which statehood is a requirement."[40] The enunciation of these points reassured the Chinese that the United States was not abandoning its one-China policy, despite the democratization of Taiwan and the visit by Taiwan President Lee Teng-hui to his alma mater, Cornell University.[41] During this thaw in Sino-American relations, the Clinton administration provided a presidential waiver for American satellite launches on Chinese rockets.[42] The United States and China also commenced high-level military-to-military exchanges. According to defense officials in the Clinton administration, these exchanges were not just confidence-building measures, but also ways to enhance deterrence by convincing the Chinese military of America's overwhelming military superiority.[43]

At a basic level, Japanese officials welcomed the improvement in Sino-American relations in the wake of the two Clinton-Jiang summits. The last thing they wanted was for Japan to become entrapped in a military conflict between the United States and China over Taiwan. But there were several aspects of America's engagement of China that made Japanese leaders uneasy. Japanese journalists and Republican critics of the administration made much of President Clinton's failure to stop in Tokyo before or after his June 1998 trip to China, suggesting that the United States was bypassing Japan, an ally, to placate the Chinese. But beyond this symbolism, there were substantive issues that bothered the Japanese.

First, although the Clinton administration embraced the notion of the United States and China "working toward a constructive strategic partnership in the twenty-first century,"[44] while in China the president never publicly emphasized the importance of the U.S.-Japan security alliance for regional and global security and stability. Japan had been taking a lot of heat from China about the new 1997 U.S.-Japan defense cooperation guidelines, but Tokyo had resisted Beijing's pressure to explicitly exclude Taiwan from the scope of the guidelines. Moreover, Tokyo was beginning to be receptive to Washington's requests to cooperate with research on theater missile defense, despite Beijing's strong opposition. Japanese leaders would therefore have appreciated firm public backing from President Clinton about the reinvigorated U.S.-Japan alliance in the context of Sino-American interactions. Instead of providing this kind of moral support, Clinton confused the Japanese by referring to a strategic partnership with China and going beyond the Japanese statements on the Taiwan question with the so-called three no's.[45]

Second, on the economic front, the Japanese were miffed by what they interpreted as China and the United States ganging up against Japan.

When Japanese finance officials proposed the Asian Monetary Fund in the wake of the 1997 East Asian financial crisis, the two countries that vigorously opposed this idea were the United States and China. During a joint press conference with Jiang on his June 1998 trip to China, President Clinton praised China's willingness to forgo devaluation of the Chinese *yuan*, while criticizing Japan for not doing enough to deal with the regional economic crisis by reviving its own economy.[46]

Finally, President Jiang's repeated harping on Japan's militaristic past during his stay in Japan irritated the Japanese—even those who had heretofore harbored friendly views toward China. Jiang seemed to be personally bitter that Prime Minister Obuchi refused to give him the same sort of written apology for Japan's past that was given to South Korean President Kim Dae Jung a month earlier. Therefore, despite the sweeping Japan-China agreement to move forward on thirty-three areas of cooperation, the November 1998 summit appeared to leave Sino-Japanese relations in a worse state than Sino-American relations. To the extent that there is a triangular logic to U.S.-Japan-China interactions, the improvement in Sino-American relations may have steered China to take a tougher posture toward Japan. Indeed, American insensitivity toward Japan may have encouraged the Chinese to move in this direction. For example, when Jiang made his state visit to the United States, his first stop was Pearl Harbor—a gesture interpreted by many Japanese as a slap in the face. Although the U.S. government stayed clear of the Sino-Japanese tensions about history, American intellectual and journalistic circles tended to be critical of Japan's unwillingness to fully acknowledge and atone for its misdeeds.

According to Japanese officials who manage relations with China, the concern was not that the United States might abandon Japan in favor of China. These officials knew full well that the deeply rooted common interests between the United States and Japan made the bilateral alliance robust enough to withstand some slights caused by American interactions with China. What bothered Japanese diplomats was the volatility of and wide swings in U.S.-China relations. To compensate for a deterioration in Sino-American relations, Washington sometimes overindulges Beijing to the detriment of Tokyo. For Japan, what is most desirable is a stable Sino-American relationship.[47]

To prevent U.S. and Japanese interactions with China from having a negative effect on U.S.-Japan relations, as well as to avoid misunderstandings among the three countries, Japan discreetly proposed in September 1997 a trilateral dialogue among Japan, the United States, and China. Initially, U.S. Secretary of State Madeline Albright reacted coolly to this proposal by simply noting that the Chinese would be unlikely to accept it. In 1998, however, National Security Advisor Samuel "Sandy"

Berger was more receptive and proceeded to propose the idea to the Chinese. Sure enough, Chinese Foreign Minister Qian Qichen did reject an official trilateral dialogue, arguing that such a process was "premature." But Qian did agree to a high-level Track II dialogue that might involve officials participating in their private capacity as well as influential scholars and former officials.[48] The process was inaugurated in summer 1998 with the Japan Institute of International Affairs (JIIA), a research institute affiliated with the Ministry of Foreign Affairs, hosting the first meeting in Tokyo. By the end of 2001, five of these trilateral sessions had been convened, with the location rotated among the three countries. Although these discussions do not have the weight of official meetings, the forum has provided an important venue for a frank exchange of views that are no doubt conveyed to the respective governments. The advantage of these trilateral talks is that they mitigate the distrust that sometimes arises from one country saying different things to the other two countries.[49] According to one analyst, China might eventually agree to upgrade these discussions to the official level if Beijing became anxious enough about U.S.-Japanese collaboration on theater missile defense.[50]

Engagement Adrift and Revived: 1999–2001

After the sour Jiang-Obuchi summit in November 1998, Sino-Japanese relations appeared to be headed on a downward slide while Sino-American relations seemed to be on an upward track. But again, as in 1992, these two sets of bilateral relations took an opposite turn.

In the years 1999–2001, numerous developments had the potential of reinforcing the deterioration in Sino-Japanese relations and undermining the domestic political foundation in Japan for a cooperative engagement policy toward China. On the security front, in addition to China's military modernization programs that could threaten Japan, the Chinese irritated Japan by escalating their so-called maritime research activities in the waters claimed by Tokyo as its exclusive economic zone (EEZ). Japanese analysts interpreted these intrusions as a Chinese fait accompli strategy to gain leverage in the Sino-Japanese dispute regarding their respective EEZ boundaries. Moreover, Chinese warships stepped *up* their activities in the East China Sea (including near the disputed Senkaku/Diaoyu Islands), and their intelligence-gathering vessels in May and June 2000 circumnavigated Japan. All of this behavior suggested to the Japanese a troubling shift in Chinese naval strategy from coastal to offshore defense.[51]

Concerning the Sino-Japanese economic relationship, the Japanese public became increasingly aware through various journalistic accounts that

the Chinese had been less than appreciative of Japan's large economic assistance to China. In fact, the Chinese government had done little to publicize to its own people Japan's contribution. For the first time since the beginning of Japan's yen loan programs, Japanese political leaders and
influential commentators began to question whether to continue this economic assistance on such a large scale. When China's economy is booming
and its defense budget is expanding in ways that could threaten Japan,
why should the Japanese provide aid to China when Japan is having economic problems at home and when the Chinese are not even grateful? In
addition to the aid issue, the rapid increase in Chinese exports to Japan im-
pressed upon the Japanese that China's economic miracle could be more of
a threat than an opportunity for Japanese commercial interests.

Finally, on the history issue, more and more Japanese began to believe
that Japan had done enough to atone for its past wrongs. But whereas
South Korean President Kim Dae Jung had publicly stated his intention
to look toward the future rather than dwell on the past, Chinese leaders
appeared unwilling to give up the "history card" against the Japanese,
despite Japan's willingness to accommodate Chinese sensitivities regarding such matters as history textbooks, provocative remarks by nationalist politicians, and visits by Japanese leaders to the Yasukuni Shrine. Indeed, the willingness of Japanese officials to accommodate Chinese
pressure on history provoked the rise of a neo-revisionist movement in
Japan that promoted a more nationalistic reading of history. In this context, a conciliatory policy toward China was becoming much harder to
sustain politically in Japan.

What has been remarkable, however, is that these issues have not had
the negative effect on Sino-Japanese relations that one might expect. A
major reason for this is the conciliatory attitude that Beijing developed
toward Tokyo beginning in spring 1999. After President Jiang vented his
frustration about history during his visit to Japan and subsequently won
approval from the People's Liberation Army for being firm with the
Japanese, Chinese diplomats and Japan experts in China gradually per-
suaded Jiang and the top leadership that a hard-line posture toward
Tokyo would only drive the United States and Japan closer together in an
alliance against China. In a sense, the strong rhetoric while in Tokyo was
a catharsis for Jiang. Consequently, the Chinese leadership made at least
a tactical shift in its dealings with Japan. The first outward sign of this
change came in April 1999, when Jiang gave an especially warm recep-
tion for a visiting Japanese parliamentary delegation and a large group of
Japanese tourists. On this occasion, Jiang issued an important statement
in the *People's Daily* highlighting China-Japan cooperation.[52]

This trend was soon reinforced by developments in Sino-American relations. In April 1999, the Clinton administration unsuccessfully attempted to get the UN Human Rights Commission in Geneva to pass a resolution condemning China's human rights record. About the same time, China made breathtaking concessions in its negotiations with the United States on the terms of China's accession to the WTO, only to be rebuffed by President Clinton during Premier Zhu Rongji's trip to Washington. But most damaging of all to Sino-American relations was the U.S.-led NATO military campaign on behalf of Kosovo. The United States not only bypassed the United Nations (and therefore China), but also mistakenly bombed China's embassy in Belgrade in May 1999. The combination of these events provoked a groundswell of anti-American sentiment in China.[53] For the Jiang government, the strategy of putting America first in its foreign policy was not working. With the Sino-American relationship so fragile, China could not afford to have Sino-Japanese relations deteriorate as well.

China's recalibration of its America and Japan policies permitted Beijing and Tokyo to deal with issues in a cordial, business-like manner and weather controversies without destabilizing their bilateral relationship. Numerous examples fit this pattern. When Tokyo decided to reevaluate its yen loans to China, Beijing expressed understanding rather than show irritation. When Japan protested the intrusion of Chinese research vessels in the EEZ claimed by Japan, China agreed to defuse the issue by negotiating a prior notification regime. When Tokyo decided to allow former Taiwan president Lee Teng-hui to visit Japan for medical reasons, Beijing's protests were muted and perfunctory.

When Japanese finance officials tried to persuade their Chinese counterparts about China's stake in regional financial stability, the Chinese were quite responsive. In sharp contrast to their earlier opposition to Japan's Asian Monetary Fund concept, the Chinese endorsed regional financial cooperation with Japan and supported Japan's Chiang Mai Initiative, which involved a multilateral currency swap arrangement. When Japan invoked safeguard measures against Chinese agricultural imports, China retaliated with tariffs against Japanese manufactured products, but resolved the dispute with Beijing agreeing to a form of voluntary export restraints, and with Tokyo lifting its safeguard measures, as Pekkanen describes in Chapter 10 of this volume. In April 2002, Japan and China agreed to institutionalize a dialogue to manage the bilateral economic relationship in a cooperative manner.

Even the history issue did not derail the improvement in Sino-Japanese relations. When the Japanese government approved a history textbook that played up Japanese achievements while downplaying Japanese militarism and atrocities against the rest of Asia, Chinese criticisms were much less extreme than those coming from South Korea. When Prime Minister Junichiro Koizumi announced his intention to visit the Yasukuni Shrine in 2001, China hands in the Japanese Foreign Ministry attempted to persuade him to do otherwise. When this failed, Japanese and Chinese diplomats worked together to soften the blow of such a visit by having Koizumi go to the shrine before August 15, 1945—the official termination date of the Pacific War. After the visit, the two governments collaborated to restore the positive momentum in bilateral relations by arranging for Koizumi to go to China in September 2001 prior to the Shanghai APEC meeting hosted by China and having him ameliorate Chinese public feelings by visiting Marco Polo Bridge—the site of the military clash that triggered the Sino-Japanese war in 1937.

The improvement in Sino-Japanese relations did not come at the expense of Sino-American relations. Rather, the deterioration of Sino-American relations on their own terms encouraged China to keep Sino-Japanese relations on an even keel. Moreover, the stabilization of Sino-Japanese relations did not have a negative effect on U.S.-Japanese relations, because Tokyo had not appeased Beijing to the detriment of Washington's interests. On security issues critical to the United States (such as bilateral defense cooperation, Taiwan, and theater missile defense), Japan did not budge in its relations with China. In short, the improvement in Sino-Japanese relations reflected less a Japanese appeasement of Chinese interests and more a Chinese conciliatory attitude toward Japan. What appeared to be happening was a gradual evolution of this bilateral relationship from an emotional and guilt-ridden interaction (at least from the Japanese side) to a normal and business-like relationship based on mutual interests.

One caveat may concern the terms of China's accession to the WTO. From America's viewpoint, it might have been helpful if Japan had held off on finalizing its negotiations with China until China was ready to make the necessary concessions to the United States. A joint, coordinated strategy probably would have enhanced America's leverage over China, but there was no evidence that U.S. trade negotiators sought such coordination from their Japanese counterparts. And in the end, even without a coordinated approach, Washington and Beijing ultimately reached an agreement on WTO accession.

The 2000 election of George W. Bush as president of the United States certainly made Sino-American relations much more problematic than Sino-Japanese relations. Rather than talking about constructing a strategic partnership with China, Bush referred to China as a "strategic competitor" and criticized the Clinton administration for bypassing Japan. Although the Japanese appreciated the Bush administration's emphasis on the importance of the U.S.-Japan alliance, they worried that Sino-

American relations might deteriorate so much as to entrap Japan in a Sino-American conflict. The tensions between Washington and Beijing over the upgrading of U.S. arms sales to Taiwan and over the air collision off of Hainan Island made the Japanese especially anxious. In the end, however, both Chinese leaders and the Bush administration recognized that a more stable bilateral relationship was in their mutual interest and proceeded to manage the air collision crisis in such a way as to avoid an irreparable rupture between China and the United States. By the time the September 11th terrorist attacks occurred, Sino-American relations were on the upswing. The terrorist attacks only reinforced this trend, and remarkably China did not protest Japan's bold move to provide rear-area support for U.S. military operations in Afghanistan.

At least for the moment, the trilateral interaction among China, Japan, and the United States appears to display a rare and delicate balance in which Sino-American and Sino-Japanese relations are both relatively stable and the U.S.-Japanese alliance has been strengthened.

Conclusion

In its basic character, the structure of China, Japan, and U.S. interactions is an isosceles triangle in which the U.S.-Japan side is much shorter than the U.S.-China and the Japan-China sides. As the narrative presented in this chapter demonstrates, despite the continuing differences between Japan and the United States on perspectives, priorities, and approaches to China, they share common interests vis-à-vis China at the fundamental level. Therefore, Japanese and American policy differences on China have on the whole been complementary rather than conflictual, despite the remarkable absence of explicit policy coordination. This does not mean that Japan and the United States are not at times suspicious of or irritated by the other's dealings with China. The triangular logic among these three countries makes a certain amount of U.S.-Japanese friction over China inevitable.

For Japan, the most desirable situation is one in which Sino-American relations are neither so good that Japan's importance relative to the other two (especially the United States) is diminished, nor so bad that Japan might get caught in the crossfire between China and the United States. Given the fragility and volatility of Sino-American relations and China's geographic proximity, Japan is loathe to be an American partner in a containment strategy against China. The danger here is that America might abruptly shift course and reach out to China, leaving Japan (perhaps alone) in a hostile relationship with its giant neighbor. Therefore, even at the risk of American irritation at certain moments, the Japanese prefer to nurture a stable relationship with China.

For the United States, some analysts, such as Henry Kissinger, argue that America has a strategic interest in maintaining a balance between Japan and China. Others believe that the United States should have better relations with both Japan and China than Japan and China have with each other.[54] Still others feel that America's role is to temper the incipient yet inevitable competition between Japan and China for regional leadership. From the Japanese perspective, however, these arguments are confusing, if not contradictory. In many ways, Japan's willingness to be an active ally of the United States is what has exacerbated tensions between Japan and China. Moreover, if the United States is worried about Sino-Japanese rivalry in Asia as a destabilizing factor, then from the Japanese viewpoint, Washington should not be so concerned about improvements in Beijing-Tokyo relations.

Finally, China prefers a certain amount of tension between the United States and Japan so it can play the two off of each other in promoting its own national interest. What the Chinese want to prevent is a situation in which the United States and Japan collaborate tightly to contain China. Thus far, China has had little success in driving a wedge between the United States and Japan, but it has pursued another version of triangular diplomacy rather effectively: avoid having bad relations with both Washington and Tokyo at the same time.

American and Japanese Strategies in Asia

DEALING WITH ASEAN

ANDREW MACINTYRE

Introduction

The steady widening and deepening of U.S.-Japan relations affects not only the way these two countries interact with each other, but also the way they interact with other parts of Asia. This chapter traces out and examines the broad patterns of American and Japanese efforts to engage with Southeast Asia, and in particular with the Association of Southeast Asian Nations (ASEAN). This is a useful optic for considering the changing dynamics of U.S.-Japan relations, because it magnifies the areas of both shared and competitive interests, as well as the differing approaches that Tokyo and Washington have pursued. This chapter focuses on government-to-government relations, and although the distinction is sometimes elusive, particular attention is given to efforts to engage ASEAN as a regional collective rather than to bilateral efforts to engage the individual member states.

This turns out to be a more revealing exercise than expected. ASEAN is usually viewed as a weak and rubbery organization, known more for its airy dialogue than for concrete and coordinated policy adjustments. Easy rhetoric rather than consequential policy action has been its hallmark. Yet in spite of this, ASEAN remains central to virtually all multilateral strategies in Pacific Asia. For their own reasons, Tokyo and Washington have each long been interested in engaging with ASEAN. This interest has strengthened over time, even as ASEAN itself has had to grapple with increasingly serious internal problems. Along with the United States and Japan, China and then India have also recently sought to develop their institutionalized relationships with ASEAN.

For all its well-recognized weaknesses, ASEAN has two important advantages. One is that to date it is still the only well-established multilateral framework in Asia. Precisely because it has been so difficult for the big powers in Asia—particularly in Northeast Asia—to come together on a collective basis, ASEAN has served as a makeshift extended table around which everyone can gather. A second advantage that ASEAN enjoys is that it comprises nearly all of the potential "swing states" in Asia. From the viewpoint of the big powers, none of the individual ASEAN states—not even Indonesia—is really critical, but united they form a crucial voting bloc in regional affairs. Both of these considerations matter to Japan and the United States as they seek to pursue, jointly and separately, their core economic and security interests in Asia. But there is also an important trade-off here: while there is clear value in having the support of the Southeast Asian states, ASEAN's composition and organizational rules make it a frustratingly weak framework for serious multilateral cooperation. For Japan, and particularly for the United States, this trade-off is likely to become increasingly pointed.

This chapter is organized into three main parts. It begins by tracing the broad outlines of U.S. and Japanese approaches to ASEAN since the late 1960s, highlighting shifts over time. This is followed by a more analytic discussion of the various factors lying behind the increasing emphasis on engaging Southeast Asia multilaterally, as well as by some reflections on the paradoxical asymmetries of Japanese and American influence in Southeast Asia. The final section asks why Southeast Asia in general and ASEAN in particular receive as much attention as they do from Washington and Tokyo.

The Evolution of U.S. and Japanese
Approaches to ASEAN

The United States has had a consistently positive view of ASEAN since its inception in 1967. Although there was very little to the fledgling organization in the late 1960s, from Washington's viewpoint it was a welcome diplomatic initiative that promised to institutionalize greater trust and cooperation among the anti-Communist states of Southeast Asia, as well as to assist the rehabilitation of Indonesia following the turbulence and socialist leanings of the Sukarno period. In the high Cold War context of 1960s Asia, the building of ASEAN was a positive if modest development for the United States. But the bedrock of U.S. relations with Southeast Asia remained unambiguously bilateral, as analyzed at length in the chapters by Pempel and Ikenberry in this book. Without question, the

bulk of serious government-to-government business continued to be handled bilaterally, in dealings with the individual states of the region.
ASEAN, the collective, was very much an afterthought. This picture began to shift in the latter 1970s, as Washington gradually began to invest
significant diplomatic capital in the fledgling regional organization. In
part this was a function of the geopolitical need to help shore up the regional balance of power in Southeast Asia in the wake of the Communist
victory in Vietnam and the withdrawal of U.S. troops from Indochina
and Thailand, and in part it reflected the fact that slowly there was coming to be more substance to ASEAN itself as member states overcame
their mutual suspicions of one another and began to give more serious
consideration to issues of regional cooperation.

The first ASEAN leaders' summit in February 1976 and the accompanying Treaty of Amity and Cooperation were welcome signs of growing
ASEAN solidarity. This was an initial indication that the regional grouping might in fact prove durable. Less welcome to the United States was
ASEAN's move to enshrine the earlier enunciated doctrine of Southeast
Asia as a Zone of Peace, Freedom and Neutrality (ZOPFAN) in the Declaration of ASEAN Concord. Washington explicitly opposed any suggestion of Southeast Asia as a nuclear weapons free zone, as well as the call
to terminate foreign military bases and external security links.[1] Neither
provision, however, ever proved to be a source of serious concern. The
former remained simply a statement of hope and the latter was little more
than a doctrinal fiction maintained out of deference to Indonesian sensibilities on the part of its Southeast Asian neighbors.

An important step in the gradual ratcheting up of U.S. diplomatic engagement with ASEAN came with the launching in 1977 of the U.S.-
ASEAN Dialogue as an annual meeting of senior U.S. officials (usually including the secretary of state) and ASEAN foreign ministers. As part of
this launch, Washington granted association status to ASEAN to enable
cumulative rules of origin under the terms of the U.S. generalized system
of tariff preferences.[2] ASEAN governments used these regular high-level
meetings to push for an extensive agenda of economic policy concessions
ranging from increased aid to ASEAN (as distinct from individual members) through dealing with falling prices for ASEAN commodity exports
to U.S.-based market-access problems. On the security front, Washington
was sympathetic to ASEAN's independent diplomatic efforts to promote
a resolution of the Vietnam-Cambodia problem.

Conversely, notwithstanding the increased rhetorical support of
ASEAN and the growing commitment of diplomatic resources in this
heightened pattern of formal interactions, there were clearly limits in the
extent to which Washington was willing to go in backing ASEAN. The

menu of items on the ASEAN economic wish list shifted over the years, but the general pattern was for Washington to shower ASEAN members with rhetorical praise and encouragement while giving them very little in the way of significant policy concessions. Hopes for increased aid to Southeast Asia (above and beyond bilateral assistance) went largely un-requited (indeed, U.S. aid was generally of declining significance); ASEAN was unable to secure any special economic relationship with the United States along the lines of the European Economic Community's Lome Convention with parts of the developing world; and ASEAN com-plaints about rising U.S. protectionism through the 1980s (even as South-east Asia itself increasingly liberalized) had little impact. In short, on the economic issues on which ASEAN focused in discussions with the United States, it encountered frustration.[3] And while Washington celebrated ASEAN's enhanced diplomatic cohesion and activism and was happy to endorse its efforts on the Cambodia problem, post-Vietnam, it was not about to weigh in on ASEAN's side in a serious way.[4] In effect, the United States delegated real control over the Cambodia problem to China.

In sum, through the 1970s and 1980s, Washington welcomed and val-ued the rise of ASEAN, but ASEAN and Southeast Asia more broadly were of only moderate significance in the wider scheme of thought on U.S. foreign policy. This is not surprising given both the declining strate-gic importance of Southeast Asia to Washington post-Vietnam and the re-gion's still modest economic significance. More broadly, notwithstanding its growing cohesiveness, ASEAN's institutional capabilities were clearly very limited. In security terms, ASEAN's contribution was welcome but modest, as summed up by Leifer's designation of it as a diplomatic rather than a security community.[5] And in economic terms, ASEAN had yet to demonstrate any serious interest in or ability to promote forms of in-traregional economic cooperation of real interest to new categories of traders and investors in the United States.

As the 1980s progressed into the 1990s, the level of U.S. engagement with ASEAN continued to ratchet up gently. This movement reflected the accelerating industrial transformation of the region and the maturing of ASEAN as an organization. With Southeast Asian industrial exports booming and the United States increasingly preoccupied with Asian trade imbalances, ASEAN governments found themselves subjected to some of the same pressures directed at Japan, Korea, and Taiwan. Washington made use of ASEAN as a multilateral forum to drive home its concerns about traditional trade barriers as well as newer trade-related issues in-volving intellectual property rights, labor, and environmental standards.[6] On the security front, when Washington sought to become involved with specific regional challenges or crises, such as the political settlement in

Cambodia in 1992, the South China Seas tensions in 1995, and the East Timor rescue operation in 1999, it found ASEAN to be a useful interlocutor.[7] Conversely, when ASEAN first formally announced its plan to use its Post-Ministerial Conference (PMC) as an institutional framework for a wider East Asian multilateral security forum, the United States was initially opposed, fearing that this would undercut the core bilateral security alliances it had in place across the Pacific, as Ashizawa discusses in Chapter 11 of this volume.[8] But American resistance eased as the United States became more engaged in the wider process of multilateral economic cooperation through Asia-Pacific Economic Cooperation (APEC) under the Clinton administration, and as the utility of engaging a reemergent China became increasingly evident.

The 1997–98 financial crisis constituted a sharp disjuncture in the trend toward gradually deepening U.S. engagement with ASEAN—both in the extent to which the organization was ignored and in the ill-will that Washington's tough policy stance ultimately generated. In the period since, particularly with the advent of the George W. Bush administration, we have seen a renewal of interest in ASEAN. The primary driver for this was a desire to employ ASEAN as a partial regional balancing force in the face of heightened concerns about China. Also relevant were lesser concerns about both the growth of transborder problems and the development of the ASEAN+3 framework. It remains to be seen whether engagement via ASEAN as a whole will be of any benefit in Washington's campaign against terrorism following the September 11 attacks.

Japan's approach to and engagement with ASEAN have differed from those of the United States in important ways. Japan has focused more intensely on engagement with ASEAN as a collective entity than has the United States. It has been more heavily, though by no means exclusively, concerned with economic issues, and it has placed higher policy priority on Southeast Asia than has the United States.

Interestingly, Japan was initially slower than the United States to take an interest in ASEAN. Yamakage reports that in the 1960s, Tokyo simply did not take ASEAN seriously, because it was more concerned with promoting its own institutional vehicle for multilateral cooperation in the region—the Ministerial Conference for Economic Development in Southeast Asia (MCEDSEA), launched in 1966.[9] Apart from its interest in the short-lived MCEDSEA, Tokyo's attention during the early years of ASEAN was overwhelmingly on the bilateral relationships, particularly with Indonesia and Thailand, with a view to ensuring access to key natural resources.[10] Japan did not really engage substantively with ASEAN until 1973, and then it did so at the initiative of ASEAN rather than Tokyo. Moreover, the early engagement was not particularly cordial. ASEAN states were angered by the damage being done to their natural rubber sales by Japan's export of synthetic rubber. In response to this focused criticism, both sides agreed to set up the Japan-ASEAN Forum on Rubber to discuss the problem. Although a significant step toward a constructive dialogue, this initiative did not prevent the emergence of wider criticism of Japan's economic behavior within Southeast Asia, which culminated in violent demonstrations during Prime Minister Kakuei Tanaka's disastrous 1974 visit to Bangkok and Jakarta.

From this point on, a number of factors came together and led to a basic shift in Japan's approach to ASEAN. At the most immediate level, it was clear that not all was well in Tokyo's relations with Southeast Asia. There were lingering resentments from World War II, and Japanese firms were the subject of nationalist protests. Both of these resentments stood as possible irritants for Japan's growing industrial investments in the region. Other factors were at work as well, further encouraging Tokyo to engage ASEAN in a serious fashion. The wider geopolitical context was changing. On one hand, Japan had normalized relations with China and was thus more confident about its immediate Northeast Asian environment; but on the other hand, Communism had triumphed in Indochina, and the United States had withdrawn militarily from mainland Southeast Asia.[11] In these new circumstances, assisting the development of a stable and prosperous Southeast Asia became a more pressing foreign policy priority for Japan. Reinforcing the shift in this direction was U.S. pressure for Japan to share more of the burden of promoting regional security, which fed directly into the growth of Japanese Official Development Assistance (ODA) to Southeast Asia.[12] Finally, also significant was that, as in the earlier discussion of deepening U.S. engagement with ASEAN around this time, ASEAN itself was beginning to emerge as a more cohesive regional organization that might warrant more sustained attention, and Tokyo's originally preferred vehicle for multilateral engagement in Southeast Asia—MCEDSEA—had passed from the scene.

The cumulative effect of these developments became plain from 1977 on, as Tokyo moved to overhaul its relationships with Southeast Asia and engage seriously with ASEAN. The first step was the establishment in March 1977 of a new Japan-ASEAN Forum as a framework to facilitate high-level communication between senior Japanese officials and their ASEAN counterparts. This was followed in August by the watershed regional tour by Prime Minister Takeo Fukuda, during which he outlined Tokyo's desire to forge a new and supportive partnership with ASEAN. The shift in policy that Fukuda's trip presaged paved the way for a rapid broadening and deepening of official engagement with ASEAN. Japanese aid to ASEAN soon rose dramatically, new venues for official dialogue were institutionalized, and visits by Japanese prime ministers and foreign ministers became a matter of routine.

To be sure, ASEAN had various complaints through the 1980s on issues ranging from technology transfer and restrictive aid to concerns about overall economic dominance. Japan too was concerned about a variety of market-opening issues, but there was now much more scope for extensive and substantive dialogue.[13] As we have already seen, Washington was also engaging more with ASEAN through the 1980s. However, by comparison, Japanese involvement was much more intensive both quantitatively and qualitatively. The dramatic transformation of Japan's relations with ASEAN was perhaps best symbolized by the fact that Japanese Prime Minister Noboru Takeshita was the sole foreign leader invited to attend the Third ASEAN Leaders' Summit in 1987.

Japan's engagement with ASEAN was by no means limited to purely economic issues; it was also making steady efforts to help shape the wider politico-security environment in Southeast Asia through nonmilitary means. Vietnam's invasion of Cambodia quickly became a focal point for ASEAN diplomatic activity during the 1980s. Japan sought to assist the cause of regional stability by offering ODA to Vietnam, in the hope of preventing its complete diplomatic isolation from the West. In the face of stiff protests from ASEAN (through the ASEAN-Japan foreign ministers' meetings), however, Japan backed off and suspended its aid to Vietnam following the latter's invasion of Cambodia.[14] Japan renewed its involvement in the Indochina problem in the latter part of the 1980s, when the loss of Soviet aid to Vietnam triggered a realignment of the forces at play. Tokyo carefully secured ASEAN agreement at the outset, outlining proposals for financial assistance for an international peacekeeping force (including the dispatch of Japanese personnel) at an ASEAN foreign ministers' meeting in July 1988. This paved the way for an unprecedented burst of Japanese diplomatic activism on a Southeast Asian security problem.[15]

As the 1990s progressed, Japan became increasingly active in pursuing broad politico-security goals involving Southeast Asia. All of these goals involved direct engagement and cooperation with ASEAN. Two factors in particular facilitated this wider Japanese-ASEAN cooperation. One was a shared resentment of what was seen as economic bullying and diplomatic heavy-handedness by Washington. The other was a shared concern about the rise of China in the context of what initially appeared to be declining U.S. military engagement in the region following the 1991 closure of the U.S. bases in the Philippines. Much more than the United States, Japan worked through and with ASEAN. However, in the absence of ASEAN concurrence, Japanese proposals could not proceed.

One key instance of this was Tokyo's interest in promoting a multilateral regional security dialogue. The idea was first floated in 1990 by Australia and Canada. ASEAN reacted coldly. In July 1991, at an ASEAN PMC, Japanese Foreign Minister Taro Nakayama floated another version of the idea, one that was more consistent with ASEAN sensibilities. Nakayama proposed that the ASEAN-PMC be the vehicle for a region-wide security dialogue.[16] ASEAN still reacted coolly. Despite this official reaction, a month earlier a similar concept had been adopted by ASEAN's Track II security dialogue—the ASEAN Institutes for Strategic and International Studies (ISIS) network—as part of a set of recommendations that ISIS was tasked to prepare for the upcoming fourth ASEAN leaders' summit the following year. In due course, notwithstanding the earlier reluctance of the foreign ministers, at the January 1992 Summit ASEAN leaders adopted the recommendation to inaugurate what was to become known as the ASEAN Regional Forum (ARF).

Another major instance of Japan-ASEAN interaction of this sort was the founding of what grew into the ASEAN+3 framework for annual summit meetings of Northeast Asian and Southeast Asian heads of government. During a January 1997 visit to Southeast Asia, Japanese Prime Minister Ryutaro Hashimoto gave a speech about the need for an institutionalized meeting of Japanese and ASEAN leaders to discuss regional developments. The Southeast Asian leaders reacted skeptically. However, by the end of the year, their preferences had shifted markedly and they were keen to endorse such a plan. The change came, of course, as a result of the Asian financial crisis and Southeast Asia's radically altered economic circumstances. With the crisis spinning out of control and Washington insisting on a prescription of bitter policy medicine, ASEAN leaders were only too happy to commence the dialogue that grew into the wider "Asians only" ASEAN+3 framework.

Working in close conjunction with ASEAN, Japan has made unprecedented headway in the region with politico-security initiatives since the early 1990s. But there is an irony in this, for the headway on this front stands in remarkable contrast to developments on the economic front. In Southeast Asia, Japan was the subject of intense criticism during the financial crisis, both for its inability to help the region by getting its own economic house in order, and more pointedly, for its inability to assume a leadership role in responding to the crisis.[17] Japan was seen as too easily deterred by Washington from its proposal for the Asian Monetary Fund, which promised to provide emergency financial assistance on much less onerous terms than the International Monetary Fund (IMF); and then, in the subsequent watered-down and Washington-approved Miyazawa initiative, it was seen as too willing to allow emergency assistance to be tied to Japanese commercial interests. (On these topics, see the Amyx and Katada chapters in this volume.)

In the period since the Asian financial crisis, notwithstanding the disarray within the Southeast Asian region, Tokyo has continued to work quietly to expand its engagement of ASEAN. Notable here was the currency swap agreement (the so-called Chiang Mai Initiative) made through the ASEAN+3 framework, as well as the broadening of multilateral cooperation on other transborder problems, such as drug trafficking and terrorism.[18]

U.S. and Japanese Approaches Compared

Several points emerge from this comparison of the evolution of Japanese and U.S. engagement with ASEAN. The first point is that for all the familiar and real weaknesses of ASEAN as a multilateral institution, what is striking about the record of the past three decades is the extent to which both Washington and Tokyo have in fact invested serious diplomatic resources in engaging with it, rather than simply relying on their individual bilateral relationships. It goes without saying that both Washington and Tokyo retain muscular bilateral relationships with the various Southeast Asian states (including treaty relationships in two cases). The converse is also the case: while the states of Southeast Asia have certainly found increasing advantage over time in presenting a common front in their dealings with both Japan and the United States, all have pursued much of their national business—and certainly the most important items on their respective national agendas—bilaterally. To be clear, then, there is no suggestion here that the relationships through the regional organization have come to overshadow the relationships between the individual Southeast Asian states and the United States and Japan. Yet, having reminded ourselves of that basic (and familiar) truth, the more surprising point is the extent to which the United States and Japan have engaged with ASEAN on economic, security, and now new transborder issues. Okawara and Katzenstein's language of "incipient multilateralism" emerging within a context of "entrenched bilateralism" captures the situation neatly.[19]

What accounts for this movement toward greater multilateral engagement with Southeast Asia by both the United States and, particularly, Japan? A shifting mix of causal factors has been involved. Certainly it would be a serious mistake to see this as simply a function of the ending of the Cold War and the passing of a tensely bipolar world. The collapse of the Soviet Union and the changing relationship between Tokyo and Moscow did indeed play into the story by easing somewhat Japan's acute security dependence on the United States. This afforded greater room for diplomatic maneuver. It also encouraged Tokyo to seek out multilateral options in the Pacific so as to simultaneously restrain and engage the United States, and thereby reduce the risk of having to choose between Japan and Asia.[20] But geopolitical considerations other than the ending of the Cold War have also been very important. For instance, the earlier American defeat and withdrawal from Indochina prompted Washington and Tokyo to reach out to ASEAN in diplomatic support from the mid-1970s on, and indeed prompted ASEAN itself to pursue intraregional cooperation more vigorously. These considerations were further strengthened subsequently by concerns about a possible U.S. disengagement from the region following the closure of the Philippine bases. And more recently the rise of an increasingly muscular and assertive China has separately but similarly motivated Japan, the United States, and the Southeast states to explore enhanced multilateral engagement through the vehicle of ASEAN.

While we can see these changing geopolitical considerations affecting the incentives of the various players over time, it is also plainly the case that a powerful economic dimension has been at work. Critical to the deepening engagement between Japan and ASEAN through this period were the strong underlying economic complementarity between their economies as well as the policies facilitating trade and investment linkages that they adopted. Also important here was U.S. economic behavior. Macroeconomic policy developments in the United States along with retaliatory trade measures against Asian economies through the 1980s and early 1990s further encouraged Japan and ASEAN to come together. Reciprocally, American fears about restrictive commercial policy practices in Asia and about being left out of the Asian economic boom impelled Washington to respond to the so-called Asian Challenge. And then, in the 1990s, in the wake of the Asian economic meltdown and Washington's unbending insistence on orthodox economic remedies, Japan and Southeast Asia found powerful common cause to push further in pursuing multilateral economic collaboration.

Also bearing on the evolution of Japanese and U.S. engagement with ASEAN were the specific dynamics of the bilateral U.S.-Japan relationship. U.S. trade pressures on Japan of the sort just mentioned, as well as U.S. efforts to push Japan to take on a greater share of the regional security burden separately, encouraged Tokyo to reach out to ASEAN. Finally, we need to take account of intraregional political and economic developments within Southeast Asia itself and the preferences of the individual ASEAN states in encouraging collective efforts to engage Tokyo and Washington, as well as to push for wider multilateral engagement of the Pacific region as a whole.

If we draw back from the causal factors lying behind the growth of U.S. and Japanese engagement with ASEAN, a further general observation to emerge from this overview is the striking asymmetry of their involvement. Although both countries have seriously engaged ASEAN as a collective, as well as the individual states of the region, Japan has clearly done so in a much more intensive fashion. This is scarcely surprising because, quite simply, Southeast Asia matters much more to Japan than it does to the United States. Perhaps the easiest indicator of this difference is the vast disparity in their ODA commitments to Southeast Asia. Nevertheless, notwithstanding the asymmetry of their interests in and commitments to Southeast Asia, Washington exerts much greater influence on ASEAN than Tokyo does.

Tokyo has great difficulty getting ASEAN as a collective (or the individual ASEAN states) to do anything they do not wish to do. We saw this illustrated earlier in the way ASEAN was able to exercise veto power over the pace and direction of plans to develop a multilateral framework for regional security discussions. But it applies to the bilateral relationships as well. In the early 1990s, when Japan appeared to be at the height of its economic powers, the Indonesian government had a large telecommunications infrastructure project to allocate. A range of foreign corporations vied for the contract, but NEC of Japan came out on top. Amid American fears that Japan's large aid contributions to Indonesia had undermined AT&T's prospects, Washington swung into action. Following a telephone call from George Bush to Indonesian President Suharto, Indonesian authorities moved to split the contract between the two companies.[21] Whatever advantage Japanese economic presence had brought to NEC was apparently undercut by a short telephone call from the U.S. president.

Similarly, vastly greater Japanese aid counted for little in Thailand when Washington decided to press the Thai government on behalf of a U.S. glass manufacturer whose entry into the Thai market was being thwarted by an investment ban designed to protect a near-monopoly enjoyed by a Japanese joint venture.[22] Conversely, whereas Washington has not hesitated to pursue ASEAN governments aggressively over what it regards as unfair trade practices, Tokyo has been much more circumspect. It took an extraordinarily egregious breach of WTO rules by Jakarta— the awarding of exorbitant privileges to a car assembly joint venture between a Suharto son and the Korean Kia group in 1996—and, moreover, an act that flagrantly struck at core Japanese corporate interests in the Indonesian automotive sector, to trigger serious policy countermeasures from Tokyo. Following protracted efforts by the Ministry of International Trade and Industry (MITI) to persuade the Indonesian government to reconsider its position, and a declared preparedness to take the matter to the WTO, not only did Jakarta not accede, but in April 1997 Suharto bluntly rebuffed the entreaties and ordered that the project in fact be accelerated.[23] These were scarcely the actions of a government fearing significant bilateral sanctions.

Stated simply, despite Japan's much bigger direct economic presence in Southeast Asia, Washington has much greater ability than Tokyo to induce policy adjustments. The most dramatic evidence of this is, of course, provided by the financial crisis of 1997–98. As I have tried to show, however, viewed from a Southeast Asian perspective, the underlying pattern was evident much earlier, when Japan still seemed to be on an upward trajectory. None of this is to say that Tokyo is without influence in the region; a range of policy outcomes it sought have ultimately come to pass, but only when ASEAN agreed. Nor is it to suggest that Tokyo is unhappy with the situation. ASEAN cannot impose initiatives on Japan (to say nothing of the United States), but it does seem to exercise a surprising degree of veto power and agenda control.

Note how different this picture is—both in terms of the asymmetry between U.S. and Japanese leverage with ASEAN and in terms of Japan-ASEAN relativities—from that in the important literature that focuses on production networks and ODA and concludes that Southeast Asia is locked "in Japan's embrace."[24] Southeast Asian firms may well have had to adjust to the needs of their giant Japanese counterparts, but at the government-to-government level the asymmetries have been much less clear-cut or consequential. Despite the vast disparities in economic stature between Japan and the Southeast Asian states, Japan's economic might translates into much less policy leverage in Southeast Asia than might be expected. And with the prolonged economic malaise in Japan and the slowed flows of private Japanese capital to Southeast Asia (see Chapter 6 in this volume, by Hamilton-Hart, for details), the relative importance of Tokyo and Washington in ASEAN eyes has only tilted further in favor of the latter.

What explains the fact that Japan's regional economic leadership has never really translated into strong policy leadership or leverage? Why should the policy influence of Washington be so much stronger than that of Tokyo? A number of factors seem relevant. A frequently heard argument is that Tokyo is constrained by its past, and that bitter memories of World War II in Asia compel it to tread gently.[25] Certainly Japan's diplomatic style in Asia contrasts sharply with that of Washington, but war memories alone seem an unsatisfactory explanation, both because residual resentment toward Japan from the 1940s is much less strong in Southeast Asia than in Northeast Asia, and more broadly, because Japan appears to assume the same soft-spoken approach in, say, Latin America or the Middle East as it does in Asia. It is not evident that Japan pursues a significantly more assertive diplomatic strategy in these other regions than it does in Northeast Asia. A second layer of explanation relates to the economic disparities. While it is true that Japan has been a more important source of capital—whether through bank lending, direct investment, or development assistance—the United States has been the more important market for exports.

Finance and sales both matter, but in ASEAN eyes the danger of Washington restricting access for particular products or imposing punitive measures in response to some Southeast Asian business practice has seemed much greater than the danger of Tokyo moving to discourage private capital flows or redirect aid flows. Notwithstanding the fact that the U.S. market is by far the more open of the two, for ASEAN countries it is U.S. policymakers who wield the greater capacity to inflict economic costs.

A third and still more basic layer of explanation relates to geopolitics and military power. It matters that the United States is the ultimate guarantor of security for ASEAN (and of course for Japan). Notwithstanding periodically intense policy and even ideological disagreements with Washington, ASEAN members well understand that it is the U.S. military that has been critical to a satisfactory regional balance of power. This has been true both during the Cold War and subsequently with the rise of China. This fundamental fact is neither seldom discussed explicitly nor directly related to economic policy issues by ASEAN, either as a collective or by its individual members, but its significance is far-reaching.

Southeast Asia and ASEAN-Centric Multilateralism in Pacific Asia

Why do Southeast Asia and ASEAN feature as prominently as they do in the efforts of both Japan and the United States to engage Pacific Asia on a multilateral basis? None of these states—not even Indonesia—has the economic weight or military capabilities of, say, South Korea or Australia. More broadly, in both economic and military terms, it is quite clear that the main game for both the United States and Japan is in Northeast Asia, not Southeast Asia. Yet it is ASEAN that is central to so much of the multilateral activity in the region. Why is this?

Part of the explanation is that in both political and economic terms the Southeast Asians are the key swing states in Pacific Asia. If the Southeast Asians were to move closer to any one of the three big Pacific states—the United States, Japan, and China—it would have important implications for the overall regional balance. From the perspectives of Washington, Tokyo, and Beijing, ASEAN constitutes most of the rest of Pacific Asia.

None of the three major powers wants to see the ten ASEAN states be drawn more closely into the economic or security orbit of any one of the others. The United States does not want them to become too close to China or Japan, either in security or economic terms. The reciprocal is true for both China and Japan as well. Engaging the Southeast Asians multilaterally is a way of helping to reduce any such risk. This is an important part of why we encounter so many ASEAN+X arrangements. Japan favors ASEAN+3 (or ASEAN+Northeast Asia); the United States favors APEC, and failing that, ARF (or ASEAN+the whole Pacific), and China favors ASEAN+1 (or ASEAN+China Free Trade Area).[26] The Southeast Asian states understand the interests the major powers have in their region's orientation, and they seek to play on it.

But if Southeast Asia holds some enduring value as an economic and strategic balancing chip, it is less clear that ASEAN—the multilateral organization itself—will be of enduring value, at least in its current form. Aside from the inherent value of its member states to the big powers, the other reason that ASEAN is so prominent as a forum for multilateral interaction in Pacific Asia is that developing an effective and stable basis for government-to-government interactions in Northeast Asia has proved so difficult. In the absence of any solid institutional basis for the major players in Northeast Asia—Japan, China, and the United States—to enjoy stable, multilateral dialogue, meetings built around the good offices of ASEAN remain a useful instrument—but only up to a point.

How much longer the major players, particularly the United States, will find ASEAN's discursive and inconclusive modus operandi satisfactory is unclear. ASEAN is a deeply limited organization, fundamentally because of the differences in the core preferences of its now quite diverse member states. Campbell and Reiss have pointed to the need to create new multilateral frameworks to tackle pressing problems specific to Northeast Asia, recognizing that the ASEAN-based ARF is unable to deal adequately with these issues.[27] Already there are various exploratory moves in this direction, but along with frustration with ASEAN on the part of the major Northeast Asian players there is also considerable frustration within ASEAN itself. Well prior to the financial crisis, Jakarta already regarded ASEAN as limiting. (But given all of Indonesia's internal problems, international strategy is not a priority at present.) And at the other end of the scale, Singapore is now actively pursuing a range of bilateral Pacific free trade arrangements, out of frustration with the sclerotic condition of the existing regional multilateral frameworks.

The Southeast Asian states all understand that united as ASEAN they are much more than the sum of their individual parts. This makes the grouping worth having. But whether they can fashion the organization into a form in which it can make meaningful decisions remains an open question. As Japan and the United States contemplate engaging Pacific Asia, they will face an increasing sense of trade-off between the coalitional advantages of having all the ASEAN membership lined up with them, and the organizational disadvantages of living with ASEAN's very limiting organizational procedures.

More broadly, with the multiplication of ASEAN+X-type frameworks, it is becoming increasingly apparent that the decisive participants are not the ASEAN states but X. Yet until the other states—principally the major players in Northeast Asia—can generate a viable multilateral framework of their own, ASEAN will remain an indispensable element in the multilateral equations of Pacific Asia.

PART II

ECONOMIC FLOWS

Capital Flows and Financial Markets in Asia

NATIONAL, REGIONAL, OR GLOBAL?

NATASHA HAMILTON-HART

Introduction

Changes in capital flows and national financial markets in Asia are likely
to exert some influence on the Japan-U.S. relationship as it moves toward
a more multilateral future. A commonly held view is that Asian markets
are losing any distinct regional identity they had, as Western investors
and financial firms move into a cash-strapped and politically complaisant
region. In this view, Asian countries will initially have little choice and
subsequently little interest in resisting such change, creating the grounds
for greater cooperation among the United States, Japan, and the rest of
Asia, in both pan-Pacific and global arenas. Alternative analyses have
generally been based on political considerations, such as the likelihood of
a nationalist backlash in many countries and regional resentment at the
way the United States and global institutions such as the International
Monetary Fund (IMF) managed the crisis.[1] Following such analyses,
Japan's relationship with the United States can be expected to be increasingly conflictual as it works out either a nationalist or a regionalist solution to the problems of managing an internationalized financial sector.

It is clearly possible for politics to trump economics when it comes to determining which rules will govern capital flows and financial markets.
Hence, even assuming a decisive shift toward increasingly globalized capital markets in Asia, both possibilities for U.S.-Japan relations remain open.
But it is also the case that economic conditions differentially empower political actors and create incentives for them to pursue particular agendas.
Of course, market developments will not have a determinative effect on

U.S.-Japan relations, but they will make up a set of incentives and constraints to which we can expect economic and political actors to respond.

The next section presents a brief overview of precrisis economic flows and linkages in Asia, describing the degree of regionalization that existed before the crisis. The following sections describe three major trends in capital flows and financial markets since 1997. The first trend is a sharp decline in Japan's financial ties with the region, in both absolute and relative terms. The second is the move toward an increasingly open and global orientation in some markets. Mergers and acquisitions in Asia by non-Asian companies have increased significantly and the pattern of bank lending to the region has also taken on a more globally diversified structure as Japanese banks retreat and their role is taken up by European and American lenders. In contrast, the third trend points to a continuing regional concentration with regard to some financial ties, and to an overall decline in the level of financial internationalization in some markets. Japanese manufacturing investment and official aid retain a significant regional orientation, but on other indicators regionalization trends increasingly bypass Japan. Finally, this chapter assesses the implications of these developments for U.S.-Japan relations in Asia.

Before the Crisis: Growing Regionalization

Before the crisis of 1997–98 there was some regional concentration in the trade and financial links of Asian countries.[2] Trade was increasingly intraregional, and inward foreign direct investment (FDI) was dominated by regional sources. To the extent that local banking markets in Southeast Asia were open to foreign banks, non-Asian banks with long histories in the region had a significant presence. Banks from Asia were generally increasing their share of local banking assets at a faster rate than non-Asian foreign banks. Table 6.1 provides some indicators of the degree of regionalization in Asian countries' international transactions before the crisis.

The picture of outward investment from Asian countries is not fully captured in Table 6.1, however. The country with by far the largest stock of outward foreign investment was Japan, which has always directed most of its outward FDI to non-Asian countries. Between 1971 and 1980, Japan directed more than a quarter of its FDI to Asia. Asia's share dropped to an average of 12 percent of FDI outflows in the late 1980s (when nearly half of Japanese FDI went to North America), then rose to about 20 percent in the first half of the 1990s.[3] Conversely, Japan remained the single most important source of FDI for the rest of the region.

TABLE 6.1
*International Transactions
of Non-Japan Asia, 1996 (%)*

	Asia	U.S.	E.U.
Exports	53.5	19.8	13.7
Imports	55.4	14.3	14.0
FDI inflows	67.9	10.7	12.1
Bank lending	35.4	6.2	43.2

SOURCE: Masahiro and Akiyama, "Implications of the Currency Crisis," 47.
NOTE: Non-Japan Asia (NJA): China, Hong Kong, Taiwan, Korea, Indonesia, Malaysia, Philippines, Singapore, Thailand, Vietnam; Asia: NJA plus Japan, except for bank lending (Japan only).

Furthermore, this investment played a pivotal role in the creation of region-wide, integrated production structures in many industries.[4]

For most other Asian countries, international bank lending, bank branching, and outward FDI had a definite regional orientation. Much of this activity was carried out by ethnic Chinese businesspeople in the greater China area (Hong Kong, Taiwan, and the People's Republic of China) and in Southeast Asia, where ethnic Chinese account for a disproportionate share of corporate wealth. Many studies of Chinese business in Asia in the 1990s suggest that transnational interfirm linkages and business-government ties influenced the trade and investment patterns of ethnic Chinese living in the region.[5] Together, the distinctive corporate strategies and regionally based networks of both Japanese and ethnic Chinese businesses contributed to the regionalization of Asian economies and made up a largely informal set of transnational regional ties and institutions.[6] While far from complete, the trend in the decade up to 1996 was toward increased economic regionalization in Asia. As described in the next section, this picture has changed in some significant ways since 1997.

Japan and Asia: Reduced Ties

One of the major changes in the nature of capital flows and financial markets in Asia since the crisis is the decline in Japanese investment in the region. Japanese capital flows to the rest of Asia have fallen both absolutely and relatively, as the country has disinvested from the region and diversified its overseas investment portfolio. Japanese banks have drastically reduced their exposure to Asia since 1997. From about $275 billion in outstanding loans to the region in 1997, Japanese banks cut their regional loans to $99.8 billion in mid-2002. Asia now accounts for 9.4 per-

TABLE 6.2
FDI Outflows from Japan, US$ Billions

	1997	1998	1999	2000	2001
Asia	12.181	6.528	7.162	5.931	2.762
	(24%)	(16%)	(11%)	(12%)	(20%)
NEA	3.574	2.194	2.987	3.254	1.345
SEA	7.520	3.976	3.838	2.459	1.319
U.S.	20.769	10.316	22.296	12.136	3.140
	(38%)	(25%)	(33%)	(25%)	(23%)
Europe	10.963	13.850	25.191	24.406	4.966
	(20%)	(34%)	(38%)	(50%)	(36%)
World	53.972	40.747	66.694	48.580	13.699

SOURCE: Japan External Trade Organization (JETRO), *JETRO White Paper on Foreign Direct Investment 2001*, Table 11 and *JETRO White Paper on Foreign Direct Investment 2002*, Table 4.1.

NOTE: Year is the financial year (1 April–31 March); NEA: Korea, Taiwan, HK, China; SEA: Malaysia, Thailand, Indonesia, Singapore, Philippines. Based on Ministry of Finance reports and notifications. FDI figures based on alternative measurements vary widely; see, for example, Table 6.7.

cent of total international lending by Japanese banks, compared to about 25 percent before the crisis.[7]

Japanese direct investment outflows have seen a similar shift away from Asia since the crisis. Table 6.2 reports the declining Asian share of Japan's total outward FDI. Absolute levels of outward FDI have fluctuated since 1997, but outflows did not decline decisively until the first half of FY2001. The proportion of Japanese FDI now going to Asia is about the same as in the late 1980s, but Europe rather than the United States is now receiving the greatest share of outward FDI from Japan. While declining exposure to Asia is a clear trend, aggregate capital flows from Japan (dominated by capital movements by financial investors and banks) show a high degree of volatility over recent years in terms of geographical destination.[8]

It is possible that the decline in Japanese lending and investment in Asia is simply a product of short-term contingencies. Japanese banks remain distressed and falling corporate profitability in Japan has constrained outward investment.[9] Early in the crisis, there was some evidence that the drop in exposure to the region could be expected to be temporary. An example of Japanese banks' readiness to put relationships over returns can be seen in the Industrial Bank of Japan's role in raising $500 million for the Thai export-import bank during the crisis. U.S. lenders stayed out of the syndication on the grounds that it was not profitable enough.[10] Similarly, loans and equity recapitalization of Japanese affiliates in Asia and the buyout of joint-venture partners in the region accounted for much of Japan's direct investment in Asia in 1997 and 1998.[11] Along with the maintenance of local employment levels in crisis-affected countries despite the economic contraction, these moves have been taken to indicate a concern with maintaining supply and distribution networks rather than short-term profits, a pattern of responses that reflects the governance structure of Japanese corporations.[12]

As discussed in a later section, Japanese manufacturing investment and official aid flows do retain a strong regional orientation. In other respects, however, the trend is toward reduced financial ties with Asia. Far from maintaining corporate relationships, Japanese banks have demanded more in the way of loan repayments than banks from any other country except the United Kingdom.[13] Further, it is not just the level of Japanese lending and investment to Asia that has declined; the *share* of Japan's outward capital flows directed to Asia has also declined markedly.

A More Globalized Region

The second major change in the nature of capital flows and financial markets in Asia since the crisis is the development of more extensive and diversified linkages with the rest of the world. Non-Asian investors and financial intermediaries are playing much more significant roles in the region, especially in Japan, Taiwan, and Korea. While the following section discusses exceptions to this trend of increasing openness, this section presents evidence of an increasingly open and global orientation in certain markets and categories of investment.

In terms of bank lending, Table 6.3 shows that the region has increased its reliance on European creditors, who now hold $376 billion in loans to non-Japan Asia. Japanese banks, with $99.8 billion in loans outstanding in non-Japan Asia, are now less important to the rest of the region than are U.S. banks, which hold $103 billion in outstanding loans. U.S. banks are also increasing their exposure to Asia whereas Japanese banks are still withdrawing loans from the region, although at a much slower rate than in the late 1990s. U.S. banks now have a larger proportion (12 percent) of their international loan portfolio allocated to non-Japan Asia than do Japanese banks (9.4 percent), if loans to the offshore centers of Hong Kong and Singapore are included.

In the case of direct investment flows, the pattern for the Northeast Asian countries suggests a shift to a more globally open orientation. Table 6.4 shows the trend in inward FDI on a country-by-country basis, as well as documenting a sharp rise in mergers and acquisitions (M&A) transactions as a component of total FDI inflows to Japan and Korea. In

TABLE 6.3
Bank Lending to Asian Countries by
Nationality of Lending Bank

	Total	Japan	U.S.	Europe
Japan	582.817	—	76.210	297.773
			(13.1%)	(51.1%)
China	53.211	10.123	6.375	25.698
		(19%)	(12%)	(48.3%)
Taiwan	43.500	3.346	16.707	18.567
		(7.7 %)	(38.4%)	(42.7%)
South Korea	86.268	9.650	22.054	36.632
		(11.2%)	(25.6%)	(42.5%)
Indonesia	35.108	7.142	3.025	19.796
		(20.3%)	(8.6%)	(56.4%)
Malaysia	51.535	5.701	8.047	21.787
		(11.1%)	(15.6%)	(42.3%)
Philippines	22.535	2.700	4.979	11.021
		(12%)	(22.1%)	(48.9%)
Thailand	41.275	10.300	4.137	16.319
		(25%)	(10%)	(39.5%)
Vietnam	2.454	0.238	0.369	1.335
		(9.7%)	(15%)	(54.4%)
Burma	0.689	0.026	—	0.630
		(3.8%)	—	(91.4%)
Hong Kong	268.864	32.091	21.008	168.572
		(11.9%)	(7.8%)	(62.7%)
Singapore	122.894	18.457	16.386	55.991
		(15%)	(13.3%)	(45.6%)
U.S.	2778.103	441.566	—	1825.053
		(15.9%)		(65.7%)
Total		1064.921	858.017	6816.142

SOURCE: Bank for International Settlements, "BIS Consolidated Banking Statistics,"
Table 9.
   NOTE: Consolidated foreign claims of BIS reporting banks, as of June 2002, in billions
of U.S. dollars; Europe comprises Austria, Belgium, France, Germany, Netherlands,
Switzerland, and the UK; total: total claims vis-à-vis all countries; claims on Hong Kong
and Singapore include claims on the offshore banking market.

contrast, China and the Southeast Asian countries, which received high
levels of FDI before the crisis, have either maintained FDI inflows at
roughly precrisis levels or have experienced a drop in inflows.

   In some cases, nonregional investors have become more important,
with an increase in M&A purchases by U.S. and European actors. At
$5.8 billion in 1999, M&A purchases by U.S. firms in non-Japan Asia
represented only 5 percent of all cross-border M&A purchases by U.S.

TABLE 6.4
Total FDI Inflows and Cross-Border M&A Sales

	1988–95*	1996	1997	1998	1999	2000	2001
Japan	0.563	0.228	3.224	3.193	12.741	8.322	6.202
M&A	0.401	1.719	3.083	4.022	16.431	15.541	15.183
China	26.163	40.180	44.237	43.751	40.319	40.772	46.846
M&A	0.226	1.906	1.856	0.798	2.395	2.247	2.325
Hong Kong	5.910	10.460	11.368	14.770	24.596	61.938	22.834
M&A	1.725	3.267	7.330	0.938	4.181	4.793	10.362
Taiwan	1.365	1.864	2.248	0.222	2.926	4.928	4.109
M&A	0.015	0.050	0.601	0.024	1.837	0.644	2.493
Korea	1.101	2.325	2.844	5.412	9.333	9.283	3.198
M&A	0.104	0.564	0.836	3.973	10.062	6.448	3.648
Indonesia	2.575	6.194	4.677	−0.356	−2.745	−4.550	−3.277
M&A	0.205	0.530	0.332	0.683	1.164	0.819	3.529
Malaysia	4.572	7.296	6.324	2.714	3.895	3.788	0.554
M&A	0.227	0.768	0.351	1.096	1.166	0.441	1.449
Philippines	1.273	1.520	1.249	1.752	0.578	1.241	1.792
M&A	0.321	0.462	4.157	1.905	1.523	0.366	2.063
Singapore	6.579	8.608	10.746	6.389	11.803	5.407	8.609
M&A	0.445	0.593	0.294	0.468	2.958	1.532	4.871
Thailand	1.747	2.271	3.626	5.143	3.561	2.813	3.759
M&A	0.104	0.234	0.633	3.209	2.011	2.569	0.957
Vietnam	1.535	1.803	2.587	1.700	1.484	1.289	1.300
M&A	—	0.006	0.063	—	0.059	0.019	0.004
U.S.	49.549	84.455	103.40	174.43	283.38	300.91	124.43
M&A	44.58	68.07	81.71	209.55	251.93	324.35	184.88

SOURCE: United Nations Conference on Trade and Development, *World Investment Report 2000*, Annex Table A.IV.6; and *World Investment Report 2002*, Annex Table B.2 and B.7.
*Annual average (1987–95 for M&A sales).

firms, but 23 percent of all M&A sales in non-Japan Asia.[14] U.S. direct investment in Asia (including Oceania and South Asia) increased from an average of $14.6 billion each year between 1996 and 1998 to an average of $21.4 billion between 1999 and 2001, with Japan, Hong Kong, China, Australia, Indonesia, and Singapore the largest investment sites. Reciprocally, investors from Singapore and Malaysia showed a new interest in the United States in 2000.[15]

For Japan, FDI inflows, concentrated in the services sector, increased after 1997. These inflows were dominated by large M&A deals involving U.S. and European investors. Major transactions have been GE Capital's purchase of Japan Leasing Corporation (with a transaction value of $6.6 billion) and Toho Mutual Life Insurance (valued at $2.32 billion), the acquisition of a 37 percent stake (valued at $5.4 billion) in Nissan by Renault, and a large investment by Vodafone in Japan Telecom. The United States accounted for nearly all of M&A sales in Japan in 1998 and 55 percent in 1999.[16] While the United States accounted for only 10 percent of total inward FDI in Japan in FY1999, this increased to 32 percent in FY2000 and the first half of FY2001.[17] The increase in inflows marks a significant change from Japan's earlier extraordinarily low levels of inward FDI.

Foreign investors have also made inroads into the domestic financial markets of some countries in Asia. Most countries in the region liberalized foreign access to the financial sector either as a result of general financial reform or as part of crisis-related relaxation of foreign investment rules.[18] Indonesia, Thailand, and Korea substantially liberalized policies governing the entry of foreign banks and raised limits on foreign ownership of domestic banks after the crisis. The Philippines had liberalized foreign entry to the banking market in 1994.

These policy shifts have brought about some significant changes. In the Philippines, ten new foreign banks were admitted to a previously highly protected domestic market in 1995, and the foreign share of bank assets increased to 15 percent by 1998, from 9 percent in 1990–94.[19] In Indonesia, the number of substantially foreign-owned banks increased from forty-one in November 1999 to fifty-two a year later, while the number of local private banks decreased from ninety-two to eighty-one over the same period.[20] Overall, the foreign bank share of commercial bank lending increased from 9 percent in 1996 to 28 percent at the end of 2000. In Korea, foreign control of domestic banking assets increased from less than 1 percent in 1994 to 16 percent at the end of 1999. The sale of Korea First Bank to U.S.-based Newbridge Capital in December 1999 accounts for most of the increase in foreign control of bank assets.[21]

The Japanese financial sector also registered a significant increase in foreign control as a result of record levels of inward FDI and ongoing rationalization of the financial industry. Investment in the financial industry accounted for 21 percent of inward FDI in 1999 and 33 percent in 2000.[22] Japanese financial institutions are still in the process of major consolidation exercises, most of which involve mergers among domestic players. Some significant purchases, however, have been made by foreign institutions. These include the acquisition of the nationalized Long-Term Credit Bank (LTCB) by a U.S. investment consortium and insurance industry purchases by U.S. companies.[23]

The nonbanking financial sector, particularly in the area of advisory and investment banking services, is another area that has seen an influx of non-Asian players. Until the downturn in the second half of 2001, the market for these services expanded after 1997 and American firms have been preeminent in Asia, a reflection of their almost complete dominance of investment banking worldwide.[24] Their business has in part been fed by governments in the region as they have gone increasingly to bond markets to raise the funds for crisis-related spending, begun to divest nationalized financial sector assets, and devolved the management of many nationalized commercial assets to private players. The involvement of foreign financial advisers and investment bankers in private sector restructuring has also been significant.[25]

A few anecdotal examples point to the predominant role of the big U.S. firms in providing these financial services. The leading investment banks and other advisers involved in the upsurge of M&A activity in Japan (deals worth $34.7 billion were reported in the first half of 2000) are American: Merrill Lynch was at the top of the table for Japanese business in 2000, Goldman Sachs in 1999. PricewaterhouseCoopers increased its Japan-based staff tenfold from mid-1999.[26] In the first half of 2000, the lead arrangers in the market for M&As completed by non-Japanese Asian target companies were all Western firms, mostly American. The top bookrunners for all bond issues were all Western (the top four were American), except for Nomura Securities, which ranked seventh. In contrast, four of the top five arrangers of syndicated loans were Japanese.[27] U.S. investment banks have also been engaged since 1998 to advise Indonesia's bank restructuring agency on its protracted efforts at selling nationalized banking assets. Lucrative as such deals are, Asia as a whole is still a small market for these American firms. For Morgan Stanley, for example, about 5 percent of its global staff are employed in Asia, which accounts for about 5 percent of its global income. Merrill Lynch's staff in Asia (excluding Japan and Australia) accounted for 3.5 percent of its global workforce.[28]

Overall, there have been some clear changes since 1997. Japan, Korea, and Taiwan have become more open to foreign investors, and these investors have largely been from the United States and Europe. The United States has increased its investment and lending to Asia significantly, and European, not Japanese, banks are the largest lenders to the region. Together these changes point to a more open and globally oriented region.

Countervailing Trends: Going National, Staying Regional

This section discusses two trends that are somewhat at odds with the deregionalization of Japanese outward investment and the increasingly global and open nature of regional financial markets just described. The first trend is the declining aggregate importance of some of the region, particularly Southeast Asia, to global investors. The second trend is the continuing dominance of regional players in some markets.

Going National

The turnaround in private capital flows to non-Japan Asia in 1997–98 was dramatic. As shown in Table 6.5, countries that had registered high levels of capital inflow suddenly experienced large capital outflows. The reversal in capital flows was registered mainly by the crisis economies of Korea, Thailand, Indonesia, Malaysia, and the Philippines, largely in terms of the withdrawal of bank lending and portfolio flows.[29] The decline of bank lending and portfolio flows may signal a more durable and stable set of linkages with the rest of the world, because direct investment has been demonstrably less volatile than other types of capital.

Overall, however, Southeast Asia is now more peripheral to global investors and banks than it was in the early and mid-1990s. While the immediate economic consequences of the crisis in affected countries included changes that were expected to have a positive effect on foreign investment, other effects (such as the ongoing currency volatility, the contraction of domestic consumption, and increased import costs) reduced incentives for foreign investment.[30] Political instability and security risks, most obviously those affecting Indonesia but also an issue in the Philippines, have also been cited by foreign companies as deterrents to investment. Other deterrents mentioned by foreign companies were the same regulatory, infrastructural, and human resource problems that were evident in Southeast Asia before the crisis.[31]

These factors can be seen at work in cases where proposed foreign takeovers of banks and other firms did not go through. While there were foreign takeovers in many Asian markets, this increase in foreign participation was much smaller than many had anticipated. An initial postcrisis feeding frenzy of announced mergers and acquisitions involving financial institutions turned to disenchantment among foreign players as relatively few deals got off the ground.[32]

In Indonesia, one of the few foreign banks to express an early interest in acquiring a midsize Indonesian bank was Standard Chartered. This acquisition was derailed at a relatively late stage as a result of a corruption scandal involving the then-ruling party, the central bank, and the bank restructuring agency.[33] The affair led to the suspension of IMF and World Bank loans to Indonesia and worsened the country's image: economic growth remained low, political instability appeared to be worsening, and reforms aimed at improving legal and regulatory institutions

TABLE 6.5
Net Capital Flows to Emerging Asia, US$ Billions

	1995	1996	1997	1998	1999	2000	2001	2002	2003
Private capital	96.9	122.1	7.1	−45.9	6.8	−12.9	16.7	31.6	7.9
Direct	52.6	53.4	56.8	59.7	61.2	54.2	47.1	58.7	59.0
Portfolio	22.7	32.8	7.3	−17.9	14.4	4.3	−13.5	0.7	−9.7
Other (loans)	21.6	35.9	−56.9	−87.7	−68.8	−71.4	−16.8	−27.8	−41.3
Official capital	4.5	−12.4	16.9	26.1	4.4	5.1	−5.7	−1.4	3.3
Reserves	−43.3	−46.9	−15.4	−67.4	−78.9	−48.7	−84.7	−97.4	−67.8

SOURCE: International Monetary Fund, *World Economic Outlook September 2002*, Table 1.3.
NOTE: Data for 2002 and 2003 are estimates. Reserves: change in reserves. A minus sign denotes a rise in reserves.

were having, at best, no effect at all. Despite lifting restrictions on foreign ownership, there was no rush of foreign investment in the country's distressed banks, although the Indonesian government did eventually sell down its nationalized stake in what had been the largest private bank in Indonesia, with an American investment fund taking up a major share in 2002 in conjunction with a local partner.[34] As noted earlier, there has been a significant increase in foreign banks' share of the Indonesian banking market, but this has occurred in the context of an extraordinary contraction in the Indonesian market: total loans outstanding held by all banks in Indonesia decreased in nominal rupiah terms by 45 percent between the end of 1998 and the end of 2000. Foreign banks are now playing a larger role in Indonesia, but Indonesia is less important to foreign banks.

In the Thai case, although the country has maintained direct investment inflows, the financial sector has not been attractive to foreign banks, despite liberalization and the desperate need of Thai banks for new equity. In one instance, protracted negotiations over the sale of Bangkok Metropolitan Bank to HSBC were eventually abandoned early in 2001 when, according to a source close to the negotiations, it appeared that the Thai agency responsible for bailing out banks and finance companies "would virtually have to pay HSBC to take the bank off its hands. That was politically unacceptable."[35] At the time, 58 percent of the bank's loan portfolio was classified as nonperforming. The previous year, extended negotiations to sell another Thai bank, Siam City Bank, to Newbridge Capital collapsed, apparently over the issues of price and arrangements for dealing with nonperforming loans (NPLs).[36] While four commercial banks did pass into foreign hands, these were relatively small players. After asset write-downs, the foreign share of domestic banking assets was only 7 percent, which according to some estimates is actually

a decrease from their immediate precrisis share.[37] This level of foreign
control of domestic banking assets remains far lower than in most other
non-Asian emerging markets.[38]

In Malaysia, the share of commercial banking assets accounted for by
foreign-owned banks in mid-2001 was the same as it had been for several
years before the crisis: about one quarter of total bank assets.[39] Malaysia
retains a foreign ownership ceiling for domestic banks, and its radical financial sector restructuring involves mergers of its domestic institutions.
No foreign takeovers have occurred. In the Philippines, the capital and
equity markets have seen a decline in foreign participation, and twelve
foreign brokerages (including Merrill Lynch, which had been the largest
operator in Manila) had closed or planned to close their operations in the
country by the end of 2001.[40] Finally, some of the new wave of FDI into
the Japanese financial services sector has already begun to retreat. For example, at the end of 2001 Merrill Lynch was in the process of disman-
tling the major retail brokering business it had acquired from Yamaichi
Securities in 1998. Like several other foreign brokerages in Japan that
were also scaling back operations, lack of profitability was the reason for
the withdrawal.[41]

Staying Regional

There remains a significant regional concentration to some types of
capital flow and in some financial markets. In contrast to trends in Korea
and Japan, inroads by foreigners in the Southeast Asian banking markets
have largely involved established regional players, despite the retreat of
Japanese institutions.[42] Taiwanese investors have in some cases moved in
where the Japanese left, as with the purchase of the Hong Kong branch
of Yamaichi Securities in 1998 by Taiwanese investors. Prior to the crisis,
Taiwanese banks had only twelve branches or subsidiaries in the whole
of Southeast Asia, and acquisitions in the financial sector are very much
a new development.[43] However, despite cabinet-level support for a private pooled investment fund for Southeast Asia, Taiwanese investments
in the region's financial industry remain very modest.

Singaporean banks and investors are a more significant source of an ongoing regional aspect to cross-boarder investments in the financial sector.
Singapore's largest local bank, DBS, has continued its precrisis expansion
in Asia, acquiring majority shares in a small bank in Thailand (Thai Danu)
in 1998 and in Hong Kong (Kwong On) in 1999. It has also bought a 20
percent share in a large local bank in the Philippines (Bank of the Philippine Islands).[44] It lost out to Standard Chartered in its bid for Chase Man-
hattan's Hong Kong credit card business but succeeded in its $10 billion

bid for a majority share in Hong Kong's fourth largest local bank, Dao Heng, in 2001.[45] According to its chief executive, the purchase was part of DBS's drive to be a regional bank "run by Asians or Asia-philes."[46]

Another bank from Singapore, United Overseas Bank (UOB), also bought a small Thai bank in 1999 (Radanasin, the smallest of the thirteen Thai banks by asset size in 2001, after NPL write-downs) and a share in a small Philippine bank. In addition, Singapore government investment holding companies have acquired stakes in two large Thai banks, Bangkok Bank and Thai Farmers Bank, as well as other Thai firms over the last three years. Thailand's largest brokerage, already substantially owned by foreign investors (from Taiwan), also came under majority Singaporean ownership as a result of a cross-shareholding agreement between a Singaporean and a Taiwanese firm.[47]

Banks with long histories in the region have also been prominent among foreign investors in Southeast Asian financial markets. For example, the two other Thai banks to come under majority foreign control after the crisis were bought by ABN-Amro (Bank of Asia) and Standard Chartered (Nakornthon). Both of these European banks have had extensive operations in Asia (including Thailand, in the case of Standard Chartered), since the nineteenth century. A similar consolidation or increase in the role of foreign players already established in Southeast Asian banking markets has occurred in Indonesia, Malaysia, and Singapore, where Citibank, HSBC, and Standard Chartered remain among the largest foreign banks.

The pattern of investment flows more generally has a regional aspect for some countries, including China. Inward FDI in China retains a strong regional element and, although this is declining, Asia remains the largest source of FDI. As shown in Table 6.6, Asian sources accounted for more than 80 percent of actually utilized inward FDI between 1979 and 1998, and still accounted for 61 percent over 2000–01. Outward investment by non-Japan Asia has declined in some cases since the crisis, as shown in Table 6.7, but appears to have maintained much of its regional orientation.[48] One indicator that direct investment from non-Japan Asia is directed to the region is the concentration of M&A purchases by so-called developing Asian countries in other developing countries.[49] Given precrisis investment patterns and media reports of individual investment deals since the crisis, most of this investment in developing countries is likely to be in Asia.

Market imperfections in Southeast Asia may be less of an issue for investors from the region. According to a long-term Singaporean investor in Indonesia, conditions had not deteriorated to anything like the extent implied in media reports.[50] Bearing out the idea that proximity and familiarity can encourage investment, Singaporean and Malaysian investors

TABLE 6.6
*Sources of Actually Utilized
FDI Flows to China (%)*

	1997–98	1999	2000	2001
Hong Kong	59	41	38	36
Taiwan	8	6	6	7
Japan	8	7	7	10
Singapore	3	7	5	5
Korea	2	3	4	4
U.S.	8	10	11	10

SOURCE: *Almanac of China's Foreign Economic Relations and Trade*, (later, *Yearbook of China's Foreign Relations and Trade*), 2000, 2001, and 2002. Data for 1979–98 as calculated by Wang, "Informal Institutions and Foreign Investment in China," 525–56, 545.

have accounted for most of the large sales of Indonesian assets since the crisis.[51] In 1999, 59 percent of Singapore's direct equity investment abroad was held in Asia.[52] This is the last year for which aggregate figures on stocks of outward direct investment by Singaporeans are available, but outward FDI from Singapore has almost certainly increased its regional concentration since then, with the two largest foreign investment deals ever undertaken by Singaporean firms being acquisitions by DBS of Dao Heng Bank in Hong Kong and by Singapore Telecom of a telecommunications provider in Australia, both in 2001. Later that year, Singapore Telecom also took a significant stake in an Indonesian telecommunications provider.

For Thailand and Malaysia there is some regional concentration in capital flows. In Thailand, the percentage of capital flows accounted for by Asian sources or destinations has been rising, with Asia accounting for 50 percent of inward FDI and 56 percent of outward investment over 1998–2000.[53] For Malaysia, as shown in Table 6.8, Asia is the most important source and destination for both equity and portfolio flows. The regional concentration of portfolio flows could reflect the roles of Hong Kong and Singapore as intermediating points, rather than an actual predominance of Asian investors or investment sites. However, data on the Singapore fund management industry suggests that this is not completely the case. Of the $166 billion in discretionary assets managed from Singapore at the end of 2000, 36 percent came from Asia (16 percent from North America and 27 percent from Europe), while 81 percent was invested in Asia.[54] Furthermore, portfolio flows to Asia from outside the region are on the whole lower than they were before the crisis.[55]

There may even be a regional element to bank lending to Asia. While European banks are clearly the region's largest creditors, the Bank for In-

TABLE 6.7
FDI Outflows from East Asia

	1996	1997	1998	1999	2000	2001
Japan	23.428	25.993	24.153	22.743	31.558	38.088
China	2.114	2.563	2.634	1.775	0.916	1.775
Taiwan	3.843	5.243	3.836	4.420	6.701	5.480
Hong Kong	26.531	24.407	16.978	19.336	59.374	8.977
Korea	4.670	4.449	4.740	4.198	4.999	2.600
Indonesia	0.600	0.178	0.044	0.072	0.150	0.125
Malaysia	3.768	2.675	0.863	1.422	2.026	0.267
Philippines	0.182	0.136	0.160	0.030	0.107	0.161
Singapore	6.827	9.465	0.795	4.277	4.966	10.216
Thailand	0.816	0.447	0.123	0.344	0.052	0.171

SOURCE: United Nations Conference on Trade and Development, *World Investment Report 2002*, Annex Table B.2.

NOTE: FDI flows in billions of U.S. dollars, measured on a balance of payments basis.

ternational Settlements figures used in Table 6.3 leave a large portion of lending to countries such as China unattributed. Loans from the financial centers of Hong Kong and Singapore may not be fully captured in these figures. As of mid-2002, loans from the Singapore offshore market to Asia (China, Hong Kong, Japan, South Korea, Taiwan, and Southeast Asia excluding Singapore) totaled U.S.$149 billion.[56] Locally incorporated Singapore banks are also active lenders to regional countries, accounting for a significant share of total international lending to Thailand and Malaysia in particular.[57]

Finally, a distinctively Asia-regional orientation characterizes two components of Japanese capital flows: its manufacturing investment and its Official Development Assistance (ODA). Japan is by far the world's largest aid donor and it continues to direct the greater part of its ODA to Asia.[58] Japan's crisis-related aid to the region halted what had been a clear trend toward Asia receiving a reduced proportion of Japanese ODA and other assistance.[59] Between 1995 and 1997, Asia received 50 percent (on average) of Japanese ODA. In 1998 this increased to 62 percent.[60] Japan's official aid plans clearly give priority to Asia. In one estimate a total of $48 billion had been committed to Asia as of January 1999 under the New Miyazawa initiative and other schemes to provide financial support to crisis-affected countries.[61]

Some of this assistance has been channeled to Japanese firms in the region, enabling them to reduce debt, buy out distressed joint venture partners, and maintain operations. ODA has thus supported a second strand of Japanese economic regionalization, the maintenance of regional pro-

TABLE 6.8
Malaysia: Distribution of Capital Flows

	Asia 1998–2000	U.S. 1998–2000	Europe 1998–2000
Inflows from:			
Portfolio	103.2	13.31	25.36
Loans	19.15	23.42	8.22
Equity	6.95	4.12	6.53
Outflows to:			
Portfolio	112.9	13.46	27.1
Loans	4.67	3.63	1.19
Equity	5.00	2.93	3.04

SOURCE: Bank Negara Malaysia, *Monthly Statistical Bulletin* (March 2001).

NOTE: Capital flows on a balance-of-payments basis, in billions of Malaysian ringgit, Asia portfolio: Hong Kong, Taiwan, Singapore, Japan; loans: Hong Kong, Singapore, Japan; equity: Brunei, Cambodia, Indonesia, Laos, Myanmar, Philippines, Singapore, Thailand, Vietnam, China, Hong Kong, Japan, Korea, Taiwan. Europe portfolio: U.K., Switzerland, Germany; loans: U.K., Germany, Switzerland; equity: UK, France, Germany, Netherlands, Denmark, Sweden. All significant sources and destinations of capital flows are included, except for loans from the offshore centre of Labuan, which is Malaysia's most important source of new lending.

duction systems characterized by dense supply and distribution networks.[62] According to postcrisis surveys of Japanese manufacturers, strengthening and expanding overseas production is now their most commonly cited priority, and Asia and the United States are seen as the most favorable destinations for this outward expansion.[63] China is consistently rated the most promising overseas investment site, the United States is rated second, followed by Thailand and Indonesia. For the last two years, the ten most promising countries for manufacturing FDI, aside from the United States, have all been in Asia. Japanese manufacturing FDI, which accounted for 25 percent of total outward FDI in 2000, is thus much more regionalized than aggregate FDI outflows or other forms of capital outflow.[64] Given relatively high levels of interfirm trade in manufactures, this helps explain why Asian exports to Japan have continued to increase, accounting for 42 percent of Japanese imports in 2000 compared to 37 percent in 1995.[65]

Implications: U.S.-Japan Relations in Asia

Broadly speaking, there have been a number of new developments and some continuity in capital flows and financial markets in Asia since the crisis. Japan, Taiwan, and Korea have become more open to FDI, which has come mostly from non-Asian sources. Foreign players are now more significant in local financial markets in most countries. This new openness, however, coexists with lower overall capital flows to Southeast Asia. Further, on certain measures, economic regionalization remains significant: Japan has drastically cut its financial links with Asia, but its involvement in regional manufacturing production systems looks set to be sustained. Along with trends in Japanese official aid flows and outward investment from other Asian countries, this creates a regional dimension to current trends toward greater openness. This section looks at how these changes could affect U.S.-Japan relations in three related areas: market access, the rules governing international finance, and intra-Asian regional cooperation.

Access to local financial markets by foreign investors and intermediaries has long been a source of friction between the United States and Asian countries. Overt barriers to entry are now much lower due to liberalization; and alleged implicit barriers to entry, such as incompatible corporate governance codes, interfirm networks, and firm-level management and financing practices, now appear less significant. Whether the allegations were justified or not, these host country factors had the potential to provoke conflict and charges of unfair competition or exclusion. Given the inroads made by Western firms and investors into previously relatively closed markets since the crisis, conflict over access issues may recede.

Policy change and corporate restructuring in many countries are definitely moving the regulatory framework and business sector in the direction of U.S. standards.[66] Governance (corporate and other) is a postcrisis buzzword in the region. The recent upsurge in M&As was made possible by changes to the regulatory environment and by corporate need for outside investors. This kind of change is significant in that M&As have been a significant form of FDI in the Northeast Asian countries traditionally closed to foreign investment, and a significant vehicle for increased U.S. investment in Asia. Because such investment carries with it active control over the acquired asset and (in contrast to greenfield FDI, or investment in mainly new assets, the main form of FDI in Southeast Asia before the crisis) less of a role for local actors, it may also have a significant impact on corporate practices and on the regulatory environment in the host country.[67]

Conversely, many reform programs have met serious implementation obstacles as a result of political opposition or inadequate administrative capacity. While the incentives arising from the recent burst of foreign activity in Asian markets may override these obstacles, there are several reasons to believe that the increased role of nonregional investors will have only limited effects. First, the ratio of M&A sales to total FDI inflows is still at very low levels in many Asian countries, and on the whole the region remains much more closed to this form of foreign investment than the United States. Second, FDI remains the category of capital flows most dominated by regional sources. Third, it is not clear how much foreign investors export their corporate strategies and governance structures to host countries, even where such investment is sustained at high levels.[68] Fourth, although the evidence is limited, the particular firms acquired by foreign investors since the crisis seem to be those that already have corporate profiles at odds with the archetypal highly leveraged, nontransparent, and family- or network-oriented Asian firm. An analysis of recent M&A sales in Korea suggests that foreign purchases targeted Korean companies that had low debt levels and were already larger, more profitable, and more export-oriented than other Korean firms. Rather than revolutionizing Korean practices and bringing them into line with more efficient foreign standards, this study concluded that foreign investment in Korea was induced by favorable firm-level characteristics and economic growth, rather than the other way around.[69]

It is still too soon to say whether these new types and sources of investment will do much to bring about a trans-Pacific convergence in corporate practices and governance. Even if such convergence occurs, however, conflict over issues associated with increased foreign activity in local markets is not likely to go away. While U.S. firms and investors are not likely to complain about being excluded from Asian markets at present (both because the barriers they face are lower and because these markets are currently not very attractive), their presence could generate resistance if domestic losers from corporate restructuring press their interests politically. There is a great deal of political contention over issues associated with foreign penetration and globalization more generally in Asia.[70] This chapter has ignored the interests of domestic actors who are on the receiving rather than the driving end of recent trends, but in many cases these actors are important politically.

Cooperation over the international rules governing finance is a second area in which U.S. and Japanese interests may be converging as a result of recent changes. If the foreign investment and lending strategies of American and Japanese firms are basically the same, commercial competition may be intense, but they have no material basis for conflict over the rules under which investment occurs or over how financial crises are managed. Further, globally diversified and interlinked financial markets arguably require global governance structures. Attempts to reform the framework governing international finance gained a new level of attention as a result of the financial crises of 1997–98.[71] While many of the issues under consideration in the so-called international financial architecture remain contentious, the crisis itself may have prompted a change in thinking among both Japanese and American players, bringing their ideas about financial regulation closer together.[72]

Again, however, there are some reasons to doubt that ideas and interests on global financial regulation have in fact converged. Japanese policymakers and Japanese financial institutions clearly have an interest in global rules governing finance. It does not follow, however, that they have an interest in the same global rules that American policymakers and financial firms support.[73] The Washington consensus may be severely dented but the IMF has shown signs of returning to its precrisis stance of wanting to make capital account liberalization one of its official goals.[74] Also, influential Japanese actors have voiced preferences that are distinctly different from those prevailing among American policymakers and American financial sector firms.[75] Former Ministry of Finance official Eisuke Sakakibara may represent only one set of views among many in Japan, but his proposals for international financial reform place more emphasis on the inherent instability of international capital flows than is reflected in the American position on the issue.[76] Although Sakakibara is no longer in a policymaking position, he was nominated as a contender to be the new IMF managing director in February 2000.

A third area in which recent investment trends may have implications for U.S.-Japan relations is the issue of regional cooperation on an intra-Asian basis. Demand for regional solutions to problems of monetary and financial management has risen in Asia since the crisis. A range of initiatives for greater cooperation are currently on the regional agenda, covering joint monitoring of capital flows, coordination of financial standards, crisis management facilities, and studies of currency collaboration.[77] At first glance, these proposals are somewhat paradoxical, given the decisive weakening of Japan's financial links with Asia. Viewed from one perspective, reduced economic ties with the region should reduce incentives to support regional cooperation initiatives.

In fact, Japanese interest in regional cooperation is not related in a straightforward way to the distribution of outward investment from Japan. The Japanese government and agencies such as the export-import bank have delivered a large amount of crisis-related funding to the region since 1998. These resources were made available without the conditionalities associated with IMF lending and thus made it easier for some countries to avoid the policy prescriptions associated with IMF loans. Malaysia, for example, received pledges of $6 billion in loans from the government of Japan and two Japanese banks when it was searching for ways to fund its heterodox crisis-management program.[78] The nature of much of the Japanese support—in the form of human resources training, trade credits, and assistance to Japanese firms in the region—also made it likely to strengthen corporate and human networks between Japan and Southeast Asia.[79]

These initiatives may mean that Japanese investment in the region retains a degree of distinctiveness, even if it suffers an absolute and relative decline. They also suggest that Japan has diplomatic and political reasons to remain engaged in the region, even if its official initiatives are becoming increasingly peripheral to the core interests of Japanese investors. Outward investment may be distributed globally, but Japan is part of Asia and has a particular interest in the political and financial stability of its neighbors. Japan has also positioned itself diplomatically as a country with particular responsibilities with regard to Asia and thus will pay a price if it ignores demands for cooperation coming from the rest of the region. Although the United States opposed proposals for intra-Asian cooperation during the crisis, such cooperation need not be a source of friction between the United States and Japan in the future if the American position continues to be accepting of regional initiatives.

The prospect that intra-Asian regional cooperation could occur without a central Japanese role cannot be dismissed. The concentration of financial ties in non-Japan Asia described here is consonant with the recent decision by Southeast Asian countries and China to pursue a free trade agreement among themselves. If this caused some anxiety in Japan, it may also be a reason why Japan will not give up on a regional agenda. The complexity of Japanese interests with regard to regional cooperation and international financial governance may help explain why Japanese foreign policy in the region often appears indecisive and falls short of expectations on both sides of the Pacific.

Conclusion

While the U.S.-Japan relationship is complex and cannot be reduced to any one dimension, economic and political actors in both countries are sensitive to the incentives and constraints created by financial markets. Trends in capital flows and financial markets since 1997 suggest that these incentives and constraints have changed in some important ways. The most important change since the crisis is the opening of many Asian economies and financial markets to higher levels of foreign participation. American investors and financial firms are now playing more of a role in much of the region and have more of a stake in developments there. In contrast, Asia is now less important for Japanese banks. With more equivalent stakes, the two countries may find more common ground in their policies toward the region. Further, postcrisis restructuring and re-form have lowered many of the barriers to entry that allegedly restricted American firms in the past and occasionally caused friction in diplomatic relationships between the United States and Asian countries. Conversely, when disaggregated, the type of investment relations linking Japan to Asia are different from those of the United States. American firms have made inroads in the financial and services sector and in bank lending; Japanese firms are much more engaged in the manufacturing sector. This means that their interests are likely to diverge in some respects, particularly in the event of a future financial crisis.

The likelihood of such crises has not diminished much since 1997. Although international bank lending is lower, loans and portfolio flows remain significant and demonstrably volatile. Asian financial systems thus remain vulnerable to shifts in investor sentiment, a vulnerability that is only partly reflected in ongoing efforts to develop more effective crisis management and financial governance systems. Developing regional institutions could complement global regimes for crisis management and prevention, but given the high level of exposure to the region on the part of European and American lenders, crisis management cannot be fully devolved to the regional level without creating severe moral hazard effects. Furthermore, because Asia is no longer dominated by Japanese sources of investment and bank lending, more diversified webs of interdependence will shape both intraregional cooperation and American engagement in Asia.

When Strong Ties Fail

U.S.-JAPANESE MANUFACTURING RIVALRY IN ASIA

WALTER HATCH

Introduction

Competition between Japanese and U.S. manufacturers used to be a simple game. In highly stylistic terms, it worked something like this: members of each team battled among themselves for position on the home court and, via exports and foreign direct investment (FDI), on the opposing team's court; the winning team was the one that, in the aggregate, controlled the largest share of sales in the two markets.[1]

Today, however, the game has become much more complex—thanks in large part to the emergence of Asia as a global center for the production and export of manufactured products.[2] (In 2000, even as it struggled to overcome the lingering effects of the Asian financial crisis of 1997–98, the region—not including Japan—accounted for 17 percent of global exports.[3]) Over the past fifteen years, Japanese and U.S. manufacturers have shifted a significant share of their production capacity to places such as Taipei and Tianjin, Bangkok and Batam, and have tried to build competing networks across the region. In short, the contest between Japanese and U.S. producers has spilled over into Asia.

Who is winning and why? In this chapter, I try to answer those questions by examining two very different industries in Asia: automobiles and computer peripherals. In both of these industries, Japanese multinational corporations (MNCs) tried to replicate the close, mutually reinforcing, and exclusionary ties they had constructed at home, but they achieved much more success in the automobile sector. The uneven outcomes can be attributed to two factors: host country policies, particularly trade and industrial policies; and technological conditions. While strong network ties have given Japanese MNCs an edge in the auto sector, which has been heavily protected and subsidized by host governments in Asia and tends to evolve through incremental innovation, they actually have hindered the performance of Japanese MNCs in the computer industry, which has been relatively unprotected by governments in Asia and, as a "new" industry, is still developing in sudden bursts of innovation.[4] Put simply, strong ties work in a closed regime facing a relatively stable technological environment but fail in an open regime facing a relatively unstable technological environment.

For U.S.-Japan bilateral relations, this analysis suggests a significant departure from the past. In the 1980s and early 1990s, government officials from the two countries routinely squared off, face to face, over contentious trade issues in these critical sectors. The United States demanded, for example, that Japan impose voluntary restraints on its automobile exports to the United States, and pushed Japan to reserve a share of its semiconductor market for "Made in the U.S.A" chips. Today, the two states enthusiastically support (and in Japan's case, even coordinate and guide) their own multinationals as they compete for market share in neutral Asia, but they do so largely from the sidelines—as cheerleaders (the U.S.) and coaches (Japan), not as combatants. A battle still rages, only now it assumes the shape of a private contest.

The chapter is organized as follows: The next two sections present a cursory analysis of the costs and benefits of different kinds of business networks, and then briefly discuss the multinationalization of such networks. This discussion is followed by a case study of the automobile industry in Southeast Asia, which has been dominated by Japanese MNCs, and a case study of the computer industry in Asia, where Japanese MNCs are now struggling to catch up with U.S. rivals. The final section concludes the chapter with a discussion of the analytic insights that flow from these two case studies.

Business Networks

Economic sociologists have demonstrated that most transactions do not occur in the atomistic, impersonal market of neoclassical economic theory or inside the expanding hierarchies described by neo-institutionalists such as Williamson;[5] rather, they occur in the large, gray domain of social relationships that exists between these two extremes.[6] That is, exchange usually takes place in some kind of relational network.

A network conditions and is conditioned by individual and corporate behavior. It does not merely respond to price signals from outside or to commands from above; rather, it generally reflects the specific configuration of ties that bind its members. In more technical terms, a network is a relatively durable governance structure linking three or more actors, each of whom occupies a node or point of contact. Relationships among these actors are reciprocal or interdependent, but not necessarily equal. That is, each actor is able to access the others inside the network, although often not instantly and often not without passing through other nodes.

Much of the empirical study of business networks has targeted East Asia[7] and, above all, Japan. For example, Gerlach[8] as well as Imai and Kaneko[9] have written about the Japanese economic system as a web of mutually reinforcing networks held together by cooperative ties between nominally independent firms. They focus their attention on *keiretsu*, business groups whose members are linked through cross-shareholding, interlocking directorates, personnel transfers, and interfirm transactions. The Japanese government, which has helped launch and sustain a variety of interfirm networks,[10] openly endorses this view. Japanese capitalism, according to one government study, is different in that it "emphasizes the merits of cooperation based on long-term relationships between economic actors and within economic institutions. In this way, each economic actor has been able to avoid the risks associated with fierce competition, maximizing its self-interest by forging alliances within the market."[11]

But business networks are not confined to Japan, or even to East Asia. They appear throughout the world, and scholars have studied manifestations of relational or informal contracting in, for example, Silicon Valley's software industry, Sweden's special steel industry, and northern Italy's bicycle, food processing machinery, and woodworking tool industries.[12] What distinguishes Japan (and perhaps South Korea and Taiwan as well) is not the presence of business networks, but the durability and intensity of interfirm ties. In a nutshell, these ties tend to be much stronger in Japan than in the United States and, to a lesser extent, Europe. Aldrich and Sakano conducted a cross-national survey of small business networks in Japan, the United States, Italy, Northern Ireland, and Sweden, and concluded that Japanese networks make up "a more closely tied, relatively circumscribed system than networks in other nations. Once a relationship is established, consultation and information-seeking go around within the circumscribed network."[13]

Business networks present a trade-off between transaction costs and information costs. By forging stable relationships, firms are able to curb the costs of securing, monitoring, and enforcing contracts; at the same time, however, they face higher costs to obtain information about economic opportunities outside the network. The stronger the relational ties are, the lower will be the transaction costs and the higher the information costs.[14]

Mindful of this trade-off, Håkansson notes that strong ties facilitate trust and interdependence, binding members of the network to one another, but they may also yield a lock-in effect, inhibiting members from assimilating new information and discouraging them from exploring and utilizing alternative resources. In such cases, the network will serve as an "obstacle to change."[15]

Likewise, in his study of the apparel industry in New York City, Uzzi finds that firms characterized by "embeddedness" (strong, mutually reinforcing ties with one another) outperformed other, more independent firms—but only up to a threshold point, when the positive effect suddenly turned sharply negative. He concluded:

A crucial implication is that embedded networks offer a competitive form of organizing but possess their own pitfalls because an actor's adaptive capacity is determined by a web of ties, some of which lie beyond his or her direct influence. Thus a firm's structural location, although not fully constraining, can significantly blind it to the important effects of the larger network structure, namely its contacts' contacts."[16]

In his study, Uzzi does not identify this threshold point where the costs of strong ties begin to overwhelm the benefits. In general, though, we can assume that the information impactedness[17] associated with strong ties will become too costly when a firm finds itself in a market characterized by a high level of uncertainty—a result of either fierce price competition or rapidly changing technology.

Cross-Border Networks

In their foreign as well as their domestic operations, firms routinely use networks to reduce transaction costs. Manufacturers, in particular, often allocate different production processes to different locations, "slicing up the value chain" according to the comparative advantage (and more specifically, the technological endowment) of each location.[18] For example, a multinational corporation may allocate its most labor-intensive activity to a host economy with a relatively large supply of cheap labor, and may establish other affiliates—or contract with suppliers—to produce key components in different economies with relatively large supplies of skilled engineers and technicians. Parts are then shipped across borders.

This pattern of networking is particularly common in Asia, where indigenous technical skills vary dramatically from one economy to the next.

TABLE 7.1

Thai Automobile Sales (January–June 1997)

Maker	Passenger Vehicles	Commercial Vehicles	One-Ton Pickups	Total Vehicles	Percentage of Market
Toyota	35,235	5,299	37,022	77,556	31.2
Isuzu	595	6,861	46,628	54,084	21.8
Nissan	6,760	2,469	22,011	31,240	12.6
Mitsubishi	6,842	2,272	16,132	25,246	10.2
Honda	21,002	n/a	719	23,084	9.3
Mazda	1,142	1,502	6,968	9,612	3.9
All Others	16,191	11,079	1,456	27,363	11.0
Total	87,767	29,482	130,936	248,185	100.00

SOURCE: Automotive Resources Asia (Bangkok).

Both Japanese and U.S. MNCs have established intrafirm production networks in the region, especially in the electronics industry. But empirical studies repeatedly show that Japanese affiliates in Asia are tightly tethered to the parent company in Japan. That is, they belong to vertically organized intrafirm networks that are held together by extraordinarily strong relational ties, and thus are, according to Itami, "integrated extensions of domestic production systems."[19] Indeed, Sedgwick suggests that Japanese manufacturers in Thailand "are part of a tightly controlled and rigorously hierarchical organizational structure extending down from Japan."[20]

Compared with their U.S. counterparts, Japanese manufacturing affiliates operating overseas also tend to forge stronger interfirm ties—usually with other Japanese MNCs (including, on occasion, erstwhile competitors) and often with the Japanese state acting in a supporting role as a kind of broker. In some cases, Japanese manufacturers have tried to draw on horizontal keiretsu ties, hooking up with the local or regional affiliate of their Japanese main bank to borrow funds or using the overseas affiliate of the general trading company in their group for logistical support. In many other cases, they have tried to recreate vertical keiretsu ties, encouraging their Japanese subcontractors to follow them in locating abroad and to continue supplying components from these new overseas manufacturing facilities. These parts supply networks have become widespread in Asia, which is by far the favorite destination for Japanese subcontracting firms investing overseas.[21]

Observed behavior thus indicates that Japanese regional production networks differ from their American counterparts in much the same way that domestic network structures in Japan differ from those in the United States. Simply stated, the former are held together by stronger ties. Given

TABLE 7.2
Indonesian Automobile Sales (January–July 1997)

Maker	Passenger Vehicles	Commercial Vehicles	Total Vehicles	Percentage of Market
Toyota	4,711	52,760	57,471	23.5
Mitsubishi	1,029	44,271	45,300	18.5
Suzuki	5,904	37,601	43,505	17.8
Isuzu	None	31,889	31,889	13.0
Daihatsu	5	24,420	24,425	10.0
Timor	11,785	None	11,785	4.8
All Others	16,191	11,079	27,363	12.4
Total	42,015	202,637	244,652	100.00

SOURCE: Gaikindo (Indonesian Automobile Manufacturers Association).

what Doremus, Keller, Pauly, and Reich refer to as "the enduring influence" of national institutions and norms on the behavior of multinational corporations, this conclusion should not surprise us.[22] Even as they expand into Asia, Japanese and American MNCs remain fundamentally Japanese and American.

The Automobile Industry in Asia

For the past three decades, Japanese MNCs have dominated the automobile industry in Asia, particularly Southeast Asia.[23] In the combined markets of the four core members of the Association of Southeast Asian Nations, or the ASEAN 4 (Thailand, Indonesia, Malaysia, and the Philippines), Japanese manufacturing affiliates accounted for as much as 95 percent of local production in 1970 and for 91 percent in 1997,[24] and their parent companies in Japan accounted for the lion's share of imports. As Table 7.1 shows, in the first half of 1997, just before the Asian economic crisis erupted, five Japanese firms controlled 85 percent of the Thai market for vehicles. Table 7.2 provides comparable data for Indonesia, where the former Suharto regime contracted with a Korean automaker for production of a national car, the Timor.[25] Although the Timor enjoyed a number of advantages, five Japanese firms still controlled about 83 percent of the Indonesian automobile market in the first half of 1997.[26]

Japanese automakers initially acquired such a dominant position in this region because their primary rivals at the time, the former Big Three of the United States (General Motors, Ford, and Chrysler), abandoned it in the 1970s as they scrambled to defend market share at home, where cheaper

Japanese imports were becoming increasingly popular. Southeast Asia seemed relatively inconsequential at the time, but eventually came to boast the world's fastest growing automobile market. Domestic production in the ASEAN 4 nearly quadrupled between 1985 and 1996, increasing from 365,000 units to 1.42 million units.[27] Thailand in particular emerged as an important center of automobile assembly and parts production.

Unsurprisingly, the region's phenomenal growth attracted the attention of non-Japanese manufacturers. At the lower end of the market, Korean automakers, led by Daewoo, moved aggressively into transitional economies such as Vietnam, where Japanese firms did not already have a chokehold, and tried to gain sufficient production experience and scale for a broader offensive in the region. The Asian financial crisis, however, stymied these plans. In 1999, Daewoo went bankrupt after failing to service the huge debt it had incurred in its massive expansion program.

A more serious and sustained threat came from U.S. automakers, which struggled in the late 1980s and throughout the 1990s to return to the region. But as we shall see, they began to acquire a foothold only at the very end of the decade, when they purchased significant shares in a few financially strapped Japanese firms.[28] How did Japanese automakers continue to dominate markets in the region for so long? The answer is that they built production networks based on strong, even exclusionary ties that held up over time, thanks in large part to host-country policies.

Intrafirm Networks

To be competitive, automobile manufacturers must achieve economies of scale, which means that the marginal cost of production declines as total output increases. Until the late 1980s, the nationally organized automobile industries of Southeast Asia fell woefully short of fulfilling this requirement. Due to import substitution policies adopted by governments in Thailand, Indonesia, Malaysia, and the Philippines, each industry was highly protected and thus cut off from others in the region, leaving manufacturers to sell virtually all of their output in relatively small, well-protected domestic markets. Most factories produced fewer than 10,000 vehicles a year—well below the 200,000 units that industry analysts consider necessary to achieve economies of scale and thereby efficient mass production.[29]

Beginning in the late 1980s, Japanese automakers tried to overcome this constraint by building intrafirm networks across the region. These networks treat all of Southeast Asia as a single market and allocate different production functions to different plants in the region based on an intrafirm division of labor. Toyota, for example, produces diesel engines and pressed parts in Thailand, gasoline engines in Indonesia, steering gears and electronics in Malaysia, and transmissions in the Philippines. Parts are swapped between the different affiliates, which then assemble them—along with other components—into finished cars and trucks. Toyota's regional network has expanded dramatically since 1993, when it handled only $25 million in parts. Three years later, in 1996, it was moving nearly $200 million in parts.[30]

Although Toyota has set up a regional trading center in Singapore to oversee the daily movement of these standardized parts, the parent company in Japan continues to coordinate the overall network. One way it does this is by rotating key personnel in and out of Toyota affiliates in Asia and requiring them to communicate daily with headquarters. "Even in cases like Indonesia and the Philippines, where we do not have a majority of the equity, we are able to aggressively send in our own management team and maintain control," boasts Yokoi Akira, Toyota's vice president for international affairs.[31]

Toyota is not unique in this regard; all parent companies in the Japanese automobile industry try to maintain strict control over their operations in Asia. Nakashima, who studied operations inside the Thai affiliate of Mitsubishi Motors, notes that the affiliate (Mitsubishi Sittipol) slavishly followed the parent company's human resource rules and procedures. "This is not because the local department and other managers lack the ability to devise a new system, but because they are not given the authority to do so."[32]

To support the creation of cross-border production networks, Southeast Asian governments have adopted a series of regional trade promotion schemes, each one more ambitious than the last.[33] All of these schemes benefit well-established insiders at the expense of outsiders trying to export into the region. In 1988, for example, the four core members of ASEAN approved the Brand-to-Brand Complementation (BBC) scheme, which gave automakers a 50 percent tariff reduction on parts exchanged between their Southeast Asian plants for the production of a particular kind of vehicle.[34] Then, in 1996, association members enacted the ASEAN Industrial Cooperation (AICO) scheme to further trim tariffs on approved products traded within the region. (Most of the applications for AICO status have come from Japanese automakers or parts suppliers.) They have also endorsed the ASEAN Free Trade Agreement (AFTA), which will cut tariffs on most products imported from other countries in the region to 5 percent or less. More recently, ASEAN agreed to study the option of expanding its free trade agreement to include Japan, China, or both.[35]

Japanese MNCs have led efforts to implement not only these trade initiatives but also a number of ASEAN-wide industrial promotion efforts that treat automobile manufacturing as a regionally rather than nationally organized industry. As Legewie puts it, they "have become the decisive actors over time by partly taking over the formulation of industrial policies at the ASEAN level."[36] One must note, however, that Japanese firms have been strongly supported in these efforts by the Japanese state, which has assumed a kind of coordinating role.[37]

For example, the Ministry of Economy, Trade, and Investment (METI)—better known by its former name, the Ministry of International Trade and Industry, or MITI—has sponsored an annual meeting of automobile experts from Japan and ASEAN countries to discuss regionwide promotional policies for this industry.[38] It has also prodded the Japan Automobile Manufacturers Association (JAMA) to organize a regionwide trade association—the ASEAN Automotive Federation (AAF)—"with a view to enhancing the intra-regional cooperation of automobile industries."[39] According to industry representatives, AAF is JAMA's voice in Southeast Asia; indeed, its first president was the head of Toyota Motors Thailand.[40]

Interfirm Networks

Economies of scale are not enough to ensure competitiveness in automobile manufacturing. Business scholars suggest that efficient automakers must now go beyond large-scale mass production ("Fordism"); they must demonstrate an ability to engage in flexible specialization ("post-Fordism")—the careful production and assembly of thousands of high value-added components.[41] This requires backward linkages to upstream suppliers of parts.

But supporting industries in Southeast Asia have been woefully underdeveloped. Until the 1990s, assemblers in Indonesia, for example, could choose from only a few dozen parts suppliers located in that country while their counterparts in Japan could call on a few thousand. "We had a very narrow supply base," says Herman Latif, chairman of Gaikindo (the Association of Indonesian Automotive Industries).[42] As a result, he says, the industry in Indonesia had been made up of firms that screw together imported parts rather than firms that actually manufacture vehicles.

Japanese automakers have not only built elaborate production networks spanning national borders in Southeast Asia; but within the region's different economies, they have also forged increasingly strong ties with local parts suppliers—most of which happen to be Japanese transplants. Indeed, these assemblers have tried to replicate, wherever practical, the vertical keiretsu networks they built so carefully, over so many years, at home in Japan. In the 1990s, as they struggled to comply with domestic content requirements and to reduce their own production costs, Japanese MNCs operating in places like Jakarta and Bangkok leaned hard on their domestic suppliers to follow them into Southeast Asia. This pressure yielded dramatic results: in just seven years (1991 through 1997), Japanese auto parts producers made 223 investments in the ASEAN 4 countries of Indonesia, Thailand, Malaysia, and the Philippines; earlier they had taken twenty-nine years (1962 through 1990) to make only 182 investments in those countries.[43]

Japanese transplants quickly came to dominate supporting industries in each of these countries. One statistic from Indonesia may put this in perspective. In the late 1990s, fifty-three joint ventures with foreign capital accounted for virtually all of the production of key components for that country's automobile industry; of these supply firms, forty-six (or 85 percent of the total) were Japanese joint ventures.[44]

At the same time, supply clubs emerged throughout Southeast Asia. Organized by Japanese assemblers and filled with Japanese subcontractors, these clubs carry the same name as the vertical keiretsu in Japan after which they are patterned. Thus, in Thailand, Nissan has its Thai Takara-kai, made up almost entirely of the local affiliates of its most trusted Japanese subcontractors; Mitsubishi Motors has its Thai Kashiwa-kai; Toyota has its Thai Kyōhō-kai; and so on.

Because of the limited size of the automobile market in each host country in the region, Japanese subcontractors who invested in Southeast Asia would never have been able to achieve their own economies of scale by supplying only their main keiretsu customer. By necessity, then, they supplied multiple customers—at least at first. But by the mid-1990s, when auto markets in host countries began to expand quite rapidly, transaction patterns long established in Japan began to take shape in the region. Nishioka concludes that, "with the exception of those cases in which an established supplier has stayed home, we find very few examples of Japanese automakers [in Southeast Asia] engaging in transactions outside their established keiretsu groups."[45] This trend was particularly evident in Thailand, the region's fastest growing automobile market. Thus, Kasahara argues that Japanese automakers in Thailand are seeking to capture "relational quasi-rents" by conducting almost all of their business with Japanese subcontractors who belong to their parent firm's keiretsu network.[46]

Consider the case of Toyota Motors Thailand, which relies almost exclusively on parts produced by its keiretsu suppliers in Japan or on parts produced by the transplants of those suppliers in Thailand. Table 7.3 lists the thirty-two Japanese members of the Toyota supply club in Thailand in 1997. The list includes the Thai affiliates of most of Toyota's major sub-

TABLE 7.3
Japanese Members of Toyota Supply Club in Thailand

Name of Thai Affiliate	Parts Produced	Year Established in Thailand	Name of Japanese Parent	Does Parent Belong to Toyota Keiretsu?
Aoyoma Thai	Metal fasteners	1965	Aoyama	Y
Bangkok Foam	Interior trim	1971	Inoac Corporation	Y
Thai Bridgestone	Tires, tubes	1969	Bridgestone	Y
CI-Hayashi	Carpeting	1993	Hayashi	Y
Denso Thailand	Alternators, regulators	1974	Denso	Y
Enkei Thai	Aluminum wheels	1987	Enkei	N
Siam GS Battery	Batteries	1970	Nihon Denchi	Y
Inoue Rubber	Industrial rubber parts	1970	Inoac Corporation	Y
Kallawis Autoparts	Wheels	1973	Chuo Hatsujo	Y
NHK Spring Thailand	Seats, springs	1963	Nihon Hatsujo	Y
Nippon Paint Thailand	Paint	1968	Nippon Paint	Y
National Thai Co.	Car radios	1961	Matsushita	Y
Ogihara Thailand	Pressed parts	1990	Ogihara	N
Pioneer Electronics	Car stereos	1991	Pioneer	Y
Sunstar Chemical	Pressed parts	1989	Sunstar Engineering	N
Siam Aishin	Brake drums	1996	Aishin	Y
Siam Furukawa	Batteries	1992	Furukawa Denchi	Y
Siam Kayaba	Shock absorbers	1996	Kayaba	Y
SNC Soundproof	Soundproofing	1994	Nihon Tokushu Toryo	Y
Thai Auto Works	Body parts	1988	Toyota Autobody	Y
Thai Arrow Products	Wire harness	1963	Yazaki	Y
TCH Suminoe	Upholstery	1995	Suminoe Orimono	Y
TG Pongpara	Steering wheels	1995	Toyoda Gosei	Y
Thai Koito	Headlamps	1986	Koito	Y
Thai Kansai Paint	Paint	1970	Kansai Paint	Y
Thai Parkerizing	Metal coating	1979	Nihon Parkerizing	N
Thai Seat Belt	Seat belts	1994	Tokai Rika Denki	Y
Thai Steel Cable	Control cables	1981	Nihon Cable Systems	Y
Thai Stanley Electric	Signal lamps	1981	Stanley	Y
Thai Safety Glass	Windshield, windows	1988	Asahi	Y
Toa Shinto	Paint	1989	Shinto Toryo	Y
Yuasa Battery	Batteries	1963	Yuasa	Y

contractors in Japan—from Denso to Kallawis, from Aishin to Kayaba, from NHK Spring to Koito. In fact, the parents of all but four of these affiliates belong to Toyota's supply club in Japan.

Toyota and other Japanese automakers in Southeast Asia do purchase parts from indigenous suppliers that are not joint ventures with foreign firms. But even these suppliers are, for the most part, tied to Japan because they produce the specified part under a strict technology licensing agreement with the assembler's preferred keiretsu supplier in Japan. In the late 1990s, Siam Motors—Nissan's affiliate in Thailand—bought only one item (a muffler-tail pipe unit) from a completely independent supplier.[47]

Host states in Southeast Asia have tried hard to promote supporting industries in their own countries. In doing so, however, they have relied heavily on Japanese policy advice—a fact that has tended to benefit those local suppliers already holding, or willing to cultivate, strong equity or technical ties with Japanese suppliers. Thailand's Board of Investment (BOI), for example, has established its own BOI Unit for Industrial Linkage Development (BUILD) with offices in Tokyo and Osaka as well as Bangkok. In the automobile sector, "we try to encourage joint ventures that will improve our supply base by attracting investment and technology from Japan," according to a BUILD official.[48]

For its part, the government of Japan has acted as a kind of matchmaker, fostering ties between host country firms hoping to improve their capabilities and Japanese firms offering capital, technology, or both. This objective is reflected in the names of regional schemes pursued by METI: Local to Local Meetings, the Asia Industrial Network Project, the Asia Supporting Industry Action (ASIA) Program, the Supporting Industry Promotion Project, and the Roving Automotive Expert Dispatch Scheme.[49] Under this last program, the Japanese state is tapping its Official Development Assistance (ODA) to underwrite the cost of sending Japanese engineers and managers to Thailand, Indonesia, Malaysia, and the Philippines to advise local parts suppliers on ways to upgrade production and management practices.

The Effect on Competition

For outsiders attempting to set up competing operations in Southeast Asia, these exclusionary network structures built by Japanese MNCs represented a significant barrier to entry.[50] Consider the case of Chrysler (now Daimler-Chrysler), which wanted to set up its own production facilities in several locations throughout the region in the early 1990s. It approached leading parts suppliers, all of which happened to be Japanese

transplants belonging to various keiretsu groupings, but was repeatedly
stymied in efforts to negotiate solid contracts. Tim Suchyta, then director
of Chrysler's regional operations, tells what happened:

We had some outright rejections that made absolutely no business sense at all. In
Malaysia, for example, we had an AC [air conditioning] supplier who simply refused to have anything to do with us. It seemed pretty clear that he had been instructed to just say no.[51]

In the mid-1990s, General Motors (GM) encountered a similar problem when it tried to set up a factory in Thailand. The U.S. manufacturer
went from breathless enthusiasm (announcing at the outset that it would
assemble eighty thousand units of the Opel Zafira in 1996 and eventually
capture as much as 10 percent of the region's auto market) to bitter dis-
appointment. "A number of suppliers said they could not do business
with us," recalls a GM executive.[52] The firm was so frustrated that it decided to ask the Thai government to waive a stringent (54 percent) requirement for domestic content, thereby allowing GM to source components from around the world. To the surprise of many,[53] the Thai
government agreed. This decision reflected the government's growing
frustration with the reluctance of Japanese MNCs to transfer technology
and localize management. Indeed, in 1995, the Thai Board of Investment
had begun to complain openly about this and invited Western MNCs to
enter the Thai automobile market "through joint ventures with wholly
owned Thai firms with minimal keiretsu ties."[54]

To hold onto their strong positions in the face of persistent efforts by
U.S. and European MNCs to enter markets in Southeast Asia, Japanese
MNCs began to collaborate with one another in ways they would not or
could not in Japan. For example:

- In 1995, Toyota, Nissan, and Isuzu agreed to jointly establish
  casting plants and other facilities in Thailand to produce cylinder
  heads, cylinder blocks, connecting rods, camshafts and crankshafts
  used there in the assembly of pickup trucks. "To compete against
  American and European producers, we needed to find a way to
  reduce costs even further," explained Hiroyuki Tezuka, president of
  Siam Toyota Motors, which produces cylinder blocks for the three
  automakers.[55]
- In 1994, Mitsubishi Motors and Suzuki Motors teamed up to use
  common components for the passenger trucks they
  independently—and competitively—assemble in Indonesia.
  Mitsubishi agreed to contribute left-side doors, while Suzuki
  agreed to contribute right-side doors.[56]

- In 1993, Honda and Isuzu reached an agreement to compensate for weaknesses in their respective menus of automobile models. In Thailand, this means that Honda sells a repackaged Isuzu pickup called the Tourmaster while Isuzu offers a born-again Honda Civic called the Vertex.[57]

These horizontal ties raised entry barriers even higher for non-Japanese MNCs. But in the late 1990s, U.S. and European automakers finally found a way to crack the Japanese-dominated markets of Southeast Asia: they bought major, often controlling interests in Japanese automobile firms that had run up staggering debts and thus desperately needed capital. Renault purchased 37 percent of the outstanding shares of Nissan, which had fallen into a $21 billion debt.[58] Daimler-Chrysler bought 37 percent of the shares of Mitsubishi Motors, which had fallen into a $14 billion debt. General Motors likewise increased its stake in Suzuki (20 percent) and Isuzu (49 percent), while Ford did the same with its investment in Mazda (33 percent). After years of struggling, mostly in vain, to enter the region via "greenfield" investments (investments in mainly new assets), Western MNCs became, almost overnight, well-established insiders through these mergers and acquisitions.

The competition is far from over, however. Toyota and Honda, now Japan's number one and number two automakers, respectively, and the only remaining purely Japanese vehicle manufacturers, continue to use strong ties to compete in Asia. This was especially evident during the region's fiscal crisis, when Toyota and Honda rushed to the defense of their beleaguered keiretsu suppliers in Southeast Asia. Both companies provided financial assistance to regional subcontractors in the form of advance payments and cash for short-run expenses, such as the lease of equipment; they assigned to Asian affiliates some of the production chores that had until then been done entirely in Japan; and they dramatically boosted the import of parts from struggling parts suppliers in Asia.[59] This allowed Toyota and Honda to maintain or even strengthen their positions in the region. Meanwhile, some of the newly Westernized automakers retreated a step or two. Nissan, for example, yielded control of its affiliate in the Philippines to Yulon Motors, Nissan's joint venture partner in Taiwan.[60]

The Computer Industry in Asia

Asia has become the low-cost production center for world-class electronics firms from Japan and the United States (as well as Korea and Taiwan), and now accounts for 51 percent of global exports in this field.[61] Like the automobile sector, the region's electronics industry is growing rapidly. But unlike the automobile industry, it is not—with the glaring exception of consumer electronics—wholly dominated by Japanese MNCs.[62] Indeed, in personal computers and some computer-related subsectors such as semiconductors, information storage devices (hard disk drives, floppy disk drives, and CD-Rom drives), keyboards, and power supply units, Japanese manufacturers have, since the late 1980s, lost ground to U.S. rivals at the higher end of the market and to Korean and Taiwanese rivals at the lower end. This has occurred in spite of efforts by the Japanese government to support and, in some cases, even subsidize Japanese electronics firms expanding into Asia, and to provide guidance to host countries formulating policies for the information technology sector.[63]

Consider the hard disk drive (HDD) industry. U.S. producers dominate the global market—thanks in large part, according to McKendrick, Doner, and Haggard, to the fact that they moved early into Southeast Asia (and then China) and established dynamic networks in a region blessed with relatively productive labor and relatively high agglomeration economies.[64] In 1990, U.S. manufacturers like Seagate, Connor Peripherals, Unisys, and Western Digital were using their plants in Southeast Asia, especially in Singapore, to assemble more than half of all their HDDs; by 1995 that percentage had climbed to 67 percent. Japanese firms, by contrast, began the decade producing only a tiny fraction of their HDDs in Southeast Asia; 90 percent of their global production remained in Japan. Over the next five years, Japanese producers like Fujitsu, NEC, Hitachi, and Toshiba rushed into the region (especially Thailand and then later the Philippines), which by 1995 came to account for 55 percent of their global output.[65] But these Japanese networks in the HDD industry have been unable to close the gap with their American-owned competitors. Japanese firms still account for only 15 percent of global output in the HDD industry; American manufacturers account for 85 percent.[66]

While the HDD case is revealing, it is also somewhat exceptional in that U.S. producers never faced a serious challenge. This was quite different in the case of semiconductors (or integrated circuits). In the late 1980s, it looked like this industry would go the way of televisions, VCRs, and stereo systems—industries in which U.S. producers established dominant positions in global markets, only to be edged out by Japanese rivals enjoying access to cheap capital. But U.S. semiconductor manufacturers have staged a dramatic comeback. By 1998, they accounted for 33.9 percent of global production capacity, while Japanese firms accounted for 29.6 percent. (Asian firms, primarily Taiwanese and Korean manufacturers, accounted for another 27.3 percent, while European firms accounted for the remaining 9.2 percent).[67] In 1999, three of the five biggest semiconductor manufacturers in the world (Intel, Motorola, and Texas Instruments) were headquartered in the United States, and they alone accounted for nearly a quarter of global sales.[68] U.S. chipmakers managed to achieve this success by moving into more complex, more technology-intensive lines such as flash memory; by forging ties with offshore foundries, especially in Taiwan; and by establishing their own facilities in Asia. Leachman and Leachman estimate that by 2004, U.S. semiconductor manufacturers will have twice as much production capacity in Asia as their Japanese rivals.[69]

Why have Japanese manufacturers of computer peripherals failed to keep up with, let alone outpace, their American rivals in Asia? McKendrick, Doner, and Haggard, focusing on the HDD industry, conclude that it was merely a strategic oversight: "Although Japanese companies were aware of the U.S. production shift to Southeast Asia and the resulting competition in their domestic market, they did not follow suit."[70] As a result of slow (or late) movement, the Japanese ostensibly missed a critically important business opportunity. Conversely, Borrus argues, the answer has more to do with the continued use of now-outmoded business practices in an increasingly global industry characterized by shorter and shorter product cycles: "Japanese production networks boasted redundant investment and remained relatively closed, even as the U.S. networks became more open and entwined with indigenous producers, with each link in the U.S. network chains becoming more specialized."[71] The evidence gathered for this study supports Borrus's conclusion. It suggests rather clearly that the strong, even exclusionary ties that aided Japanese automakers in Asia have simultaneously hurt Japanese producers of computer peripherals in the region.

Intrafirm Networks

To an even greater extent than their counterparts in the automobile industry, Japanese firms in the computer industry have built tightly integrated production networks across Asia that link the parent company's technology-intensive, prototype manufacturing plant in Japan to moderately sophisticated facilities in such places as Taiwan and Singapore, as well as to low-cost facilities in such places as Thailand and the Philippines. The cohesive nature of these networks can be seen in the high level of intrafirm trade between parent companies and their affiliates in Asia, as well as between related affiliates located in different countries in the region. In a 1998 study of sales and procurements by Japanese electronics affiliates in Asia, MITI found that intrafirm channels handled 88.9 percent of electronics exports to Japan and 59.5 percent of such exports to third countries in Asia. It also found that these channels absorbed 86.6 percent of electronics imports from Japan and 45.9 percent of such imports from third countries in Asia.[72]

In most cases, the parent company in Japan carefully controls this vertically organized network of complementary and specialized production nodes across the region. As a result, local affiliates usually cannot exercise decision-making authority over critical issues such as procurement and sales, technology licensing, financing, and long-term business strategy. Ernst, for example, notes that Japanese electronics firms in Asia have, at least in the past, sought to "minimize risk and organize their production networks in a highly centralized manner."[73]

This tight control is clearly evident in personnel practices. The parent company in Japan tends to dispatch its own trusted managers to run operations in Asia, relegating local staff to supporting roles. In Singapore, Chia conducted a comparative study of Japanese and U.S. electronics manufacturers and found that the American firms had proceeded much more quickly to localize management: "Most of the senior management of [U.S.] companies surveyed were completely non-U.S., with positions filled by Singaporeans and other Asians. For the Japanese firms, however, top management was invariably Japanese."[74] Wong came to the same conclusion: "Still today, there is not a single Japanese electronics manufacturing plant in Singapore where the topmost manager is not a Japanese. . . . In contrast, many U.S. electronics firms in Singapore have promoted indigenous Singaporeans to the most senior management post in their Singaporean manufacturing operations. . . . "[75]

This contrast between American and Japanese electronics manufacturers is evident in other host countries as well. In Thailand, the leading HDD manufacturer—Seagate, a U.S. firm—relies heavily on local Thai managers, as well as on Singaporeans, to run its facility, while Fujitsu, the number two producer of HDDs, continues to use primarily Japanese staff dispatched from the home office.

Interfirm Networks

Computers have far fewer and far more standardized parts than automobiles. Thus, it should come as no surprise to learn that Japanese manufacturers of computer peripherals have not built the same kind of extensive, multitiered subcontracting networks that Japanese automakers have built. But compared to their U.S. counterparts, Japanese computer parts producers do forge very strong ties with key suppliers—even as they operate overseas. In Asia, this characteristic manifests itself in close relationships between Japanese transplants.

In Singapore, where indigenous suppliers tend to possess solid technical skills, Wong reports that such firms have faced greater difficulty securing contracts with Japanese electronics firms than with U.S. firms. While the latter have shown "greater willingness to try out local indigenous suppliers of various precision engineering parts and contract manufacturing services," Japanese firms have preferred to use their own suppliers who have set up operations in Singapore.[76] In the Philippines, Tecson notes, Japanese MNCs in the HDD industry rely almost exclusively on other Japanese MNCs, including fellow keiretsu members, for components and subassemblies.[77] And in Thailand, the author's own fieldwork revealed the same. Japanese affiliates contract routinely with local or regional suppliers, but these suppliers are in almost all cases Japanese transplants, and many of them are affiliates of keiretsu members in Japan.

Consider the case of Melco Manufacturing Thailand (MMT), which in the late 1990s was producing 600,000 floppy disk drives per month. It was importing high-tech electronic components such as semiconductors, stepper motors, and condensers from Japanese affiliates in Singapore, and obtaining magnetic parts, resistors, and cable from Japanese affiliates in the Philippines and Thailand. Many of these Japanese suppliers, such as Mitsubishi Metals, are the Thai affiliates of Melco keiretsu members in Japan. "In recent years, as supporting industries have expanded into Thailand from Japan, we have had a growing contribution from Japanese suppliers," explains MMT's managing director.[78] "For the most part, these suppliers are very familiar with the way we do things because their parent companies work with our parent company in Japan."

The Effect on Competition

In Asia, which is rapidly emerging as the leading production center for the global personal computer (PC) industry, Japanese manufacturers of computer peripherals have pursued a losing strategy by building relatively closed networks based on strong relational ties. They have failed to tap into a low-cost supply base composed of indigenous producers, and until quite recently have also failed to forge synergistic linkages with technically sophisticated Taiwanese and Korean producers in the OEM (Original Equipment Manufacturing) market. By contrast, U.S. MNCs have pursued a winning strategy by setting up more open and flexible networks based on what Takeuchi refers to as "growing complementation with Asia."[79] That is, American manufacturers have specialized in high value-added operations such as integrated circuit (IC) design and delegated less knowledge-intensive functions to their Asian partners. Borrus describes the payoff in the following terms:

[T]he turn to skilled but cheaper Asian suppliers helped to lower overall production costs, fierce competition within the supply base helped to reduce turnaround times, and specialization and diversity within the network permitted U.S. producers to keep better pace than Japanese rivals with rapid technological and market shifts. Growing Asian technical capabilities freed U.S. firms to focus their efforts (and scarce resources) on new product definition and standards competition, systems integration, software value-added and distribution. In the bargain, the U.S. networks helped to spawn and sustain direct Asian competition to Japanese firms in several of their stronghold markets. . . . [80]

Japanese electronics firms have lost some ground in Asia, but they have not been entirely eclipsed in the region—or in the rest of the world. Indeed, they seem to have made some progress in recent years by moving, at the margins, to open up their networks. Although Japanese affiliates in the region continue to obtain most of their parts from Japanese sources (either via imports from the Japanese parent company and its home country suppliers or from Japanese parts suppliers in the host country), they now contract more often with Asian firms for OEM supplies.[81] In the mid-1990s, for example, Taiwanese manufacturers began producing monitors, motherboards, and other computer parts for Japanese computer giant NEC, while Taiwanese foundries began churning out memory chips for Japanese producers such as Toshiba and Fujitsu.[82]

It might be wise, however, to question how robust this trend really is. Evidence indicates that Taiwan and Silicon Valley are far more tightly integrated than Taiwan and Tokyo; in 1998, 51 percent of Taiwan's semiconductor foundry capacity was used to serve clients in the United States, while less than 7 percent served clients in Japan.[83] It also seems that some Japanese MNCs used outsourcing merely as a stopgap measure until they could forge their own strategic alliances,[84] or until Japanese-owned production facilities in China came on line in the late 1990s.[85]

Conclusion

Paradoxically, strong ties allowed Japanese automakers to hold onto market power in Southeast Asia, keeping U.S. rivals at bay for many years; but such ties also served to undermine the competitive position of Japanese manufacturers of computer peripherals in the region. This paradox is explained by the different characteristics of the two industries— characteristics that determine the net impact of strong ties.

Closed Versus Open Regimes

Host states in Southeast Asia have protected and nurtured national automakers, including the manufacturing affiliates of foreign firms. Tariffs on automotive imports have been high, and only recently have begun to fall. In Indonesia, for example, the tariff on fully assembled passenger cars was 200 percent, until June 1999, when it fell to 65–80 percent (depending on engine size). The tariff is now 35–50 percent on knocked-down vehicles (assembled as a kit) and 15 percent on automotive parts used in local assembly.[86] Indonesia, as well as neighboring states in Southeast Asia, did agree in 1992 to establish an ASEAN Free Trade Area, an ambitious scheme to sharply reduce tariffs on most trade within the region. But in the wake of the Asian fiscal crisis, members of ASEAN (with the exception of Thailand) reneged on their pledge to liberalize auto trade. Malaysia was particularly concerned about the impact of liberalization on its national brands, Proton and Perodua. Likewise, the Philippines delayed the elimination of local content requirements in the automobile industry, originally scheduled for January 2000, until the end of 2004.[87]

In the computer and semiconductor industries, by contrast, Asian states imposed relatively light tariffs through most of the 1990s, and then, with the advent of the WTO's Information Technology Agreement, agreed to eliminate them completely in January 2000.[88] Interestingly, the crisis of 1997 and 1998 did not dissuade them. Unlike the way they have waffled on measures to open up automobile markets, host states have not abandoned their commitment to free trade in computer-related industries.

This difference in levels of protection reflects the fact that the automobile industry in Asia is geared primarily for domestic and, to a lesser extent, regional markets, while the electronics industry is geared for regional and global markets. In other words, the latter is far more export-oriented. In Thailand, for example, manufacturers of electronic components export about 95 percent of their total output, while automakers—who have struggled mightily to cultivate overseas markets since 1997, when the domestic market collapsed—now export 38 percent.[89]

Stable Versus Unstable Technological Conditions

Vehicle manufacturing, while relying on an increasingly large number of electronic inputs, remains a relatively stable, oligopolistic industry requiring economies of scale and thus mass production. It belongs to the "old economy" of capital-intensive production.

The manufacturing of computer peripherals, however, is different. Consider the HDD industry. It is characterized by extremely short product cycles, now estimated to be six to nine months, and rapidly declining unit prices. McKendrick, Doner, and Haggard note that prices of 3.5 disk drives have fallen at a rate of 1 percent per week, "prompting some managers to complain that they are in the fish business: products on the shelf begin to stink."[90] Technology changes constantly, and often does so in dramatic fits and starts. Design improvements have expanded storage capacity at lower and lower costs: a little more than a decade ago, the average per-megabyte cost of a disk drive was $11; in 1998, it was less than 5 cents.

The Net Impact of Strong Ties

While strong ties generate familiarity and trust, and thereby reduce transaction costs, they also generate a "stickiness" that translates into higher information costs as firms respond more slowly to price signals and technological change. In the case of the automobile industry in Southeast Asia, which is relatively closed and characterized by technological stability, the strong ties of Japanese MNCs yielded greater transaction cost reductions than information cost increases. But in the computer peripherals sector, which is relatively open and characterized by technological uncertainty and uneven development, a similar set of strong ties yielded greater information cost increases than transaction cost reductions. Thus, strong ties helped Japanese firms edge out their American rivals in the automobile industry in Asia but hurt them in their efforts to compete effectively in computer-related industries.

U.S.-Japan Relations

The U.S. and Japanese governments, aware of the large and growing consumer markets and export platforms for automobiles and computer peripherals in Asia, have tried to help their own multinational corporations (that is, MNCs headquartered in their respective countries) compete in these key sectors. The U.S. government's role, to be sure, has been far more circumscribed. Unlike Japanese bureaucrats, who have aggressively and proactively used industrial policies to guide and coordinate manufacturing FDI to and in the region, U.S. officials have resigned themselves to playing firemen by trying to help private firms and their executives fix problems after they have already occurred.[91]

Neither government, however, has managed to win the game for its home team. In the computer sector, a highly globalized industry, Japanese guidance did not boost the competitive position of Japanese firms in the region. Indeed, by encouraging strong ties between Japanese firms, state guidance may have weakened the position of Japanese MNCs in Asia.

The Japanese government was far more successful with automobiles—but only because it operated under the protective shade of host governments trying hard to build up national auto industries. Even then, Japan was unable to stop U.S. and European automakers from eventually buying their way into Japanese automobile networks.

This suggests that while Japanese and U.S. firms will continue to wage a pitched battle for pivotal markets in Asia, the Japanese and U.S. governments may gradually assume a lower profile. This is especially true as industries, including automobiles, become less and less national. Indeed, the two home governments may have to withdraw entirely from the field, acting, if at all, only through host governments that can actually influence the outcome of a private competition. Thus, as Japanese and U.S. MNCs expand further and further into neutral (or third) territories such as Asia, the bilateral bargaining that characterized the 1980s and early 1990s is likely to become less and less common.

Japan's Counterweight Strategy

U.S.-JAPAN COOPERATION AND COMPETITION IN INTERNATIONAL FINANCE

SAORI N. KATADA

Introduction

International relations are full of asymmetrical relationships and political environments under which weaker partners search for strategies that will enable them to avoid overdependence and loss of autonomy even as they maintain collaborative and often beneficial bilateral ties with the strong. Japan's asymmetrical relations with the United States, which have given Japan the reputation of being a reactive state, are an example that sheds light on such strategies.

What recourses are available for the Japanese government when it objects to U.S.-led policies in the regional and international arenas? Due to the overwhelming importance of cooperation with the United States to achieve collective goals, the Japanese government has often played a supporting role in the international arena. However, when Japan's interests diverge significantly from those of the United States, the Japanese government faces the challenge of circumventing the "cooperative" binds without creating a major fissure in its bilateral relationship. In short, how can the Japanese government go beyond bilateralism.

The Japanese government's actions in response to the Asian financial crisis, and its participation in the debate over New International Financial Architecture (NIFA), show the emergence of a policy direction that can be labeled as Japan's *counterweight strategy*. This strategy involves a mixture of bargaining plus institution- and coalition-building efforts designed to increase regional and international support for Japan's position, particularly when it contrasts with the U.S. position. Needless to say, Japan has no intention of directly confronting the United States, especially at the possible cost of bilateral ties. The counterweight strategy, however, helps tip the power balance between the two countries, bolstering Japan's position, or so the Japanese government hopes.

The Asian financial crisis provides an interesting case to analyze how this counterweight strategy came about and the instruments to which the Japanese government has resorted. When the Asian financial crisis broke out during the summer of 1997, efforts to restore Asia's regional financial stability, a type of regional public good, came in various and often conflicting forms. They included, on the one hand, U.S.-Japanese cooperation, a coordination, and unequivocal support by the two governments of the solution led by the International Monetary Fund (IMF). On the other hand, the Japanese government explicitly attacked the U.S.-led neoliberal approach to the Asian crisis, the causes of which, according to many analysts in Japan, were closely tied to short-term capital movements. In this context, the Japanese government began to face the challenge of creating a counterweight to the U.S.-dominated international financial policy-making structures, thereby enabling Japan to address the crisis more independently. Strengthening regional institutions and forming coalitions with Western European countries (hereafter Europe) have become important instruments for Japan.

On the surface, the Japanese government's position is puzzling. The Japanese government fully supported IMF involvement in the crisis, while Japanese analysts became the most vocal critiques of IMF solutions. Japan has been a supporter of nonexclusive regionalization in Asia; the Japanese government actively opposed the establishment of the exclusive East Asian Economic Group proposed by Malaysian Prime Minister Mahathir in 1990, and it supported the Asia-Pacific Economic Cooperation (APEC), which includes the United States and several non-Asian countries. In the aftermath of the Asian crisis, however, Japan advocated Asia-only financial institutions in the form of the Asian Monetary Fund (AMF) and subsequently helped launch the Chiang Mai Initiative under the Association of Southeast Asian Nations (ASEAN)+3 framework. Both structures excluded the United States. Furthermore, in the aftermath of the Asian crisis, the Japanese position on the NIFA debate was clearly against rapid capital mobility, which also challenges the dominant American position. Yet the Japanese government also actively engaged in collective management of the Asian crisis with the United States, as it in-

creased the exclusivity of its aid program by requiring that aid money be
received in yen and used for projects performed by Japanese companies.

The evolution of events and Japan's ambivalence underscore the bilateral binds that Japan confronts vis-à-vis the United States. The counterweight strategy has emerged in response. Because of the importance of its
bilateral relations with the United States, the Japanese government has
opted for the most part to collaborate on global issues. While that collaborative tendency remained a prominent feature of Japan's actions
during the Asian crisis, as discussed shortly, the Japanese government
demonstrated hints of competition and resentment against what was perceived to be U.S. hegemonic abuse of the international financial system.[1]
It struggled to address such frustration through concrete actions.

This chapter argues that the Japanese government began to use a counterweight strategy by resorting to regional institutions and by allying with
the Europeans and the Asians to promote positions that challenged the
United States. It claims that conflicting sets of behavior on the part of the
Japanese government, especially within the Ministry of Finance (MOF), indicate how the Japanese government tries to go beyond the role of mere
supporter to the United States. Now the Japanese government hopes to expand its options. Through the counterweight strategy, Japan challenges
and attempts to modify the dominant U.S.-led international financial system, which includes issues such as appropriate modes of financial crisis response, international financial institution (IFI) reform, permissibility of
capital control, hedge fund regulation, and regional financial and exchange
rate mechanisms. By strengthening the regional cooperation framework in
the postcrisis period, the Japanese government has achieved a certain level
of leadership in regional financial matters. Conversely, the alliance between
Japan and the Europeans on certain aspects of international financial debate has enhanced support of Japan's position in international arenas.

The chapter first analyzes three aspects of U.S.-Japanese tensions in the
face of the Asian financial crisis that led the Japanese government to move
beyond U.S.-Japan bilateralism, even though during the height of the Asian
crisis from mid-1997 to 1998, signs of strong bilateral collaboration continued. It then lays out two policy directions that have contributed to
Japan's creation of counterweight strategies. One is Japan's effort to generate regional alternatives by fostering strong regional financial cooperation. The other is the strategy of the Japanese government to ally with Europeans on certain contentious issues. These policies are not strictly for the
purpose of circumventing the bilateral binds, but because they have
changed Japan's position in the international system, they have increased
the cards in the hands of the Japanese government vis-à-vis the United
States. Despite its economic recession, Japan remains the largest creditor

and the second largest economy in the world. Despite such strengths, it was usually a predictable U.S. supporter (with few exceptions) in the international arena. That Japan is willing to go beyond bilateralism has major implications for the formation of international financial arrangements and for global power structures. As a partial conclusion, the chapter assesses the implications and potentials of Japan's counterweight strategies on U.S.-Japan relations and international financial relations.

The United States and Japan in the
Asian Financial Crisis

U.S.-Japanese dynamics in the management of the Asian financial crisis is itself a fascinating subject that is fully covered in the chapter by Amyx in this volume. The present chapter in turn focuses on Japan's long-term foreign policy strategy in the area of finance after its struggle in the Asian financial crisis. It is nevertheless important to discuss the central areas of tension between Japan and the United States surrounding the Asian crisis, because these struggles made it critical for the Japanese government to go beyond bilateral binds after the crisis. The tension can be clustered into three broad themes: debate over the causes of the crisis, debate over international financial management, and problems in Japanese domestic politics.

Debate over the Causes and Nature of the Crisis

The debate over the causes and nature of the Asian crisis can be divided into two camps. Their respective understandings of the crisis had major implications for their supporters' behavior as they attempted to contain the crisis and to modify the existing international financial architecture.

Both the U.S. government and its financial sector are major shapers and beneficiaries of the financial globalization of the 1990s. The United States was therefore a leading actor in diagnosing what went wrong in the financial crisis that hit the (former) miracle economies in Asia. Despite some variations, the dominant and widely accepted explanation was that the Asian crisis was a crisis of *fundamentals*. According to such views, the major causes of the crisis were the declining export competitiveness of these Asian economies and inefficiency and mismanagement of Asia's financial sector due in turn to a false sense of security that arose from fixed or near-fixed exchange rates.[2] Some went even further and blamed the corrupt and often inefficient "crony capitalism" of many Asian economies.[3] Thus, people in the fundamentals camp have de-

manded stabilization, economic reform, and the adaptation of flexible exchange rates. In its Asian crisis management strategies, the Clinton administration actively supported the inclusion of structural reform components in IMF conditionality.[4]

With its strong interest in the Asian economies but with a troubled
economy and relatively weak currency of its own at the time of the crisis,
Japan had a different view. The Japanese government, and analysts sympathetic to its position, insisted that the financial crisis experienced by
Asian countries was one of *liquidity* arising mostly from the flaws associated with the prevailing international financial structure. The rapid and
massive inflow and outflow of foreign capital, led by highly leveraged institutions (HLIs) such as hedge funds, and supported by ongoing financial
liberalization in the region, led to this temporary imbalance.[5] The pre-
scriptive implication of this understanding was therefore to help increase
short-run liquidity available to these countries in crisis. Added liquidity
should be bolstered in the medium and long-run by some reform of the
domestic financial sector and some changes in international regulations
on the detrimental activities of the HLIs. Furthermore, Japanese analysts
were quite concerned about the impact of foreign exchange volatility on
Asian economies that are highly dependent on imports and exports.

In short, this tension regarding ideas between the two camps constituted an important aspect of Japan's position as a major creditor government engaged in discussions on the NIFA. Moreover, the liquidity camp
has become the ideational backbone that pushed the Japanese government to cast doubt on the international financial paradigm dominated by
the United States.

Politics of International Financial Crisis Management

Politics on both the international and the domestic levels is an important component of international financial crisis management. Due to
Japan's economic dependence on the United States, Japanese businesspeople have always felt vulnerable to the effects of U.S. domestic politics.
The U.S. Congress supported political attacks on Japan when the dollar-
yen exchange rate was perceived to be out of line, or when Japan was accruing a large trade surplus.

Domestic and international politics were also important influences on
U.S. behavior at the time of the international financial crises. The contrast between the United States' involvement in the Mexican peso crisis
and its involvement in the Asian crisis provides the most indicative illustration of this fact. During the Mexican peso crisis (1994–95), the Clin-

ton administration took clear leadership in solving the crisis. When opposition from the U.S. Congress as well as skepticism among the Europeans stalled the Mexican rescue package at the end of January 1995, the Clinton administration bypassed Congress and set up a $50 billion rescue package.[6] Yet the United States did not contribute financially to the first rescue package of the Asian crisis to Thailand, partly because of the implications of this Mexican rescue, but mostly due to the lack of political will on the part of the U.S. administration.[7]

The United States began to pledge financial support to the countries that went into crisis after Thailand, namely Indonesia and South Korea, in the form of the second line of defense.[8] But damage was already done to U.S. credibility among Asian elites. Despite being a model student of the IMF-led reforms after the crisis, Thailand repeatedly criticized U.S. unwillingness to come to its aid.[9] In addition, the idea of the AMF, analyzed by Amyx in Chapter 9 of this volume, also excluded the United States, partly because it was not a member of the "Friends of Thailand"—mostly Asian countries that contributed funding to the country's rescue in August 1997. Furthermore, economic reforms demanded by the IMF, which became the central piece of the Asian crisis solution, incurred suspicion that the IMF was taking advantage of this "opportunity" to pry open the Asian economies.[10]

The actions taken by the United States and Japan during the Asian crisis presented a set of new challenges for their bilateral relationship when their trade tension was relatively low. As the Asian crisis began to rattle global finance, U.S. criticism of Japan began in earnest. It focused no longer on the U.S.-Japan trade imbalance, but on Japan's failure to stimulate its own economy and to help Asian countries out of their economic turmoil.[11] The United States' criticism infuriated Japanese leaders, including then Prime Minister Hashimoto Ryūtaro, who included an Asian rescue component in the country's manifold and multibillion dollar economic stimulus packages. Japanese frustration was further exacerbated by the Clinton administration's praise over China's policy in mitigating the crisis.[12]

For most of the Japanese leaders, the politics of managing the Asian financial crisis were clear. Under a monolithic U.S.-led approach among the creditors, the Japanese were, as always, expected to provide money to ensure liquidity and funding (and, it was hoped, a larger Japanese market for Asian goods). Furthermore, and in connection with the ideational tension between the United States and Japan discussed earlier, U.S. policymakers had much to gain by labeling Japan and the Japanese economic model a major cause of the Asian crisis, thus discrediting alternative plans advocated by Japan.

Politics of Resentment in Japan's Domestic Politics

Japanese financial policymakers' resistance to American positions arose partially from "the politics of resentment."[13] Because of the highly visible role that American government and business both played in financial liberalization, economic globalization, and the IMF-led crisis solution, the United States became a target of criticism. In the face of major economic decline and social instability, Asian leaders (including the Japanese) found the United States to be a convenient villain. These leaders "rediscover[ed] the rhetoric of popular nationalism as a way of deflecting domestic criticism," a rhetoric that has not been "heard since the years of the immediate postcolonial era."[14]

For Japan, latent antagonism against American-led neoliberal policies predates the Asian crisis. It arises from the popular prediction among the Japanese that inequality in U.S.-Japan relations caused Japan's domestic economic problems of the 1990s. Many popular books came out during the course of the "lost decade," blaming the United States for Japan's deep recession. One of the most influential, by Mototada Kikkawa, explicitly argues that Japan's recession originated from its deference to the U.S. macroeconomic policies in the 1980s; that Japan's low-interest rate policy was designed to increase Japanese purchase of U.S. stocks and bonds but also led to Japan's "bubble economy"; and that Japan's strengthening yen since the 1985 Plaza Accord weakened Japan's economy by encouraging capital and production to exit the country.[15] The cumulative effect was a weakening of the Japanese finance and productive base into the 1990s. Furthermore, what is perceived as the U.S. imposition of a global standard on Japan's unique economic model of permanent employment and main-bank system, has stirred up some fear among the Japanese public (mostly among the "salary men"), whose life plans rely totally on job security.

In the late 1990s, when both the MOF and the Liberal Democratic Party (LDP) were suffering from mounting criticisms and loss of public support, they took the opportunity to play on such anti-American sentiments.[16] Of course, the use of such "politics of resentment" has been quite subtle; it has not placed the United States explicitly in the position of scapegoat. The U.S.-Japanese bilateral relations are much too important to be harmed in this way, particularly as their security relations were being transformed after the Cold War. Nevertheless, it became not only acceptable, but also appealing, to say no to the United States, and to criticize its policies, and those of the IMF, particularly after the onset of the Asian crisis.

In addition to existing ideational differences and the political power play between the two countries, many Japanese resented U.S. criticism of Japan's inaction during the crisis, and what was perceived as the U.S. imposition of its economic interests on Japan. Such emotions provided the support base for Japanese policymakers to seek alternative financial frameworks that go beyond U.S.-Japan interdependence. Alternative views concerning U.S.-Japanese relations and the fostering of independent Japanese actions in Asia have become persuasive.

Bilateral Cooperation in Asian Crisis Management

The Japanese government has seen the same detrimental effects from its overdependence on bilateral relations with the United States and has sought to cultivate alternative paths. Interestingly enough, however, Japan's search for an alternative by no means precluded cooperation with the United States. Both Japan and the United States were fully involved in attempting to solve the Asian crisis. There they demonstrated clear signs of collaboration, designed to contain the crisis at the earliest stage and to minimize the bargaining leverage of the debtors, especially vis-à-vis the most problematic case of Indonesia.

The first signs of collaboration came in the very early stage of the crisis, when the Japanese government insisted on the IMF-based solution. The leaders of three crisis countries—Thailand, Indonesia, and South Korea—first hoped to get bilateral assistance directly from Japan so as to avoid the intrusive IMF. But all three failed to achieve that goal, because the Japanese government repeatedly urged the leaders of those countries to turn to the IMF first.[17] Being the second largest shareholder in the IMF, the Japanese government (especially the MOF) had been an unequivocal supporter of the IMF prior to the Asian crisis. As a result, Japanese policy in financial crisis management and development finance had fairly high coherence with that of the United States.

Second, after the Japanese government retracted its AMF idea during the fall of 1997, Japanese support for U.S. initiatives vis-à-vis problem countries, especially Indonesia, was fairly consistent. The tension between Indonesia and the IMF emerged as Indonesia's president, Suharto, announced on January 6, 1998, his FY1998 national budget, which included a large public-spending program. This program conflicted with the budget austerity conditions of the IMF loans. As a result, the Indonesian currency took a nosedive until a new agreement between the Indonesian government and the IMF was announced ten days later. This was but one of Indonesia's rebellious attempts against the IMF-led prescription to its economic crisis. Economically damaged by the ever-declining rupiah, Suharto in February revealed his interest in pursuing the idea of a "currency board," a foreign exchange pegging mechanism used by Argentina, Hong Kong, and others.[18] The plan was strongly criticized by the IMF and the U.S. government as an unfeasible scheme that would be detrimental to Indonesia's already depressed economy. Because Indonesia's economic reforms agreed upon under IMF loan conditions were not making progress, there was also skepticism about Suharto's commitment to carry out the IMF-led reform. The IMF came to a decision on March 6 to suspend its second loan installment of $3 billion. Along with the IMF loan suspension, loans from the World Bank and other bilateral donors such as Japan were also frozen. Soon after, Suharto abandoned the currency board idea.

With the aim of persuading President Suharto, who was reelected for the seventh time on March 10, 1998, to cooperate with the IMF, special envoys and top officials from both the United States and Japan flew to Jakarta during the first weeks of March. During these missions, both the United States and Japan urged the government to stick to the IMF reforms so that the country could restore market confidence in its currency. Nevertheless, the manner in which this message was conveyed varied between the two creditor governments. When U.S. special envoy Walter Mondale, a former vice president, visited Jakarta, his message was strong and clear—the United States would not support Indonesia if it continued to resist IMF reforms. Conversely, in his March 14 meeting with Suharto, Japanese Prime Minister Hashimoto promised additional food and financial aid amounting to several billion dollars if Suharto cooperated with the IMF and smoothly enacted the promised economic reforms.[19]

Finally, the APEC forum was used to address the Asian crisis. It was during the annual APEC summit, held in Malaysia from November 14 through 18, 1998, that the two governments announced a $10 billion joint initiative on debt restructuring and refinancing titled the Asia Growth and Recovery Initiative (AGRI).[20] In addition, during the first meeting between incoming Japanese Prime Minister Keizō Obuchi and President Clinton in September 1998, both agreed to some "geographical division of labor" between the two countries in managing the financial crises of emerging market countries. This discussion occurred when both Russia and Brazil were showing signs of distress.[21]

In short, there are solid indications of collaboration and coordination between the United States and Japan as they faced the series of financial crises in the emerging market countries from 1997 through 1998. Sometimes their collaboration took the form of a division of labor, while at other times it involved a unified front. Regardless of format, it is clear that the Japanese government went along with U.S. interests. Conversely and as discussed later, there were concomitant elements of competition in the region. The Japanese government's fear of U.S. dominance in regional financial matters led Japan to pursue an alternative course in Asia, sometimes in competition with the United States.

Regional Financial Cooperation as a Counterweight

Japan's AMF proposal—an idea that at the time was dubbed the Asian version of the IMF, with an expected $100 billion contribution in emergency funding mostly from the Japanese government for the crisis economies in Asia—excluded the United States. The AMF was also perceived by many as a sign of Japan's willingness to take independent regional leadership. The set of ideas that led to the AMF proposal survived even after the AMF itself, due to opposition by the United States and China, was put to rest. Through this idea, the Japanese government (particularly the International Bureau of the MOF) advocated for the importance of pursuing mutual interests among the members of the region by providing both financial and social safety nets against the overwhelming forces of mobile cross-border capital.

The AMF idea first emerged after the Asian countries pitched in behind the package assembled by the IMF and Japan to support Thailand in August 1997. The idea was repeatedly discussed during the Asia-Europe Meeting (ASEM) of finance ministers in Bangkok and the World Bank/ IMF annual meeting in Hong Kong, both in September 1997. The exact format of the AMF was never clearly outlined, but it aimed to establish a standing regional institution among Asian members that would provide financial support to Asian countries in financial crisis through balance-of-payments support, short-term liquidity, and long-term development finance. According to an MOF official, four major factors motivated the Japanese government to push this proposal forward:

1. Concerns about the possibilities of contagion
2. Awareness that limited money sources were available outside of Asia
3. Awareness that access to the IMF funds was limited, particularly for Asian countries, due to their small IMF quotas.
4. Difficulty of some countries, such as Australia, in justifying case-by-case bilateral support of rescue packages in domestic political arenas, thus creating the need for an established regional fund.[22]

The Asian countries in crisis as well as some parts of Japan's private sector welcomed the idea. Both hoped that Japan's official financial contribution would put an end to the financial crisis and check the regional contagion. Some Asian leaders also hoped that establishment of such a regional funding mechanism would enable them to avoid intrusive involvement by the IMF. The exclusion of the United States was in fact key to creating an IMF alternative.[23]

Opposition from the United States, the IMF, and many European governments, as well as from China, forced the Japanese government to give up pursuing the AMF by the end of October 1997. Indonesia had to resort to the IMF rescue package and accept IMF conditionality. On November 19, 1997, at a meeting of central bankers and finance ministers in Manila, the Manila Framework was set up. It emphasized a regional economic monitoring and surveillance mechanism and introduced the Supplemental Reserve Facility (SRF). The SRF would enable the IMF to respond to short-term financial crises with greater flexibility. The AMF idea was thus "subsumed under Manila Framework,"[24] leaving the central tools for solving the Asian financial crisis in the hands of the IMF.

The Japanese government had to retract the AMF idea, partly due to strong international opposition and partly to its own domestic economic and financial problems, which worsened in November 1997.[25] But the desire to stabilize regional finance under Japanese leadership, even in competition with the United States, died hard among Japanese policymakers, and expectation of an active Japanese role lingered among some Asian leaders from 1997 through 2000. In October 1998, the Japanese government responded to Asia's continuing call for financial leadership by launching the New Miyazawa Initiative (formally known as the New Initiative to Overcome the Asian Currency Crisis). This plan committed a total of $30 billion to Asia's economic recovery—half in the form of medium and long-term funding and half for short-term lending. At the end of 2000, the Japanese government announced that it had provided $80 billion to support the Asian countries in crisis via various funding facilities.[26]

Along with increased official funding, which demonstrated the high level of the Japanese government's resolve to take financial leadership, some Japanese policymakers and some Asian leaders persistently revisited the idea of the AMF. By March 1999, the Japanese government used a part ($3 billion) of the fund set aside for the New Miyazawa Initiative to set up the Asian Currency Crisis Support Facility (ACCSF) in the Asian Development Bank (ADB). During 1999, the ASEAN+3 (China, Japan, and South Korea) leaders discussed a regional financial framework to provide a quick response to financial crises. This scheme was discussed at the APEC symposium in July 1999, supported by Asian deputy ministers at the ASEAN+3 meeting in Manila in November, and finally and officially announced in the form of the Chiang Mai Initiative on May 6, 2000. Although this initiative calls for a regional financial mechanism in the form of bilateral swap agreement networks among central banks, and not for the establishment of a formal regional institution, Japanese policymakers remained hopeful that it would create the basis for an institution like the AMF.[27]

Finally, in May 2001, the ASEAN+3 members formalized the Chiang Mai Initiative in Honolulu and pushed forward their drive to strengthen regional financial cooperation. Throughout the process, the Japanese government emphasized that the swap arrangement has to complement the IMF-centered global financial framework. In the Honolulu meeting, the member countries agreed that only 10 percent of the bilateral swap agreement can be drawn before involving the IMF; the remaining 90 percent will require IMF involvement. Despite this condition, the creation of a "supplementary" regional financial framework should increase Japan's leverage over regional financial matters in the near future. Japan and the Asian countries have subsequently engaged in discussions to establish a regional monitoring and surveillance mechanism separate from the Manila Framework.[28] This movement indicates a long-term and future-looking view among the member countries toward enhanced regional financial cooperation.[29]

One noteworthy player throughout the creation of this regional arrangement has been China. After strongly opposing the Japanese AMF proposal, the Chinese government gradually began to see the utility of an Asia-based financial arrangement. Facing the eminent accession to the World Trade Organization that would require financial liberalization, and having observed the impact of the financial crises in Asia, the Chinese government became increasingly concerned about its own challenges. Because the Japanese government proposed the AMF without consulting the Chinese government, the AMF was a nonstarter. However, as Japanese and ASEAN officials began discussing the ASEAN+3 framework in full collaboration with the Chinese, the regional arrangement became an attractive choice. Nevertheless, Chinese suspicion of Japan's hegemonic intentions led China to press for IMF involvement in the Chiang Mai arrangement to check any Japanese unilateralism.[30] From Japan's point of view, China's participation in the regional arrangement is essential. In this way, one of the region's most influential members is included while the United States is precluded from playing Japan against China—the tactics that the Japanese government observed at the height of the Asian crisis.

Regionalization of the financial framework in Asia thus constitutes one wing of Japan's counterweight strategy vis-à-vis the United States. Concomitantly, and as discussed in the following section, the Japanese government has also allied with the Europeans in the hope of reshaping international and regional financial arrangements. This creates another counterweight enabling Japan to go beyond U.S.-Japan bilateralism. The Japanese government is now creating means through which it can push forward its agenda independently of the United States, but without antagonizing the bilateral relationship.

Allying with Europe as a Counterweight

Multilateralism and trilateralism that include the active participation of European countries have always been important in order for Japanese policymakers to go beyond bilateral constraints. The alliance with the European governments in the field of international finance became increasingly critical for Japan in the aftermath of the 1997 Asian crisis, as differences in the views of the United States and Japan appeared stark. Since then, more than ever the Japanese government has pursued European support and collaboration to counter U.S. dominance in international financial management.

There has also been resonance between the Japanese and European positions. European policymakers had reasons to respond positively to Japan's overtures. Since the mid-1990s, the Europeans have indicated discontent over U.S. dominance of the IMF and overtly self-interested U.S. calls for the reform of the international financial architecture. U.S. triumphalism and the rise of economic unilateralism under the Clinton administration were the foundation of such frustration. Several events in the second half of the 1990s convinced European leaders that they needed to enhance mechanisms and political weight to check U.S. hegemonic abuse of the international financial system.

One of the most striking events emerged during the rescue drama over the Mexican peso in January 1995. Due to overwhelming political necessity to contain the Mexican crisis fast, the Clinton administration used the U.S. Treasury's Exchange Stabilization Fund (ESF) to put up $20 billion for the U.S. bilateral rescue package. At the same time, as Mexico's external imbalance hit the crisis stage in late January, the administration managed to get the IMF to approve $17.8 billion in loans to the country. This IMF package was 688.4 percent of Mexico's IMF quota, an amount vastly beyond the maximum 300 percent ceiling and the highest proportion ever allowed to any member country up to that point. Resenting the U.S. government's actions to ram this unusually large Mexican rescue package down the IMF's throat, on January 31, six European countries (Germany, the United Kingdom, Switzerland, the Netherlands, Belgium, and Denmark) abstained from supporting the package.[31]

The second tension between the United States and Europe arose over how the U.S. government led "vetoing schemes" against various plans advocated by the Europeans for financial crisis resolution during the debate over the NIFA from 1997 through 1999.[32] For the European leaders, case-by-case financial crisis strategies supported by the United States would "simply allow the Americans to dictate which countries are helped and under what conditions."[33]

Finally, the initiation of the European Monetary Union and the arrival of the euro has increased the region's resentment against the U.S. position in favor of a flexible foreign exchange rate regime. Sustaining the credibility of the euro, which admittedly had a rocky start, became a critical issue for the European leaders, and "prompted a desire to play a greater role in international economics."[34] French President Jacques Chirac demonstrated such a desire clearly when he openly split with U.S. policy and promoted the idea of three specific foreign exchange zones during a speech to the World Bank and the IMF in February 1999.[35] These three zones, according to Chirac, were to be maintained by respective regional powers—the United States, Europe, and Japan.

Given the European position on the NIFA debate and on the U.S.-domination of international finance and financial crisis management, the Japanese government, particularly after the Asian crisis, began to see the increased utility of improved links with Europe. One way to influence the United States was to ally with European leaders in the multilateral forums, such as the G7 summits and the IMF. The other was by linking Asian regionalization efforts to those in Europe. The European Union (EU) is increasingly seen as a model of regional integration and as a counterpart through which the Asian countries can shape the region's positions on specific issues in the international economy.

Europe as a Political Ally in the Global Economic Forums

For the Japanese government, the G7 summits have been forums for high-profile diplomacy.[36] From the early years of the G7, Japanese leaders were hopeful that these summits would allow Japan to build strong, substantive, top-level ties with major nations beyond the United States. The Japanese government hoped to expand its scope for political maneuvering, and create more opportunities for Japan to be a rule-shaper in international issues, in ways that would have been impossible in the context of U.S.-Japan bilateral relations.[37] The Japanese government also hoped to rely on active European support at the G7 economic forum in the aftermath of the Asian financial crisis to reshape an international financial structure that, in the predominant Japanese understanding, threatened the viability of the relatively healthy economies in Southeast and East Asia.

The 1998 Birmingham Summit became the first G7 battleground for Japan in debating the international financial architecture.[38] The contrast between the United States and Japan's respective understanding of the nature of the Asian crisis had a major impact on this debate. The Japanese government emphasized that the new structure would not only increase international financial stability, but also provide better chances for the Asian countries, including Japan, to compete.

It is quite obvious that the Asian crisis was behind Japan's increased interest in soliciting European support on international financial issues. Before the crisis, the Japanese government had been quite a reliable supporter of U.S. initiatives on international financial matters at the G7 meetings. This tendency was visible when IMF reform was put on the table during the 1994 Naples Summit. The Japanese government also welcomed initiatives by Canada and the United States during the 1995 Halifax Summit on the increased capital subscription to the IMF in the aftermath of the Mexican peso crisis.

The G7 Summit held at Birmingham, United Kingdom, on May 15–17, 1998, launched a new discussion on the NIFA. At the meeting of the finance ministers held a week before the summit, the issue of international finance was at the center of the agenda. The Japanese media emphasized the prospect that a certain level of regulation would be imposed on short-term capital flows, including those of the hedge funds.[39] The real focus of discussion, however, proved to be different from what the Japanese had wished or expected. Rather than discussing the activities of the hedge funds, the G7 leaders, especially those from the United States, focused on Japan's problematic financial reform as an essential threat to global economic stability.[40] The summit statement emphasized that it was important for the G7 to maintain and expand the global economy. The statement also stressed that each country had to continue efforts to reform its economy in order for the global market to function smoothly. The statement was an explicit confirmation that the G7 governments were not about to agree to regulate certain cross-border financial activities, although some efforts would be made to increase the efficiency and transparency of international financial activities. Furthermore, the G7 members confirmed that the IMF should continue to lead the efforts to support and reform those Asian economies affected by the crisis.

Thus the discussion on the NIFA remained mostly on the same footing as the issues put on the table by the 1995 Halifax Summit. The U.S. Treasury was already taking initiative in several areas—including "initiatives to enhance disclosure and transparency, initiatives to strengthen national financial sectors, and mechanisms to ensure that the market more fully bore the consequences of its credit and investment decisions."[41] It was these areas that drew the greatest concentration of U.S. effort. Conversely, the Clinton administration stuck mostly to the status quo ante on issues of crisis resolution and showed little interest in discussing new exchange rate regimes, monetary union or target zones.[42]

The series of financial crises in the latter half of 1998 changed the attitudes of the G7 members, especially among the European leaders, and they became more critical of unregulated international financial markets. As a partial outgrowth of the Asian financial crisis in August, Russia, which had already suffered from a myriad of difficulties during its transition to a market economy, devalued its currency and partially defaulted on its external debt. It did so despite the financial support of the IMF and other creditors. In addition, Brazil faced financial turmoil before and after its presidential election in October 1998. Despite the IMF-led precautionary rescue package provided to Brazil in November, the country was later forced to abandon its currency peg to the dollar and to devalue the *real*, triggering further capital outflows and declines in its stock market in January of 1999. In addition to these international financial crises, the United States experienced a domestic financial crisis arising from the dramatic decline of its stock market in the late summer of 1998, and the failure and bailout of the hedge fund Long Term Capital Management (LTCM) in the fall.

These crises consequently created a political environment in which Japan's position urging increased caution on certain types of international financial activities attracted sympathy, particularly among the Europeans. Leaders of major European countries, which had just launched the euro in January 1999, emphasized the importance of stable exchange rates and the danger of HLIs, such as hedge funds.[43] Such institutions can impose massive pressure on exchange rates and create large capital outflows from countries in distress. Conversely, the United States, whose financial institutions dominate this type of business, insisted on maintaining the principles of open market and financial liberalization, albeit with adequate supervision and transparency.

Encouraged by increased support from both the Asians and the Europeans, however, the Japanese government promoted the idea of curtailing short-term capital outflows. The proposal emphasized that countries in financial crisis should be allowed to suspend their external payment temporarily, and that non-national financial institutions have to maintain a certain level of outstanding claims to countries in crisis.[44] The Japanese government promoted these ideas at the G7 financial ministers' meeting in April 1999. Although this plan was not taken as proposed, the Japanese government saw it as progress when other G7 members (though not so much the United States) endorsed the idea of checking and regulating short-term capital flows across borders.

The 1999 Köln Summit addressed the direction of the new international financial system. The finance ministers of the G7 countries had already conducted the bulk of their discussions on the NIFA in the newly created and European-supported Financial Stability Forum in February of 1999 and during the meeting of the finance ministers two weeks prior to the leaders' summit. The division was always clear. Even after the events of October 1998, which President Clinton himself called "the biggest crisis of the past fifty years," the U.S. administration was reluctant to address the increased regulation of hedge funds. The Clinton administration was allegedly "under considerable pressure from the U.S. financial community, which was typically suspicious of official interference in the design of its contracts and vocal in its insistence that any such measures should be purely voluntary."[45] Conversely, the Europeans and the Japanese were concerned about both the unregulated and the volatile nature of those funds and in favor of exchange rate management (rather than total flexibility) for many countries.

What came out of the meetings of the financial specialists were plans to further strengthen the international financial system. These plans involved the participation of the private financial sector. Emphasis was on the co-responsibility of the lenders (rather than only on the borrowers). Interviewed by the *Nihon Keizai Shinbun* on June 8, Japan's vice minister of finance, Eisuke Sakakibara, noted:

There has been an increase in the awareness regarding the crisis in global capitalism even in the United States as the Asian crisis has spread to Latin America and Russia, and as the major American hedge fund has failed. The United States, Europe, and Japan *all now agree* that the center of the causes of these crises lies in capital movements. We have to strengthen our capacity to monitor short-term capital movement in particular. In that context, the G7 members all acknowledge the possibility of regulating movement (entrance and exit) of capital at the time of crisis.[46]

The redirection of the international financial system toward stability rather than growth was further helped by the host of the G7 Summit, German Chancellor Gerhart Schröder, who captioned the summit as seeking "globalization with a human face." Chancellor Schröder also stressed the need for regulating the activities of institutional investors at times of international financial instability. Taking up the opportunity, the Japanese leaders cautioned against the predominant force of U.S.-led "market fundamentalism."[47] The Japanese government also insisted on the need to respect other cultures when universal values are promoted via alleged global standards.

The resulting document on financial issues includes (a) discussion of the adverse effect of policy biases in favor of short-term capital flows, (b) a caution against the drastic capital account liberalization, and (c) examination of the justifiability of the use of controls on capital inflows.[48] Furthermore, the G7 members agreed to turn interim committees at the IMF into a permanent standing committee called the International Financial and Monetary Committee (IFMC). They also agreed to set up the so-called Group of Twenty (G20), consisting of the G7 members and emerging market countries, "to establish an informal mechanism for dialogue among systemically important countries within the framework of the Bretton Woods institutional system."[49] On a limited scale, the Japanese government accomplished some of what it had set out to do. It managed to convince the G7 members that the international financial system, particularly the activities of the hedge funds, and other short-term capital flows deserved partial blame for past crises. Further, the influence of developing countries—obviously some from Asia—in the debate over the new international financial architecture was enhanced.[50]

Nevertheless, it is too soon to judge whether the Japanese government actually succeeded in influencing the U.S. position. The U.S. government had on its own begun to show increasing concern over financial fragility, especially due to the crisis in Brazil and the failure of LTCM. However, the Clinton administration, unlike Japanese and European financial leaders who supported increased regulation, focused on IMF reform. The United States supported the creation of a new funding facility called the Contingent Credit Line (CCL) to provide short-term lines of credit to preapproved countries pursuing strong policies. Nevertheless, heightened American concerns led to the commissioning of a report by the International Financial Institution Advisory Commission (the Meltzer Commission) to deliberate the future roles of IFIs in exchange for delayed approval by Congress of $18 billion in additional funding to the IMF.[51]

Countering the United States and Solidifying Asian Positions

U.S. administrations have been quite vigilant against being excluded from any Asian efforts to create regional institutions. At least until the Asian financial crisis, this U.S. attitude prevented Japan from promoting any exclusive regional arrangements in Asia. Japan's reluctance was illustrated when Malaysian Prime Minister Mohamad Mahathir proposed the East Asian Economic Caucus (EAEC). Because the U.S. opposition was quite explicit, despite some support from pro-Asia Japanese officials, the Japanese government refrained from supporting EAEC. Increased regionalization in Europe and the Western Hemisphere in the 1990s and Japan's experience through the Asian crisis changed Japan's attitudes toward Asia's exclusive regionalization in the field of international finance. To facilitate the regionalization process, Japanese leaders' counted on Europe on two accounts: to counter U.S. opposition by gaining European support, and to enhance Asia's regional identity by learning from European regionalization efforts. For both reasons, the relatively low profile and seemingly unimportant ASEM became an important forum for the Japanese leaders.

The achievements of ASEM thus far are quite limited, but the very existence of a multilateral forum that explicitly excludes the United States constitutes an essential element in Japan's post-Asian crisis counterweight strategy. One of the major implications of the ongoing ASEM process on Japan's regional position is closely linked to the country's bilateral interests with the United States: "[B]y locating itself within the ASEM perimeter fence, Japan is not seen to contradict its Security Treaty partner. In this way, Japan is also given opportunities to challenge the U.S. position without open bilateral disagreement."[52]

Japan's interests correspond to those of the Europeans. For Europe, besides avoiding the region's total geo-economic marginalization in the so-called Pacific Century (a vision that died in the Asian crisis), ASEM was seen to have geostrategic utility. In Dent's words, "[f]ortifying the Eurasian axis in this way would side East Asia and Europe together to potentially counter any perceived U.S. hegemonic misbehavior in international affairs."[53]

ASEM is a relatively new cross-regional forum. It is truly Eurasian, including all fifteen EU members and ten Asian members.[54] The twenty-five ASEM member countries first met in March 1996 in Bangkok, Thailand, following a strong call by Singaporean Prime Minister Goh Chok Tong. The forum came into being under the initiative of ASEAN leaders, and European leaders agreed so as "not [to miss] the Asian boat."[55] This forum was created explicitly to exclude the United States, and the Japanese government was at first very cautious in supporting this interregional arrangement. But as Japan found that the United States was not vehemently opposed to the establishment of ASEM, the Japanese government became more enthusiastic in its support of the Asia-European framework.[56]

Started as a group of "fair-weather friends," ASEM shifted its focus dramatically at its second meeting in London in April 1998 due to the financial crisis. As the Asian economies stagnated, the Europeans committed to the region's economic recovery by setting up a £30.9 million Asian Trust Fund in April 1998 in return for the promise of the Asian countries to allow continued European access to their markets. At that point, the Europeans seemed to have missed a grand opportunity to take a strong lead in international financial matters by working to contain the crisis. Their actions, though quite substantial in terms of providing foreign aid and debt write-offs, were in accordance with the U.S./IMF-led crisis solution and failed to provide an original alternative.[57]

Conversely, ASEM has gradually become a suitable forum for Japan's activism. During the 1998 London meeting, Japan's Finance Minister Kiichi Miyazawa floated the idea of the new Asian currency regime consisting of a basket of currencies, including a higher proportion of the yen. The ASEM Vision Group submitted its first report, which emphasized the "sustaining economic partnership between Asian and Europe," to ASEM's foreign ministers' meeting in March 1999. The report included a point on enhanced cooperation for financial stability, and emphasized the region's need for "management of exchange rates, substantial reduction in the volatility of short-term capital flows and the strengthening of domestic long-term financial markets."[58] Finally, during the ASEM financial ministers meeting in Kobe, Japan, in January 2001, Japan, with support from France, proposed a research project to study the feasibility of an Asian monetary union (AMU) in the foreseeable future.[59] The report from this research initiative, which came out in July 2002, recommended three phases: a monetary integration process in phase one (to be completed by 2010), preparation for a single currency in phase two (to be completed by 2030), and the launching of a single currency in phase three, which would start in 2030.

An additional benefit of the ASEM process is that Japan has been able to help develop Asia's regional identity without provoking either the suspicion of Asian countries themselves, including China, or the opposition of the United States.[60] Because each ASEM discussion requires Asia to develop a coordinated regional position vis-à-vis the more experienced and relatively uniform EU, the incentive for Asian countries to discuss issues openly and create a collective Asian identity is increased. From the Japanese policymakers' standpoint, such an exercise has been invaluable.[61] Particularly in the area of foreign exchange, the EU hopes to serve as a model of regional integration from which the Asian leaders can learn and to which they can also provide support. ASEM is now functioning as a forum where such cooperation and learning can occur between Europe and Asia without fundamentally threatening the United States.

Japan's strategy was again facilitated partly by the shifting U.S. attitude toward regionalism in Asia and by the proposals for an Asia-centered financial framework. The U.S. opposition to Japan's alternative at the time of the Asian crisis seemed adamant, but as Asian expert Walden Bello testified to Congress in April 1998, the opposition came as a result of domestic political maneuvering within the Clinton administration:

The Clinton administration, without consulting Congress, backed the IMF leadership and "made considerable efforts to kill Tokyo's proposal." One of the key reasons is that, with Congress' assertiveness in foreign economic policy using its power of the purse, the Clinton administration sees the IMF as an increasingly important instrument to push key initiatives without having to submit them to Congressional oversight.[62]

Thus the Clinton administration could not let the AMF jeopardize the IMF's monopoly over international financial crisis management. However, not too long after the United States shot down the AMF, many American experts criticized the U.S. government for having killed an invaluable regional initiative on the part of Japan.[63] In addition, and due to the changing of the guard in the IMF from former managing director Michele Camdessus to new director Horst Köhler, the IMF moved toward less conditionality and a more restricted role. Köhler also appears much more supportive of regional integration and efforts toward regional financial frameworks than Camdessus was.[64]

All in all, alliance with the Europeans has given increased weight to Japan's position in the U.S.-centered international financial framework. The Japanese government has managed to influence agenda setting in the international finance discussion because its competing ideas were introduced in a trilateral forum that was beyond the U.S.-Japan bilateral framework. The Japanese government managed to advocate its views and policies regarding the regional and international financial architecture, and managed to gain support from the Europeans and Asians in international and cross-regional forums without provoking the United States.

Assessment

The Asian crisis revealed a stark contrast in ideas between Japan and the United States on the one hand and the overwhelming power of the United States along with the central role of the IMF on international financial matters on the other. With underlying resentment and frustration among the Japanese elite toward the United States as a backdrop, the Japanese government has struggled to gain supporters for its policy preferences and thus to circumvent U.S. opposition. For such efforts, the Japanese government has relied on both the Asian region and European counterparts to enhance Japan's political power and the international credibility of its positions.

Although the emergence of Japan's new counterweight strategy as a device to allow it to go beyond U.S.-Japanese bilateralism is clear, assessing the effectiveness of this strategy is still quite difficult. As discussed earlier, U.S. policymakers are also shifting their attitudes from opposition to accommodation of Asia's regionalism, and U.S. lawmakers are currently rethinking the NIFA debate and associated questions on the country's financial sector and the role of the IFIs.[65] Conversely, the U.S. government is taking an uncompromising position on hedge fund regulation, in support of flexible exchange rates. The gradual changes in the international debate on these areas indicate evolution in the global financial environment and some achievement by the counterweight strategy, especially as Japan has allied with its European counterparts.

The implications of Japan's efforts on the U.S.-Japan relations as well as on the international financial system are important. Japan is now much more capable than before of opposing U.S. positions. Understanding the strong need for regional alternatives (or at least supplements) to the IMF, the Japanese government is less likely to give up on institutions like the AMF and arrangements that would increase financial stability in the region (including an AMU). As the result of these measures, plus the already quite strong regional integration on the trade and investment fronts, the economic integration of Asia should continue either with or without the U.S. blessing. The former is obviously preferred by the Asian countries, including Japan, but Japanese policymakers seem to have realized and acted on the regional card and gone beyond the constraints of U.S.-Japan bilateralism.

As for international financial arrangements and the IFIs, the power of the United States and its ideas is still dominant. However, the uncontested leverage over international financial matters that the United States once had, partly thanks to consistent support by the Japanese government (and its funds), has waned. The competition of ideas and policies between Japan and the United States, which the Japanese government cannot effectively address on a bilateral basis, has increased the importance of alternative arenas. The triangular dynamics among the United States, Japan, and Europe are now becoming more significant as Japan becomes willing to align itself with the Europeans, in some cases opposing the United States. Having gradually realized the utility of counterweights, the Japanese government seems ready to implement its independent initiatives.

These trends are quite healthy for U.S.-Japan bilateral relations. The Japanese government now has various avenues through which it can address its differences with the United States, acquire counterparts in Asia and in Europe, and indirectly influence U.S. decisions. This development is a good start toward a more well-balanced relationship between the two major economic powers.

Japan and the Evolution of Regional Financial Arrangements in East Asia

JENNIFER A. AMYX

Introduction

Financial crises are endemic to the nature of capitalism, striking advanced industrial as well as emerging market economies. They have become particularly frequent in recent decades, raising the importance of international financial crisis management. Some governments are able to resolve their crises without external intervention; many others must rely on outside assistance. The most frequent source of such assistance has been the International Monetary Fund (IMF), established in 1944 and dominated since its founding by the United States. By itself the United States holds enough votes to prevent any change in the fund's organizational structure or in the distribution of quotas.[1] Although Japan is the second largest paid-in-capital contributor to the fund and thus plays an indirect role in international financial crisis management, its voice within the organization has historically been weak.[2]

In August 1997, in the wake of Thailand's financial crisis, Japanese officials put forward an informal but highly publicized proposal to establish a new regional monetary fund—temporarily dubbed the Asian Monetary Fund (AMF). This move drew a great deal of attention and seemed to signal an important departure in both substance and style from Japan's prior regional institution-building initiatives that included the United States. Japan's proposal to establish the Asian Development Bank (ADB) in 1966, for example, called for the United States to assume equivalent equity and voting standing with Japan.[3] More recently, when Malaysia's prime minister called in 1990 for the establishment of an East Asian Economic Caucus (EAEC) that excluded the United States, Japan's reluctance to join doomed the idea to failure for the time being.[4] Implicit in Japan's 1997 AMF proposal, however, was the creation of a regional institution that did not include the United States.

The AMF proposal also seemed to signal an aberration in Japan's style of economic diplomacy in the region. Japan has been characterized as exercising "leadership from behind," inhibited from taking a more overt leadership role by lingering memories of its invasion and colonization of many Asian nations.[5] This leadership style was reflected, for example, in Japan's critical behind-the-scenes role with Australia in establishing the Asia-Pacific Economic Cooperation (APEC) forum.[6] With the bold AMF initiative, however, Japanese government officials made little attempt to mask Japan's efforts to exert overt leadership.

Thus, to many observers, Japan's pursuit of an AMF independent of U.S. influence signaled a possible turning point in Japan's foreign economic diplomacy. Some also interpreted the proposal as Japan's assumption of a competitive stance vis-à-vis the IMF and the United States in the management of financial relationships in the region. After all, philosophical and policy disagreements within the World Bank between the United States and Japan are well documented.[7] With Japan's distinctive development model largely discredited by the nation's prolonged economic stagnation, might Japan be attempting to present instead to its Asian neighbors a distinctive model of financial crisis management or regulation? Some observers suggested that such philosophical motivations lay behind the AMF proposal.

The AMF proposal encountered a number of obstacles, the most formidable of which was opposition by the United States and the IMF. Consequently, in 1997, Japanese officials aborted the initiative for a new region-based multilateral monetary institution. The notion of an AMF resurfaced in a variety of forms thereafter, however, and a top-ranking Ministry of Finance (MOF) official would later describe a network of bilateral currency swap arrangements agreed to by the Association of Southeast Asian Nations (ASEAN)+3 nations in May 2000 as a "functional equivalent" to the original AMF idea.[8] In an ironic twist, however, when the ASEAN+3 nations announced more details of this swap facility in April 2001, they revealed a key point of departure from the original AMF plan. Under a proposal put forward by Japan, the release of all but 10 percent of the funds in the facility was made contingent on recipient countries having an IMF program in place. Thus, rather than representing an alternative to the IMF or a new regional institution devoid of U.S. influence, the currency swap arrangements seemed to reassert the IMF's centrality in international financial crisis management and to ensure continued American influence over the way such crises are managed.

A number of explanations might be offered for Japan's seeming about-face. For example, a realist interpretation focusing on simple power relations would argue that Japan's desire to play a greater leadership role in the region—and in regional multilateralism in particular—remains stifled by the power imbalance in U.S.-Japan relations. In this interpretation, the U.S.-Japan alliance continues to constrain Japanese behavior in critical ways, despite the end of the Cold War and the decline of U.S. hegemony. Alternatively, one might argue that the outcomes to the present situation represent a redefinition of Japanese interests and an ideational or philosophical shift in thinking within Japan's MOF. In this interpretation, American pressure is of peripheral importance and evolutionary thinking within Japan takes center stage.

Determining the true motivations for Japan's shift first to exclude and then to indirectly include the United States (through close IMF linkage) in regional institution-building efforts is important. Different motivations imply not only different directions for U.S.-Japan relations but also different expectations for Japan's role in multilateral institutions in the years to come. It would be difficult to point to another policy realm where Japan is better positioned to assume a leadership role on the international stage. In international finance, the types of domestic constraints that hinder Japan from taking a greater leadership role in many other multilateral institutions are noticeably absent. We know, for example, that Japan's distinctive peace constitution has constrained its exercise of a greater leadership role in the United Nations (UN) by impeding the full participation of the Japanese in peacekeeping operations. We also know that domestic political structures and the configuration of domestic interests impose considerable constraints on government leaders in multilateral trade forums such as the World Trade Organization (WTO), leading some to label it a "reactive state" in the realm of foreign economic policy.[9] Japanese elected officials pay little attention to exchange rates or international financial crisis management, however, granting the MOF and the Bank of Japan (BOJ) considerable policy autonomy in these areas.[10] In addition, Japan's status as the world's largest holder of foreign exchange reserves suggests that if there is any policy arena where Japan might take a leading role, international financial crisis management is it.[11] Accordingly, if the message from recent developments is simply that Japan has bowed to U.S. pressure, then the prospects for moving beyond bilateralism appear extremely bleak.

This chapter argues that despite the appearance of simple power politics, there is a more complex story to be told. Through an examination of the political dynamics surrounding the Japanese government's initial proposal in 1997 for the creation of an AMF and for the arrangements that emerged in its place, the chapter argues that Japan has not simply given in to its more powerful alliance partner. Rather, the outcomes to date reflect two equally important forces.

First, the outcomes reflect a reassessment of national interests and an adjustment of strategies on both sides of the Pacific since the outbreak of the Asian financial crisis. Deeper consideration of the practical limitations inherent in a truly independent regional institution, as well as recognition of progress made with innovations and reforms in the IMF and other existing institutions, have led Japanese officials to view linkage with the IMF differently than they did in 1997. At the same time, changes in U.S. behavior, spurred by the AMF proposal and by the signs of growing Asian solidarity since, have lent support to the aforementioned innovations and reforms in the IMF and have served as a check to some degree on U.S. monetary unilateralism via the IMF.

Second, the tight linkage of current regional financial arrangements to IMF facilities and conditionalities reflects Japan's attempt to reconcile the wide range of preferences within Asia concerning the form and function of a regional monetary institution. The evolution of a more independent regional institution is hindered as much by widely divergent views held by countries within the region as it is by U.S. objections. In this way, the outcomes to date cannot be fully understood only through the lens of the bilateral U.S.-Japan relationship. Analysis of the interaction of interests among the larger group of actors who will constitute the membership of the new regional monetary institution is also necessary.

To make these arguments, the chapter first examines the original motivations and catalysts for Japan's 1997 AMF proposal and the objections that this proposal raised. The chapter then examines the evolution of other mechanisms for regional cooperation that arose in place of the AMF. Next, the chapter explores the difficulties inherent in delinking the evolving network of bilateral currency-swap arrangements in the region from IMF facilities and conditionality. The chapter closes with a summary of the findings and implications.

The AMF Proposal

Pre-crisis Roots

The idea for creating a regional monetary fund first arose with the establishment of the ADB in 1966. Proponents of the idea saw an IMF equivalent in Asia as complementing the activities of the ADB in the same way as the IMF complements the activities of the World Bank. The idea failed to gain currency, however, and was not actively pursued for some decades. While the demand for a development fund was constant and the need obvious, the various actors involved in the founding of the ADB found it difficult to envision clearly the role that a regional monetary fund would play. In the early years of the ADB, the pattern of currency crises seemed to suggest that such crises were limited to industrialized countries. Most of Asia did not yet fit into this category.

As Asia's emerging markets began to attract foreign capital in the late 1980s, however, the idea of an AMF reemerged within Japan's MOF. This was particularly true after the outbreak of the Mexican peso crisis in 1995, when Japanese officials realized that Asian nations probably would not qualify for IMF loans proportionate to the ones received by Mexico because the Asian countries' IMF quotas had not been adjusted to reflect their rapid economic development.[12] A group of incumbent and former MOF officials began to meet regularly in private forums to discuss the idea.[13] Yet within the ministry—and even within the ministry's International Finance Bureau—there were a variety of views on what an AMF would be like and how it would function. Differences of opinion centered primarily around whether or not the United States should be included in such a regional institution.[14] Some in the MOF, resentful of American domination of the IMF and perceiving the United States as a competitor in the financial arena and as hindering the pursuit of Japanese national interests in Asia, sought to preclude involvement by the U.S. Treasury. Others in the ministry, however, who viewed America as more of a cooperative ally in the region, felt that the United States ought to be included in a regional fund. Thus, although the idea for an AMF was brewing within the Japanese government long before the eruption of the 1997–98 financial crisis, consensus was lacking on the scope of the fund's membership or on its precise nature.

Crisis Provides a Rationale

The collapse of the Thai baht in the summer of 1997 created an opportunity to move forward with the AMF idea because the IMF was unable alone to provide funds sufficient to rescue Thailand from the throes of crisis. The amount of aid an IMF member country could obtain from the fund was determined by that country's quota. Thailand's need for funding was triple its quota and the Thai government appealed to Japan for assistance. Japan responded by taking the lead in organizing bilateral aid packages to make up the difference. This effort complemented the IMF response, and Japan and the other bilateral aid donors relied on IMF information gained through its regular surveillance of member countries as they worked out these aid packages.[15]

The ad hoc effort to organize bilateral aid packages proved successful in quelling the Thai crisis. Yet other countries in the region feared attacks on their own currencies. Setting up individual aid packages and accumulating money to fend off currency attacks were time-consuming endeavors and a great deal of economic and financial damage could be incurred as arrangements were being made. Furthermore, just as in the case of Thailand, it was clear that the IMF quota on aid amounts would be too small to prevent crisis if the currencies of other nations in the region were similarly attacked. Given this situation, the time seemed ripe for Japanese officials to advance the AMF idea.

As noted earlier, varying ideas of what an AMF would be like circulated within the MOF at this time. The domestic and international context in August 1997 helped determine which of the conceptualizations of an AMF would emerge as the official government proposal. Japan's vice minister of finance for international affairs at the time was Eisuke Sakakibara, whose personal view was that Japan should pursue a greater leadership role in Asia independently of the United States.[16]

America's total refrain from contributing to the bilateral aid effort for Thailand effectively lent support to Sakakibara's personal bias of setting up a regional institution not including the United States. The American government's passive stance on Thailand surprised MOF officials, particularly because the United States had played the key role in providing bridging funds to IMF loans for Mexico in 1995.[17] Although U.S. State Department and National Security Council officials argued for at least a modest U.S. contribution to maintain America's image as a leader in the region, U.S. Treasury Secretary Robert Rubin rejected the idea.[18] Securing the funds for the Mexican peso bailout had involved a tough political battle in the United States. Another substantial commitment to bailing out an economy in which America clearly had a lesser stake would have been hard to sell to Congress.[19]

The initial proposal for an AMF also came amid rising resentment within the Japanese government of U.S. criticism of Japan's own financial and economic problems. For most of the postwar period, U.S.-Japan financial relations focused on exchange rate management; while sound management of national financial systems was considered important, it was simply not part of the bilateral agenda. Japan's irresolution of its nonperforming loan problem after six years, however, was now a topic

pursued by American officials in bilateral meetings. An increasingly defensive mood within the bureaucracy thus provided a supportive context
for an initiative that excluded the United States.

Sakakibara's conceptualization of a regional monetary institution that
did not include the United States was thus adopted in Japan's initial formulation of the idea, put forward on August 11, 1997, at a meeting in
Tokyo of the countries that had contributed to the rescue package for
Thailand. Since the United States was not a contributor to this package,
American officials were absent from these initial discussions. Sakakibara
then raised the idea informally with other financial agencies and central
banks in the region during the remainder of the month and into September
1997. Most notably, on September 10 he sent a confidential and unofficial
memo outlining his idea to officials in South Korea, Malaysia, Hong Kong,
Singapore, and Indonesia.[20] Although he didn't cite specific figures, he let
it be known that he was contemplating a fund in the magnitude of tens of
billions of dollars that would be used to provide trade finance and balance-
of-payments support to the Asian economies hit by crisis, while also acting
as a pooled reserve for currency defense.

The Opposition

While Malaysia enthusiastically embraced the AMF idea and most
ASEAN member countries, such as the Philippines and Thailand, were
generally supportive, China and Singapore were reluctant to lend their
support. As the second largest holder of foreign exchange reserves in the
region, China's participation in any regional fund was particularly key.[21]
Its failure to lend support was interpreted as opposition to the creation of
a regional institution not including the United States. Some other countries in the region with close ties to the United States were also concerned
about the exclusion of the United States and informed American officials
of Japan's lobbying activities within the region.[22]

U.S. Treasury Secretary Robert Rubin and Federal Reserve Chairman
Alan Greenspan responded with a counterattack on September 17, writing
a letter to their Asian counterparts and sending U.S. Treasury and Federal
Reserve representatives to Asian capitals to lobby against Sakakibara's
plan.[23] For the IMF and the U.S. government, fear that the importance of
their respective roles in Asia would diminish with the advent of such a
fund provided one unspoken motivation to object. Since the Mexican peso
bailout in 1995, the White House had become increasingly constrained by
Congress from committing financial resources to international initiatives.
As a result, the IMF's importance as a mechanism for U.S. influence in international monetary affairs and international financial crisis management

had risen significantly.[24] In addition, the presence of an alternative funding source threatened IMF potency. The proposed fund's duplication of IMF functions, however, was the primary reason formally given by the United States and the IMF for their opposition. Because an increase in IMF resources was pending for 1998, IMF officials argued that it was unnecessary to augment the IMF with a separate fund.[25]

The United States, as well as many European nations, also suspected that Japan would attach softer conditionality to aid from any fund it helped create and argued that doing so would simply promote moral hazard and do little to help the crisis countries in the long run. Sakakibara's idea at this point had moved little beyond an abstract concept and, as a result, its details were not only unavailable to the public but also unclear to its architects. Thus, suspicion spread concerning whether the new fund might bypass the IMF. While MOF officials downplayed the possibility of weaker conditionality attached to an AMF, conditions within Japan lent credibility to the suspicion.[26] Many of Japan's own standards of financial regulation failed to conform to internationally recognized best standards in 1997, and while the government had officially embraced market capitalism in its adoption of legislation to move forward the so-called Big Bang financial reforms, these reforms had yet to be implemented.[27] Moreover, many of the fundamentals on which the IMF focused in establishing conditions for the receipt of funds had fallen into severe disrepair in Japan.[28]

After encountering strong opposition from their U.S. and European counterparts at a meeting of G7 finance ministers and after failing to win a statement of Chinese support by the time of the meeting to discuss the proposal held in conjunction with the IMF-World Bank meeting on September 21, Japanese officials realized that the creation of a regional fund was impossible for the time being. Plans to make a formal proposal for the creation of an AMF were therefore abandoned, for the time being. Few countries in the region wished to move forward with the idea in the face of strong U.S. objections, fearing a souring of relations with the United States. Even Malaysian officials, the most enthusiastic initial supporters of the idea, thought it best not to move forward in the face of U.S. opposition.[29] After all, U.S.-ASEAN relations were viewed as equal in importance to Japan-ASEAN relations. Additionally, contagion had not yet surfaced in Asia, nor had the Russian or Brazilian crises yet occurred.

A More Inclusive Guise for Regional Cooperation:
The Manila Framework

Despite its rejection, the AMF proposal did serve as a wake-up call to U.S. officials, forcing a change in behavior. Treasury Secretary Rubin and

Federal Reserve Chairman Greenspan argued in mid-September that an increase in IMF quotas and new procedures to make loan approval easier in emergencies would sufficiently boost the fund's ability to quell future crises. Yet antipathy towards the United States was high enough at the end of September that some Asian nations sought to exclude American officials from participating in the meeting to discuss Japan's AMF proposal.[30] Also, memos from the U.S. Treasury to high-level administration officials sent at the end of September revealed a new awareness that the measures outlined by Rubin and Greenspan would alone be insufficient to stem the momentum in the region stimulated by the AMF proposal.[31] Nations in the region clearly wished to establish a regional financing mechanism for mobilizing resources to augment IMF support.

With the spread of crisis to Indonesia in October, concerns about the adequacy of the IMF intensified. This spurred U.S. officials, now in agreement on a new strategy for crisis management that involved larger IMF rescue packages plus promises of bilateral aid, to support a more collaborative response to financial crisis within the region. In November 1997, U.S. and Japanese senior finance and central bank officials gathered with counterparts from twelve other countries in the Asia-Pacific region to establish a group to facilitate bilateral financing between countries in the region and to discuss a framework for strengthening regional cooperation toward currency stability.[32] With the spread of crisis beyond Thailand, the IMF's weakness in carrying out regional surveillance became increasingly evident. The assembled countries decided that their finance and central bank deputies would meet biannually to discuss international finance and the conduct of monetary surveillance in the region. Programs of technical support to strengthen the financial sectors and market management in member nations were also proposed. The new forum for collaboration was known thereafter as the Manila Framework Group (MFG). The most notable development to come out of the MFG was the establishment of the Cooperative Financing Arrangement (CFA). Members of this group shared an understanding that each would assist other members who fell into crisis. In this way, the MFG represented a move toward ensuring coordinated bilateral support in case of a future crisis. All assistance would be carried out after an IMF agreement was in place and the CFA would be activated only if IMF resources were found to be inadequate.

Although the CFA involved no permanent pool of funds—or even a secretariat to coordinate responses—it addressed to a limited extent the two problems that had generated earlier demand for a regional fund: resource inadequacy and the speed at which financing could be provided in the case of crisis. Japanese officials stated at the time that they considered "the objective of the Asian Monetary Fund concept to be in line with the newly agreed [upon] Cooperative Financing Arrangement."[33] They would reiterate this sentiment in January 1998.

Resurgence of Support for a More Exclusive Regional Fund

As 1998 progressed, however, the idea of establishing a framework that did not rely on U.S. involvement began to reemerge within Asia. Although the United States participated in the MFG, American officials were seen to convey little "softness" toward the crisis-hit countries.[34] The U.S. government's attitude toward Indonesia, as expressed through the IMF, was perceived among Asian countries as particularly harsh. The IMF allowed Indonesian banks to fail without any system of deposit insurance in place, thereby triggering financial panic in that country. As a result, many banks not initially in dire straits collapsed, with significant repercussions for the populace, a large proportion of whom were just above the poverty line prior to the onset of crisis. Thus, conditions imposed by the IMF in return for its assistance increasingly became a focus of criticism within the region. The perception within Asia by late 1998 to early 1999, furthermore, was that U.S. concern about the crisis in Asia failed to deepen until problems spread beyond the region, affecting Russia and Brazil.[35]

In 1998, Japanese officials also became increasingly outspoken in their criticisms of the IMF. Toyo Gyohten, a former MOF vice minister of finance for international affairs, argued that Japan should play a more prominent role in regional affairs. He further noted that Asia's $600 billion dollars in foreign exchange reserves would have been sufficient to deal with problems had a framework for regional cooperation been established prior to the collapse of the baht.[36] In July 1998, Japan's ambassador to Korea also advocated for the creation of a new Asian fund in an article arguing that the crisis showed the need for East Asian countries to come together.[37]

Japan's diplomatic efforts also revealed attempts to draw closer to its Asian neighbors. In March 1998, Japanese Prime Minister Ryutaro Hashimoto became the first head of state to visit Indonesia after the crisis, while the United States sent a senior cabinet minister. In May of the same year, Foreign Minister Keizō Obuchi also visited Thailand, Malaysia, and Singapore. Japan's drawing closer to Asia in these ways came at the same time as Finance Minister Kiichi Miyazawa hotly contested the IMF's revised growth projections for Japan, announced in July 1998. The

launching of the euro, set for January 1999, heightened fears of the yen's marginalization.

A prerequisite for the receipt of support through the New Miyazawa Initiative was simply "economic reform, taking into account the situation in each country."[41] In those countries with IMF programs in place, this new source of aid complemented IMF assistance. Funds dispersed to Malaysia, Vietnam, and Myanmar, where IMF programs were not in place, however, substituted for rather than supplemented IMF aid. Malaysian officials, having rejected IMF support and imposed capital controls in September 1998, were particularly eager to gain access to another source of funds that was not linked to IMF conditionality.[42]

Notably, the spread of financial weakness across the globe influenced the way U.S. officials perceived such Japanese efforts. With the eruption of financial crisis in Russia in the summer of 1998, the rescue of the mammoth U.S. hedge fund Long-Term Credit Management (LTCM) in September 1998, and serious problems looming in Brazil, the United States now prioritized international financial system stability over more dogmatic concerns. Furthermore, as the scale of financial crisis expanded and the threat of resource inadequacy for dealing with these crises rose, U.S. officials began to better appreciate Japan's provision of financing to the region. Thus, changed circumstances in the international system helped muffle potential U.S. or IMF criticism of Japan's new aid program.

Because the Miyazawa Initiative represented Japan stepping out on its own, however, American and Japanese officials concurred that it was desirable to establish a cooperative scheme, even if in name only. Out of this sentiment arose the Asian Growth and Recovery Initiative, announced jointly by the United States and Japan in November 1998. A major component of this initiative was the establishment of the Asian Currency Crisis Support Facility within the ADB, which was funded solely by Japan, drawing on New Miyazawa Initiative funds. The cooperative nature of the Asian Growth and Recovery Initiative was aimed at countering perceptions of rising tensions between American and Japanese responses to the crisis.[43] In April 1999, Japan and the United States also announced new joint projects to address human security in Asia under the rubric of the U.S.-Japan Common Agenda.

Notably, in this same period, the United States and Japan also worked together within the G7 framework to enhance regional stability and reform the international financial architecture. In October 1998, the G7 endorsed the creation of the Contingency Credit Line (CCL) within the IMF. This mechanism aimed primarily at crisis prevention was then established in April 1999. In the same month, financial authorities from the G7 countries held the first meeting of the Financial Stability Forum (FSF), aimed at making the international system less vulnerable by strengthening regulatory and supervisory measures on highly leveraged hedge funds, offshore markets, and short-term capital flows.

ASEAN+3 and the Chiang Mai Initiative

In 1999, the New Miyazawa Initiative was expanded beyond loans and credit guarantees to include the establishment of backup facilities in the form of currency swap agreements, with the central banks of Korea and Malaysia. The currency swap innovation represented a shift from simply providing aid to assist the crisis-stricken countries in overcoming ongoing economic difficulties to establishing an institutional framework to prevent contagion. This development thus represented another step toward the realization of an AMF as originally conceptualized.

Enhanced sentiment in favor of cooperation within the region in 1998 and 1999 also encouraged the strengthening of a new regional grouping that brought the ASEAN member countries together with Japan, China, and Korea into the ASEAN+3. ASEAN member countries were particularly interested in maximizing the benefits of aid from Japan for all members, including those not hit by crisis. In addition, the multilateral platform of ASEAN+3 was seen as a springboard for strengthened bilateral ties in the region—particularly between Japan and Korea and Japan and China. This strengthening was in turn seen to promote greater overall regional stability.

In January 1999, the ASEAN+3 first met to discuss the establishment of a permanent regional fund. While the ASEAN nations increasingly welcomed a greater leadership role for Japan, they at the same time heightened their expectations that Japanese officials would engage more actively in a process of consultation with regional leaders so as to represent the region in G7 discussions. The administration of Prime Minister Keizō Obuchi was the first to respond to these expectations, and Obuchi's decision in April 1999 to hold the July 2000 G7 summit in Okinawa, closer to the ASEAN nations, was interpreted as symbolic of a shift in Japanese attitudes.

In August 1999, Prime Minister Obuchi also dispatched the Mission for Revitalization of the Asian Economy to the countries hit by crisis to assess Japan's aid programs and identify key areas where Japan might play a role. This mission's findings led Obuchi to announce at the end of November 1999 the Plan for Enhancing Human Resource Development and Human Resource Exchange in East Asia—otherwise known as the Obuchi Plan. This plan would support more people-focused cooperation and aid in the region. Thus, Japan's ties with its Asian neighbors deepened in 1999 as the AMF idea was being reconsidered.

Beginning in 1999, the ASEAN+3 countries expanded their level of co-operation to include an annual finance minister's meeting held back to back with the annual ADB meeting. At an informal ASEAN+3 summit meeting in November 1999 in Manila, member country leaders also is-sued the Joint Statement on East Asia Cooperation, agreeing to use the ASEAN+3 framework to strengthen self-help and mutual support mech-anisms for regional cooperation on monetary and financial matters. In essence, this joint agreement called upon the region's finance ministers to produce something tangible when they met the following year. While countries in the region recognized that the original AMF idea had prob-lems, they now called on Japan for leadership in establishing a regional fund that would supplement the IMF.

One of the greatest criticisms of the IMF was its lack of country exper-tise and its common template for all countries. A regional arrangement was thought to imply superior knowledge of specific events and needs within the region, enabling prescriptions for crisis management to be han-dled with more nuance. In this way, a regional fund was envisioned as more receptive to Asian needs than the generic prescription used by the IMF.[44] A report issued in January 2000 by the Prime Minister's Commis-sion on Japan's Goals in the 21st Century reinforced this sentiment:

If the IMF can be likened to a major hospital caring for the world as a whole, then we should consider supplementing it with the establishment of an Asian Monetary Fund to serve as a "family physician" to provide care at a more inti-mate level. We have reached the stage at which we should take a multilevel ap-proach in the field of finance as well, responding both globally and locally.[45]

At the ASEAN+3 finance ministers' meeting in Chiang Mai, Thailand, in May 2000, views on economic and financial cooperation were ex-changed and a framework for strengthening East Asian financial cooper-ation was announced. The framework centered on currency swaps and had two components: the expansion of an existing ASEAN swap agree-ment (ASA), and the establishment of a network of bilateral swap arrangements (BSAs). Both components were expected to aid in protect-ing against future speculative currency attacks.

The first component, however, was more symbolic than substantial. The ASA expanded an existing swap network among the top four ASEAN countries to all ten ASEAN member nations and increased the amount of funds in this network from $200 million to $1 billion. Yet even this amount remained relatively trivial and the conditions sur-rounding the implementation of these agreements undermined any credi-ble defense against a speculative attack. For example, once a country in the network withdrew funds, other countries in the network were required to wait for six months before being permitted to withdraw funds.[46] Thus, the arrangement did little to stem the chances of contagion. The critical advance made in the Chiang Mai Initiative (CMI)—the network of bilateral currency swaps that included Japan, China, and Korea—was therefore its second component. Participation by these three countries, each a major holder of foreign exchange reserves by this time, enabled a considerable expansion in the scale of the swap facility.

The CMI stated that the arrangement would "supplement existing international facilities."[47] Press guidance on the initiative further stated, however, that the purpose of the BSA was to provide short-term financial assistance to a country "in need of balance-of-payment support *or short-term liquidity support*" (italics added).[48] The need for balance-of-payment support implied a situation in which something was wrong with the recipient country's macroeconomic policy and thereby implied that IMF programs had a relevant role to play. The need for short-term liquidity support, however, implied that for some reason—perhaps unrelated to macroeconomic management—capital was rapidly exiting the country and thus a liquidity injection was required. In such cases, an IMF program was not necessarily relevant. Although Japanese officials argued that the second line of reasoning was invalid—that is, they argued that crisis was never brought about solely by contagion and without any relationship to macroeconomic mismanagement—the ASEAN countries pushed strongly for the latter provision for short-term liquidity support.[49]

Over the following year, the ASEAN+3 countries grappled with contentious issues related to the swap network, such as the degree of linkage with the IMF, the rate of interest, and the strictness of guarantee and disclosure requirements. In April 2001, the finance ministers of the ASEAN+3 countries agreed that disbursement of the swap funds would be conditioned on the swap partner borrowing the equivalent of 90 percent of the swapped amount from the IMF. Only the initial 10 percent of amounts drawn would be provided in the absence of linkage to IMF facilities. Yet even in this case, the swap-providing countries would judge whether the requesting country faced a short-term liquidity problem. Implicit in the conditions therefore is the requirement that recipient countries must fundamentally abide by the strict economic and fiscal conditions attached to lending by the IMF.

Explaining the Reversion

What explains the close linkage today between the IMF and the AMF-like CMI arrangement? The change in approach from the initial AMF idea may now seem even more puzzling, given the previous discussion of rising concerns within the region in 1998–99 about the appropriateness of IMF conditionality. The fact that the CMI built on existing swap arrangements that were not explicitly linked to the IMF also suggests that the linkage was not inevitable. As noted earlier, a currency swap mechanism was already in place among ASEAN core member countries. Furthermore, under the New Miyazawa Initiative, BSAs were already in place between Malaysia and Japan (in the amount of $2.5 billion) and between Korea and Japan (in the amount of $5 billion).

The solution to this puzzle becomes clearer in light of the prerequisites for the sound functioning of any multilateral financing arrangement and the formidable political impediments to putting these elements in place in the near future. As in the case of regional financial institution-building efforts in Europe, countries in Asia began to tackle the critical practical issues of how a new regional financing facility might actually function only *after* making the political decision to move forward with regional financial cooperation. Transforming a new sense of community into a concrete scheme would prove difficult, because it would necessitate reconciliation of the widely varying interests of countries within the region.

Preferences of China and Korea

Under the BSAs, any of the ASEAN+3 countries can be a fund recipient and any can be a donor. Given economic realities, however, the potential donors are essentially only those with substantial foreign exchange reserves—that is, Japan, China, and Korea.[50] In a crisis, Korea and China, as well as Japan, would be called upon to mobilize their reserves.[51] Japan would never be the sole donor. Consequently, China and Korea adopted a conservative stance in the negotiations among the ASEAN+3 countries, favoring close linkage to IMF programs. Doing so minimized the potential demand for capital from their own coffers and ensured that funds lent had a better chance of being repaid. China in particular insisted that the arrangements be closely linked to IMF programs, arguing even for 100 percent linkage.[52]

Preferences of the ASEAN nations

At the other end of the spectrum, Malaysia insisted that no linkage to the IMF was necessary. Because Malaysia already had a swap in place with Japan that was not linked to the IMF and because it had avoided IMF involvement in rebuilding after its crisis, Malaysian officials were particularly upset by the introduction of the IMF at this stage. Other

ASEAN countries, with the exception of Singapore, also preferred weak IMF linkage because the economic realities underlying the bilateral swap agreements meant they were unlikely to be anything but fund recipients.[53] Given this fact, weaker rather than tougher conditions attached to funds meant easier access in times of need. Yet the ASEAN countries were in a weak bargaining position. Although a currency swap facility was already in place among ASEAN member countries, this arrangement lacked anywhere near the level of funds—and hence the level of defense from contagion—that a swap arrangement involving Japan could provide. Thailand and the Philippines in particular recognized that they had no possibility of mounting a credible currency defense without swap agreements. They were thus eager to move ahead and work out agreements with Japan. Malaysia therefore became totally isolated in its opposition to any IMF linkage.[54]

Japanese Arbitration of Divergent Preferences

Having proposed the CMI, Japan played the pivotal arbitrating role in working out the general conditions and principles for the currency swap network. Japanese officials initially assumed a stance in the middle, desiring some—but not necessarily full—linkage to IMF programs. This stance represented a shift from attitudes reflected in Sakakibara's 1997 AMF proposal and a process of reexamination of Japan's national interests. Japan's new stance furthermore reflected the recognition that the IMF had undergone significant reform since the outbreak of the crisis in 1997. The official IMF consensus on many crisis management-related issues and the nature of the fund's response at the outbreak of crisis in the region had evolved over time. Accordingly, IMF linkage in 2001 meant something different than it had in 1997.

The emergence in 1999 of new leadership within Japan's MOF on the backdrop of IMF reform and enhanced Asian representation in other existing multilateral finance-related institutions served as a catalyst for the reevaluation of Japanese national interests. Redefined, these interests resonated more closely with U.S. desires that new regional mechanisms for financial cooperation should supplement existing international institutions.

As noted earlier, the MOF held various conceptualizations of the AMF at the time of the initial proposal in 1997. The domestic and international context at the time lent support to those who envisioned an AMF independent of any U.S. influence, so it was this conceptualization that Japan initially pursued. In 1999, however, Haruhiko Kuroda replaced Sakakibara as the MOF's vice minister of finance for international affairs.

Kuroda also had a long-standing interest in the establishment of an AMF—an interest that in fact predated Sakakibara's.[55] Yet Kuroda's view of the IMF was less critical than the view held by Sakakibara, and his conceptualization of the AMF was of an institution that cooperated rather than competed with the IMF.

One of the weaknesses of the initial AMF proposal was its underdeveloped form.[56] Kuroda felt that the IMF (and the U.S. government) had learned lessons from their mistakes. The IMF's failures with conditionality in Asia were widely recognized and reforms were under way by the time Japanese officials began to work out the terms of the BSAs. Kuroda and his MOF colleagues also acknowledged that IMF involvement was necessary for any new institutional framework to be successful. Not only were the United States and Europe unlikely to support a new framework in the absence of any linkage, but a new regional fund would lack the capacity to carry out needed surveillance of member countries—at least initially. The IMF possessed institutionalized surveillance measures and better information on undertakings in particular countries. Since Japan would be the main provider of funds in any regional institution, having access to the best possible intelligence was in Japan's national interest. Understandably, concern over credible surveillance mechanisms was shared as well by China, Korea, and Singapore—the other top holders of foreign exchange reserves in the ASEAN+3. Today the surveillance issue stands as the largest barrier to any regional monetary institution more independent of the IMF.

Although the May 2000 joint ministerial statement of the ASEAN+3 finance ministers emphasized the important role of surveillance in strengthening East Asian financial cooperation, little progress was made in that area between May 2000 and May 2001.[57] Regardless of how necessary it might be, surveillance such as that carried out by the IMF in its annual Article 4 review of member countries is seen by many countries as intrusive and politically sensitive. Gaining domestic support for the conduct of separate surveillance activities by another agency is extremely difficult, in particular for less politically open countries such as China, Indonesia, and Singapore.[58] In lieu of such surveillance, the presence of a "bad guy" in the form of the IMF is seen as helpful in combating moral hazard and ensuring that borrowed funds are repaid.[59]

Delinkage from the IMF of 10 percent of the assets mobilized under the CMI represented a compromise to placate Malaysia and some of the other ASEAN member nations. As part of the compromise, Japanese officials pledged to work for reform in the IMF quota structure, in the voting system, and in the composition of its board of directors. These reforms were important because East Asia's IMF quotas account for less than 15 percent of the fund's total, despite the fact that the region accounts for more than 20 percent of global gross domestic product, almost a quarter of world trade, and almost half of the world's foreign exchange reserves. Notably, Japan's efforts to spur review of the quota system and increase the strength of the region's representation in the IMF are strongly supported by the United States.[60] Due to the zero sum nature of fund shareholder arrangements, however, an increase in Asian representation necessitates a decrease in the representation of European members.[61] As a result, Japanese and American efforts in this area have encountered strong European resistance.

Japanese officials have also sought to loosen conditions underlying use of the IMF's CCL by member countries. The CCL was established by the fund in the wake of Brazil's crisis in April 1999 and is intended to provide precautionary short-term financing to countries with balance-of-payment problems arising from a sudden loss of market confidence. CCL's aim is to protect countries that are vulnerable to contagion. Yet countries must apply in order to have access to the CCL, and the conditions surrounding application are so unattractive that no country has yet applied. As with the quota issue, U.S. officials have joined Japan in pushing hard for making the facility easier and more attractive for countries to use. In addition to working to advance the aforementioned IMF reforms, Japan has made concerted efforts to address problems with hedge funds and capital movement in its interactions with other G7 nations within the FSF.

American and IMF officials have also expressed support of the network of currency swaps being constructed under the CMI.[62] By May 2001, Japan had reached substantial agreements over the terms and conditions for bilateral swap arrangements with Thailand, South Korea, and Malaysia.[63] The conclusion of swap arrangements with the Philippines and with China followed in July 2001 and March 2002. By September 2002, agreements were also in place between South Korea and the Philippines, China and the Philippines, and China and Thailand. Each agreement enables parties to borrow between $1 and $3 billion dollars in reserves from partners, with the exception of the Japan-China accord, which enables China to borrow yen reserves.[64] Although many would argue that the amounts involved under the CMI remain inadequate for stopping speculative attacks, actors in the region emphasize that the simple process of negotiating and concluding these agreements has had a major impact on the ability of countries in the region to fend off future speculative attacks by giving rise to dense networks of communication—networks that did not exist at the time of the Asian financial crisis—between central bankers and finance ministers in the region.[65]

Conclusion

Japan's 1997 AMF proposal was clearly premature. The original conceptualization of a regional monetary fund was put forward without serious consideration of its practical workings and without significant prior consultation with potential member countries. Given the widely disparate levels of economic development represented among countries in the region and the corresponding variation in their interests, it is difficult to imagine how an AMF could possibly have worked—even in the absence of U.S. opposition.[66]

It is wrong, however, to view the AMF proposal simply as a failure. As this chapter has shown, the proposal forced a shift in U.S. policy despite the failure to establish a concrete institution. Moreover, it helped spur dialogue and debate over the prerequisites for successful regional financial cooperation. In addition, current institution-building efforts by the ASEAN+3 nations in the form of a network of regional currency swap continue to influence U.S. and IMF behavior in important ways, even though these arrangements remain closely linked to IMF conditionality. Moreover, the process of negotiating the CMI arrangements, led by Japan, has served to build strong networks of communication among central bankers and finance ministers in the region—networks that alone go a long way toward preventing a reoccurrence of regional financial crisis.

This chapter has also shown that there were significant examples of cooperation in U.S.-Japan relations after the eruption of the Asian financial crisis. Despite the bitter fight over the AMF in August and September 1997, Japanese officials ultimately joined forces with the U.S. administration during the Asian crisis. As time progressed, U.S. officials became increasingly appreciative of Japan's willingness to take a more proactive role in helping to maintain regional financial stability. Moreover, the evidence suggests that Japan has no intention of abandoning participation in existing institutions such as the IMF. Japanese officials have actively worked to reform existing institutions while at the same time leading efforts to establish a new framework for regional monetary cooperation. In these ways, the increased utilization of multilateral forums need not be incompatible with strengthened bilateral relations.

Nonetheless, the adoption of close linkage to IMF programs by the ASEAN+3 countries in their network of BSAs to date does not guarantee close linkage into the future, nor does it symbolize an end to efforts to create the AMF. If the ASEAN+3 nations are able to develop an independent surveillance capacity, then future delinkage from the IMF is entirely possible. Such delinkage would in turn likely mean a loss of American influence in the region. Japanese officials continue to aggressively pursue the idea of an Asian regional monetary institution and have obtained considerable support from their Asian neighbors.[67] Given that East Asia holds the largest pool of foreign exchange reserves of any region in the world, and given that an inherently different cost-benefit structure arises from geographical proximity, some regional actors foresee a time when IMF primacy may no longer be taken for granted and when an IMF and AMF might function in separate but equal fashions.[68]

Even so, there is no indication that a truly independent regional monetary institution would represent an alternative model to financial crisis management that is distinctively Asian on an ideological level. Dramatically different stages of economic development in the region, combined with disparate political regimes, present East Asia with particularly daunting challenges to institution building compared to the challenges experienced by Europe. These factors also limit the degree to which Japan can effectively lead in the region, even if such leadership is encouraged by the United States as a form of burden sharing by Japan in the provision of the public good of regional financial stability.

While a clear consensus has emerged in East Asia that a global or U.S.-determined solution to financial problems in the region is insufficient, regional actors face difficulties in creating an alternative institution. Presently, lacking an institutionalized mechanism for surveillance of member countries, the ASEAN+3 group has no other choice but to rely heavily on the IMF. Competence building in this area and in intervention and other aspects of currency management over time might be expected to decrease the need for future reliance on the IMF. Yet the prospects for significant capacity building in the near future remain hindered by the resistance of many of the ASEAN+3 countries to opening up their books and domestic affairs to another actor in addition to the IMF. Without greater receptivity to surveillance activities, any new regional institution will lack the capacity to tailor crisis management prescriptions to particular country contexts—an objective that appeared to be foremost in the minds of many regional actors during the Asian financial crisis.

Monetary cooperation within East Asia has clearly moved beyond the embryonic stage. Yet the evolution of greater independence from the IMF for a new regional monetary institution remains impeded by a number of factors. Among these, U.S. objection represents one of the less formidable barriers. The most prominent limitations to regional institution building today are to be found within Asia.

PART III

MULTILATERAL ORGANIZATIONS

At Play in the Legal Realm

THE WTO AND THE CHANGING NATURE OF
U.S.-JAPAN ANTIDUMPING DISPUTES

SAADIA M. PEKKANEN

In a public statement released on October 20, 1999, the Japanese minister of international trade and industry put the U.S. government on alert about a bilateral trade dispute involving the steel industry. Japan, the statement proclaimed, would be challenging U.S. final antidumping determinations on certain hot-rolled steel from Japan, not bilaterally as it had done in the past but rather under the legal auspices of the World Trade Organization (WTO).[1] Two days later, a more caustic letter emerged from the vice minister of international affairs, again directed at the United States.[2] The heart of the letter was concerned with some inflammatory remarks made by the U.S. undersecretary of commerce for international trade, who had allegedly criticized Japan's ambitions to further antidumping discipline in the WTO and also Japan's status as the "'greatest dumping country in the world.'" Pointing out that Japan and the United States suffered almost equally from antidumping cases, the letter suggested that the United States, like Japan and other developing countries, should pay serious attention to strengthening the antidumping agenda in the next WTO round.

All this rhetoric was designed to signal Japan's strong interest in using a rule-based approach to resolving trade disputes, particularly those with the United States. Since 1995, Japan has followed up this rhetoric with both offensive and defensive action in the high-profile legal setup of the WTO across a number of cases and issues. This WTO activity is unusual given Japan's nonlegalistic and nonconfrontational trade policy in the past.[3] In addition, the emphasis on legalistic tactics in a global multilateral setting stands in marked contrast to Japan's nonlegalistic activities in regional multilateral settings, as traced by Ashizawa and Krauss and in Chapters 11 and 12, respectively, in this volume. Yet given the actions against the United States thus far, there is little question that the Japanese government has put increasing and deliberate emphasis on legalization in the global multilateral context. By legalization is meant the overall emphasis on the precision of the legal rules of the WTO, the obligations they engender, and their central role in WTO panel and appellate body adjudication of trade disputes.[4] One of the main reasons for the emphasis on legal rules in the WTO is that there is no other forum—multilateral, regional, bilateral, or otherwise—that allows Japan to deal with the United States in an area of concern to both the Japanese government and industry, namely dumping and antidumping. Dumping, as understood in the WTO agreements, is when an exporter sells goods in a market at a price less than the price at which the goods are sold in the exporter's home market or less than the cost of production of the goods. The difference in either the price or the cost is called the *margin of dumping*, and under the WTO agreements members have the right to counter such practices legally, such as through antidumping remedies. Unlike other areas that lack legalized multilateral discipline, such as international finance, where the Japanese are reluctant to confront the United States, the antidumping issue under the auspices of the WTO provides an excellent illustration of the way U.S.-Japanese trade relations have been changing as a whole. In fact, the way in which antidumping disputes are increasingly being resolved between the two countries is a harbinger of things to come in the context of U.S.-Japan trade disputes more generally.

This chapter therefore focuses exclusively on longitudinal and substantive changes in U.S.-Japan trade relations in the context of antidumping disputes, although it also highlights the burgeoning importance of such disputes in Japan's trade relations with other Asian countries, especially China. For most of the postwar period, Japan did not overtly challenge the internal means and procedures by which the United States determined antidumping measures against Japanese products. Japanese discontent, in both the public and private sectors, existed but was almost always handled strictly bilaterally by the two countries. Since the birth of the WTO in 1995, however, Japan has taken up the banner against antidumping in the WTO arena far more forcefully. Thus far, Japan's legal complaints and actions concern the United States most directly, and they have already had an important impact on the way Japan intends to push antidumping disputes out of the previously U.S.-Japan bilateral context and under the fully legalized multilateral auspices of the WTO.

The focus here is on tracing the chronological and legal developments that signify the emergence of what I call a new "legalized paradigm" for trade relations between the United States and Japan. The main argument, in brief, is that the substantive and procedural rules of the WTO at the heart of this emerging paradigm have changed the way antidumping disputes now unfold between the United States and Japan. As this chapter demonstrates, the presence of international law—more specifically, the legalized multilateral system of the WTO with formal adjudication processes at its core—has increasingly become a source of national power for countries with relatively weak bargaining powers in the global trade arena. This in turn holds important policy implications not only for the future of U.S.-Japan trade relations as a whole, but also for the resolution of similar trade conflicts in the WTO system in the future.

The remainder of this chapter is organized into four main parts. The first part begins by demonstrating the centrality of antidumping disputes in the broader context of U.S.-Japan relations in the WTO. It then lays out an overview of the key longitudinal and cross-sectional trends pertaining to U.S. antidumping measures. This constitutes the departure point for the rest of the analysis, especially because, as the historical data across a number of foreign exporters show, U.S. remedies have been invoked most consistently and frequently against the Japanese steel industry over the postwar period. This data examination leaves no doubt that the political actions of the steel industry in the United States, and consequently the reactions of the steel industry in Japan, have been central to antidumping disputes. This much has not changed in the post-WTO world, and even today the steel industry continues to play this key role. But as the broader U.S.-Japan relations in the WTO dispute settlement processes show, the main change is that the Japanese government is no longer butting heads bilaterally with the United States, but rather is using the legal rules of the WTO to challenge the antidumping determinations of the U.S. government.

The second part outlines the specifics of the Antidumping Agreement (AD Agreement) overseen by the WTO that are relevant to antidumping determinations and implementations, and also highlights the problematic significance of the "standard of review" concept to the adjudication process as a whole. Apart from this technical legal background, this part also provides a brief overview of all antidumping disputes in the WTO within which U.S.-Japan interactions are embedded.

The third part then zeroes in on Japanese actions against the United States. While Japan has generally taken a keen interest in pushing for the antidumping area in conjunction with other members of the WTO, it has also been unilaterally active in two distinct ways within the formal dispute settlement processes. For one thing, since 1998 Japan has been carefully appearing as a third-party in a range of antidumping disputes, most of which involve complaints against U.S. procedures and implementations. For another, Japan is increasingly aggressive in challenging U.S. antidumping measures more directly. On this front, it has already prevailed legally in two cases against the United States, one concerning the Antidumping Act of 1916 and the other related to antidumping determinations on imports of hot-rolled steel from Japan. More recently, as part of a nine-member team, it is also engaged in consultations regarding controversial practices under the U.S. Continued Dumping and Subsidy Offset Act of 2000, better known as the Byrd Amendment. The larger point is that the United States has been suffering legal setbacks with respect to antidumping disputes as a whole, and doing so especially when Japan has been involved as a third party or direct complainant. These "wins" further legitimate Japan's legal tactics in the WTO arena, and this legitimacy extends to disputes beyond the antidumping arena, and even beyond disputes with the United States. As sketched out briefly in this section, the use and abuse of trade remedies is also becoming an important part of Japanese trade diplomacy toward its Asian neighbors, such as China.

The fourth part concludes the chapter with an overall assessment of the argument that Japan uses WTO rules to challenge the legality of U.S. antidumping actions in a multilateral setting, a strategy that is far removed from the overall bilateral U.S.-Japan paradigm that many observers still continue to stress. The chapter then extracts policy implications for both the United States and Japan for antidumping disputes in particular, and from these implications draws broader conclusions about the impact of the WTO rules on the future of U.S.-Japan trade diplomacy in general. Despite the ongoing trend in which the WTO is becoming the centerpiece of Japan's foreign trade diplomacy, the United States continues to view its trading relations with Japan through an outmoded bilateral prism. The chapter ends by summarizing and discussing how and in what ways Japan has moved beyond bilateralism, and why the United States should do the same in order to handle future trade disputes with Japan more effectively.

U.S.-Japan Antidumping Disputes and the Role of the Steel Industry

Antidumping duties have been a long-standing means of redress for goods and products imported into the United States. Along with countervailing duties, antidumping duties are regarded as part of the process of administered protection under U.S. "fair" trade laws, through which industries have increasingly sought import relief vis-à-vis their competitors. In fact, administered protection is now widely regarded as *the* "protectionist weapon of choice."[5] Because of the emphasis on unfair foreign trade practices, administered protection also has the advantage of appearing consistent with U.S. liberal trade stances while at the same time appearing to head off domestic demands for protection. Due to their increased use, U.S. antidumping practices have become a key source of concern to the major trade partners of the United States. Not surprisingly, in June 2000, the U.S. General Accounting Office reported that within the WTO's dispute settlement system, antidumping complaints were among the two most important sources (the other being textiles) of cases against U.S. practices.[6]

It is helpful to place antidumping disputes in the broader context of U.S.-Japan relations within the WTO. To many observers, a cursory overview of the WTO dispute settlement process would seem to confirm the perception that Japanese trade policy as a whole is nonlegalistic. Within the WTO, the United States makes up the lion's share of the dispute settlement process, followed by the European Union (EU). Of the 187 complaints filed by WTO members between the start of 1995 and the end of 2000, 30 percent have been brought by the United States, 26 percent by the EU, and a mere 4 percent by Japan.[7] But broad numbers do not capture the whole story, and the concentration of cases is of the utmost importance in forecasting the fault lines, as far as the future of U.S.-Japan trade relations is concerned.

The United States has been most interested in pursuing cases related to agriculture, intellectual property, and taxes and subsidies.[8] Of the five complaints it has filed against Japan since 1995 to the present, two were concerned with agricultural disputes.[9] The United States managed to prevail in both cases, but lost badly in the high-profile Fuji-Kodak dispute that may well have deterred it from dealing with Japan in the WTO on related issues of concern in the domestic Japanese marketplace. The 1996 Fuji-Kodak case essentially involved issues of competition policy that Kodak alleged were causing it market-access problems in Japan. Because the WTO rules on competition policy are rudimentary, and because the Japanese government strenuously maintained that the marketplace and not the government was determining outcomes in this case, it was able to shield its domestic practices from rigorous foreign scrutiny.

If the Fuji-Kodak case was disappointing from the U.S. perspective, it served only to galvanize Japan's interest in legalizing its trade disputes with the United States.[10] To borrow from Katada's chapter in this volume, Japanese government officials quickly came to perceive of WTO legal rules as a "counterweight strategy" for dealing with the United States. Japan then went on the offensive, focusing on antidumping disputes, which have long been a major bone of contention between the two coun-

IMF's downward revision to o percent growth for Japan came just as the Liberal Democratic Party headed into a tough battle in the Upper House Diet elections. Such pessimistic growth projections undermined the credibility of the government's less-than-aggressive policies toward the banking sector's nonperforming loan problem.

Criticism of the IMF's handling of the crisis in Asia and perceptions that America lacked appropriate levels of concern for the crisis-stricken countries thus helped revive regional interest in establishing a non-U.S.-dominated lender of last resort. Whereas in 1997 many countries in the region had been wary of excluding the United States from any new regional institution, these same countries now welcomed Japanese leadership in setting up an institution focused more narrowly on Asia. There was a growing conviction that Asia needed a champion with a loud voice and that this champion could only be Japan.

The New Miyazawa Initiative

Since the outbreak of crisis in Thailand in July 1997, Japan had funneled huge amounts of aid to the crisis-stricken countries through the IMF and existing aid mechanisms.[38] In October 1998, however, Miyazawa announced a new program of bilateral aid—dubbed the New Miyazawa Initiative—that would provide up to $30 billion in loans and loan guarantees to help revive the five countries hit by crisis.[39] Most countries were out of acute crisis by this time but still needed funds to proceed with economic development and to deal with ongoing economic difficulties.

The New Miyazawa Initiative was seen as an initial step toward the revival of attempts to establish the AMF. Through bilateral programs of aid to countries in the region, Japanese officials hoped to foster greater trust between Japan and its regional neighbors. Strengthened trust was in turn seen as a prerequisite for the future realization of a Japan-led multilateral regional institution.[40]

The new program of aid was also seen as furthering more tangible Japanese interests. By strengthening market confidence in recipient countries and thereby spurring the resumption of private lending in these economies, the aid was intended to help restore sound trade and investment ties between the crisis-hit countries and Japan. Through the extension of yen-denominated loans to the region, the New Miyazawa Initiative was also seen as furthering long-standing efforts to internationalize the yen. Since the 1980s, MOF officials had argued for the need to encourage more widespread use of the yen around the globe. Despite Japan's having the second largest economy in the world, its currency failed to figure prominently into international financial markets, and the tries. Japan has not only been active in terms of sponsoring negotiations concerned with strengthening antidumping remedies in the WTO, but it has also filed cases that demonstrate its substantive interest in the matter, especially vis-à-vis the United States. Five of the eight complaints filed by Japan have been against the United States, and three of those five have been high-profile cases in which Japan has concentrated its legal firepower against U.S. antidumping practices. From Japan's perspective, as from that of many other countries, there have been and continue to be significant abuses of U.S. antidumping remedies by U.S. industry.

This situation necessitates a look at domestic U.S. processes from the perspective of both the government and industry. For both antidumping duties and countervailing duties, the process of establishing whether an imported product is being dumped or subsidized is carried out by both the International Trade Administration (ITA) at the U.S. Department of Commerce (USDOC) and the United States International Trade Commission (USITC).[11] Both make a preliminary and final determination, with the ITA concentrating on sales of import at less than fair value (LTFV) and the USITC concentrating on material injury to the domestic industry.[12] The key issue is whether or not a duty is ordered, after either a positive preliminary determination at the ITA or a positive final determination by both the ITA and the USITC. Both of these, from the perspective of government-supplied protectionism, are important regardless of whether the supposed benefit accruing to the domestic industry is temporary or not.[13]

In the context of U.S.-Japan trade relations, there are of course a few sensational cases that have allowed the antidumping issue to take center stage. Among the most well-known was the severe trade friction and subsequent antidumping petition activity in the semiconductor industry.[14] The early 1980s saw cyclical downturns in the semiconductor industry, and the astonishing rise and domination of the Dynamic Random Access Memory (DRAM) market by Japanese companies. The Semiconductor Industry Association (SIA), formed in 1977, first began to lobby the U.S. government for trade relief between 1981 and 1982, but it was not until 1985 that the industry went into a severe recession and turned to bilateral recourses for trade relief specifically vis-à-vis Japan. In June 1985, the SIA filed a section 301 petition—in essence a complaint about market barriers in Japan—at the U.S. Trade Representative (USTR).

More pertinent to this analysis, a number of the major companies filed antidumping petitions between July and September 1985 (Micron on 65K DRAMS; Intel, AMD, and National Semiconductor on EPROMS, or Erasable, Programmable, Read-Only Memory chips), and the Commerce Department initiated investigations in that year (on 256K and DRAMS). In May 1986, the House of Representatives voted 408 to 5 to recommend retaliation under Section 301 unless there was a market access agreement. In June 1986, the USITC issued its final ruling of affirmative material injury in the case of 64K DRAMS, which would remain the last word on the dispute until the final ruling by the USDOC.

Because of the large preliminary antidumping findings and material injury decisions, U.S. negotiators were able to demand very specific bilateral trade relief from Japan. Confronted with the automatic and non-negotiable imposition of these duties as well as by the possibility of Section 301 action, both of which strengthened the United States' negotiating position, Japan had to settle the case. This resulted eventually in the first five-year semiconductor agreement in 1986. This agreement was concerned with the dumping of Japanese semiconductors in the American market as well as in the third market, but it was also, in departure from previous approaches, concerned with the access of American companies to the Japanese market. This process of extreme political pressure at the domestic level in the United States followed by judicialized antidumping petition activity appeared to pave the way for some sort of direct bilateral agreement with foreign trade partners. More important, this process established a pattern for other U.S. industries to follow suit.

Or did it? Apart from the celebrated semiconductor case, what exactly are the facts with respect to antidumping petition activity and U.S. government responses, especially where Japan is concerned? The answer to this question relies on a simple statistical examination of the cross-sectional and longitudinal data derived from official U.S. compilation from 1960 to the late 1990s.[15] One phenomenon that instantly commands our attention across the data is, contrary to widespread perceptions, the overall lack of U.S. government protection provided through these trade remedies. Actual antidumping duty orders relative to total number of petitions fell to 33 percent in the early 1980s and did not do hugely better at 54 percent in the late 1980s.[16] The other salient factor is the petition activity by industry. Here, the historical data show that such activity is highest in the steel-related industry that has been at the heart of most of the controversial U.S.-Japan disputes in the antidumping arena. The U.S. steel industry has accounted for about 45 percent of all manufacturing antidumping petitions filed between 1960 and 1997. In the aggregate, however, it has benefited from the imposition of antidumping duty orders only 48 percent of the time.[17]

The regional aspect is similarly concentrated, and it is here that Japan begins to stand out most visibly. Antidumping duty orders against Japan have been strikingly high across all industries, especially in comparison to the EU and Western European countries. Actual antidumping duty orders peaked in the late 1980s and early 1990s when the debates over U.S. "declinism" (the relative economic decline of the United States in comparison to the other advanced industrial countries) and unfair Japanese trade practices were in full force. Of the 111 antidumping petitions filed against Japanese industries from 1960 to 1997, 67 percent actually saw antidumping duty orders imposed. The petition activity was also especially concentrated in the steel-related industries, and resulted in antidumping duty orders being imposed about 60 percent of the time, compared to 40 percent for the European cases.

Since the steel industry appears to be central to U.S.-Japan antidumping disputes in general, it is important to understand its role in the domestic political process. In both the United States and Japan, the steel industry is widely regarded as an economically influential and politically powerful actor. This domestic fact remains central to understanding the interest that both governments show in the fate of their steel industries, whether they are butting heads in a bilateral or a multilateral arena.

In the United States, the steel industry has long been one of the most influential and powerful sectors in the American political arena. "Big Steel" has referred to the giant, vertically integrated firms such as US Steel, LTV Steel, and Bethlehem Steel, and their union counterpart, the United Steelworkers of America.[18] Along with steel-community congressional representatives, the integrated steel firms and steelworkers have formed a "steel triangle" that has been particularly active in terms of garnering protection. The standard way in which this triangle has attempted to influence steel import policy is to use, or threaten to use, antidumping or countervailing duty processes in order to obtain some agreement that would help stabilize U.S. prices. To make a long story short, the U.S. domestic, rule-based antidumping processes have allowed the industry to credibly deter their rivals and to force a series of quantitative settlements of steel disputes from the late 1960s onward.[19] Despite the fact that employment is on the decline in the steel industry as a whole, going from about 512,000 workers in the mid-1970s to only about 140,000 in the early 1990s, and despite the fact that mammoth steel companies no longer dominate the domestic markets due to the rise of minimills, Big Steel retains considerable political clout and is very effective at making its views known to politicians.

As in the past, so today the U.S. steel industry's lobbying efforts stem from its well-publicized arguments that unfair foreign competition is the root cause of its economic demise. One of its most consistent arguments is that overcapacity in foreign countries is the principal cause of dumping in the United States. Apart from demanding direct legislative relief or apart from participating in talks about multilateral steel agreements (MSAs), the data, as discussed earlier, certainly show that the U.S. steel industry has been most active in attempting to use trade remedy laws concerned with antidumping and countervailing duties. Much the same story remains true even today.

After the 1997 Asian financial crisis, it was widely expected that there would be a surge of protectionist pressures in the United States. Such a surge was not long in coming. There was intense anxiety, articulated especially well by the U.S. steel industry, about the likelihood of dumping by Asian exporters.[20] By September 1998, major U.S. steel companies and their unions had announced plans to seek government protection against allegedly unfair and illegal dumping practices, singling out Japan in particular, among other countries.[21] As the pressures from the steel industry mounted, the Clinton administration began to move toward concrete action, including expedited antidumping investigations, to protect the domestic industry.[22]

In the meantime, the Japanese steel industry, now reeling under the twin effects of the domestic recession and the Asian financial crisis, began also to voice its concerns zealously to the Japanese government about the potential loss of the U.S. export market and the discriminatory import treatment that would result from that loss.[23] This brings us to the other part of the domestic political argument, this time in Japan. Like the U.S. steel industry, the Japanese steel industry enjoys considerable political clout. At the heart of the major antidumping disputes are some of Japan's largest steel makers—Nippon Steel Corporation, NKK Corporation, and Kawasaki Steel Corporation. Together, these firms account for 90 percent of all known exports of steel during the more recent antidumping disputes.[24] By all accounts, these are some of the most politically powerful firms in Japan. Together they boast sales levels of about half a billion dollars, and employment levels nearing at least a hundred thousand people. In addition, they hold tremendous lobbying power through their industry association, which as a further sign of the industry's political influence is only one of three industries whose offices are located in the Keidanren (Japan Federation of Economic Organizations) Building, which hosts the most influential players in Japanese business. An additional well-documented fact is that the Japanese steelmakers are also patriotically supported by Japanese domestic steel users, making them even more potent in terms of their influence.[25]

Thus, the steel industries in both the United States and Japan are the major actors in the unfolding disputes over antidumping. The ongoing disputes are not new. The arena in which they are battling and the legal ways in which they are battling, however, are new. As traced below across a number of antidumping disputes, the new context makes all the difference. The simple point is that the substantive and procedural rules of the WTO change the ways in which the bilateral conflicts are handled and tensions diffused. To get to that story, we turn next to the WTO's AD Agreement and to what it potentially means for handling trade disputes related to antidumping between member states.

The AD Agreement and the Standard of Review

Dumping, and more specifically antidumping, has been enshrined in the General Agreement on Tariffs and Trade (GATT) since its inception in 1947 in the form of Article VI, which addresses antidumping and countervailing duties.[26] Article VI, which defines dumping in terms of price and cost differentials, remains today the core international rule regarding dumping. It specifically allows members to offset or prevent dumping through the imposition of an antidumping duty that is not greater than the margin of dumping. In general, however, members can do so only in the event that the dumping causes or threatens material injury or material impediments.

In addition, because of procedural differences in the calculations of dumping margins and because of widespread concern that these may lead to new trade barriers, there has also been a stand-alone "antidumping code" that resulted from both the Kennedy Round in 1967 and the Tokyo Round in 1979.[27] Finally, at the conclusion of the Uruguay Round in 1994, the 1979 code was subsumed formally under the GATT as the Agreement on Implementation of Article VI of the General Agreement on Tariffs and Trade 1994, or AD Agreement or Code, for short. The AD Agreement consists of eighteen articles and two annexes. It starts by stating clearly that antidumping measures are to be applied only under the circumstances laid out in Article VI of GATT 1994, and then proceeds to explicate procedural elements such as the determination of dumping, determination of injury, definition of domestic industry, and so on.

Apart from its legal clarity, the AD Agreement also has a direct bearing on the issue of sovereignty. This is because WTO panels, in their deliberations, are confronted with national procedures and acts, such as for determining antidumping duties, which may conflict with the WTO rules. In these cases, the issue is whether such national determinations should prevail, and to what extent, in the adjudication of the disputes. In other words, panels have to know when to approach a dispute de novo and when to respect national government determinations. This process is known as the *standard of review* and is regarded as central to the sovereignty debate in a WTO world because it is fundamentally about the allocation of power between an international tribunal and national government authorities when visible economic interests are at stake.[28]

Article 17.6 of the AD Agreement lays out the two-part antidumping standard of review. This states clearly that the panel cannot overturn a national government evaluation if the establishment of facts was proper and the evaluation was unbiased and objective, even though the panel might have reached a different conclusion.[29] Practically, what this means is that if a national government imposes an antidumping order, it has to prove that such an order is based on processes that are unbiased and objective, and that, more broadly, such processes do not favor the interests of the domestic industry. In the context of antidumping complaints against the United States, this is the most contested provision, especially when duties have been imposed. What this means is that Japan, for example, can directly challenge the internal means and procedures through which the United States both determines and imposes duties, and it can do so because of the underlying rule-based claim that the U.S. government shows bias and partiality in determining antidumping margins for Japanese firms. While Japan certainly did protest bilaterally against the imposition of antidumping duties by the United States in the past, it is only now, in the context of the WTO rules, that it is directly butting heads with the United States on this front.

From the perspective of domestic industries in the United States, such as steel, that have made heavy use of antidumping petitions, having a stringent standard of review is important because an international body cannot overturn domestic outcomes that could be more favorable to them. This is why antidumping disputes in the context of the WTO dispute settlement processes can be heavily politicized, especially in a case involving the United States in which there was a spate of domestic antidumping activity, as in the aftermath of the Asian financial crisis.

Some of this activity also inevitably spilled over into the legalized dispute settlement arena of the WTO. From the inception of the WTO in 1995 through October 2001, a total of 239 disputes were brought either partially or fully to the WTO dispute settlement system.[30] Of these disputes, approximately 30 have involved antidumping measures of some sort across a range of industries and countries. Not surprisingly, given the centrality of administered protectionism in its domestic processes, as traced in the previous section, the United States stands out here as a defendant. Of the 30 complaints, almost half were concerned with challenges by other countries against U.S. antidumping measures. Thus far, the complainants have been Latin American and, especially, Asian countries. Notably, the United States has brought only one related complaint against Mexico, regarding high-fructose corn syrup, and this complaint was allowed to lapse initially and then was reinstated formally a year later. In short, the United States remains a defender rather than a challenger of antidumping practices in the dispute settlement processes of the WTO.

There are as yet no antidumping complaints against Japan, which gives it the moral high ground in challenging U.S. measures in this area. Although the Japanese government understands that challenges to the U.S. antidumping procedures and the whole issue of standard of review are politically sensitive and can potentially cause backlashes at the domestic level, this has not stopped it from attempting to legalize antidumping conflicts. In stark contrast to its behavior in the past, Japan also does not appear to step back when the politically powerful interests of the U.S. steel industry are at stake. In fact, as the next section traces more closely, Japan, which has helped lead the antidumping crusade against the United States at a macro level, has brought three direct complaints and been involved in four others concerning U.S. antidumping measures. Almost all of these complaints are related directly or indirectly to the economic fate of the Japanese steel industry, which is one of the U.S. steel industry's most serious competitors.

Japan's Antidumping Agenda at the WTO

Both the history of antidumping disputes between the United States and Japan and the surge of U.S. antidumping activity against Japan in the aftermath of the Asian financial crisis brought home to the Japanese government the importance of conflicts in this area. At the Seattle talks in 1999, Japan moved formally, visibly, and with some seriousness to pursuing the antidumping agenda. The two main ministries involved in the process—the Ministry of Economy, Trade, and Industry (METI, formerly and at that point the Ministry of International Trade and Industry, or MITI) and the Ministry of Foreign Affairs (MOFA)—agreed in principle that antidumping discipline in the WTO needed to be strengthened and clarified, but they disagreed on the extent to which this new agenda could be pushed in the WTO, especially because the United States was both passive and recalcitrant on the subject.[31] Although the antidumping agenda ultimately moved from the principal negotiators to the executive level, involving President Clinton and Prime Minister Obuchi, there is also disagreement about the extent to which it was the principal cause for the breakdown of the Seattle talks.[32]

Whatever the points of disagreements, however, the fact is that the antidumping agenda continues to loom large for the Japanese side. In fact, antidumping is one of the most important agenda items for the next WTO round as far as Japan, in conjunction with both the EU and other developing countries, especially in Asia, is concerned. Working in the multilateral context, Japan has won the full backing of both the EU and other

Asian countries, such as Korea, which are likewise concerned about rampant antidumping duties, especially in the United States. The ever-present danger, as in the U.S. domestic arena, as described earlier, is that antidumping measures can also become the protectionist weapon of choice in the multilateral WTO system. This is something that Japan is adamant about preventing.

If rhetoric alone is not convincing enough, then Japan's use of the WTO dispute settlement system to address antidumping measures should be proof enough of the seriousness with which Japan takes the matter. In addition to pushing for enlarging and strengthening the WTO's underlying antidumping rules, Japan has also been engaged in deliberate tactics to deal with related disputes. Specifically, within the WTO dispute settlement processes it has moved toward emphasizing legalization of its trade disputes on two fronts—as third-party and as direct complainant. Both of these efforts highlight the emerging emphasis on the legalized paradigm between the United States and Japan.[33] This section also sketches the Sino-Japanese dispute of 2001 and ends by showing the importance of antidumping disputes beyond the narrow confines of the U.S.-Japan relationship.

Third-Party Rights and Learning

On one front, Japan has been almost conscientious in learning about and voicing opinions in formal cases brought by other member states against U.S. antidumping practices. It has done this predominantly by asserting its legal rights as a third party, allowed for under the rules of the Dispute Settlement Understanding (DSU).[34] As a third party to antidumping disputes at the WTO, Japan can claim, according to the DSU rules, a "substantial interest" in a matter before a panel and thereby have its opinions heard by the panel. It also has the right to make written submissions to the panel, which are then reflected in the final report. As a third party to a dispute, at the first meeting of the panel it can also receive submissions from the two parties directly engaged in the dispute as complainant and defendant. This process potentially allows a third party, such as Japan, to assess the legal merits of cases that are similar to those it is interested in pursing in formal panel processes later on.

The third party can then, if it so desires, go on to initiate its own panel proceedings regarding the disputed measure if it believes that the same measure is nullifying or impairing benefits accruing to it under any covered agreement. Such a dispute is referred to the original panel whenever possible. This means that if a favorable precedent is set from the perspective of an interested third party in another dispute, then, other things being equal, that third party is likely to prevail in a similar dispute with the same panel of judges. This is essentially one of the main advantages for countries with weak legal resources, such as Japan, which can weigh the outcome of a similar legal case without having to go through the expense and time required to mount a legal challenge. At least four antidumping cases presented at the WTO after the Asian financial crisis stand out in this respect. Each is discussed briefly here.

In April 1998, Japan became interested in a case in which Poland challenged the imposition of Thai antidumping duties on a range of steel products.[35] Japan subsequently joined the case as a third party in November 1999. In that case, the panel questioned not just the objectivity of the calculations carried out by the Thai authorities, but also, thereby, the causal relationship between the dumped products and domestic injury. Overall, the panel concluded, and upon appeal the Appellate Body later concurred, that Thailand had acted inconsistently with provisions of the AD Agreement and had thereby nullified and impaired benefits to the complainant. This was among the first cases from which Japan could learn about panel deliberations and treatment of national procedures regarding implementation.

In November 1998, Japan requested and was denied "enhanced third-party rights" in an EU complaint against the U.S. Antidumping Act of 1916.[36] Japan did, however, become a third party to the dispute. In this case, the EU challenged the act as an antidumping measure that targeted imports and price discrimination, contrary to the provisions allowing such actions in the AD Agreement. The panel ruled that the United States was indeed contravening key aspects of the AD Agreement, and as such was nullifying and impairing benefits to the EU. Because Japan went on to establish another panel in respect to the 1916 act, the EU case set an important precedent with respect to the same contested measure that almost guaranteed that Japan would similarly prevail.

In September 1999, India initiated a formal complaint against the EU's antidumping duties on imports of cotton bed linens from India.[37] In this case as well Japan reserved its third-party rights. India charged that both the procedures and the findings were inconsistent with the provisions of the AD Agreement. Although the panel dismissed some aspects of India's case, it also found some legal contraventions on the EU's part. Like the other cases, this case also highlighted the fact that even if complainants did not prevail outright in antidumping disputes, they could at least do so partially.

Finally, in November 1999, Japan also appeared as a third party in Korea's case against US antidumping measures on certain steel products.[38]

Korea's claim was that the U.S. procedural determinations of antidumping duties were not only erroneous but also inconsistent with provisions of the AD Agreement. As in other similar cases, the Panel found that while not all of the challenged actions by the US constituted breaches of the AD Agreement, there were some important legal violations. In large part, the panel upheld the legal charges brought by Korea and set an important precedent for weaker actors confronting U.S. antidumping measures in a legal setting. This case in particular set an important precedent for the subsequent Japanese cases regarding the steel sector, which has been at the heart of many trade disputes between the United States and Japan.

Complainant Rights and Confrontation

In addition to learning from antidumping cases against both the United States and other countries, Japan has also directly confronted the United States in the WTO dispute settlement processes. At least two cases stand out in this respect: the U.S. Antidumping Act of 1916 and the U.S. antidumping duties on hot-rolled steel from Japan. In conjunction with other complainants, Japan has also recently challenged the Byrd Amendment. These cases are discussed here, with a focus on highlighting the way Japan has been legalizing antidumping disputes with the United States.

Japan's first formal complaint against U.S. antidumping measures concerned a U.S. statute originally enacted as Title VIII of the Revenue Act of 1916 and more commonly known as the Antidumping Act of 1916 (hereafter called the 1916 Act), about which the EU had also complained.[39] The provision under challenge dealt specifically with "Importation or Sale of Articles at Less Than Market Value or Wholesale Price."[40] This provision essentially prohibits dumping undertaken in the United States provided that such dumping is carried out with the intent of destroying or injuring U.S. industries. A key element of the 1916 Act, apart from criminal penalties such as fines or imprisonment in actions brought by the U.S. government, is that it allows the injured private party to sue for and receive treble damages in a U.S. federal court. Thus far, however, no such criminal penalties have been imposed by the U.S. government. Almost all of the cases brought to court have involved civil complaints, but no complainant has ever recovered treble damages and the cost of the suit.

Japan's formal complaint, therefore, centered not on any particular instance of application of the 1916 Act but rather on the entire nature and substance of the Act's provisions. The departure point for the case was that the mere existence of the 1916 Act violated key legal elements of both Article VI of the GATT and the AD Agreement. Some of the more salient aspects of Japan's complaint were as follows: To start, Japan claimed that the imposition of civil and criminal penalties was inconsistent with specific WTO provisions that allow for the imposition of duties as the only remedy to counteract dumping. Moreover, the 1916 Act did not provide for ease of comparison across elements in order to establish the dumping margin, determine material injury, or initiate and conduct dumping investigations. The Act also violated the national treatment clause of the GATT because it discriminated between imported and U.S. goods. Finally, it was inconsistent with GATT provisions on quantitative restrictions.

By May 2000, the panel had rendered its judgment. It found that certain aspects of the 1916 Act were in fact inconsistent with U.S. legal obligations under both the GATT and the AD Agreement. As a result, the panel concluded that the benefits accruing to Japan under the WTO agreements were nullified. Going further, the panel also boldly recommended that one way for the United States to bring the 1916 Act into conformity with its WTO obligations would be simply to repeal it altogether because in comparison to other antidumping instruments it was hardly ever used. This constituted an outright legal victory for Japan.

The United States then moved to appeal the decision, but the appellate body largely upheld the conclusions of the panel.[41] In September 2000, the dispute settlement body adopted the two panel reports and the appellate body report for both Japan and the EU. In October 2000, the United States informed the WTO that it would implement the rulings but it would require a "reasonable period of time." Both Japan and the EU, which had already responded jointly to the U.S. appeal, balked at this move and countered with a request for binding arbitration.[42] While the United States requested that a reasonable time frame would be fifteen months, given lengthy legislative realities, both the EU and Japan requested instead that it be set for about six months, given that the United States had demonstrated that it could legislate rapidly in trade-related matters when it so chose. Given the extreme arguments on both sides, the arbitration determined in February 2001 that ten months from the date of the adopted panel report was the most reasonable time frame for the United States to fulfill its legal obligations. Expiration was set for July 26, 2001, but the period was subsequently extended until the end of the U.S. Congress session on 12 December 2001.

The United States is thus legally obliged to implement the ruling—an outright repeal of the 1916 Act. Japan's actions in this case have shown that it can prevail in such disputes within the WTO framework—something it had difficulty doing in a strictly bilateral context. The 1916 Act case was essentially a warm-up to a more substantive second case in which Japan also directly filed a complaint against U.S. antidumping measures.

Here the interests of the powerful steel industry were at stake in both countries, and both governments were under intense domestic pressure. Here too Japan was able to prevail legally, though not to the extent desired by the Japanese government.

The story in this case can be traced to the Asian financial crisis. Because of the crisis, and because of the fear of cheap exports being dumped into the U.S. marketplace, U.S. steel producers and steelworkers' unions filed a large number of antidumping petitions, especially against Japan. According to Japan, this resulted in either antidumping investigations or duty impositions on about 80 percent of Japanese steel exports to the United States since 1997, the year that marked the start of the crisis.[43] In November 1999, Japan requested consultations with the United States, and then, because these proved to be unsatisfactory, proceeded to request the establishment of a panel.[44] In March 2000, a panel was established to examine the dispute between the United States and Japan. At issue was the WTO consistency of U.S. antidumping calculations and procedures carried out by both the USITC and the USDOC.

A little of the background related to the dispute is in order.[45] In quick succession both the USITC and the USDOC had rendered preliminary and final verdicts that charged Japanese exporters with dumping. In November 1998, the USTIC issued an affirmative preliminary determination that the U.S. industry was threatened with material injury. By February 1999, the USDOC, which had restricted its investigated respondent sample to three Japanese producers, issued its preliminary affirmative dumping determination. Since the USDOC had determined earlier that critical circumstances existed for imports of hot-rolled steel from Japan, it then directed the U.S. Customs Service to suspend liquidation and posting of cash deposits or bonds retroactive to the November date of the preliminary determination of dumping. In early May 1999, the USDOC made final determinations of dumping margins ranging from 17 to 67 percent. In June 1999, the USITC also determined that the U.S. steel industry was materially injured or threatened with material injury because of Japanese hot-rolled steel imports. By the end of June 1999, the USDOC had announced the imposition of antidumping duty orders against Japan. Much of this was reminiscent of the way that antidumping disputes between the United States and Japan had unfolded in the past.

What was different this time, however, was that Japan was willing to challenge the U.S. antidumping investigation and orders within the legal framework of the WTO. Japan advanced two main sets of legal arguments. First, it argued that specific aspects of the U.S. antidumping measures, as well U.S. antidumping law, regulations, and administrative procedures in general, were inconsistent with key provisions in the AD

PEKKANEN

Agreement. Second, it charged that some of the actions undertaken by both the USITC and the USDOC violated GATT Article X, the transparency clause that requires any instituted government measure to be clear to all concerned. Japan also requested that if the panel did not find dumping or injury to U.S. domestic industry, it should ask the United States to revoke its antidumping orders and reimburse any antidumping duties collected.

In its conclusions, the panel did find that some of the U.S. actions were inconsistent with certain aspects of the AD Agreement as Japan had claimed, which makes both the determination of U.S. dumping duties and the findings of injury suspect. The panel also, however, dismissed part of the Japanese legal claim concerning U.S. violations of the AD Agreement, particularly those claims concerned with the alleged lack of procedural transparency in the United States. In addition, the panel was willing to recommend, as is generally the case when legal infringement is found, that the United States bring its offending measures into conformity with its obligations under the AD Agreement. The panel was circumspect, however, because it chose not to recommend the remedies sought by Japan, that is, the revocation of duty and the reimbursement of amounts collected by the United States. This was certainly a weaker conclusion than Japan had wanted. Subsequently, both the United States and Japan moved to appeal certain aspects of the ruling.[46] While the appellate body reversed some aspects of the panel's rulings, there were no major upsets as far as Japan was concerned. Since the appellate report was adopted on August 23, 2001, this case has served as an important cautionary note for the United States because it cannot completely disregard the very same WTO legal commitments it signed on to uphold. The United States has also been cautioned that, given the precedents being set, a future panel or appellate body might well deem it possible to rule for the reimbursement or outright revocation of the United States' domestically calculated antidumping duties.

A final case that also shows Japan's efforts to legalize antidumping disputes and move them out of the strictly bilateral context concerns the U.S. Continued Dumping and Subsidy Offset Act of 2000, better known as the Byrd Amendment.[47] Essentially, this act allows antidumping and countervailing duties collected in U.S. unfair trade cases to be given to injured U.S. domestic companies. Because U.S. companies can thus collect duties, they are given a second remedy beyond the initial remedy of remitting the funds to the U.S. Treasury, and this second remedy violates WTO rules.[48] In December 2000, Japan planned to file a complaint in conjunction with the EU, but to increase pressure on the United States, it asked other countries, including South Korea, India, and Brazil, to join the complaint.[49] Eventually, a nine-member coalition that included Japan filed a consultation request with the United States on December 21, 2000. These consultations were further joined by Argentina, Canada, and Mexico. Because no mutually agreed-upon solution emerged, the original nine complainants then requested the establishment of a panel, and one was constituted by August 23, 2001. Meanwhile, direct pressure from other countries also mounted against the United States, and both Canada and Mexico, the United States' NAFTA partners, directly filed a complaint with respect to the same measure in May 2001 and then requested the establishment of a formal panel. On September 10, 2001, a single panel was constituted to deal with the complainants, both those of the original nine-member coalition, including Japan, and the later complainants, including Canada and Mexico.

The essence of the complaints in this case is that the Byrd Amendment constitutes mandatory legislation, and that it also constitutes a specific action that is not allowed under WTO rules. In addition, the offsets provide incentives for U.S. domestic industries to instigate antidumping or antisubsidy petitions, because they have a strong interest in collecting duties. This case is currently under way at the WTO, and the eleven-member coalition is likely to prevail. The United States will probably be faced with an adverse ruling because, as the complainants point out, the Amendment violates several provisions of the GATT, the AD Agreement, and the Agreement on Subsidies and Countervailing Measures. Like the outcome in the 1916 Act case, it is entirely possible that both the panel's and the appellate body's rulings may recommend a repeal of this Amendment. If they do, this case may end up providing another favorable outcome for the Japanese. As a result, Japan may push even further, either alone or in conjunction with others as in this case, for the legalization of future antidumping disputes with the United States.

Antidumping Disputes with Asian Neighbors

Japan's emphasis on legalization in antidumping disputes with the United States is also a harbinger of changes in its trade relations with its Asian neighbors. These changes are due to recent concerns that Japan is no longer a victim of antidumping remedies, as it had been in its relations with the United States, but is also potentially a user of them. A flood of cheap exports from Asian countries, especially China, in products ranging from textiles to mushrooms, has alerted the trade-related policy establishments in both Japan and China about the importance of antidumping and safeguard measures in protecting the fate of politically powerful domestic industries.[50]

Because of the burgeoning importance of antidumping to Japan-Asian trade relations as a whole, it is all the more important to understand the motivations and actions of Japan in this area and what they might mean for U.S.-Japan trade relations. A series of events in Sino-Japanese trade relations makes this point clear. In June 1999, Chinese authorities began an investigation concerning dumping by Japanese and Korean firms. In April 2000, the Chinese government issued a statement that nine Japanese companies were engaged in dumping, with margins ranging from 26 to 75 percent.[51] As the result of investigations in November and December 2000, the Chinese Ministry of Foreign Trade and Economic Cooperation (MOFTEC) issued further rulings that Japanese makers of chemical materials and cold-rolled stainless sheet were dumping their products in China.[52] On December 18, the Chinese government concluded, in what the Japanese press dubbed an opaque process, that eight Japanese companies had dumping margins ranging from 17 to 58 percent.[53] The Chinese remained unwilling to discuss how these rulings could be compatible with the rules of the WTO. More worrisome is that the Japanese concern about Chinese antidumping measures has not receded. Even as China moved definitively toward WTO accession, there was a general concern among Japanese chemical and steel makers that a decrease in formal tariffs as a means of protecting domestic industries could lead to further Chinese reliance on antidumping measures.[54]

Beginning in early 2001, this basic Sino-Japanese tussle over antidumping concerns also spilled into other areas as a range of producers in Japan began demanding import protection. On January 22, 2001, the Ministry of Agriculture, Forestry, and Fisheries (MAFF) announced its intention to investigate the import levels, market shares, and profit-and-loss situations of nine agricultural products in Japan.[55] This was the first indication that there could be a generalized turn toward protectionism in Japan as well, and that protectionism could well become a reality given the dire economic situation and competitive pressures from abroad. On February 26, 2001, the Japan Towel Industrial Association filed a petition with METI, seeking to have a textile safeguard invoked.[56] Around that time, MAFF officials began to meet with Chinese officials to explain why they had begun investigations to restrict imports of certain agricultural items, such as mushrooms and leeks. Domestically, the agricultural, finance, and trade ministries, along with LDP officials, with their electoral concerns, began deliberations on import restrictions on Chinese eels and seaweed.[57] Subsequently, Japan announced that it would be invoking WTO-consistent safeguard action against three Chinese agricultural products, namely spring onions, shiitake mushrooms, and igusa rushes, that would go into effect for a two-hundred-day period beginning April 23. This action would involve tariffs ranging up to 266 percent on trade in the three agricultural goods, worth approximately $100 million. The Chinese condemned these moves as unilateral decisions that went against the rules of fair play and that would prove to be detrimental to Sino-Japanese trade relation in the long run.[58]

As cautioned by the finance minister, Japan's safeguard actions on the agricultural products encouraged other import-competing sectors to do the same.[59] The government then also began to consider the alarming possibility of import restrictions on a range of other agricultural and textiles goods. MAFF officials, for instance, considered the possibility of investigating import levels and conditions on additional goods, such as eels, seaweed, and garlic. Similarly, accepting the tremendous increase in towel imports and their impact on decreasing shares of the Japanese market by Japanese makers, METI announced that in the middle of April it would begin a textile safeguard investigation.[60] Japanese necktie producers, complaining similarly of foreign producers holding an increasing number of domestic market shares, also moved to have textile safeguards invoked.[61] One of the most interesting trends in Japan today concerns producer opposition to onrushing cheap imports even as consumers and discount retailers, such as Uniqlo, protest protectionist moves and tout the virtues of free trade.[62]

China has had its own trade grievances, however, and has proved willing to butt heads directly with Japan.[63] On February 9, 2001, the Chinese government announced that it would conduct an antidumping investigation against three Asian polystyrene makers, among them Japan, Thailand, and Korea.[64] Although China continued to hold talks with Japan concerning its displeasure over Japanese emergency safeguard actions regarding agricultural products, it also moved to retaliate in other sectors as well. In early June, China began to threaten restrictions on imports of Japanese automobiles, and by June 20 it had placed punitive tariffs of 100 percent on imported Japanese cars, mobile phones, and air conditioners valued at around $500 million.[65] Japanese officials, in keeping with the larger trend toward a WTO-based trade strategy, criticized China for making this move even as China was about to accede to the WTO, and urged it to follow measures based on WTO rules in the future.

Two days of talks between the two sides in early July followed by another set of talks in late September failed to resolve the trade disputes, and by the end of August Japan was considering a move to compensate Japanese companies affected by the Chinese import restriction policies.[66] Japan also took some conciliatory moves, such as delaying its decision regarding import restrictions on towels from China because import levels had stabilized, to improve the atmosphere of impending public- and private-sector trade talks between the two countries.[67] The goal for the talks was to have a resolution before November 8, when Japan would decide whether to renew the controversial import tariffs on Chinese agricultural goods for up to four years.[68] The talks failed to achieve a breakthrough. As the safeguard restrictions expired on November 8, and China refused to consider the Japanese proposal for "orderly trade," Japan could only agree to put off extending the four-year limit to December 21, 2001.[69] In late December, Japan agreed not to invoke full-scale import curbs on farm products from China. Yet this may be just the tip of the trade-friction iceberg between Japan and China. There is little question that agricultural as well as industrial disputes will continue, and that they may ultimately be resolved to both sides' satisfaction only by relying on WTO dispute settlement processes, with which Japan is increasingly comfortable and to which China will be a newcomer. But like Japan, China too may use the rules instrumentally, both as a sword with which to ward off foreign pressures and as a shield to protect home industries.[70] This legal tactic has served Japan quite well thus far in its relations with the United States, and it is entirely possible that it will serve China just as well vis-à-vis Japan. There are already indications that China may use legal protectionist devices such as antidumping laws once it does join the WTO and thereby protect some of its key industries.[71]

In all, what the ongoing Sino-Japanese trade conflict shows is that even as Japan criticizes U.S. antidumping measures as a protectionist device that serves the interests of a powerful domestic lobby, it too is beginning to invoke the same kinds of arguments in defending its tactics in other cases. Indeed, the Japanese legal right to protect domestic industries that have been unduly and unfairly harmed by import competition is very much the same as the right invoked by the United States in support of its steelmakers.[72] This has important policy implications for U.S.-Japan trade relations as well, as discussed shortly.

More worrisome, perhaps, is the possibility that Japan will move increasingly toward the use of antidumping measures as a form of legal protectionism. Thus far, Japan has adopted antidumping measures only rarely in its postwar history.[73] In 1983 and 1989, antidumping petitions against Korean cotton yarn and Korean knitwear, respectively, were withdrawn when the Korean industries offered voluntary export restraints. An antidumping petition against Norwegian and French ferrosilicon measures was similarly withdrawn in 1984 after import prices improved and the aforesaid industries engaged in extensive political statements. Things changed, however, in the early 1990s as Japan's economic problems continued and as cheaper imports from China kept rushing in. In October 1991 the Japan Ferroalloy Association filed antidumping petitions against China, Norway, and South Africa. To make a long story short, the Japanese government determined that it was necessary to impose antidumping duties against China only for the purpose of protecting the home industry for an indeterminate period. In 1995, use of such remedies continued and Japan imposed antidumping duties on cotton yarn imports from Pakistan.

This trend toward the use of antidumping has not necessarily ended. In fact, Japanese companies are becoming as vociferous as U.S. corporations about antidumping allegations. At the end of September 2001, Japanese cold-rolled steelmakers were cited among twenty others in antidumping actions undertaken by U.S. companies.[74] About a month later, Japanese semiconductor companies moved similarly to file antidumping petitions against foreign, especially Korean, rivals operating in Japan.[75]

As these ongoing trends suggest, antidumping measures have become one of the key bones of contention in the WTO system as a whole; and as a negotiating agenda they will no doubt remain on the table for some time to come. Japan, along with a host of developing countries, continues to seek ways to limit the uses and abuses of antidumping measures in the context of the WTO arena, even as it is beginning to pursue unprecedented parallel regional options in its foreign trade diplomacy.[76] Despite the rhetoric of common interests with developing countries, the United States is not necessarily Japan's major or only target, although as this chapter has shown the United States has thus far borne the brunt of Japan's legal wrath within the WTO. Rather, the target is also, as the brief sketch of the unfolding Sino-Japanese trade tensions shows, China and other competitive Asian neighbors in Japan's immediate vicinity. The China reality is increasingly as important a component of Japan's larger trade diplomacy as the United States is, and it is another concrete reason for thinking beyond the narrow confines of bilateral U.S.-Japan trade relations.

Conclusion and Policy Implications

As this chapter has shown, antidumping disputes between the United States and Japan are now constrained by a legalized paradigm. A set of substantive and procedural WTO rules increasingly affects both the development and the resolution of U.S.-Japan trade disputes. In fact, the emphasis on the legalization of trade disputes extends beyond the narrow confines of the U.S.-Japan relationship and affects the interaction of all members of the WTO.

As the longitudinal changes traced earlier show, Japan is not only keen

on pushing the antidumping agenda in the next WTO round in conjunction with other countries, but also increasingly willing and able to take
on the United States both indirectly and directly. Indirectly, Japan challenges the United States as a third party in a range of antidumping-related
complaints brought by other parties. Perhaps more important, however,
is that it also directly confronts U.S. administrative means and procedures
that bear on the determination of antidumping fines and duties. All of
these cases show Japan's interest in legalizing disputes in the context of a
multilateral forum that spotlights both Japan's and, equally important,
the United States' commitment to upholding international legal rules.

To conclude, Japan's legal tactics with respect to the United States in the
framework of the WTO, its desire also to deal with China in the same forum, as well as worrisome protectionist trends in its domestic political
economy all merit attention. For those monitoring current trends in
Japan's trade diplomacy, there is no question that the presence of the
WTO rules is increasingly helping to move U.S.-Japan trade relations as a
whole toward interaction in a rule-based multilateral framework. In fact,
the emphasis on the legalization of trade disputes extends beyond the narrow confines of the U.S.-Japan relationship, and affects the conduct of all
members of the WTO as well as the substantive nature and governance of
the global trade regime at large. The very presence of the WTO legal rules
has already had a transformative impact on state-to-state relations, constraining the behavior of the strong, such as the United States, and empowering the actions of weaker powers, such as Japan. Despite the ongoing rhetoric about free trade agreements with South Korea and China, the
WTO arena is where Japan can hope to legitimately affect the course of
Sino-Japanese disputes as well. These trends hold the following important
policy implications for both the United States and Japan:

- First and foremost, the United States has to recognize the changing
  nature of Japan's trade diplomacy. As a case, the legalization of
  U.S.-Japan antidumping disputes constitutes an important break
  from the strictly bilateral relationship that governed trade conflicts
  between the two countries during much of the Cold War. It will no
  longer be easy for the United States to impose antidumping duties,
  negotiate voluntary restraints, conduct bilateral agreements, or
  engage in aggressive unilateralism, because Japan can, as it has
  done in many cases since the birth of the WTO in 1995,
  legitimately challenge the WTO-legality of such acts. Nor will
  foreign pressure (*gaiatsu*) have much of an impact across many
  trade issues, because it can also be reversed and manipulated
  within the parameters of the existing legal rules.

- Second, the United States has to recognize that today Japan not only has a vision of legal equality with respect to the United States, but also possesses the means with which to try to achieve such equality in the context of the WTO. Again, antidumping disputes are the most important, though not the only, arenas in which Japan is attempting to change the terms of debate. If the rule-based resolution of these disputes is a test of strength for the Japanese, especially when issues of U.S. compliance come to the fore, then it is also a showcase for the United States' long-term commitments to the rule of law in the international trading system. When the United States chooses to flout or evade WTO rulings, it sets an important precedent not just for how the United States may deal with Japan but also for how it may deal with other countries. After all, it is not just Japan that is watching, but also China, with which the United States will no doubt down the line have trade disputes in the framework of the WTO. Committing itself more solidly to the rule of WTO law will make it much easier both tangibly and morally for the United States to deal with Japan as well as with China in the framework of the WTO.
- Third, Japan's tactic of increasingly relying on the legal rules of the WTO to indict foreign practices or thwart foreign measures is a double-edged sword. This is where the argument extends beyond the antidumping issue, where Japan has been particularly adroit, if not always successful, at parlaying the rules to its advantage. If Japan gets tough with a legal stance, its trade partners can turn around and do the same in sectors that are politically sensitive, such as agriculture and textiles. At that point, Japan, which has embarked on the road to high legalization as a trade strategy, cannot then turn around and refuse to deal with its trade partners precisely on the basis of those same rules. Moreover, Japan's safeguard and antidumping actions can also be legitimately scrutinized under the WTO framework, as China has recently threatened to do. This emphasis on the legal rules in a multilateral setting where reputation matters to future interaction remains the main legitimate option for dealing with and cracking open Japan in the near future.
- Fourth, Japan has to recognize the potential for political backlash in countries such as the United States, especially as the result of legal losses in the WTO for domestically powerful industries such as U.S. steel. A succession of what are perceived as failures by either the U.S. domestic industry or the U.S. media, especially in the context of antidumping disputes, could destabilize U.S.

commitments to the future of the WTO. This is certainly an important worry. To counter these trends, the United States needs to publicize more fully the many cases in which it has also been able to prevail in the WTO, against both Japan and the EU. This is especially true for the agricultural sector, in which both Japan and the EU have suffered legal setbacks. Yet the potential for backlash exists increasingly in Japan as well. The United States also needs to be aware that it is no longer alone with respect to sectoral pressures on trade policy. Japan too has transnationalized and pluralized, and there are now increasing divisions between competitive world-class manufacturers and inward-oriented producers. In many instances, just as in the United States, the sorry plight of such inward-oriented producers can become fodder for anti-WTO or antiglobalization sentiments. At this stage, however, the real worry with respect to Japan is that such industry pressures are behind the turn toward legal forms of protectionism, such as in the recent use of safeguards and antidumping provisions. As competitive pressures from China and other Asian countries continue, Japan may invoke such measures more frequently. The point, in short, is that METI is increasingly and visibly subject to political pressures, with the result that its trade policy is far more politicized than ever before. These pressures will make it even more difficult for the United States to deal with Japan bilaterally in the future, because in the event of safeguard or antidumping actions METI will be careful to make its actions WTO-consistent. Thus the only way to deal with backlashes is to recognize that they are a reality for both the United States and Japan, and no longer something that only the United States can use to demand trade concessions.

- Finally, both the United States and Japan need to reaffirm their interest in upholding the multilateral and legalized framework of the WTO. Even if recent moves toward free trade areas—stretching from Canada to Argentina, and between China, South Korea, and Japan—evolve into tangible realities for both the United States and Japan, they will remain stepping stones for both countries' larger global ambitions. This is particularly true for the United States, which is the largest user of the WTO dispute settlement process and, despite flamboyant outcries every now and then about eroding U.S. sovereignty, one of its chief beneficiaries. More important, the WTO remains the main *legitimate* legal vehicle for great economic powers such as the United States and Japan to resolve their trade disputes with countries both within and outside the proposed regional blocs. In the ongoing moves toward closer cooperation among Japan, China, and Korea, it is clear that the countries involved see these areas as more generalized forums for cooperation rather than as specific arenas for resolving bilateral disputes. In fact, in the Sino-Japanese trade dispute, both Japan and China made heavy mention of their intention to rely on the rules of the WTO to resolve their differences. This also serves as an important lesson for the United States, because it suggests limitations in the bilateral approach to dealing with China in the future over antidumping or other disputes. It is important for the United States and Japan to remain fully and vigilantly engaged with the WTO dispute settlement process, whether they win outright, lose badly, or suffer partial setbacks. It is the WTO process alone that will help deflect criticisms of high-handedness in dealing with up-and-coming countries such as China and allow both the United States and Japan to pursue their future economic interests under a legitimate legal sheen. To step out of the WTO framework, then, for both the United States and Japan, is to step toward less certain means, if any exist, of dispute resolution in the global trading regime.

Japan, the United States, and Multilateral Institution-Building in the Asia-Pacific

APEC AND THE ARF

KUNIKO P. ASHIZAWA

Introduction

During the last decade, the Asia-Pacific region witnessed a vast increase in regional multilateral institution-building over a range of economic, energy, political, and security issues, and consisting of minilateral, subregional, and regionwide arrangements.[1] Despite persistent skepticism about their effectiveness and significance, these developments can be regarded as a new regional trend for the Asia-Pacific countries. Only fourteen years ago Japan's foreign policymaking was largely confined within its bilateral relationship with the United States. U.S. foreign policymakers viewed the U.S.-Japan bilateral relationship as the key component in their overall approach to Asia, an approach that is often defined as hub-and-spoke bilateralism centered around the United States. This recent growth in multilateral institution-building involving Japan and the United States may indicate a change in the two countries' regional orientations away from the previous, almost exclusive dependence on bilateral approaches to intraregional management.

To what extent has their approach to the region actually changed? How have the two countries perceived and reacted to this new development of regional institution-building, and why? And how has the emergence of such institutions affected the U.S.-Japan relationship? To explore these questions, this chapter examines Japanese and U.S. foreign policymaking toward the Asia-Pacific Economic Cooperation (APEC) forum and the ASEAN Regional Forum (ARF). APEC was launched in 1989 as the first multilateral forum in the Asia-Pacific region to focus primarily on economics. The ARF, the regionwide forum for security dialogue, was established in 1994 and has been seen as a major breakthrough in the security sphere in the Asia-Pacific, where such multilateral arrangements were previously almost nonexistent and seen as difficult to achieve. Examining U.S. and Japanese policymaking toward these forums may shed light on their general approaches toward multilateral institutions in the region, as well as on their general attitude toward intraregional relations in the Asia-Pacific over the past decade. Comparing the U.S. and Japan in APEC and the ARF affords an opportunity to contrast their respective approaches to regional multilateralism and to ascertain the extent to which these approaches are similar or different in the economic and security arenas.

This chapter finds that Japan and the United States displayed particular behavior patterns across the two regional institution-building cases. Japan found the creation of APEC and the ARF a desirable and practical option for advancing a vision of new regional order—something beyond the hub-and-spoke system. It came to see the promotion of regional multilateral arrangements as a new foreign policymaking agenda, while still firmly acknowledging the primacy of bilateral relations with the United States. The United States, on the other hand, at first did not hide its reservations or skepticism about the multilateral frameworks proposed by other countries. Shortly thereafter it began to see them somewhat favorably and sought ways to make them better serve U.S. interests. The U.S. attitude toward regional multilateral initiatives has been largely reactive and often ambivalent in both security and economics.

The United States' and Japan's particular attitudes suggest that the impact of the creation of APEC and the ARF was far greater for Japan than for the United States. Given the disparity, it can be said that the emergence of multilateral institutions has affected U.S.-Japan relations at least at the *management level*, by increasing uncertainties for the United States in dealing with Japan on regional issues. Although it has brought little fundamental change in the nature of U.S.-Japan relations, the influence of APEC and the ARF can be regarded as indirect and probably long-term— affecting bilateral relations in the manner in which the overall relationship is ultimately managed by offering each country more complex options with which to relate to and influence the other.

The Creation of APEC and the ARF

This section briefly reviews the creation of APEC and the ARF, with a specific focus on U.S. and Japanese foreign policymaking. To be sure, the review is not intended to serve as a definitive analysis of how and why

APEC and the ARF were established. Rather, it focuses on how foreign policymakers in Tokyo and Washington perceived and accepted multilateral frameworks for both economic and security issues as policy options for managing intraregional matters.

APEC

In June 1988, the Ministry of International Trade and Industry (MITI) of Japan completed an internal report that proposed the idea of creating ministerial-level formal arrangements for regional economic cooperation among the Asia-Pacific countries.[2] After its release, the report was conveyed by MITI officials to eleven Asia-Pacific countries, all of which became the original members of APEC a year later.[3] MITI envoys met their official counterparts—some at the director-general and ministerial levels—and presented the internal report to gauge each country's reaction. When the MITI official met his counterpart in the office of the U.S. Trade Representative (USTR), the latter showed little interest in the proposal and never responded to it afterward. Only Australia responded with considerable enthusiasm, and since then, quiet collaboration has taken place between Australia and MITI to gradually shape and promote the idea of a regional economic forum at the ministerial level.

In January 1989, in Seoul, Australian Prime Minister Robert Hawke officially called for the founder's meeting of a ministerial-level forum to promote Asia-Pacific economic cooperation. MITI was generally pleased with Hawke's proposal, despite the abruptness of the timing, but found one crucial difference between MITI's proposal and Hawke's—whether to include the United States in the proposed regional forum. Hawke's proposal did not assume U.S. participation, but for MITI officials U.S. participation was crucial. In the following months, MITI undertook a threefold strategy to realize the proposed economic forum: (1) promoting the proposal for an official multilateral economic forum to other prospective members, namely the ASEAN countries and the United States; (2) persuading Australia as well as ASEAN countries to include the United States; and (3) supporting Australia in taking official initiatives to establish a new institution.[4]

The initial U.S. reaction to the Hawke proposal was "restrained," largely because the proposal was announced after President Bush had been in office only two weeks, making it difficult to respond quickly before the formulation of his administration's comprehensive Asia policy.[5] In the following months there were discussions within the administration on how to respond to the Hawke proposal, and the State Department, headed by new Secretary of State James Baker, tended to be at the center of such discussions.[6] During this time, MITI sent its officials to Washington to keep its American counterparts informed of the new developments, such as ASEAN's reaction to the proposal, and sought to reassure Washington that the new forum should include the United States.[7]

Baker's address at the Asian Society in New York in June 1989 formally endorsed the proposal of creating a ministerial-level economic forum among Asia-Pacific countries, stating that "the need for a new mechanism for multilateral cooperation among the nations of the Pacific rim is an idea whose time has come." Baker confirmed American involvement in creating such a new institution, and gave credit to both Australia and MITI for their initiatives.[8] By late July, all prospective members finally reached a consensus, despite persistent resistance from some ASEAN countries. The first meeting of APEC was held on November 6 in the Australian capital, Canberra.

ARF

Calls for the creation of an Asia-Pacific regionwide framework for regional security were first expressed in the late 1980s by some influential statesmen, including Mikhail Gorbachev and Australian Foreign Minister Gareth Evans. The United States and Japan were both skeptical about multilateral approaches to regional security, and concerned that such a multilateral security framework would weaken the existing U.S.-Japan alliance. The United States also worried that the multilateral security approach could lead to naval arms control between the United States and the Soviet Union in the Asia-Pacific region, which the United States viewed as unacceptable given the U.S. global military strategy at that time.[9]

In the summer of 1991 Japan officially shifted its policy toward favoring the ongoing discourse over regionwide multilateral security arrangements. At the ASEAN Post-Ministerial Conference (ASEAN-PMC) in July 1991, Foreign Minister Taro Nakayama proposed a multilateral forum for security dialogue in the Asia-Pacific, suggesting the use of existing ASEAN-PMC for this new function of "a process of political discussions designed to improve the sense of security" among members.[10] Initially, Nakayama's proposal received little enthusiasm from either the United States or the ASEAN countries. Baker expressed strong concern, saying, "we ought to be careful about changing those [existing bilateral] arrangements and discarding them for something else unless we're absolutely certain that the something else is better and will work."[11] As for ASEAN's indifferent reaction, it is thought that this was partially because the Ministry of Foreign Affairs (MOFA) did not inform the ASEAN members with enough advance notice that Nakayama would introduce the proposal at this meeting.

Nevertheless, Japan did not have long to wait to see its proposal take off. Six months later, in January 1992, at the fourth summit meeting, ASEAN announced that it would use the ASEAN-PMC for security dialogue for issues covering the Asia-Pacific region. At this point, Japan's initial objective was largely attained. Thus, after ASEAN's announcement, MOFA officials took a wait-and-see stance toward further ASEAN initiatives to more concretely develop the new proposal. Meanwhile, they sought to make the United States more receptive to the proposal, because the United States had not yet made clear whether it would accept the creation of such a security forum.[12]

Until it left office in January 1993, the Bush administration remained skeptical of multilateral approaches to regional security in the Asia-Pacific. The Clinton administration, however, soon changed the course. In his policy statement before the Senate Foreign Relations Committee in March 1993, Winston Lord, assistant secretary of state for East Asian and Pacific affairs, officially endorsed the proposal by including "developing a multilateral forum for security consultations" as one of ten major goals for U.S. policy in the Asia-Pacific.[13] In July, President Clinton himself stated the necessity of new regional security dialogues in the Asia-Pacific in his remarks to the Korean National Assembly in Seoul.

ASEAN carried forward this security dialogue scheme in a careful manner and decided to create a new forum, to be named the ASEAN Regional Forum, or ARF, that would include China, Russia, and other Indochina countries as members.[14] At the ASEAN-AMM in July 1993, the ASEAN foreign ministers formally announced the creation of the ARF. In the following ASEAN-PMC, all members, including Japan and the United States, approved the ASEAN-AMM decision and agreed to convene the first meeting of the ARF within a year in Bangkok. The main stage for the regionwide security dialogue shifted from the ASEAN-PMC to the newly created ARF. The first meeting was convened in July 1994, in Bangkok, where eighteen foreign ministers gathered to exchange their opinions on regional security in the Asia-Pacific.[15]

Motive for and Interests in Institution-Building

As the brief history just presented shows, Japan and the United States displayed different behavior patterns across the two cases of regional institution-building. Japanese policymakers conceived the idea of the regionwide arrangements early. At around the same time, other Asia-Pacific countries arrived at similar proposals, and Japan favored these countries—namely Australia for APEC and ASEAN for the ARF—to play leadership roles to actualize the proposals. Tokyo consistently supported the process to establish these institutions, conducting quiet diplomacy to persuade other prospective members to join. The U.S. government, conversely, took no formal initiatives for the creation of both APEC and the ARF.[16] Its initial response to the proposals was either reserved or skeptical. Yet when a new administration came to office—that is, in the case of APEC, when Bush replaced Reagan, and in the case of the ARF, when Clinton replaced Bush—Washington began to view more favorably the creation of a new multilateral forum in the Asia-Pacific, and then officially announced its approval.

This section explores how and why the two countries acted as they did during the course of the creation of APEC and the ARF, in order to understand the goals and interests that each country pursued.

Japan: Taking the Initiative for Multilateralism

In Japan, elite bureaucrats of the related ministry (of MITI for APEC and of MOFA for the ARF) were primarily responsible for Japan's policymaking toward the creation of APEC and the ARF. Examining how these elite bureaucrats rationalized the need for APEC and the ARF reveals that Japanese policymakers envisioned a regionwide multilateral forum in connection with their new perspectives on a regional order of the Asia-Pacific.

In the case of APEC, MITI's internal report argued that the region's economic structure should be shifted from "development through U.S. dependency (*beikoku-izongata-hatten*)" to "development through role-sharing (*yakuwari-buntangata-hatten*)."[17] Given the persistent trade and budget deficits of the United States and the perspective that redressing such deficits would inevitably lead to slowdown of the U.S. economy, the report argued that the existing system of U.S.-led development of the regional economy, in which the economic development of Asian countries depended exclusively on the U.S. market, would no longer be sustainable. Meanwhile, the prospect of emerging regional blocs in the world economy at the time was another concern for the Asia-Pacific economy, which was largely export-oriented and took great advantage of the postwar free-trading system.[18] Japan and other Asian countries were told in the report that they should contribute to the expansion of intraregional trade, to the increase of domestic consumption, to the opening of markets, and to the establishment of economic cooperation, while the U.S. economy continued to play a considerably important role. To achieve this shift to a development-through-role-sharing structure, MITI officials keenly felt the need for some type of policy coordination among the Asia-Pacific countries, in addition to national-level efforts. It was in this context that

MITI suggested establishing a governmental-level multilateral forum in which the economic ministers of Asia-Pacific countries would participate.

As for the ARF, in the latter part of 1990, MOFA officials became aware that the impact of the end of the Cold War was at last reaching the Asia-Pacific region, when they saw that the reduction of U.S. forces in Asia had begun. The Bush administration publicly stated that it would reduce U.S. forces in East Asia by fourteen to fifteen thousand personnel.[19] MOFA officials viewed this development as a serious challenge to the fundamental security structure in the Asia-Pacific, which had long been described as a hub-and-spoke bilateral system led by the United States. They began formulating their own perspective on an emerging regional security structure for the post-Cold War Asia-Pacific. They conceived of a *multi-tiered* structure involving different levels of coordination among states to comprehensively maintain security of the region.[20] Such levels of engagement are generally categorized within four tiers: (1) bilateral alliances as a core security function; (2) subregional, ad-hoc arrangements; (3) a region-wide security dialogue; and (4) nonsecurity arrangements, such as the APEC forum, for increasing communication among regional countries. All levels should be complementary to one another, and the primacy of the first tier's function, namely U.S.-Japan bilateral alliance, should remain intact. Obviously the third tier lacked any existing arrangements at the time. Thus, in the Nakayama proposal of 1991, MOFA suggested using the ASEAN-PMC as a regionwide forum for security dialogue among the Asia-Pacific countries.

In addition to conceiving of the creation of a regionwide multilateral forum as a key part of regional order, Japanese policymakers in both cases also found new regionwide institutions to be a useful policy option for responding to three challenges that the country was facing at the time. The first challenge was to *assume an active role in bringing a new order into the region without arousing the fear of Asian countries.* When they perceived ongoing changes in the regional order, in both the economic and the security realms, Japanese policymakers sought to take certain initiatives to bring order and stability into the region during a period of transition. Conceptualizing their vision of a new regional order was part of such efforts. Meanwhile, given the negative historical record of Japan's own aggressions against other Asian countries during World War II, policymakers contended that any initiative should not arouse Asian neighbors' fears about the possibility of Japan's resurgence as a dominant power, politically or militarily, in the region. Proposing a regionwide multilateral forum through the conduct of low-profile diplomacy was seen as one of few options for Japan to play a more active role without making its Asian neighbors too nervous about Japan's activism. MITI officials, for example, saw the relation between "major" and "small" countries as less hierarchical in multilateral settings than in bilateral settings, and they expected that their proposed multilateral framework would make the small countries, namely the ASEAN countries, raise their voices more comfortably.[21] MOFA officials repeated that the objective of a regionwide security forum is to foster security dialogue to enhance "a feeling of mutual reassurance" among the countries, because they expected increasing multilateral dialogue to help reduce Japan's Asian neighbors' long-standing suspicion of Japan.[22]

The second challenge was to *keep the U.S. involved in the Asia-Pacific region*. Given Japan's inherent dependence on U.S. military capability for its national defense, along with the United States' considerable influence over regional stability as well as economic development, Japanese policymakers were strongly convinced that the U.S. presence in the region was indispensable. Keeping the United States as an Asia-Pacific country would best serve Japan's national interests. To have the United States involved in the regionwide multilateral forum, though loose and weak as an institution, thus had both practical and symbolic importance. One MITI official said, "we thought it would offer a kind of foothold for the U.S. to stay in the Asia-Pacific."[23] Facing the U.S. force reductions from the region, MOFA officials believed that the creation of a regionwide security forum for security dialogue would help keep the United States involved in Asia by engaging it in a new multilateral framework.

The third challenge was to *cope with ongoing problems within U.S.-Japan relations*. MITI officials were frustrated with the continuous bilateral trade disputes with the United States, which had become increasingly tense since the mid-1980s. Foreseeing that such bilateral trade negotiations would be further intensified in the near future, MITI officials needed to find a way out of this deadlock. They thought that a regional multilateral framework, though far from a panacea, might offer a buffer against the increasing bilateral pressures from the United States.[24] MOFA officials in 1991 were also coping with a problem in the security relationship. They were very concerned that the Gulf War crisis revealed Japan's inability to support its most important ally, the United States, militarily in a situation of crisis. Frustrated by Washington's and other governments' lack of appreciation for Japan's huge financial contribution to the U.S.-led multinational military operation against Iraq, MOFA officials felt desperate to play more politically visible roles, internationally as well as within the U.S.-Japan alliance. Burden sharing became a common conclusion in writings and comments about post-Gulf War U.S.-Japan relations at that time.[25] In this context, given Japan's considerable domestic constraints in pursuing a military role, MOFA officials viewed proposing a regionwide security forum as one of few options for Japan to play a constructive role in regional security management, so as to indirectly contribute to the U.S. security role in the region.

Overall, for both APEC and the ARF, Japan conceived the creation of regionwide multilateral forums as an important part of the country's vision of a new regional structure. Japan also found regionwide institution-building as a useful, though limited, policy option for dealing with several challenges the country faced in relations with the United States and with Asian countries.

United States: Cautious Moves Toward Regional Multilateral Institution-Building

In the initial stages of both APEC and the ARF, the U.S. government responded either reservedly (to APEC) or negatively (to ARF) to the proposals for creating these regionwide multilateral frameworks in the Asia-Pacific. Later, however, under new administrations, Washington grew more positive to the proposals and decided to join the new regional economic and security forums. Why was the United States' initial reaction to the proposals for APEC and the ARF reserved or skeptical and why did the U.S. government then alter its previous attitude and decide to join these new regional institutions?

Behind the United States' initially reserved response to the proposals for multilateral regional institutions was a latent preference for bilateral approaches for dealing with issues and problems in Asia. Throughout 1988 and early 1989, when proposals for possible regional multilateral arrangements for economic cooperation had initially been floated, the U.S. government appeared more interested in bilateral free trade arrangements as possible policy options for its economic policy toward Asia. Facing a worsening trade deficit in the late 1980s, Washington made several attempts, both formally and informally, to explore bilateral free trade agreements (FTAs), beginning with Australia and New Zealand, and then with ASEAN, South Korea, and Japan. For instance, Senator Byrd proposed the joint study of a U.S.-Japan FTA to then Prime Minister Noboru Takeshita, who was visiting Washington, D.C., in January 1988. As for ARF, when responding to the series of proposals for regional multilateral security frameworks in the early 1990s, the U.S. government adamantly maintained the hub-and-spoke, U.S.-led bilateral system as a basic organizing principle for regional strategic matters. In his *Foreign Affairs* article of late 1991, Secretary of State Baker plainly presented such a view toward Asia by describing the relations between the United States and its allies in Asia as "spokes in the fan."[26]

The U.S. preference for the bilateral option in its policymaking toward

Asia is understandable, because for a powerful country such as the United States, the process would usually be faster, and negotiation to gain its desired outcomes would be easier to control in a bilateral setting than in a multilateral one. Compared to U.S. trans-Atlantic relations, the large disparity in power between the United States and other Asian countries (except Japan) can add further rationale for the U.S. preference for bilateral frameworks for dealing with regional affairs in the Asia-Pacific. Given such a latent preference, the U.S. government tended to be instinctively displeased with other countries' initiatives for multilateral institution-building.

There has also been an underlying tendency to view the issues of the Asia-Pacific as secondary to other U.S. foreign policy priorities. When the ideas of creating APEC and the ARF were floated, the focus of Washington's foreign relations was mainly on supporting a peaceful transition in Europe after the dramatic changes in the Soviet regime. At the same time, in terms of economic regional cooperation, Washington became enthusiastic about realizing a regional grouping in its own backyard, beginning with Canada and later including Mexico in the North American Free Trade Agreement (NAFTA).[27] Furthermore, the Persian Gulf War and the subsequent Middle East peace talks also largely occupied U.S. foreign policymaking during the period leading up to the ARF's establishment.

As these examples illustrate, the United States, as a global power, almost always faced several issues in different regions simultaneously. Issues of the Asia-Pacific, particularly regional cooperation, did not receive the highest priority on the U.S. foreign policymaking agenda. Given this general tendency, Washington tended to be less responsive than other Asia-Pacific countries to ongoing changes in intraregional relations and to pay little concentrated attention to the issue of regional cooperation in the Asia-Pacific. Consequently, the United States was not prepared to think beyond the usual pattern of regional management—U.S.-led bilateralism—when the ideas for regionwide multilateral institution-building were proposed by some Asia-Pacific countries.

Why then did the U.S. government change course and decide to participate in the proposed regional multilateral institutions? The U.S. policymakers primarily involved in decision making about the founding of APEC and the ARF were a virtual handful of high-ranking officials, most of whom were newly appointed to their State Department posts when the new administration came into office. As part of a series of comprehensive policy reviews by the new administration during its first few months in office, these newly appointed officials closely looked at the proposals for regionwide multilateral forums in the Asia-Pacific in the process of overall review of the government's Asia policy. In the case of APEC, the transition from the Reagan administration to the Bush administration offered James Baker an opportunity to examine the concept of creating a regional economic association in the Asia-Pacific—an idea that Baker himself had been interested in when he was in the Treasury Department but was not able to put forward before he moved to the State Department.[28] Winston Lord also reviewed the option of a multilateral framework for regional security dialogue when formulating the Clinton administration's overall Asia policy.

Through these examinations, neither Baker's nor Lord's team found any necessary contradiction between the proposed multilateral frameworks' loosely institutionalized forum style and the existing U.S. bilateral relations with other Asian countries, particularly the relationship with Japan. This was an important recognition for U.S. foreign policymakers, especially for security policymakers, because the view that multilateral frameworks would jeopardize existing bilateral relations had been pervasive and had prevented U.S. policymakers from considering a multilateral framework as an option.[29] Having recognized the proposed multilateral framework as an acceptable option, both Baker's and Lord's teams sought to define how the new institutions could serve U.S. interests.

The primary objective defined for both frameworks was a quite modest one—to reinforce the U.S. link with Asia. The Hawke proposal's exclusion of the United States as a prospective member of APEC induced Baker to want the United States to be included in order to establish it as a member of the Asia-Pacific community.[30] Further, he felt that U.S. exclusion should be avoided in order to maintain the country's economic access to the region. In ARF's founding, Lord clarified U.S. participation as essential in order to assure other Asian countries of America's continued commitment to the security of the region.[31] Assurance of the United States' continuous commitment would in turn help strengthen the existing bilateral security arrangements between the United States and key Asian countries.

Behind such immediate goals were long-term, strategic objectives. Baker and his staff viewed the creation of an Asia-Pacific economic grouping as a possible vehicle for advancing regional and global economic liberalization. They also expected that, in the multilateral context, the United States could mobilize positive pressures on Japan to further Japan's economic liberalization.[32] Similarly, though to a lesser extent, Lord and his staff expected the ARF to produce, over time, some concrete "preventive diplomacy" measures to head off regional conflicts before they arise.[33]

In reviewing these proposals, U.S. policymakers recognized the nonconflicting relationship between the proposed multilateral institutions and existing bilateral relations. They also realized that participating in the new regional institutions, both APEC and the ARF, might allow the United

States to attain both immediate goals and long-term objectives without jeopardizing the continuing bilateralism that favored U.S. interests.

After Creation: Expectation, Disappointment, and New Interests

As discussed in the preceding sections, Japan and the United States had quite different attitudes and expectations toward the creation of region-wide multilateral forums in the Asia-Pacific. Analyzing the subsequent developments of APEC and the ARF is as important as discerning the interests and strategies of both the United States and Japan in the creation of these institutions. This section first addresses whether Japan and the United States achieved what they expected by building and participating in these new institutions and whether any further changes or developments were observed in their respective attitudes toward, expectations for, or interests in these institutions. The section then assesses whether the creation and development of APEC and the ARF have had any impact on the two countries' bilateral relationship.

Subsequent Developments of APEC and the ARF

Since its first meeting in 1989, APEC's size and scope of activities have developed more quickly than those involved in its founding had expected, despite persistent skepticism and occasional criticism of its significance and of its capability in dealing with regional economic relations. The membership expanded from twelve to twenty-one, including Russia. High-level activities include annual summit meetings, annual meetings of foreign and trade ministers, and other ministerial-level meetings on twelve different subjects, such as finance, telecommunications, energy, and the environment. APEC now has four standing committees, eleven working groups, and various task forces and other groups.

The story of APEC's development can be divided into four phases. The first three years were the phase of institutionalization of the APEC forum. At the first four ministerial meetings from 1989 to 1992, APEC members regularized the annual ministerial meeting, formulated APEC's objectives and principles, and established a small secretariat in Singapore. The successful admission of China, Taiwan, and Hong Kong at the 1991 Seoul meeting was the most significant achievement during this institutionalization phase, given the fact that regional economic issues could not be meaningfully discussed without their participation and that this was the first organization to formally include both Taiwan and China.

Quite comfortable with this gradual formalization process, Japanese policymakers emphasized the significance of APEC as a symbol of an emerging new Asia-Pacific era and stressed the promotion of APEC as a key Japanese foreign policy objective. Obviously their emphasis was on economic cooperation, and they nurtured this first regionwide institution in Asia-Pacific with considerable care.[34] These policymakers' views were largely shared by the general public, although public attention to this matter was quite limited during this period.[35]

Meanwhile, the U.S attitude toward this first stage of APEC was largely reserved, a matter of trying to "avoid imposing a 'made in America' blueprint for the trans-Pacific grouping."[36] U.S. foreign policy officials at the time were aware of the importance of APEC's growth and careful about some ASEAN countries' fear of being subordinated by the interests of the big powers. These officials therefore stopped short of addressing the subject of trade liberalization, particularly region-level arrangements.[37]

The next three years constituted the second phase of APEC development, during which time the first Asia-Pacific economic institution received a great deal of attention. APEC's visibility grew due to the initiative of newly elected President Clinton to convene the first summit meeting of APEC in 1993 in Seattle, bringing together the leaders of the Asia-Pacific countries for the first time in history. Introducing the annual summit meeting was certainly not the only factor to make this phase of APEC development distinctive. It was the conspicuous shift of APEC's main focus from economic cooperation to trade and investment liberalization. Thanks to the strong leadership and personal ambition of President Suharto of Indonesia, the 1994 APEC Summit meeting at Bogor announced APEC's new goal of trade and investment liberalization within the region by the year 2020 (by 2010 for industrialized countries). Not surprisingly, the Bogor Declaration was enthusiastically backed by the Clinton administration, which was more economics-oriented than the previous administration had been. This alteration of the previously rather reserved U.S. attitude toward APEC was accomplished by defining participation in APEC as a key U.S. policy toward the region aimed at increasing access to markets in Asia for American goods.[38] The dramatic shift of APEC's main focus onto trade and investment liberalization was to a considerable extent due to the Clinton administration's formulation of its new policy toward APEC.

Japanese policymakers viewed this new development with ambivalence. On the one hand, they welcomed Clinton's initiative for a summit meeting as giving this relatively new institution further importance and international recognition. On the other hand, the Bogor Declaration not only made Japanese policymakers, particularly MITI officials, feel uneasy about this rapid shift toward making trade and investment liberalization

APEC's main focus,[39] but also posed a difficult task for the Japanese government because, as the Osaka meeting's host the next year, Japan had to set concrete measures to materialize this ambitious political goal. It was also a goal for which the Japanese government felt enormous leadership constraints because of the strong power of the agriculture sector, notably rice production, in its domestic politics. The result was the introduction of the *concerted, unilateral approach* (CUA), invented by Japanese officials for the 1995 Osaka meeting, as an organizing principle for APEC's trade and investment liberalization goal. This concept gives members a certain degree of freedom to choose a pace and a sector to liberalize. Despite criticism of the CUA as jeopardizing the momentum of APEC's liberalization initiative, the Japanese government self-justifiably defined the CUA concept as reflecting the interests of developing countries in Asia, and emphasized Japan's role as building bridges between those developing countries and industrialized countries in the region.

After the Osaka meeting, Japanese policymakers tended to expect the main focus of APEC to return to issues related to economic cooperation, such as technical assistance and standardization, while U.S. policymakers, unsatisfied with the results of the Osaka meeting, sought a way to push APEC's trade liberalization agenda further. This difference in expectations epitomized the third phase of APEC's development between 1996 and 1998. Evaluating the 1996 meeting held in Manila, both MITI and MOFA reaffirmed the importance of economic and technology cooperation as one of the important outcomes of the meeting.[40] By contrast, U.S. policymakers viewed APEC's endorsement of the WTO's initiative for Information Technology Agreement (ITA), which called for gradual elimination of tariffs on high-tech products by the year 2000, as the most significant positive achievement.[41]

The issue of trade liberalization again began to receive extensive attention after the Manila meeting, this time in the form of the Early Voluntary Sectoral Liberalization (EVSL) initiative. As Krauss's chapter in this volume describes, between late 1997 and 1998 Japan and the United States severely confronted each other on how to implement the EVSL initiative, especially in the forestry and fishing products sectors. In the end, no compromise was possible and the issue moved to the WTO. The failure of the EVSL negotiation, together with APEC's inability to deal with serious economic problems after the Asian financial crisis of 1997 and 1998, considerably discredited APEC's significance and diminished enthusiasm for and expectations of APEC among many policymakers and the general public as well.

The fourth phase, from 1999 onward, can be seen as a search for the *raison d'être* of APEC itself, which has appeared to run out of momentum.

The trade liberalization agenda has stagnated and the outcomes of the annual summit and ministerial meetings have often been treated as inconspicuous or merely diplomatic rhetoric. Despite this obvious setback, however, the annual summit meeting has become a fairly routine event in the diplomatic schedule of each member. In this context, the inclusion of Russia as the newest member in 1998 helped add political weight to the summit meetings per se, and the meeting's attention has further shifted more toward political and security matters rather than focusing exclusively on trade and economic concerns since the September 2001 terrorist attacks in the United States. Also, bilateral summit meetings during the APEC gatherings have come to be seen as useful opportunities to achieve the respective foreign policy agendas of APEC members.

In Japan, during this fourth phase, MITI officials understandably have became less enthusiastic about APEC and have begun discussions with Singapore and South Korea on the possibility of concluding bilateral FTAs, which the Japanese government had consistently opposed until late 1998.[42] In contrast, MOFA officials and foreign policy specialists still appear to be relatively sympathetic to APEC—repeating the importance of APEC's framework to Japanese foreign policy on the region while pragmatically placing more emphasis on the bilateral summit talks during the APEC annual meetings. As for the United States, though it is considerably disillusioned by APEC's inability to achieve a concrete trade liberalization agenda, Washington has nevertheless stopped short of downgrading APEC completely, by at least sustaining efforts to send the president to the organization's annual summit meetings.[43] For example, despite growing concern for his safely abroad shortly after initiating the U.S. war on terrorism, President Bush chose to attend the 2001 Shanghai summit meeting in October, enabling him to secure support from APEC members (particularly from China) for the U.S. military operation against the Taliban and al-Qaeda in Afghanistan.

The story of the ARF has been less dramatic so far. Its development appeared fairly slow, however steady, and its main activities centered around the annual foreign ministers' meeting for discussing regional security matters, together with intersessional meetings and seminars as part of confidence-building measures (CBMs). At the second meeting in 1995, the ARF members adopted a three-stage approach for organizing subsequent meetings of the ARF. Three agenda items corresponding to each stage are set: (1) confidence building, (2) preventive diplomacy, and (3) conflict resolution.[44] Although the ARF began to discuss preventive diplomacy in 1997, the progress of the discussions has been slow.[45] In terms of membership, the ARF expanded from its original eighteen members to twenty-four, including North Korea, which was admitted in 2000. Another noteworthy development is China's increasingly constructive participation in the ARF despite its initial reluctance.

The Japanese government has consistently referred to the creation of the ARF as a significant development in post-Cold War Asia and has positively participated by co-chairing several intersessional meetings and seminars. Japanese policymakers, as well as foreign policy experts, hardly ever fail to designate Japan's participation in ARF's security dialogues as one of the keys to the country's Asia-Pacific policy, particularly in the context of the multi-tiered approach to regional security.[46] Engaging China and North Korea is increasingly seen as an important ARF function. As for the ongoing discussion on preventive diplomacy, MOFA officials face the constant dilemma that slow progress lessens U.S. interest in the ARF, while progress deemed too hasty might result in China's defection.[47]

When the ARF was established, the expectation of U.S. policymakers about its utility was quite modest, as suggested by Winston Lord's statement that the U.S. government viewed U.S. participation in the ARF as essentially to assure other Asian countries of America's continued commitment to the security of the region. Nevertheless, it did not take long for Washington to begin to expect the ARF to progress much faster and to play more concrete roles in regional security concerns. At the third ARF meeting in 1996, for example, Secretary of State Warren Christopher referred to his government's hope that the ARF would soon move to the second stage of its agenda—preventive diplomacy. He further enumerated several areas in which the U.S. would like to see the ARF play positive roles, including the territorial disputes in the South China Sea, stability on the Korean peninsula, limits on arms exports, and the human rights and democracy concerns of Myanmar—issues that for some members were too sensitive to discuss in the ARF setting. The U.S. government also played the central role in bringing India into the ARF despite some resistance expressed by certain member states.[48] This tendency to expect the ARF to play more concrete functions, in accordance with U.S. foreign policy objectives in the region, is also illustrated by the Bush administration's successful push to place the issue of antiterrorism measures at the top of the agenda at the 2002 Brunei meeting.

Evaluating Achievements and Policy Changes: Japan

What have Japan and the United States achieved in APEC and the ARF given their original expectations, and have their respective attitudes toward and interests in these institutions changed over the course of their development?

When conceiving the idea of the APEC forum in early 1988, MITI officials conceptualized a new regional economic order in the Asia-Pacific—an order based on *development through role-sharing*, in which Asian countries would help absorb exports from other Asian countries as well as from the United States, thus shifting from *development through U.S. dependency*, which relied heavily on the U.S. market. To realize this shift, APEC needed to help the Asian countries advance their economic capabilities by promoting economic and technical cooperation. Japan's main focus was thus economic cooperation. This goal has been somewhat achieved. Many activities of economic and technical cooperation within APEC continue in the form of studies and seminars.[49] However, the current picture of a regional economic order is far from what the MITI officials depicted.

MITI officials chose the APEC option to realize their new regional economic order, expecting that it could help Japan *play a more active role without arousing the fear of Asian countries, keep the U.S. involved in the region*, and *mitigate strained relations with the United States*. Were these goals achieved? For the first goal, the answer is mixed. The ASEAN countries, as well as South Korea and China, have gradually become receptive to Japan's activism in regional matters. Meanwhile, APEC has ironically revealed Japan's inability to take a decisive leadership position on the regional trade liberalization agenda.

For the second goal, the answer is fairly positive. The participation of high-profile U.S. policymakers, including the president, in Asia-Pacific multilateral activities has increased U.S. involvement in the region, if only superficially. Also, compared to the time of APEC's founding, the fears of U.S. withdrawal from Asia have largely subsided.

The third goal appears to be barely achieved. Although bilateral trade frictions have become less significant in recent years than they were in the late 1980s, this is largely due to the dramatic recovery of the American economy in the mid-1990s, which helped to redress somewhat the previous excessive, bilateral trade imbalance. Furthermore, the two countries occasionally clashed over trade policies, even in multilateral settings, as discussed in other chapters of this volume.

Meanwhile, the interest of Japanese policymakers in some of these objectives has shifted. Their interest in building a new regional economic order—development through role-sharing—slipped away when APEC shifted its central focus to trade liberalization. Given the sharp decline of Japan's own economy, the goal of regional economic order-building became largely irrelevant in Japanese economic policymaking.

In contrast, promoting economic cooperation remains an important objective in Japan's policymaking on APEC, because it is linked to Japan's policy on the ASEAN countries and offers ground where Japan can play some leading roles. To keep the United States in Asia also remains an important role of APEC, particularly from MOFA's perspective, given that only APEC holds Asia-Pacific summit meetings. In this context, MOFA became more receptive to APEC as an important framework for Japanese foreign policy—an interesting shift from its original reluctance to create the APEC forum. Unsurprisingly, the expectation that it would mitigate bilateral frictions with the United States was in vain. Throughout the EVSL negotiation and after, the Japanese government persistently repeated that negotiations for trade liberalization, notably in the agriculture sector, should be carried out only in WTO, not in APEC. This firm Japanese attitude toward dealing with trade liberalization may again lead to future confrontations with the United States within APEC.

When conceiving the idea of building a regionwide security forum, MOFA officials, like MITI officials, also conceptualized their version of a new regional order for coping with security challenges in the Asia-Pacific. They viewed the regional security order as evolving into a multi-tiered structure in which different types of frameworks (for example, bilateral, minilateral, and multilateral) would function for different objectives (defense and deterrence, conflict management, and security dialogue). In this context, a regionwide multilateral framework should serve security dialogue functions such as confidence building among the region's countries.

Slowly but only partially, these goals have been achieved. The existing bilateral security alliance and cooperation have been quite sound in recent years, as the Hughes and Fukushima chapter in this volume indicates, and the ARF has modestly established itself as the regionwide framework for security dialogue. Yet the region still lacks effective minilateral frameworks for dealing with particular security-related problems, such as the South China Sea territorial disputes and North Korea's instability, though there has been an increasing number of calls for such subregional arrangements.

Overall, the regional security order has seemed to be gradually moving toward what MOFA officials conceptualized a decade ago. The importance of the security dialogue and confidence building cannot be underestimated, precisely because these functions hardly existed before the ARF's creation.

Like MITI officials in the case of APEC, MOFA officials' view was that pursuing a regionwide security forum would help Japan play a more active role without arousing the fear of Asia's countries, keep the United States involved in the region, and contribute to the U.S. security role in the region. On all three of these goals Japan has been largely successful. The Japan Defense Agency (JDA) has actively organized a series of seminars, studies, or simply friendly exchanges with their counterparts in

Asia, both bilaterally and multilaterally, since 1996. ASEAN countries have expressed few concerns about the activities of Japan's Self-Defense Forces (SDF) outside the country, such as participating in the Cambodian peacekeeping operation and supporting the U.S. military operation in Afghanistan. South Korea's and China's sentiments were similar, though to a lesser extent. Lining up the U.S. secretary of state with his or her Asian counterparts at the ARF meetings, not to mention at APEC meetings, also has symbolic meaning in that it represents the United States as an Asia-Pacific country. Mitigating other Asian countries' fear against SDF activities has indirectly resulted in a favorable impact on the U.S.-Japan alliance in that it has enabled Japan to offer greater support to the U.S. military operation in the region and to increase Japan's burden sharing within the bilateral relationship.

Have Japan's objectives changed? Not significantly. Japan formally endorsed the ASEAN+3 framework to deal with future security issues,[50] and MOFA officials began to discuss the possibility of establishing a Northeast Asian multilateral security framework.[51] These actions reflect Japan's consistent, if cautious, pursuit of a multi-tiered approach. Promoting CBMs remains a central focus of the ARF. The ARF's framework is still helping Japan play constructive roles in regional matters and keeping the United States involved in the region. The role of ARF as supplementary to, not supplanting, U.S.-Japan bilateral security relations has become firmly ensconced in Tokyo's thinking.

Evaluating Achievements and Policy Changes: The United States

When the first APEC meeting was convened, the United States was neither a sponsor nor an organizer, but merely another invitee. Given this level of involvement, the United States naturally viewed its goal of participating in the forum in a limited manner. The primary concern of U.S. policymakers at the time was to be included. Beyond this, they saw APEC as a potentially helpful instrument to advance the U.S. general interest to increase American access to markets everywhere, in line with its liberal grand strategy orientation, described by Ikenberry in Chapter 2 of this volume. Overall, the expectation at the time was relatively modest.

Were these objectives achieved? Certainly being a member of APEC helped the United States establish itself as a member of the Asia-Pacific community—thus achieving its primary goal. APEC is still the only regional multilateral economic forum in which the United States is a member. As for trade liberalization, the answer is mixed. The Bogor Declaration was seen as a symbolically significant achievement. APEC also has helped to apply political pressure for liberalization to global trade negotiations, namely the GATT Uruguay Round and the WTO, especially the ITA case, which Washington sees as a significant achievement. But as seen in the failed EVSL negotiation, the APEC principle of voluntarism posed an inherent difficulty for APEC to carry out the ambitious liberalization agenda, including the 2010 and 2020 goals of the Bogor Declaration.

On the question of whether U.S. objectives have changed, the answer is complicated by the fact that the U.S. government originally did not seem to have an underlying, overall policy toward APEC. Rather, Washington defined and formulated a separate, ad hoc agenda in preparation for each APEC meeting. As a former State Department official points out, given the relative low priority of Asia-Pacific cooperation within the U.S. foreign policy agenda, there has been "little concentrated or continuous attention to Asia-Pacific regional cooperation, or the specific institutions, such as APEC."[52]

Less attention from top policymakers could also be attributed to different actors, such as the State Department and the USTR, pursuing different APEC agendas in the U.S. policymaking process. As a result, there has been a strong tendency for the United States to seek from each APEC meeting some short-term, concrete outcomes that would contribute to the general U.S. foreign policy objectives at the time. In other words, U.S. policymakers have been little interested in APEC for its own sake. This tendency is likely to continue.

Similarly, the United States participated in the first ARF meeting only as an invitee and with fairly modest expectations. The last-minute cancellation of Secretary of State Warren Christopher's attendance at this meeting, due to his involvement in the Middle East Peace talks at that time, reflected the level of U.S. expectation about the ARF. As discussed earlier, U.S. policymakers viewed U.S. participation in the ARF as serving to ensure other Asian countries of continued U.S. commitment to the region. In this regard, the U.S. objective has certainly been achieved.

Once the ARF was set on its way, U.S. policymakers came to expect, as they did with APEC, more concrete outcomes from each ARF meeting. Advancing preventive diplomacy as a major agenda for the ARF as well as producing some concrete measures for dealing with specific security issues, such as the antiterrorism measures, became new areas of focus in Washington's approach to the ARF meetings. Further, given China's increasingly positive participation in the ARF activities, engaging China, as well as North Korea, became another positive role of the ARF in U.S. thinking. Such expectations inevitably led U.S. policymakers to feel rather disappointed with the considerable slowness of the ARF's development. On balance, the significance of the ARF in the thinking of Asian and security specialists in Washington is largely limited.

ASHIZAWA

Conclusion

Examining Japanese and American policymaking on the founding and development of APEC and the ARF allows us to compare the two countries' respective approaches to and strategies on Asia in general and regional multilateral institutions in particular. Despite APEC's and the ARF's considerable limitations in problem solving, Japan viewed their creation as significant for its foreign policy on Asia, because these regionwide multilateral frameworks were key to realizing Japanese policymakers' earlier concepts of a new regional order in both economics and security. The pan-Pacific framework of these institutions is quite important, because due to its status as a major regional power and junior partner of the United States, Japan cannot afford to focus exclusively on either Asia or the United States. Although Japan benefited considerably from the U.S.-led hub-and-spoke system during the Cold War, it came to see such a rigid bilateral system as inherently contradictory to Japan's particular status in the long run. The more frameworks that exist, the better it may be for Japan to maneuver in its regional relations while still keeping U.S.-Japan relations as the very basis of its global and regional policymaking. Therefore, once regionwide frameworks were safely established in the Asia-Pacific, Japan could begin to move cautiously into other types of regional frameworks that excluded the United States, such as the ASEAN+3, the Asia-Europe Meeting (ASEM), and bilateral FTAs with other Asian countries.

The United States' initial indifference toward and subsequent acceptance of the proposals to create APEC and the ARF highlight the reactive nature of U.S. general attitudes toward the regional initiative for multilateral institution-building in the Asia-Pacific. Given the United States' global power status, along with the considerable power disparity between the United States and most countries in the region, it instinctively prefers bilateral or unilateral options in its policymaking on Asia. At the same time, however, it also intuitively recognizes the inherent value of multilateral activities and cooperation among the region's countries. The issue of multilateral institutions in Asia, or general regional cooperation, does not receive high priority within overall U.S. foreign policymaking. Despite some occasional rhetoric expressed by U.S. policymakers, little concentrated or continuous attention has been given to these institutions, except when they can attain immediate ad hoc results, for example, for trade liberalization or a pressing security problem.

In contrast to Japan, the United States has not been interested in these new institutions for their own sake; instead, it has concentrated on the pursuit of limited concrete results from them in a way that serves the U.S.

foreign policy agenda in a global context at a given time. All in all, the U.S. attitude toward the regional multilateral initiatives has been ambivalent. In the years following the creation of APEC and ARF, the United States, on the one hand, adamantly opposed the proposal of the East Asian Economic Caucus and initially the establishment of the Asian Monetary Fund (see Chapter 9, by Amyx, in this volume), both of which excluded U.S. membership. On the other hand, however, the United States did not resist the establishment of other U.S.-excluded frameworks, such as ASEM and ASEAN+3.

As for U.S.-Japan relations, neither APEC nor the ARF has thus far affected the bilateral relationship in a fundamental manner. As the stories of their creation show, neither institution was designed to alter U.S.-Japan relations. Although the EVSL negotiation at the 1998 APEC meeting, for instance, brought serious tension between the two countries, it nevertheless harmed each country's expectation toward APEC itself more than the overall bilateral relationship (see Chapter 12, by Krauss, in this volume). The ARF, conversely, has indirectly contributed to improving the U.S.-Japan security relationship by enabling the Japanese SDF to assume a more active role, though limited, outside the country; yet it has done little to alter the essential nature of the relationship.

Nevertheless, the impact of APEC's and the ARF's creation on Japanese foreign policymaking should not be dismissed. The successful launching of the two regionwide institutions made Japan view its horizon of maneuvering in dealing with regional matters as gradually expanding outside the long-standing U.S.-Japan bilateral framework. Japan began to see intraregional management functions as increasingly multi-tiered, as shown in its growing activism in regional institution-building over the past few years. Such Japanese multilateral and bilateral initiatives that exclude the United States would not have been possible without the prior establishment of the Asia-Pacific frameworks known as APEC and the ARF. This change in the Japanese side of the relationship has in turn posed new uncertainties for the United States in dealing with Japan and with policymaking on regional matters.

Moreover, the increasing availability of different frameworks, though still limited, brings about an environment in certain issue areas that may introduce game-like elements into the diplomatic maneuvers of the two countries, such as Japan's counterweight strategy, as Katada calls it in Chapter 8 of this volume. Considering these developments, the impact of APEC and the ARF on U.S.-Japan relations can be regarded as indirect and long-term—affecting bilateral relations in the manner in which the overall relationship is ultimately managed, by giving each country more complicated options with which to relate to and influence the other.

From the theoretical viewpoint of international relations scholarship, this chapter leads to the following three points about the existing theories of international institutions. First, it clearly shows a conspicuous limitation of hegemonic stability theory, which contends that a most powerful state (hegemon) creates and shapes international institutions to help maintain an international order. Besides the absence of U.S. hegemonic leadership in the formation of APEC and the ARF, the theory of hegemonic stability leaves us to wonder why Japan, a regional hegemonic power in East Asia (not in the megaregion of the Asia-Pacific), failed to pursue an institution exclusive to the East Asia region from the outset.

Second, the chapter also points to the inherently limited focus of the cost-benefit calculation thesis advanced by the neoliberal institutionalist theory, which argues that states create international institutions when the benefits to be derived from the political exchanges in newly established institutions (for example, alteration of transaction costs, provision of information, and reduction of uncertainty) are relatively high compared to the attendant costs (communication, monitoring, and enforcement). To be sure, the costs attendant to the creation of APEC and ARF were considerably modest due to their underinstitutionalized designs, such as the absence of a headquarters secretariat and domestic ratification requirements, as well as little need for enforcement and monitoring mechanisms based on voluntary and consensus-based principles.

Yet closer examination suggests that Japanese policymakers in fact consciously sought to reduce the very costs of institution-building by, for example, proposing to use an existing framework for a new institutional function (in the case of ARF) and advancing a loosely structured style— a forum for ministerial-level gathering—that basically eliminates the issue of monitoring and enforcement costs, as in the case of APEC. This implies that states seeking to build new institutions may deliberately try to reduce prospective costs in order to realize their goals. The cost-benefit calculation thesis does not exactly explain when and under what conditions states sometimes put extra effort into reducing prospective costs, but they sometimes do not. The discussion in this chapter illustrates underlying conditions and particular motivations that may lead states to initiate their new institution-building efforts.

Third, tracing the subsequent development of APEC and the ARF in this chapter preliminarily serves as supporting evidence for another argument suggested by the neoliberal institutionalist: international institutions often persist and tend to evolve rather than die, because of "organizational inertia, consideration of reputation, and connections to domestic politics," even when the condition and momentum for their creation have disappeared.[53] Although how the two institutions will sustain their institutional vigor remains to be seen, no member states at the time of this writing showed an inclination to abandon them.

Finally, this analysis helps to highlight certain differences between the economic and security realms. Although Japan and the United States behaved similarly in the creation of both APEC and the ARF, their relationship in the two institutions' subsequent development appears different from what it was earlier. The relationship between the U.S. and Japan in the APEC forum has tended to be confrontational and shaky, while in the ARF it has been more cooperative and stable. The two countries' expectations and objectives for APEC have fluctuated over the course of the forum's development, while those for the ARF have been constant, albeit modest. Further, the number of actors involved in the APEC projects since its inception has increased (for example, several ministries, such as finance, energy, environment, and education, and business interest groups, have joined), while such change has been quite limited (to foreign and defense officials) in the ARF.

These differences can be attributed to a general difference in the strategic environment between the economic and security realms in U.S. and Japanese foreign policymaking, and they may serve as interesting subject matter for future studies on APEC, the ARF, and U.S.-Japan relations.

12

The United States and Japan in APEC's
EVSL Negotiations

REGIONAL MULTILATERALISM AND TRADE

ELLIS S. KRAUSS

EVSL: From Bilateral to Multilateral Trade Friction

Since the mid-1990s, there seems to be a marked decline in U.S.-Japan bilateral trade friction. Although there are many reasons for this decline, it
coincides with the rise of an increasing number of regional multilateral forums, including the primary one in the Asia-Pacific, the Asia-Pacific Economic Cooperation forum, or APEC. When the U.S.-Japan political economic relationship becomes embedded in such a multilateral forum, how
does it change? Is U.S.-Japan friction necessarily diminished as a result?
How are the negotiation strategies, processes, and outcomes changed by
the multilateral context, and with what consequences? These are the main
questions raised in this chapter through the analysis of a single but crucial
case of negotiations in APEC.

As Ashizawa indicates in Chapter 11 of this volume, from the beginning Japan's goals in APEC were to legitimize its participation and leadership among Asian countries and to mitigate U.S.-Japan bilateral trade
friction while keeping the United States involved in the region. In contrast, the goals of the United States were to avoid being seen as "abandoning" Asia after the Cold War and to find a less conflict-prone arena
within which to advance trade liberalization with Japan. Thus both
hoped that APEC would facilitate their individual national goals in the
region while simultaneously mitigating the bilateral trade friction that
had plagued their relationship during the 1980s.

Early Voluntary Sectoral Liberalization (EVSL) was the major initiative at the APEC forum's 1997 Vancouver meetings. APEC's Bogor Declaration in 1994 promised trade liberalization in the region by 2010 for the developed countries and by 2020 for the developing countries.[1] EVSL's origins lay in the desire of the "free trader" nations, such as the United States and Canada, to ensure speedier implementation of Bogor in selected sectors. The United States wanted the nine initially designated sectors—environmental goods and services, fish and fish products, toys, forest products, gems and jewelry, energy, medical equipment and instruments, chemicals, and a telecommunications mutual recognition arrangement—to be considered as a complete package. Japan refused to participate in the tariff and nontariff measure portions of two sectors—forestry and fishing; the result was APEC's most intense conflict and most public "failure" in the trade arena. EVSL was one of the first occasions when U.S.-Japan negotiations resulted in a failure to reach any agreement through even a face-saving compromise, and the first such failure in a multilateral context. The EVSL negotiations thus represent an interesting and important case study of U.S.-Japan trade conflict in a regional multilateral context, and of one of the worst outcomes of the two countries' many negotiations, all within the normally consensual politics of APEC.

The case thus raises an important puzzle. One would expect that a consensual multilateral body such as APEC, resting on the principle of "voluntarism" with no enforcement mechanisms, would have mitigated economic tension more than bilateral negotiations. In EVSL, did the context instead contribute to conflict? If so, how and why?

Although the United States pushed hard for the package, this conflict was not simply the result of a blind American ideological crusade for trade liberalization. The United States had several allies in its strong push for liberalization in the natural resource sectors; at one point, all of the other APEC members, except Japan, were in agreement with the basics of the entire package.

This is also not a simple case of Japan resisting only because of the great hardships that the proposed liberalization would have imposed on important domestic groups. Japan already had one of the region's lower tariff structures on fish products.[2] In forestry products, too, Japan's tariffs were relatively low, except on such products as plywood.[3] An independent analysis of the economic effects of the proposed forestry and fish products liberalization shows almost no impact at all in these sectors, only a moderate *increase* in real income in forestry and a moderate decrease in real income in the fishing industry.[4] On the one hand, the difficulties of liberalization should not have been anywhere near as great as they were in the case of rice, considering the large numbers of rice farmers, their nationwide distribution, Japan's malapportioned electoral districts, and the importance of the rural vote to the Liberal Democratic Party (LDP). On the other hand, Japan paid a price to its international interests because of its die-hard resistance, most notably a loss of credibility to its recently hard-won political legitimacy in Asia-Pacific affairs, attained in part through its support of such regional forums as APEC and its support for that body's consensual norms.

EVSL poses the general puzzle of why a multilateral forum that could have reduced bilateral U.S.-Japan trade friction failed to do so in this case. In addition, however, several specific paradoxes are posed: Japan signed onto the Vancouver Declaration that included the nine-sector EVSL initiative, but then refused to make any concessions in forestry and fishing; the United States rejected Japan's compromise, even though it thus risked dooming the whole package; Japanese agricultural interests were fiercely resistant to any concessions, despite the minor domestic economic consequences of doing so; and the Japanese government surrendered to those interests, despite great and embarrassing international consequences. The rest of this chapter seeks to explain these puzzles and explores some of their implications for the U.S.-Japan trade relationship when it becomes embedded in a regional multilateral context.

The conclusion of this chapter argues that the global and regional multilateral context itself, the particular norms of the APEC forum, and the strategies that Japan and the United States each adopted to push their interests in this milieu exacerbated the differences of interest between them and doomed the initiative. It further concludes that not only is the U.S.-Japan relationship still important to each of the partners, but the future of APEC and of regional economic multilateralism itself depends a great deal on the two countries' being able to work out the differences in their political economies, interests, and goals. In this sense, the bilateral relationship may be said to have become more, not less, important in the new multilateral Pacific era.

EVSL: Early Preferences and Processes

Getting EVSL on the Agenda

APEC is explicitly designed to rest on three "pillars"—trade liberalization, trade facilitation, and economic and technical cooperation (ecotech). In trade liberalization, the 1995 Osaka Action Agenda attempted to implement the momentous but vague statement of the Bogor Declaration that the APEC economies should identify industries in which the reduction of both tariff and nontariff barriers "may have positive impact on trade and on economic growth in the Asia-Pacific region or for which there is regional industry support for early liberalization."[5] The following year, the Leaders' Declaration at Subic Bay in the Philippines specifically instructed trade ministers to identify and recommend those sectors in which such early liberalization could be achieved.[6]

The United States had pushed to get this language into the declaration, in part because, with Japan's cooperation and help, it had succeeded at the same meeting in getting APEC to support the Information Technology Agreement (ITA), which called for the substantial elimination of tariffs in that sector by the World Trade Organization (WTO) by the year 2000.[7] In ITA, the United States had for the first time successfully used the promise of liberalization in Asia's important information technology markets to exert leverage over the European Union (EU) during WTO negotiations to liberalize this market. U.S. officials thus became convinced that APEC was a promising new venue for concrete liberalization through sectoral negotiations that would also produce synergy for American negotiations in the WTO. U.S. negotiators consistently cited ITA as the "model" when publicly discussing EVSL.[8]

The APEC Trade Ministers' Meeting in Montreal in May 1997 provided one of the real breakthroughs in creating the EVSL initiative. U.S. Trade Representative (USTR) Charlene Barshefsky and Malaysia's Minister of International Trade and Industry Rafida Aziz succeeded in getting their colleagues to agree on the EVSL goal and on implementation through a process in which all countries would first nominate sectors they wished to include.[9] The trade ministers instructed their officials to report to them by the end of August so that they in turn could make specific recommendations for the November meetings in Vancouver. Among other instructions, officials were told to include tariff, nontariff, facilitation, and ecotech cooperation when considering the sectors. They were also urged to pay attention to "critical mass" by "significant groups of APEC members," "and where appropriate," to set the stage for EVSL's incorporation into the WTO.[10] An important liberalization initiative had thus developed from the "thin reed of language"[11] contained in the leaders' earlier statement at Subic.

The Inclusion of Fish and Forestry Products

The EVSL initiative reflected the generic American preferences and agenda for trade liberalization, but the politics of how forest and fish products specifically came to be included reflects a much more complicated process. Developing countries were primarily interested in lowering barriers and facilitating trade and technological advancement in primary products such as fruits, vegetables, and wood products. Clearly reflecting its

own regional manufacturing and processing interests in the region, Japan
nominated eight sectors, including film, pharmaceuticals, transportation
equipment, investment regulations, gum products, and fertilizer, and with
the United States, Taiwan, and Canada, environmental equipment.[12]

Even after senior officials in Singapore in late October had winnowed
out overlapping nominations and those for which there was little support, forty-one sectors were still on the table as candidates—far too many
to deal with efficiently.[13] Then, with host Canada's leadership, senior officials narrowed the field to fifteen sectors, among them forestry products
and fish products, a larger final group than most had expected.[14] The free
trader nations, including the host country, had concluded that a larger
package might be easier to get through than a smaller one, and at the last
minute a number of sectors, including natural resources, were added to
the priority list.[15]

The ministerial meeting endorsed the fifteen, but gave priority to the
nine largest (the remaining six sectors would be taken up later) as well as
to balancing primary and manufacturing products so as to bridge the gap
in concerns between developed and developing countries. Forestry and
fish products were both on the priority list. On some products, members
were asked to go to zero tariffs within a fixed deadline, as well as to remove some nontariff measures (NTMs) such as quotas.

Japan's proposals were hardly reflected in the final list. The country
was particularly disappointed that transportation equipment, namely automobiles, was not included in the list of the first nine priority sectors,
even though it was in the remaining six to be taken up later. It was also
frustrated that the United States would not include textiles, which Japan
felt was a key sector for many developing Asian nations. According to
one Japanese official, this made EVSL a case of "damage control" from
the beginning.[16]

Japan also had not at all wanted forestry and fish products to be included. Some American officials think that the NTMs were at least as
much of a problem for the Japanese as the zero-tariff targets were.[17]
Japanese MITI Minister Horiuchi was quoted as saying that Japan would
not agree to early liberalization of these sectors, and that "[w]e ought to
consider the standpoint of importing countries and avoid the subtle sectors."[18] Yet Japan accepted the Vancouver Declaration, which identified
the nine priority sectors, including the two natural resources areas Japan
had opposed. This was an action that would haunt Japanese officials
thereafter, and today "they admit it was probably the biggest mistake
they ever made."[19]

The United States had strongly supported Canada and the push for
EVSL in general, and undoubtedly worked behind the scenes for the sectors it wanted to include. After the Vancouver meeting, President Clinton

touted the EVSL's initiative as a "crossroads," because it had the potential for $1.5 trillion in market-opening results and because it affirmed lib-
eralization despite Asia's economic problems.[20]

America was not responsible, however, for at least part of what riled
the Japanese. The United States had nominated and wanted, for example,
sectors such as forestry products and chemicals, where its industries were
interested and active. It also supported sectors, such as energy, scientific
equipment, and toys, that others had nominated.[21] But the United States
had not nominated fish products. U.S. officials had considered and discussed the possibility, but wound up not nominating it. Australia, New
Zealand, Thailand, and Indonesia were among the nominating countries,
and although the U.S. fish industry was quite supportive throughout the
EVSL negotiations, it had not taken the initiative in this area.[22]

The situation was different for forestry products. The United States
was a nominating country and quite active in pushing this sector onto the
agenda, in part because of its global strategy: "A lot of the target of the
forest products initiative was Europe. . . . "[23] In this sector, previous U.S.
bilateral attempts to open Japan's market were also relevant. In the mid-
1980s, tariffs and nontariff barriers on wood product and building standards and on some paper products were one of the four sectors in the
MOSS (market-oriented, sector-specific) talks, with the agreement
reached having "disappointing" results, according to the evaluation of
the American Chamber of Commerce in Japan. In 1990, the USTR
named wood products under the Super 301 (provisions of the Omnibus
Trade and Competitiveness Act of 1988) procedure as having "unreasonable restrictions." This led to the Wood Products Agreement of 1990,
and a follow-up 1997 agreement on graded lumber. American industry,
however, still considered the level of protectionism on value-added
forestry products such as plywood to be substantial, but Japan had refused any further tariff reductions on a bilateral basis.[24]

U.S. government agencies and major American forestry groups, along
with their powerful supporters on Capitol Hill,[25] were thus keen to open
the Japanese market further and to take advantage of the opportunity afforded by the EVSL. Not only did the U.S. forestry interest groups push
for the inclusion of forestry products in the initiative, but throughout the
meetings between Vancouver and Kuala Lumpur, they were heavily involved in lobbying other countries' delegations, and "spent a lot of time,
a lot of money, a lot of hours in Asia, maybe meeting with government
people in Asia, whoever," including the Japanese.[26]

Thus, of the two sectors, the Americans gave a higher priority to
forestry; they also thought that the fish products sector would be a tougher
sell in APEC. The big producers of forest products were pushing for liberalization, but the largest producers of fish products—China, Japan,

Korea—were unenthusiastic about EVSL. "Fish we thought from the beginning was probably going to be the toughest."[27]

Thus, the preferences of the actors alone shed little light on why the
Japanese agreed to EVSL in the first place and why the United States
didn't offer to drop or make major concessions in the fishing products
area in subsequent negotiations. Answering these questions requires looking at the strategic multilateral environment, and at how the institutional
settings at home and in APEC influenced the choice of actions and shaped
the information available to the two countries during the negotiations.

The Problem of "Voluntary"

Why did Japan agree to the Vancouver Declaration if it didn't plan to
implement EVSL in forestry and fishing products? Japanese officials today
claim that it was clear in Vancouver, especially from discussions with the
Canadian hosts and the Australians, that EVSL would be "voluntary":

If you look at the ministers' statement in Vancouver, it is clearly written that ministerial leadership of member economies were free to choose sectoral initiatives or
something like that. . . . That phrase was introduced by the MITI minister himself. So we thought that the voluntary aspect of EVSL was really clearly established. Also Barshefsky said to Japan that if Japan cannot do anything about forest groups or fisheries group, but please don't disturb other member economies
on forest groups or fisheries group. So we understood that this meant that if
Japan had a problem, it was free to choose. . . . [28]

The phrase in the ministerial declaration to which this official refers
states, "Recognizing the need for a balanced and mutually beneficial
package, and recalling that *the process of early liberalization is conducted
on the basis of the APEC principle of voluntarism, whereby each economy remains free to determine the sectoral initiatives in which it will participate . . .* " (emphasis added).[29]

The italicized phrase just quoted was inserted into the statement at the
insistence of the Japanese minister of international trade and industry.[30]
For the Japanese, the "principle of voluntarism" meant exactly that: that
Japan would be free to choose the time frame, that it would enjoy some
flexibility in which products were to be liberalized, and that it could
choose the sectors in which it would participate. Thus, Japanese officials
assumed that if they wished to participate in the ecotech or trade facilitation part of any of the EVSL sectors, they could and would do so, but
they could also opt out of tariff liberalization in any particular sector.[31]
At the close of the Vancouver meetings, American and Canadian officials
touted EVSL as the "medicine of market stability" in the midst of the

Asian economic crisis, and made comparisons to the previous year's ITA. Japanese newspapers, undoubtedly based on information provided by trade officials, emphasized, however, that "[e]ven if the members reach an agreement on the issue, the plan does not carry any formal obligation."[32]

The ITA analogy also meant different things to the countries that pushed for liberalization than it did to the Japanese. For the Americans, it was the model of sectoral liberalization that could move WTO negotiations forward. The Japanese instead may have been focused on the voluntary nature of participation in ITA and on the assurances of especially Canada and Australia that

"after all this is voluntarism. No strong commitment, so please don't pull out from the forestry and fisheries sectors because that will discredit this initiative." That was the reason why MAFF decided to participate. Their understanding was that they weren't going to do anything in the tariff measures of the . . . forestry and fishing sector, but they would do something in the facilitation and eco-tech sectors, and that's how they explained it to the politicians.[33]

Neither Japanese officials nor politicians expected a problem.

The American Position and Strategy

A Balanced Package

For the Americans, EVSL was about a total package of sectors that had to be negotiated and accepted *in toto* if it was going to work.[34] After mentioning the free rider problem of liberalization, an American official said:

It was always based on the idea of critical mass, for one thing. . . . We're not going to liberalize unless there are enough countries in the world willing to join us—critical mass. For us, this includes generally the EU and always Japan, too, especially if there are barriers there we are interested in. There are a lot of developing countries involved in this process, we knew there was going to have to be a certain amount of flexibility built in with respect to some of their products maybe, maybe in terms of staging, and how we go about this meant that there was going to have to be a voluntary process. That's how we interpreted voluntary. . . . [35]

The Americans were willing to accept some flexibility in the details of participation in products and time frames, and even in the participation of some developing nations; however, they felt that Japan, as the second-largest economy in the world, had to shoulder its responsibility and make some concessions in all nine trade liberalization sectors, especially during the developing Asian economic crisis.

In all my interviews about EVSL in different departments of the American government, there was total consistency in the view that EVSL was a "package." At no time in the entire process was any attempt made to sacrifice a specific sector so that the others could go forward. Although there was linkage in negotiations among the nine sectors insofar as they were put together as a package, there was no linkage in making trade-offs among the sectors: "We wanted to make sure that there was no linkage; that was very, very high on our list of priorities."[36]

Some officials dealing with fish products suspected that the forestry industry occasionally thought that if they could only get rid of fish, their sector could be pushed through; but this was not discussed in the interdepartmental meetings: " . . . we didn't sort of amongst ourselves talk about dropping one for the other," in part because the Department of Agriculture "does do some stuff on fish also, and they also do forest products, so it would not really have made sense for them to drop one and not the other. Politically it would not have been good."[37]

The main reason, however, was strategic. It was clear that if the fish products sector was dropped, fish exporting countries such as Indonesia and Thailand, who were making major concessions in other sectors, would not see the whole package as sufficiently in their interest to make the compromises necessary for agreement in the other sectors.[38] And if that occurred, the entire initiative might well be jeopardized: "[B]asically it became clear to everybody that this EVSL would only work if we could keep the package together. Economies would start to opt out of sectors, and then the whole thing would quickly unravel."[39] This, of course, was the reason that a package of nine sectors rather than a smaller priority list had been generated in the first place. If the Americans had originally not expected such a large number of sectors to be included, and if they hadn't nominated, pushed for, or placed a high priority on all of them, they nonetheless subsequently found themselves committed for strategic reasons to ensuring that all would be kept in the package. The Americans felt that in order to get liberalization in the sectors they cared about most, they could not allow any trade-offs among the sectors.

In addition, if the Japanese could point to wording in the ministerial statement that participation in sectors is voluntary, the Americans could point to the Vancouver Leaders' Declaration, which, after endorsing the EVSL initiative, stated, "We find this package to be *mutually* beneficial and to represent a *balance of interests*."[40] This was to be the legitimation of the American and proliberalization countries' position. Despite the apparent contradiction of the ministerial and leaders' declarations, because of the latter, Japanese officials were told that their participation was necessary in order to keep the package "balanced," and that not participating in all sectors was not within the purview of the meaning of "voluntary."[41]

Peer Pressure

There was another important aspect to the American strategy—using APEC to bring peer pressure to bear on Japan while giving Japanese officials "cover" to make concessions without appearing to be bullied by the United States:

We thought . . . one of the problems with Japan, especially as this has gotten to be the mid- to late '90s, Japan has been saying, "The U.S. is bullying us. The U.S. is bullying us." Well, here's a forum that is multilateral, where there's a number of countries expressing interest in it, and Japan wants an excuse to be able to go to its people with an excuse and say, "We've got to liberalize in this sector. There's a number of countries that want us to do it, it's not just the U.S., but Indonesia, New Zealand." . . . That's the reason for playing—for taking the strategy. The other way of putting it is that you get more leverage on Japan because it's a multilateral initiative. But if they wanted to use it cleverly internally, it would've provided them with some political cover.[42]

The salience of this strategy increased after Vancouver as officials in both the forestry and fishing sectors were busy trying to come up with an acceptable package. It was at one of these meetings that MITI first realized that the Americans, Canadians, and others did not have the same interpretation of "voluntary" as they did. Instead, they considered all of EVSL to be a package and they were going to push zero-tariff targets within a fixed number of years.[43]

At first Japan was not the only member resisting tariff and NTM liberalization in these agricultural areas. In fishing, Chinese Taipei, Korea, and China were unhappy. At the first meeting in Malaysia, a Japanese representative even stood up in front of the fisheries working group meeting that was discussing EVSL and "said they could not support the tariffs and NTM portions of the initiative, and that, oh, by the way, they would speak for China, Korea, and Taiwan—Chinese Taipei—too."[44] The Japanese, however, underestimated these countries' willingness to negotiate, not to mention their bridling at Japan's presumption that it would represent them in this matter. For example, as an American official present at the meeting reported to me, "at that same meeting later on the Koreans came up and said, 'Excuse me. But you can talk to us.' And there the fun began, I guess you could say."[45]

"The fun" involved the Americans and other members favorable to fishing and forestry liberalization working hard to bring all the resisting countries around to their point of view. By spring of 1998, particularly after the February changeover in Korea to the Kim Dae-jung administration, the Koreans became much more flexible. China also moved toward some acceptance of the package, although not so much as Korea. Although Chinese Taipei remained closest to Japan in resisting liberalization, it too made some concessions. The same thing happened in forestry.[46] For varying reasons, Japan was rapidly losing its APEC "allies." Regardless of how much these other countries initially sympathized with Japan's argument about "voluntarism," they began to make concessions, a development that, according to some American officials, "drove the Japanese crazy."[47]

As the APEC Trade Ministers' Meeting in Kuching in late June 1998 was approaching, the American strategy of isolating Japan was working. Even the host country, Malaysia, could not be counted on to support Japan.[48] Nevertheless, the Japanese government was unified in sticking to its position that APEC was not the place for such tariff negotiation and that it could not make any concessions in natural resource products beyond those made in the previous Uruguay Round of global trade negotiations.

By the afternoon of June 22nd, during the Trade Ministers' Meeting at Kuching, it was clear that Japan was effectively isolated. Almost all of the other members were willing to make some concessions, and none supported the Japanese position. MITI minister Horiuchi and the other MITI officials were having a very rough time standing up to the pressure. The tenor of the discussions became unusually testy.[49] In fact, although not immediately, the MITI minister was so angry that he left the meetings early and returned to Japan ahead of schedule, refusing to endorse the chair's declaration of support for the package, calling it "insufficiently practical."[50]

The Americans, however, saw as effective their strategy of isolating Japan. As one American official put it:

. . . we were basically able to neutralize the likely supporters and Japan was left out there hanging. . . . [A]pparently it was a quite contentious meeting. The Japanese were under quite a deal of pressure at that meeting. . . . Maximum heat on them, as being the ones hanging out there. . . . They were very uncomfortable. This was basically the way we had wanted things to work out. The only way we were going to get them on board was to make them feel this heat. And it worked at that meeting, but they were very upset.[51]

The Japanese Strategy

Exploring Compromise

The Japanese had not expected such pressure or collective antipathy to their position in these sectors. Although some countries were later to waffle on their Kuching position, during the meeting the Japanese were "shocked" by the "magnitude" of their isolation.[52]

Negotiations continued in September at a senior officials' meeting in Malaysia, with no movement on either the exporting countries' position or Japan's.[53] Immediately after, in late September, President Clinton turned up the pressure during his Washington summit meeting with Prime Minister Obuchi. There he made a direct appeal for Japan to respond positively on the natural resources issues. Obuchi instead talked about taking up the issue at the next stage of the WTO. He passed the buck to his deputy chief cabinet secretary, who provided no response except to repeat the Ministry of Agriculture, Forestry, and Fisheries (MAFF) line that importation of foreign wood products would somehow lead to the destruction of Japan's forests.[54] On the same day, the LDP opened its Special Committee on Trade Countermeasures in Agriculture, Forestry, and Fishing Products. It discussed the "crisis," pointedly noting to the representatives of the three ministries in attendance—MITI, the Ministries of Foreign Affairs (MOFA), and MAFF—the Committee members' resolve to maintain unity in the government in resisting the pressures for liberalization.[55]

Despite this urging, however, the debacle at Kuching had for the first time stimulated a break in the previously unified Japanese government ranks against any concessions. Although MAFF was to remain consistently and adamantly opposed to any concessions from beginning to end,[56] both MITI and MOFA sought to find a compromise that would allow them to sign on to the initiative in these sectors: "after July we thought of the necessity for some sort of compromise."[57] Clinton's pressure had also set off alarms in the prime minister's office.[58]

MAFF apparently decided that its position needed bolstering a few days after the summit when the LDP's "agricultural policy tribe" (*nōrin seisaku zoku*) began to weigh in for the first time, mobilizing industry and public allies. MAFF also sent its minister and two political vice ministers off to Europe and Asia to gain support, possibly in an attempt to shore up resistance for the forthcoming Kuala Lumpur APEC meetings in November. Parallel to Katada's findings in Chapter 8 that Japan has shown increasing interest in coalitions with Europe against the United States on some issues, this move was probably also intended to signal to the United States and other domestic actors that MAFF could play the "European card" as well.[59]

The split among ministries surfaced clearly a few weeks later, in the third week of October, as the government attempted to "coordinate" its policies for the forthcoming Kuala Lumpur meeting. At a special meeting between ministers related to APEC and Prime Minister Obuchi, MITI Minister Yosano argued that Japan should study the impact of the liberalization measures on specific products (especially in the fish products sector) and possibly respond favorably by the abolition of tariffs. Obuchi requested that the ministers work hard to find a resolution, and at a press conference following the meeting, Chief Cabinet Secretary Nonaka even hinted that Japan might have to attempt liberalization.[60]

The Domestic Counterattack

The reaction from both MAFF and the LDP was almost instantaneous. At a press conference after the meeting with Obuchi, MAFF Minister Nakagawa reiterated his ministry's firm opposition to any concessions and indicated his displeasure at MITI and MOFA's moves toward compromise.[61]

A day later, forestry and fisheries interest group leaders met at LDP party headquarters in an emergency meeting with agriculture, forestry, and fishing "tribe" (*zoku*) leaders, as well as some executives from the party's executive council (*Sōmukai*), such as Etō Takami, a leader of the Etō-Kamei faction, who was also high in the LDP's agricultural "policy tribe." These politicians took the lead in angrily denouncing the search for concessions and in demanding that the prime minister refuse to respond to liberalization efforts in these areas.[62] They then took their demands to the prime minister's office, where there was reportedly at least one heated exchange.[63]

For a bit more than a week following this meeting, the LDP exerted enormous pressure on the prime minister and the wavering ministries—especially, it appears, on MOFA. On November 5, the representatives of the three ministries were called before an LDP committee on trade to reaffirm the prior policy of no concessions, particularly with an eye toward pressuring MOFA for its changed policy.[64] At that meeting, a MOFA division director was repeatedly asked to confirm that every member at the Vancouver meeting had told Japan it did not have to participate in every sector of EVSL.[65]

Meanwhile, on November 4, fish and forestry groups held rallies in Tokyo that were attended by thirty LDP representatives.[66] There was pressure on MITI as well. A MITI official told me that every week during 1998 there had been repeated calls from LDP politicians asking for details about Japan's position and that the issue had become very politicized.[67] MAFF too was trying to influence the other ministries in a "double attack" with the LDP.[68] It was also conducting its own foreign policy initiatives, including sending the agriculture minister along with the foreign minister to Southeast Asian countries. It is possible that it was during these MAFF tours, or perhaps during the preceding summer, that alarm bells began to go off in Washington that Japan was trying to "buy" support on EVSL in Southeast Asia using its aid money. Details are scarce, and who was doing the buying seems to vary with each American official, but many believe it to be true:

> We got reports from some of our places in Southeast Asia that the Japanese were throwing around all kinds of aid money all of a sudden, big bucks. I mean, there at least was the impression that they were trying to buy support. . . .
>
> Well actually where we . . . it was like Malaysia, Thailand . . . yeah, a lot of people thought they were trying to buy support. There's no proof. It just seems that there was more aid available then. . . . [69]

Other American officials thought it might have somehow involved the $30 billion of Miyazawa aid money that Japan was promising Asian nations in the grip of the economic crisis.[70] This might all be dismissed as rumor or misunderstanding except that some U.S. officials say they were told privately by Southeast Asian nations that it had indeed occurred.[71] There is also some indirect evidence in the Japanese press linking the dispatching of the agriculture and foreign ministers to EVSL support in return for more Japanese aid.[72] Such reports incensed the Americans. Japanese officials deny them or are skeptical that it happened.

After his swing through Southeast Asia, Agriculture Minister Nakagawa also went to Washington to consult with USTR Barshefsky and White House and Department of Agriculture officials, while the two MAFF vice ministers went to Asian countries to obtain their "understanding" of Japan's position and to inform them that Japan would make no concessions.[73] When Nakagawa returned home, he reported that Barshefsky's response was "unconvincing and unreasonable." He recommended to Prime Minister Obuchi in a cabinet meeting on the sixth that Japan not change its policy of refusing to participate in the two sectors' liberalization, a position that Obuchi and the MITI and MOFA ministers also accepted. He also told the House of Representatives Committee on Agriculture, Forestry, and Fisheries that there were now no differences of viewpoint on the issue within the government. It was all over except for the official announcement a few days later that Japan would go into the Kuala Lumpur APEC meeting with no concessions on these issues.[74]

Was the result merely a question of overwhelming political pressure on MITI and MOFA? That can be only part of the story. First, pressure alone would not explain their retreat. Surely the two ministries knew from the beginning that in searching for concessions they would have to stand up to pressure from MAFF and its agricultural *zoku* allies. Second, after the Kuching meeting and Clinton's personal pressure on him, Obuchi and some other LDP leaders had also been concerned about the damage to Japan's international and regional position. Why hadn't this concern carried the day over the parochial pressure of agricultural interests? In previous trade frictions with the United States, prime ministers had been able to bring along powerful parochial interest groups in support of agreements designed to avoid major friction with the United States. In this case the United States was joined by several other countries.[75]

Finally, why were the agricultural interests and their LDP allies so angry and so able to mobilize the entire agricultural *zoku* at the prospect of these concessions, seemingly out of proportion to any economic impact such concessions might bring? And what arguments could they make to the prime minister and other government officials to convince them to override the important concerns of MITI and MOFA?

The answer to these questions lies in a combination of Japan's WTO strategy regarding agriculture, the symbolism of the issue to broader agricultural interests, and the inability of Japan to get the free trader group in APEC to make any concessions at all.

When Japan began to realize that it might be isolated in APEC on this issue, even before Kuching, the Japanese agricultural press, MAFF officials, and agriculture politicians had consistently seen EVSL in the natural resource sectors as a "preliminary skirmish" before the next WTO round of negotiations. They further saw the U.S. strategy to include these sectors in EVSL as a threat to Japan's own strategy for that global multilateral body. Thus, they argued repeatedly that Japan could not liberalize agriculture beyond the previous Uruguay Round concessions it had made.[76] The latter was due in part, according to some American officials, to a promise made to the LDP *zoku* politicians that after the Uruguay Round concessions there would be no more for a while.[77] A MAFF official indirectly alluded to this when he explained that even "nuisance tariffs" could become symbolic, and if officials decided to lower them immediately they couldn't because it would take a great deal of time to get the politicians and industry groups to agree. It couldn't be done until perhaps a new comprehensive round of global negotiations.[78]

A senior Japanese government official involved in APEC indicated that some countries proposed to Japan that it should merely offer to "cut" the parts of its fishing tariff that were already zero or offer to cut its already low tariffs in the 1 to 2 percent range over an eight-year period. The official said, however, that they could not easily accede even to that because it would go against the language of voluntarism that the MITI minister had inserted into the Vancouver declaration. He then went on to elaborate on the strategic calculations involved:

And also our people in forestry and fishery products were fearful that if we say something, . . . by doing so we will invite further interest. "Okay you mentioned 50 percent, but this is really nothing. Is that a really responsible attitude from

Japan?" etc. Then we'll enter into another political pressure, "Why didn't you propose a meaningful position?" etc., etc. . . .

And also our agriculture people thought that the real battle might be coming in the WTO negotiations; APEC is not the place of tariff negotiations. So under the politically difficult situation, they couldn't say anything about the possibility of making tariff reduction in these difficult sectors. But if they make something in APEC, then people in WTO will ask for further concessions. . . . So from the strategic perspective of trade negotiators on fishery and forest products, they didn't have a full margin of maneuver. So they are really fearful of incomplete tariff negotiation, or too early tariff negotiation in the forum of APEC, which isn't basically considered as a forum of negotiation.[79]

Japanese officials thus feared that any concessions in EVSL fish and forestry products would leave Japan open to further pressure for even more concessions, as well as leaving it with little with which to negotiate within these sectors in the next WTO round. Finally, there was the added problem that differences in tariff rates and the equity of reductions can be negotiated before substance in the WTO, but could not be accomplished in APEC.[80]

Early concessions in any agricultural sector also carried wider strategic symbolism. When asked directly if the EVSL conflict was in fact connected to the issue of rice, most Japanese officials, including those in MAFF, said it was not.[81] In the strict sense of a direct connection, this is literally true. It is clear from press reports and officials' statements, however, that agricultural interests and their governmental supporters feared that EVSL was but the opening wedge for a broader attack on agriculture in the next WTO round. This made forestry and fish products the symbolic first line of defense against similar pressures in rice. As an article in the agricultural press put it, "Within the Ministry, a strong, dangerous feeling is spreading also to agricultural products [*nōsan butsu*] not confined to the forestry and fish products which are targeted"; and the United States and other agricultural exporters will make the focus of the next stage of WTO negotiations "large scale reduction of farm product tariffs."[82]

Another article at the time of the mobilization against MITI and MOFA concessions argued directly, using the metaphor of the storming of a *daimyō* (feudal lord) castle, that "[it] is de facto the first skirmish of the next stage of WTO negotiations. If Japan stumbles here it will generally destroy the WTO strategy, and inevitably we will stand in a difficult position in the agricultural sector, starting with rice, the 'castle's keep' [*honmaru*]."[83] This perception led to agricultural interests and their political and bureaucratic allies opposing even the mildest concessions in fish and forestry products in APEC lest the defense against rice liberalization in the WTO be symbolically and strategically undermined.

MAFF's consistent hard line against concessions in EVSL, and the instantaneous and fierce counterattack by *zoku* politicians, MAFF, and interest groups against MITI's and MOFA's wavering, can be explained only by reference to this strategic calculation concerning the next round of WTO negotiations, both in these specific sectors and in agriculture more broadly. It was undoubtedly these arguments as well as the ferocity of the pressure that finally convinced Prime Minister Obuchi to adopt a hard line, too.

A final factor was the American response to attempted concessions. The Japanese had indicated to the Americans that even cuts to 1 percent tariffs, for example, in the fishing products sector, might be much more doable than going to zero, as the United States and other exporting countries were demanding; but the Americans would not accept that.[84]

Some Japanese officials feel that this and other concessions offered by Japan were never considered seriously and that the Americans were rigid in sticking to their view that the whole package was necessary. When MITI and MOFA realized that the Americans and Australians would rebuff their concessions, by the beginning of November even these ministries gave up their attempt to find a resolution. After mentioning the MITI and MOFA's moves toward concessions, a government official told me that Japan realized that "incremental compromise" made no sense in this case in dealing with the United States, Australia, and New Zealand. Thus, Japan stopped considering compromise. He further confirmed that these other countries' uncompromising attitude legitimized MAFF's successful defense of no concessions at all.[85]

So the American strategy of demanding cuts to zero and making no exception to these demands in the case of Japan helped confirm MAFF's claims that a hard-line stance of making no concessions at Kuala Lumpur and toughing out the international consequences was the right position for Japan.

Kuala Lumpur: Confrontational Anti-Climax

The Americans, however, still held out some hope that the Japanese might concede if President Clinton could use his considerable persuasiveness at the leaders' meeting to convince Prime Minister Obuchi that it was in Japan's best interest to go along.[86] Other American officials are a bit more skeptical and think that even for Clinton it really would have been "sort of a Hail Mary pass at that point."[87] Japanese officials are certain it wouldn't have made a bit of difference, because Obuchi had already made his final decision more than a week before at the cabinet meeting, and by then even MITI and MOFA had fallen into line.[88] In any event, when President Clinton decided not to make the trip and sent Vice President Gore in his place, all American officials gave up any hope, knowing that any prospect for success would have to be at the WTO.[89]

The meetings turned nasty anyway. According to the Japanese press, a bilateral meeting between USTR Barshefsky and MITI Minister Yosano was quite confrontational.[90] Barshefsky also then publicly accused Japan of trying to induce Indonesia, Thailand, and the Philippines to reject participation as well, touting their refusal to be influenced: "[T]hree of the ASEAN countries who had been visited by Japan and urged to withdraw not only did not withdraw, they improved their tariff cut offers across the board in all nine sectors." She also made it clear that the United States had to keep forestry and fish products in the package because otherwise the ASEAN countries and New Zealand would not get what they wanted from EVSL and it would have unraveled: "You would have no initiative left. You have nothing left."[91] As another official put it to me:

You have to remember that the other economies, particularly the ASEAN members, they relied on us to push Japan, because they knew they couldn't push them themselves. Charlene thought it was her responsibility, that the others were counting on her.[92]

Barshefsky also stated publicly that "Japan has gone around the region offering assistance in the form of money to countries willing to back away from the [trade] initiative." A Japanese Foreign Ministry spokesperson denied Barshefsky's charges.[93] Combined with Vice-President Gore's attack on the meeting's Malaysian host Mahatir, the Kuala Lumpur meeting proved to be the most contentious in APEC's history.

EVSL, APEC, and U.S.-Japan Relations: The Implications

What went wrong in these EVSL negotiations with the United States and Japan at the center of the conflicts? How did the multilateral, rather than bilateral, context affect the conflict? What are the consequences of the friction? The implications of EVSL for U.S.-Japan relations in APEC and other multilateral negotiations can be seen in at least six areas.

Trade Friction

Most simply and obviously, two current ideas—that U.S.-Japan trade friction has become obsolete because of multilateralism, and that America can engage in "Japan passing," concentrating on China and Southeast

Asia and ignoring Japan because its economy is no longer dynamic and because it is too difficult to open its markets—are myths. The two political economies are still divergent in many respects, and APEC and other multilateral bodies have not eliminated the frictions that can result from that divergence, even if they have changed the process by which they are handled. Similarly, any Japanese hope that APEC and other multilateral bodies would provide a complete buffer against U.S. pressure and friction is also belied. The United States cannot ignore Japan, and Japan is not safe from U.S. pressure, not despite but *because* there are more multilateral trends in the Asia-Pacific today. To accomplish its goals, each country must take into account how to get the agreement of the other. Multilateral bodies require coalition building, but because each of the two largest economies in the region can abort or block any of the other's initiatives,[94] resolving or managing the differences between them remains as important as ever.

The Potential for Conflict in Multilateral Settings

The issue of forestry and fishing products might not have put the two countries on a collision course were it not for the new multilateral context. Of course, the United States and Japan had previously fought and negotiated bilaterally over these products; there had been a history of American dissatisfaction with Japan's barriers to imports of forestry products as well as some aspects of fishing products. As a result of previous bilateral negotiations, however, despite continuing dissatisfactions, a modus vivendi had been reached in both sectors. Placing the two sectors on the EVSL agenda in APEC, however, gave American domestic groups, both commercial and bureaucratic, the opportunity to push for further openings in the Japanese market. These sectors might not have been given such a priority in bilateral negotiations.

The multilateral setting of APEC also gave American bureaucratic players the opportunity to use a strategy vis-à-vis Japan that could not have been employed in a bilateral context. Although the United States was keenly aware of the domestic political consequences and controversy of raising a trade issue that involved both zero tariffs and nontariff measures in any primary sector product, it forged ahead and insisted that Japan participate in a way it might not have in bilateral negotiations. The multilateral context provided both countries with political cover. The U.S. negotiators' explicit strategy was to use the peer pressure of almost all other Asia-Pacific countries to give their Japanese counterparts the excuse to make concessions they would have found difficult to do bilaterally. The U.S. negotiators, however, benefited too from the political cover of multilateralism. After a decade of criticism and reaction within Japan about U.S. "bullying" in bilateral trade negotiations, pressure could be brought to bear on Japan within a multilateral context in which the United States couldn't be singled out for blame or overbearing unilateralism. Without the opportunity provided by the multilateral forum, the Americans might not have put either sector on their negotiating agenda or considered them targets of likely success worth the attempt.

Both countries made crucial strategic errors during the negotiations. Indeed, it was probably more the clash of their strategies than the gap between their preferences that doomed EVSL negotiations.[95] Japan's agricultural interests were so focused on the next round of WTO negotiations and how concessions in APEC might affect these that they could not look beyond that narrow perspective to see how little the fish and forestry sectors would actually be harmed. Nor were they particularly concerned about how much Japan's other national interests—its newly won reputation for leadership in Asia and its important relationship with the United States— would be hurt by refusing to make some concessions in both sectors.

There may have been validity to the concern of agricultural interests and the government that the Americans would try to discount any Japanese concessions in APEC in subsequent WTO negotiations. But its better strategy might have been to make some minimal concessions in trade liberalization in these two sectors to satisfy the United States and then to fight the battle against further concessions at the WTO. There Japan could have counted on the EU as an ally. As it turned out, the EU at Seattle refused to go along with the whole EVSL package anyway, but Japan had already paid a political cost to both its Asian leadership image and to U.S.-Japan relations.

The Americans may have made their most important strategic error in pushing a multisector initiative without allowing for bargaining over trade-offs among sectors. As rational as it was for the United States to use peer pressure and to tie together all sectors as a package to prevent selective defections, its approach ultimately failed for a simple political reason: all negotiators in all countries must have some room to maneuver and to justify concessions made in politically sensitive areas by showing that they achieved greater gains, or fewer concessions, in others. A package, multisector initiative without the possibility of bargaining across sectors was too rigid to enable the kind of sensitive domestic political concessions in forestry and fish products that Japan was being asked to make. This was particularly true because Japan's high-priority sectors, such as automobiles, had not been included in the original nine-sector package. Thus there was even less incentive to accept, and little ability to justify, the package in toto. Had such sectors been included, they might have helped offset and balance out the natural resource sector defeat.

Costs of Failing to Reach an Agreement

Japan spent a good deal of political and financial resources trying to legitimize its participation in and leadership of Asia during the previous decade. Indeed, it played a major role in founding APEC itself. One of Japan's aims in supporting multilateral forums was to create something of a buffer for itself and other Asian countries against bilateral American trade pressures (and potential American protectionism) and to legitimize its leadership role in Asia.[96] Yet in EVSL, Japan found itself isolated with few allies within the very forum it had helped to build. Instead, it was being pressured by a large coalition, including its Asian trading partners, who were acting as allies of the United States, to liberalize in a politically sensitive sector. As it turned out, Japan's simultaneous initiative in proposing the Asian Monetary Fund in response to the East Asian financial crisis (see the Amyx and Katada chapters in this volume) probably mitigated some of the collateral damage to Japan's reputation from the EVSL debacle. But for APEC, the failure of EVSL was worse, and relatively unmitigated. APEC lost its momentum as an organization, and because it no longer seemed to be a good location for "forum shopping" on trade liberalization, for a few years the United States seemed to lose interest in it.[97]

The Negotiating Process and Outcomes

That negotiation led to complete stalemate was also affected by the multilateral context. In previous bilateral negotiations over the years, the United States had almost always succeeded in wresting some domestic concessions from Japan, but it had almost never achieved all of its original aims. In this case, the American's ability to compromise was severely constrained by the multilateral context of the negotiations. The United States could not allow Japan either to opt out of either sector or to accept a compromise on the tariff and nontariff barrier elimination without threatening the entire negotiations, because forestry and fish product exporters like Thailand and Indonesia might defect from other sectors of even more importance to the United States and other countries. The multilateral context tied American negotiating hands to an all-or-nothing position, and in the process also tied the hands and unintentionally undermined the efforts of those Japanese players—MITI, MOFA, and the prime minister's office—that were prepared to compromise.

Another clear implication of both countries' strategies in the EVSL case is that, much more than has been recognized in the rhetoric or literature, APEC in the area of trade is very much a "nested game"[98] within the larger WTO. This is true to a greater extent than bilateral negotiations have been. Note that the American strategy of accepting EVSL as only a package and the need to get Japan to agree in all sectors was rooted in the U.S. desire for a critical mass of countries to create leverage on Europe in the next WTO negotiations. Also, Japan's ultimate resistance to concessions in the two primary sectors was intimately linked to its fear of undercutting its own WTO strategy in agriculture.

The United States faces a dilemma with regard to agriculture and APEC and WTO negotiations. Clearly, on the one hand, Japan will never negotiate liberalization in agricultural products in APEC, but only in the WTO. On the other hand, the United States fears that without prior agreements in an Asian forum like APEC, Japan and Europe may make a common cause of resistance in the WTO, making it more difficult to gain concessions. Recent thorough research by Christina Davis, however, indicates that trade agreements in agriculture are more likely to occur when there is strong, cross-sector linkage and legal framing, which by and large means in the General Agreement on Tariffs and Trade/WTO framework, than in any other negotiating context.[99]

APEC's Consensual Norms

Both countries, in different ways, counted too much on APEC's vaunted Asian norms. Since its inception, APEC has prided itself on its "soft" norms of voluntarism and peer pressure rather than binding force or "hard" legalism to bring about progress and agreements. Indeed, it has often been assumed that voluntarism and peer pressure are synonymous. EVSL showed these norms to be overly vague and potentially contradictory. Japan relied so heavily on the concretely undefined norm of voluntarism that it either misunderstood from the beginning or failed to see the possibility that others might eventually interpret this norm differently.

The United States, conversely, put its faith in the tremendous peer pressure that it thought would eventually force Japan to go along by allowing its negotiators the political cover to concede. It failed to realize that the perceived costs of conceding completely were too great for Japanese domestic interests and the government, given their linkage to the next WTO round and their inability to show any real concrete sectoral gains. EVSL showed that APEC's vague, consensual norms have the potential, through failures of information and coordination, to handicap agreements and contribute to conflict as much as they might foster harmonization.

U.S.-Japan Relations in APEC

The EVSL conflict had important negative consequences for U.S.-Japan relations and APEC. As a Japanese official made clear,

First is that it has destroyed completely the constituency for APEC in the Japanese government and Japanese political policy making area. It really made our job—my job—more difficult after everything. And the Japanese attitude toward APEC became really negative, within the government and within the members—the MPs [members of Parliament]. It's true that has really destroyed the support for APEC in Japan. . . . [100]

There was particular bitterness toward Canada and especially Australia because the latter had been the main beneficiary of APEC. Yet instead of trying to mediate in this negotiation, Australia completely sided with the United States. Because of the experience with EVSL, it would take a full two years before MITI made any new initiative in APEC.[101]

There was an equally negative consequence on the American side—bitterness and a hesitancy to use APEC again as a vehicle for trade liberalization. As an American official succinctly put it to me, "I think that there's a real reluctance to try to do that again."[102] The negative reverberations from EVSL at the domestic level in both nations does much to explain the apparent loss of attention and perception of APEC's significance in recent years.

The combination of the failure of APEC to play a more central role in managing the East Asian financial crisis and EVSL the same year fundamentally altered the key players' attitudes toward the organization. Both the United States and Japan (and Singapore and other countries) are now pursuing bilateral free trade agreements rather than concentrating on using APEC to attain ambitious, mutually beneficial trade outcomes. In game-theoretic terms, each has decided to pursue its own selfish "rabbit hunt" instead of the cooperative "stag hunt."

Conflict, however, can also perform a positive function if it results in the realistic adjustment of the adversaries' relationship.[103] Ironically, the EVSL conflict may have moved both countries' officials closer on their views of APEC's proper, if much more limited, role in the trade area. After EVSL, MITI's discussions about APEC's function led them to believe that it can best play a role in the area of trade implementation and capacity building for application of WTO agreements. There was an emerging consensus within the Japanese government that this was in the best interests of Japan. Japan's first initiative in APEC after EVSL, in 2000 at Brunei, was along these lines.[104] The Americans have also moved in the direction of using APEC less for trade liberalization and more for trade facilitation to lower transaction costs, including customs issues: "I think tariffs and some of these agricultural policies, countries are only going to address those in a multi—the WTO forum. And that would be the U.S. policy as well."[105]

Given the independent but similar responses of both governments to the EVSL case, it is clear that their preferences about the role and function of APEC in trade now may be much more realistic and overlapping.[106] This bodes well for future cooperation between the United States and Japan in APEC should they choose to take advantage of this unintentional synergy. Whether APEC can keep the interest of the U.S. government without an active trade liberalization agenda, however, is another question.

The growing interaction of the United States and Japan within a multilateral context can thus change and complicate the parameters of their relationship. It influences what issues get on the agenda, the strategies of each toward the other, how and whether those issues are managed well, and the outcomes of negotiation. The EVSL case does not prove that the relationship is always better off in a bilateral mode, but it does demonstrate that embedding it in a multilateral venue need not in the short term always consistently move it in a more positive and efficacious direction for either country.

Conclusion

BEYOND BILATERALISM —
TOWARD DIVIDED DEPENDENCE

ELLIS S. KRAUSS AND T. J. PEMPEL

The individual chapters in this volume have examined how three deep-rooted changes have affected the U.S.-Japan relationship: (1) serious reconfigurations of geopolitical power, especially in Asia; (2) the dramatic rise in the power and mobility of privately held capital; and (3) the expanded number and institutionalization of various multilateral organizations. These three changes have combined to reshape the previously bilateral linkage.

All three changes are essentially global or regional. As such, their genesis and influence have been largely independent of domestic political and economic trends within the two countries, and global structures are now vastly less conducive to bilateralism than they once were. Without a doubt the bilateral relationship has continually shifted, tilted, and been recalibrated in response to a bevy of ongoing alterations in domestic political, economic, and societal conditions within both Japan and the United States. However, a central message of this volume is that leaders in both countries now confront deep structural challenges that are far less subject to governmental intervention and manipulation than the much more politically malleable conditions that emerge out of domestic shifts. Leaders are still free to make choices, and actors' choices still count, but today they face new constraints and opportunities that will predispose them to behave quite differently from their bilaterally driven predecessors. The chapters in this book have focused on changes that are largely outside the realm of manipulation by the two governments. They can shape these changes only minimally; instead, they must respond to them constantly. They have choices in the ways they respond, but the broad changes themselves remain largely impervious to governmental manipulation, whether by one government alone or by both in cooperation.

Nevertheless, governments can realign their strategies, their policies, and even the trajectories of their institutionalized relationships to cope with the new changes they now face. Thus both countries can buffer a bilateral security alliance that was "adrift"; Japanese elites can take initiatives in founding multilateral regional institutions to deflect a negative spiral of routinized bilateral trade friction; and American policymakers can shift attitudes and policies to offset severe criticism of their actions during the East Asian economic crisis. This book has not only been about the challenges facing American and Japanese policymakers as they cope with changes that are not under their control; but it has also been about how they have shifted policies and positions in response to these new challenges. This has often involved preserving their fundamental goals and perceived interests even as they have sought to manage new changes. Finally, this book has addressed some of the consequences of these shifts.

This volume has analyzed the impact of these global and regional changes on the U.S.-Japan relationship in terms that are comprehensible to policymakers as well as scholars. Though informed by studies in the field of international relations and foreign policy, neither the individual chapters nor the volume as a whole has sought primarily to advance theory. Our goals have been more analytically modest. Nevertheless, the preceding chapters, and this conclusion, have provided empirical case material that bears on a number of the most significant questions in contemporary international relations. Hamilton-Hart and Amyx have asked, How do sovereign states cope with the consequences of rapid transnational capital flows? Similarly, Hatch and MacIntyre have asked, What does the growing economic power of Japan in Asia suggest about the fungibility of economic and political power?

In the aftermath of the major geopolitical changes of the past two decades, the current transitional security context of the Asia-Pacific raises the interesting question, addressed by Ikenberry and by Hughes and Fukushima, of why and how an alliance that was created to balance against a very specific enemy acquires new functions once the original enemy is no longer considered a threat. In a related vein, Mochizuki has asked, How do two powerful states linked in a major bilateral relationship cope with the rise of a new and potentially destabilizing economic and security power?

The rather sudden proliferation of multinational organizations within a region in which they were particularly scarce also raises important questions. Ashizawa has asked, How do powerful states determine whether or not to encourage new multilateral organizations? Krauss has wondered, If a country joins such an organization, how much of its sovereignty will it willingly surrender? And does a bilateral relationship become more or less cooperative in a regional or global multilateral context? Katada and Pekkanen have both asked the question, What strategies for dealing with each others' demands do bilateral partners adopt once the global and regional context has changed? This volume has thus provided our partial answers to these questions in terms of the U.S.-Japan relationship.

In this conclusion, we deal with four key aspects of the transformations wrought by geopolitical changes, financial flows, and new multilateral forums. First, we compare the ways that the three key, independent changes have influenced the different dimensions of the U.S.-Japan relationship. Second, we examine how these key trends have combined to change the management of the relationship. We argue that the bilateral cohesion that prevailed during the Cold War has given way to what we have called *divided dependence*. Divided dependence involves a relationship of great fluidity that ranges over a wide range of issues. The third section examines the new potential constraints as well as the enhanced opportunities that are now available to policymakers. Finally, we assess the implications for the region of the changes in the U.S.-Japan relationship.

How Far Beyond Bilateralism?

The three sweeping forces have combined, we argue, to move the U.S.-Japan relationship beyond bilateralism in several important ways. Nevertheless, while all three have challenged past patterns, their particular impacts have been refracted in quite different ways.

Alterations in geopolitics, for example, have meant that the previously clear-cut targets of the U.S.-Japan security alliance as well as the strategies designed to deal with them have given way to a much more complex and shaded pallet of allies and foes, along with a more nuanced set of tools by which the two governments seek to influence one another. Today, Japan and the United States respectively assess the Asia-Pacific geopolitical matrix quite differently from each other on several potentially problematic cases. North Korea, Vietnam, and Burma provide easy examples of countries whose strategic significance and geopolitical intentions are assessed differently by Japan and the United States, despite the overall agreement of both countries on many other key security threats. Both countries also have multifaceted and often incompatible views of long-term Chinese intentions, and of the best means for dealing with China's rapid resurgence as a regional power.

On security tactics as well, the differences between the two countries are quite disparate. Japan has been far quicker than the United States to pursue diplomatic and security advantages through behind-the-scenes negotiations, with a heavy reliance on economic rather than military or diplomatic pressures. Its stated objectives have long centered on a "comprehensive security" that includes a wide range of targets and tactics, with a great deal of emphasis on ensuring economic security.[1] The United States, in contrast, is far quicker to focus on security concerns and to rely on overt demands that make the most of its own diplomatic leverage and military might. These traditional instruments have become increasingly important in United States policymaking during the Bush administration. The results of the two different strategies are apparent in Southeast Asia, where, as MacIntyre has made clear, U.S. power remains considerably greater than that of Japan, despite the latter's massive economic contributions to the area. Both Japan and the United States have agreed to cooperate in missile defense development, but the United States is a far more committed advocate than its Asian partner. Japan's Prime Minister Koizumi sought to use quiet bargaining and the promise of economic assistance to move toward normalizing relations with North Korea. George W. Bush opted out of the economic agreements of Korean Peninsula Energy Development Organization (KEDO) in favor of direct diplomatic and military threats.

Finally, to add one more dimension, Japan and the United States have also taken far different approaches to the proliferation of weapons of mass destruction and global terrorism. Again, the United States has taken by far the harder line. Japan has felt itself far less directly threatened by foreign terrorist attacks and has been muted in its public criticism of suspected violators of nonproliferation norms, particularly with regard to China and North Korea. Moreover, rumors abound that the Japanese government has engaged in bribery with terrorist groups to ensure the release of captured Japanese citizens. In addition, Japan is reluctant to engage in organized sanctions against such alleged terrorist states as Libya or Syria.

In short, the new global and Asian regional security context has done a great deal to break down the previously clear lines of strategic cooperation between Japan and the United States. At the same time, however, as Hughes and Fukushima have made clear, the new geopolitical relationship in the region has bolstered many elements of the bipolar relationship, such as the rearticulation of the main goals of the Security Treaty, and the revisions of the U.S.-Japan Guidelines for Defense Cooperation in September 1997. These reinforced bilateral trends have been supplemented by subordinate movements relying on new multilateral organizations such as the ASEAN Regional Forum (ARF) and the Track II dialogues. The result has been the creation in security of what has been called "bilateralism plus." In essence, bilateralism has strong institutional roots in the security area, giving bilateralism incredible staying power in U.S.-Japan relations. Consequently, although the strategic relationship has been altered in important ways, security remains an arena in which the continuing legacies of previous eras and elites' responses have exhibited the strongest bilateralism.

After September 11, nonstate groups such as terrorist organizations have further transformed international politics and the security agendas of many states, making clear the broader ability of nonstate actors to shape the U.S.-Japan relationship. This ability can be seen even more clearly, if less suddenly, in global finance. There the institutional pattern established by the International Monetary Fund (IMF), the World Bank, the Asian Development Bank (ADB), the Group of Eight (G8), and other groupings has been far from state-driven and bilateral, as was the case in security. Most dramatically, the rise in the rapidly moving amounts of capital under private control has made it increasingly difficult for either the Japanese or U.S. governments to create a clear-cut and enforceable "national financial policy." The worldwide powers of private holders of capital have eroded the once overwhelming economic primacy of governments. In addition, within both countries there has been a substantial jump in the power of private sector players such as banks, brokerages, hedge funds, and the like to shape national behaviors. All have enhanced their independence from and influence over their respective national governments. Thus, a fixed exchange rate regime, such as that which prevailed between the United States and Japan until 1971, has become all but impossible in today's world of global currency arbitrage. Similarly, efforts to control the investment activities of global corporations, regardless of the location of their national headquarters, have proved increasingly futile. The major influence of global capital markets on bilateralism has been to increase the number of relevant players and to reduce the ability of either government to coordinate its economic actions domestically as well as to coordinate their joint economic and financial actions with each other. In this sense, it is in the areas of economics and finance that bilateralism has been subject to perhaps the most acute challenges.

Finally, the rise in multilateral forums has generated still a third and different type of challenge to bilateralism. The primary influence of multilateralism has been to create arenas, often on an issue-specific basis, within which the members will meet and bargain regularly. Most of these organizations are new, with only the most thinly developed institutional roots. But they create new arenas with new decision rules that have the potential to gain increased influence with time. Most, though not all, of the relevant multilateral organizations of which both the United States and Japan are members have sovereign governments rather than private groups as their members.[2] Short of ongoing and enforceable commitments to act as a single bloc, this means that, within these new multilateral institutions, any two government members can pick and choose their allies and opponents on a case-by-case basis. They are also far more likely to bundle together a mixture of issues rather than bargain them out sequentially. This has certainly been the case in the Asia-Pacific Economic Cooperation forum (APEC), the World Trade Organization (WTO), and as best we can tell so far, ASEAN+3 (APT). This emerging multilateralism has consequently generated important alterations from prior bilateralism.

Most conspicuously, as Katada has suggested about the finance area in Chapter 8, multilateral organizations allow Japan to pursue a "counterweight" strategy that is different from, and that helps to alleviate, some of its earlier dependence on, and inability to bargain as an equal with, the United States. This also is particularly noteworthy in areas such as global trade. As Pekkanen has shown in Chapter 10 for the WTO, Japan has become willing and able to initiate cases against the United States in ways that it previously avoided completely, even when it might have had a good legal case. Such new forums by no means favor Japan one-sidedly, however, as Krauss's analysis of Asia-Pacific Economic Cooperation (APEC) forum's EVSL negotiations in Chapter 12 makes clear. Japan is by no means assured of more favorable outcomes within the new multilateral arenas, particularly when its claims are patently self-serving and antiglobal.

To sum up, all three of these changes create a complex arena for the bilateral relationship, but they do so in very different ways. If one thinks of the bilateral ties between the United States and Japan as a game, changes in geopolitics have only slightly altered, and in some cases actually reinforced, the previous strategies of both players, even if the shape of the board has been transformed. Global finance, in contrast, has vastly increased the number of powerful players and given a premium to their economic resources in playing the game. Finally, multilateralism has expanded the arenas within which the game is played, along with the possibilities for the players to pursue far more complex and multilayered strategies as the game evolves.

There is also a clear continuum in the extent to which the relationship has gone beyond bilateralism across the three arenas of security, finance, and trade. The security arena remains by far the arena most characterized by bilateralism, while global finance is the least. Trade relationships fall somewhere between these two. There may be various reasons for this pat-

tern, but two clear contributions emerge from our analysis: first, the preexisting level of institutionalization of bilateral versus multilateral relationships;[3] and second, the current incentives for each country to move
away from bilateralism.

In security relations, the two countries long ago achieved rather high
levels of convergence and bilateral institutionalization involving coordination and harmonization of security forces and force structures. Military
elites in the two countries consequently had a greater rationale to resist
moving toward multilateralism than was true in other arenas. In economics and finance, by contrast, such bilateral coordination had not been
achieved and institutionalized; instead, lower levels of "mutual recognition" and "monitored decentralization"[4] were the modus operandi.
Whether to institute even these limited forms of cooperation was a major
source of conflict and bargaining during several 1980s trade disputes.

There are also far fewer incentives in the security than in the economic
arena for the United States to move away from bilateralism. Because the
United States has a greater relative dominance and more leverage in security than it has in finance or trade, it gains comparatively far more than
its partners, including Japan, from the continuation of bilateralism in the
security arena. The United States today has a military budget equal to
that of the next twenty largest spenders; its technological lead militarily
is probably even greater. Whatever financial or trade advantage the
United States enjoys is far less dramatic. As Hughes and Fukushima have
made clear in Chapter 3, in today's more fluid regional security situation
Japanese elites may be tempted by the "collective security" option of UN
multilateralism; however, Japan still has exceptionally strong incentives
to retain the assurances of the U.S. security blanket. A multilateral alternative or the UN option might forestall Japan's becoming entrapped in
U.S. regional strategy, but at a terribly high cost to the fundamental bilateral core on which Japan has for so long depended.

Vestiges of the Cold War in Northeast Asia add to the persistence of bilateralism in security. There is a real threat of traditional military instability on the Korean peninsula. North Korea may also have the ability to
build and deliver nuclear weapons or to sell fissile material. China remains a potential military destabilizer and the Taiwan issue has yet to be
resolved. Russia remains heavily nuclear. In short, though the Cold War
has ended in Europe, certain vestiges remain salient in Asia.

It has thus been in the interests of both the United States and Japan to
keep security relations primarily bilateral, despite the changing and increasingly complex alignment of nations in the region. Both countries have
moved gingerly to add a regional dimension to the alliance's coverage.
ARF, Track II dialogues, and multinational confidence-building measures

have gained important toeholds that supplement the prior, more restrictive bilateralism. The United States has also pressed for a multilateral approach to the 2003 North Korean nuclear crisis, in contrast to its approach in regions such as the Middle East, for example. But on balance, U.S.-Japan bilateralism continues to be relatively pervasive in the security arena.

In global finance, the relationship had a long history of global or regional institutionalization with the IMF, the World Bank, or the G7 or G8. Thus, with the explosion of currency and investment across borders in the past decade and a half, both the precedent of working through multilateral organizations and the incapacity to reach effective bilateral solutions have led both countries to seek nonbilateral solutions at both the global and regional levels.

Finally, trade has fallen somewhere between the other two arenas in the persistence of bilateralism. For the most part, trade long proceeded along two tracks simultaneously. The General Agreement on Tariffs and Trade (GATT) provided a global multilateral forum for trade, albeit, as Pekkanen has pointed out in Chapter 10, a weak one, and one in which Japan has had little confidence in neutrality. But parallel to multilateral GATT procedures, trade has also shown strong residual bilateralism, largely with the United States pressing Japan for ad hoc concessions in specific economic sectors. Japan's dissatisfaction with American trade pressure has encouraged it to move toward managing trade through multilateral venues. This includes its newfound activism within the WTO. There Japan has enjoyed considerable success in the few cases it has brought against trading partners such as the United States. Moreover, Japan has been a prime mover in creating multilateral forums for handling trade and other economic relationships, such as APEC and APT. More recently, Japan's proactive strategy of searching for alternatives to U.S.-Japan bilateralism has also been shown in its increased interest in negotiating bilateral free trade agreements (FTAs) with other countries. Nevertheless, bilateral trade negotiations continue on selected items, and other than the WTO, regional multilateral organizations such as APEC tend to reflect "soft" multilateralism without legalization or binding rules of arbitration. Such soft multilateralism allows larger powers to retain disproportionately high levels of influence, leaving elements of bilateralism to exert notable pull, even in multilateral settings, as Krauss's chapter on EVSL demonstrates.

Thus, security was the earliest arena deeply institutionalized in a bilateral fashion; as such it remains the arena in which both countries have the most incentive to continue established bilateral patterns. Soft multilateralism is only a supplement. Finance was long ago institutionalized primarily at the multilateral level; multiple private actors have gained power to shape finance, and both countries have had incentives to move even more so in that direction. Trade was only partially and weakly multilateralized, and while the United States has had little incentive to move away from bilateralism on trade matters, the incentives for Japan to do so are far greater.

These disparate findings across sectors also support those who have decried the sometimes rigid and artificial distinctions among the different schools of international relations theory. Rather than lending support to any one predetermined deductive approach, the chapters in this book have suggested instead the merit of a problem-centric approach in which complementary theories provide alternative lenses through which to understand specific empirical puzzles. Clearly, no one approach seems to explain all of the U.S.-Japan relationship in its multiple dimensions across the several issue-areas explored here. Constructivists, for example, would find support for their theories in Japan's quest for a new regional identity in economics, but much of Japan's reaffirmation of the security alliance was apparently based on well-institutionalized continuations of much earlier rational strategic calculations that were congruent with institutionalist perspectives. Realists, by contrast, might see the reaffirmation of bilateralism in security as a response to the continuing, and indeed intensifying, insecurity resulting from the breakdown of the previously stable structures of the Cold War, including the rise of China that Mochizuki has described in Chapter 4. Yet greater institutionalization in finance seems a more likely response to the need for coordination in a functionally integrated world of mobile capital, described by Hamilton-Hart in Chapter 6, which is quite consonant with the assumptions of liberal institutionalism. Finally, the establishment of many new but weak multilateral enforcement organizations in the Asia-Pacific is an apt showcasing of neoliberal assumptions about institutional "insurance regimes" aimed at decreasing uncertainty but also revealing an underlying failure to solve the problem of commitments.[5]

Yet the theoretical evidence is mixed even within each issue-area. The norms and institutionalized relationships of the U.S.-Japan alliance, as Hughes and Fukushima's chapter has mentioned, have also motivated Japan's hedging of its security through bilateralism in addition to any purely realist search for security in an anarchic world. The attempt to coordinate increasing interdependence in finance, while heavily supportive of liberalism, also contains elements of realist conflict over relative gains that would follow the establishment of an Asian monetary fund, as both the Katada and Amyx chapters describe. In addition, Krauss's chapter on EVSL reveals an interplay between Japan's "mercantile realism"[6] and the United States' use of presumptive multilateral norms to assert its primacy within APEC.

Each country's strategies also intentionally mix and match elements that political scientists like to keep separate. Thus what Ikenberry calls the United States' "liberal grand strategy" works side by side with a realist-oriented military hegemony that utilizes America's security capabilities to gain economic advantage in areas such as Southeast Asia (as noted by MacIntyre). Japan has hedged its dependence on the United States by creating multilateral regimes in the Asia Pacific (see Ashizawa's chapter), by enacting a "counterweight strategy" in finance (as noted by Katada), and by competing fiercely with the United States to develop manufacturing networks in Southeast Asia (as per Hatch). For Japan's elites, these strategies coexist comfortably alongside "bandwagoning" with the United States on security matters. Like most countries, Japan wields a self-interested economic sword in the midst of the most legalistic and normative regime, the WTO (as Pekkanen has noted), even as it winds up cooperating with the United States to maintain the latter's preexisting dominance in international global financial regimes such as the IMF (see Amyx's chapter).

For the most part, particularly in conjunction with changes in global finance, these patterns have made bilateral bargaining, especially on economic and trade matters, less probable. As Yoshihiro Sakamoto, vice minister for international affairs of the Ministry of International Trade and Industry (MITI) put it in a speech to the Foreign Correspondents Club of Japan, "In . . . considering the globalization of industrial activities, it is no longer relevant to negotiate and have an agreement on issues related to global industrial industries in a limited bilateral context such as between Japan and the U.S. The era of 'bilateralism' is over. This is not to say that bilateral frictions will disappear. But any such friction from now on will have to be solved in accordance with the WTO and other international rules and by following market mechanisms."[7]

From Cold War Cohesion to Divided Dependence

These major changes in the context of the relationship have reshaped the ways in which the relationship is now managed. Both governments now interact with one another in far more complex ways. Six main consequences flow from this mix of geopolitical, financial, and multilateral shifts: (1) potential allies and opponents are more fluid, (2) nonstate actors have become more influential, (3) issues are managed within new forums, (4) military and economic relations have become more independent of one another, (5) cumulative friction has declined, and (6) issues have become fragmented and depoliticized. Each of these outcomes derives from a combination of at least two of the structured changes we have described, and each deserves attention.

More Fluidity of Potential Allies and Opponents

First, there has been a substantial challenge to the relationship between allies and opponents. Geopolitics in Asia no longer carries the open-and-shut, black-and-white certainties of the past. Almost no problem in the bilateral relationship, whether military or economic, can currently be discussed or managed without China or ASEAN looming as an important conditioning factor. South Korea and Taiwan also play significantly into the regional equation, in ways that are no longer simple extensions of Cold War contestations.

As Mochizuki's chapter has made clear, China has at least two faces—economic and military—and either face can be smiling or frowning autonomously and in rapid succession. This is particularly true with the increasing separation of the military and economic spheres in the US-Japan relationship. Both countries now have wary, though diverse, military relationships with China that often move quite independently of their economic interactions.[8]

Complex multinational economic ties have proceeded principally through private trade and investment involving U.S., "Greater Chinese," Southeast Asian, and Japanese firms. The increased influence of autonomous nonstate actors is beyond question. All of them have incentives to monitor and meddle in the U.S.-Japan relationship. Along with the stagnation of Japan's economy and perceptions of declining or stable opportunities in Japan, there has been a phenomenal rise in interest about China within the Washington Beltway and a concomitant decline in attention to Japan. Simultaneously, both Japan and China have become increasingly interested in one another economically, as well as in ASEAN, both Koreas, and the individual nations of Southeast Asia.

China also has come to play a larger role in Japan's economy and its politics. The recent trade war between Japan and China over agricultural products that Pekkanen has described in Chapter 10 is only one manifestation of this trend. So is the increasing U.S. focus on the rising bilateral trade deficit with China. Japanese-owned firms are now also heavily investing in China. Undoubtedly we will see more instances where U.S.-Japan trade friction will be displaced by Japan-China or U.S.-China conflicts. In both countries, nonstate actors will increasingly shape not only each country's views and actions toward China but also the other country's policies as well.

China is the most important potential ally for each country given the more complicated and fluid geopolitical and economic conditions now prevailing in Asia. This generates diverse patterns of cooperation and rivalry, like three ever-shifting legs on a triangle. While reaffirming and regionalizing the alliance with the United States, Japan has nonetheless adopted a more wary policy than the United States has adopted over Taiwan. Nor did Japan follow the U.S. sanctions on human rights following the Tiananmen Square incident for as long as the United States did.[9] Even though the United States and Japan are as close as ever economically, and perhaps even closer militarily, each must now consider the other's actual and potential relationship with China on most issues that arise between them. No longer can either presume agreement with its long-time partner, nor can either assume that the two countries' joint relations will be the primary shaper of events across Asia.

South Korea is unquestionably an ally of the United States and important for Japan economically and strategically, but its growing economic prowess, particularly in some fields of information technology, simultaneously makes many of its companies powerful economic competitors. Meanwhile, its policies toward North Korea often differ from and constrain the ways in which the United States would like to respond toward alleged provocations from the Democratic People's Republic of Korea (DPRK), particularly when South Korea gains support from Japan. Both Japan and the United States have many reasons to want ASEAN to serve as a unified voice for Southeast Asia. But on occasion each country also has strong reasons to return to bilateral country-to-country actions with one or more of ASEAN's member countries, as MacIntyre's chapter has discussed.

The examples can be multiplied. Japan gained allies in its contest against U.S. protection of steel, particularly the European Union (EU) and Brazil. The United States had many Southeast Asian allies, all challenging Japan's position on EVSL. Japan was much closer than the United States to President Kim Dae-jung in his "sunshine policy" toward North Korea, as well as to his successor, Roh Moo-hyun, and it had more support from the region than the United States did in its attempt to establish the Asian Monetary Fund (AMF) after the East Asian financial crisis. The United States and Japan remain genuinely close on most big issues, but on numerous other issues they have become far freer to pursue separate and sometimes conflicting agendas involving diverse allies and opponents.

The Increasing Importance of Nonstate Actors

Nonstate actors, once constrained to advancing their policy agendas through bargaining with, or within, government agencies, are now far more capable of acting unilaterally, with important consequences for the bilateral relationship. Capital flows have become denationalized while private finance, portfolio managers, banks, bond ratings agencies, and global accounting standards have gained increasing scope and heightened levels of autonomy. Furthermore, globally invested corporations headquartered in the United States, Japan, or elsewhere now have enhanced capabilities to make important financing, production, and even taxation decisions that are less nationally exclusive and more independent of government controls. Even nongovernmental organizations (NGOs) have gained enhanced importance in global negotiations, from trade, labor standards, and the environment to whales, land mines, and women's rights.

The Increasing Number of New Arenas

The rising number of actors is further complicated by the increasing number of arenas within which policy problems that affect both Japan and the United States are now addressed. As several of this book's chapters have made clear, more and more global and regional multilateral organizations have been woven into the policy process. It is now increasingly easy for both the Japanese and the U.S. government to engage in "forum shopping." This was illustrated clearly in Pekkanen's chapter on Japan's increasing use of the WTO process both to defend its protected sectors from U.S. pressure and to attack American trade practices. The rules and regulations of such forums can be invoked in support of one or another party to the dispute, mitigating any simple disparities in power between the two countries as the key factor in negotiations.

The Separation of Military and Economic Issues

There has been an increased separation of the military and economic dimensions of the bilateral relationship. In the years immediately following World War II and continuing through the end of the Cold War, the economic and military dimensions of both countries were intimately connected in service of a common goal—military security. The United States was anxious to ensure its global and regional alliance structure and was convinced that Japan's economic recovery would help Japanese supporters of that alliance retain their grip on government power. As a result, the United States retained largely open markets at home while remaining generally quiescent about the closed nature of the Japanese market, from which American exports and investment were largely blocked. In Japan, this linking of security and economics fit well with the prevailing Yoshida Doctrine, allowing the country to hold down its military expenditures and to rely on U.S. military guarantees while devoting its scarce capital resources to industrial recovery and to rapid growth in manufactured goods.[10] In fact, as Hughes and Fukushima have indicated in Chapter 3, this doctrine sought to do just enough militarily to keep the United States from abandoning its important protection of Japan, but not enough to interfere with Japan's other goals of maximizing economic growth, avoiding entrapment in any U.S. regional conflict, or acting in ways that would pose a threat to its Asian neighbors.

Subsequently, as Japan's economy soared and numerous U.S. firms began to confront substantial competition from foreign manufactures, the relationship went through a number of bilateral clashes over both structural economic differences and specific sectoral conflicts. Many American business and congressional leaders contended that Japan's growing economic prowess in the U.S. market meant that the country was getting a free ride on defense. Meanwhile, many of Japan's most successful commercial products could be traced back to readapted military technologies, and many U.S. military advances owed a considerable debt to Japanese civilian technological breakthroughs. Certain Japanese elites were not above raising such linkages as a bargaining tool on bilateral economic frictions.[11] Throughout these economic skirmishes, U.S. military leaders consistently argued that the security relationship should not be held hostage to "narrow economic interests." In Japan, meanwhile, officials, particularly in the Ministry of Foreign Affairs, also sought to put together packages of economic accommodation by Japanese firms that would reduce economic threats to the broader alliance.

What is clear is that through the mid- to late 1980s, even though the once-unquestioned linking of security and economics was no longer so tight, the military and economic components of the relationship were explicitly, and usually favorably, integrated to serve a common purpose. This has changed. The reduction in overt military threats to Japan, along with rapid economic development of most of the Asian region, catalyzed a recalibration by American leaders of the relative importance of "military security" versus "economic security," particularly under the Clinton administration.

Japanese elites also began to decouple economics from dependence on American security. Particularly after the fierce semiconductor dispute of the mid- to late 1980s, many MITI officials became more willing to resist American demands and to look for different, more multilateral ways to handle trade friction and pressure from the United States rather than automatically making concessions for the sake of the broader relationship.[12] National economic well-being has always been a critical component of Japanese leaders' definition of "national security." Indeed, Japan was one of the first countries to articulate explicitly a policy of "comprehensive security." Not surprisingly, Japanese officials have come to resist many American economic demands, thus showing little concern that military security commitments might consequently be threatened. Similarly, American policymakers, concerned about Japan's failure to deal more aggressively with the nonperforming loans at the heart of Japan's financial crisis and its global implications, have quietly pressured Japan without any linkage of finance to the security ties.

Further, as the Cold War thawed, the presence of U.S. bases on Okinawa became more fractious, particularly in response to specific well-publicized criminal actions by individual U.S. military personnel, as well as to such issues as noise pollution and the confiscation of valuable land areas. With Japan having attained affluence, the necessity of accepting the costs of keeping U.S. military bases on Japanese soil has become less pressing to many Japanese citizens, especially on Okinawa. Economic interests in both counties no longer remain easily subordinated to security concerns, whereas military cooperation can increasingly be divorced from economic competition, often resulting in increased economic tensions.

The once-unquestioned linking of security and economics began to be questioned in the economic competition of the 1980s. It became even less tightly coupled by the early 1990s, as no common, overriding purpose arose to require continued subordination of economic differences to Cold War security concerns. The increasingly separate dimensions of security and economics were most dramatically manifested in the breakdown of talks between Prime Minister Hosokawa and President Clinton in 1994. For the first time in the postwar period, the two countries failed to come to some sort of resolution over a potentially divisive economic issue. Hughes and Fukushima's chapter has graphically illustrated how, by the early 1990s, this separation of economics and security led many elites in both countries to see the alliance as unraveling and adrift.

It was largely to protect the security component of the relationship that the two countries engaged in the discussions that eventually led to the so-called Nye Initiative and to Japan's updating of its National Defense Program Outline. The bilateral security relationship was reinforced in ways that had little linkage to their more conflictual economic ties.

More than a decade of slow to no growth in Japan has transformed American leaders' thinking from worries about the economic threat posed by Japan's presumed economic prowess into concerns about a potential global meltdown due to Japan's anticipated financial collapse or to its potential to trigger a wave of global deflation. Furthermore, under the Bush administration, and particularly after September 11, military concerns have again taken center stage for the U.S government. America's bipartisan commitment to balanced budgets of the mid- to late 1990s has ended and the military budget has gained its largest increases in twenty years. For the Bush administration, military concerns trumped economics for at least the early years. American attention to Japan's economy had a similarly low profile. It is unlikely that U.S.-Japan relations will ever again see economics as closely linked, and subordinated to, security matters as it once was. The continuing bifurcation of military issues and economics is apparent as the United States pressures Japan to undertake structural reform within its failing domestic economy, while Japan quickly, and with little overt U.S. pressure but with its warm acceptance, has dispatched Maritime Self-Defense Force ships to the Indian Ocean in close cooperation with the U.S. war on terrorism, launched its own spy satellites, engaged in fleet modernization, entertained joint research on missile defense, and talked about preemptive strikes against any North Korean missile threats.

If the previous four points stress greater complications and potentially new types of disagreements in managing the bilateral relationship, two others promise to diminish certain tensions that bedeviled the relationship in the past.

The Decline of Cumulative Friction

By the late 1980s, years of friction over trade had led gradually but inexorably to the buildup of bilateral tensions that radiated well beyond simple economics. In Japan, America's continued emphasis on trade friction came to be perceived as a constant barrage of "Japan-bashing," with the United States portrayed as using Japan as a scapegoat to avoid focusing on its own domestic economic problems. Such generalized resentments, especially among the young, led to a new word in the Japanese lexicon: *kenbei*, "despising America." In the United States, meanwhile, Japan's closed markets and export drives were associated with bankruptcies and layoffs in traditionally American industries and companies. Japan was viewed as an "unfair" but unstoppable economic juggernaught and as an increasing threat to U.S. economic well-being.[13] The accuracy or validity of these perceptions or responses was less relevant than that increasing numbers of each country's mass public saw the other country as a threat while their political elites took policy stances that, for better or worse, exacerbated conflicts in the overall relationship. Thus, Prime Minister Hosokawa found it popular to say no to the United States in the Framework Talks on autos.

As the EVSL negotiations in APEC along with Japan's AMF proposal made clear, multilateralism is no panacea for such differences of interest and approach, or for misunderstanding and miscommunication. Multilateralism does not automatically prevent conflicts; indeed, it may even have negative spillover effects on bilateral cooperation. Yet the type of intense and generalized country-to-country friction that characterized the bilateral relationship in the late 1980s and early 1990s had virtually disappeared by the early 2000s and is unlikely to be repeated within the new, more multilateral East Asian environment. Eight years of U.S. economic growth in the 1990s, plus Japan's parallel economic woes, have undoubtedly reduced earlier economic frictions. Still, Japan's trade deficit with the United States remains large, and Japanese companies still dominate many sectors of manufacturing. Nevertheless, many issues that during the heyday of the bilateral relationship would have been channeled through the two governments are now being settled within the private sector. Both because of transnational integration in the industries and because many of the issues have become more market-based and governments have ceded much of their previous sectoral monitoring to the private sector, intergovernmental negotiations and consequent frictions have often been bypassed and government-to-government economic frictions have been largely replaced by market competition.

Both governments also have been less willing to intervene in sectors where multinational tie-ups and successful market penetration have made the definition of "national interest" more complicated. Despite a continuing lopsided trade deficit in autos and auto parts, it is much more difficult for the U.S. government to take action against Japan when Mazda is partially owned by Ford, when General Motors has a joint venture with Toyota in California, and when Honda is a major employer of Ohio workers. Additionally, the 1986 and 1991 semiconductor agreements gave U.S. manufacturers enough of a market share in Japan that government attempts to open the market further are increasingly viewed as unnecessary and even as jeopardizing the success of American companies now ensconced in the Japanese market. In financial services, previously bilateral conflicts are being fought through mergers and acquisitions and third-market competition.

Even where issues are raised intergovernmentally, they are increasingly taken up in any one of several multilateral venues, giving each government the opportunity to "forum shop," as mentioned previously. Governments can now pick the forum where they believe they have the best chance for success. If either government does not like the other's trade policies, the WTO becomes a logical venue within which to seek resolution. If the United States wants Japan to reflate, it can use the G8 summits or work with private currency speculators to increase pressure. If Japan doesn't like the United States' stance on the AMF, it can endeavor to push a less objectionable version through APT. Thus multilateralism provides an often tension-reducing alternative to bilateralism on potentially conflictual issues. Surrounded by several third parties lining up fluidly on different issues, neither country can as easily blame the other exclusively for any single problem or for the nature of its eventual resolution.

A long-term reduction of tensions is also more probable with the increase in the variety and number of potential allies and opponents throughout the region. A government that supports Japan's position in one forum can support the U.S. position in another while the United States and Japan may be on the same side in still a third. China, for example, supported the U.S. position on the AMF when it was first raised, but then agreed with Japan's altered version in ASEAN +3. Japan and the United States opposed each other in APEC's EVSL, but they cooperated on finance after settling the AMF controversy, as well as on security within KEDO and ARF.

Negotiating issues and adjusting grievances in various multilateral forums is much less likely to allow any one country to become the prime target of the other's resentments. Grievances are less likely to accumulate, and neither country is likely to feel itself a permanent winner or loser. Labels such as "unfair" or "bully" are less likely to stick. Today, brinkmanship must be tempered and generalized conflicts avoided, because each government knows that the other may be a potential ally in the same or a different forum tomorrow.[14]

Fragmentation and Depoliticization of Issues

Tensions are now defused in another way: by becoming so fragmented and technical that they are less likely to attract the attention or energy of politicians in either the United States or Japan. Issues can increasingly be dealt with by both countries with low to no linkage whatsoever. In the absence of such linkages, functional differentiation prevails. Individual government agencies gain greater management over ever more technically specific issues. When trade issues arose in the 1980s, the Department of Defense was likely to be the moderating voice resisting American retaliation against Japan for fear of alienating an important security partner, and the U.S. Trade Representative sought to link bargaining on multiple sectors. In Japan, the Foreign Ministry was likely to play the same role as the Department of Defense, while MITI sought to link industrial and agricultural bargaining. In addition, on most big issues, politicians in each country often resorted to generalized grandstanding.

Today, larger numbers of issues are addressed technically, narrowly, and outside the legislatures of either country. The finance, information, defense, and even agricultural industries have become vastly more globalized, sophisticated, and technical. The greater the technicalities, the more their management is driven by bureaucrats and interest groups with particularistic expertise, instead of by politicians better equipped to deal with more general and symbolic issues.

The growing importance of multilateral forums exacerbates this trend. Trade issues in the WTO often involve highly technical legal issues. The IMF, global bond rating agencies, GAPP accounting practices, and Basel Capital Accord, while not above politics, all rely on highly technical criteria for numerous actions. Regional forums in the Asia-Pacific tend to be organized along functional lines, with APEC handling trade and development, the ARF (and previously KEDO) dealing with security, and APT focusing on financial matters. Within these organizations, separate issues are usually devolved to even narrower functional committees. Thus APEC has developed more than a dozen specialized committees and working groups for particular types of trade and development concerns. Even when the leaders of the member economies decide the general upcoming agenda for the organization, the details and management of most issues are handled by experts within such specialized groups.[15]

Specialized bureaucrats, and in many cases their affiliated interest groups, therefore shape much of the most important decision making in such multilateral organizations. It is much more difficult for politicians to become involved, unless the issue is so general and important that it promises strong political payoffs. The EVSL case for Japan or sovereignty and nationalist outbursts over American cases lost in the WTO show that politicians will seize moments when possible. But compared to the earlier bilateral era, increasingly specialized issues are less likely to become generalized and politicized. This too should reduce the possibilities for intense, general, and cumulative conflict between the two countries.

The puzzle, of course, is that despite the very obvious challenges and changes it has recently faced, the relationship between the United States and Japan has survived, and even been strengthened. The answer to this puzzle rests in the fact that by going beyond bilateralism and toward multilateralization, trilateralization, complex functional differentiation, and depoliticization, the relationship has gained new forms and depths of integration. The old relationship rested primarily on simple and unequal pursuit of an exceptionally limited set of common goals. Interactions were ritualized in symbolic affirmations of the United States' commitment to defend Japan, its democracy, and its status as an important ally in the Cold War. Japan in turn affirmed America's importance to Japan's security and economy, and Japan's loyalty to the West. Yet the downside of such simplicity was that whatever conflicts arose, they were intensified by the symbols and rhetoric of invasion, unfairness, free rides, dominance, and bullying.

The increasing complexity, specialization, and fragmentation of the relationship enhances the complex interdependence between the two countries. Each has goals and interests that on many issues coincide only partially. Each also pursues many of its goals and interests in venues other than bilateral governmental agencies. Both countries can cooperate when their mutual interests coincide, and come into conflict when they do not, with the reduced likelihood that any specific issues will threaten the overall relationship. The relationship has now become so complex and multi-dimensionally dependent across a range of issues that no single conflict is sufficiently consuming or intense to threaten the total relationship. U.S.-Japan ties, once based primarily on an overriding security goal, have given way to a more "organic" relationship that involves complex roles, inter-linked issues, and ongoing interactions. Each nation depends on the other in increasingly complex ways that maintain the relationship but make it vastly more complex and encompassing of greater divergence in interests and strategies.[16] Divided dependence now characterizes the relationship.

Costs and Benefits, Constraints and Opportunities

As the relationship has moved beyond bilateralism and toward divided dependence, policymakers have faced a new distribution of costs as well as benefits, and new constraints and opportunities. Several of these are common to both sides. It is now much tougher, for example, for either government or both in coordination to settle the issues between them. The actors who affect the relationship have become more numerous, the tools that governments control are no longer as robust, and official regulations and admonitions are less controlling. The military dimensions of the bilateral relationship are substantially less affected by such change than are other dimensions; nevertheless, the capacity of the two governments to monopolize control of the terms of their relationship has clearly been diminished.

Each government can also now use China against the other in erstwhile bilateral disputes. The United States did so when it got China to agree to concessions in the EVSL dispute (see Krauss, Chapter 12). Conversely, Japan got China to go along with a revised version of its AMF idea, even though China had originally sided with the United States (see Amyx, Chapter 9). Naturally, China may also be able to play Japan and the United States against one another. Thus, in negotiations for China's ascension to the WTO, Japan agreed earlier and on easier terms than did the United States.

For both countries as well, the participation of private actors in the new East Asian context provides a greater opportunity than previously to bring these actors into the policymaking process. Perhaps the most rational way for policymakers to manage their own loss of control over market actions is to co-opt the most important private actors. This has already happened to some extent in multilateral forums such as the North American Free Trade Agreement (NAFTA), where labor and environmental groups are now being increasingly consulted, and in APEC, where representatives of private telecommunications firms sat behind U.S. policymakers, and Japanese trade association organizations provided input to their government on APEC's Mutual Recognition Arrangement.[17] This approach has several advantages. First, it enables the governments to gain needed private sector information and expertise. Second, it enables policymakers to influence private actors. Finally, it gives private actors a stake in the outcomes, ultimately facilitating the implementation of any multilateral agreements that are reached.

Both governments now also have enhanced opportunities and incentives to increase the density and intensity of their cooperative and consultation efforts. The stakes in doing so are higher than ever in the new multilateral context, because failure to do so can result in publicly embarrassing and costly outcomes. The United States learned this in the EVSL negotiations, Japan learned it in its precipitous proposal for the AMF. Given that Japan and the United States are typically key pivot points around which multilateral regional organizations revolve, little progress will occur unless they cooperate; each, as Krauss has pointed out in Chapter 12, can veto the other's unilateral moves in such forums. Fortunately, as Amyx's chapter suggests, both countries may be learning this lesson.

If both the United States and Japan confront certain common constraints and opportunities, other costs and benefits, as well as constraints and opportunities, are also different for each country.

The United States

There is no denying that the United States, with its predominant military power, is likely to have more leverage in any bilateral relationship than it does in any multilateral context. MacIntyre, in Chapter 5, has provided graphic cases showing how this plays out in Southeast Asia. On negotiations over any particular issue with another country, American power is likely to force at least a compromise. Further, on any issue that is confined primarily to the two countries, it would be far more efficient for the United States to negotiate bilaterally.

The U.S.-Japan trade negotiations of the late 1980s are a good example of such an American advantage. Regardless of how stubborn and resistant Japan was and no matter how short of original U.S. demands eventual decisions proved to be, it was almost invariably Japan that wound up making the greatest concessions. Compare this to negotiations in multilateral forums. In a "soft" institution such as APEC, Japan was often able to refuse U.S. demands completely; and in the binding panel decisions of the WTO, if U.S. arguments are dismissed, nothing need be forthcoming from Japan.

Despite its many appeals to a preeminent power such as the United States, bilateralism has its costs. Backlash against U.S. unilateralism and its use of predominant military power and large economic markets was substantial in Japan and elsewhere even before the 1990s. That backlash was even greater in America's unilateral run-up to the war against Iraq in 2003. Conversely, a more complicated, multilateral world empowering larger numbers of private actors and more governments helps to mitigate that reaction against American power. As Ikenberry has pointed out in Chapter 2, when America "binds" itself to multilateral forums, it reassures both friends and potential adversaries about the limits of American power. Such binding can constrain one form of power, but it often allows the exercise of other forms of less costly influence. A genuine multilateral coalition, even when led by the United States, can usually press its claims with greater leverage while provoking less America-specific resentment. Because host country Indonesia and others pushed the trade liberalization agenda at the Bogor summit of APEC in 1994, the United States was ultimately successful despite the reservations of many member countries, including Japan.

Indeed, in the new conditions of divided dependence, U.S. attempts to act unilaterally often help Japan whether the United States obtains most of its objectives or not. Faced with such unilateralism, other Asian countries have greater incentives to welcome Japan's political leadership in the region as a counterweight against the United States. This was clearly shown in the wake of the 1997–98 economic crisis. Resentment against the loan conditions imposed by Washington and the IMF was vital to Japan's ability to mobilize subsequent support for the Miyazawa initiative and for the creation of APT. As China becomes increasingly stronger, Japan as well as other Asian countries will also seek to enlist it as a counterweight to any negative manifestations of U.S. unilateralism.

The United States also gains another advantage in the world beyond bilateralism when it does not have to expend its full power and credit in pursuit of its objectives. On many issues where U.S. and Japanese goals coincide, Japan can do some of the heavy lifting. The Chiang Mai initiative was sufficiently synergistic with U.S. goals and IMF prerogatives that Japan could pursue that course in an effort to head off future Asian financial crises without triggering a negative American or IMF response. Japan's actions cost the United States very little. Although American policymakers may not be completely happy with their progress so far, security dialogues in the ARF, a forum to whose founding Japan contributed, also support broad American goals.

Finally, Asian regional multilateralism also gives American policymakers a new tool with which to advance U.S. interests elsewhere in the world. As Krauss has reminded us in Chapter 12, if the United States can gain agreement in regional forums from many Asian nations, its bargaining power vis-à-vis the EU in the WTO is thereby enhanced on many issues. This was true of the successful International Technology Agreement and might have worked had EVSL been carried through. In a host of ways, therefore, greater U.S. acceptance of multilateralism can lead to serious forms of burden sharing without undermining the basic American aims of its liberal grand strategy.

Japan

Similarly for Japan, the move beyond bilateralism brings both gains and losses. At first blush it appears that Japan has gained more than the United States. American pressure for Japan to open its markets has decreased as multilateral forums and global capital flows have made such a strategy increasingly ineffective. The ability of the United States to link and deal with a full package of issues has also been reduced.

Japan has gained new tools to reduce its vulnerability in the face of American unilateralism and to advance its own interests independently of the United States. As Pekkanen's chapter has made clear, Japan has found it more efficacious to deal with U.S. trade barriers and with trade pressure within the WTO than to negotiate bilaterally with the United States. The lack of rules and allies in bilateral bargaining left Japan at a disadvantage from the outset. In finance as well, Japan has also found regional forums useful as a counterweight to the United States and as a means to pursue its own goals for leadership in Asia. And if the United States can use success in Asian forums to pressure the EU on certain issues, Japan can also ally itself with the EU when both have common objectives that deviate from those of the United States.

The rise of China as an economic and potential major military power in the region has certain advantages for Japan too; it no longer suffers the unwanted attention it previously received as an export-driven economic threat during the 1980s. China helps Japan become as normal to the United States as such countries as Germany or Britain.

There are many downsides for Japan, however. Complex, multilateral forums have removed Japan from the protective umbrella of the United States. They frequently expose certain Japanese policies, such as protection of its domestic agriculture, fishing, and insurance markets, as globally reactionary rather than as the targets of U.S. bargainers acting at the behest of American special interests. If U.S. policymakers are willing to put the time and energy into building coalitions and alliances, these can create a broader challenge, whether regional or global, to previously sacrosanct areas of Japan's political economy. No longer does Japan get the satisfaction of being of unquestioned importance to the United States, as Mochizuki has noted in Chapter 4. Unilateral Japanese intransigence can enhance American influence in the region by reinforcing distrust of Japan as a "taker" and not a "maker" of regional multilateralism.

Because the U.S.-Japan alliance has become a common asset for the whole region's security, Japan is expected to take more responsibility and risks than it used to. Previously it could rely on the Yoshida Doctrine and its Peace Constitution to justify making minimal concessions to the United States on defense and other regionally relevant issues. Even if Japan was not the free rider that some charged, bilateral arrangements allowed Japan a low-cost defense and a sustained focus on economic growth. As the U.S.-Japan alliance takes on a broader regional role, Japan is finding it increasingly difficult not to accept responsibility for both its own defense and the region's. This may ultimately involve Japan in the risk of armed conflict.

Economically, Japan now assumes much more of a burden in the region than it did previously. Even during its decade-long recession, Japan continued to provide far more official development assistance (ODA) than the United States did, as well as more aid to Asia, until 2002. The U.S. government also provides far fewer financial resources than Japan does to the rising number of multilateral organizations in the region. At the same time, Japan comes in for far more sustained and regionwide criticism than does the United States for alleged insensitivity to its militaristic history, for failing to rectify its domestic economic problems, and for not absorbing a larger portion of Asian exports.

Japan also gains a great deal, however. The new world of multilateralism it helped to create provides Japan with the opportunity to become a more "normal" nation, not only in security, but equally important, politically and diplomatically. One of Japan's major goals in the last forty years has been to legitimize itself as a player, and indeed as a leader, in Asia, overcoming the fears and enmity of its neighbors. Still snuggled within the U.S.-Japan alliance that reassures those neighbors, it has earned a measure of regional trust, respect, and leadership by helping to found and support several new multilateral organizations in the Asia-

Pacific. Lacking the United States' security capabilities and open markets, Japan uses ODA funds and financial leverage to gain enhanced influence within those organizations. In many ways, "bilateralism plus" in security combined with multilateralism in the economic realm provide Japan with the best of both worlds: continued reassurance that the United States will be seen as the "cork in the Japanese military bottle" while the country remains free to take policy initiatives and even to provide a counterweight to the United States among Japan's Asian neighbors.

In summary, in the new East Asia, the United States has lost some of its past power and incentives to exert unilateral actions. Yet if the United States so chooses, it can still exercise extensive leverage through bilateralism. To the extent that it operates through other channels and shares with Japan some of the burdens of leadership, however, it gains political cover for accomplishing its general aims. Japan in turn has lost the exclusivity of the bilateral relationship and must now bear greater political, military, and economic burdens. In return it has gained the potential for enhanced respectability with reassurance, and for autonomy without arrogance.

Beyond Bilateralism: Implications Beyond the Two Countries

The expression "beyond bilateralism" carries one meaning related to the increasingly complicated ties between the United States and Japan, and to the efforts of governments in both countries to manage their relations. But as was noted in the introduction, the phrase carries a second meaning as well. As the bilateral U.S.-Japan relationship changes, there are further regional and global implications. This last section of this chapter explores several of the most prominent of these implications, highlighting both the positive and negative aspects that are now developing.

Regional

The U.S.-Japan relationship has had an important stabilizing effect on security relationships across Asia particularly from the mid-1970s onward. These relationships have in turn contributed at least indirectly to a reduction in overt military conflicts and the creation of a broader regional consensus on the merits of and means by which to generate rapid, export-led growth. That consensus has even expanded to include the once vitriolically hostile China. As the U.S.-Japan relationship has become more complex, however, there have been even greater spillover effects on the economic growth for the region as a whole.

Since the mid-1980s in particular, ever larger numbers of U.S.-based and Japanese-based firms have felt it safe and advisable to invest heavily in Southeast Asia and in China as part of an expanding base of corporate competition. As Hamilton-Hart, Hatch, and MacIntyre have demonstrated in their respective chapters, companies headquartered in both countries have sought access to the other's market through Asian investments. Japanese companies in particular have sought to bypass rising U.S. protectionist barriers against trade from Japan by increasing production by Japanese-owned firms in other parts of Asia. Similarly, Japanese banks have loaned considerable funds to Southeast Asian borrowers, in part because of exchange rate changes wrought by the Plaza Accord of 1985. U.S. portfolio managers, convinced that many of Asia's tigers would follow in Japan's high-growth footsteps, also made substantial bets of equity capital on those emerging markets. Such investments and expanded production networks helped move the relationship beyond bilateralism.

As the bilateral relationship changed, there were rippling economic effects across the region. Thus, financial liberalization has been pressed in different ways in various countries of Asia by the banking, insurance, and brokerage institutions of both Japan and the United States. The corporate webs being spun across the Asia-Pacific increasingly include companies and capital from Singapore, South Korea, Taiwan, and Hong Kong, among others.[18] Moreover, in the aftermath of the Asian economic crisis, considerable debate has gone on not only between U.S. and Japanese policymakers, but also across Asia, over the most appropriate regional and global mix of institutions that could serve as "lenders of last resort" that might prevent a repetition of the economic crisis.[19]

In all of these ways, there has been, as there was with the U.S.-Japan trade relationship more generally, a growing denationalization of production, investment, and trade in Asia. Increasing numbers of products are now being manufactured from parts made and assembled in several different countries. Just as the U.S.-Japan relationship has shed its bilateral character, so has much of the rest of the Asia-Pacific. Dense networks of economic interdependence are making it increasingly difficult to identify many products as starting and ending in any single country. With this has come a decline in explicit country-to-country trade frictions and a greater intraregional openness to trade liberalization. Yet this also exposes the entire region to downturns in the Japanese domestic economy to a much greater extent than was true a decade or two ago. As a result, Japan and its protectionism have come in for criticism from various quarters across the Asia-Pacific.

Such changes might well be scored as victories for U.S.-style globalization across the region. But as Hatch's chapter has made clear, it was U.S.

companies that structured industrial developments in computers and hard disk drives, while it was Japanese business networks that structured much of the production in automobiles. Meanwhile, in still other industries, ethnic Chinese businesses with separate models of corporate organization have prevailed. Thus, there has been a denationalization of many aspects of economic competition across Asia, and the region is now marked by multiple competing models of how best to organize businesses and financial institutions.

Worth noting in this regard is the fact that as the region has become increasingly integrated, the speed of the Schumpeterian process of "creative destruction" has increased.[20] Today's economic winners may now rapidly gain market shares across the entire trans-Pacific region instead of being restricted to a single national market. But equally as rapidly, economic losers risk being marginalized by higher social and political costs than was previously the case.

A second major regional consequence of the move beyond bilateralism has to do with the way in which the new U.S.-Japan relationship embeds the United States in Asia. It has long been noted that the bilateral ties between Japan and the United States solidified the U.S. commitment to remain active diplomatically and militarily in Asia. They also served as checks against potential Japanese military expansion, and worked to keep China from entering a bilateral power struggle with its major Asian competitor, Japan. All of these elements have been deepened by recent developments.

APEC was one semiformalized process that kept the United States involved in Asia. The ASEAN Regional Forum is another. Track II processes now take place on a regular basis on numerous issues, weaving the United States and Japan into complex formal and semiformal links. Moreover, trans-Pacific links have been strengthened, even by such seemingly all-Asian bodies as the APT, for Japan has worked to keep the United States informed about APT developments.[21] In all of these ways, the bilateral relationship has shifted many of both Japan's and America's ties in Asia beyond the formerly dominant hub-and-spoke system, more firmly embedding the two countries (as well as a host of others) in a web of formal and informal Asian connections.

A third regional consequence can also be cited. Between 1995 and 1997, as a result of the Nye Initiative—and of Japan's updating of its National Defense Program Outline, in which the two countries reaffirmed and revised many of the specific details associated with implementation of their treaty arrangements—the treaty has taken on a more explicitly regional role, as Ikenberry and Hughes and Fukushima have made clear. Both countries agreed to cooperate to achieve stability in the Asia-Pacific

Region rather than simply to defend Japan. The reinterpreted treaty added an explicit security dimension to the emergence of regional multi-lateralism in the Asia-Pacific. It also expanded the scope of military activities by Japan, dovetailing with ongoing efforts from within Japan to expand its own national defense perimeter.

To some extent this new security arrangement strengthened the probabilities for bilateral U.S.-Japan cooperation on military matters and potential confrontations in Asia. The new arrangement builds Japanese military cooperation into U.S. regional security plans, making Japan's future behavior in potential crisis situations far more predictable. Cooperation by these two powers also works to create a sense of shared destiny and permanent partnership that helps toward building a democratic peace across the region.[22] To the extent that the United States and Japan cooperate within the region, they can bring to bear a mixture of military and economic pressures against individual countries that conspicuously resist accommodating their common goals. In turn, those countries' risk of regional isolation is enhanced. To some extent this has happened to the Democratic People's Republic of Korea (DPRK) and Myanmar. The new arrangements, however, will also highlight differences between the United States and Japan in goals and approaches to security. As noted by Mochizuki in Chapter 4, Japan and the United States differed on, among other issues related to China, how best to deal with China following Tiananmen. Moreover, Japan has been far less willing than the United States to confront the DPRK as an integral element in an "axis of evil," or to insist on rigid DPRK inspections, at the risk of undermining Japan's improving ties with South Korea and its efforts to normalize ties with the North. Japan has also been far friendlier toward Myanmar than has the United States. And clearly, despite the quickness with which the Japanese government approved the movement of Japanese ships into the Indian Ocean as part of the U.S. war in Afghanistan or the speed with which it came to the support of the United States in Iraq, it is not at all clear that Japan would be quite as willing as the United States to risk its relations with China, let alone Japanese lives, should a clash develop between China and Taiwan.

In short, as the U.S.-Japan relationship has moved beyond bilateralism, overall economic and military cooperation within the Asian region has been enhanced, serving as an important cornerstone around which additional relations can be structured. At the same time, however, such cooperation is far from an unalloyed benefit. Economically less-competitive firms and countries are likely to suffer more quickly and severely than they would have under earlier arrangements. Most nation-states in the region will find it more difficult to challenge Japanese-U.S. positions when the two countries are unified. Nor are differing national interests in either country likely to disappear, making it equally plausible that any particular differences they may have in approaches to regional foreign policy will become more glaringly exposed and regionally relevant than they previously were.

The regionalization of the U.S.-Japan security alliance also poses major potential risks and problems across Asia. Under the new security guidelines, Japan, as Hughes and Fukushima and Mochizuki have indicated, has intentionally kept vague the meaning of its regional commitment, leading to the belief that Japan might be willing to defend Taiwan. The Nye-Armitage Report of 2000 further pushed Japan toward becoming the "Britain of the Pacific."[23] Whatever deterrence these moves may have exerted on China, and in whatever way they underline the importance of Japan to the United States, they also create a disparity between Japanese governmental elites and the general public, possibly raising false expectations within American policy circles. It is quite unclear whether the Japanese public is prepared to risk war with China over Taiwan. If a military crisis occurs in the Straits, a very nervous Japanese public is likely to resist any Japanese government support of U.S. actions. If that were to happen, reaction in the United States would almost certainly be fiercely negative, possibly threatening the alliance. Such an unraveling of the alliance, especially in a tense period, could destabilize the entire region.

Similarly, other Asian nations, especially South Korea, could increasingly resent a bilateral relationship that undertakes regional security with limited participation by or input from the very countries whose fates would be most deeply affected by the actions of the two principals. Whereas in economics both private and public sector regionalization have been accompanied by more extensive regional participation through the creation of explicit and institutionalized multilateral forums, in security, "bilateralism plus" remains a vague and problematic stage between bilateralism and the development of regional institutions.

Global

The global implications of moving beyond bilateralism are perhaps less immediate and direct than are those in the Asia-Pacific. Yet several implications warrant highlighting.

Enhanced regionalism in Asia has been part of a far more global trend toward closer ties among geographic neighbors. The EU and NAFTA are the most well-known of such arrangements. However, a host of additional configurations has been put into place in Central America, the Latin

American southern cone, several sections of the African continent, the Middle East, and elsewhere.[24] These arrangements vary greatly in character. However, as the U.S.-Japan relationship has moved beyond bilateralism, it has struck an important blow for open as opposed to closed regional arrangements.

From the end of the 1980s into the early 1990s, there was considerable concern that the United States, Germany, and Japan, as the world's three most important economies, would form the anchors of closed regional arrangements. Initial enthusiasm in Asia for an East Asian Economic Caucus (EAEC) was congruent with this evolution. EAEC quickly lost pride of place to the more open APEC. If the process of globalization is increasingly being intermediated by regional organizations, the now-more-complex bilateral relationship between Japan and the United States further reinforces the probability that any such Asian regional arrangements will be open rather than closed. As the linkage between the world's two largest economies moves beyond bilateralism, that connection "Asianizes" the United States, inducing it to maintain and enhance its deep interests in the Asia-Pacific. Simultaneously it "NAFTA-izes" Japan, forcing it to become more deeply involved in trade liberalization extending across the Asia-Pacific. Failure to do so would cause Japan to lose important markets in North America. While as much as a quarter of outgoing Japanese foreign direct investment goes to Asia, an even larger 40 percent goes to North America, and 30 percent of Japan's exports go there as well. Japanese efforts to negotiate a Mexico-Japan free trade arrangement represent but one recent manifestation of corporate Japanese involvement in the Mexican and Latin American markets.[25]

The new relationship, and the cross-Pacific regionalism it fosters, meshes well with Japan's own autonomous efforts to tiptoe from beyond its primarily intra-Asian regional role and to embrace larger global linkages, particularly but not exclusively in economics and finance. Expanding ODA combined with financial support in dealing with the Latin American debt crisis of 1995–96 are but two examples of such broader global efforts.[26] Yet the slowness of Japan's domestic economic recovery is a stumbling block preventing Japan from taking, and the rest of the world from recognizing, such a larger role.

"Beyond bilateralism" has another set of global implications, namely in the now broad reconsideration of the New International Financial Architecture. The chapters by Amyx and Katada have analyzed intra-Asian battles over the AMF and the APT. Hamilton-Hart has demonstrated the more important ways in which bank funds and investment flows in Asia have shifted with time. As capital flows have expanded in and across Asia, there have been escalating debates about existing structural arrangements anchored in the IMF versus possible alternatives. As is widely noted among Asians, the Japanese and collective Asian representation on key IMF boards is based on weightings that no longer accurately reflect Asia's massive economic development. Furthermore, Japan, China, Taiwan, Hong Kong, and South Korea each have more than $100 billion in foreign reserves, giving them individually and collectively incredible potential to assist economies facing short-term liquidity problems. An increasingly debated issue both within Asia and globally has become how best to take advantage of these collective capital resources. The problem drove a wedge between the United States and Japan during the Asian crisis of 1997–98 and is likely to continue to be a part of relations between the two countries as they move further beyond bilateralism. As Amyx has indicated in Chapter 9, eventual adjustments ultimately provided some compatibility between Japan-led regional efforts and the U.S.-led global financial architecture. At the same time, the broader debate remains unresolved; evolving U.S.-Japan-Asian financial arrangements are almost certain to have extensive global implications.

It is also important to note that the general peace across Asia has emerged in part due to the U.S.-Japan relationship, as well as to broader Asian economic development. This frees up both U.S. and Japanese resources for use in other problem areas of the world. This was most recently seen in the Afghan War as various U.S. forces deployed quickly from Northeast Asia to South Asia, with Japan sending several Maritime Self-Defense Forces ships to the region as well. Calm in Asia frees up military resources from both the United States and Japan for redeployment elsewhere; the same will be true for economic resources to the extent that Asian growth continues.

Finally, it is valuable to recognize that the enhanced role for Asian regional institutions can be conducive to similarly enhanced roles for global multilateral bodies such as the WTO, the IMF, the World Bank, and the G8. At bottom, cooperation in one forum and among one set of countries makes further cooperation in other forums and among different sets of countries more plausible to larger numbers of actors. As the process of bilateral and multilateral cooperation goes forward, further trust in the process is more generally enhanced. The overall result is greater institutional proliferation, depth, and capacity worldwide. As global and regional organizations gain the reputation for effective problem solving, membership in them becomes ever more desirable, not only to the countries that gain official membership, but also to nonstate actors operating in those countries.

This last point can be seen particularly in the ways in which China (and Taiwan) became integrated into the world trading system through membership in the WTO. While the governments of both countries were anxious to advance their membership claims, those claims were bolstered by the pressures for membership being exerted by both Japanese and U.S.-based companies with substantial Chinese and Taiwanese investments and trade. Specific corporate interests are increasingly protected, to the extent that global standards and norms are institutionalized in the locations of their business dealings. Conversely, as global organizations such as the WTO gain influence, as Pekkanen has noted in Chapter 10, pressures also increase for existing member countries to abide by WTO standards and norms. It thus becomes increasingly difficult for countries such as Japan or regions such as the EU to resist broad global pressures for economic liberalization of currently protected agricultural sectors, or for the United States to engage in unilateral protectionism on items such as steel or textiles.

In all of these ways, therefore, it becomes clear that as the U.S.-Japan relationship moves beyond bilateralism, the shift affects not only the two countries most immediately involved. The changing relationship in the narrowest sense has broader implications that affect regional and global politics and economics as well. The ripple effects of the changing relationship between Japan and the United States are increasingly influenced by, but also are affecting, conditions well outside the elite policy circles in Tokyo and Washington. It is increasingly imperative that officials within these two narrow spheres be particularly sensitive to those far more complex causes and consequences. The current condition of divided dependence places challenging new demands on policymakers in both Japan and the United States, in ways that bilateralism did not. Failure to recognize this new context and continuing to operate out of anachronistic presuppositions is a formula for failure. An acceptance of divided dependence, in contrast, allows both sides to build on existing strengths while meeting unforeseen challenges within the new Asia-Pacific, in ways that are likely to benefit both countries and the region.

REFERENCE MATTER

Notes

1. Ikenberry, "America's Liberal Grand Strategy"; see also Ikenberry, Chapter 2, this volume.

2. Among the better works in this genre are the following: Ōtake, *Nihon no Bōei to Kokunai Seiji*, 1986; Destler, Fukui, and Sato, *The Textile Wrangle*; Destler et al., *Managing an Alliance*; Kusano, *Nichi-Bei*; Buckley, *U.S.-Japan Alliance Diplomacy*; Pyle, *The Japanese Question*; Cohen, *Uneasy Partnership*; Vogel, *U.S.-Japan Relations in a Changing World*.

3. This literature is too extensive to cite here but includes Ruggie, *Multilateralism Matters*; Mansfield and Milner, *The Political Economy of Regionalism*; Ravenhill, *APEC and the Construction of Pacific Rim Regionalism*; Alagappa, *Asian Security Practice*; and Lake and Morgan, *Regional Orders*.

4. This focus began with the conflict over Japanese textile exports to the United States in the early 1970s, as described in Destler, Fukui, and Sato, *The Textile Wrangle*; from the early 1980s to the mid-1990s, this aspect of the relationship took center stage in such works as Kusano, *Nichi-Bei*; three works by Cohen: *Uneasy Partnership*, *Cowboys and Samurai*, and *An Ocean Apart*; and Schoppa, *Bargaining with Japan*. An important subcategory of this genre was the attention given to Japan's industrial policy, beginning with Chalmers Johnson's seminal *MITI and the Japanese Miracle*, and the myriad works that plumbed the policy and business-government relations sources of Japan's success and its perceived (usually disastrous) implications for the United States (such as job losses, factory closings, and regional dislocation).

5. Among the better works in this genre are the following: Ōtake, *Nihon no Bōei*, 1986; Destler et al., *Managing an Alliance*; Buckley, *U.S.-Japan Alliance Diplomacy*; Pyle, *The Japanese Question*; Green, *Arming Japan*; and Green and Cronin, *The U.S.-Japan Alliance*.

6. For example, Scalapino, *The Foreign Policy of Modern Japan*; Curtis, *Japan's Foreign Policy After the Cold War*; Blackwill and Dibb, *America's Asian Alliances*.

Notes to Pages 3-12

7. Among the best are Katzenstein and Shiraishi, *Network Power*; Lincoln, *Japan's New Global Role*; Green, *Japan's Reluctant Realism*; and Fukushima, *Japanese Foreign Policy*. A very recent addition is Inoguchi, *Japan's Asia Policy*.

8. See, for example, the following otherwise excellent works: Vogel, *U.S.-Japan Relations in a Changing World*; and Iriye and Wampler, *Partnership*. A partial exception, because it contains a section called "The Strategic Context" on how changes in that context have affected and should affect the relationship between Japan and the United States, is Mochizuki, *Toward a True Alliance*.

9. Cumings, *Parallax Visions*.

10. The defining nature of the security arrangements are explored, inter alia, in Watanabe, *San Francisco Kōwa*; Iokibe, *Sengo Nihon Gaikoshi*.

11. Ikenberry, Chapter 1, this volume.

12. For an excellent analysis of the origins and consequences of the Yoshida Doctrine, see Pyle, *The Japanese Question*, chap. 2.

13. On differences among approaches to capitalism, see, for example, Albert, *Capitalism vs. Capitalism*; and Dore, *Stock Market Capitalism*. See also Pempel, *Regime Shift*.

14. Dower, *Empire and Its Aftermath*; Katzenstein and Okawara, *Japan's National Security*; Ōtake, "Bōei Futan o meguru Nichibei Masatsu"; Ōtake, *Nihon no Bōei to Kokunai Seiji*, 1983; and Ōtake, *Nihon ni okeru 'Gunsankan Fukugoeai' Keisei no Zasetsu*; and Pyle, *The Japanese Question*, inter alia.

15. One indicator is that Japanese voting patterns matched those of the United States almost 100 percent for the first fifteen years of Japanese membership; and as recently as 1975–80, agreement levels were in the range of 75–80 percent. Hook et al., *Japan's International Relations*, 311–12.

16. Pempel, *Uncommon Democracies*.

17. Nau, *At Home Abroad*, 153.

18. Destler et al., *The Textile Wrangle*; Kusano, *Nichi-Bei*; Ōtake, *Gendai Nihon no Seiji Kenryoku Keizai Kenryoku*; Watanabe, *Sengo Nihon no Taigai Seisaku*, inter alia.

19. Gould and Krasner, "Germany and Japan."

20. Samuels, *Rich Nation, Strong Army*, 46.

21. Japan External Trade Organization, "Nihon no Kuni, Chiiki betsu Bōeki no Suii," and *White Paper of International Trade 2001*; U.S. Department of Commerce, Office of Japan, "U.S.-Japan Merchandise Trade Data"; Mansfield University, "Appendix C."

22. U.S. Department of Commerce, Bureau of Economic Analysis, *Foreign Direct Investment in the U.S.* (Washington, D.C.: Bureau of Economic Analysis, annual).

23. Ministry of Finance, "Tainaigai Minkan Tōshi Tokushu."

24. The one exception involved the massive Japanese protests against the Security Treaty in 1960, when it became linked to perceived undemocratic methods for ratifying the revised version.

25. Green, *Arming Japan*; Katzenstein and Okawara, *Japan's National Security*.

26. Lincoln, *Japan*, 4.

27. Destler et al., *The Textile Wrangle*.

28. Kusano, *Nichi-Bei.*

29. Dwyer, "U.S.-Japan Financial-Market Relations"; Henning, *Currencies and Politics*; and Volker and Gyohten, *Changing Fortunes.*

30. "Defense of Japan, 1985," 86–87.

31. Desmond Ball, "September 11," 1.

32. Rozman, "Japan's Quest for Great Power Identity," 78.

33. For an extremely prescient (in the wake of September 11) analysis of what the Aum attacks represented in terms of changes in the nature of modern terrorism, see Hughes, "Japan's Aum Shinrikyo."

34. Leheny, "The War on Terrorism in Asia."

35. Data from Bank for International Settlements as reported in Simmons, "The International Politics of Harmonization," 589.

36. Greider, *One World, Ready or Not,* 245; "Financial Indicators: Trade, Exchange Rates and Reserves," 97.

37. Cohen, *The Geography of Money,* 132.

38. Pempel, *Regime Shift* and "Structural 'Gaiatsu.'"

39. "Financial Indicators: Foreign Assets," 123.

40. Hatch and Yamamura, *Asia in Japan's Embrace.*

41. Fallows, *Looking at the Sun,* 264.

42. "Financial Indicators: Trade," 119.

43. Kawakami, "Exporting a Surplus," 45.

44. Frieden, "Domestic Politics and Regional Cooperation, 434.

45. Kato, "Open Regionalism and Japan's Systematic Vulnerability," 38.

46. Kanabayashi, "Japan's Appetite for Chinese Goods Boosts Ties."

47. Solingen, *Regional Orders at Century's Dawn* and "ASEAN, Quo Vadis?"

48. See Bobrow, Chan, and Reich, "Southeast Asian Prospects and Realities."

49. Henning, *Currencies and Politics*; Nau, *At Home Abroad,* 80–81.

50. Henning, *Currencies and Politics.* For a less sanguine interpretation, see Dore, *Stock Market Capitalism.*

51. Pempel, *The Politics of the Asian Economic Crisis,* esp. chaps. 2–5; Haggard, *The Political Economy.*

52. Ikenberry, "Rethinking the Origins of American Hegemony," 381.

53. Raum, "Talk of U.S. Isolation Increasing."

54. NAFTA has an institutional basis for dispute settlement. Chapter 20 sets forth a generally applicable procedure in which the third party's ruling is nonbinding and without proper enforcement authority. In addition, chapter 19 establishes a separate dispute settlement mechanism for antidumping and countervailing duties. Panel decisions are binding and have "direct effect" in domestic laws, creating such a "binding obligation." Abbott, "NAFTA and the Legalization of World Politics."

55. Green, *Japan's Reluctant Realism,* 193.

56. Ministry of Foreign Affairs, "Preamble."

57. Green, "The Challenges of Managing U.S.-Japan Security Relations," 244.

58. Green, *Japan's Reluctant Realism,* 193.

59. Heginbotham and Samuels, "Mercantile Realism and Japanese Foreign Policy," 179.

60. Harding, "Asia Policy to the Brink," 57.
61. Bergsten, Ito, and Noland, *No More Bashing*.

CHAPTER 2

1. On the idea floated by the United States in the early 1940s and during 1950–51 of a multilateral security institution in Asia that was to be a counterpart to NATO, see Crone, "Does Hegemony Matter?"
2. See Schaller, *Altered States*; and Bruce Cumings, "Japan's Position in the World System."
3. See Auerbach, "The Ironies That Built Japan Inc."
4. This argument is made in Gilpin, *The Challenge of Global Capitalism*, chap. 2.
5. This logic of "security binding" is discussed in the next section.
6. See Lundestad, "Empire by Invitation?"
7. This argument is explored in Ikenberry, *After Victory*.
8. Ikenberry, "Institutions, Strategic Restraint, and the Persistence of American Postwar Order."
9. This "liberal grand strategy" is discussed in Ikenberry, "America's Liberal Grand Strategy."
10. For recent suggestions that strategic interdependence is working, see Smith, "Signs in China and Taiwan"; and Kynge, "China Puts Business Before Politics."
11. Quoted in Kynge, "China's Binding Ties."
12. This is discussed in Ikenberry, *After Victory*, chap. 3.
13. For a discussion on this basic difference between Japan and Germany, see Gould and Krasner, "Germany and Japan."
14. See Tamamoto, "A Land Without Partiots."
15. An American strategy toward Asia was spelled out in a February 1995 Defense Department report that emphasized four overriding goals: maintain a forward presence of 100,000 in the region, put America's alliances with Japan and Korea on a firm basis, develop multilateral institutions such as the ASEAN Regional Forum to foster security dialogue, and encourage China to develop a position of strength by defining its interests in ways that are compatible with those of its neighbors and the United States. See Department of Defense, *United States Strategy for the East-Asia Pacific Region*, 1995. This view is echoed in the last Defense Department strategic report on East Asia of the 1990s, *United States Security Strategy for the East-Asia Pacific Region*, 1998.
16. Institute for National Strategic Studies, "The United States and Japan."
17. See Slevin, "Powell Offers Reassurance to South Korea."
18. Funabashi, *Asia Pacific Fusion*; and Pempel, "Gulliver in Lilliput."
19. Yamamura, "The Deliberate Emergence of a Free Trader; and Pempel, *Regime Shift*.
20. Johnston, "Socialization in International Institutions."
21. Schmitter, "Three Neo-Functional Hypotheses."
22. See Nye, "East Asia." For later reflections, see Nye, "The 'Nye Report.'" For background, see Funabashi, *Alliance Adrift*.

23. Department of Defense, *U.S. Security Strategy*, 1998, 9.
24. White House, Office of the Press Secretary, "Remarks by the President."
25. Department of Defense, *U.S. Security Strategy*, 1998, 61.
26. Blair and Hanley, "From Wheels to Webs."
27. This argument is presented in Ikenberry, "American Grand Strategy."
28. See for example, Erlanger, "In Europe, Some Say"; and Sciolino, "Who Hates the U.S.?" For imperial views of American power, see Johnson, *Blowback*; and Hardt and Negri, *Empire*.

CHAPTER 3

1. Okawara and Katzenstein, "Japan and Asian-Pacific Security."
2. Ibid.; Katzenstein and Okawara, "Japan, Asian-Pacific Security and the Case for Analytical Eclecticism"; Maull and Harnisch, "Embedding Korea's Unification Multilaterally"; Wah and Fong, *Relating the US-Korea and US-Japan Alliances.*
3. Alagappa, "Rethinking Security."
4. Green, "Balance of Power," 14.
5. Sakamoto, *Nichibei Dōmei no Kizuna*, 198; Welfield, *An Empire in Eclipse*, 108.
6. Ibid, 104–5.
7. Hemmer and Katzenstein, "Why Is There No NATO in Asia?" 578–79.
8. Green, "The Search for an Active Security Partnership," 138.
9. Green, *Arming Japan.*
10. Katahara, "Japan," 87–88.
11. Hughes, *Japan's Economic Power and Security*, 88–96.
12. Christopher W. Hughes, "Japan's Aum Shinrikyō."
13. Ozawa, *Nihon Kaizō Keikaku.*
14. Mochizuki, "American and Japanese Strategic Debates," 63.
15. Ibid, 59–62.
16. For an example of this type of view from the U.S. side, see Institute for National Strategic Studies National Defense University, *INSS Special Report*, 3–4.
17. Advisory Group on Defense Issues, *Modality of the Security and Defense Capability of Japan.*
18. Funabashi, *Alliance Adrift.*
19. Hughes, *Japan's Security Policy and the War on Terror.*
20. Hook et al., *Japan's International Relations*, 66.
21. Samuels, *Rich Nation, Strong Army.*
22. Green, "The Challenges of Managing US-Japan Security Relations," 248.

CHAPTER 4

The author expresses his deep appreciation to the Smith Richardson Foundation for generously supporting the research project on which this chapter is based.

1. Good references to this concept and the debate about it include Khalilzad et al., *The United States and a Rising China*; and Szayna et al., *The Emergence of Peer Competitors.*

2. Mann, *About Face.*

3. Although the term *engagement* was explicitly used by the Clinton administration to characterize its policy toward China, the Japanese government has not officially used this term. It has, however, invoked many of the ideas implicit in the engagement concept. For example, Tokyo has repeatedly referred to the importance of encouraging "China to become an even more constructive partner in the international community," of supporting "China's open and reform policy," and of promoting "bilateral and multilateral dialogue and cooperative relations." See "Japan's Basic Policy Toward the People's Republic of China" on the Japan Foreign Ministry Web site [http://www.mofa.go.jp/region/asia-paci/china/index.html].

4. Glenn Snyder, "The Security Dilemma in Alliance Politics."

5. Ross, "National Security, Human Rights, and Domestic Politics," 291–96.

6. Tanaka, *Nit-chuū Kankei 1945–1990*, 173–77; and Ijiri, "Sino-Japanese Controversy," 656–57.

7. Kotake Kazuaki, "Ten'anmon Jiken to Nit-chū Gaikō," 130–31.

8. Tanaka, *Nit-chū Kankei*, 177–80; and Ijiri, "Sino-Japanese Controversy," 658.

9. Tanaka, *Nit-chū Kankei*, 181–83.

10. Ibid., 183–84.

11. Ibid., 185–86.

12. Kojima, *Gendai Chugoku no seiji*, 366.

13. One source on the Chinese use of the notion of "the revival of Japanese militarism" is Ijiri, "Sino-Japanese Controversy Since the 1972 Diplomatic Normalization," 61, 64–68.

14. Tanaka Akihiko, "Tai-Nichi Kankei," 145–48; and Kojima, "Sino-Japanese Relations," 85.

15. Kojima, *Gendai Chugoku no seiji*, 366.

16. Tanaka, "Tai-Nichi Kankei," 150.

17. Kakizawa, "Tennō Ho-Chū-go no Nit-chū Kankei," 45–51.

18. Harwit, "Japanese Investment in China," 983–84.

19. Kobayashi, "Japan's Need for Re-Asianization"; and Ogura, "Ajia no Fukken' no tame ni."

20. Armacost, *Friends or Rivals?*, 137.

21. Baker, *The Politics of Diplomacy*, 588–94; and Lampton, "China and the Strategic Quadrangle," 80.

22. Oksenberg, "China and the Japanese-American Alliance," 101.

23. Kojima, "Sino-Japanese Relations," 86–87.

24. Tanaka, "Tai-Nichi Kankei," 151.

25. Quoted in Kojima, "Sino-Japanese Relations," 92.

26. Wakisaka, "Japanese Development Cooperation for China," 119–20.

27. Quoted in Kojima, "Sino-Japanese Relations," 97.

28. Okazaki and Nakajima, *Nihon ni Ajia Senryaku wa arunoka*, 10–23.

29. Funabashi, *Alliance Adrift*, 80–81.

30. Available at [http://www.mofa.go.jp/region/n-america/us/security/security.html]. See also Defense Agency, *Defense of Japan 1998*, p. 322.

31. Funabashi, *Alliance Adrift*, 399.

32. Ibid, 400.
33. Ibid, 400.
34. National Institute for Defense Studies, *East Asian Strategic Review 1997–1998*, 106–7.
35. Mann, *About Face*, 345–56.
36. Hashimoto, "Seeking a New Foreign Policy Toward China."
37. Interview with official from the Japanese Ministry of International Trade and Industry, Tokyo, 11 May 2001; and press conference by the Press Secretary, 9 September 1997 [http://www.mofa.go.jp/announce/press/1997/9/909.html#2].
38. Tucker, "The Clinton Years," 60.
39. Mann, *About Face*, 355–62.
40. Ibid, 330.
41. Tucker, "The Clinton Years," 62.
42. Lampton, *Same Bed, Different Dreams*, 93–94; and Tucker, "The Clinton Years," 62–63.
43. Interview with former Clinton administration defense official involved in Asian affairs.
44. Tucker, "The Clinton Years," 59–60.
45. Ibid, 59.
46. Johnstone, "Strained Alliance"; Green, "Managing Chinese Power," 162; and Watanabe, "The Asian Financial Crisis," 61–65.
47. Interviews with Japan Ministry of Foreign Affairs officials involved in relations with both the United States and China.
48. Interview with Japanese diplomat involved in China policy. See also Green, *Japan's Reluctant Realism*, 104; and Christensen, "China, the U.S.-Japan Alliance, and the Security Dilemma in East Asia," 159–60.
49. Kunihiro, "Nichi-Bei-Chū Sangoku Kankei wa Torakku 2 kara"; and Nakayama, "Nichi-Bei-Chū Kaigi dai-4 kai Kaigō."
50. Christensen, "China, the U.S.-Japan Alliance, and the Security Dilemma in East Asia," 160.
51. National Institute for Defense Studies, *East Asian Strategic Review 2001*, 199–202.
52. Interviews with Chinese diplomats involved in Japan policy.
53. Lampton, *Same Bed, Different Dreams*, 55–61.
54. Armacost and Pyle, "Japan and the Engagement of China," 41.

CHAPTER 5

1. Alagappa, "A Nuclear Weapons Free Zone."
2. Krause, *U.S. Economic Policy Toward the Association of Southeast Asian Nations*, 73.
3. Chia, "Development and Issues in U.S.-ASEAN Economic Relations"; Morrison, *Japan, the United States, and Changing Southeast Asia*; Krause, *U.S. Economic Policy*; Tan and Akrasanee, *ASEAN-U.S. Economic Relations*.
4. Alagappa, "The Major Powers and Southeast Asia" and *U.S.-ASEAN Security Cooperation*.

5. Leifer, *ASEAN and the Security of South-East Asia*, 8–9, 66–67.

6. Lee, "History of U.S.-ASEAN Trade Relations," 37.

7. Interview with Kurt Campbell, former deputy assistant secretary for East Asian security, Department of Defense, 14 June 2001.

8. See also Bresnan, *From Dominoes to Dynamoes*, 89–90.

9. Yamakage, "Japan's National Security and Asia-Pacific's Regional Institutions," 283, 290.

10. Ikema, "Japan's Foreign Relations with ASEAN."

11. Yamakage, "Japan's National Security," 284.

12. Alagappa, 1989, 570.

13. Weinstein, "ASEAN and Japan"; Sudo, "From Fukuda to Takeshita."

14. Sudo, "From Fukuda to Takeshita," 125, 137; Yamakage, "Japan's National Security," 290.

15. Peng, "Japanese Relations with Southeast Asia," 254–56; Sudo, *Southeast Asia in Japanese Security Policy*, 341–42.

16. Fukushima, *Japanese Foreign Policy*, 138–44.

17. MacIntyre, "Japan, Indonesia and Policy Leadership in the Pacific."

18. Okawara and Katzenstein, "Japan and Asian-Pacific Security," n. 39; Tsunekawa, "Classifying Japan's Efforts."

19. Okawara and Katzenstein, "Japan and Asian-Pacific Security."

20. Yamakage, "Japan's National Security"; Fukushima, *Japanese Foreign Policy*.

21. "Jakarta Shifts Stance on Telephone Contract."

22. "Thailand Finally OKs Joint Glass Venture."

23. "MITI Miffed by Jakarta's National Car Policy"; "Jakarta Ups Ante with Tokyo on Car Project," *Business Times* (Singapore), 22 April 1997.

24. See, most notably, Hatch and Yamamura, *Asia in Japan's Embrace*; Pempel, "Trans-Pacific Torii"; Doner, "Japan in East Asia"; Arase, *Buying Power*; Fallows, *Looking at the Sun*.

25. Perhaps the clearest statement of this view comes from Drifte, *Japan's Foreign Policy for the Twenty-First Century*, 160–161: "The legacy of the past, and particularly the way this issue is handled by the Japanese, is what still weighs most heavily on Japan's relations with Asia. It casts a shadow over every positive aspect of Japan's relations with Asia, and it worsens every aspect of the relationship which is considered by the Asians as less welcome. It is thwarting Japan's natural political and economic leadership in Asia."

26. Most recently there is an interesting proposal for an ASEAN + India framework.

27. Campbell and Reiss, "Korean Changes, Asian Challenges and the U.S. Role," 65–66.

CHAPTER 6

1. Higgott, "The Asian Economic Crisis."

2. See Pempel, chap. 1, this volume; and Hamilton-Hart, "Regional Capital and Cooperation in Asia," 127–35.

3. Masuyama, "The Role of Japan's Direct Investment," 217.

4. Bernard and Ravenhill, "Beyond Product Cycles and Flying Geese." See also Hatch, chap. 7, this volume.

5. For example, Department of Foreign Affairs and Trade, *Overseas Chinese Business Networks in Asia.*

6. Katzenstein and Shiraishi, *Network Power*; Hamilton, "Asian Business Networks in Transition."

7. Hamilton-Hart, "Regional Capital and Cooperation," 133; and Bank for International Settlements, "BIS International Consolidated Banking Statistics," table 9.

8. As recorded in the financial and capital accounts of Japan's balance of payments, reported by the Ministry of Finance's Regional Balance of Payments series [http://www.mof.go.jp].

9. Masuyama, "The Role of Japan's Direct Investment," 231–32.

10. Sender, "Out of Asia."

11. Japan External Trade Organization, *JETRO White Paper on Foreign Direct Investment 2001*; United Nations Conference on Trade and Development, *World Investment Report 2000*, 39.

12. Masuyama, "The Role of Japan's Direct Investment," 247.

13. Ramkishen and Siregar, "Private Capital Flows in East Asia," 22.

14. United Nations Conference on Trade and Development, *World Investment Report 2000*, 33 and Annex Table A.IV.6.

15. Figures for 1996–98 from U.S. Department of Commerce, "U.S. Direct Investment Abroad," Table 16, and "Foreign Direct Investment in the United States," Table 16. Figures for 1999–2001 from U.S. Department of Commerce, "BEA Current and Historical Data," Table G.2 and Table G.4. The increase in Malaysian investment is not recorded in this source but shows up in Bank Negara Malaysia, *Annual Report 2000*, Table A.22. The Malaysian figures on outward investment aggregate bank lending and other forms of investment, while the U.S. figures are for direct investment only.

16. United Nations Conference on Trade and Development, *World Investment Report 2000*, 38 and 33; JETRO, *White Paper*, 2002, 23.

17. JETRO, *White Paper*, 2001, Table 15; and JETRO, *White Paper*, 2002, Table 6.1. These figures do not fully reveal the origin (by ownership) of inward FDI, because inward FDI by foreign-affiliated companies in Japan is reported as coming from Japan.

18. Masuyama, "The Role of Japan's Direct Investment, 244–45; and Petri, "Foreign Direct Investment," 191–93.

19. Unite and Sullivan, "Reform and the Corporate Environment in the Philippines," 208.

20. The source for this information on Indonesia is Bank Indonesia, *Indonesian Financial Statistics.*

21. International Monetary Fund, *International Capital Markets*, 153–55.

22. United Nations Conference on Trade and Development, *World Investment Report 2000*, 38; JETRO, *White Paper*, 2002, Table 6.2.

23. International Monetary Fund, *International Capital Markets*, 196.

24. In the global market for underwriting international bond issues, the top four or five bookrunners are generally U.S. investment banks. Nomura Securities, well down on the list of the top twenty firms, is the only significant Asian firm in this market.

25. For example, Sara Webb, "Foreign Banks Alter Asian Growth Model," *Asian Wall Street Journal*, 23 August 1999.

26. Andrew Cornell, "Merger Activity an Inside Job," *Australian Financial Review*, 13 July 2000.

27. Henny Sender, Bill Spindle, and Douglas Appell, "Chase Manhattan-J.P. Morgan Merger Complements the Firms in Asia," *Asian Wall Street Journal*, 14 September 2000, p. 5.

28. "Investment Banks Not Planning to Cut Asian Staff," *Business Times*, 11 May 2001.

29. International Monetary Fund, *World Economic Outlook*, May 2000, 51–52.

30. Petri, "Foreign Direct Investment."

31. Masuyama, "The Role of Japan's Direct Investment," 251–54.

32. Sara Webb, "Foreign Banks Alter Asian Growth Model," *Asian Wall Street Journal*, 23 August 1999.

33. Booth, "Survey of Recent Developments," 3–38, 5–6.

34. Initially, foreign investor interest in this bank had been low. See McLeod, "Survey of Recent Developments," 5–40, 24–26.

35. Davies, "Foreign Takeover of BMB Scrapped?"

36. Ibid.

37. In one account, foreign firms controlled 9 percent of banking assets in Thailand in 1997, and this figure was considered on the low side because it excluded the operations of foreign banks operating out of Thailand's offshore center. See International Monetary Fund, *International Capital Markets*, 211.

38. Ibid, 153. The same study (153–56) estimated foreign control of bank assets at more than 50 percent in central Europe and between 18 and 54 percent in Latin American countries. These figures, however, underestimate the level of foreign control in Asia because they exclude the assets of foreign bank branches, a major mode of entry to many Asian markets.

39. Bank Negara Malaysia, *Monthly Statistical Bulletin*, various issues.

40. "HSBC to Shut Philippine Brokerage," *Business Times*, 14 November 2001.

41. "Merrill Lynch 'May Sack Hundreds of Financial Consultants' in Japan," *Straits Times*, 7 December 2001.

42. In 1998, Daiwa Bank, Fuji Bank, Hokuriku Bank, Nomura Securities, and Daiwa Securities all announced plans to close half or more of their overseas branches. See Peter Landers, "Headlong Retreat," *Far Eastern Economic Review*, 5 November 1998.

43. Julian Blum, "On the Prowl," *Far Eastern Economic Review*, 2 April 1998, 49.

44. This bank was the second largest in the Philippines in 1998, with 14 percent of total banking assets. See Unite and Sullivan, "Reform and the Corporate Environment," 207.

45. After acquiring the stake in Dao Heng held by Malaysia's Guocco Group, DBS will hold 71 percent of the bank. See Hugh Chow, "DBS Bank Offers $10b for Dao Heng," *Straits Times*, 12 April 2001.

46. Haddock, "DBS Thinks Big in Asia."

47. Siow Li Sen, "S'pore Banks Keen to Muscle in on a Slice of Thai Action," *Business Times*, 8 May 2001; Serena Ng, "Kim Eng Bags Top Thai Brokerage for $45m," *Business Times*, 18 May 2001; Nikomborirak and Tangkitvanich, "Corporate Governance in Thailand," 76–77; Petri, "Foreign Direct Investment," 195. Taiwanese investors were also involved in providing new equity to the Bangkok Bank, Thailand's largest.

48. Because of very limited capital account monitoring by some countries and the use of the regional centers of Hong Kong and Singapore as intermediating points for investment, these figures almost certainly underestimate outward investment, particularly for Indonesia and Thailand.

49. Of total cross-border M&A purchases by these Asian countries of $17.9, $6.0, and $10.6 billion in 1997, 1998, and 1999, 73 percent, 67 percent, and 84 percent respectively were made in other developing countries. See United Nations Conference on Trade and Development, *World Investment Report 2000*, 122 and Annex Table A.IV.7. Developing Asian countries included in this report are Taiwan, Singapore, Hong Kong, and Korea. Although South Asia is also included, its share of total M&A purchases is negligible.

50. Comment made at a public seminar, Institute of Southeast Asian Studies, Singapore, March 2001.

51. These sales have been of nationalized corporate assets held by the Indonesian Bank Restructuring Agency. They have included the partial sale of Indonesia's largest vehicle manufacturer and distributor to a consortium led by Singaporean investors, and the sale of plantation assets to a Malaysian company, although the latter deal was overturned by the Indonesian parliament after it had supposedly been finalized.

52. Singapore Department of Statistics, *Yearbook of Statistics 2002*, Table 5.14.

53. Bank of Thailand, Economic Data Tables 58, 60.1, 62.1, and 64.1 [http://www.bot.or.th].

54. Monetary Authority of Singapore, "2000 Survey."

55. U.K. investment funds, for example, had 3.3 percent of their total investment portfolio in Asia (including Japan) as of mid-2000, compared to 6 percent in the mid-1990s. See Neil Behrmann, "UK Funds Shying Away from Asia-Pac Equities," *Business Times*, 14 August 2000.

56. Monetary Authority of Singapore, *Monthly Statistical Bulletin*, Table I.16. Full details on the geographic distribution of external assets of banks operating from Hong Kong are no longer available, but regional lending is significant. For example, as of mid-2002, claims on banks and nonbank institutions in mainland China alone totaled $17 billion. In mid-2001, loans from Hong Kong to Asia totaled $205 billion. See Hong Kong Monetary Authority, *Monthly Statistical Bulletin*, 2002, Table 2.9.1; and Hong Kong Monetary Authority, *Monthly Statistical Bulletin*, 2003), Table 3.11.3. These amounts cannot simply be added to those in Table 6.3 because of the degree of double-counting that would be involved.

57. Full figures on Singapore banks' overseas lending are not disclosed. For details on their exposure to Korea, Indonesia, Thailand, Malaysia, the Philippines, and Thailand, see Monetary Authority of Singapore, "Regional Exposure and NPLs."

58. In 2000, the world's top five ODA donors were Japan ($13.5 billion), the United States ($9.9 billion), Germany ($5 billion), the United Kingdom ($4.5 billion), and France ($4.1 billion). See Organization for Economic Cooperation and Development, "ODA Steady in 2000," Table 1.

59. A summary of the changing orientation of Japanese aid and official assistance is given in Katada, *Banking on Stability*, 41–47.

60. Ministry of Foreign Affairs, *Japan's ODA Annual Report 1999*, Chart 42.

61. Masuyama, "The Role of Japan's Direct Investment," 243–46; Ministry of Economy, Trade and Industry, "Present State of MITI-Related Economic Cooperation." Details of Japan's aid to Asia under the New Miyazawa Initiative and the Chiang Mai Initiative are available at [http://mof.go.jp/english/if/if.htm#uu].

62. See Hatch, chap. 7, this volume.

63. These details are based on annual surveys of manufacturing sector companies by the Japan Bank for International Cooperation (formerly the EXIM Bank). The survey is relatively large (501 companies with 7,710 overseas affiliates responded in 2001) and has a comparatively good response rate (63 percent in 2001). See Japan Bank for International Cooperation (JBIC), "JBIC FY2001 Survey," 1–57.

64. JETRO, *White Paper*, 2002.

65. International Monetary Fund, *Direction of Trade Statistics Yearbook 2001*.

66. Drysdale, *Reform and Recovery in East Asia*; Haggard, *Political Economy of the Asian Financial Crisis*.

67. Mody and Negishi, "Cross-Border Mergers and Acquisitions."

68. Encarnation, *Rivals Beyond Trade*; Mason and Encarnation, *Does Ownership Matter?*

69. Freund and Djankov, "Which Firms Do Foreigners Buy?"

70. Kim, *East Asia and Globalization*.

71. Noble and Ravenhill, *The Asian Financial Crisis*.

72. Amyx, chap. 9, this volume.

73. For an earlier analysis of why Japanese banks have different interests but were unable to prevail against American proposals for international bank regulation, see Oatley and Nabors, "Redistributive Cooperation."

74. See the managing director's statement to the executive board of the International Monetary Fund, Camdessus, "Statement to Board," 143–44.

75. Katada, chap. 8, this volume.

76. Sakakibara, "End of Market Fundamentalism."

77. For example, Rajan, "Financial and Macroeconomic Co-operation in ASEAN"; Kawai and Akiyama, "Implications of the Currency Crisis"; Kawai and Takagi, "Proposed Strategy."

78. Eddie Toh, "KL Says It Has Access to RM62b Needed to Finance Recovery," *Business Times*, 12 January 1999; Athukorala, "The Malaysian Experiment."

79. Masuyama, "The Role of Japan's Direct Investment," 243–46.

CHAPTER 7

1. This stylistic description ignores the obvious fact that Japanese and U.S. firms also compete on "neutral" courts, especially in Europe.

2. Unless otherwise indicated, "Asia" here is the aggregate of ten economies: China, Hong Kong, South Korea, Taiwan, Singapore, Malaysia, Thailand, Indonesia, the Philippines, and Vietnam. Note that Japan is *not* included in this definition.

3. See World Trade Organization, *International Trade Statistics 2001*.

4. One must be careful not to overdraw this distinction between the automobile and computer peripheral industries. I agree with an anonymous reviewer who notes that computer peripherals, like autos, are commodities that rely on well-developed manufacturing processes. But I also disagree that both industries enjoy a predictable technological trajectory. If this were true, we should expect them both to have relatively long product cycles. In fact, however, the product cycle of computer peripherals (such as HDDs) is notoriously short.

5. Williamson, *Markets and Hierarchies*.

6. The seminal statement is Granovetter, "Economic Action and Social Structure."

7. Fruin, in *Networks, Markets, and the Pacific Rim*, 3, has asserted that business networks are "uncommonly abundant and influential among rapidly growing Pacific Rim economies." Meanwhile, Biggart and Hamilton, in "On the Limits of a Firm-Based Theory to Explain Business Networks," 50–53, argue that these social structures, not utility-maximizing individuals, have organized markets in the region.

8. Gerlach, *Alliance Capitalism*.

9. Ken'ichi and Ikuyo, *Nettowāku Soshiki-ron*.

10. In the 1950s and 1960s, Japanese government bureaucrats encouraged major firms to cement existing ties through intensified cross-shareholding, personnel and technology exchanges, and other forms of mutual "hostage-taking." See Vestal, *Planning for Change*, 53.

11. Economic Planning Agency of Japan, *Kōzō Kaikaku ni Chōsen, Keizai Shakai ni Dainamizumu o*.

12. See Saxenian, *Regional Advantage*; Axelsson, "Supplier Management and Technological Development"; and Brusco, "The Emilian Model."

13. Aldrich and Sakano, "Unbroken Ties," 51.

14. In his pioneering work on "getting a job," Granovetter found that people tend to learn about employment opportunities from more distant rather than closer contacts. His argument makes intuitive sense: individuals tend to congregate in social networks held together by strong ties. Members of such networks tend to know what other members know. To obtain new information, they must rely on weaker ties connecting them to members of other social networks. See Granovetter, "The Strength of Weak Ties," and *Getting a Job*. Burt extends this analysis by introducing the concept of "structural holes" that link nonredundant contacts. See Burt, *Structural Holes*.

15. Håkansson, "Product Development in Networks," 92. Regarding product development, he notes (on p. 91) that the network may "act as a control mechanism. . . . It makes certain changes easier and others more difficult. The resources

are structured in relation to the network and they are more easily mobilized if the development is in accordance with the structure of the network compared to the case when the development implies structural change."

16. Uzzi, "The Sources and Consequences of Embeddedness," 694.

17. Williamson, *Markets and Hierarchies.*

18. See Krugman, "Growing World Trade: Causes and Consequences."

19. Itami, a master of understatement, adds parenthetically that Japanese affiliates in Asia "are not very independent." See Hiroyuki Itami, "Overview," 21. Itagaki offers a helpful explanation for the "strong authority" that Japanese parent companies exercise over their foreign affiliates: "This tendency stems from one particular characteristic of J companies, at home or abroad, which is to rely to a considerable extent on human networks within companies and on information shared by employees, rather than on a standardised and integrated mechanism." See Itagaki, *The Japanese Production System,* 372–73. Although his work is now dated, Yasumuro provides a similar explanation. See Yasumuro, *Kokusai Keiei Kōdōron.*

20. See Sedgwick, "Does Japanese Management Travel in Asia?"

21. In the mid-1990s, Asia attracted as much as 81 percent of all FDI by Japanese small and medium-size firms.

22. Doremus, *The Myth of the Global Corporation,* 3.

23. Northeast Asia has presented a more challenging environment for Japanese automakers. While they gained market power in Taiwan, they did not in South Korea, where the government imposed tight restrictions on both direct investment by foreign manufacturers and the export of CBU (completely built-up, or finished) vehicles from Japan. For all its supposed independence, however, the auto industry in South Korea is deeply dependent on Japan for technology. China is the only Asian country that does not depend heavily on Japan for either capital or technology. But Japanese automakers have recently stepped up investment activity in China, with Mitsubishi Motors opening a new engine factory in Heilongjiang, and Honda tripling its production of passenger cars outside Guangzhou.

24. Fourin, *Tōnan Ajia-Taiwan-Taishū no Jidōsha Buhin Sangyō.* Domestic production here includes the assembly of imported kits, known as CKD (completely knocked down) units.

25. The Timor was a pet project of the former president, who authorized the tariff-free import of vehicles manufactured in South Korea by Kia Motors under a contract with PT Putra Timor Nasional, an Indonesian firm controlled by one of the president's sons.

26. For years, automobile manufacturing has been Indonesia's most highly concentrated industry (along with flour and liquor), according to at least one economic analysis. See Bird, "Concentration in Indonesian Manufacturing, 1975–93," 60.

27. Fourin, *Tōnan Ajia-Taiwan-Taishū.*

28. Nissan and Mitsubishi Motors, the most troubled Japanese firms, were actually rescued by French and German-American automakers (Renault and Daimler-Chrysler, respectively). Mazda and Isuzu also found themselves in need of capital injections, which they received from their leading foreign shareholders—Ford and General Motors, respectively.

29. In 1985, automobile manufacturers in the Philippines collectively produced only twenty thousand vehicles. Even their relatively busy counterparts in Indonesia, which led the ASEAN region in the production of automobiles that year, managed to manufacture only 139,000 units. See Fourin, *Tōnan Ajia-Tai-wan-Taishū.* For the sake of comparison, one might note that Japan's domestic production in 1985 reached 12.27 million vehicles (or eighty-eight times Indonesia's total production volume). See Nikkan Jidōsha Shimbunsha, *Jidōsha Sangyō Handobukku, 2000 Nenpan,* 2.

30. Matsuoka, "Accord Drives Change to Asian Carmaking."

31. "Ajia no Jidōsha Sangyō."

32. Nakashima, "Industrial Relations and Ethnicity," 14.

33. Maruyama and Legewie do a good job of describing these schemes, and an even better job of documenting the role of Japanese MNCs in formulating them. See Maruyama, *Ajia no Jidōsha Sangyō,* 27–30; and Legewie, "Driving Regional Integration."

34. Indonesia did not actually agree to participate until 1995.

35. *Kyodo News Service,* 28 April 2001; *China Daily,* 6 March 2002.

36. Legewie, "Driving Regional Integration," 2.

37. It is sometimes difficult to distinguish between Japanese government and business activities in Southeast Asia. Consider this example: in 1991, when Tokyo was still honoring a U.S.-led trade embargo against Hanoi, the Mitsubishi Corporation delivered to Vietnamese officials a "master plan for the automobile industry in the Republic of Vietnam." It recommended various industrial policies and listed the names of numerous auto parts manufacturers—almost all of them Japanese—that could serve as a supply base for the industry. See Hatch and Yamamura, *Asia in Japan's Embrace,* 34–35, 136–37.

38. CLM Working Group (MITI Japan), "Chairman's Summary."

39. Ibid., 2.

40. Interviews, September 1997, Bangkok and Jakarta.

41. The definitive source here is the International Motor Vehicle Program at MIT, located on the Web at [http://web.mit.edu/ctpid/www/imvp]. It was this program that produced Womack, Jones, and Roos, 1990.

42. Interview, Jakarta, 17 September 1997.

43. These data come from Fourin, *Tōnan Ajia-Taiwan-Taishū.*

44. Association directory and interview, Gabungan Industri Alat Mobil & Motor (GIAMM / Indonesia Auto Parts and Components Industries Association), Jakarta, 15 September 1997.

45. Nishioka, "ASEAN ni okeru Jidōsha Sangyō no Dōkō," 66.

46. Kasahara, "Transfer and Adaptation of Manufacturer-Supplier Relationships," 22.

47. Interview with Ozaki Tetsuo, general manager of Asian operations, Nissan Motors, Bangkok, 23 September 1997.

48. Interview with Wisarn Tanthawichian, director of Board of Investment Unit for Industrial Linkage Development, Bangkok, 2 September 1997.

49. "MITI Helps JAMA, JAPIA Send Advisers to Southeast Asia," *Japan Digest,* 20 October 2000; "Joint Programme to Strengthen Auto Parts Suppliers,"

The Nation (Bangkok), 2 February 2000; "Japan to assist streamline of electrical, auto sectors," *Bangkok Post*, 19 September 1997; and Japan Automobile Manufacturers Association, "Dispatch of Experts to Thailand."

50. Ford is perhaps the exception to this rule. In 1998, it began producing one-ton pickups at a $750 million plant in Thailand's Eastern Seaboard Industrial Park. But the U.S. automaker was able to penetrate the Southeast Asian market because it was, even then, closely allied with Mazda.

51. Interview, Bangkok, Thailand, 12 July 1995. For more on Chrysler's experience in Southeast Asia, especially in Thailand, see Yamamura and Hatch, "A Looming Entry Barrier," 15–16.

52. Telephone interview with Ronald Frizzell, president, GM Thailand, 23 September 1997.

53. Until then, the Thai government had demonstrated rather strong favoritism toward the Japanese MNCs that had come to dominate Thailand's automobile industry. One example stands out. In 1991, Chrysler tried to introduce the Jeep Cherokee into Thailand. The Thai government labeled the 4x4 sport utility vehicle a luxury car and imposed a hefty excise tax of 38 percent, even though it had already labeled Mitsubishi's competing 4x4, the Pajero, a pickup truck, thus qualifying it for a lower tax of only 10 percent. U.S. officials ultimately intervened on Chrysler's behalf and managed to persuade Thai officials to give the two utility vehicles equal treatment. But the negotiations dragged on for three years, during which time Mitsubishi enjoyed a substantial price advantage over Chrysler.

54. Thai Board of Investment, "Investment Opportunities Study."

55. *Asahi Shinbun*, 4 January 1995, 9.

56. *Nikkei Weekly*, 20 June 1994, 24.

57. Siam Future Development Company, Ltd. [http://www.siamfuture.com/WorldInThai/isuzu.asp].

58. Thornton, "The Debt That's Dragging Nissan Downhill."

59. *Nikkei Weekly*, 5 October 1998, 19 October 1998, and 21 December 1998; also *Nihon Keizai Shinbun*, 5 February 1998.

60. *Nikkei Weekly*, 15 November 1999.

61. Mikami, "Asia's PC and Semiconductor Industries," 79.

62. Japanese firms are by far the leading producers of audiovisual equipment and many other forms of consumer electronics in the world, not just in Asia. Although Samsung of Korea is a rising challenger, Japanese giants such as Matsushita, Sony, Toshiba, and Hitachi continue to dominate this subsector.

63. Government-affiliated financial institutions, such as the Export-Import Bank of Japan and the Japan Finance Corporation for Small Business, provide low-interest loans to many Japanese firms—including electronics manufacturers—hoping to establish production facilities in Asia. In addition, the Japanese state has used ODA to influence the development of the electronics industry in Asia. For example, in 2001, as part of its $15 billion program to help reduce the "digital divide" in Asia, Tokyo began working with Jakarta to develop IT policies for Indonesia and agreed to set up the Southeast Asia Engineering Education De-

velopment Network (SEED-NET) to foster closer professional and research ties between Japanese and Southeast Asian universities.

64. McKendrick, Doner, and Haggard, *From Silicon Valley to Singapore.*

65. Ibid., 98–111.

66. Gourevitch, "Globalization of Production," 305.

67. See Leachman and Leachman, "Trends in Worldwide Semiconductor Fabrication Capacity," 16.

68. See Arnold, "Top Global Semiconductor Companies."

69. Leachman and Leachman, "Trends," 18.

70. McKendrick, Doner, and Haggard, *From Silicon Valley to Singapore,* 105.

71. Borrus, "Resurgence of U.S. Electronics," 71.

72. Ministry of International Trade and Industry, *Wagakuni Kigyō no Kaigai Jigyō Katsudō, Dai 26-Kai,* 213, 220.

73. He also predicts, however, that this characteristic will change as Japanese MNCs acquire greater expertise in operating overseas. See Ernst, "From Partial to Systemic Globalization."

74. Chia, "Singapore," 55.

75. Wong, "Globalization of U.S.-Japan Production Networks," 96.

76. Ibid., 94–95.

77. Tecson, *Hard Disk Drive Industry in the Philippines.*

78. Interview with Hosaka Shuroku, Bangkok, 9 September 1997.

79. Takeuchi, "Comparison of Asian Business."

80. Borrus, "Left for Dead."

81. Like U.S.-based MNCs, then, they became increasingly enmeshed in what one anonymous reviewer of this chapter called "a complex network of networks."

82. Ernst, "From Partial to Systemic Globalization," 30; and Matthews and Cho, *Tiger Technology,* 180–83.

83. Chen and Chen, "Global Production Networks and Local Capabilities," 14.

84. For the development of System LSI (large-scale integrated) circuits, Mitsubishi Electric and Matsushita joined forces in December 1998. For the development of DRAM (Dynamic Random Access Memory) chips, Toshiba and Fujitsu hooked up in December 1998, while NEC and Hitachi hooked up in June 1999. *Yomiuri Shinbun,* June 24, 1999.

85. Ernst, "Partners for the China Circle?," 25.

86. U.S. Embassy, Jakarta, "Indonesia."

87. Fourin, *Kaigai Jidōsha Chōsa Geppō,* 7.

88. China, which joined the World Trade Organization in December 2001, has agreed to eliminate IT tariffs by 2005. As of 2000, the key tariffs were 5 percent for semiconductors and 9 percent for computers.

89. U.S. Embassy, Bangkok, *Country Commercial Guide;* and Japan Research Institute, "Automakers Unveil New ASEAN Strategies."

90. McKendrick, Doner, and Haggard, 30–31.

91. This observation is based on numerous interviews conducted with Commerce Department officials at U.S. embassies throughout Asia in 1995. One offi-

cial even confided that his role was to "put out fires" caused by unsuspecting or undiplomatic U.S. business officials in the region.

CHAPTER 8

The author thanks Len Schoppa, Nobuhiro Hiwatari, and all the participants of the Beyond Bilateralism conference for their helpful comments and suggestions, as well as Pablo Heidrich and Andrew Blum for their excellent research assistance.

1. Susan Strange, in *Casino Capitalism*, predicted even before the Asian crisis that European and Japanese governments might seek to increase their own financial powers as a means of trying to "nudge" the United States toward less unilateral behavior. See Helleiner, "Still an Extraordinary Power," 240.

2. The most prominent U.S. figure who has taken this position is Alan Greenspan, governor of the U.S. Federal Reserve Board. The reasons for the Asian countries' loss of export competitiveness are as follows. First, it was competition from China, due to its low labor cost and currency devaluation in 1994, in the labor-intensive goods. Second, the rapid depreciation of the Japanese yen vis-à-vis the U.S. dollar curtailed the competitiveness for high-end manufactured goods (especially for South Korea). Finally, Japan's recession shrank export markets. On the other hand, the Asian countries pegged rates to the U.S. dollar under rapid liberalization of the financial sector invited massive foreign capital inflows, much of them used for speculative purposes (especially in Thailand).

3. The term, originally used for the case of the Philippines under Marcos, is now used as a generic term for collusion and corruption that occur in many of Asia's "developmental state"-led economies.

4. DeLong and Eichengreen, "Between Meltdown and Moral Hazard," 45 and n. 63. They argue, "Not surprisingly, financial reform—closing bad banks, recapitalizing the survivors, and strengthening prudential supervision—were key elements of the IMF's crisis programs in Asia."

5. For a recent and influential piece on this view, see Yoshitomi and Shirai, "Technical Background Paper for Policy Recommendations." Some American scholars are sympathetic to this view. See Stiglitz, "Boats, Planes and Capital Flows."

6. Having supported the North American Free Trade Agreement, Clinton's political credibility was at stake. For more discussion on the political dynamics of the Mexican rescue package, see Katada, *Banking on Stability*; and Lustig, "Mexico in Crisis, U.S. to the Rescue."

7. After bypassing the Congress, the Clinton administration faced mounting criticism for its disregard of Congressional concerns and its unilateral conduct of the Mexican rescue. The U.S. Senate passed an amendment to the Treasury Appropriations Bill for fiscal year 1997 that prevented the Clinton administration from committing more than $1 billion in aid in any one year without congressional approval, unless the administration could prove it was vital to U.S. interests. This made it difficult for the administration to provide bilateral financial contributions to Thailand. The amendment expired on September 30, 1997.

8. The second line of defense is a promise in which a central bank of a country in balance-of-payments difficulty could request a loan in reserve currency (usually in U.S. dollars). The central banks of the participating countries then deposit the amount of reserve currency committed to the other party's central bank account. This idea was convenient for both the United States, because the U.S. executive branch could commit a certain amount of money to the financial crisis management of Indonesia and still avoid a major fight with the Congress. Japan Economic Institute of America, *JEI Report*, no. 42B.

9. "Generosity of the United States, Our Great Friend, Is Even More Scarce in Time of Crisis," *Bangkok Matichon*, FBIS, 15 January 1998.

10. For example, *Korean Times*, 20 April 1998; and *Maeil Kyongje Sinmun*, 10 February 1998.

11. David E. Sanger, "U.S. Sees New Villain in Asia Crisis: Tokyo's Leadership," *New York Times*, 22 February 1998.

12. Johnstone, in "Paradigms Lost," notes that "even as Washington denounced Japan's failure to implement domestic reforms, President Clinton publicly praised Beijing for its refusal to devalue the *renminbi* [China's Currency]" (p. 381). He also argues that because China contributed only limited funds to rescue packages ($1 billion each to Thailand and Indonesia) compared to the $80 billion contribution by Japan, the Japanese officials could not swallow the biased attitude of American leaders.

13. Higgott, "Asian Economic Crisis."

14. Ibid., 347.

15. Kikkawa, *Monē Haisen*, 102–52.

16. For the MOF, the collapse of Hyogo Bank and the scandal surrounding Daiwa Bank rocked Japan's financial sector along with corruption charges against MOF officials in 1995. The major case of MOF's mismanagement came at the time of the Jusen (housing loan companies) rescue, which required ¥685 billion of taxpayers' money from FY1996. For the LDP, the temporary loss of its Diet majority in 1993 was only a beginning. The public began to lose confidence in the LDP as it consistently failed to boost the economy over several years. The public was also resentful of the party's collusive relationship with special interests, as well as its misjudgment on Japan's economy, represented by Prime Minister Hashimoto's decision to increase the sales tax from 3 to 5 percent in April 1997 (which halted and reversed Japan's economic upswing).

17. See Katada, *Banking on Stability*, 174–79.

18. In this system, the country fixes its exchange rate per dollar and determines the country's domestic supply of rupiah based on the amount of foreign currency it holds. This system, in effect, makes the country abandon all flexibility on its monetary policy, and provides a full commitment to its fixed exchange rate.

19. *Nihon Keizai Shinbun*, 14 March 1998. Although Washington reportedly feared Japan's "soft" stance vis-à-vis Indonesia, one newspaper speculated that when U.S. envoy Mondale made a several-hour stopover in Tokyo on his way to Jakarta there was consultation between the United States and Japan regarding their respective negotiation strategies with Indonesia (that is, playing good cop and bad cop roles) (*Nihon Keizai Shinbun*, 3 March 1998). Later, the Japanese government

also pledged $1 billion in JEXIM Bank untied loans to Indonesia on 6 April in order to entice the Indonesian government to reach an agreement with the IMF, which was realized two days later (*Nihon Keizai Shinbun*, 7 and 8 April 1998).

20. The total amount of this so-called AGRI fund included contributions from the World Bank and the ADB. The U.S. money would support trade and investment in these countries, and Japan would provide at least $3 billion in addition to the already announced $30 billion aid package through the New Miyazawa Initiative. *New York Times*, 18 November 1998; *Nihon Keizai Shinbun*, 17 November 1998; and Japan Economic Institute of America, *JEI Report*, no. 44B.

21. *Asahi Shinbun*, 25 September 1998. The United States discussed a similar arrangement at the time of the Brazilian crisis. *The New York Times* reported a comment of a U.S. official claiming that as Germany and Japan were reluctant to take part in its financial rescue package, Latin America was becoming chiefly Washington's problem. David E. Sanger, "U.S. Plans to Send Billions to Shield Brazil's Economy," *New York Times*, 25 October 1998.

22. Interview with an MOF official, Tokyo, June 1998.

23. Interview with Eisuke Sakakibara (then vice minister of MOF and considered to be the intellectual and political force behind the AMF), Tokyo, 19 July 2001. Sakakibara noted that the U.S. exclusion was intentional so that the Asian leaders could discuss regional financial problems without U.S. pressure.

24. Interview with an IMF official, Tokyo, June 1998.

25. Collapse of Japan's two major financial institutions, Hokkaido Takushoku Bank and Yamaichi Securities, in November shook the foundation of Japan's financial health. For an explanation of how Japan's domestic financial problems influenced the Japanese government's behavior in the Asian financial crisis in fall 1997, see Amyx, "Political Impediments."

26. See Web sites of the Ministry of Finance [http://www.mof.go.jp] and the Ministry of Foreign Affairs [http://www.mofa.go.jp] for the updated details of the New Miyazawa Initiative.

27. Interview with an MOF official, Tokyo, November 2000.

28. Interviews with high-ranking Thai government advisor, Bangkok, June 2001. An MOF senior official commented on the same point in an interview in Tokyo, June 2001.

29. In Japan, the relatively new Office of Regional Financial Co-operation in the International Bureau of the MOF, created after the Asian financial crisis to deal with the regional financial issues, was upgraded to Regional Financial Co-operation Division in July 2001. This indicates a long-term commitment by the MOF and Japanese government to this issue.

30. Summary of quotes from Premier Zhu Rongji's speech at the ASEAN+3 summit on 25 November 2000. [http://www.fmprc.gov.cn/eng/6063.html], 27 April 2001.

31. *Nihon Keizai Shinbun*, 4 February 1995.

32. DeLong and Eichengreen, "Between Meltdown and Moral Hazard," 57, provides examples of such a scheme:

[The Clinton a]dministration officials played a role in the rejection by the G-10 in 1996 of a mechanism akin to an international bankruptcy court for resolving sovereign debt problems. They torpedoed France's proposal in 1998 for a "financial safeguard clause" . . . under whose umbrella countries might impose temporary capital controls. They resisted Canadian and British calls for an international standstill mechanism for sovereign debt.

33. "Tensions Under the Table."
34. Ibid., 72.
35. David E. Sanger, "Chirac, in U.S., Offers Alternative Approach to Economic Crisis," *New York Times*, 19 February 1999.
36. Because membership of this summit formally included Russia since the 1997 Denver summit, "Group of Eight" or G8 is often used to address this association of world leaders. I maintain, however, that the title G7 is more appropriate because most of the top-level discussions on economic and financial issues are still carried out without the participation of Russia.
37. Inoguchi, "Changing Significance of the G7 Summits," 30–33. She also notes that the G7 helped strengthen Japan's position on its own foreign policy concerns, and gave a salutary "deadline effect" on Japanese domestic decision making.
38. The 1997 G7 summit in Denver was held in June, before the Thai crisis.
39. *Nihon Keizai Shinbun,* 8 May 1998.
40. *Nihon Keizai Shinbun,* 16 May 1998.
41. DeLong and Eichengreen, "Between Meltdown and Moral Hazard," 55.
42. Ibid., 57–60.
43. Within Europe, France was the strongest promoter of direct regulation on HLIs. Coere and Pisani-Ferri, "Events, Ideas, and Actions," 57, n. 87.
44. *Nihon Keizai Shinbun,* 15 April 1999.
45. Coere and Pisani-Ferry, "Events, Ideas, and Actions," 23; and DeLong and Eichengreen, "Between Meltdown and Moral Hazard," 58.
46. *Nihon Keizai Shinbun,* 8 June 1999. Translated by author, emphasis added.
47. Kondo, "Kerun Samitto no Seika to Nippon," 19–20.
48. "Report of G7 Finance Ministers to the Köln Economic Summit," 18–20 June 1999. [http://www.g8kyushu-okinawa.go.jp/e/past_summit/25/e25_e.html].
49. From Point 7 of Köln Summit Conference G7 Statement [http://www.g7. utoronto.ca/summit/1999koln/g7statement june18.htm], 18 June 1999. Besides the G7 members, countries such as Russia, Saudi Arabia, Australia, Brazil, Argentina, China, Indonesia, and South Korea were invited. See Kirton, "What Is the G20?" [http://www.library.utoronto.ca/g7/g20/g20whatisit.html], 31 July 2000.
50. The Asian countries, including Thailand, South Korea, Malaysia, and China, all welcomed the progress even though some urged further regulation in the capital market. *Asahi Shinbun,* 19 June 1999.
51. The Meltzer Commission Report was delivered in March 2000. It recommended that the IMF serve as a de facto international quasi-lender of last resort, and that IMF loans should be given on a preapproved basis. It also argued in favor of eliminating the IMF conditionality. The report is available at [http://www. house.gov/jec/imf/meltzer.htm]. In June 2000, the U.S. Treasury published its response, mainly disagreeing with the elimination of the IMF conditionality, and emphasizing the transparency and accountability issue (1 October 2001) [http://www. treas.gov/press/releases/reports/response.pdf].

52. Julie Gilson, "Japan's Role in the Asia-Europe Meeting."

53. Dent, "ASEM and the 'Cinderella Complex,'" 34.

54. Importantly, ASEM's Asian membership is almost identical to that of the ASEAN+3 countries. The countries from Asia consist of the ASEAN+3 members except the least developed three (Myanmar, Cambodia, and Laos).

55. France President Jacque Chirac made the forum an important part of France's Asian policy. Europeans were concerned about the energized APEC discussion and rapid economic expansion of the Asian countries, which seem to have benefited both Japan and the United States, but not Europe. Gilson, "Japan's Role in the Asia-Europe Meeting," 737.

56. Bobrow, in "The U.S. and ASEM," argues that the reason "the hegemon [United States] did not bark" was because ASEM did not pose any threat to U.S. interests in Asia or in the world. The ASEM process was seen by America's internationalists as some modest help to liberalize and stabilize Asia.

57. Dent, "ASEM and the 'Cinderella Complex,'" 41–42.

58. Ibid., 44–45. See also 1999 ASEM Vision Group, "Asia-Europe Partnership in the 21st Century." [http://europa.eu.int/comm/external_relation/asem/asem_process/vg.pdf].

59. See "Chairman's Statement, Third Asia-Europe Finance Ministers' Meeting," point 29, [http://www.mof.go.jp/english/asem/aseme03j.htm], 25 February 2001; also Anthony Rowley, "Exploring Alternative Asian Currency Regime," *Business Times* (Singapore), 18 January 2001.

60. Dent, "ASEM and the 'Cinderella Complex,'" 50.

61. Interview with a Ministry of Foreign Affairs official, Tokyo, 5 June 2001.

62. Testimony of Walden Bello before Banking Oversight Subcommittee, Banking and Financial Services Committee, U.S. House of Representatives, 21 April 1998. [http://www.hartford-hwp.com/archives/25/058.html].

63. Well-known economists with policy impact such as Jeffrey Sachs, C. Fred Bergsten, and Nobel Prize-winning economist Robert Mundell all support the establishment of the AMF, but mostly including the United States.

64. "Interview: Horst Köhler: Focusing the Fund on Financial Stability," *Far Eastern Economic Review*, 14 June 2001 (13 November 2001). [http://www.feer.com/2001/0106_14/p048money.html].

65. The most recent of such efforts is summarized in the Joint Economic Committee Study "Recent Bailouts and Reforms of the International Monetary Fund," chaired by Congressman Jim Saxton, published July 2001. [http://www.house.gov/jec/imf/roth.htm].

CHAPTER 9

The author thanks Muthiah Alagappa, Gordon de Brouwer, Natasha Hamilton-Hart, John Ikenberry, Saori Katada, Ellis Krauss, Hugh Patrick, T. J. Pempel, and Leonard Schoppa for their helpful criticism and comments. Sincere thanks go as well to the many government officials who granted interviews for this study. The chapter also benefited from comments received at presentations at Griffith University, the Australian National University, the University of Pennsylvania, Stanford University's Asia/Pacific Research Center, and the 2002 Annual Meeting of the Association for Asian Studies. An earlier version of the chapter received the 2001 J. G. Crawford Award, given by the Australia-Japan Research Centre.

1. Krieger, *Oxford Companion to World Politics* (New York: Oxford University Press, 1993), s.v. "International Monetary Fund," by Don Babai.

2. Japan joined the Fund in 1952.

3. Japan, however, has staffed the top position of president since the ADB's creation. Moreover, with the exception of one, all of the presidents have been former high-ranking Finance Ministry officials. Lincoln, "Asian Development Bank."

4. Many see the ASEAN+3 framework for regional cooperation, discussed later in the chapter, as a resurfacing of the EAEC in another form.

5. Rix, "Leadership from Behind."

6. Terada, "Creating an Asia Pacific Economic Community."

7. Rapkin and Strand, "The United States and Japan in the Bretton Woods Institutions: Sharing or Contesting Leadership?" *International Journal* 52, no. 2 (1997): 265–96.

8. The remarks were made by Zenbee Mizoguchi, International Bureau Director-General, Ministry of Finance, Japan. Foreign Exchange Deliberation Council, *Gaikoku Kawase-to Shingikai Dai 53-kai Sokai Gijiroku.*

9. Calder, "Japanese Foreign Economic Policy Formation."

10. Author interviews with numerous Japanese Diet members and Ministry of Finance officials, 2000.

11. As of 31 July 2003, Japan's foreign exchange reserves totaled $556.836 billion. Ministry of Finance, Japan, "Foreign Exchange Reserves at the end of periods."

12. Blustein, *Chastening,* 165. The Mexican bailout would not have succeeded without, in addition to IMF support, unprecedented amounts of assistance from the United States—assistance that President Bill Clinton confided would not have been politically possible had Mexico not shared a border with the United States. Woodward, *Maestro,* 141–42.

13. Interview with Ministry of Finance, Japan, official, 2000.

14. Ibid.

15. In fact, the IMF package agreed to by the Thai government was also a result of close Japanese collaboration between the Japanese and Thai governments, because the Japanese ambassador to Thailand had a close relationship with Prime Minister Chavalit Yonchaiyudh of Thailand. Tanaka, "Press Conference by the Press Secretary."

16. Sakakibara's ascension to the position of vice minister of finance for international affairs was due in at least some part to domestic political events that spurred an unusual political intervention in MOF personnel affairs. While this intervention was made with little, if any, consideration of policy issues, it nonetheless had a significant impact on the evolution of the AMF idea.

17. Interview with Ministry of Finance, Japan, official, 2000. Notably, the IMF was not yet being showered with criticism concerning the conditions it attached to its rescue packages.

18. Blustein, *Chastening*, 79.

19. Altbach, "Asian Monetary Fund Proposal." For the 1995 Mexican bailout, the Treasury slyly drew on a special pool of money to extend credit to Mexico, thereby circumventing Congress. See Blustein, *Chastening*, 79; and Woodward, *Maestro*, 138–44.

20. Blustein, *Chastening*, 165.

21. Sakakibara's circulation of the confidential memo outlining his plan to Hong Kong but not Chinese officials was undoubtedly one reason for China's cold and suspicious reaction to the initial proposal. Hong Kong had only reverted to Chinese rule on July 1, 1997, and was being governed by China under a "one China, two systems" philosophy.

22. Interview with Ministry of Finance, Japan, official, 2000.

23. Blustein, *Chastening*, 166.

24. Altbach, "Asian Monetary Fund Proposal," 9.

25. Ibid.

26. IMF conditionality had not yet emerged as a major issue within the region.

27. Implementation of these reforms began in April 1998.

28. For example, the Japanese government had gone from having a balanced budget in 1990 to having one of the worst budget deficits in the advanced industrial world by 1997.

29. Interview with official in Ministry of Finance, Malaysia, 2000.

30. Blustein, *Chastening*, 167. Blustein notes that in the end American representatives were permitted by Japan's Finance Ministry to sit in as observers.

31. Ibid, 168.

32. The fourteen countries that gathered were Australia, Brunei, Canada, China, Hong Kong SAR, Indonesia, Japan, Korea, Malaysia, New Zealand, the Philippines, Singapore, Thailand, and the United States.

33. Hashimoto, "Press Conference."

34. Interview with Stephen Leong, deputy director-general, Institute of Strategic and International Studies, Malaysia, 2000.

35. Interview with officials of Ministry of Finance, Japan, 2000.

36. See Gyohten, "East Asian Initiative Needed in Crises."

37. See Ogura, "Atarashii Ajia no Sozo"; an abridged version appeared as Ogura, "Creating a New Asia." The article was notable because it was the first written by an incumbent government official to argue that the United States had no right to protest being left out of such an arrangement.

38. Between July 1997 and November 1998, Japanese aid funneled through existing mechanisms totaled $44 billion.

39. The initial proposal for an AMF was considered to be the first Miyazawa Initiative. In fact, both the initial proposal for an AMF and the New Miyazawa Initiative were the brainchildren of MOF bureaucrats in the International Finance Bureau. Haruhiko Kuroda, who would replace Sakakibara as vice minister of finance for international affairs in 1999, was well-versed in drafting such plans. At the time of the Mexican debt crisis in the 1980s, when Kiichi Miyazawa was serving his first stint as finance minister, Kuroda drafted the Miyazawa Plan proposed by Japan to deal with the Mexican crisis. The United States rejected the plan as

too stringent but in the end put forward a very similar plan, dubbed the Brady Plan. Interview with Ministry of Finance, Japan, official, 2001.

40. Kishimoto, "Shin Miyazawa Kōsō no Shinei to Ajia Tsuka Kikin," 42.

41. Ministry of Finance, Japan, "Q&A About the New Initiative."

42. Interview with Ministry of Finance, Japan, official posted to Japanese Embassy in Kuala Lumpur, 1999.

43. Interviews with Ministry of Finance, Japan, officials and U.S. Treasury officials, 1999.

44. Cornell, "Japan Pushes for Asian version of IMF," citing the *Asahi Shinbun.*

45. Prime Minister's Commission on Japan's Goals in the 21st Century, *The Frontier Within.*

46. Interview with officials of Ministry of Finance, Japan, 2001.

47. "Joint Ministerial Statement of the ASEAN+3 Finance Ministers Meeting." A document distributed to the press at the time this statement was issued adds, "including those provided by the IMF," thereby making the complementary nature of the arrangement clear. See "Press Guidance on Chiang Mai Initiative."

48. "Press Guidance on Chiang Mai Initiative."

49. Interview with official of Ministry of Finance, Japan, 2001.

50. China was the second largest holder of foreign exchange reserves in the world at end-June 2003, with $346.5 billion. Korea had $131.66 billion in foreign exchange reserves as of end-June 2003, ranking it the fourth-largest holder in the world. Although Taiwan and Hong Kong ranked third and fifth in the world, respectively, political sensitivities have precluded Taiwan from being admitted into membership of the ASEAN+3. Hong Kong's return to China in July 1997 also makes it somewhat beholden to Chinese desires.

51. An exception is made if multiple countries, including one of the donor countries, are under attack. For example, if Thailand and Korea were both hit by liquidity crises, Korea would withdraw as a donor to Thailand. The maximum amount that countries may draw from the swap facility is determined by bilateral negotiation, but if the swap mechanism is activated, funds are drawn on a pro rata basis.

52. Interviews with officials of the Ministry of Finance, Japan, and of the Ministry of Finance and Economy, Korea, 2001.

53. Singapore, a holder of sizeable foreign exchange reserves, supported IMF linkage.

54. Interview with official of the Ministry of Finance, Japan, 2001.

55. Ibid.

56. Kuroda was widely recognized as being more pragmatically minded than Sakakibara, whose tendency to focus on lofty ideals resulted in his original AMF proposal, which lacked the answers to many questions about the proposed fund's actual operation.

57. The little progress related to competence-building for surveillance activities made to date includes the establishment of the Japan-ASEAN Financial Technical Assistance Fund, which has been used to strengthen systems of monitoring capital flows within ASEAN. A number of countries in the region have also agreed to exchange data on short-term capital flows. The possibility of establish-

ing an early warning system in the region that might require the monitoring of balance of payments, exchange rate regimes, levels of foreign borrowing, and the activities of currency hedge funds in each country was under consideration in 2002, but no concrete progress was made toward achieving such a system.

58. In May 1999, the IMF and World Bank launched the Financial Sector Assessment Program as a means to boost the IMF's surveillance capacity, which had obviously proven too weak in the crisis-stricken countries. While the introduction of this program has been viewed as a positive step forward in helping countries to address problems before they reach crisis proportions, the Financial Sector Assessment Program has also become renowned for the heavy burden it places on the host country's regulators. The assessment is said to essentially require host country regulators to halt their normal activities for approximately two weeks, to translate all laws and documents into English, and to engage in intense discussion and debate in English with IMF assessors about their findings. The resistance of Japan's own Financial Services Agency in September 2001 to acceding to an IMF request for such an assessment was motivated largely by the disruptive nature of this assessment. Interview with official of the Financial Services Agency, Japan, September 2001.

59. Interview with official of the Ministry of Finance, Japan, 2000.

60. Both countries wish to see an increase in the IMF funding contributed by Asian nations (as well as by emerging market nations in Central America and South America). "IMF Eyes Revising Formula for Member Contributions," *Nikkei Net Interactive*, 29 June 2000.

61. The Fund allocates much higher quotas to European countries, and membership of the IMF Executive Board is likewise weighted in favor of Europe. Eight of the twenty-four executive directors are from Europe.

62. In May 2002, for example, former IMF First Deputy Director Stanley Fischer expressed support for the network of currency swap arrangements, first at a meeting of the ASEAN+3 finance ministers on the sidelines of an Asian Development Bank meeting in Shanghai, and then in a speech at the Hong Kong Monetary Authority.

63. Ministry of Finance, Japan, "Joint Ministerial Statement."

64. Because China already has large holdings of U.S. dollars, Japan has pledged to provide the Chinese central bank with yen if Beijing needs to defend its currency by selling yen for yuan.

65. Japan's former vice minister for international finance, Eisuke Sakakibara, notes that before the crisis he regularly communicated with individuals at the U.S. Treasury about yen-dollar movements and could easily pick up the phone and call the Treasury Secretary. Yet the same kind of constant contact, personal familiarity, or flow of information was absent in relations between Japanese officials and central bankers / finance ministers in other countries in East Asia. Author interview, 1999. Numerous central bankers and finance ministry officials interviewed for this project throughout the region emphasized the important role that the simple strengthening of such communication networks should have in fending off speculative attacks in the future and in coordinating responses. Author interviews, 1999–2002.

66. Notably, regional financial arrangements evolved over a thirty-year period in Europe and, even then, were carried out on the backdrop of a level of integration in the real economy not yet seen in Asia. European nations also shared much more similar economic structures and stages of development.

67. In 2002, for example, elected officials in Thailand and representatives from that nation's bankers' association urged Japanese officials to increase their efforts at realizing the AMF initiative. Koji Nozawa, "AMF Safety Net Plans Snag on Details," *Nikkei Net Interactive*, 25 February 2002.

68. Sentiment expressed by government representatives at a third-track conference, Conference on Regional Financial Arrangements in East Asia, October 2002, Canberra, Australia.

CHAPTER 10

The author thanks all the participants at the first conference for their helpful comments, especially Nakagawa Junji, Glenn Fukushima, Saori Katada, Akiko Fukushima, and the book's editors, Ellis Krauss and T. J. Pempel.

1. Statement of Takashi Fukaya, minister of international trade and industry, "On Request for Consultation of Antidumping Duties on Certain Hot-Rolled Steel from Japan," 20 October 1999. [http://www.meti.go.jp].

2. "Letter of October 22 from Vice-Minister Arai Against Under Secretary of Commerce, Mr. Aaron's remarks made at National Press Club in Washington D.C. on October 19," 22 October 1999. [http://www.meti.go.jp].

3. Saadia M. Pekkanen, "Aggressive Legalism: The Rules of the WTO and Japan's Emerging Trade Strategy," *World Economy* 24, no. 5 (2001): 707–37; Saadia M. Pekkanen, "International Law, the WTO, and the Japanese State: Assessment and Implications of the New Legalized Trade Politics," *Journal of Japanese Studies* 27, no. 1 (2001): 41–79.

4. Goldstein et al., "Introduction"; Abott et al., "Concept of Legalization," 401.

5. Krueger, "Introduction," 8.

6. U.S. General Accounting Office, *World Trade Organization: Issues in Dispute Settlement*, 11–12.

7. The 187 cases exclude 5 cases in which there were co-complainants. Figures for the United States and Europe are from U.S. General Accounting Office, *World Trade Organization: U.S. Experience*, 3–4. Figures for Japan are based on calculations by the author of WTO dispute settlement data from 1995 to the present, and they include both cases in which Japan is a single complainant and those in which it is a co-complainant.

8. U.S. General Accounting Office, *World Trade Organization: Issues*, 9–12.

9. Based on calculations by author.

10. Pekkanen, "Aggressive Legalism."

11. This information about the investigative process is based on Louth and Rogers, "Import Administration."

12. Several steps need to be taken before the industry petitioners can expect to see favorable outcomes, meaning here the imposition of either a preliminary or a

final duty. After a petition is accepted by the ITA, it moves to the USITC, which makes a preliminary determination. If the preliminary injury determination at the USITC is negative, the petition is dismissed. If not, it reverts back to the ITA for a preliminary determination, and if that determination is positive, petitioners can expect to see the alleged dumping margin or subsidy rate temporarily equalized through cash deposits or bonds collected by U.S. Customs. The investigation then proceeds onward to final determinations by both the ITA and the USITC sequentially; if either determination is negative, the case is dismissed. If the ITA finding is positive, the case continues on at the USITC, and both determinations have to be positive in order for the imposition of a duty order, in which case U.S. Customs can collect the duties.

13. Staiger and Wolak, "Differences in the Uses and Effects of Antidumping Law." The authors separate petitioners into "outcome filers" (those who file because they expect to benefit from the final outcome of an antidumping order at the end of the investigation) and "process filers" (those who file because they expect to benefit from the nonduty effects of the investigation process regardless of whether a final antidumping duty is imposed). As Kala Krishna points out in his comments on the authors' essay, however, it is very difficult to attribute motivations based on outcomes alone, and there may well be mixed motives for the filing that can be gauged only using case studies and interviews. Moreover, it is difficult to see how the negative preliminary findings fit into the authors' framework. I concentrate here simply on the assumption that all industries file with the expectation of seeing an antidumping or countervailing duty imposed.

14. Irwin, "Trade Politics and the Semiconductor Industry."

15. Data on rulings of antidumping duties and countervailing duties petitions from 1960 onwards are from the official compilation of the U.S. Department of Commerce's International Trade Administration, available at [http://www.ita.doc.gov]. Data for both have been broken down by commodity, time, and countries. All calculations have been made by the author. For accuracy, some of the data between 1980 and 1990 have been checked against those published in Destler, *American Trade Politics*, Appendixes B and C. The analysis here concentrates largely on ADs.

16. Countervailing duty petitions fared the same, with only about 50 percent of the total petitions actually resulting in the imposition of duties during the decade.

17. A similar story is true for countervailing duties. Here too the steel-related industries filed the largest number of petitions, accounting for more than 56 percent of the total filed between 1970 and 1997. Yet the overall imposition of the countervailing duty rate in the face of this lobbying onslaught stood at a mere 51 percent return.

18. Moore, "Steel Protection in the 1980s," 73–77.

19. Interview with MITI official, June 1997. The competitiveness of the Japanese steel industry led to severe trade friction with the United States, resulting in VERs between 1984 and 1989, and subsequently from 1989 to 1992. There was also movement toward multilateral settlements in the 1990s. Yet, as a rule, MITI officials describe the negotiations over the Multilateral Steel Agreement (MSA) in October 1990 between the United States, Canada, and the European Union as

conflictual and prone to tremendous domestic political pressures that made a mockery of just such a solution. Although the parties could consent to a general agreement, the negotiations fell apart six years later, in October 1996, due to the different interests of the integrated carbon steel producers and due to sheer finger pointing among the governments involved. Negotiations over the Multilateral Specialty-Steel Agreement (MSSA), principally between the United States and the European Union, also soured after two years, in 1997. The stance taken by the Japanese on the MSSA represents, according to some MITI officials, the first visible shift toward multilateral commitments on the part of the Japanese government. One of the principal reasons for Japan's opposition to the MSSA was MITI's larger contention that this was a sector-specific solution that went against the very grain of the WTO rules that had come into existence in January 1995. This was also the position taken by the domestic Japanese steel industry as a whole. Most officials argue that because of the extreme lobbying power of steel in the United States, as well as its political power in Japan, this industry will not be amenable to multilateral solutions.

20. Edward Nielan, "Dumping Steel," *Journal of Commerce Newspaper*, 28 August 1998.

21. Paul Blustein, "Steel Industry Plans to Fight Imports," *Washington Post*, 11 September 1998. Other countries specifically mentioned were South Korea and Russia.

22. Deborah McGregor, "US Pressure Mounts for Steel Curbs," *Financial Times*, 15 January 1999; "U.S. Vows to Protect Steel Industry; Promises Faster Action When Imports Surge," *Plain Dealer*, 27 July 2000.

23. Alexandra Harney, "Troubles Grow for Japanese Steel Executives," *Financial Times*, 20 November 1998.

24. NKK steel and Kawasaki Corporation unveiled a merger plan in the middle of April 2001.

25. Tilton, "Regulatory Reform and Market Opening in Japan," 176–77.

26. Information on provisions in Article VI and the AD Agreement are directly from the published WTO Agreements.

27. Jackson, "Dumping in International Trade," 6–9.

28. Croley and Jackson, "WTO Dispute Procedures," 193–95.

29. The standard of review also carries over into the interpretation of international law. Here the Panel has to defer to national government interpretations as long as they are based on those that are within the permissible interpretations in cases where there are more than one, even if the Panel prefers another.

30. This information comes directly from WTO documents numbered WT/DS/OV/1 ("Update of WTO Dispute Settlement Cases, New Developments Since Last Update, Up Until 16 October 2001"); and WT/DSB/26/Add.1 ("Dispute Settlement Body, Annual Report 2001, Overview of the State of Play of WTO Disputes—Addendum"). [http://www.wto.org].

31. Interview with director, First International Organizations Division (WTO Division), Economic Affairs Bureau, MOFA, March 2001.

32. Interview with Masakazu Toyoda, director-general, Multilateral Trade System Department, METI, March 2001.

33. Unless otherwise indicated, all information, references, and data on the trade dispute cases are from official published WTO documents known as Panel Reports, Appellate Body Reports, and Arbitration Reports.

34. Third-party rights are laid out in Article 10 of the DSU, one of the four annexes overseen formally by the WTO.

35. *Thailand—Anti-Dumping Duties on Angles, Shapes and Sections of Iron or Non-Alloy Steel and H-Beams from Poland: Report of the Panel*, WTO WT/DS/122/R28 [http://www.wto.org], September 2000.

36. *United States—Anti-Dumping Act of 1916, Complaint by the European Communities: Report of the Panel*, WTO WT/DS136/R [http:/www.wto.org], 31 March 2000.

37. *European Communities—Anti-Dumping Duties on Imports of Cotton-Type Bed Linen from India: Report of the Panel*, WTO WT/DS141/R [http://www.wto.org], 30 October 2000.

38. *United States—Anti-Dumping Measures on Stainless Steel Plate in Coils and Stainless Steel Sheet and Strip from Korea: Report of the Panel*, WTO WT/DS179/R [http://www.wto.org], 22 December 2000.

39. The following discussion is drawn exclusively from *United States—Anti-Dumping Act of 1916, Complaint by Japan: Report of the Panel*, WTO WT/DS162/R [http://www.wto.org], 29 May 2000.

40. 15 U. S. C. § 72.

41. The Appellate Body heard a joint appeal by Japan and the European Union, as shown in *United States—Anti-Dumping Act of 1916, AB-2000-5—AB-2000-6: Report of the Appellate Body*, WTO WT/DS136/AB/R and WT/DS162/AB/R [http://www.wto.org], 28 August 2000.

42. There was also a joint arbitration report for Japan and the EU, namely *United States—Anti-Dumping Act of 1916, Arbitration Under Article 21.3(c) of the Understanding on Rules and Procedures Governing the Settlement of Disputes: Award of the Arbitrator*, WTO WT/DS136/11 and WT/DS162/14 [http://www.wto.org], 28 February 2001.

43. Statement of Mr. Takashi Fukaya, Minister of International Trade and Industry, "On Request for Consultation with the United States Regarding the Imposition of Antidumping Duties on Certain Hot-Rolled Steel from Japan." [http://www.meti.go.jp], 20 October 1999.

44. The facts and information are drawn exclusively from *United States—Anti-Dumping Measures on Certain Hot-Rolled Steel Products from Japan: Report of the Panel*, WTO WT/DS184/R [http://www.wto.org], 28 February 2001.

45. Russian and Brazilian steel exports were also investigated by the United States, but the analysis here concentrates only on the Japanese exports.

46. *United States—Anti-Dumping Measures on Certain Hot-Rolled Steel Products from Japan—AB-2001-2: Report of the Appellate Body*, WTO WT/DS184/AB/R [http://www.wto.org], 24 July 2001; "U.S. Files Appeal on WTO Steel Dumping Ruling," *Japan Economic Newswire*, 25 April 2001.

47. See WTO document *United States—Continued Dumping and Subsidy Offset Act of 2000, Constitution of the Panel Established at the Request of Aus-*

tralia, Brazil, Canada, Chile, the European Communities, India, Indonesia, Japan, Korea, Mexio, and Thailand: Corrigendum, WT/DS217/6/Corr.1 and WT/DS234/14/Corr.1 [http://www.wto.org], 12 November 2001.

48. "EU Could Move Against 'Byrd Amendment' in WTO as Early as This Week," *International Trade Reporter Current Reports,* 26 October 2000.

49. "Japan, EU to Bring U.S. Byrd Law to WTO Shortly," *Jiji Press Ticker Service,* 19 December 2000.

50. "Japan Starts Picking on China," *Economist,* 10 February 2001; "Chugoku no Danpingu Chōsa: Kokunai Porisuchirin meka ni Hamon" (Chinese dumping investigation: ripples for domestic polystyrene makers), *Nihon Keizai Shinbun,* 15 March 2001.

51. "China Penalizes Japan Firms for Dumping Steel," *Japan Times,* 14 April 2000.

52. "China Rules Japanese Sheet Steel Dumped on Market," *Japan Economic Newswire,* 17 December 2000.

53. "Chugoku Tekkō Danpingu Kettei: Nihon Kigyō 8 Sha ni Saikō 58% Kazei Tsūchi" (China's steel dumping decision: Eight Japanese companies with highest 58% duties notice], *Mainichi Shinbun,* 19 December 2000. According to the press reports, China was the world's largest target of antidumping complaints, with forty countries issuing about four hundred such complaints.

54. "Chugoku WTO: Kitai to Gimon no Koe, Nihon Kigyō Hannō" (China WTO: Japanese companies express expectations and doubts), *Mainichi Shinbun,* 4 July 2001.

55. "Nōsuishō: Seefugaado Kanshi Taisei o Kyōka, Hitsuyō na Jyōhō o Jyōji Suru" (Agricultural ministry: Strenghtening safeguard supervision arrangement; usual gathering of necessary information), *Mainichi Shinbun,* 23 January 2001.

56. Enami Mamoru, "Seefugaado: Nihon Taoru Kōgyō Kumiairen ga Hatsudō o Yōsei" (Safeguards: Towel industry association requests operation], *Mainichi Shinbun,* 26 February 2001; Tamaki Aikyo and Yuichiro Onda, "Towel Makers Disagree on WTO Safeguard," *Daily Yomiuri,* 18 February 2001; Ken Hijino, "Tokyo May Restrict China Imports," *Financial Times,* 26 February 2001.

57. Tsukamoto Hiroki and Takahashi Hideo, "Seefugaado: Zantei Sochi Katsudō de Kihon Gōi, Nōshōra 3 Kakuryō" (Basic Agreement on Temporary Steps, 3 Cabinet Members), *Mainichi Shinbun,* 31 March 2001.

58. Takekawa Masaki, "Negi Nado Nōsanbutsu 3 Himmoku o 23 Nichi Kara Zantei Katsudō e" (Toward temporary operation on three agricultural items], *Mainichi Shinbun,* 17 April 2001; Anthony Rowley, "China-Japan Onion Spat Could Spark More Rows," *Business Times Singapore,* 16 April 2001; Miki Tanikawa and Don Kirk, "Mushrooms with Garlic and Tariffs," *New York Times,* 17 April 2001.

59. "Seefugaado: Taishō Kakudai no Ugoki o Kensei, Miyazawa Zaimushō" (Safeguard: Checking the Movement of the Enlarging Subject, Miyazawa Finance Minister), *Mainichi Shinbun,* 17 April 2001; Takekawa Masaki, "Negi Nado Nōsanbutsu 3 Himmoku o 23 Nichi Kara Zantei Katsudō e (Toward temporary operation on three agricultural items]," *Mainichi Shinbun,* 17 April 2001; Shinji

Kayano, "Protectionist Clamor Damaging Japan," *Daily Yomiuri*, 8 May 2001; "Seefugaado: Wakame ni mo Katsudō Yōbō, Iwateken Engan 5 Shichōsonchō (Safeguard: Demands for operation in Wakame as well, mayor of five coastal municipalities in Iwateken," *Mainichi Shinbun*, 17 April 2001.

60. "Seefugaado: Taoru ne Tsuite Kichōsa e, Keizai Sangyōshō" (Safeguard: Basic Investigations Concerning Towels, MITI), *Mainichi Shinbun*, 6 April 2001. Estimates provided by the Japanese towel association suggest that domestic demand was being met 60 percent by foreign products.

61. Takekawa Masaki, "Seefugaado: Katsudō Shinsei Hōshin o Hyōmei, Zen Nihon Nekutai Kōgyō Renmei" (Safeguard: Application action plan stated, all Japan necktie industry association], *Mainichi Shinbun*, 13 April 2001.

62. Interview, Riwa Sakamoto, deputy director, Manufacturing Industries Bureau, METI, March 2001; Araki Isao, "Uniclo Shachō: Safugaado Hatsudō no Seifu Kentō o Karatsu ni Hihan" (Uniclo president: Severe criticism of government safeguard investigation), *Mainichi Shinbun*, 22 May 2001; and Takekawa Masaki, "Yasai Shushi Yushutsu Jishuku: Shubyō Kyokai 'Kokunai Nōgyō Hakai'no Hihan Uke (Vegetable seed export controls: Nursery association criticism of domestic agriculture collapse], *Mainichi Shinbun*, 30 May 2001.

63. Clay Chandler, "Asia-Pacific Nations Urge New Trade Talks," *Washington Post*, 8 June 2001.

64. "Chugoku no Danpingu Chōsa: Kokunai Porisuchirin meka ni Hamon" (Chinese dumping investigation: Ripples for domestic polystyrene makers], *Nihon Keizai Shinbun*, 15 March 2001.

65. Akira Fujino, "China Planning Retaliation Against Japanese Goods," *Daily Yomiuri*, 20 June 2001; Craig S. Smith, "China: Trade Dispute with Japan," *New York Times*, 20 June 2001; Ken Hijino, James Kynge, and Gillian Tett, "Beijing Hits Back on Japan Import Tariffs," *Financial Times*, 20 June 2001; James Kynge and Richard McGregor, "China Imposes 100% on Japan, Retaliatory Moves Growing Assertiveness in Trade Relations," *Financial Times*, 22 June 2001; and Statement by Mr. Takeo Hiranuma, Minister of Economy, Trade and Industry on China's Announcement Regarding Imposition of Special Duties on Japanese Products [http://www.meti.go.jp], 21 June 2001.

66. "Nicchū, Safugaado Taiōsaku De Minkan Reburu Kyōgi" (Private sector conference on Japan-China safeguard countermeasures], *Nikkei Net*, 24 September 2001, [http://www3.nikkei.co.jp]; David Ibison, "Japan to Compensate Companies in Trade Pact," *Financial Times*, 20 August 2001.

67. Ken Hijino, "Japan Delays Import Rulings," *Financial Times*, 12 October 2001.

68. "Settle Disputes Under WTO Rules," editorial, *Daily Yomiuri*, 4 November 2001; "Nōgosanhin Safugaado, Nichū no Kanmin Kyōgi de Gōi Dekizu" (Agricultural safeguards, Japan-China official talks fail], *Yomiuri Shinbun*, 8 November 2001; "Temporary Restrictions on Farm Imports Expire," *Japan Times*, 9 November 2001.

69. "Japan-China Trade Row Lives On," BBC News [http://news.bbc.co.uk], 8 November 2001.

70. Pekkanen, "Sword and Shield."

71. "Trading Troubles," *South China Morning Post*, 21 June 2001.

72. Clay Chandler, "Asia-Pacific Nations Urge New Trade Talks," *Washington Post*, 8 June 2001.

73. Komuro, "Japan's First Antidumping Measure," esp. 13–14, 26–29; "Textile Makers Seek Antidumping Duties on Polyester Imports," *Japan Economic Newswire*, 28 February 2001.

74. "Diary: Steel," *The Plain Dealer*, 29 September 2001.

75. Robert A. Guth and Terho Uimonen, "Japan's Chip Firms Consider Filing Dumping Complaint," *Asian Wall Street Journal*, 25 October 2001.

76. James Brooke, "Ready for WTO Talks, and Ready to Deal," *New York Times*, 9 November 2001; and Joseph Kahn, "A Trade Agenda Tempts Murphy's Law; U.S. Sees Talks as a Test of Leadership, but the Road to Qatar was Rocky," *New York Times*, 9 November 2001.

CHAPTER I I

For their many helpful comments on earlier versions of this paper, the author would like to thank the participants in this project, especially Ellis Krauss, Akiko Fukushima, and Glen Fukushima, as well as Greg Noble and other participants in a seminar held at the Institute of Social Sciences, University of Tokyo, in December 2001.

1. Those at the official level include, for example, APEC, the ARF, AFTA, the KEDO, ASEAN+3, Trilateral Coordination and Oversight Group (TCOG) meeting, and the annual Chiefs of Defense Conference.

2. Ministry of International Trade and Industry, *Arata naru Ajia-Taiheiyo Kyoryoku o Motomete*.

3. The original APEC members include Japan, the United States, South Korea, Australia, New Zealand, Canada, and six ASEAN members.

4. MITI faced resistance domestically from MOFA, partly because of the ministerial rivalry over foreign policy affairs and MOFA's strong sensitivity to the ASEAN countries' concern about Japan's activism for regional affairs. See Krauss, "Japan, the U.S., and the Emergence of Multilateralism in Asia," 479–80.

5. Baker, "The United States and APEC Regime Building," 168.

6. Baker, *The Politics of Diplomacy*, 609–13; and Krauss, "Japan, the U.S., and the Emergence of Multilateralism in Asia," 481.

7. Interview with Shigeo Muraoka, then Deputy Vice-Minister of MITI, 12 June and 10 July 2001.

8. U.S. Department of State, "Secretary Baker's Address."

9. For example, see Solomon, "Asian Security in the 1990s," 245–46.

10. Nakayama, "Statement by His Excellency Dr. Taro Nakayama."

11. U.S. Department of State, "Settlement to Cambodia Problem Needed, Baker Says."

12. For example, when President Bush visited Tokyo in January 1992, the Japanese government pushed the idea of a security dialogue through the ASEAN-PMC to be included in the joint announcement at the end of the summit meeting.

Tokyo partly succeeded in achieving this, but given U.S. reluctance, they avoided using the term *security dialogue* and instead used *political dialogue*.

13. U.S. Department of State, "Winston Lord Assistant Secretary-Designate for East Asian and Pacific Affairs, Statement."

14. Two reasons for not using the ASEAN-PMC came into consideration. The first was that given the increasing importance of economic management in Southeast Asia, ASEAN needed to keep the ASEAN-PMC as a framework not solely for security issues, but for economic cooperation with non-ASEAN members. The second reason was membership. China, the most crucial security concern for ASEAN, was not a member of ASEAN-PMC, and the inclusion of Vietnam surfaced as another issue.

15. The original members of the ARF include ASEAN, Australia, Canada, China, Japan, Laos, New Zealand, Papua New Guinea, Russia, South Korea, the United States, and the European Union.

16. Although the idea of an Asia-Pacific multilateral economic cooperation had been floated among some influential Americans, such as George Shultz, the U.S. government took no formal initiatives to follow up or implement it.

17. Ministry of International Trade and Industry, *Arata naru*, 25.

18. The U.S.-Canada Free Trade Agreement was signed at the beginning of that year, and the creation in 1992 of a single European market, often noted as "Fortress Europe," was in sight.

19. U.S. government, *A Strategic Framework for the Asian Pacific Rim*. Although the scale of the reduction was still limited, there was a general perception among Japanese policymakers that a further reduction would be carried out, including the possible closure of U.S. military bases in the Philippines and elsewhere.

20. Yukio Satoh, then director-general of the Information and Analysis Division at MOFA, first conceptualized this framework in mid-1991, although he used the term *multiplex*. Satoh, "Asia-Pacific Process for Stability and Security," 34–45. Since then, the concept had been cited in the speeches and writings of other foreign policy officials, beginning with the Nakayama proposal, which used the English translation "multilayered." When referring to the concept, MOFA usually uses the Japanese term *juso-teki*, but the English translation in official documents is either "multilayered" or "multi-tiered." In this chapter, I use "multi-tiered" in order to avoid confusion.

21. Interview with Muraoka.

22. Interview with Satoh Yukio, MOFA, 23 and 26 February 2001.

23. Interview with Shinji Fukukawa, then senior vice minister of MITI, 22 May 2001. Some MITI officials became concerned about the possible decrease of U.S. involvement in the region at that time, given the conclusion of the U.S.-Canada Free Trade Agreement of 1988 and the preparation of another arrangement between the United States and Mexico.

24. Interview with a MITI official who was closely involved in the process, 10 January 2001. Also, "Mebuku Chiikishugi, Ajia-taiheiyo Kyoryokukousou," *Nikkei Shinbun*, 11 May 1989.

25. "Zadankai: Meiyo aru Chii o Erutameni"; and "Zadanakai: Jinrui ni tot-teno Nichibei Doumei towa."

26. Baker, "America in Asia."

27. For example, in his memoir, James Baker III, then secretary of the treasury and later secretary of state, expressed an enthusiastic attitude toward the realiza-tion of NAFTA, in contrast to his reserved tone in his discussion of the Asia-Pa-cific grouping in the same volume. Baker, *Politics of Diplomacy*, 604–9.

28. When Baker was secretary of the treasury in the Reagan administration, he and his staff members explored the idea of Asia-Pacific grouping on macroeco-nomic issues but did not go further. Krauss, "Japan, the U.S., and the Emergence of Multilateralism in Asia," 481.

29. Interview with Winston Lord, 16 April 2002. Lord particularly empha-sized his attempt to define the multilateral security dialogue as a supplement to existing bilateral arrangements, in contrast to the previous administration's atti-tude toward them.

30. Interview with Sandra Kristoff, then assistant U.S. trade representative for Asia and the Pacific, 19 March 2002; and with Robert Fauver, then deputy assis-tant secretary of state for East Asian and Pacific Affairs, 21 February 2002.

31. U.S. Department of State, "USIA Foreign Press Center Briefing."

32. For the U.S. strategic interests, see Krauss, "Japan, the U.S., and the Emer-gence of Multilateralism in Asia," 481–82.

33. Interview with Winston Lord.

34. For a useful summary to see how MITI officials viewed the APEC forum during those years, see the serial articles in the *Tsusan Journal*: Tsushoseisakuk-yoku Ajia-Taiheiyo Chiikikyoryokusuishinshitsu, "APEC Nau, 1"; and "APEC Nau, 2."

35. For example, the editorial coverage of major newspapers (*Asahi*, *Yomiuri*, *Mainichi*, *Nikkei*, and *Sankei*) on the APEC issues from 1990 to 1992 was counted as 4, 19, and 26 respectively. It increased dramatically in 1993, counted as 56 (and 47 in 1994 and 110 in 1995).

36. Comments by Richard Solomon, then assistant secretary of state for East Asian and Pacific affairs. U.S. Department of State, "Hearing on the East Asian and Pacific Affairs Subcommittee."

37. The U.S. expected APEC to succeed in advancing trade liberalization among members in the long run. See, for example, U.S. Department of State, "Background Briefing."

38. Although when describing its policy toward APEC as well as Asia in gen-eral the Clinton administration's use of "New Pacific Community" appeared to promote genuine multilateralism and community building within the region, many pointed out that the underlying motivation for the administration's New Pacific Community was to open Asian markets for American products. See, for example, Bodde, "Managing APEC."

39. Japanese officials of both MITI and MOFA who were interviewed said uniformly that they thought the issue of liberalization would be taken up at APEC someday in the future, but not as early as had happened.

40. For example, see METI [http://www.meti.go.jp/press/past/dbap09/html] and MOFA [http://www.mofa.go.jp/mofaj/gaiko/apec/97/2.html].

41. Baker, "The United States and APEC Regime Building," 182. See also Krauss, chap. 12, this volume.

42. This shift in Japan's policy toward bilateral and regional FTA was formerly stated in the 1999 MITI White Paper, 295–96. The significance of this shift was discussed, for example, in "Gurobaru-ka suru Sekaikeizai no nakade Nihon to Ajia wa Douarubekika."

43. It should be noted that before this phase Clinton in fact cancelled his participation in APEC summit meetings twice, in 1995 and 1998. Yet since 1999 onward (at least until 2002, at the time of this writing), Washington managed to send the president to all of the summit meetings.

44. ASEAN [http://www.aseansec.org/3635.htm].

45. It took four years for the ARF to agree on the definition of *preventive diplomacy.*

46. The concept of a *multi-tiered approach* for regional security frequently came into play in the discussion of the ARF by MOFA officials as well as by political leaders. See, for example, Yanai, "Reisengo no Wagakuni no Anzen-hoshouseisaku," 48–49.

47. Hiramatsu Kenji, "Ajia-Taiheiyo-gata no Anzenhoshoukikou wa Seiritsu Suruka."

48. Interview with Winston Lord.

49. Ieppei Yamazawa, "APEC's Economic and Technical Cooperation."

50. In Prime Minister Mori's speech at ASEAN+3 meeting in 2000; see MOFA [http://www.mofa.go.jp/region/asia-aci/asean/conference/asean3/state0011.html].

51. For example, see "Zadankai: Ugokidashita Hokutouajia, Shinraijosei ka Tairitsukouzou ka." Until the mid-1990s, MOFA officials were largely hesitant to discuss the issue in a clear manner.

52. Baker, "The United States and APEC Regime Building," 186.

53. Keohane, "Institutionalist Theory and the Realist Challenge After the Cold War," 295.

CHAPTER 12

The author would like to thank John Ravenhill, Aurelia George-Mulgan, Greg Noble, Jennifer Amyx, Dick Samuels, the other members and discussants in this project—especially Saadia Pekkanen, Saori Katada, Akiko Fukushima, Glen Fukushima, and Nobuo Tanaka—and the anonymous Stanford University Press reviewers for their useful feedback on earlier versions of this chapter. The author is also grateful to the Center for Global Partnership and the Social Science Research Council for an Abe Fellowship that provided the funding for the field research done in 1998–2000 on the United States and Japan in APEC, on which the empirical sections of this chapter are based.

1. The U.S. emphasis on a sectoral approach dates back to the Uruguay Round of GATT. See Ravenhill and Aggarwal, "Undermining the WTO," 2ff.

2. Japan's tariff range is below 20 percent, lower than the ranges of the United States, Indonesia, the Philippines, and Korea, and far lower than the ranges of China, Chinese Taiwan, and Malaysia. Its average tariffs on fish products are around 5 percent, lower than those of many other countries in the region. Chart and data provided by "C," a U.S. Commerce Department official involved in EVSL negotiations, during an interview, 3 April 2000. See also the import weighted tariffs and average tariff rates in Dee, Hardin, and Schuele, "APEC Early Voluntary Sectoral Liberalization," tables 1 and 2.

3. American officials believe that, had they wanted to, the Japanese could have come up with a package in EVSL on forestry products that could have satisfied the exporting countries. Interview with "J," U.S. Agriculture official knowledgeable about EVSL, 6 April 2000.

4. The economic effects measured were those on allocative efficiency, real GDP, and terms of trade. Dee, Hardin, and Schuele, "APEC Early Voluntary Sectoral Liberalization," tables 4 and 6.

5. APEC Secretariat, "The Osaka Action Agenda," Section C, 1b and 2b.

6. APEC Secretariat, "APEC Economic Leaders' Declaration," item 8.

7. Ibid., item 13.

8. See, for example, U.S. Trade Representative Charlene Barshefsky's citation of ITA as the stimulus to EVSL at the Vancouver APEC meetings, "'97 APEC Bankūba: Jiyūka Iji de Kiro ni. Sōki Bunya Kōsoku ryoku naku. Russia Sanka de Henshitsu mo ('97 APEC Vancouver: A fork in the road for liberalization: Early liberalization with commitment; A qualitative change also with Russian participation)," *Nihon Keizai Shinbun*, 24 November 1997, p. 9.

9. Interview with "G," U.S. official knowledgeable about trade, 5 April 2000.

10. U.S. Department of State, "Statement of the Chair," especially p. 2. See [http://www.usinfo.state.gov/regional/ea/apec/montreal.htm].

11. Interview with "G."

12. "APEC Shijo Kaihō. 8-Bunya Maedaoshi Teian. Nihon, Kankyō Kiki Gakki nado" (APEC market liberalization: Proposal to speed up in eight sectors, Japan—environmental equipment, pharmaceuticals, and others), *Nihon Keizai Shinbun*, 25 October 1997, p. 4.

13. Ibid.; also "Shijo Kaihō maedaoshi. 41-Bunya wo Kōho ni" (Early market opening: Forty-one candidate sectors), *Nihon Keizai Shinbun*, 29 October 1997, p. 9; and interview with "C," Department of Commerce official involved in EVSL negotiations.

14. APEC's private sector advisory committee, the APEC Business Advisory Council, had weighed in with a proposal to seek agreement in eight priority areas, including pulp and wood products. "Kagaku nado 8-Bunya Kaihō e Yūsen wō APEC Shimon'i Teigen" (APEC advisory committee proposal for prioriy to eight sectors, for example, chemicals), *Nihon Keizai Shinbun*, 4 November 1997, p. 5.

15. Interview with "J."

16. Personal communication from METI official, 8 April 2002.

17. Interviews with "J" and "C."

18. "APEC Kakuryō Kaigi Kaimaku. Sōki Jiyūka 9-Bunya Teiji. Rainen 6-gatsu

ni Gutaisaku Kettei" (APEC ministerial meeting opens: Proposes nine sectors for early liberalization), *Nihon Keizai Shinbun*, evening edition, 22 November 1997, p. 3; see also, among others, "Kankyōkiki, Kagaku Seihin, Suisanbutsu nado. 15-Bunya wo Yūsen Jiyūka. Vietnam, Peru, Russia 98-nen Dōji Sanka mo" (Priority liberalization in fifteen sectors, for example, environmental machinery, chemical products, fishing products; Vietnam, Peru, Russia also simultaneous participation in 1998), *Nihon Keizai Shinbun*, 21 November 1997, p. 8.

19. Interview with "J."

20. "Shijo Kaihō no Kōka 1-chō 5000 oku doru Sōtō—Bei Daitōryō Kyōchō" (Results of market opening equals $1.5 trillion—American president claims), *Nihon Keizai Shinbun*, evening edition, 26 November 1997, p. 2.

21. Interview with "G."

22. Interview with "C." One reason that the United States did not nominate fish products was that it would have had a harder time getting it through the interagency process than it would have had with some other sectors. Another reason was a simple miscommunication between the Department of Commerce and the USTR about administrative leadership.

23. Interview with "G."

24. American Chamber of Commerce in Japan, *Making Trade Talks Work*, 2000, 141–47.

25. Altbach, "AUSTR Charges That Japan May Undercut APEC Trade Talks."

26. Interview with "J."

27. Ibid.

28. Interview with "Ka," Japanese government official involved in APEC, 27 May 1999.

29. Japan Ministry of Foreign Affairs, "Early Voluntary Sector Liberalization," p. 3.

30. Interview with "Ka."

31. The six aspects of fishing products at EVSL were tariffs, non-tariff measures, subsidies, SPS (sanitary and private sanitary standards), ecotech, and cooperative international fisheries management. The latter was put in at Japan's insistence. Interview with "C."

32. "97 APEC Bankūba-," *Nihon Keizai Shinbun*, 24 November 1997, p. 9.

33. Interview with "Shi," Japanese government official involved with APEC trade issues, 1 June 2000.

34. Wesley, "APEC's Mid-Life Crisis?" See also the contrasting approaches in EVSL, represented by the Japanese and American differences discussed here, as a fundamental issue in APEC: an "inductive" approach of gradual consensus building over time versus a deductive approach of setting a general goal and then providing "deliverables," in part to keep the forum's momentum going.

35. Interview with "G."

36. Quotation from interview with "C"; also interviews with "G" and "J."

37. Interview with "C."

38. Ibid.

39. Interview with "G."
40. APEC Secretariat. "The APEC Economic Leaders' Declaration." Emphasis mine.

41. Interview with "Ka."   42. Interview with "G."
43. Interview with "Shi."   44. Interview with "C."
45. Ibid.

46. Ibid. Korea's initial position was that they could not make many concessions in fish tariffs, but they then moved toward eliminating all tariffs by the year 2005, with just five low-level exceptions.

47. Interview with "J"; interview with "G."

48. "APEC, Jiyūka meguri Chōsei e, 22, 23 nichi Daijin Kaigo" (APEC: Ministers' meeting on 22nd, 23rd; toward coordination concerning liberalization)," *Nippon Nogyō Shinbun*, 13 June 1998, p. 2; interview with "Shi."

49. Interview with "Shi."

50. "Suisanbutsu nado Yūsen 9-Bunya. Shijō Kaihō Gōi Sakiokuri. APEC Bōekishō Kaigō ga Heimaku. Asia, Uchimuki ni" (Nine priority sectors such as fish products agreement postponed; APEC trade ministers' meeting closes: Asia, turning inward)," *Nihon Keizai Shinbun*, 24 June 1998 , p. 5.

51. Interview with "G."
52. Interview with "Shi."

53. "APEC Kōkyū Jimureberu Kaigo Heimaku, Jiyūka Mondai wa Ketchaku sezu" (APEC high SOM-level meeting closes, without resolving liberalization issue), *Nippon Nogyō Shinbun*, 17 September 1998, p. 2.

54. "Beikokugawa ni Irei no Api-ru, Nichibei Shunō Kaidan ([Unusual appeal to the American side; Japan-U.S. summit meeting)," *Nippon Nogyō Shinbun*, 26 September 1998, p. 2.

55. "Rin, Suisanbutsu de Jimin Bōeki Jiyūka Soshi wo Kakunin" (LDP trade countermeasures committee confirms obstruction of liberalization in forestry, fish products)," *Nippon Nogyō Shinbun*, 26 September 1998, p. 2.

56. Interview with "Nu," a MAFF official responsible for international relations.

57. Interview with "Shi."

58. "Nyūsu no Tansō: Yuragu WTO Senryaku, Seifunai ni Jōho no Ugoki" (Depth news: Tottering WTO strategy, concession movement in the government)," *Nippon Nogyō Shinbun*, 30 October 1998, p. 3.

59. Ibid.; "WTO Nirami Gaikō Honkakuka, Renkei Kyōka de Nōshō Hōō" (Getting to basic WTO foreign policy rules: Agriculture minister visits Europe to strengthen cooperation), *Nippon Nogyō Shinbun*, 20 October 1998, p. 1.

60. "Suisanbutsu no Jiyūuka. Shina goto no Kyōgi mo. Tsūsanshō. APEC Taisaku Kaigi" (Liberalization of fishing products. Discuss each good: MITI minister. APEC strategy meeting), *Nihon Keizai Shinbun*, 24 October 1998, evening edition; also "APEC Jiyūka Mondai, Shushō Chōsei wo Shiji, Tsūsan, Gaimushō ni Nōshō Hanpatsu (APEC liberalization issue, indicates prime minister's coordination, agriculture minister opposes MITI, MOFA)," *Nippon Nogyō Shinbun*, 24 October 1998, p. 2; "Nyūsu no tansō," p. 3.

61. "Kanzei Sage Jōho Sezu, Rin/Suisanbutsu Jiyūka Mondai de Nōsuishō" (No concessions on reducing tariffs, MAFF on the issue of fish/forestry product liberalization), *Nippon Nogyō Shinbun*, 27 October 1998, p. 1.

62. "Jiyūka Maedaoshi Kyohi wo, APEC Kyōgi de Jimin Nōrin Suisandantai" (LDP, agriculture, forestry, fisheries organizations reject early liberalization at APEC meetings), *Nippon Nōgyō Shinbun*, 28 October 1998, p. 2.

63. "Nyūsu no Tansō," p. 3.

64. "Gaimushō no Sekinin Tsuikyū e, APEC Jiyūka Kyōgi de Nanka, Jimin Bōtaii" (LDP trade countermeasures committee toward pursuing MOFA responsibility on making APEC liberalization discussions flexible), *Nippon Nogyō Shinbun*, 1 November 1998, p. 1.

65. "Jimin Bōtaii, Rin/Suisanbutsu no Jiyūka Fusanka, Jūrai Hōshin wo Kakunin" (LDP trade countermeasures committee confirms prior policy of nonparticipation in forestry and fish product liberalization), *Nippon Nogyō Shinbun*, 6 November 1998, p. 2.

66. "Jiyūka Soshi e Kekki, APEC Rin/Suisanbutsu, Gyogyo Dantai ga Kinkyū Shūkai" (Action to stop liberalization, forestry fish industry organizations have emergency meeting on APEC forestry, fish products), *Nippon Nogyō Shinbun*, 5 November 1998, p. 1.

67. Interview with "Ka."   68. Interview with "Shi."
69. Interview with "J."   70. Interview with "G."
71. Ibid.

72. "Rin-suisanbutsu. Sakiokuri Shiji Uttae. APEC Kakkoku ni. Mikaeri ni enjo" (Appeal to support putting off forestry, fishing products. Aid to guarantee to each APEC country), *Nihon Keizai Shinbun*, 31 October 1998, p. 5.

73. Interview with "Shi."

74. "Jiyūka Kyohi de Seifu Itchi, APEC Rin-suisanbutsu Kyōgi" (APEC forestry, fishing product meetings: Government united in rejecting liberalization), *Nippon Nogyō Shinbun*, 7 November 1998, p. 1; "Rinsan-suisanbutsu. Kanzei Teppai ni ōjizu. APEC e Seifu Hōshin" (No responding to complete tariff elimination: government policy toward APEC), *Nihon Keizai Shinbun*, 8 November 1998, p. 3.

75. See Krauss, "U.S. and Japanese Negotiations on Construction and Semiconductors"; former Prime Minister Hosokawa had also made major concessions on rice as well as fishing and forestry in the previous GATT round.

76. See for example, "APEC, Jiyūka Meguri Chōsei e, 22, 23 nichi Daijin Kaigo."

77. Interview with "I," State Department official knowledgeable about Japan, 23 May 2000.

78. Interview with "Nu."

79. Interview with "Ka," May 18, 2000.

80. Ibid.

81. Interview with "Nu"; interview with "Ka," 2000.

82. "Nyu-su tansō: APEC Bōeki Daijin Kaigo no Shōten" (A depth news: The focus of the APEC trade ministers' meeting), *Nippon Nogyō Shinbun*, 18 June 2000, p. 3.

83. "Nyūsu no Tansō: Yuragu WTO Senryaku."

84. Interview with "C."

85. Personal communication with "Shi," May 2001; and interview with "Shi."

86. Interview with "J."

87. Interview with "G."

88. Interview with "Shi."

89. The United States and other countries would have had to get agreement at WTO to have participated in EVSL in any case. The question was whether EVSL went to the WTO with or without a "critical mass" that included Japan.

90. "APEC Kakuryō Kaigi, Kanzei Teppai Kyohi ni Beikoku wa Kankan" (APEC ministerial officials meeting, U.S. flies into rage at tariff elimination refusal), *Nippon Nogyō Shinbun*, 15 November 1998, p. 2.

91. See U.S. Department of State, "Transcript."

92. Interview with "S," a high-level Commerce Department official who has dealt with both APEC and Japan, 15 November 1999.

93. "Trade Meeting Opens with a Spat," *Los Angeles Times*, 14 November 1998, p. C1.

94. On the "blocking" capabilities of the United States and Japan in multilateral initiatives, including EVSL, see Rapkin, "The United States, Japan, and the Power to Block." The author thanks Rapkin for providing a draft copy of this article before publication.

95. On distinguishing preferences from the strategic environment to explain outcomes, see Lake and Powell, *Strategic Choice in International Relations*, esp. 4–29.

96. Krauss, "Japan, the U.S., and the Emergence of Multilateralism in Asia."

97. Thus, the recent concerns of some observers that the United States was in danger of being left out of East Asia and the world were divided trilaterally. See, for example, Bergsten, "America's Two-Front Economic Conflict."

98. Tsbelis, *Nested Games*.

99. Davis, "Trade Rules and Political Persuasion."

100. Interview with "Shi."

101. Ibid.

102. Interview with "G."

103. This is one of George Simmel's classic insights into the functions of conflict. See Coser, *Functions of Social Conflict*.

104. Interview with "Shi."

105. Interview with "G."

106. For a somewhat different view, that EVSL indicates the possible emergence of "rival blocs" in APEC, see Wesley, "APEC's Mid-Life Crisis?"

CHAPTER 13

1. For example, see Nakasone, "Toward Comprehensive Security."

2. Although because of the problem of recognition of Taiwan, arrangements are often covered with the fig leaf of "economies" being members, as in the case of APEC.

3. The authors thank Verena Blechinger for suggesting how the pattern of prior institutionalization created varying impacts on these dimensions.

4. See Kahler, *International Institutions and the Political Economy of Integration*, xxi–xxii.

5. The term *insurance regime* is from Keohane, "The Demand for International Regimes," esp. 121–22.

6. The term *mercantile realism* is from Heginbotham and Samuels' classic article, "Mercantile Realism and Japanese Foreign Policy."

7. Sakamoto, "Moving to an Era of Cooperation."

8. Heginbotham and Samuels, in "Japan's Dual Hedge," have referred to this separation of security and economics whereby Japan relies on the United States as a "hedge" against military threats, but relies on other economic partners as a hedge against economic threats.

9. On why Japan suspended foreign aid in the first place, see Saori Katada, "Why Did Japan Suspend Foreign Aid to China?"

10. See Pyle's excellent chapter on the Yoshida doctrine in *The Japanese Question*, 20–41.

11. In one well-cited passage, for example, Liberal Democratic Party power broker Ishihara argued in *The Japan That Can Say No*, 21, that U.S. missiles could be rendered completely ineffective if Japan chose to deny the United States access to certain Japanese semiconductor technologies. The Japanese version, published with Sony president Morita Akio, was *"No" to ieru Nihon*.

12. Schoppa, "The Social Context in Coercive International Bargaining," esp. 323–25. On how these changing attitudes contributed to APEC's founding, see Ashizawa, chap. 11, this volume; and Krauss, "Japan, the U.S., and the Emergence of Multilateralism in Asia," 478.

13. In 1994 more than half of Americans saw Japan as a rival and only 19 percent saw it as a friend, compared to 27 percent of Japanese who saw the United States as a rival and 38 percent who saw it as a friend. Also in the early 1990s, Americans' "unfavorable" or "mostly unfavorable" view of Japan had risen to about half of those surveyed, surpassing the negative evaluation given to China. See Ladd and Bowman, *Public Opinion in America and Japan*, 52 and 58.

14. Repeating, or in social science jargon, "iterative," games in which the adversary or partner may switch sides in the future are more likely to provide incentives to keep hostilities in check and to manage them.

15. On committees and working groups as of 2001, see Taiwan Studies Institute, "APEC Committees and Working Groups."

16. The intended, if stretched, analogy is of course to Emile Durkheim's distinction between the "mechanical" solidarity of preindustrial society, based on commonalities and common rituals and routines, and the "organic" solidarity of industrialized societies, with the divergences among individuals in a complex division of labor into specialized roles that nonetheless made each person dependent on the others for survival. See Durkheim, *The Division of Labor in Society*.

17. Interviews by Krauss in Washington and Tokyo.

18. For example, Hamilton, "Asian Business Networks in Transition"; and Pempel, "Regional Ups, Regional Downs," 45–61, 62–78.

19. Eichengreen, *Toward a New International Financial Architecture*.

20. Joseph A. Schumpeter, *Capitalism, Socialism, and Democracy*.

21. Webber, "Two Funerals and a Wedding?"

22. Nau, *At Home Abroad*.

23. The specific wording of the report is, "We see the special relationship between the United States and Great Britain as a model for the (Tokyo-Washington) alliance." Institute for National Strategic Studies, "The United States and Japan," p. 6.

24. For example, Solingen, *Regional Orders at Century's Dawn*; Thomas and Tétreault, *Racing to Regionalize*; Adler and Barnett, *Security Communities*; Mansfield and Milner, *The Political Economy of Regionalism*, inter alia.

25. Bergsten, "America's Two-Front Economic Conflict."

26. Katada, *Banking on Stability*.

References

CHAPTER I

Abbott, Frederick M. "NAFTA and the Legalization of World Politics." *International Organization* 54, no. 3 (2000): 535–43, cited in Young J. Choi and James A. Caporaso. *Comparative Regional Integration: Overview and Assessment.* Unpublished manuscript, University of Washington, 2001.

Alagappa, Muthiah, ed. *Asian Security Practice: Material and Ideational Influences.* Stanford, Calif.: Stanford University Press, 1998.

Albert, Michel. *Capitalism vs. Capitalism.* New York: Four Walls Eight Windows, 1993.

Ball, Desmond. "September 11: Political and Security Impact and Changes in the Strategic Balance of the Asia Pacific Region." Paper presented at the sixteenth Asia-Pacific Roundtable, Kuala Lumpur, June 2–5, 2002.

Bergsten, C. Fred, Takatoshi Ito, and Marcus Noland. *No More Bashing: Building a New Japan-United States Economic Relationship.* Washington, D.C.: Institute for International Economics, 2001.

Blackwill, Robert D., and Paul Dibb, eds. *America's Asian Alliances.* Cambridge, Mass.: MIT Press, 2000.

Bobrow, Davis, Steve Chan, and Simon Reich. "Southeast Asian Prospects and Realities: American Hopes and Fears." *Pacific Review* 9, no. 1 (1996): 1–30.

Buckley, Roger. *U.S.-Japan Alliance Diplomacy.* Cambridge: Cambridge University Press, 1992.

Cohen, Benjamin J. *The Geography of Money.* Ithaca: Cornell University Press, 1998.

Cohen, Stephen D. *Uneasy Partnership: Competition and Conflict in U.S.-Japanese Relations.* Cambridge, Mass.: Ballinger, 1985.

———. *Cowboys and Samurai: Why the United States Is Losing the Battle with the Japanese, and Why It Matters.* New York: Harper Business, 1991.

———. *An Ocean Apart: Explaining Three Decades of U.S.-Japanese Trade Frictions.* Westport, Conn.: Praeger, 1998.

Cumings, Bruce. *Parallax Visions: Making Sense of American-East Asian Relations at the End of the Century.* Durham, N.C.: Duke University Press, 1999.

Curtis, Gerald L., ed. *Japan's Foreign Policy After the Cold War: Coping with Change*. Armonk, N.Y.: Sharpe, 1993.

Defense Agency. *Defense of Japan 1985*. Tokyo: Japan Times, 1985.

Defense Agency. *Defense of Japan 1998*. Tokyo: Japan Times, 1998.

Destler, I. M., et al. *Managing an Alliance: The Politics of U.S.-Japanese Relations*. Washington, D.C.: Brookings Institution, 1976.

Destler, I. M., Haruhiro Fukui, and Hideo Sato. *The Textile Wrangle: Conflict in Japanese-American Relations, 1969–1971*. Ithaca: Cornell University Press, 1979.

Dore, Ronald. *Stock Market Capitalism: Welfare Capitalism—Japan and Germany Versus the Anglo-Saxons*. Oxford: Oxford University Press, 2000.

Dower, John. *Empire and Its Aftermath: Yoshida Shigeru and the Japanese Experience, 1878–1954*. Cambridge, Mass.: Harvard University Press,1979.

Dwyer, Jennifer Holt. "U.S.-Japan Financial-Market Relations in an Era of Global Finance." In *New Perspectives on U.S.-Japan Relations*, edited by Gerald Curtis, 82–128. Tokyo and New York: Japan Center for International Exchange, 2000.

Fallows, James. *Looking at the Sun: The Rise of the New East Asian Economic and Political System*. New York: Random House, 1994.

"Financial Indicators: Trade." *Economist*, 23 November 1996, 119.

"Financial Indicators: Foreign Assets." *Economist*, 9 November 1996, 123.

"Financial Indicators: Trade, Exchange Rates and Reserves." *Economist*, 23 May 1998, 97.

Frieden, Jeffry A. "Domestic Politics and Regional Cooperation: The United States, Japan, and Pacific Money and Finance." In *Regionalism and Rivalry: Japan and the United States in Pacific Asia*, edited by Jeffrey A. Frankel and Miles Kahler, 423–44. Chicago: University of Chicago Press, 1993.

Fukushima, Akiko. *Japanese Foreign Policy: The Emerging Logic of Multilateralism*. New York: St. Martin's Press, 1999.

Gould, Erica R., and Stephen D. Krasner. "Germany and Japan: Binding Versus Autonomy." In *The End of Diversity? Prospects for German and Japanese Capitalism*, edited by Kozo Yamamura and Wolfgang Streeck. Ithaca, N.Y.: Cornell University Press, 2003.

Green, Michael J. *Arming Japan: Defense Production, Alliance Politics, and the Postwar Search for Autonomy*. New York: Columbia University Press, 1995.

———. "The Challenges of Managing U.S.-Japan Security Relations After the Cold War." In *New Perspectives on U.S.-Japan Relations*, edited by Gerald L. Curtis. Tokyo and New York: Japan Center for International Exchange, 2000.

———. *Japan's Reluctant Realism*. New York: Palgrave, 2001.

Green, Michael J., and Patrick M. Cronin, eds. *The U.S.-Japan Alliance: Past, Present, and Future*. New York: Council on Foreign Relations, 1999.

Greider, William. *One World, Ready or Not: The Manic Logic of Global Capitalism*. New York: Simon and Schuster, 1997.

Haggard, Stephan. *The Political Economy of the Asian Financial Crisis*. Washington, D.C.: Institute of International Economics, 2001.

Harding, Harry. "Asia Policy to the Brink (U.S. Relations with Asia)." *Foreign Policy* 96 (fall 1994): 57–74.

Hatch, Walter, and Kozo Yamamura. *Asia in Japan's Embrace*. Cambridge: Cambridge University Press, 1997.

Heginbotham, Eric, and Richard J. Samuels. "Mercantile Realism and Japanese Foreign Policy." *International Security* 22, no. 4 (spring 1998): 171–203.

Henning, C. Randall. *Currencies and Politics in the United States, Germany and Japan*. Washington, D.C.: Institute for International Economics, 1994.

Hook, Glenn D., Julie Gilson, Christopher W. Hughes, and Hugo Dobson. *Japan's International Relations: Politics, Economics and Security*. London: Routledge, 2001.

Hughes, Christopher W. "Japan's Aum Shinrikyo, the Changing Nature of Terrorism, and the Post-Cold War Security Agenda." *The Pacific Review* (February 1998): 39–60.

Ikenberry, G. John. "Rethinking the Origins of American Hegemony." *Political Science Quarterly* 104, no. 3 (autumn 1989): 375–400.

———. "America's Liberal Grand Strategy: Democracy and National Security in the Post-War Era." In *American Democracy Promotion: Impulses, Strategies, and Impacts*, edited by Michael Cox, G. John Ikenberry, and Takashi Inoguchi, 103–26. New York: Oxford University Press, 2000.

Inoguchi, Takashi. *Japan's Asia Policy: Revival and Response*. New York: Palgrave, 2002.

Iokibe, Makoto. *Sengo Nihon Gaikōshi* (A history of postwar Japanese foreign policy). Tokyo: Yuhikakusha, 1999.

Iriye, Akira, and Robert A. Wampler, eds. *Partnership: The United States and Japan, 1951–2001*. Tokyo: Kodansha International, 2001.

Japan External Trade Organization. "Nihon no Kuni, Chiiki betsu Bōeki no Suii" (Changes in Japanese foreign trade by country and region). [http://www.jetro.go.jp/ec/j/trade/excel/40w01.xls], 2003.

———. *White Paper on International Trade 2001*. Tokyo: Japan External Trade Organization, 2001.

Johnson, Chalmers. *MITI and the Japanese Miracle*. Stanford, Calif.: Stanford University Press, 1982.

Kanabayashi, Masayoshi. "Japan's Appetite for Chinese Goods Boosts Trade Ties." *Asian Wall Street Journal*, 22 February 2001, 4.

Kato, Kozo. "Open Regionalism and Japan's Systematic Vulnerability." In *Asian Regionalism*, edited by Peter J. Katzenstein, Natasha Hamilton-Hart, Kozo Kato, and Ming Yue, 35–87. Ithaca, N.Y.: Cornell University, East Asia Series, 2000.

Katzenstein, Peter, and Nobuo Okawara. *Japan's National Security: Structures, Norms and Policy Responses in a Changing World*. Ithaca, N.Y.: Cornell University, East Asia Series, 1993.

Katzenstein, Peter, and Takashi Shiraishi. *Network Power: Japan and Asia*. Ithaca, N.Y.: Cornell University Press, 1997.

Kawakami, Sumie. "Exporting a Surplus." *Far Eastern Economic Review*, 4 July 1996, 44–46.

Kusano, Atsushi. *Nichi-Bei: Masatsu no Kōzō* (Japan-U.S.: The structure of friction). Tokyo: PHP Kenkyujō, 1984.

Lake, David A., and Patrick M. Morgan, eds. *Regional Orders: Building Security in a New World*. University Park: Pennsylvania State University Press, 1997.

Leheny, David. "The War on Terrorism in Asia and the Possibility of Secret Regionalization." Paper presented at Remapping Asia Workshop, organized by T. J. Pempel, Portland, Oregon, 15 May 2002.

Lincoln, Edward J. *Japan: Facing Economic Maturity*. Washington, D.C.: Brookings Institution, 1988.

———. *Japan's New Global Role*. Washington, D.C.: Brookings Institution, 1993.

Mansfield University. "Appendix C: Highlights of U.S. Foreign Trade." [http://www.mnsfld.edu/depts/lib/highlights-trade.txt], 2003.

Mansfield, Edward D., and Helen V. Milner, eds. *The Political Economy of Regionalism*. New York: Columbia University Press, 1997.

Ministry of Finance. "Tainaigai Minkan Tōshi Tokushū" (Special edition: Incoming and outgoing foreign direct investment). Tokyo: Ministry of Foreign Affairs, 2003. [http://www.mof.go.jp/kankou/hyou10.htm].

Ministry of Foreign Affairs. "Preamble." *Diplomatic Blue Book* (Tokyo: Ministry of Foreign Affairs, 1957).

Mochizuki, Mike M., ed. *Toward a True Alliance: Restructuring U.S.-Japan Security Relations*. Washington, D.C.: Brookings Institution Press, 1997.

Nau, Henry R. *At Home Abroad: Identity and Power in American Foreign Policy*. Ithaca, N.Y.: Cornell University Press, 2002.

Ōtake, Hideo. *Gendai Nihon no Seiji Kenryoku Keizai Kenryoku* (Political and economic power in contemporary Japan). Tokyo: San'ichi Shobo, 1979.

———. "Bōei Futan wo meguru Nichibei Masatsu: Sono Keika to Haikei" (Japan-U.S. conflict over the defense burden: Development and background). *Keizai Hyoron* (July 1980): 14–25.

———. *Nihon no Bōei to Kokunai Seiji: Detanto kara Gunkakue* (Japanese defense and domestic politics: From detante to military buildup). Tokyo: San'ichi Shobo, 1986.

———. "Nihon ni okeru 'Gunsankan Fukugoeai' Keisei no Zasetsu" (The failure to form a 'military-industrial complex' in Japan). In *Nihon Seiji no Soten-Jirei Kenkyū ni yoru Seiji Taisei no Bunseki* (Problems in Japanese politics: Analysis of the political system through case study), edited by Ōtake Hideo, 13–69. Tokyo: San'ichi Shobo, 1984.

Park, Gene. "Policy Ideas and Crisis: The Making of Japan's Regional Economic Policy." Unpublished paper, University of California, Berkeley, May 2001.

Pempel, T. J. *Regime Shift: Comparative Dynamics of the Japanese Political Economy*. Ithaca, N.Y.: Cornell University Press, 1998.

———. "Structural 'Gaiatsu': International Finance and Political Change in Japan." *Comparative Political Studies* 32, no. 8 (December 1999), 907–32.

———, ed. *Uncommon Democracies: The One-Party Dominant Regimes*. Ithaca, N.Y.: Cornell University Press, 1990.

———, ed. *The Politics of the Asian Economic Crisis*. Ithaca, N.Y.: Cornell University Press, 1999.

Pyle, Kenneth. *The Japanese Question: Power and Purpose in a New Era.* Washington, D.C.: American Enterprise Institute, 1992.

Raum, Tom. "Talk of U.S. Isolationism Increasing." PNL TV, 26 July 2001. [http://www.pnltv.com/NewsStories/July%2026%20Talk%200f%20U.S.%20 Isolationism%20Increasing.htm].

Ravenhill, John. *APEC and the Construction of Pacific Rim Regionalism.* Cambridge and New York: Cambridge University Press, 2001.

Rozman, Gilbert. "Japan's Quest for Great Power Identity." *Orbis* 46, no. 1 (winter 2002): 73–91.

Ruggie, John Gerard, ed. *Multilateralism Matters: The Theory and Praxis of an Institutional Form.* New York: Columbia University Press, 1993.

Samuels, Richard J. *Rich Nation, Strong Army: National Security and the Technological Transformation of Japan.* Ithaca, N.Y.: Cornell University Press, 1994.

Scalapino, Robert A., ed. *The Foreign Policy of Modern Japan.* Berkeley: University of California Press, 1977.

Schoppa, Leonard J. *Bargaining with Japan: What American Pressure Can and Cannot Do.* New York: Columbia University Press, 1997.

Simmons, Beth A. "The International Politics of Harmonization: The Case of Capital Market Regulation." *International Organization* 55, no. 3 (summer 2001): 543–602.

Solingen, Etel. *Regional Orders at Century's Dawn: Global and Domestic Influences on Grand Strategy.* Princeton, N.J.: Princeton University Press, 1998.

———. "ASEAN, Quo Vadis? Domestic Coalitions and Regional Cooperation." *Contemporary Southeast Asia* 21, no. 1 (April 1999): 30–53.

U.S. Department of Commerce, Bureau of Economic Analysis. *Foreign Direct Investment in the U.S.* Washington, D.C.: Bureau of Economic Analysis, annual. [http://www.bea.gov/bea/di/di1fdibal.htm].

U.S. Department of Commerce, Office of Japan. "U.S.-Japan Merchandise Trade Data (1970–2002)." [http://www.mac.doc.gov/japan/source/menu/trade/usjmt .html], 2002.

Vogel, Steven K., ed. *U.S.-Japan Relations in a Changing World.* Washington, D.C.: Brookings Institution, 2002.

Volker, Paul, and Toyoo Gyohten. *Changing Fortunes: The World's Money and the Threat to American Leadership.* New York: Times Books, 1992.

Watanabe, Akio, ed. *Sengo Nihon no Taigai Seisaku* (Postwar Japanese foreign policy). Tokyo: Yuhikaku, 1985.

———, ed. *San Francisco Kōwa* (The San Francisco peace). Tokyo: Todai Shuppan kai, 1986.

CHAPTER 2

Auerbach, Stuart. "The Ironies That Built Japan Inc." *Washington Post*, 18 July 1993, H1.

Blair, Dennis C., and John T. Hanley Jr. "From Wheels to Webs: Reconstructing

Asia-Pacific Security Arrangements." *Washington Quarterly* 24, no. 1 (2001): 7–17.

Crone, Donald. "Does Hegemony Matter? The Reorganization of the Pacific Political Economy." *World Politics* 45, no. 4 (1993), 501–25.

Cumings, Bruce. "Japan's Position in the World System." In *Postwar Japan as History*, edited by Andrew Gordon, 34–63. Berkeley: University of California Press, 1993.

Department of Defense. *United States Security Strategy for the East Asia-Pacific Region*. Washington, D.C.: Department of Defense, 1995.

———. *United States Security Strategy for the East Asia-Pacific Region*. Washington, D.C.: Department of Defense, 1998. [http://www.defenselink.mil/pubs/easr98].

Erlanger, Steven. "In Europe, Some Say the Attacks Stemmed from American Failings." *New York Times*, 22 (September 2001), B12.

Funabashi, Yōichi. *Asia Pacific Fusion: Japan's Role in APEC*. Washington, D.C.: Institute for International Economics, 1995.

———. *Alliance Adrift*. New York: Council on Foreign Relations, 1999.

Gilpin, Robert. *The Challenge of Global Capitalism: The World Economy in the 21st Century*. Princeton: Princeton University Press, 2000.

Gould, Erica, and Stephen D. Krasner. "Germany and Japan: Binding Versus Autonomy." In *The End of Diversity? Prospects for German and Japanese Capitalism*, edited by Wolfgang Streeck and Kozo Yamamura. Ithaca, N.Y.: Cornell University Press, 2003.

Hardt, Michael, and Antonio Negri. *Empire*. Cambridge, Mass.: Harvard University Press, 2000.

Ikenberry, G. John. "Institutions, Strategic Restraint, and the Persistence of American Postwar Order." *International Security* (winter 1998/1999), 43–78.

———. "America's Liberal Grand Strategy: Democracy and National Security in the Post-War Era." In *American Democracy Promotion: Impulses, Strategies, and Impacts*, edited by Michael Cox, G. John Ikenberry, and Takashi Inoguchi, 103–26. New York: Oxford University Press, 2000.

———. *After Victory: Institutions, Strategic Restraint, and the Rebuilding of Order After Major War*. Princeton: Princeton University Press, 2001.

———. "American Grand Strategy in the Age of Terror." *Survival* 43, no. 4 (2001/2002), 19–34.

Institute for National Strategic Studies. "The United States and Japan: Advancing Toward a Mature Partnership." *INSS Special Report*, 11 October 2000.

Johnson, Chalmers. *Blowback: The Costs and Consequences of American Empire*. New York: Henry Holt, 2000.

Johnston, Iain. "Socialization in International Institutions: The ASEAN Regional Forum and I.R. Theory." In *The Emerging International Relations of the Asia-Pacific Region*, edited by G. John Ikenberry and Michael Mastanduno. Forthcoming.

Kynge, James. "China's Binding Ties." *Financial Times*, 10 May 2001, 16.

Kynge, James. "China Awards Landmark Telecoms Deal." *Financial Times*, 16 May 2001, 13.

Lundestad, Geir. "Empire by Invitation? The United States and Western Europe, 1945–1952." *The Journal of Peace Research* 23, no. 3 (1986): 263–77.

Nye, Joseph S. "East Asia: The Case for Deep Engagement." *Foreign Affairs* 74, no. 4 (1995), 90–102.

———. "The 'Nye Report': Six Years Later." *International Relations of the Asia-Pacific* 1, no. 1 (2001): 95–103.

Pempel, T. J. "Gulliver in Lilliput: Japan and Asian Economic Regionalism." *World Policy Journal* 13, no. 4 (1996/1997): 13–26.

———. *Regime Shift: Comparative Dynamics of the Japanese Political Economy.* Ithaca: Cornell University Press, 1998.

Schaller, Michael. *Altered States: The United States and Japan Since the Occupation.* New York: Oxford University Press, 1997.

Sciolino, Elaine. "Who Hates the U.S.? Who Loves It?" *New York Times*, 23 September 2001, sec. 4, 1.

Schmitter, Philippe C. "Three Neo-Functional Hypotheses About International Integration." *International Organization* 23, no. 1 (1969), 161–66.

Slevin, Peter. "Powell Offers Reassurance to South Korea." *Washington Post*, 2 February 2002, A19.

Smith, Craig. "Signs in China and Taiwan of Making Money, Not War," *New York Times*, 15 May 2001, A1.

Tamamoto, Masaru. "A Land Without Patriots: The Yasukuni Controversy and Japanese Nationalism." *World Policy Journal* 18, no. 3 (2001): 33–40.

White House, Office of the Press Secretary, "Remarks by the President in Address to the National Assembly of the Republic of Korea," Seoul, Korea, 10 July 1993. [http://www.ibiblio.org/pub/archives/whitehouse-papers/1993/Jul/Presidents-Remarks-to-Korean-National-Assembly-71093].

Yamamura, Kozo. "The Deliberate Emergence of a Free Trader: The Japanese Political Economy in Transition." In *Japan: A New Kind of Superpower?* edited by Craig C. Garby and Mary Brown Bullock. Washington, D.C.: Woodrow Wilson Center Press, 1994.

CHAPTER 3

Advisory Group on Defense Issues. *The Modality of the Security and Defense Capability of Japan: The Outlook for the Twenty-First Century.* Tokyo: Ōkurashō Insatsukyoku, 1994.

Alagappa, Muthiah. "Rethinking Security: A Critical Review and Appraisal of the Debate." In *Asian Security Practice: Material and Ideational Influences*, edited by Muthiah Alagappa, 27–64. Stanford, Calif.: Stanford University Press, 1998.

Funabashi, Yōichi. *Alliance Adrift.* New York: Council on Foreign Relations, 1999.

Green. Michael J. *Arming Japan: Defense Production, Alliance Politics, and the Postwar Search for Autonomy.* New York: Columbia University Press, 1995.

———. "The Challenges of Managing U.S.-Japan Security Relations After the Cold War." In *New Perspectives on U.S.-Japan Relations*, edited by Gerald

Curtis, 241–64. Tokyo and New York: Japan Center for International Exchange, 2000.

————. "The Search for an Active Security Partnership: Lessons from the 1980s." In *Partnership: The United States and Japan 1951–2001*, edited by Akira Iriye and Robert A. Wampler, 135–60. Tokyo: Kodansha, 2001.

————. "Balance of Power." In *U.S.-Japan Relations in a Changing World*, edited by Steven K. Vogel, 9–34. Washington, D.C.: Brookings Institution Press, 2002.

Hemmer, Christopher, and Peter J. Katzenstein. "Why Is There No NATO in Asia? Collective Identity, Regionalism, and the Origins of Multilateralism." *International Organization* 56, no. 3 (summer 2002): 575–607.

Hook, Glenn D., Julie Gilson, Christopher W. Hughes, and Hugo Dobson. *Japan's International Relations: Politics, Economics and Security*. London: Routledge, 2001.

Hughes, Christopher W. "Japan's Aum Shinrikyō, the Changing Nature of Terrorism, and the Post-Cold War Security Agenda." *Pacifica Review* 10, no. 1 (1998): 39–60.

————. *Japan's Economic Power and Security: Japan and North Korea*. London, Routledge, 1999.

————. *Japan's Security Policy and the War on Terror: Steady Incrementalism or Radical Leap?* University of Warwick CSGR Working Paper 104.02. [http://www.warwick.ac.uk/fac/soc/CSGR/wpapers/wp10402.pdf], 2002.

Institute for National Strategic Studies National Defense University. *INSS Special Report. The United States and Japan: Advancing Toward a Mature Partnership*. Institute for National Strategic Studies National Defense University, 2000.

Katahara, Eiichi. "Japan: From Containment to Normalization." In *Coercion and Governance: The Declining Political Role of the Military in Asia*, edited by Muthiah Alagappa, 69–91. Stanford, Calif.: Stanford University Press, 2001.

Katzenstein, Peter J., and Nobuo Okawara. "Japan, Asian-Pacific Security and the Case for Analytical Eclecticism." *International Security* 26, no. 3 (winter 2001–2002): 164–65.

Maull, Hanns W., and Sebastian Harnisch. "Embedding Korea's Unification Multilaterally." *Pacific Review* 15, no. 1 (2002): 29–6.

Mochizuki, Mike M. "American and Japanese Strategic Debates: The Need for a New Synthesis." In *Toward a True Alliance: Restructuring U.S.-Japan Security Relations*, edited by Mike M. Mochizuki, 43–82. Washington D.C.: Brookings Institution Press, 1997.

Okawara, Nobuo, and Peter J. Katzenstein. "Japan and Asian-Pacific Security: Regionalization, Entrenched Bilateralism and Incipient Multilateralism." *Pacific Review* 14, no. 2 (2001): 165–94.

Ozawa, Ichirō. *Nihon Kaizō Keikaku* (Japan Reconstruction Plan). Tokyo: Kōdansha, 1993.

Sakamoto, Kazuya. *Nichibei Dōmei no Kizuna: Anpo Jōyaku to Sōgosei no Mosaku* (Ties of the Japan-U.S. alliance: Searching for mutuality in the Japan-U.S. security treaty). Tokyo: Yūhikaku, 2000.

Samuels, Richard J. *Rich Nation, Strong Army: National Security and the Technological Transformation of Japan*. Ithaca, N.Y.: Cornell University Press, 1994.

Wah, Chin Kin, and Pang Eng Fong. *Relating the U.S.-Korea and U.S.-Japan Alliances to Emerging Asia-Pacific Multilateral Processes: An ASEAN Perspective.* A/PARC Alliances Working Paper, Stanford University, March 2000.

Welfield, John. *An Empire in Eclipse: Japan in the Postwar American Alliance System—A Study of the Interaction of Domestic Politics and Foreign Policy.* London: Athlone Press, 1988.

CHAPTER 4

Armacost, Michael H. *Friends or Rivals? The Insider's Account of U.S.-Japan Relations.* New York: Columbia University Press, 1996.

Armacost, Michael H., and Kenneth B. Pyle. "Japan and the Engagement of China: Challenges for U.S. Policy Coordination." *NBR Analysis* 12, no. 5 (December 2001, entire issue).

Baker, James A., III. *The Politics of Diplomacy.* New York: Putnam, 1995.

Christensen, Thomas J. "China, the U.S.-Japan Alliance, and the Security Dilemma in East Asia." In *The Rise of China*, edited by Michael E. Brown et al., 135–66. Cambridge, Mass.: MIT Press, 2000.

Funabashi, Yōichi. *Alliance Adrift.* New York: Council on Foreign Relations, 1999.

Green, Michael J. "Managing Chinese Power: The View from Japan." In *Engaging China: The Management of an Emerging Power*, edited by Alastair Iain Johnston and Robert S. Ross, 152–75. London: Routledge, 1999.

Green, Michael J. *Japan's Reluctant Realism.* New York: Palgrave, 2001.

Harwit, Eric. "Japanese Investment in China." *Asian Survey* 36, no. 10 (October 1996).

Hashimoto, Prime Minister Ryutaro. "Seeking a New Foreign Policy Toward China." Speech, Tokyo [http://www.mofa.go.jp/region/asia-paci/china/seeking.html], 28 August 1997.

Ijiri, Hidenori. "Sino-Japanese Controversy Since the 1972 Diplomatic Normalization." In *China and Japan: History, Trends, and Prospects*, edited by Christopher Howe, 60–82. Oxford: Clarendon Press, 1996.

Johnstone, Christopher. "Strained Alliance: U.S.-Japan Diplomacy in the Asian Financial Crisis." *Survival* 41, no. 2 (summer 1999): 121–38.

Kakizawa, Koji. "Tennō Ho-Chū-go no Nit-chū Kankei (A new stage in Sino-Japanese ties). *Chūō Kōron* (December 1992): 202–10.

Khalilzad, Zalmay M., and Abram N. Shulsky, Daniel Byman, Roger Cliff, D. Orletsky, David A. Shlapak, and Ashley J. Tellis. *The United States and a Rising China: Strategic and Military Implications.* Santa Monica, Calif.: RAND, 1999.

Kobayashi, Yotaro. "Japan's Need for Re-Asianization." *Foresight* (April 1991).

Kojima, Tomoyuki. "Sino-Japanese Relations: A Japanese Perspective." *Asia-Pacific Review* 3, no. 1 (spring/summer 1996).

Kojima, Tomoyuki. *Gendai Chugoku no seiji: Sono riron to jissen* (Contemporary Chinese politics: Theory and practice). Tokyo: Keio Gijuku Daigaku Shuppankai, 1999.

Kotake, Kazuaki. "Ten'anmon Jiken to Nit-chū Gaikō" (The Tiananmen incident and Japan-China diplomatic relations). In *Ajia Jidai no Nit-chū Kankei* (Japan-

China relations in the Asian era), edited by Kojima Tomoyuki, 120–35. Tokyo: Saimaru Shuppankai, 1995.

Kunihiro, Michihiko. "Nichi-Bei-Chū Sangoku Kankei wa Torakku 2 kara" (Japan-U.S.-China trilateral relations starts with Track II). *Gaikō Forum* 148 (November 2000): 48–53.

Lampton, David M. "China and the Strategic Quadrangle." In *The Strategic Quadrangle*, edited by Michael Mandelbaum. New York: Council on Foreign Relations Press, 1995.

———. *Same Bed, Different Dreams: Managing U.S.-China Relations, 1989–2000*. Berkeley: University of California Press, 2001.

Mann, James. *About Face: A History of America's Curious Relationship with China, from Nixon to Clinton*. New York: Knopf, 1999.

Nakayama, Toshihiro. "Nichi-Bei-Chū Kaigi dai-4 kai Kaigō" (4th meeting of the Japan-U.S.-China conference). *Japan Institute of International Affairs Newsletter* no. 104 (February 2001).

National Institute for Defense Studies. *East Asian Strategic Review 1997–1998*. Tokyo: National Institute for Defense Studies, 1998.

National Institute for Defense Studies. *East Asian Strategic Review 2001*. Tokyo: National Institute for Defense Studies, 2001.

Ogura, Kazuo. "'Ajia no Fukken' no tame ni" (A call for a new concept of Asia). *Chūō Kōron* 108, no. 7 (July 1993): 60–73.

Okazaki, Hisahiko, and Nakajima Mineo. *Nihon ni Ajia Senryaku wa arunoka* (Does Japan have a strategy for Asia?). Tokyo: PHP Kenkyujo, 1996.

Oksenberg, Michel. "China and the Japanese-American Alliance." In *The United States, Japan, and Asia: Challenges for U.S. Policy*, edited by Gerald L. Curtis. New York: Norton, 1994.

Ross, Robert. "National Security, Human Rights, and Domestic Politics: The Bush Administration and China." In *Eagle in a New World: American Grand Strategy in the Post-Cold War Era*, edited by Kenneth Oye, Robert Lieber, and Donald Rothchild. New York: HarperCollins, 1992.

Snyder, Glenn. "The Security Dilemma in Alliance Politics." *World Politics* 36, no. 3 (1984): 461–95.

Szayna, Thomas S., Daniel L. Byman, Steven C. Bankes, Derek Eaton, Seth G. Jones, Robert E. Mullins, Ian O. Lesser, and William Rosenau. *The Emergence of Peer Competitors: A Framework for Analysis*. Santa Monica, Calif.: RAND, 2001.

Tanaka, Akihiko. *Nit-chuū Kankei 1945–1990* (Japan-China relations 1945–1990). Tokyo: Tokyo Daigaku Shuppankai, 1991.

———. "Tai-Nichi Kankei" (Relations with Japan). In *Chūgoku Sōran*, edited by Chūgoku Sōran Henshu Iinkai, 144–52. Tokyo: Kazankai, 1994.

Tucker, Nancy Bernkopf. "The Clinton Years: The Problem of Coherence." In *Making China Policy: Lessons from the Bush and Clinton Administrations*, edited by Ramon H. Myers, Michel C. Oksenberg, and David Shambaugh, 45–76. Lanham, Md.: Rowman & Littlefield, 2001.

Wakisaka, Noriyuki. "Japanese Development Cooperation for China." In *Chal-*

lenges for China-Japan-U.S. Cooperation, edited by Ryosei Kokubun, 114–29. Tokyo: Japan Center for International Exchange, 1998.

Watanabe, Koji. "The Asian Financial Crisis and the Trilateral Relationship." In *New Dimensions of China-Japan-U.S. Relations*, edited by Japan Center for International Exchange, 61–70. Tokyo: Japan Center for International Exchange, 1999.

CHAPTER 5

Alagappa, Muttiah. *U.S.-ASEAN Security Cooperation: Limits and Possibilities.* Kuala Lumpur, Malaysia: Institute for Strategic and International Studies, 1986.

———. "A Nuclear Weapons Free Zone in Southeast Asia: Problems and Prospects." *Australian Outlook* 41 (1987): 173–80.

———. "The Major Powers and Southeast Asia." *International Journal* 44, no. 3 (1989): 541–97.

Arase, David. *Buying Power: The Political Economy of Japan's Foreign Aid.* Boulder, Colo.: Lynne Riener, 1995.

Bresnan, John. *From Dominoes to Dynamos: The Transformation of Southeast Asia.* New York: Council on Foreign Relations Press, 1994.

Campbell, Kurt, and Mitchell Reiss. "Korean Changes, Asian Challenges and the U.S. Role." *Survival* 43, no. 1 (2001): 53–69.

Chia, Siow Yue. "Development and Issues in U.S.-ASEAN Economic Relations." In *ASEAN Security and Economic Development*, edited by K. Jackson and H. Soesastro, 117–40. Berkeley: Institute of East Asian Studies, University of California Berkeley, 1984.

Doner, Richard. "Japan in East Asia: Institutions and Regional Leadership." In *Network Power: Japan and Asia*, edited by Peter Katzenstein and Takashi Shiraishi. Ithaca, N.Y.: Cornell University Press, 1997.

Drifte, Reinhard. *Japan's Foreign Policy for the Twenty-First Century: From Economic Superpower to What Power?* 2nd ed. New York: St. Martin's Press, 1998.

Fallows, James. *Looking at the Sun: The Rise of the New East Asian Economic and Political System.* New York: Pantheon, 1994.

Fukushima, Akiko. *Japanese Foreign Policy: The Emerging Logic of Multilateralism.* New York: St. Martin's Press, 1999.

Hatch, Walter, and Kozo Yamamura. *Asia in Japan's Embrace: Building a Regional Production Alliance.* Melbourne: Cambridge University Press, 1996.

Ikema, Makoto. "Japan's Economic Relations with ASEAN." In *ASEAN in a Changing Pacific and World Economy*, edited by Ross Garnaut, 453–80. Canberra: Australian National University Press, 1980.

"Jakarta Shifts Stance on Telephone Contract," *Far Eastern Economic Review*, 9 August 1990, 54–5.

Krause, Lawrence. *U.S. Economic Policy Toward the Association of Southeast Asian Nations: Meeting the Japanese Challenge.* Washington, D.C.: Brookings Institution, 1982.

Lam, Peng Er. "Japanese Relations with Southeast Asia in an Era of Turbulence." In *Japanese Foreign Policy Today*, edited by Takashi Inoguchi and Purnendra Jain, 251–65. New York: Palgrave, 2000.

Leifer, Michael. *ASEAN and the Security of South-East Asia*. London: Routledge, 1989.

MacIntyre, Andrew. "Japan, Indonesia and Policy Leadership in the Pacific: Economic Crisis and Foreign Policy Opportunities." In *Japan's Asia Policy: Revival and Response*, edited by Takashi Inoguchi, 153–69. New York: Palgrave, 2002.

"MITI Miffed by Jakarta's National Car Policy." *Japan Times Weekly* (International Edition), June 1996, 24–30.

Morrison, Charles. *Japan, the United States, and Changing Southeast Asia*. Lanham, Md.: University Press of America, 1985.

Okawara, Nobuo, and Peter Katzenstein. "Japan and Asian-Pacific Security: Regionalization, Entrenched Bilateralism and Incipient Multilateralism." *Pacific Review* 14, no. 2 (2001): 165–94.

Pempel, T. J. "Trans-Pacific Torii: Japan and the Emerging Asian Regionalism." In *Network Power: Japan and Asia*, edited by Peter Katzenstein and Takashi Shiraishi. Ithaca, N.Y.: Cornell University Press, 1997.

Sudo, Sueo. "From Fukuda to Takeshita: A Decade of Japan-ASEAN Relations." *Contemporary Southeast Asia* 10, no. 2 (1988): 119–43.

———. *Southeast Asia in Japanese Security Policy*. Singapore: Institute of Southeast Asian Studies, 1991.

Tan, Loong-Hoe, and Narongchai Akrasanee, eds. *ASEAN-U.S. Economic Relations: Changes in Economic Environment and Opportunities*. Singapore: Institute of Southeast Asian Studies, 1988.

"Thailand Finally OKs Joint Glass Venture," *Journal of Commerce*, 28 June 1990, 5A.

Tsunekawa, Keiichi. "Classifying Japan's Efforts for Regional Cooperation in Asia." Paper presented to the Social Science Research Council Conference on Remapping Asia, Hayama, Japan, 15–18 March 2001.

Wang, Lee Meng. "History of U.S.-ASEAN Trade Relations." In *U.S.-ASEAN Relations: Implications for Business*, edited by Teck Meng Tan et al., 19–38. Singapore: Prentice Hall, 1997.

Weinstein, Franklin. "ASEAN and Japan." In *ASEAN Security and Economic Development*, edited by K. Jackson and H. Soesastro, 167–79. Berkeley: Institute of East Asian Studies, University of California Berkeley, 1984.

Yamakage, Susumu. "Japan's National Security and Asia-Pacific's Regional Institutions in the Post-Cold War Era." In *Network Power: Japan and Asia*, edited by Peter Katzenstein and Takashi Shiraishi. Ithaca, N.Y.: Cornell University Press, 1997.

CHAPTER 6

Almanac of China's Foreign Economic Relations and Trade, 2000. Beijing: China Foreign Economic Relations and Trade Publishing House, 2000.

Almanac of China's Foreign Economic Relations and Trade, 2001. Beijing: China Foreign Economic Relations and Trade Publishing House, 2001.

Athukorala, Prema-chandra. "The Malaysian Experiment." In *Reform and Recovery in East Asia: The Role of the State and Economic Enterprise*, edited by Peter Drysdale, 169–90. London: Routledge, 2000.

Bank Indonesia. *Indonesian Financial Statistics* [http://www.bi.go.id/bank_indonesia_english/main/publication/], March 2001.

Bank for International Settlements. "BIS International Consolidated Banking Statistics for the Second Quarter of 2002." Press release [http://www.bis.org], 23 October 2002.

Bank Negara Malaysia (BNM). *BNM Annual Report 2000* [http://www.bnm.gov.my], 2001.

Bank Negara Malaysia (BNM). *Monthly Statistical Bulletin*, March 2001 [http://www.bnm.gov.my], 2001.

Bernard, Mitchell, and John Ravenhill. "Beyond Product Cycles and Flying Geese: Regionalization, Hierarchy, and the Industrialization of East Asia." *World Politics* 47 (1995): 171–209.

Blum, Julian. "On the Prowl." *Far Eastern Economic Review*, 2 April 1998, 49.

Booth, Anne. "Survey of Recent Developments." *Bulletin of Indonesian Economic Studies* 35 (1999): 3–38.

Camdessus, Michel. "Statement to Board." *International Monetary Fund Survey* 28, no. 9 (10 May 1999): 143–44.

Davies, Ben. "Foreign Takeover of BMB Scrapped?" *Asiamoney*, February 2001, 8, 45.

Department of Foreign Affairs and Trade. *Overseas Chinese Business Networks in Asia.* Canberra, Australia: East Asia Analytic Unit, Department of Foreign Affairs and Trade, 1995.

Drysdale, Peter, ed. *Reform and Recovery in East Asia: The Role of the State and Economic Enterprise.* London: Routledge, 2000.

Encarnation, Dennis. *Rivals Beyond Trade: America Versus Japan in Global Competition.* Ithaca, N.Y.: Cornell University Press, 1992.

Freund, Caroline, and Simeon Djankov. "Which Firms Do Foreigners Buy? Evidence from Korea." IMF Discussion Paper. Washington, D.C.: International Monetary Fund, 20 July 2000.

Haddock, Fiona. "DBS Thinks Big in Asia." *Asiamoney*, February 2001, 100.

Haggard, Stephan. *The Political Economy of the Asian Financial Crisis.* Washington, D.C.: Institute for International Economics, 2000.

Hamilton, Gary. "Asian Business Networks in Transition, or What Alan Greenspan Does Not Know About the Asian Business Crisis." In *The Politics of the Asian Economic Crisis*, edited by T. J. Pempel, 45–61. Ithaca, N.Y.: Cornell University Press, 1999.

Hamilton-Hart, Natasha. "Regional Capital and Cooperation in Asia." In *Asian Regionalism*, by Peter J. Katzenstein, Natasha Hamilton-Hart, Kozo Kato, and Ming Yue, 115–69. Ithaca, N.Y.: Cornell University East Asia Program, 2000.

Higgott, Richard. "The Asian Economic Crisis: A Study in the Politics of Resentment." *New Political Economy* 3 (1998): 333–56.

Hong Kong Monetary Authority. *Monthly Statistical Bulletin* [http://www.info.gov.hk/hkma/eng/site/site_b.htm], November 2002.

Hong Kong Monetary Authority. *Monthly Statistical Bulletin* [http://www.info.gov.hk/hkma/eng/site/site_b.htm], January 2003.

International Monetary Fund. *International Capital Markets: Developments, Prospects, and Key Policy Issues.* Washington, D.C.: International Monetary Fund, 2000.

International Monetary Fund. *World Economic Outlook.* Washington, D.C.: International Monetary Fund, May 2000.

International Monetary Fund. *Direction of Trade Statistics Yearbook 2001.* Washington, D.C.: International Monetary Fund, 2002.

International Monetary Fund. *World Economic Outlook.* Washington, D.C.: International Monetary Fund, September 2002.

Japan Bank for International Cooperation. "JBIC FY2001 Survey: The Outlook for Japanese Foreign Direct Investment (13th Annual Survey)." *JBICI Review* 6 (June 2002): 1–57.

Japan External Trade Organization (JETRO). *JETRO White Paper on Foreign Direct Investment 2001.* Tokyo: JETRO, 2001. [http://www.jetro.go.jp].

———. *JETRO White Paper on Foreign Direct Investment 2002.* Tokyo: JETRO, 2002 [http://www.jetro.go.jp].

Katada, Saori. *Banking on Stability: Japan and the Cross-Pacific Dynamics of International Financial Crisis Management.* Ann Arbor: University of Michigan Press, 2001.

Katzenstein, Peter, and Takashi Shiraishi, eds. *Network Power: Japan and Asia.* Ithaca, N.Y.: Cornell University Press, 1997.

Kawai, Masahiro, and Shigeru Akiyama. "Implications of the Currency Crisis for Exchange Rate Arrangements in Emerging East Asia." World Bank Working Paper 2502. Washington, D.C.: World Bank, 2001.

Kawai, Masahiro, and Shinji Takagi. "Proposed Strategy for a Regional Exchange Arrangement in Post-Crisis East Asia." World Bank Working Paper 2503. Washington, D.C.: World Bank, 2001.

Kim, Samuel, ed. *East Asia and Globalization.* Lanham, Md.: Rowman and Littlefield, 2000.

Landers, Peter. "Headlong Retreat." *Far Eastern Economic Review*, 5 November 1998, 57–58.

Mason, Mark, and Dennis Encarnation, eds. *Does Ownership Matter? Japanese Multinationals in Europe.* Oxford: Clarendon Press, 1995.

Masuyama, Seiichi. "The Role of Japan's Direct Investment in Restoring East Asia's Dynamism: Focus on ASEAN's Recovery." In *Restoring East Asia's Dynamism*, edited by Seiichi Masuyama, Donna Vandenbrink, and Chia Siow Yue, 213–58. Tokyo: Nomura Research Institute and Singapore: Institute of Southeast Asian Studies, 2000.

McLeod, Ross. "Survey of Recent Developments." *Bulletin of Indonesian Economic Studies* 36 (2000): 5–40.

Ministry of Economy, Trade and Industry. "Present State of MITI-Related Economic Cooperation" [http://www.meti.go.jp], 2 June 2001.

Ministry of Foreign Affairs. *Japan's ODA Annual Report 1999* [http://www. mofa.go.jp], 2000.

Mody, Ashoka, and Shoko Negishi. "Cross-Border Mergers and Acquisitions in East Asia: Trends and Implications." *Finance and Development* 38, no. 1 (2001).

Monetary Authority of Singapore. "2000 Survey of the Singapore Asset Management" [http://www.mas.gov.sg/display.cfm?id=32FBF0EA-D67E-492F-94B3 A8CC13C7F011], 2001.

Monetary Authority of Singapore. *Monthly Statistical Bulletin* [http://www. mas.gov.sg], January 2003.

Monetary Authority of Singapore. "Regional Exposure and NPLs of Singapore Incorporated Banks" [https://secure.mas.gov.sg/display.cfm?CFID= 18490& CFTOKEN=70829181&id=30AE009F-3F71-4029-B0BB9A730C5BA5E1], 2002.

Nikomborirak, Deunden, and Somkiat Tangkitvanich. "Corporate Governance in Thailand: From Crisis to Recovery." In *Restoring East Asia's Dynamism*, edited by Seiichi Masuyama, Donna Vandenbrink, and Chia Siow Yue, 69–92. Tokyo: Nomura Research Institute; Singapore: Institute of Southeast Asian Studies, 2000.

Noble, Gregory, and John Ravenhill, eds. *The Asian Financial Crisis and the Structure of Global Finance*. Cambridge: Cambridge University Press, 2000.

Oatley, Thomas, and Robert Nabors. "Redistributive Cooperation: Market Failure, Wealth Transfers, and the Basle Accord." *International Organization* 52 (1998): 35–54.

Organization for Economic Cooperation and Development. "ODA Steady in 2000; Other Flows Decline." Press release [http://www.oecd.org], 12 December 2001.

Petri, Peter. "Foreign Direct Investment in the Wake of the Asian Financial Crisis." In *Regional Co-operation and Asian Recovery*, edited by Peter Petri, 187–208. Singapore: Institute of Southeast Asian Studies, 2000.

Rajan, Ramkishen. "Financial and Macroeconomic Co-operation in ASEAN: Issues and Policy Initiatives." In *ASEAN Beyond the Crisis: Challenges and Initiatives*, edited by Mya Than, 126–47. Singapore: Institute of Southeast Asian Studies, 2001.

Rajan, Ramkishen, and Reza Siregar. "Private Capital Flows in East Asia: Boom, Bust and Beyond." Paper presented at conference on Financial Markets and Policies in East Asia, Australian National University, Canberra, 4–5 September 2000.

Sakakibara, Eisuke. "The End of Market Fundamentalism." Paper presented at the Foreign Correspondents' Club, Tokyo, 22 January 1999.

Sender, Henny. "Out of Asia." *Far Eastern Economic Review*, 16 April 1998, 12–13.

Singapore Department of Statistics. *Yearbook of Statistics, Singapore 2002*. Singapore: Department of Statistics, 2002.

Unite, Angelo, and Michael Sullivan. "Reform and the Corporate Environment in the Philippines." In *Reform and Recovery in East Asia: The Role of the State and Economic Enterprise*, edited by Peter Drysdale, 191–213. London: Routledge, 2000.

United Nations Conference on Trade and Development. *World Investment Report 2000: Cross-Border Mergers and Acquisitions and Development*. New York: United Nations, 2000.

———. United Nations Conference on Trade and Development. *World Investment Report 2002: Transnational Corporations and Export Competitiveness*. New York: United Nations, 2002.

U.S. Department of Commerce. "Foreign Direct Investment in the United States: Detail for Historical-Cost Position and Related Capital and Income Flows, 2000." *Survey of Current Business*. Washington, D.C.: U.S. Government Printing Office, September 2001 [http://www.bea.doc.gov/bea/pub/0901cont.htm].

U.S. Department of Commerce. "U.S. Direct Investment Abroad: Detail for Historical-Cost Position and Related Capital and Income Flows, 2000." *Survey of Current Business*. Washington, D.C.: U.S. Government Printing Office, September 2001 [http://www.bea.doc.gov/bea/pub/0901cont.htm].

U.S. Department of Commerce. "BEA Current and Historical Data: International Data—Investment Tables. *Survey of Current Business*. Washington, D.C.: U.S. Government Printing Office, January 2003 [http://www.bea.doc.gov/bea/ pub/ 0103cont.htm].

Wang, Hongying. "Informal Institutions and Foreign Investment in China." *Pacific Review* 13 (2000): 525–56.

Yearbook of China's Foreign Economic Relations and Trade 2002. Beijing: China Foreign Economic Relations and Trade Publishing House, 2002.

CHAPTER 7

Ajia no Jidōsha Sangyō: Zadankai (Roundtable discussion on the automobile industry in Asia)." *Asahi Shinbun* (27 November 1996), 15.

Aldrich, Howard E., and Tomoaki Sakano. "Unbroken Ties: Comparing Personal Business Networks Cross-Nationally." In *Networks, Markets, and the Pacific Rim*, edited by W. Mark Fruin, 32–52. New York: Oxford University Press, 1998.

Arnold, Bill. "Top Global Semiconductor Companies." *Electronic Business*, 1 May 1999.

Axelsson, Björn. "Supplier Management and Technological Development." In *Industrial Technological Development: A Network Approach*, edited by Håkan Håkansson. 128–76. London: Croom Helm, 1987.

Biggart, Nicole Woolsey, and Gary Hamilton. "On the Limits of a Firm-Based Theory to Explain Business Networks: The Western Bias of Neoclassical Economics." In *The Economic Organization of East Asian Capitalism*, edited by Marco Orru, Nicole Woolsey Biggart, and Gary Hamilton. London: Sage, 1997.

Bird, Kelly. "Concentration in Indonesian Manufacturing, 1975–93." *Bulletin of Indonesian Economic Studies* 35, no. 1 (April 1999): 43–73.

Borrus, Michael. "The Resurgence of U.S. Electronics: Asian Production Networks and the Rise of Wintelism." In *International Production Networks in*

Asia: Rivalry or Riches, edited by Michael Borrus, Dieter Ernst, and Stephan Haggard. London: Routledge, 2000.

———. "Left for Dead: Asian Production Networks and the Revival of U.S. Electronics." Berkeley Roundtable on the International Economy Working Paper 100. Berkeley, Calif.: Berkeley Roundtable on the International Economy, University of California, April 1997.

Brusco, Sebastiano. "The Emilian Model: Productive Decentralization and Social Integration." *Cambridge Journal of Economics* 6 (1982): 167–84.

Burt, Ronald S. *Structural Holes: The Social Structure of Competition.* Cambridge: Harvard University Press, 1992.

Chen, Tain-jy, and Shin-horng Chen. "Global Production Networks and Local Capabilities: New Opportunities and Challenges for Taiwan." Working Paper 15. Honolulu: East-West Center, February 2001.

Chia, Siow-Yue. "Singapore: Advanced Production Base and Smart Hub of the Electronics Industry." In *Multinationals and East Asian Integration*, edited by Wendy Dobson and Chia Siow Yue. Ottawa: International Development Research Centre, 1997.

CLM Working Group (MITI Japan). "Chairman's Summary of the Fourth Automobile Experts Meeting from ASEAN, CLM (Cambodia, Laos, and Myanmar), and Japan," 1997.

Doremus, Paul N., William M. Keller, Louis W. Pauly, and Simon Reich. *The Myth of the Global Corporation.* Princeton, N.J.: Princeton University Press, 1998.

Economic Planning Agency of Japan. *Kōzō Kaikaku ni Chōsen, Keizai Shakai ni Dainamizumu o* (Recommendations for structural reform and bringing dynamism to the economy). A report from the Keizai Shingikai (Deliberation Council on the Economy). Tokyo: Economic Planning Agency of Japan, June 1998.

Ernst, Dieter. "Partners for the China Circle? The Asian Production Networks of Japanese Electronics Firms." Berkeley Roundtable on the International Economy Working Paper 91. Berkeley, Calif.: Berkeley Roundtable on the International Economy, University of California, January 1997.

———. "From Partial to Systemic Globalization: International Production Networks in the Electronics Industry." Berkeley Roundtable on the International Economy Working Paper 98. Berkeley, Calif.: Berkeley Roundtable on the International Economy, University of California, April 1997.

Fourin. *Tōnan Ajia-Taiwan-Taishū no Jidōsha Buhin Sangyō* (The automobile parts industry in Southeast Asia, Taiwan, and Oceania). Nagoya, Japan: Fourin, 1998.

———. *Kaigai Jidōsha Chōsa Geppō* (Monthly report on overseas automobile manufacturing). Nagoya, Japan: Fourin, February 2000.

Fruin, W. Mark, ed. *Networks, Markets, and the Pacific Rim: Studies in Strategy.* New York: Oxford University Press, 1998.

Gerlach, Michael. *Alliance Capitalism: The Social Organization of Japanese Business.* Berkeley: University of California Press, 1992.

Gourevitch, Peter, Roger Bohn, and David McKendrick. "Globalization of Production: Insights from the Hard Disk Drive Industry." *World Development* 28, no. 2 (February 2000): 301–17.

Granovetter, Mark. *Getting a Job*. Cambridge: Harvard University Press, 1974.
———. "The Strength of Weak Ties." *American Journal of Sociology* 78 (1973): 1360–80.
———. "Economic Action and Social Structure." *American Journal of Sociology* 91 (1985): 481–501.
Håkansson, Håkan. "Product Development in Networks." In *Industrial Technological Development: A Network Approach*, edited by Håkan Håkansson. London: Croom Helm, 1987.
Hatch, Walter, and Kozo Yamamura. *Asia in Japan's Embrace: Building a Regional Production Alliance*. Cambridge: Cambridge University Press, 1996.
Imai, Ken'ichi, and Kaneko Ikuyo. *Nettowāku Soshiki-ron* (Theory of the network system). Tokyo: Iwanami Shoten, 1988.
Itagaki, Hiroshi. *The Japanese Production System: Hybrid Factories in East Asia*. Hampshire, U.K.: Macmillan Business, 1997.
Itami, Hiroyuki. "Overview: The Structural Upgrading of East Asian Economies and Industrial Networks." In *Can Asia Recover Its Vitality? Globalization and the Roles of Japanese and U.S. Corporations*, edited by the staff of the Institute of Developing Economies and Japan External Trade Organization. Tokyo: Institute of Developing Economies, 1998.
Japan Automobile Manufacturers Association. "Dispatch of Experts to Thailand Under the Roving Automotive Expert Dispatch Scheme." *Voice of Chairman* [http:www.jama.or.jp.e press/voice/20001017.html], 17 October 2000.
Japan Research Institute (JRI). "Automakers Unveil New ASEAN Strategies." *JRI Asia Monthly Report*. Tokyo: JRI, October 2001.
Kasahara, Hiroyuki. "Transfer and Adaptation of Manufacturer-Supplier Relationships from Japan to Thailand: A Case of the Automobile Industry." Unpublished paper, 1997.
Krugman, Paul. "Growing World Trade: Causes and Consequences," *Brookings Papers on Economic Activity, 1995*. Washington, DC: Brookings Institution, 1995: 327–77.
Leachman, Robert C., and Chien H. Leachman. "Trends in Worldwide Semiconductor Fabrication Capacity." Working Paper 48. Competitive Semiconductor Manufacturing Program, University of California at Berkeley, July 1999.
Legewie, Jöchen. "Driving Regional Integration: Japanese Firms and the Development of the ASEAN Automobile Industry." DIJ Working Paper 99/1. Tokyo: Deutsches Institut für Japanstudien, 1999.
Maruyama, Yoshinari, ed. *Ajia no Jidōsha Sangyō* (The Asian automobile industry). Tokyo: Akishobō, 1997.
Matsuoka, Katsunori. "Accord Drives Change to Asian Carmaking." *Nikkei Weekly* (7 April 1997), 22.
Matthews, John, and Dong-sung Cho. *Tiger Technology: The Creation of a Semiconductor Industry in East Asia*. Cambridge: Cambridge University Press, 2000.
McKendrick, David G., Richard F. Doner, and Stephan Haggard. *From Silicon Valley to Singapore: Location and Competitive Advantage in the Hard Disk Drive Industry*. Stanford, Calif.: Stanford University Press, 2000.

Mikami, Yoshiki. "Asia's PC and Semiconductor Industries and the Conditions for Their Future Development." In *Can Asia Recover Its Vitality? Globalization and the Roles of Japanese and U.S. Corporations*, edited by the staff of the Institute of Developing Economies and Japan External Trade Organization. Tokyo: Institute of Developing Economies, 1998.

Ministry of International Trade and Industry. *Wagakuni Kigyō no Kaigai Jigyō Katsudō, Dai 26-Kai* (The overseas business activities of Japanese firms, number 26). Tokyo: Ministry of Finance Printing Bureau, 1998.

Nakashima, Takamasa. "Industrial Relations and Ethnicity: The Case of MSC, a Japanese-Owned Automobile Manufacturer in Thailand." Unpublished paper for the Asian Regional Conference on Industrial Relations, Tokyo, 17–18 March 1998.

Nikkan Jidōsha Shimbunsha. *Jidōsha Sangyō Handobukku, 2000 Nenpan* (Automobile industry handbook for the year 2000). Tokyo: Nikkan Jidōsha Shinbunsha, 2000.

Nishioka, Tadashi. "ASEAN ni okeru Jidōsha Sangyō no Dōkō to Wagakuni Chūshō Buhin Meikaa e no Eikyō ni tsuite (The state of the automobile industry in ASEAN, and its influence on Japanese SME parts producers). *Chūshō Kōko Repōto*, no. 98–1 (April 1998).

Saxenian, Anna Lee. *Regional Advantage: Culture and Competition in Silicon Valley and Route 128*. Cambridge, Mass.: Harvard University Press, 1994.

Sedgwick, Mitchell W. "Does Japanese Management Travel in Asia? Managerial Technology Transfer at Japanese Multinationals in Thailand." Working Paper 96–04. Cambridge, Mass.: MIT Japan Program, 1996.

Takeuchi, Junko. "Comparison of Asian Business by Japanese and American Companies in the Electronics Sector." Tokyo: Center for Pacific Business Studies, December 2001.

Tecson, Gwendolyn R. *The Hard Disk Drive Industry in the Philippines*. Report 99–01. San Diego: University of California San Diego, Information Storage Industry Center, January 1999.

Thai Board of Investment. "Investment Opportunities Study: Automotive and Autoparts Industries in Thailand." Executive summary [www.boi.go.th/english/execsummary/f7a.html], 1995.

Thornton, Emily. "The Debt That's Dragging Nissan Downhill." *Business Week*, 5 April 1999.

U.S. Embassy, Bangkok. *Country Commercial Guide: Thailand, Fiscal Year 2000* [http://sites.usatrade.gov/imtp/thailand.doc], July 1999.

U.S. Embassy, Jakarta. "Indonesia: New Automotive Industrial Policy." August 1999.

Uzzi, Brian. "The Sources and Consequences of Embeddedness for the Economic Performance of Organizations: The Network Effect." *American Sociological Review* 61 (August 1996): 674–98.

Vestal, James. *Planning for Change: Industrial Policy and Japanese Economic Development, 1945–90*. New York: Oxford University Press, 1993.

Williamson, Oliver. *Markets and Hierarchies: Analysis and Antitrust Implications*. New York: Free Press, 1975.

Womak, James P., Daniel T. Jones, and Daniel Roos. *The Machine That Changed the World: The Story of Lean Production.* New York: Macmillan, 1990.

World Trade Organization. *International Trade Statistics 2001.* Geneva: World Trade Organization, 2001 [http://www.wto.org/english/res_e/statis_e/its2001_e/its01_toc_e.htm].

Wong, Poh-Kam. "Globalization of U.S.-Japan Production Networks and the Growth of Singapore's Electronics Industry." In *Can Asia Recover Its Vitality? Globalization and the Roles of Japanese and U.S. Corporations,* edited by the staff of the Institute of Developing Economies and Japan External Trade Organization. Tokyo: Institute of Developing Economies, 1998.

Yamamura, Kozo, and Walter Hatch. "A Looming Entry Barrier: Japan's Production Networks in Asia." *NBR Analysis* 8, no. 1 (February 1997): 5–28.

Yasumuro, Ken'ichi. *Kokusai Keiei Kōdōron: Nichibei Hikaku no Shiten Kara* (The behavior of international management: A comparison of Japanese and U.S. companies). Tokyo: Moriyama Shoten, 1982.

CHAPTER 8

Amyx, Jennifer A. "Political Impediments to Far-Reaching Banking Reforms in Japan: Implications for Asia." In *The Asian Financial Crisis and the Architecture of Global Finance,* edited by Gregory Noble and John Ravenhill, 132–51. Cambridge University Press, 2000.

Bobrow, Davis B. "The U.S. and ASEM: Why the Hegemon Didn't Bark." *The Pacific Review* 12, no. 1 (1999): 103–28.

Coere, Benoit, and Jean Pisani-Ferri. "Events, Ideas, and Actions: An Intellectual and Institutional Retrospective on the Reform of the International Financial Architecture." Paper prepared for the CDC-CEPII-CEFI international conference, Reshaping the Architecture of the International Financial System, Siena, Italy, 23–24 May 2000.

DeLong, J. Bradford, and Barry Eichengreen. "Between Meltdown and Moral Hazard: The International Monetary and Financial Policies and the Clinton Administration." Paper prepared for conference on the Economic Policies of the Clinton Administration, Kennedy School of Government, Cambridge, Mass., 26–29 June 2001.

Dent, Christopher M. "ASEM and the 'Cinderella Complex' of EU-East Asia Economic Relations." *Pacific Affairs* 74, no. 1 (spring 2001): 25–54.

Gilson, Julie. "Japan's Role in the Asia-Europe Meeting: Establishing an Interregional or Intraregional Agenda?" *Asian Survey* 39, no. 5 (September/October 1999): 736–52.

Helleiner, Eric. "Still an Extraordinary Power, but for How Much Longer? The United States in World Finance." In *Strange Power: Shaping the Parameters of International Relations and International Political Economy,* edited by Thomas C. Lawton, James N. Rosenau, and Amy C. Verdun, 229–47. Aldershot, U.K.: Ashgate, 2000.

Higgott, Richard. "The Asian Economic Crisis: A Study in the Politics of Resentment." *New Political Economy* 3, no. 3 (1998): 333–56.

Inoguchi, Kuniko. "The Changing Significance of the G-7 Summits." *Japan Review of International Affairs* (winter 1994): 21–38.

Japan Economic Institute of America. *JEI Report*, no. 42B (7 November 1997) [http://www.jei.org].

Japan Economic Institute of America. *JEI Report*, no. 44B (20 November 1998) [http://www.jei.org].

Johnstone, Christopher B. "Paradigms Lost: Japan's Asia Policy in a Time of Growing Chinese Power." *Contemporary Southeast Asia* 21, no. 3 (1999): 365–85.

Katada, Saori N. *Banking on Stability: Japan and the Cross-Pacific Dynamics of International Financial Crisis Management.* Ann Arbor: University of Michigan Press, 2001.

Kikkawa, Mototada. *Monē Haisen* (Losing a money battle). Tokyo: Bunshun Shinsho, 1998.

Kondo, Seiji. "Kerun Samitto no Seika to Nihon (The results of the Köln summit and Japan)." *Sekai Keizai Hyoron* (September 1999): 8–28.

Lustig, Nora. "Mexico in Crisis, the U.S. to the Rescue: The Financial Assistance Packages of 1982 and 1995." *Brookings Discussion Papers.* Washington, D.C.: Brookings Institution, June 1996.

Stiglitz, Joseph. "Boats, Planes and Capital Flows." *Financial Times*, 25 March 1998.

Strange, Susan. *Casino Capitalism.* Oxford: Blackwell, 1986.

"Tensions Under the Table." *Economist*, 1 May 1999, 69–73.

Vatikiotis, Michael. "Pacific Divide." *Far Eastern Economic Review* 160 (6 November 1997), 14–16.

Yoshitomi, Masaru, and Sayuri Shirai. "Technical Background Paper for Policy Recommendations for Preventing Another Capital Account Crisis." Tokyo: Asian Development Bank Institute, 7 July 2000.

CHAPTER 9

Altbach, Eric. "The Asian Monetary Fund Proposal: A Case Study of Japanese Regional Leadership." *JEI Report* 47 (19 December 1997): 9.

Blustein, Paul. *The Chastening: Inside the Crisis That Rocked the Global Financial System and Humbled the IMF.* New York: Public Affairs, 2001.

Calder, Kent E. "Japanese Foreign Economic Policy Formation: Explaining the Reactive State." *World Politics* 40, no. 4 (1988): 517–41.

Cornell, Andrew. "Japan Pushes for Asian Version of IMF." *Australian Financial Review* 12 (February 1999) [http://www.geocities.com/Eureka/Concourse/8751/edisio3/afo21201.htm].

Foreign Exchange Deliberation Council. *Gaikoku Kawase tō Shingikai dai 53-kai Sōkai Gijiroku* (Foreign Exchange, etc., Deliberation Council's 53rd General Meeting Minutes), 17 October 2000 [http://www.mof.go.jp/singikai/gaitame/gijiroku/ao53.htm], 6 February 2003.

Gyohten, Toyo. "East Asia Initiative Needed in Crises." *IIMA Newsletter*, 6 (1999): 7.

Hashimoto, Hiroshi. "Press Conference by the Japanese Delegation to the 1997 APEC Meetings in Vancouver," 21 November 1997 [http://www.mofa.go.jp/policy/economy/apec/1997/position.html].

"Joint Ministerial Statement of the ASEAN+3 Finance Ministers Meeting," Chiang Mai, Thailand, 6 May 2000 [http://www.mof.go.jp/English/if/ifo4.htm].

Kishimoto, Shuhei. "Shin Miyzawa Kōsō no Shinei to Ajia Tsuka Kikin" (The mandate of the New Miyazawa Initiative and the Asian Monetary Fund). *Fainansu* 35 (May 1999): 31–48.

Krieger, Joel, ed. *The Oxford Companion to World Politics*. New York: Oxford University Press, 1993.

Lincoln, Edward J. "The Asian Development Bank: Time to Wind It up?" In *Reconfiguring East Asia: Regional Institutions and Organisations After the Crisis*, edited by Mark Beeson, 205–26. London: Curzon Press, 2002.

Ministry of Finance. "Joint Ministerial Statement of the ASEAN+3 Finance Ministers Meeting," Chiang Mai, Thailand, 6 May 2000 [http://www.mof.go.jp/english/if/ifo14.htm].

Ministry of Finance, Japan. "The Joint Ministerial Statement of the ASEAN+3 Finance Ministers Meeting," 9 May 2001 [http://www.mof.go.jp/english/if/ekaigioo8.htm], 10 May 2001.

———. "International Reserves / Foreign Currency Liquidity." *Statistics*, 7 February 2003 [http://www.mof.go.jp/english/e1coo6.htm].

Ogura, Kazuo. "Atarashii Ajia no Sozo." (Creating a New Asia). *Voice*, March 1999, 123–35.

Ogura, Kazuo. "Creating a New Asia." *Japan Echo* 26, no. 3 (June 1999): 12–16.

"Press Guidance on Chiang Mai Initiative," ASEAN+3 Summit, Nov. 2001, on file with the author.

———. "Q&A About The New Initiative to Overcome the Asian Currency Crisis (New Miyazawa Initiative)," 7 February 2003 [http://www.mof.go.jp/english/qa/myoo1.htm].

Prime Minister's Commission on Japan's Goals in the 21st Century. *The Frontier Within: Individual Empowerment and Better Governance in the New Millennium*, 18 January 2000 [http://www.kantei.go.jp/jp/21century/report/htmls/7chap6.html].

Rapkin, David P., and Jonathan R. Strand. "The United States and Japan in the Bretton Woods Institutions: Sharing or Contesting Leadership?" *International Journal* 52, no. 2 (1997): 265–96.

Rix, Alan. "Leadership from Behind." In *Pacific Cooperation in the 1990s*, edited by Richard Higgot et al. Canberra: Australia Fulbright Commission, 1993.

Tanaka, Nobuaki. "Press Conference by the Press Secretary." *Ministry of Foreign Affairs of Japan Archives on Press Conferences*, 16 January 1998 [http://www.mofa.go.jp/announce/press/1998/1/116.html].

Terada, Takashi. "Creating an Asia Pacific Economic Community: The Roles of Australia and Japan in Regional Institution-Building." Ph.D. thesis, Australian National University, 1999.

Woodward, Bob. *Maestro: Greenspan's FED and the American Boom.* New York: Simon & Schuster, 2000.

CHAPTER 10

Abbott, Kenneth W., Robert O. Keohane, Andrew Moravcsik, Anne-Marie Slaughter, and Duncan Snidal. "The Concept of Legalization." *International Organization* 54, no. 3 (2000): 401–19.

Croley, Steven P., and John H. Jackson. "WTO Dispute Procedures, Standard of Review, and Deference to National Governments." *American Journal of International Law* 90, no. 2 (1996): 193–213.

Destler, I. M. *American Trade Politics.* Washington, D.C.: Institute for International Economics, 1992.

Goldstein, Judith, Miles Kahler, Robert O. Keohane, and Anne-Marie Slaughter. "Introduction: Legalization and World Politics." *International Organization* 54, no. 3 (2000): 385–99.

Irwin, Douglas A. "Trade Politics and the Semiconductor Industry." In *The Political Economy of American Trade Policy*, edited by Anne O. Krueger, 11–66. Chicago: University of Chicago Press for the National Bureau of Economic Research, 1996.

Jackson, John H. "Dumping in International Trade: Its Meaning and Context." In *Antidumping Law and Practice: A Comparative Study*, edited by John H. Jackson and Edwin A. Vermulst, 1–22. Ann Arbor: University of Michigan Press, 1989.

Komuro, Norio. "Japan's First Antidumping Measures in the Ferro-Silico-Manganese Case." *Journal of World Trade* 27, no. 3 (1993): 5–30.

Krueger, Anne O. "Introduction." In *The Political Economy of American Trade Policy*, edited by Anne O. Krueger, 1–10. Chicago: University of Chicago Press for the National Bureau of Economic Research, 1996.

Louth, Cydney, and Edwina Rogers. "Import Administration: Stopping Unfair Trade Practices." *Business America*, November 1990.

Moore, Michael O. "Steel Protection in the 1980s: The Waning Influence of Big Steel?" In *The Political Economy of American Trade Policy*, edited by Anne O. Krueger, 73–130. Chicago: University of Chicago Press for the National Bureau of Economic Research, 1996.

Pekkanen, Saadia M. "Sword and Shield: The WTO Dispute Settlement System and Japan." *The Japanese Economy* 28, no. 6 (2000): 3–26. Reprinted in *Japan's Managed Globalization: Adapting to the 21st Century*, edited by William Grimes and Ulrike Schaede. Armonk, N.Y.: Sharpe, 2002.

———. "Aggressive Legalism: The Rules of the WTO and Japan's Emerging Trade Strategy." *The World Economy* 24, no. 5 (2001): 707–37.

———. "International Law, the WTO, and the Japanese State: Assessment and Implications of the New Legalized Trade Politics." *Journal of Japanese Studies* 27, no. 1 (2001): 41–79.

Staiger, Robert W., and Frank A. Wolak. "Differences in the Uses and Effects of

Antidumping Law Across Import Sources." In *The Political Economy of American Trade Policy*, edited by Anne O. Krueger, 385–421. Chicago: University of Chicago Press for the National Bureau of Economic Research, 1996.

Tilton, Mark C. "Regulatory Reform and Market Opening in Japan." In *Is Japan Really Changing Its Ways? Regulatory Reform and the Japanese Economy*, edited by Lonny E. Carlile and Mark C. Tilton, 163–96. Washington, D.C.: Brookings Institution, 1998.

U.S. General Accounting Office. *World Trade Organization: Issues in Dispute Settlement.* (GAO/NSIAD-00-210) Washington, D.C.: U.S. General Accounting Office, 2000.

———. *World Trade Organization: U.S. Experience to Date in Dispute Settlement System—The First Five Years.* (GAO/NSIAD/OGC-00-196BR) Washington, D.C.: U.S. General Accounting Office, 2000.

World Trade Organization. *Report of the Appellate Body.* Various cases.

———. *Report of the Panel.* Various cases.

———. *Arbitration.* Various cases.

CHAPTER 11

Baker, James A., III. "America in Asia: Emerging Architecture for a Pacific Community." *Foreign Affairs* 70, no. 5 (1991/1992): 1–18.

———. *The Politics of Diplomacy: Revolution, War and Peace, 1989–1992.* New York: Putnam, 1995.

Baker, Richard W. "The United States and APEC Regime Building." In *Asia-Pacific Crossroads: Regime Creation and the Future of APEC*, edited by Vinod K. Aggarwal and Charles E. Morrison, 163–89. New York: St. Martin's Press, 1998.

Bodde, William, Jr. "Managing APEC." In *Whither APEC? The Progress to Date and Agenda for the Future*, edited by Fred C. Bergsten, 211–23. Washington, D.C.: Institute for International Economics, 1997.

"Gurobaru-ka suru Sekaikeizai no nakade Nihon to Ajia wa Douarubekika" (Japan and Asia in the globalizing world economy). *Tsusan Journal* (August 1999): 8–13.

Hiramatsu, Kenji. "Ajia-Taiheiyo-gata no Anzenhoshoukikou wa Seiritsu Suruka" (Can Asia-Pacific Security Institution be achieved?). *Gaiko Forum* (Special Edition 1999): 112–21.

Keohane, Robert O. "Institutionalist Theory and the Realist Challenge After the Cold War." In *Neorealism and Neoliberalism: The Contemporary Debate*, edited by David A. Baldwin, 269–300. New York: Columbia University Press, 1993.

Krauss, Ellis. "Japan, the U.S., and the Emergence of Multilateralism in Asia." *Pacific Review* 13, no. 3 (2000): 473–94.

Ministry of International Trade and Industry (MITI). *Arata naru Ajia-Taiheiyo Kyoryoku o Motomete: Konsensasu Apurochi ni yoru Tasouteki Zenshinteki Kyoryoku no Suishin* (Toward new Asia-Pacific cooperation: Promotion of multilevel gradually advancing cooperation on a consensus basis). Tokyo: MITI, 1988.

———. *Tusho Hakusho 1999* (White Paper on International Trade 1999). Tokyo: Okurasho Insatsukyoku, 1999.

Nakayama, Taro. "Statement by His Excellency Dr. Taro Nakayama, Ministry of Foreign Affairs of Japan to the General Session of the ASEAN Post Ministerial Conference, Kuala Lumpur, July 22, 1991." In *ASEAN Shiryo Shushi 1967–1996* (CD-ROM). Tokyo: Nihon Kokusai Mondai Kenkyujo, 1999.

Satoh, Yukio. "Asia-Pacific Process for Stability and Security." In *Japan's Post Gulf War International Initiatives*, edited by Japan Ministry of Foreign Affairs (MOFA), 34–45. Tokyo: MOFA, 1991.

Tsushoseisakukyoku Ajia-Taiheiyo Chiikikyoryokusuishinshitsu. "APEC Nau, 1" (APEC now, 1). *Tsusan Journal* (April 1995): 66–68.

———. "APEC Nau, 2" (APEC now, 2). *Tsusan Journal* (May 1995): 70–72.

U.S. Department of State. "Secretary Baker's Address Prepared for Delivery Before the Asia Society in New York City on June 26, 1989, 'A New Pacific Partnership: Framework for the Future.'" *Department of State Bulletin* (August 1989): 64–66.

———. "Hearing on the East Asia and Pacific Affairs Subcommittee of the Senate Foreign Relations Committee on Proposals for a Pacific Basin Forum." *Federal News Service*, 21 September 1989.

———. "Background Briefing on Secretary of State Baker's Upcoming Trip to Australia." *Federal News Service*, 30 October 1989.

———. "Settlement to Cambodia Problem Needed, Baker Says. Remarks of Secretary of State Baker Following the Association of Southeast Asian Nations Post Ministerial Conference, July 24, 1991." Available from Public Diplomacy Query (PDQ) database [http://usinfo.state.gov/products/pdq/pdq.htm].

Solomon, Richard H. "Asian Security in the 1990s: Integration in Economics, Diversity in Defense." Address given at the University of California at San Diego, October 20, 1990. *U.S. Department of State Dispatch* 1, no. 10 (1990), 243–49.

———. "Winston Lord Assistant Secretary-Designate for East Asian and Pacific Affairs, Statement Before the Senate Foreign Relations Committee, Washington, D.C., March 31, 1993." *U.S. Department of State Dispatch* 4, no. 14 (1993).

———. "USIA Foreign Press Center Briefing on Upcoming ASEAN Meetings in Bangkok by Winston Lord, July 19." *Federal News Service* (19 July 1994).

U.S. Government. *A Strategic Framework for the Asian Pacific Rim: Looking Toward the 21st Century—The President's Report on the U.S. Military Presence in East Asia*. Washington, D.C.: U.S. Government Printing Office, 1990.

Yamazawa, Ieppei. "APEC's Economic and Technical Cooperation: Evolution and Task Ahead." In *Whither APEC? The Progress to Date and Agenda for the Future*, edited by Fred C. Bergsten, 135–49. Washington, D.C.: Institute for International Economics, 1997.

Yanai, Shunji. "Reisengo no Wagakuni no Anzenhoshouseisaku" (Japan's security policy in the post-Cold War era). *Gaiko Forum* (July 1995): 44–49.

"Zadankai: Meiyo aru Chii o Erutameni" (Roundtable: To achieve honored status). *Gaiko Forum* (May 1991): 12–33.

"Zadanakai: Jinrui ni totteno Nichibei Doumei towa" (Roundtable: U.S.-Japan Alliance for Humanity). *Gaiko Forum* (November 1991): 27–40.

"Zadankai: Ugokidashita Hokutouajia—Shinraijosei ka Tairitsukouzou ka" (Roundtable: Northeast Asia in motion—confidence building or confrontation?). *Gaiko Forum* (November 2001): 24–31.

CHAPTER 12

Altbach, Eric. "Australia Charges That Japan May Undercut APEC Trade Talks." *JEI Report*, no. 42B (6 November 1998): 5.

American Chamber of Commerce in Japan. *Making Trade Talks Work, 2000.* Tokyo: American Chamber of Commerce in Japan, 2000.

APEC Secretariat. "The APEC Economic Leaders' Declaration: Connecting the APEC Community" [http://www.apecsec.org.sg/virtualib/econlead/vancouver.html], 25 November 1997.

———. "APEC Economic Leaders' Declaration: From Vision to Action," no. 8 [http://www.apecsec.org.sg/virtualib/history/mapa/leaders.html], 1996.

———. "The Osaka Action Agenda: Implementation of the Bogor Declaration" [http://www.apecsec.org.sg/virtualib/history/osaka/agenda.html], 1995.

Bergsten, Fred. "America's Two-Front Economic Conflict." *Foreign Affairs* (March/April 2001).

Coser, Lewis A. *The Functions of Social Conflict.* Glencoe, Ill.: Macmillan, 1956.

Davis, Christina. "Trade Rules and Political Persuasion: The Politics of Reforming Japanese Agricultural Policy." Paper presented at the Annual Meeting of the Association for Asian Studies, Chicago, March 2001.

Dee, Philippa, Alexis Hardin, and Michael Schuele. "APEC Early Voluntary Sectoral Liberalization." Paper presented to the Fourth APEC Roundtable: "What's APEC Worth?" sponsored by the Brandeis University Institute of Southeast Asian Studies and the Korea Institute of International Economic Policy, 26–27 May 1998 [http://www.tier.org.tw/APECC/hotnews/Discussion_Papers/ evsl2.pdf].

Japan Ministry of Foreign Affairs. "Early Voluntary Sector Liberalization: Annex to the Ministers' Joint Statement." Vancouver: 21–22 November 1997 [http://www.mofa.go.jp/policy/economy/apec/1997/statement22_6.html].

Krauss, Ellis S. "U.S. and Japanese Negotiations on Construction and Semiconductors: Building Friction and Relation-Chips." In *Double-Edged Diplomacy: International Bargaining and Domestic Politics*, edited by Peter Evans, Harold Jacobson, and Robert Putnam. Berkeley: University of California Press, 1993.

———. "Japan, the U.S., and the Emergence of Multilateralism in Asia." *Pacific Review* 13, no. 3 (September 2000): 473–94.

Lake, David A., and Robert Powell, eds. *Strategic Choice in International Relations.* Princeton: Princeton University Press, 1999.

Rapkin, David P. "The United States, Japan, and the Power to Block: The APEC and AMF Cases." *Pacific Review* 14, no. 3 (2001): 373–410.

Ravenhill, John, and Vinod Aggarwal. "Undermining the WTO: The Case Against 'Open Sectoralism.'" *East-West Center Asia Pacific Issues* 50 (February 2001), 1–6.

Tsbelis, George. *Nested Games: Rational Choice in Comparative Politics.* Berkeley: University of California Press, 1991.

U.S. Department of State. "Statement of the Chair." Meeting of APEC Ministers Responsible for Trade, Montreal, 8–10 May 1997 [http://www.usinfo. state.gov/regional/ea/apec/montreal.htm].

————. "Transcript: USTR Barshefsky Briefs on APEC Ministerial Outcomes" (APEC not going to become victim of financial crisis), 15 November 1998 [http://www.usinfo.state.gov/regional/ea/apec/wwwhbar2.htm].

Wesley, Michael. "APEC's Mid-Life Crisis? The Rise and Fall of Early Voluntary Sectoral Liberalization." *Pacific Affairs* 74, no. 2 (summer 2001), 185–204.

CHAPTER 13

Adler, Emanuel, and Michael Barnett, eds. *Security Communities*. Cambridge: Cambridge University Press, 1998.

Bergsten, C. Fred. "America's Two-Front Economic Conflict." *Foreign Affairs* (March/April 2001): 16–27.

Durkheim, Emile. *The Division of Labor in Society*, translated by George Simpson. New York: Free Press, 1997. (Originally published 1933.)

Eichengreen, Barry, ed. *Toward a New International Financial Architecture: A Practical Post-Asia Agenda*. Washington, D.C.: Institute of International Economics, 1999.

Hamilton, Gary. "Asian Business Networks in Transition, or What Alan Greenspan Does Not Know about the Asian Business Crisis." In *The Politics of the Asian Economic Crisis*, edited by T. J. Pempel, 45–61. Ithaca, N.Y.: Cornell University Press, 1999.

Heginbotham, Eric, and Richard J. Samuels. "Japan's Dual Hedge." *Foreign Affairs* 81, no. 5 (September/October 2002), 110–21.

————. "Mercantile Realism and Japanese Foreign Policy." In *Unipolar Politics: Realism and State Strategies after the Cold War*, edited by Ethan B. Kapstein and Michael Mastanduno. New York: Columbia University Press, 1999. Originally published in *International Security* (spring 1998).

Institute for National Strategic Studies. "The United States and Japan: Advancing Toward a Mature Partnership." *INSS Special Report* ["Nye-Armitage Report"]. Washington, D.C.: Institute for National Strategic Studies, National Defense University, 11 October 2000 [http://www.ndu.edu/ndu/sr_japan.html].

Ishihara, Shintaro, and Morita Akio. *"No" to ieru Nihon: Shin Nichi-Bei Kankei no Kado* (The Japan that can say no: A turning point in the new Japan-U.S. relationship). Tokyo: Kobunsha, 1989.

Ishihara, Shintaro. *The Japan That Can Say No*. New York: Simon & Schuster, 1991.

Kahler, Miles. *International Institutions and the Political Economy of Integration*. Washington, D.C.: Brookings Institution, 1995.

Katada, Saori. "Why Did Japan Suspend Foreign Aid to China? Japan's Foreign Aid Decision-Making and Sources of Aid Sanction. *Social Science Japan Journal* 4, no. 1 (2001): 39–58.

————. *Banking on Stability: Japan and the Cross-Pacific Dynamics of International Financial Crisis Management*. Ann Arbor: University of Michigan Press, 2001

Keohane, Robert. "The Demand for International Regimes." In *International Institutions and State Power*, edited by Robert Keohane. Boulder, Colo.: Westview Press, 1989.

Krauss, Ellis S. "Japan, the U.S., and the Emergence of Multilateralism in Asia." *Pacific Review* 13, no. 3 (September, 2000), 473–94.

Ladd, Everett Carl, and Karlyn H. Bowman. *Public Opinion in America and Japan: How We See Each Other and Ourselves*. Washington, D.C.: AEI Press, 1996.

Mansfield, Edward D., and Helen V. Milner, eds. *The Political Economy of Regionalism*. New York: Columbia University Press, 1997.

Nakasone, Yasuhiro. "Toward Comprehensive Security: Self-Defense and Article 9 of the Constitution." *Japan Echo* 5, no. 4 (1978): 32–39; translation of "Waga sōgō-teki anzen hoshōron." *Sekai* (September 1978).

Nau, Henry R. *At Home Abroad: Identity and Power in American Foreign Policy*. Ithaca, N.Y.: Cornell University Press, 2002.

Pempel, T. J. "Regional Ups, Regional Downs." In *The Politics of the Asian Economic Crisis*, edited by T. J. Pempel, 62–78. Ithaca, N.Y.: Cornell University Press, 1999.

Pyle, Kenneth B. *The Japanese Question: Power and Purpose in a New Era*. 2nd ed. Washington, D.C.: AEI Press, 1996.

Sakamoto, Yoshihiro. "Moving to an Era of Cooperation: The U.S. and Japanese New Relationship." 15 March 1996. Quoted in *JEI Report* 43 (14 November 1997): 3.

Schoppa, Leonard J. "The Social Context in Coercive International Bargaining." *International Organization* 53, no. 2 (spring 1999), 307–42.

Schumpeter, Joseph A. *Capitalism, Socialism, and Democracy*. New York: HarperCollins, 1950.

Solingen, Etel. *Regional Orders at Century's Dawn*. Princeton, N.J.: Princeton University Press, 1998.

Taiwan Studies Institute. "APEC Committees and Working Groups" [http://www.taiwanstudies.org/tsi_publications/view_story.php3?482], 3 October 2001.

Thomas, Kenneth P., and Mary Ann Tétreault, eds. *Racing to Regionalize: Democracy, Capitalism, and Regional Political Economy*. Boulder, Colo.: Lynne Rienner, 1999.

Webber, Douglas. "Two Funerals and a Wedding? The Ups and Downs of Regionalism in East Asia and Asia-Pacific After the Asian Crisis." *The Pacific Review* 14, no. 3 (2001), 339–72.

Index

271, 300, 302–3, 318; impact of China on, 14–15, 16–17, 33, 65, 73, 75–76, 81, 85, 86, 87–88, 90, 96, 107, 110, 112, 113–14, 121, 124, 302, 304, 306–7, 317, 318, 320; and individual self-defense, 61, 66, 72–73, 82; inequality in, 5, 6–7, 9, 41, 52–53, 61, 70, 84–85, 89, 120, 124, 308–9, 319; Japanese hedging options, 59, 60, 62–63, 75–77, 78, 84–85, 304; Japanese military policies/capabilities, 3, 6, 7, 9–10, 13–14, 18, 33, 39, 46, 52, 59, 62, 63, 65–66, 67, 70, 74, 76, 85–86; Joint Declaration on Security, 71, 72; regarding Korean Peninsula, 17–19, 38, 61, 63, 65, 72, 75, 78–79, 299, 302, 307, 311, 323; missile defense systems, 18, 19, 33, 46, 71, 76, 85–86, 107, 109, 112, 299, 311; and multilateralism, 4, 27, 28–29, 30, 32, 40, 49–50, 56, 57–58, 60, 63–65, 71, 78–84, 86, 248–50, 251–59, 262–63, 265–66, 300, 301–3, 304–5, 307, 317, 318, 334n15; Mutual Security Assistance (MSA), 63; National Defense Program Outline (NDPO), 65–66, 71, 75, 78; and Nye Initiative, 41, 49, 102, 310, 322–23; and Okinawa, 65, 68, 310; during Persian Gulf War of 1990–91, 19, 30, 67–68, 69, 70, 82–83, 255; San Francisco Peace Treaty, 1, 6; Security Treaty, 5, 6, 8, 20, 55, 56, 60–63, 322–23; separation from economic issues, 5, 8–9, 12, 30; regarding Taiwan, 61, 63, 65, 72, 75–76, 88, 107, 112, 302, 307, 323, 324; Treaty of Mutual Cooperation and Security of 1960, 61–63, 66, 67, 77; US troops based in Japan, 6, 19, 49, 52, 60, 61, 66, 68, 71, 310; and war on terrorism, 19, 38, 55, 72, 73, 76–77, 82, 83, 84, 85, 299, 300, 311, 323, 326

Sedgwick, Mitchell W., 158

Self-Defense Forces (SDF): Afghan war operations, 55, 72–73, 76–77, 82–83, 85, 113, 266, 311, 323, 326; Cambodia operations, 79, 100, 266; capabilities of, 7, 59, 62, 63, 65, 66, 67, 70, 72, 74, 76, 77, 81, 83, 85–86, 90; dispatch outside Japan, 9, 55, 62, 63, 65, 67, 71, 72–73, 76–77, 79, 83–84, 104, 113, 264, 269, 311, 323, 326; Indian operations, 73; Pakistan operations, 73

semiconductors, 155, 172, 226–27, 243, 309, 312, 347n84, 372n11; Semicon-

ductor Agreement, 12, 227; Semiconductor Industry Association (SIA), 226

Senkaku/Diaoyu Islands, 68–69, 90, 99, 109

September 11th attacks, 13, 16, 17, 19, 38, 51, 53, 69, 73, 77, 113, 119, 262, 300, 310, 333n33

Shanghai Cooperative Organization (SCO), 15, 16

Shangri-La initiative, 78

Shimamura, Yoshinobu, 102

Siam City Bank, 143

Sierra Leone, 14

SII (Structural Impediments Initiative), 12

Silicon Valley, 156

Singapore: and ASEAN, 128; during Asian financial crisis, 204, 354n32; bank lending from, 147; and Chiang Mai Initiative, 214, 215; electronics industry in, 169, 170, 171; and Five-Power Defense Arrangements, 50; foreign direct investment (FDI) from, 139, 144–45, 146, 147, 321, 341n48; foreign exchange reserves in, 215; foreign investments in, 22, 139, 145, 161, 168, 171; foreign loans to, 137, 138; Japanese investments in, 22; relations with China, 15; relations with Japan, 207, 262, 294; relations with US, 50, 53

Soeharto, 260

Solingen, Etel, 23

South Africa, 243

South China Sea, territorial disputes in, 263, 265

Southeast Asia, 289–90, 299, 305, 306, 316; automobile industry in, 154–55, 158, 159–67, 172–75, 344nn24,25,26, 345n32, 346n53; computer peripherals industry in, 154–55, 167–71, 172–75; ethnic Chinese businesspeople in, 135; foreign investments in, 142–46, 147, 149, 151–52, 154–55, 158, 159–67, 168, 169, 170–75, 321, 345n37; free trade policies in, 152. *See also* ASEAN

Southeast Asia Treaty Organization (SEATO), 62, 65

South Korea, 351n50; and APEC, 262, 264, 278, 281–82, 369n46; during Asian financial crisis, 181, 183, 204, 354n32; automobile industry in, 160, 344n23; business networks in, 156; and Chiang Mai Initiative, 216; economic development in, 13, 46–47, 168–69; electronics industry in, 167–68, 171; foreign banks in, 140; foreign direct in-

tific, and Cultural Organization (UNESCO), 27

United Overseas Bank (UOB), 145

United States: during Asian financial crisis, 25–26, 119, 122, 124, 133, 152, 177–78, 180, 181, 182–85, 190, 194, 195–96, 203–8, 217, 297, 317, 326, 348nn7,8,12, 354n32; budget deficits in, 253; Department of Commerce (USDOC), 226–27, 237–38, 368n22; Department of Defense, 8, 18; Department of State, 8, 18, 28, 48, 51, 97, 250–51, 256, 258, 263, 267, 365nn27,28; Federal Reserve system, 20, 24, 204, 348n2; fiscal policies in, 24–25; foreign investments in, 12, 136, 138, 139, 148, 312; as hegemonic power, 37–42, 52, 53–54, 178, 188, 194, 348n1; investments in Asia from, 137, 138–39, 140, 141, 146, 148, 149, 150, 153, 155, 158–59, 165–66, 167–70, 171–72, 174–75, 175; Japanese investments in, 12, 136, 148, 312; manufacturing employment in, 24; military policies/capabilities of, 6, 7, 18, 19–20, 33, 41, 52, 88–89; military spending in, 19, 41; Official Development Assistance, 342n58; relations with ASEAN, 115–19, 120, 121, 122, 123–29, 124, 194, 204, 205, 256, 306, 307, 322, 334n15, 363n12; relations with Australia, 27, 50, 53, 61, 65, 256; relations with Europe, 6, 8, 13, 43–44, 48, 51, 52, 62, 105, 111, 177, 178, 187–96, 197, 318, 348n1; relations with Indonesia, 116, 125–26; relations with Malaysia, 289; relations with Mexico, 180–81, 188, 203, 204, 348nn6,7, 353n12; relations with Myanmar, 298, 323; relations with New Zealand, 27, 50, 61, 256; relations with North Korea, 18, 38, 46, 48, 49, 53, 68, 69, 85, 102, 298, 299, 302, 303, 307, 311, 323; relations with Philippines, 50, 61, 121, 124, 364n19; relations with Russia, 48, 51, 105, 106, 302; relations with Singapore, 50, 53; relations with South Korea, 18, 38, 39, 48, 50, 51, 53, 61, 65, 78–79, 89, 118, 233, 235, 239, 256, 307, 324, 334n15; relations with Soviet Union, 6, 37, 39, 40, 65, 89; relations with Taiwan, 17, 92–93, 94–95, 101, 103–4, 106–7, 112, 118; relations with Thailand, 50, 125; relations with UN, 27; relations with Viet-

nam, 65, 117, 298; service sector employment in, 24; Trade Representative (USTR), 8, 250, 267, 275, 277, 285, 289, 313, 368n22; war on terrorism, 15, 16, 17, 19, 38, 51, 53–54, 55, 69, 72–73, 76–77, 85, 113, 119, 262, 263, 267, 299, 300, 311, 326; and WTO, 221–24, 225–26, 231, 232–33, 235–39, 243–47, 314

Uno, Sosuke, 97

U.S.-Canada Free Trade Agreement, 264n23, 364n18

U.S.-China relations, 51, 87–114, 121, 313, 334n15; air collision off Hainan Island, 113; during Asian financial crisis, 108, 181, 185, 186, 204, 313, 315, 349n12; China as threat to US, 81, 87, 89, 103–4, 299, 372n13; during Cold War, 15, 37, 39–40, 65, 88, 89, 93; containment option in, 44–45, 53, 54, 87, 88, 95, 105, 113, 114; economic relations, 16–17, 42–43, 88, 90–91, 96, 99, 108, 181, 185, 186, 204, 245, 313, 315, 349n12; impact of Japan on, 17, 52, 74, 89, 100, 114, 187, 306–7; intellectual property rights issues in, 47, 91, 100–101; regarding Korean Peninsula, 15, 89, 102; Nixon-Kissinger opening, 15, 37, 92, 93; and Northeast Asia Cooperation Dialogue (NEACD), 48; and Nye Initiative, 49; during Persian Gulf War of 1990–91, 100; role of arms sales/military technology transfers in, 89; role of democratic reforms in, 42, 47, 88, 91–92, 93, 96–98, 101, 106, 307, 323; role of engagement in, 16, 42–43, 44–45, 65, 75, 87–88, 95–101, 336n3; role of environmentalism in, 100; role of human rights in, 16, 45, 47, 91, 93, 94, 96–98, 100–102, 106, 111, 307, 323; role of labor expoitation in, 100, 101; role of rule of law reform in, 88, 92; regarding Taiwan, 17, 40, 75, 88, 89, 92–93, 94–95, 101, 103–4, 106–7, 113, 307; and terrorism, 15, 16, 17, 38, 51, 113; regarding trade and investment, 42–43, 46; US bombing of China's Belgrade embassy, 111; US investment in, 90–91; regarding WTO membership, 16, 47, 91, 111, 112

U.S. foreign policy: and Armitage Report, 45, 52; deployment of troops in Asia, 19, 49, 50, 52, 53, 71, 121, 310, 334n15, 364n19; hub-and-spokes bilat-